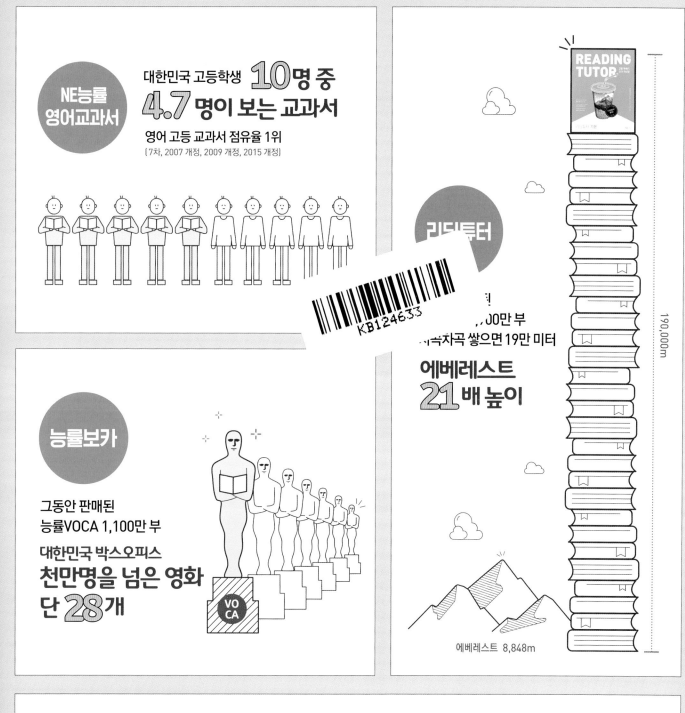

NE능률 영어교과서

대한민국 고등학생 **10명** 중 **4.7명**이 보는 교과서

영어 고등 교과서 점유율 1위

(7차, 2007 개정, 2009 개정, 2015 개정)

리딩튜터

READING TUTOR

~~1,100만 부~~

~~차곡차곡 쌓으면 19만 미터~~

에베레스트 21배 높이

190,000m

에베레스트 8,848m

능률보카

그동안 판매된 능률VOCA 1,100만 부

대한민국 박스오피스 **천만명을 넘은 영화 단 28개**

VOCA

그래머존

그동안 판매된 450만 부의 그래머존을 바닥에 쭉 ~ 깔면

1000km 서울 - 부산 왕복가능

서울

부산

KB124633

능률 중학영어 듣기 모의고사

22회 LEVEL 3

지은이	NE능률 영어교육연구소
연구원	김지현
외주 연구원	설북
영문 교열	Bryce Olk, Curtis Thompson, Patrick Ferraro
디자인	오솔길
내지 일러스트	박응식
맥편집	허문희

Let's grow together

NE능률이
미래를
창조합니다.

건강한 배움의 고객가치를 제공하겠다는 꿈을 실현하기 위해
40년이 넘는 시간 동안 열심히 달려왔습니다.

앞으로도 끊임없는 연구와 노력을 통해
당연한 것을 멈추지 않고

고객, 기업, 직원 모두가 함께 성장하는 NE능률이 되겠습니다.

NE능률

전국 16개 시·도 교육청 주관 **영어듣기평가 실전대비서**

능률 중학영어
듣기 모의고사

22회

LEVEL 3

구성 및 활용법

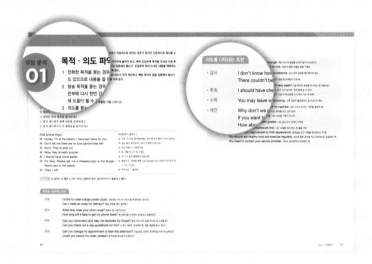

유형 분석

- 최근 〈시·도 교육청 주관 영어듣기능력평가〉에 출제되는 모든 유형을 정리하고, 각 유형에 대한 듣기 전략을 수록했습니다.

- 유형별로 자주 나오는 어휘와 중요 표현을 익힐 수 있도록 했습니다.

빠른 듣기 MP3파일 & 배속 MP3파일

실제 시험보다 더 빠른 속도의 음원을 제공하여 실전에 완벽하게 대비할 수 있도록 했습니다. 또한, 실력에 따라 듣기 속도를 다르게 하여 들을 수 있도록 배속 MP3 파일을 제공합니다.

기출문제 2회

〈시·도 교육청 주관 영어듣기능력평가〉의 최신 기출문제 2회분을 통해 실제 평가 유형을 접해 볼 수 있도록 했습니다.

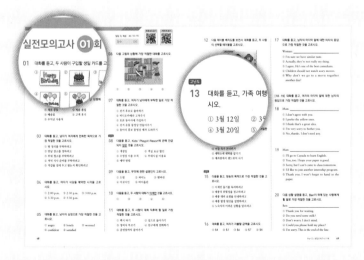

실전모의고사 18회

- 실제 시험과 유사하게 구성한 모의고사 18회분을 통해 실전 감각을 기를 수 있도록 했습니다.

- 매회 수록된 고난도 문제를 통해 실력을 한 단계 더 향상시킬 수 있도록 했습니다.

고난도 실전모의고사 2회

실제 시험보다 어려운 고난도 모의고사 2회분을 통해 실력을 보다 더 높일 수 있도록 했습니다.

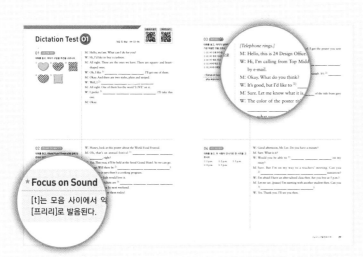

Dictation Test

모의고사 문제 전체 스크립트의 받아쓰기를 수록했습니다. 들은 내용을 한번 더 확인하며, 중요 표현들과 듣기 어려운 연음 등을 학습할 수 있습니다.

Focus on Sound

듣기를 어렵게 하는 발음 현상을 정리하여 듣기의 기본기를 높일 수 있도록 했습니다.

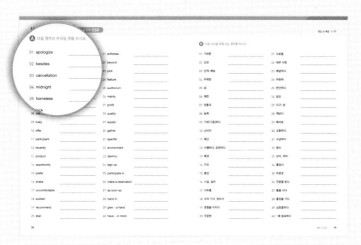

Word Test

모의고사를 통해 학습한 단어와 숙어를 문제를 통해 확인하고 정리해 볼 수 있도록 했습니다.

목차

기출 문제 유형 분석표
(2020년 ~ 2022년)

3학년	2022년 1회	2021년 2회	2021년 1회	2020년 2회	2020년 1회
목적 파악	2	2	2	2	2
그림 정보 파악	1	1	1	1	1
화제 파악	1	1	1	1	1
숫자 정보 파악	3	3	3	2	2
세부 정보 파악				1	1
심정 추론	1	1		1	1
장소 추론			1		
그림 상황에 적절한 대화 찾기	1	1	1	1	1
할 일 파악	1	1	1	1	1
부탁한 일 파악	1	1	1	1	1
한 일 파악	1	1	1	1	1
언급되지 않은 내용 찾기	2	2	2	2	2
위치 찾기		1	1	1	1
도표 파악	1				
어색한 대화 찾기	1	1	1	1	1
상황에 적절한 말 찾기	1	1	1	1	1
마지막 말에 이어질 응답 찾기	3	3	3	3	3

STUDY PLANNER

시험 전 한 달 동안 본 교재를 마스터할 수 있는 계획표입니다.
학습한 날짜와 점수를 적고 계획에 맞춰 학습하세요.

	1일차	2일차	3일차	4일차	5일차	6일차
1주	유형 분석	기출문제 01회	기출문제 02회	실전모의고사 01회	실전모의고사 02회	실전모의고사 03회
	월 일	월 일 ____점	월 일 ____점	월 일 ____점	월 일 ____점	월 일 ____점
	7일차	**8일차**	**9일차**	**10일차**	**11일차**	**12일차**
2주	실전모의고사 04회	실전모의고사 05회	실전모의고사 06회	실전모의고사 07회	실전모의고사 08회	실전모의고사 09회
	월 일 ____점	월 일 ____점	월 일 ____점	월 일 ____점	월 일 ____점	월 일 ____점
	13일차	**14일차**	**15일차**	**16일차**	**17일차**	**18일차**
3주	실전모의고사 10회	실전모의고사 11회	실전모의고사 12회	실전모의고사 13회	실전모의고사 14회	실전모의고사 15회
	월 일 ____점	월 일 ____점	월 일 ____점	월 일 ____점	월 일 ____점	월 일 ____점
	19일차	**20일차**	**21일차**	**22일차**	**23일차**	**24일차**
4주	실전모의고사 16회	실전모의고사 17회	실전모의고사 18회	고난도 실전모의고사 01회	고난도 실전모의고사 02회	어휘 총 정리
	월 일 ____점	월 일 ____점	월 일 ____점	월 일 ____점	월 일 ____점	월 일 ____점

능률 중학영어듣기
모의고사 22회
Level 3

PART
01

기출 탐구

- 유형 분석
- 기출문제 2회

목적 · 의도 파악

1. 전화한 목적을 묻는 경우, 대화의 앞부분에서 직접적으로 밝히는 경우가 많지만 간접적으로 제시될 수도 있으므로 내용을 잘 파악하며 듣는다.
2. 방송 목적을 묻는 경우, 화제가 무엇인지 파악하며 들어야 하고, 특히 도입부에 목적을 드러낸 다음 후반부에 다시 한번 강조하는 경우가 많으므로 집중해서 듣는다. 도입부의 화자 소개도 내용을 예측하는 데 도움이 될 수 있으니 놓치지 말고 듣도록 한다.
3. 의도를 묻는 경우, 누구의 의도를 파악해야 하는지 먼저 확인하고 해당 화자의 말을 집중해서 듣는다. 거절, 충고, 제안 등의 여러 상황별 표현을 익혀 둔다.

기출 맛보기 🤿

대화를 듣고, 남자가 여자에게 전화한 목적으로 가장 적절한 것을 고르시오.

① 버거 가게 위치를 확인하려고
② 제과점 영업 시간을 물어보려고
③ 원하는 버거 종류를 물어보려고
④ 참치 샌드위치 판매 여부를 문의하려고
⑤ 참치 샌드위치가 다 팔렸음을 알려주려고

....

[Cell phone rings.]
M: Honey, I'm at the bakery. I have bad news for you.
W: Don't tell me there are no tuna sandwiches left!
M: Sorry. They're sold out.
W: Wow, they're really popular.
M: I should have come earlier.
W: It's okay. Please get me a cheeseburger at the Burger World next to the bakery.
M: Okay. I will.

[휴대전화가 울린다.]
남: 여보, 저 지금 제과점이에요. 당신에게 안 좋은 소식이 있어요.
여: 남은 참치 샌드위치가 없다고 말하지 말아요!
남: 유감이에요. 다 팔렸어요.
여: 와, 정말 인기가 있나 봐요.
남: 내가 더 일찍 왔었어야 하는데요.
여: 괜찮아요. 제과점 옆에 있는 Burger World에서 치즈버거 하나 사다 주세요.
남: 알았어요. 그럴게요.

....

문제 해설 ⑤ 남자는 안 좋은 소식이 있다고 말하며 참치 샌드위치가 다 팔렸다고 했다.

목적을 나타내는 표현

• 주문	I'd like to order a large potato pizza. 포테이토 피자 큰 사이즈를 주문하려고 합니다. Can I make an order for delivery? 배달 주문을 해도 될까요?
• 문의	How long will it take to get my phone fixed? 제 전화기를 수리하는 데 얼마나 걸릴까요?
• 부탁	Can you come early and help me decorate my house? 일찍 와서 내가 집을 꾸미는 걸 도와줄래? Can you check out a Jeju guidebook for me? 나 대신 제주도 안내책자 한 권을 대출해 줄 수 있니?
• 요청	Can you change my appointment to later this afternoon? 오늘 늦은 오후로 제 예약을 바꿔 주시겠어요? Could you cancel my order, please? 제 주문을 취소해 주시겠어요?

- 감사   I don't know how to thank you enough. 뭐라 감사의 말씀을 드려야 할지 모르겠어요.
  There couldn't be a better present for me. 제게 더 좋은 선물은 없을 거예요.

- 후회   I should have checked the weather in advance. 내가 미리 날씨를 확인했어야 했어.

- 수락   You may leave whenever you want. 네가 원할 때 언제든지 가도 돼.

- 제안   Why don't we put off the meeting until next week? 다음 주까지 회의를 연기하는 게 어떨까요?
  If you want to go, we can go together. 네가 가고 싶다면, 우린 함께 갈 수 있어.
  How about going skiing this Saturday? 이번 주 토요일에 스키 타러 가는 게 어때?

- 불평   I want you to know that it was very annoying. 그게 굉장히 불쾌했다는 걸 아셨으면 해요.

- 거절   I'd like to, but I have to take care of my nephew. 나도 그러고 싶지만, 조카를 돌봐야 해.
  I don't feel like watching a movie. 나는 영화를 보고 싶지 않아.
  I'm not in the mood for shopping. 나는 쇼핑할 기분이 아니야.

- 걱정   I'm worried about my midterm grades. 나는 중간고사 성적이 걱정돼.

- 충고   You'd better do your homework first. 너는 숙제를 먼저 하는 게 좋을 거야.
  You should not judge people by their appearance. 겉모습을 보고 사람을 판단해서는 안 돼.
  You should eat healthy food and exercise regularly. 건강에 좋은 음식을 먹고 규칙적으로 운동해야 해.
  You need to contact your service provider. 서비스 공급자에게 연락해야 해.

그림 정보 파악

1 먼저 선택지 그림의 차이를 살펴보고, 주의해서 들어야 할 부분이 무엇인지 예측해 본다.
2 사물을 묘사하는 경우, 색, 무늬, 모양, 구성 요소 등을 나타내는 어휘나 표현을 익혀 두고 이를 유의하여 듣는다.

기출 맛보기 🤿

대화를 듣고, 남자가 만든 깃발을 고르시오.

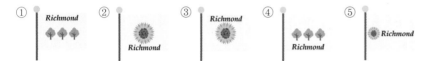

M: Mom, this is the city flag I designed for the Richmond Flag Contest.

W: It looks great! You used trees as a symbol for the city.

M: Yeah, because the city planted many trees this year.

W: That's true, but why didn't you include any sunflowers? A lot of those were planted, too.

M: I know, but I wanted to make my flag unique.

W: I see. I like your idea to put the city name above the trees.

M: Thanks, Mom.

남: 엄마, 이게 제가 Richmond 깃발 대회를 위해 디자인한 도시 깃발이에요.

여: 아주 좋아보이는구나! 도시의 상징으로 나무들을 사용했네.

남: 네, 그 도시가 올해 나무를 많이 심었거든요.

여: 맞아, 그런데 왜 해바라기를 넣지 않았니? 그것들도 많이 심었잖아.

남: 알아요, 하지만 제 깃발을 특별하게 만들고 싶었어요.

여: 그렇구나. 도시의 이름을 나무들 위에 배치한 아이디어가 좋구나.

남: 고마워요, 엄마.

문제 해설 ① 도시의 상징으로 나무를 사용했고, 해바라기는 넣지 않았으며, 도시의 이름을 나무 위에 배치했다고 했다.

사물 묘사에 쓰이는 표현

• 모양	But these animal-shaped pillows look better. 하지만 이 동물 모양의 베개가 더 좋아 보여요. I think the shorter boots would be easier to take off. 더 짧은 부츠가 벗기에 더 쉬울 것 같아요. I think these with the round top would go better with my other pots. 윗부분이 둥근 이것들은 제 다른 화분들과 더 잘 어울릴 것 같아요.
• 구성 요소	You even put a zipper on the bag. 넌 가방에 지퍼도 달았구나. I like the smiley face case with a ribbon better. 저는 리본이 달린 웃는 얼굴 모양의 케이스가 더 좋아요.
• 무늬 및 그림	How about this plate with a picture of a mountain on it? 산 그림이 있는 이 접시는 어떠세요? How about these boots with stripes? 줄무늬가 있는 이 부츠는 어떠세요? I think she would prefer the plain ones more. 그녀는 무늬가 없는 것을 더 좋아할 것 같아. Mark would prefer the polar bear to the penguin. Mark는 펭귄보다 북극곰을 더 좋아할 거야.
• 디자인 배치	Put the picture right beside the title. 그림을 제목 바로 옆에 배치하렴. You put a heart shape under the last name, KIM. 김이라는 성 아래에 하트 무늬를 넣었구나.

화제 파악

1 설명하는 대상이 무엇인지 파악하는 문제의 경우, 용도나 외양 묘사 등을 듣고 종합하여 대상을 추론해야 한다. 선택지를 미리 확인하고 듣는 내용을 예측하는 것이 도움이 된다.

2 직업이나 장소를 묻는 경우, 특정 직업이나 장소의 특징과 관련된 표현을 미리 익혀 둔다.

기출 맛보기

다음을 듣고, 어떤 직업에 관한 설명인지 고르시오.

① 수의사   ② 구조대원   ③ 치과의사   ④ 농구선수   ⑤ 동물조련사

W: People who have this job check animals' health conditions and give them proper care. When an animal needs some medical care, they check its body parts. They also give shots and perform surgeries when they are necessary. To have this job, you need to have broad medical knowledge about animals and have a license.

여: 이 직업을 가진 사람들은 동물의 건강 상태를 확인하고 적절한 보살핌을 제공합니다. 동물이 어떤 의학적 보살핌이 필요하면, 그들은 동물의 신체를 확인합니다. 그들은 또한 필요한 경우에 주사를 놓고 수술을 합니다. 이 직업을 가지려면, 동물에 관한 폭넓은 의학 지식이 있어야 하며 면허가 있어야 합니다.

문제 해설 ① 동물에게 의학적 보살핌을 제공하는 직업은 수의사이다.

화제 유형에 자주 쓰이는 표현

- 운동 경기
  You can play it both indoors and outdoors. 실내에서도, 실외에서도 할 수 있습니다.
  People score by throwing the ball into the net. 그물 안에 공을 던져 넣는 것으로 득점합니다.
  You can never touch the ball with your hands. 절대로 손으로 공을 잡아서는 안 됩니다.
  There are eleven players on each team. 각 팀에는 11명의 선수가 있습니다.

- 용도
  This is a device that is used in many different places. 이것은 다양한 장소에서 사용되는 기기입니다.
  It is a machine for measuring the weight of an object. 그것은 물건의 무게를 재는 기계입니다.
  When you need to take your temperature, you need this. 체온을 재야 할 때, 이것이 필요합니다.
  It is used for recreation, general fitness, or racing. 그것은 오락, 신체 단련이나 경주에 이용됩니다.

숫자 정보 · 세부 정보 파악

1 날짜나 요일, 시각을 묻는 경우, 대화 초반에 여러 날짜와 요일, 시각을 언급하다가 마지막에 최종 결정을 하는 경우가 많으므로 끝까지 주의해서 듣는다.
2 금액을 묻는 경우, 구입할 물건의 정가, 개수, 할인율, 쿠폰 사용 여부 등의 정보에 주의하며 듣는다.

기출 맛보기 🥽

대화를 듣고, 회사 야유회를 가기로 한 날짜를 고르시오.

① June 2   ② June 7   ③ June 9   ④ June 10   ⑤ June 19

W: Jack, we should decide on a date for our company picnic.

M: Okay, Jean. How about June 2nd or June 7th?

W: I think we need a couple more days than that to prepare for it. How about June 9th?

M: We already have a weekly meeting planned on that day at 10 o'clock.

W: I'm sure we can reschedule the meeting.

M: Okay, then let's go with your suggested date.

여: Jack, 우리 회사 야유회 날짜를 정해야 해요.

남: 알았어요, Jean. 6월 2일이나 6월 7일은 어때요?

여: 우리가 야유회 준비를 하려면 그것보다는 며칠 더 필요할 것 같아요. 6월 9일은 어때요?

남: 이미 그날 10시에 예정된 주간 회의가 있어요.

여: 우리가 분명 그 회의 일정을 다시 정할 수 있을 거예요.

남: 알았어요, 그러면 당신이 제안한 날로 해요.

문제 해설 ③ 6월 9일에 예정된 회의가 있지만 여자가 그날 야유회를 가고 회의 일정은 다시 정하자고 제안했고 남자가 동의했다.

날짜나 요일, 시각과 관련된 표현

• 날짜, 요일, 시각 정하기	Why don't we meet on Thursday? 우리 목요일에 만나는 게 어때? Let's leave on July 20 and come back on July 23. 7월 20일에 떠나서 7월 23일에 돌아오자. I have a teacher's meeting at three o'clock, so I can see you at four that day. 내가 3시에 교사 회의가 있으니까, 그날 4시에 널 볼 수 있단다.

금액과 관련된 표현

• 가격	The green one only costs $30. 초록색 상품은 30달러밖에 하지 않습니다. The adult set is $20 and the junior set is $10. 성인 세트는 20달러, 아동 세트는 10달러입니다. If he is under seven, he has free admission. 그가 7세 이하라면, 입장은 무료입니다.
• 할인	If you buy two in this design, you get $5 off of the total. 이 디자인으로 두 개를 구입하시면, 총 가격에서 5달러를 할인받습니다. You'll get 10% off the regular price if you use this coupon. 이 쿠폰을 사용하시면 정가에서 10% 할인받게 됩니다.

유형 분석 05

심정 추론

1 화자의 심정을 묻는 경우, 대상 화자의 어조에 주의하면서 전체적인 상황을 파악한다. 심정을 직접적으로 드러내는 경우도 있으니 이를 놓치지 말고 듣는다.
2 심정을 나타내는 표현을 분명하게 익혀 둔다.

기출 맛보기

대화를 듣고, 여자의 심정으로 가장 적절한 것을 고르시오.

① bored　　② happy　　③ jealous　　④ annoyed　　⑤ scared

M: Hi, Nancy. Looks like you're in a hurry.	남: 안녕, Nancy. 바쁜 것 같아 보이네.
W: Yeah. I'm on my way to get my phone back.	여: 응. 지금 내 전화기 돌려받으러 가는 중이야.
M: Did you leave it somewhere?	남: 그걸 다른 곳에 두었었니?
W: Yes, I did. I left it in a taxi last night.	여: 응, 그랬어. 어젯밤에 택시에 두고 내렸어.
M: Oh, my! Did you call your phone after you realized that?	남: 이런, 세상에! 그걸 알고 나서 네 전화기로 전화했어?
W: Yeah. The taxi driver answered and said he'd return it to me. He's at the school gate now.	여: 응. 택시 기사님이 전화를 받아서 내게 전화기를 돌려주겠다고 하셨지. 지금 학교 정문에 계셔.
M: How nice! You're very lucky to get it back.	남: 잘됐다! 전화기를 되찾다니 너 정말 운 좋다.

문제 해설 ② 여자는 어젯밤에 택시에 두고 내린 전화기를 찾게 되어 기쁠(happy) 것이다.

심정을 나타내는 어휘

• 긍정적 심정	proud 자랑스러워하는	relaxed 느긋한	peaceful 평안한	pleased 기쁜
	satisfied 만족하는	thankful 고맙게 생각하는	impressive 인상적인	relieved 안도한
• 부정적 심정	bored 지루해하는	worried 걱정하는	indifferent 무관심한	annoyed 짜증 난
	scared 무서워하는	confused 혼란스러운	frustrated 좌절한	jealous 질투하는
	embarrassed 당황한	regretful 후회되는	depressed 우울한	terrified 겁이 난

장소 추론

1 전체적인 상황을 파악해서 답을 골라야 하며, 두 화자의 관계가 힌트가 될 수 있다.
2 특정 장소에서 자주 일어나는 상황의 표현을 익혀 둔다.

기출 맛보기 🤿

대화를 듣고, 두 사람이 대화하는 장소로 가장 적절한 곳을 고르시오.

① 식당　　② 약국　　③ 카페　　④ 은행　　⑤ 보건실

W: Hello. May I have your prescription?

M: Here it is.

W: Okay. I'll be with you shortly. *[pause]* Mr. Choi, here is your medicine. Take these pills three times a day, 30 minutes after meals.

M: But the doctor said I can take them twice a day if I feel better. Is it okay?

W: Sure. In that case, you can skip the medicine after lunch. But make sure you don't take it with milk or coffee.

M: I'll keep that in mind. Thank you.

W: You're welcome. Is there anything else you need?

M: No, I'm good. How much is it?

W: It'll be five dollars.

여: 안녕하세요. 처방전 좀 볼 수 있을까요?

남: 여기요.

여: 네. 곧 오겠습니다. *[잠시 후]* 최 선생님, 여기 약 있습니다. 이 알약을 하루 세 번 식후 30분에 드세요.

남: 그런데 나아지면 하루에 두 번 먹어도 된다고 의사 선생님께서 말씀하셨는데요. 그래도 괜찮나요?

여: 물론이죠. 그런 경우에는 점심 후에는 약을 거르셔도 됩니다. 하지만 반드시 약을 우유나 커피와 함께 드시진 마세요.

남: 명심할게요. 감사합니다.

여: 별말씀을요. 필요하신 다른 게 있나요?

남: 아뇨, 괜찮아요. 얼마죠?

여: 5달러예요.

문제 해설 ② 처방전을 보여 달라고 하고 약 복용법에 대해 말하는 것으로 보아, 두 사람이 대화하는 장소로 가장 적절한 곳은 약국이다.

자주 쓰이는 표현

• 옷 가게	A: What do you think about this jacket? 이 재킷 어떤 것 같아? B: Why don't you try it on? 입어 보는 게 어때?
• 세탁소	A: I'd like to have my dress cleaned, please. When will it be done? 제 원피스 세탁을 맡기려고요. 언제 다 될까요? B: Come back Wednesday afternoon. 수요일 오후에 다시 오세요.
• 동물병원	A: My dog got away from me and was hit by a car. 제 개가 제게서 벗어나서 차에 치였어요. B: It doesn't seem that bad, but she needs to get an X-ray. 그렇게 심각해 보이진 않지만, 엑스레이를 찍어야 합니다.
• 경찰서	A: I'd like to report a theft. 도난 신고를 하고 싶은데요. B: Please sit here and fill out this form. 여기에 앉아서 이 서류를 작성해 주세요.

유형 분석

07 그림 상황에 적절한 대화 찾기

1 주어진 그림을 미리 보며, 그림의 상황에 적절한 대화를 생각해 본다.
2 그림 속 사물과 관련된 단어들을 포함한 대화가 오답으로 제시되는 경우가 많으므로, 단어 하나만 듣고 성급하게 답을 고르지 않도록 한다.
3 모든 대화를 주의 깊게 들으면서 선택지를 하나씩 지워가며 답을 고른다.

기출 맛보기 🥽

다음 그림의 상황에 가장 적절한 대화를 고르시오.

①   ②   ③   ④   ⑤

① M: Would you like to take a picture?
　 W: Not now. After I ride the bumper car.
② M: Look at the monster car over there.
　 W: Oh, it looks so scary.
③ M: How long have you been waiting?
　 W: About half an hour.
④ M: Can I see your ticket, please?
　 W: Here you are.
⑤ M: I'm sorry, but you're not tall enough to ride this.
　 W: Oh, no! I'm so sad.

① 남: 사진 찍을래?
　 여: 지금은 말고요. 범퍼카를 타고난 후에요.
② 남: 저기 몬스터 카를 좀 봐.
　 여: 아, 정말 무서워 보여요.
③ 남: 얼마나 오래 기다렸니?
　 여: 30분 정도요.
④ 남: 표 좀 보여 주시겠어요?
　 여: 여기 있어요.
⑤ 남: 미안하지만, 이것을 탈 수 있을 만큼 키가 크지 않구나.
　 여: 아, 이런! 저 너무 슬퍼요.

[문제 해설] ⑤ 놀이공원에서 놀이 기구 앞에서 여자아이가 키를 재고 있는 상황이다.

할 일 · 부탁한 일 · 한 일 파악

1 먼저 지시문을 읽고, 두 화자 중 누가 언제 할 일인지, 누가 누구에게 부탁한 일인지, 누가 언제 한 일인지 확인한다.
2 대화 중에 함께 제시되는 과거에 한 일, 어느 시점에 할 일, 또는 상대방이 할 일과 혼동하지 않도록 한다.
3 한 일을 묻는 경우, 계획에 변동이 생겼거나 상대방의 짐작과 다른 경우가 많으므로 이와 혼동하지 말고 끝까지 주의해서 듣는다.
4 부탁하는 일을 묻는 경우, 주로 마지막 부분에 부탁하는 내용이 언급되므로 이를 유의해서 듣는다.

기출 맛보기 🤿

대화를 듣고, 남자가 할 일로 가장 적절한 것을 고르시오.

① 선물 포장하기　　　② 사진 보여주기　　　③ 지갑 환불받기
④ 엄마에게 전화하기　　⑤ 가게 위치 알려주기

M: Mom, I've decided what to get Jenny for her birthday.
W: What did you decide on?
M: I think I'll get her a wallet.
W: Good idea. What kind of wallet do you have in mind?
M: I saw a nice one at the mall. I took a picture of it with my cellphone.
W: Did you? Can I see it?
M: Sure. Wait a second.

남: 엄마, Jenny에게 생일 선물로 뭘 줄지 정했어요.
여: 뭘로 결정했니?
남: 지갑을 사줄까 생각해요.
여: 좋은 생각이구나. 어떤 지갑을 염두에 두고 있어?
남: 쇼핑몰에서 좋은 걸 하나 봤어요. 휴대전화로 사진을 찍었어요.
여: 그랬니? 보여줄래?
남: 그럼요. 잠시만요.

문제 해설 ② 남자가 선물로 염두에 둔 지갑 사진을 볼 수 있을지 여자가 물었고 남자가 흔쾌히 그러겠다고 했으므로, 남자는 사진을 보여줄 것이다.

자주 쓰이는 표현

- **할 일**
Give me some of the pamphlets, and I'll pass them out to people.
팸플릿을 내게 좀 주면, 내가 사람들에게 나누어 줄게.

Today is her birthday and I'll cook for her this evening.
오늘이 그녀의 생일이어서 저녁에 내가 그녀를 위해 요리할 거야.

- **부탁한 일**
Could you read this script and correct any errors? 이 원고를 읽고 오류를 수정해 주시겠어요?
Could you bring the book to school tomorrow? 내일 학교에 그 책을 가져와 주시겠어요?
Can you book the tickets for us? 우리를 위해 표를 예매해 주시겠어요?

- **한 일**
The camp was canceled. 캠프는 취소됐어.
We visited the traditional houses in Seoul. 우리는 서울에 있는 전통 가옥을 방문했어.
I already saw the exhibition last Sunday. 나는 이미 지난 일요일에 전시회를 봤어.

유형 분석 09

언급되지 않은 내용 찾기

1 먼저 선택지를 보고, 대화나 담화에서 주의하여 들어야 할 내용이 무엇인지 파악한다.
2 대화나 담화의 내용은 보통 선택지 순서대로 언급되므로, 선택지를 하나씩 지우며 정답을 찾는다.

기출 맛보기 🎧

다음을 듣고, 음악회에 관해 언급되지 <u>않은</u> 것을 고르시오.

① 장소　　　② 시간　　　③ 입장료　　　④ 수용 인원　　　⑤ 예약 방법

M: Hello, guests. I hope you're enjoying your stay at our resort. We're going to host a music show as a special event in our grand hall today. It's located on the first floor of the main building. A famous jazz band, the Dynamic Jazz Trio will come and play some Christmas music. The show will begin at 8 o'clock in the evening. Due to the limited number of seats, we can accommodate only 100 guests. To make a reservation, please call the reception desk. Thank you.

남: 안녕하십니까, 고객 여러분. 저희 리조트에서 즐겁게 지내고 계시길 바랍니다. 저희는 오늘 그랜드 홀에서 특별 행사로 음악회를 개최할 예정입니다. 그랜드 홀을 본관 1층에 위치하고 있습니다. 유명 재즈 밴드 Dynamic Jazz Trio가 와서 크리스마스 음악을 연주할 것입니다. 음악회는 저녁 8시 정각에 시작할 예정입니다. 좌석 수가 제한적이기 때문에, 100명의 고객만 수용할 수 있습니다. 예약하시려면, 접수처로 전화 주십시오. 감사합니다.

[문제 해설] ③ 장소(그랜드 홀), 시간(저녁 8시 정각), 수용 인원(100명), 예약 방법(접수처로 전화)에 관해서는 언급되었으나, 입장료는 언급되지 않았다.

위치 찾기

1 먼저 안내도나 배치도를 보고, 입구, 무대, 화장실 등의 위치를 파악해 둔다.
2 여러 위치의 장단점을 이야기하다가 마지막에 한 곳을 선택하므로, 끝까지 주의 깊게 듣는다.

기출 맛보기 🤿

다음 배치도를 보면서 대화를 듣고, 두 사람이 선택한 사진 동아리 구역의 위치를 고르시오.

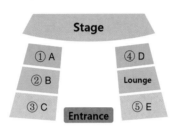

M: Ms. White, here's a map of the sections for the school festival. Which section do you think would be good for the photography club?

W: What about section B?

M: The science club has already been given that section.

W: Hmm... how about putting the photography club in a section next to the lounge?

M: Good idea! The lounge is always crowded, which can help them sell more postcards. Which is better, section D or E?

W: Why don't we give them the section near the entrance?

M: Okay. Great.

남: White 선생님, 여기 교내 축제 구역 지도예요. 어디 구역이 사진 동아리에 적합하다고 생각하세요?

여: B 구역이 어떨까요?

남: 과학 동아리가 이미 그 구역을 배정받았어요.

여: 음… 라운지 옆의 구역에 사진 동아리를 두는 게 어떨까요?

남: 좋은 생각이에요! 라운지는 항상 붐비니까, 엽서를 더 파는 데 도움이 될 수 있어요. D 아니면 E 구역 중 어디가 나을까요?

여: 입구에 가까운 구역을 주는 게 어떨까요?

남: 그래요. 좋아요.

문제 해설 ⑤ B 구역은 이미 배정이 끝났고 라운지 옆의 D와 E 구역 중 입구 근처의 구역이 좋다고 했으므로, 두 사람이 선택한 곳은 E 구역이다.

위치를 추천할 때 자주 쓰이는 표현

- 추천할 때

  It would be convenient to check in first at section B because we have a lot of baggage.
  우리가 짐이 많으니까 B 구역이 먼저 체크인하기에 편할 것 같아.

- 추천하지 않을 때

  It's too far from the entrance. 입구에서 너무 멀어.
  You can see only one side of the stage from there. 거기에서는 무대의 한쪽 면만 볼 수 있어.

도표 · 내용 일치 파악

1 화자의 선택을 묻는 경우, 도표에서 선택 사항을 하나씩 체크한 후 모든 조건을 만족하는 선택지를 고른다.
2 내용과 일치하거나 일치하지 않는지를 묻는 경우, 표의 항목 순서대로 언급되는 대화 내용을 들으며 일치 여부를 확인한다.

기출 맛보기

다음 표를 보면서 대화를 듣고, 두 사람이 관람할 쇼를 고르시오.

	Show	Length	Time
①	Magic show	1 hour	12:00 p.m.
②	Magic show	2 hours	3:00 p.m.
③	Animal show	1 hour	12:00 p.m.
④	Animal show	2 hours	1:00 p.m.
⑤	Animal show	1 hour	3:00 p.m.

M: Sarah, which show do you want to see?
W: How about an animal show? I love animals more than magic.
M: Okay. Animal shows are better for me, too. Then, which one would you like to see?
W: Well, wouldn't a two-hour show be too long for us?
M: I agree. There are one-hour shows at 12 p.m. and 3 p.m.
W: It's 11:30 a.m. now. Why don't we have lunch first and go to the show after 2 p.m.?
M: Sounds great! Let's see the show after lunch.

남: Sarah, 너 어느 쇼 보고 싶어?
여: 동물 쇼 어때? 난 마술보다 동물이 더 좋아.
남: 알았어. 나도 동물 쇼가 더 나아. 그럼 어떤 것을 보고 싶니?
여: 음, 우리한테 2시간짜리 쇼는 너무 길지 않니?
남: 동의해. 오후 12시와 오후 3시에 한 시간짜리 쇼가 있어.
여: 지금이 11시 30분이네. 점심 먼저 먹고 오후 2시 이후에 쇼를 보러 가는 게 어때?
남: 좋아! 점심 후에 쇼를 보자.

문제 해설 ⑤ 두 사람은 동물 쇼 중에서 오후 2시 이후에 하는 한 시간짜리 쇼를 보기로 했다.

어색한 대화 찾기

1 조동사, be동사, do/does/did로 시작하는 의문문은 보통 Yes/No로 대답하지만, 그렇지 않은 경우도 있으므로 주의한다.
2 의문사로 시작하는 의문문은 그 의문사가 대답의 결정적인 단서가 되므로 주의해서 듣는다.
3 여러 상황에서 자주 사용되는 관용적 대답은 미리 익혀 둔다.

기출 맛보기 🎧

대화를 듣고, 두 사람의 대화가 <u>어색한</u> 것을 고르시오.

①   ②   ③   ④   ⑤

---

① M: Have you seen my bag?
   W: Yes. It's right over there.
② M: How long will it take to get there by taxi?
   W: I haven't seen it for a long time.
③ M: I'm getting married next month.
   W: Congratulations! What is the exact date?
④ M: I'm wondering if you could send me the file again.
   W: Sure. I will send it as soon as possible.
⑤ M: Would you have dinner with me this evening?
   W: That sounds great!

① 남: 너 내 가방 봤니?
   여: 응. 바로 저기에 있잖아.
② 남: 택시로 거기에 가는 데 얼마나 걸릴까?
   여: 그걸 오랫동안 못 봤어.
③ 남: 나 다음 달에 결혼해.
   여: 축하해! 정확한 날짜가 언제야?
④ 남: 네가 그 파일을 내게 다시 보내 줄 수 있는지 궁금해.
   여: 물론이지. 최대한 빨리 보낼게.
⑤ 남: 오늘 저녁에 나와 저녁 먹을래?
   여: 좋아!

문제 해설 ② 택시 타고 가는 데 얼마나 걸릴지 물었으므로, 구체적인 소요 시간을 말하는 응답이 자연스럽다.

상황에 적절한 말 찾기

1 담화의 전반적인 상황을 이해하며 듣는다.
2 후반부에 특정 인물이 하고 싶은 말이나 원하는 바를 직접적으로 언급하는 경우가 많으니 이를 주의하여 듣는다.

기출 맛보기 🥽

다음 상황 설명을 듣고, Tina가 Mr. Duncan에게 할 말로 가장 적절한 것을 고르시오.

Tina: Mr. Duncan, _____

① I heard that the competition is delayed.
② I'm sorry, but I don't know where the gym is.
③ I think I'm almost recovered from my leg injury.
④ I believe there's something wrong with my skate.
⑤ I'm afraid I can't take part in the competition this time.

....

M: Tina is a speed skater. She is preparing for the local speed skating championship. One week before the competition, she twisted her ankle while exercising alone. She thought she would recover soon, but it got worse. So, she decides to tell her coach, Mr. Duncan that she cannot participate in the competition. In this situation, what would Tina most likely say to Mr. Duncan?

Tina: Mr. Duncan, _____

남: Tina는 스피드스케이트 선수입니다. 그녀는 지역 스피드스케이팅 선수권대회를 준비 중입니다. 대회 일주일 전에, 그녀는 혼자 연습 중에 발목을 삐었습니다. 그녀는 곧 회복할 거라고 생각했지만, 악화되었습니다. 그래서 그녀는 코치 Duncan 선생님께 대회에 참가하지 못한다고 말씀드리기로 결심합니다. 이런 상황에서, Tina는 Duncan 선생님에게 뭐라고 말하겠습니까?

Tina: Duncan 선생님, <u>유감스럽게도 저는 이번 대회에 참가하지 못할 것 같아요.</u>

....

문제 해설 ⑤ Tina는 발목 부상이 악화되어 대회에 참가하지 못한다고 말씀드리기로 결심했다고 했다.

① 대회가 연기되었다고 들었어요.
② 죄송하지만, 체육관이 어딘지 모르겠어요.
③ 저는 다리 부상에서 거의 회복된 것 같아요.
④ 스케이트에 잘못된 게 있는 것 같아요.

유형 분석 14 마지막 말에 이어질 응답 찾기

1 영어로 제시된 선택지를 먼저 보고 의미를 파악해 둔다.
2 대화의 주제와 흐름을 잘 파악하며 듣고, 특히 마지막 말을 주의 깊게 듣는다.
3 대화에 나온 단어나 표현이 포함된 오답 선택지를 성급하게 고르지 않도록 주의한다.

기출 맛보기

대화를 듣고, 여자의 마지막 말에 이어질 남자의 말로 가장 적절한 것을 고르시오.

Man: _____

① I'm sorry, but that's our policy.
② Actually, refunding takes longer.
③ Sure. People like to save money.
④ Well, would you like a larger size?
⑤ Right. This is a good place to shop.

....

M: How can I help you, Ma'am?
W: I'd like to get a refund for this dress I bought here. Here's the receipt.
M: Hmm... your receipt shows that you bought this item three weeks ago.
W: That's right. Is that a problem?
M: I'm afraid so. You can only get a refund for goods within two weeks from the date of purchase. It's clearly written on the receipt.
W: I don't understand. That's nonsense.
M: _____

남: 무엇을 도와드릴까요, 손님?
여: 여기서 산 이 드레스를 환불받고 싶어요. 여기 영수증이에요.
남: 음… 영수증을 보니 이 옷을 3주 전에 구매하셨네요.
여: 맞아요. 그게 문제가 되나요?
남: 죄송하지만 그렇습니다. 구매하신 날로부터 2주 이내의 상품에 대해서만 환불을 받으실 수 있습니다. 영수증에 명확하게 쓰여 있습니다.
여: 이해가 안 되네요. 그건 말도 안 돼요.
남: 죄송하지만, 그것이 저희의 정책입니다.

....

[문제 해설] ① 구입한 지 3주가 지나 환불을 받을 수 없다는 안내를 받고 항의하는 여자에게 할 말로 적절한 것을 찾는다.
② 사실상 환불은 더 오래 걸립니다.
③ 물론입니다. 사람들은 돈을 아끼는 걸 좋아하죠.
④ 음, 더 큰 사이즈로 원하세요?
⑤ 맞아요. 여기는 쇼핑하기 좋은 곳이죠.

• 감사하기   It's very nice of you to say so. 그렇게 말씀해 주셔서 고맙습니다.
                Thank you for helping me. 도와주셔서 고맙습니다.
                I appreciate your concern. 걱정해 주셔서 감사합니다.

• 의견 묻기   Does this suit look good on me? 이 정장이 내게 잘 어울리니?
                Do you like your soup? 네 수프 맛있니?

• 위로하기   Don't be too hard on yourself. 너무 자책하지 마.
                Cheer up! You will do better next time. 기운 내! 다음 번엔 더 잘할 거야.
                Don't blame yourself. 자책하지 마.

• 사과하기   I'm sorry for my mistake. 실수 죄송합니다.
                I apologize for the late response. 답변이 늦어 사과드립니다.

• 요청/부탁하기   Would you wrap this necklace for me? 이 목걸이를 포장해 주실 수 있나요?
                Can you recommend a nice scarf for my mom? 저희 엄마를 위한 좋은 스카프 하나 추천해 주시겠어요?

• 격려하기   I'll keep my fingers crossed for you. 잘 되길 빌게.
                Good luck to you! 행운을 빌어!

• 동의하기   I couldn't agree with you more. 네 말에 전적으로 동의해.
                I'm in favor of that. 찬성이야.

• 반대하기   I don't agree with you. 나는 너에게 동의하지 않아.
                I don't think so. / I don't see it that way. 난 그렇게 생각하지 않아.

기출문제 01회

보통속도듣기

빠르게듣기

01 대화를 듣고, 여자가 구입할 쿠션을 고르시오.

①
②
③

④
⑤

02 대화를 듣고, World Food Festival에 관해 언급되지 않은 것을 고르시오.

① 개최 시기 ② 행사 장소 ③ 프로그램
④ 참가비 ⑤ 기념품

03 대화를 듣고, 여자가 남자에게 전화한 목적으로 가장 적절한 것을 고르시오.

① 포스터 인쇄 부수를 확인하려고
② 포스터 제작 가격을 문의하려고
③ 포스터 제목 색상을 변경하려고
④ 포스터에 학교 로고를 추가하려고
⑤ 포스터에 이메일 주소를 삽입하려고

04 대화를 듣고, 두 사람이 만나기로 한 시각을 고르시오.

① 1 p.m. ② 2 p.m. ③ 3 p.m.
④ 4 p.m. ⑤ 5 p.m.

05 대화를 듣고, 여자의 심정으로 가장 적절한 것을 고르시오.

① proud ② upset ③ scared
④ relieved ⑤ grateful

06 다음 그림의 상황에 가장 적절한 대화를 고르시오.

① ② ③ ④ ⑤

07 대화를 듣고, 여자가 남자에게 부탁한 일로 가장 적절한 것을 고르시오.

① 요리하기 ② 세탁하기
③ 설거지하기 ④ 옷장 정리하기
⑤ 화장실 청소하기

08 다음을 듣고, Andy Cooper에 대해 언급되지 않은 것을 고르시오.

① 출생 년도 ② 성장 환경 ③ 취미 생활
④ 대학 전공 ⑤ 수상 경력

09 다음을 듣고, 무엇에 관한 설명인지 고르시오.

① 골프 ② 축구 ③ 배구
④ 농구 ⑤ 발야구

10 다음을 듣고, 두 사람의 대화가 어색한 것을 고르시오.

① ② ③ ④ ⑤

11 대화를 듣고, 여자가 할 일로 가장 적절한 것을 고르시오.

① 텐트 설치하기 ② 고기 구입하기
③ 여행 가방 챙기기 ④ 캠핑장 예약하기
⑤ 캠핑 의자 대여하기

12 다음 표를 보면서 대화를 듣고, 남자가 구입할 아이스크림 케이크를 고르시오.

	Ice Cream Cake	Shape	Flavor	Message
①	A	kitten	chocolate	X
②	B	kitten	chocolate	O
③	C	kitten	strawberry	X
④	D	puppy	strawberry	O
⑤	E	puppy	chocolate	X

13 대화를 듣고, 두 사람이 만나기로 한 시각을 고르시오.

① 9 a.m. ② 10 a.m. ③ 1 p.m.
④ 5 p.m. ⑤ 6 p.m.

14 대화를 듣고, 여자가 어제 한 일로 가장 적절한 것을 고르시오.

① 사진 촬영하기 ② 휴대폰 구매하기
③ 카메라 수리 맡기기 ④ 대회 참가 신청하기
⑤ 사진전 포스터 제작하기

15 다음을 듣고, 방송의 목적으로 가장 적절한 것을 고르시오.

① 학교 규칙을 설명하려고
② 학생회 가입을 홍보하려고
③ 행사 장소 변경을 공지하려고
④ 행사 참여 방법을 안내하려고
⑤ 감사 표현의 중요성을 강조하려고

16 대화를 듣고, 남자가 지불할 금액을 고르시오.

① $40 ② $70 ③ $105
④ $110 ⑤ $115

17 대화를 듣고, 남자의 마지막 말에 대한 여자의 응답으로 가장 적절한 것을 고르시오.

Woman: _____

① Okay. Let's walk to the car together.
② Yeah. I'd like to take a walk with you.
③ All right. I'll wait here until you come.
④ Good idea. I'll call a taxi to pick us up.
⑤ Sure. I'll get the car and be right back.

[18 - 19] 대화를 듣고, 여자의 마지막 말에 대한 남자의 응답으로 가장 적절한 것을 고르시오.

18 Man: _____

① Thanks. But I already have a good one.
② Don't worry. Here's my home address.
③ Not yet. I still need to practice more.
④ Sounds good. I'll be back tomorrow.
⑤ Great. Please send it to me now.

19 Man: _____

① Sure. I'll see you on Friday.
② Okay. I'll be there at that time.
③ I'm sorry. You can't join that club.
④ Yes. I'm interested in the music club.
⑤ No. The library is not open on Wednesday.

20 다음 상황 설명을 듣고, Ryan이 Ms. Amy에게 할 말로 가장 적절한 것을 고르시오.

Ryan: Ms. Amy, _____

① could you turn off the air conditioner for a while?
② I'm worried that it's too noisy in the library.
③ when did you clean the air conditioner?
④ is it okay to copy this science book?
⑤ I think the air conditioner is broken.

Dictation Test 01

정답 및 해설 pp. 02~06

보통속도듣기 빠르게 듣기

01 그림 정보 파악

대화를 듣고, 여자가 구입할 쿠션을 고르시오.

① ② ③

④ ⑤

M: Hello, ma'am. What can I do for you?

W: Hi, I'd like to buy a cushion.

M: All right. These are the ones we have. There are square- and heart-shaped ones.

W: Oh, I like 1) _____ _____ _____. I'll get one of them.

M: Okay. And there are two styles, plain and striped.

W: Well, I 2) _____ _____ _____ _____.

M: All right. One of them has the word 'LOVE' on it.

W: I prefer 3) _____ _____ _____ _____. I'll take this one.

M: Okay.

02 언급되지 않은 내용 찾기

대화를 듣고, World Food Festival에 관해 언급되지 <u>않은</u> 것을 고르시오.

① 개최 시기 ② 행사 장소 ③ 프로그램
④ 참가비 ⑤ 기념품

W: Honey, look at this poster about the World Food Festival.

M: Oh, that's an annual festival 1) _____ _____ _____ _____, right?

W: Yes. This year, it'll be held at the Seoul Grand Hotel. So we can go.

M: Great. Will there be 2) _____ _____ _____ _____?

W: Oh, here it says there's a cooking program.

M: Cool. Our kids would love it.

W: Yeah. And tickets are 3) _____ _____ _____ _____ if we get them by next weekend.

M: Okay! Let's buy them today!

03 목적 파악 🇬🇧

대화를 듣고, 여자가 남자에게 전화한 목적으로
가장 적절한 것을 고르시오.

① 포스터 인쇄 부수를 확인하려고
② 포스터 제작 가격을 문의하려고
③ 포스터 제목 색상을 변경하려고
④ 포스터에 학교 로고를 추가하려고
⑤ 포스터에 이메일 주소를 삽입하려고

★ **Focus on Sound   bright**

gh는 묵음이어서 [브라이트]로 발음된다.

[Telephone rings.]

M: Hello, this is 24 Design Office.

W: Hi, I'm calling from Top Middle School. I got the poster you sent by e-mail.

M: Okay. What do you think?

W: It's good, but I'd like to 1)_____ _____ _____ _____.

M: Sure. Let me know what it is.

W: The color of the poster title isn't *bright enough. It's 2)_____ _____ _____.

M: I see what you mean.

W: I'm thinking yellow would be better.

M: I agree. I'll 3)_____ _____ _____ of the title from grey to yellow.

W: Thanks.

---

04 숫자 정보 파악

대화를 듣고, 두 사람이 만나기로 한 시각을 고르시오.

① 1 p.m.   ② 2 p.m.   ③ 3 p.m.
④ 4 p.m.   ⑤ 5 p.m.

W: Good afternoon, Mr. Lee. Do you have a minute?

M: Sure. What is it?

W: Would you be able to 1)_____ _____ _____ on my essay?

M: Sure. But I'm on my way to a teachers' meeting. Can you 2)_____ _____ _____ _____ _____ tomorrow?

W: I'm afraid I have an after-school class then. Are you free at 5 p.m.?

M: Let me see. *[pause]* I'm meeting with another student then. Can you 3)_____ _____ _____ _____?

W: Yes. Thank you. I'll see you then.

대화를 듣고, 여자의 심정으로 가장 적절한 것을 고르시오.

① proud ② upset ③ scared
④ relieved ⑤ grateful

M: Here you are. Enjoy your meal.

W: Um... Excuse me, this isn't what I ordered.

M: Really? Let me check. *[pause]* Oh, my!

W: What happened?

M: I'm so sorry. It looks like the cook [1) _____ _____ _____ _____.]

W: Are you serious? I've already waited longer than 20 minutes.

M: Today's been really busy. I'm very sorry.

W: So, do I have to [2) _____ _____ _____ _____ _____]?

M: I'm afraid it'll [3) _____ _____ _____ _____.]

W: I can't believe it!

다음 그림의 상황에 가장 적절한 대화를 고르시오.

① ② ③ ④ ⑤

① M: Good morning, how may I help you?

　W: [1) _____ _____ _____ _____] a pizza.

② M: Can you put those books in the correct place?

　W: Sure. I'll do that right away.

③ M: Would you like to [2) _____ _____ _____] or get a refund?

　W: I'd like to return them.

④ M: These bags are so heavy.

　W: Let me help you carry them.

⑤ M: [3) _____ _____ _____]. Have a nice day.

　W: Thank you. You, too.

대화를 듣고, 여자가 남자에게 부탁한 일로 가장 적절한 것을 고르시오.

① 요리하기　　　　② 세탁하기
③ 설거지하기　　　④ 옷장 정리하기
⑤ 화장실 청소하기

M: Hey. What are you doing?

W: I'm cooking for Mom and Dad because it's Parents' Day.

M: They'll like that. I [1) _____ _____ _____ _____,] too.

W: Well, I'm also planning on doing the laundry and [2) _____ _____ _____ _____]. Would you like to do one of those things?

M: Yeah. Which should I do?

W: Can you [3) _____ _____ _____] while I clean the bathroom?

M: Sure. Of course.

다음을 듣고, Andy Cooper에 대해 언급되지 않은 것을 고르시오.

① 출생 년도 ② 성장 환경 ③ 취미 생활
④ 대학 전공 ⑤ 수상 경력

W: Hello, class. Today we'll learn about Andy Cooper, the writer of the popular novel *Miracle*. He 1) _____ _____ _____ Washington in 1969. He grew up in a poor family. But he found hope and joy in books. His hobby was 2) _____ _____ _____ _____. When he was 19, he became 3) _____ _____ _____ of the National Book Award. Now he's thought of as the best writer of the 20th century.

---

09 화제 파악

다음을 듣고, 무엇에 관한 설명인지 고르시오.

① 골프   ② 축구   ③ 배구
④ 농구   ⑤ 발야구

M: This is a team sport. It's one of the most popular sports in the world. Two teams play together. They usually play on a 1) _____ _____ _____. Players pass a ball to each other 2) _____ _____ _____. Most of them can't touch the ball 3) _____ _____ _____. Among the 11 players on a team, only one player can touch the ball with their hands. To score, players kick or head the ball 4) _____ _____ _____ _____.

---

10 어색한 대화 찾기 🇬🇧

다음을 듣고, 두 사람의 대화가 어색한 것을 고르시오.

①   ②   ③   ④   ⑤

① M: What's your favorite type of tea?
   W: They sell different kinds of tea.
② M: 1) _____ _____ _____ _____ _____ to get to Daegu?
   W: It takes about two hours by train.
③ M: I 2) _____ _____ _____ _____ my best friend this weekend.
   W: You must be happy to see her.
④ M: Can we meet at 10 o'clock?
   W: I'm afraid I can't. I have a swimming lesson.
⑤ M: I can't believe I 3) _____ _____ _____.
   W: Cheer up! You'll do much better next time.

11 할 일 파악

대화를 듣고, 여자가 할 일로 가장 적절한 것을 고르시오.

① 텐트 설치하기　　② 고기 구입하기
③ 여행 가방 챙기기　④ 캠핑장 예약하기
⑤ 캠핑 의자 대여하기

★Focus on Sound　excited to

[d]는 자음 앞에서 거의 발음되지 않아 [익싸이티드 투]가 아닌 [익싸이리투]로 발음된다.

M: Honey, I'm so ★excited to go camping tomorrow.
W: Me, too. Have you 1) _____ _____ _____ and sleeping bags?
M: Yes, I did.
W: Excellent. What about the camping chairs and table?
M: I 2) _____ _____ _____ _____ _____ already.
W: Good. We still have to get the most important thing we need, the meat for the barbecue!
M: Right. Let's 3) _____ _____ _____ _____ _____ .
W: I'll do it myself now. You've done a lot already.
M: Okay. Thanks.

12 도표 파악

다음 표를 보면서 대화를 듣고, 남자가 구입할 아이스크림 케이크를 고르시오.

	Ice Cream Cake	Shape	Flavor	Message
①	A	kitten	chocolate	X
②	B	kitten	chocolate	O
③	C	kitten	strawberry	X
④	D	puppy	strawberry	O
⑤	E	puppy	chocolate	X

W: Hi, how may I help you?
M: Hello, I'm looking for an ice cream cake for my three-year-old daughter.
W: Alright. We have these puppy- and kitten-shaped ones for kids that age.
M: She really likes cats, so I'll 1) _____ _____ _____ _____ _____ .
W: Okay. They 2) _____ _____ _____ _____ , chocolate and strawberry.
M: She 3) _____ _____ _____ _____ . So I'll take a chocolate one.
W: Sure. Do you want a message on the cake?
M: No, thanks.
W: Okay. I'll get that ready for you.

13 숫자 정보 파악

대화를 듣고, 두 사람이 만나기로 한 시각을 고르시오.

① 9 a.m.   ② 10 a.m.   ③ 1 p.m.
④ 5 p.m.   ⑤ 6 p.m.

[Cell phone rings.]

M: Hey, Sarah.

W: Hi, Andy. I was 1) _____ _____ _____ _____ _____ tomorrow. Can you join me?

M: Sounds fun. When are you going?

W: I was thinking 10 a.m. 2) _____ _____ _____ then?

M: I'm afraid not. I promised to help my sister with her project. What about 1 p.m.?

W: I'm having lunch with Emily at that time. 3) _____ _____ _____ _____ ?

M: Yeah. See you then in front of the school.

14 한 일 파악

대화를 듣고, 여자가 어제 한 일로 가장 적절한 것을 고르시오.

① 사진 촬영하기   ② 휴대폰 구매하기
③ 카메라 수리 맡기기   ④ 대회 참가 신청하기
⑤ 사진전 포스터 제작하기

W: Hey, Dan. What's up?

M: Hi, Stacy. Have you heard about the school photo contest?

W: Yeah. I saw a poster for it a couple of days ago. I'm 1) _____ _____ _____ _____.

M: I thought you would. Have you started taking pictures?

W: Not yet. I can't because the screen on my camera is broken.

M: Oh, no! Are you 2) _____ _____ _____ ?

W: Yeah. I took my camera 3) _____ _____ _____ _____ yesterday.

M: I hope they fix it quickly so you can start taking pictures.

15 목적 파악 🇬🇧

다음을 듣고, 방송의 목적으로 가장 적절한 것을 고르시오.

① 학교 규칙을 설명하려고
② 학생회 가입을 홍보하려고
③ 행사 장소 변경을 공지하려고
④ 행사 참여 방법을 안내하려고
⑤ 감사 표현의 중요성을 강조하려고

M: Good afternoon! This is Teo from the student council. This Friday is Friendship Day. There will be a special event. To take part in it, write a 1) _____ _____ _____ _____ to a friend. Then 2) _____ _____ _____ _____ before lunch. You can 3) _____ _____ _____ _____ there to give your friend with the letter. Thank you very much.

16 숫자 정보 파악

대화를 듣고, 남자가 지불할 금액을 고르시오.

① $40   ② $70   ③ $105
④ $110   ⑤ $115

W: Welcome to Blue Swimming Pool. How may I help you?

M: Hello. I'd like to sign up myself and my son for swimming classes.

W: Alright. How old is your son?

M: He's eight.

W: Okay. The adult class is ¹⁾ _____ _____ and the child class is ²⁾ _____ _____.

M: Alright. Is there a discount if we ³⁾ _____ _____ _____?

W: Yes. You'll ⁴⁾ _____ _____ _____ _____ the total.

M: Great. Then, I'll sign up both of us for the classes. Here's my credit card.

17 마지막 말에 이어질 응답 찾기

대화를 듣고, 남자의 마지막 말에 대한 여자의 응답으로 가장 적절한 것을 고르시오.

Woman: _____

① Okay. Let's walk to the car together.
② Yeah. I'd like to take a walk with you.
③ All right. I'll wait here until you come.
④ Good idea. I'll call a taxi to pick us up.
⑤ Sure. I'll get the car and be right back.

M: Nancy, I'm relieved that the doctor said your ankle isn't too bad.

W: Me, too. Dad.

M: ¹⁾ _____ _____ _____ _____ _____ while I go get the car?

W: Oh, so do you want me to stay here?

M: Yeah. This would be good for you.

W: Well, I ²⁾ _____ _____ _____ to the car.

M: You should try to avoid walking. ³⁾ _____ _____ _____ in a few minutes.

W: All right. I'll wait here until you come.

18 마지막 말에 이어질 응답 찾기

대화를 듣고, 여자의 마지막 말에 대한 남자의 응답으로 가장 적절한 것을 고르시오.

Man: _____

① Thanks. But I already have a good one.
② Don't worry. Here's my home address.
③ Not yet. I still need to practice more.
④ Sounds good. I'll be back tomorrow.
⑤ Great. Please send it to me now.

W: Tom, what after-school class did you sign up for?

M: Tennis class. How about you?

W: I'm taking that, too!

M: Great! Did you see that you need to ¹⁾ _____ _____ _____ _____?

W: Yeah. So I ²⁾ _____ _____ _____ yesterday.

M: From what website? I need to buy one, too.

W: I can't remember. ³⁾ _____ _____ _____ _____ _____ on my phone. *[pause]* Oh, I found it.

M: Great. Please send it to me now.

---

19 마지막 말에 이어질 응답 찾기

대화를 듣고, 여자의 마지막 말에 대한 남자의 응답으로 가장 적절한 것을 고르시오.

Man: _____

① Sure. I'll see you on Friday.
② Okay. I'll be there at that time.
③ I'm sorry. You can't join that club.
④ Yes. I'm interested in the music club.
⑤ No. The library is not open on Wednesday.

W: Toby, this article says teenagers don't read many books these days.

M: That's not surprising. I tried reading more books earlier this year, but I couldn't do it.

W: I've been able to read more since I ¹⁾ _____ _____ _____ _____ a couple of months ago.

M: Really?

W: Yeah. It ²⁾ _____ _____ _____ _____ because you get to share your feelings about them with others.

M: Sounds interesting! I'd like to join.

W: Everyone is welcome to join. We ³⁾ _____ _____ _____ at 3 p.m. in the library.

M: Okay. I'll be there at that time.

---

20 상황에 적절한 말 찾기

다음 상황 설명을 듣고, Ryan이 Ms. Amy에게 할 말로 가장 적절한 것을 고르시오.

Ryan: Ms. Amy, _____

① could you turn off the air conditioner for a while?
② I'm worried that it's too noisy in the library.
③ when did you clean the air conditioner?
④ is it okay to copy this science book?
⑤ I think the air conditioner is broken.

M: Ryan is a middle school student. Today, he's studying in the school library for his English test. Ms. Amy, the librarian, ¹⁾ _____ _____ _____ _____ _____ because it's too hot. After a few hours, Ryan ²⁾ _____ _____ _____. So he would like to ask Ms. Amy if she could ³⁾ _____ _____ _____ _____ for a short time. In this situation, what would Ryan most likely say to Ms. Amy?

보통 속도 듣기

빠르게 듣기

기출문제 02회

01 대화를 듣고, 여자가 구입할 자전거를 고르시오.

① ② ③

④ ⑤

02 대화를 듣고, Calming Soap에 관해 언급되지 <u>않</u>은 것을 고르시오.

① 효과 ② 무게 ③ 향기 ④ 가격 ⑤ 모양

03 대화를 듣고, 남자가 여자에게 전화한 목적으로 가장 적절한 것을 고르시오.

① 양말을 구매하려고
② 할인 쿠폰을 사용하려고
③ 신발의 사이즈를 변경하려고
④ 온라인 주문 방법을 문의하려고
⑤ 잘못 배송된 신발을 교환받으려고

04 대화를 듣고, 남자가 선택한 수업의 시작 시각을 고르시오.

① 2 p.m. ② 3 p.m. ③ 4 p.m.
④ 5 p.m. ⑤ 6 p.m.

05 대화를 듣고, 여자의 심정으로 가장 적절한 것을 고르시오.

① bored ② excited ③ concerned
④ relieved ⑤ satisfied

06 다음 그림의 상황에 가장 적절한 대화를 고르시오.

① ② ③ ④ ⑤

07 대화를 듣고, 여자가 남자에게 부탁한 일로 가장 적절한 것을 고르시오.

① 식사 주문하기   ② 예약 변경하기
③ 주방 정리하기   ④ 배달 요청하기
⑤ 재료 준비하기

08 다음을 듣고, 졸업식에 관해 언급되지 <u>않</u>은 것을 고르시오.

① 날짜   ② 장소   ③ 복장
④ 졸업 인원   ⑤ 특별 공연

09 다음을 듣고, 무엇에 관한 설명인지 고르시오.

① 김밥   ② 커피   ③ 핫도그
④ 컵라면   ⑤ 샌드위치

10 다음을 듣고, 두 사람의 대화가 <u>어색한</u> 것을 고르시오.

① ② ③ ④ ⑤

11 대화를 듣고, 남자가 할 일로 가장 적절한 것을 고르시오.

① 책 반납하기   ② 병문안 가기
③ 인터넷 검색하기   ④ 과학 과제 하기
⑤ 스케이트보드 타기

12 다음 학교 건물 배치도를 보면서 대화를 듣고, 두 사람이 선택할 동아리 부스 구역을 고르시오.

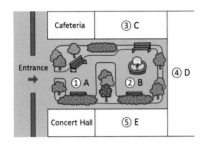

13 대화를 듣고, 두 사람이 영화를 보기로 한 시각을 고르시오.

① 1 p.m.   ② 3 p.m.   ③ 4 p.m.
④ 6 p.m.   ⑤ 7 p.m.

14 대화를 듣고, 남자가 어제 한 일로 가장 적절한 것을 고르시오.

① 쿠키 굽기   ② 생일 파티 하기
③ 생일 카드 쓰기   ④ 컵케이크 만들기
⑤ 할머니 뵈러 가기

15 다음을 듣고, 방송의 목적으로 가장 적절한 것을 고르시오.

① 특별 티켓을 홍보하려고
② 습득된 분실물을 알리려고
③ 웹사이트 주소를 안내하려고
④ 탑승 안전 수칙을 설명하려고
⑤ 운영 시간 변경을 공지하려고

16 대화를 듣고, 여자가 지불할 금액을 고르시오.

① $20   ② $30   ③ $40   ④ $50   ⑤ $70

17 대화를 듣고, 여자의 마지막 말에 대한 남자의 응답으로 가장 적절한 것을 고르시오.

Man: _____

① No, I don't like history class.
② Sure. You can go shopping now.
③ Okay. Let's talk to her this afternoon.
④ Well, I'm not sure if we can take her class.
⑤ Of course! I knew they would make a great team.

[18 - 19] 대화를 듣고, 남자의 마지막 말에 대한 여자의 응답으로 가장 적절한 것을 고르시오.

18 Woman: _____

① I'm sorry, but I can't make it to lunch.
② My friend is a famous Chinese chef.
③ I don't feel like eating noodles today.
④ Sounds great. I'll make a reservation.
⑤ I'm going on a business trip to Vietnam.

19 Woman: _____

① I think I should gain some weight.
② Sure. I'd love to play with you guys!
③ You need to control your diet to stay healthy.
④ No, thank you. I don't like to exercise in the morning.
⑤ I recommend that you start playing badminton every day.

20 다음 상황 설명을 듣고, Mr. Lee가 Mina에게 할 말로 가장 적절한 것을 고르시오.

Mr. Lee: Mina, _____

① isn't this theater too cold?
② you should believe in yourself.
③ you could have practiced more.
④ did you do your music homework?
⑤ I didn't know you joined this contest.

01 [그림 정보 파악]

대화를 듣고, 여자가 구입할 자전거를 고르시오.

① 　② 　③

④ 　⑤

M: Hello, may I help you?

W: Hi. I'm looking for a bicycle for my seven-year-old son.

M: Okay. Would you like a bicycle with or without a basket?

W: Um... I guess a 1) _____ _____ _____ would be more convenient.

M: Alright. Then, you can choose one from these. We have ones with stripes and without them. They are all popular.

W: They all look nice, but the 2) _____ _____ _____ _____ _____.

M: Good choice! Now, do you need one with training wheels in the back?

W: Yes. He just started learning how to ride a bicycle. So, I'll take the one 3) _____ _____ _____.

M: Okay. I hope your son likes this bicycle.

02 [언급되지 않은 내용 찾기]

대화를 듣고, Calming Soap에 관해 언급되지 않은 것을 고르시오.

① 효과　② 무게　③ 향기　④ 가격　⑤ 모양

★**Focus on Sound** scent

c는 묵음이어서 [쎈트]로 발음된다.

M: Hey, Laura. You've tried Calming Soap before, right?

W: Yes, I use it all the time. Why?

M: I'm thinking of getting some soap for Irene's birthday.

W: Good idea. It's well known for 1) _____ _____ _____.

M: Really? Irene said she wanted something just like that.

W: Then, she'll love it. You can find many different ★scents at the shop. All the soaps 2) _____ _____ _____, but lavender is my favorite.

M: Good to know. Do you know how much it is?

W: Yeah. It's 3) _____ _____ _____, but it's totally worth it.

M: Oh, I see. Do they come in different shapes?

W: Sure. There are 4) _____ _____ _____ _____ you can choose from.

M: Okay, thanks.

03 목적 파악 🇬🇧

대화를 듣고, 남자가 여자에게 전화한 목적으로 가장 적절한 것을 고르시오.

① 양말을 구매하려고
② 할인 쿠폰을 사용하려고
③ 신발의 사이즈를 변경하려고
④ 온라인 주문 방법을 문의하려고
⑤ 잘못 배송된 신발을 교환받으려고

[Telephone rings.]

W: Hello. This is Gentlemen Shoes Company.

M: Hello, I 1) _____ _____ _____ _____ _____ _____ online, but I got white ones instead. Can you send me the black ones that I ordered?

W: Oh, really? What is your order number?

M: Let me check. *[pause]* It's AB213.

W: *[typing sound]* Oh, I think 2) _____ _____ _____ _____ _____ . We're very sorry for the inconvenience. We'll collect the white shoes and send you a new pair of black ones as soon as possible.

M: Okay. Please 3) _____ _____ _____ _____ _____ this time.

W: Of course! And we'll also send you a 20 percent discount coupon for a future order. We apologize, again.

M: That's okay. Thanks for the coupon.

04 숫자 정보 파악

대화를 듣고, 남자가 선택한 수업의 시작 시각을 고르시오.

① 2 p.m.   ② 3 p.m.   ③ 4 p.m.
④ 5 p.m.   ⑤ 6 p.m.

W: Hi, welcome to the community center. How may I help you?

M: Hi! I hear that you offer hiphop dance classes. 1) _____ _____ _____ ?

W: Yes, they are. We have two classes on Friday. Class A begins at 3 p.m. and Class B at 6 p.m. Both last for two hours.

M: Um... I can't take Class A because I 2) _____ _____ _____ p.m.

W: Then, it looks like you have just one option. Do you want to register?

M: Yes, I'll choose Class B that 3) _____ _____ _____ p.m.

W: Good. Please fill out this form.

M: Alright.

대화를 듣고, 여자의 심정으로 가장 적절한 것을 고르시오.

① bored   ② excited   ③ concerned
④ relieved   ⑤ satisfied

M: Hello, Olivia. What's up?

W: I got selected as a member of the student council.

M: Wow! Good for you!

W: But 1) _____ _____ because I don't know anyone on the council. I've never done anything like this before.

M: Come on. You'll do great and 2) _____ _____ _____ _____.

W: What if I 3) _____ _____ _____ _____ the other members?

M: You'll be fine. You're smart, funny, and friendly. Be confident!

W: I don't know. 4) _____ _____ _____.

---

06 그림 상황에 적절한 대화 찾기

다음 그림의 상황에 가장 적절한 대화를 고르시오.

①   ②   ③   ④   ⑤

① M: Do you need any help?
  W: I want to get that book, but I 1) _____ _____ _____.
② M: Can you book the tickets for me?
  W: Sure. How many do you need?
③ M: When can you come to the bookstore?
  W: Well, I think I 2) _____ _____ _____ in 10 minutes.
④ M: What are you doing?
  W: I'm making a bookshelf for my daughter.
⑤ M: Let's start swimming now.
  W: Wait! We 3) _____ _____ _____ first.

---

07 부탁한 일 파악

대화를 듣고, 여자가 남자에게 부탁한 일로 가장 적절한 것을 고르시오.

① 식사 주문하기   ② 예약 변경하기
③ 주방 정리하기   ④ 배달 요청하기
⑤ 재료 준비하기

[Cell phone rings.]

W: Darling, have you arrived at the restaurant yet?

M: I'm almost there. How about you?

W: I'm sorry, but I think I'm going to 1) _____ _____.

M: It's okay. You don't need to hurry. Do you want me to 2) _____ _____ _____?

W: No. Can you please 3) _____ _____ _____ first? I'm so hungry.

M: Okay. What do you want?

W: I'd like roast beef and a baked potato.

M: Good. Anything else?

W: No, that's all. See you soon.

08 언급되지 않은 내용 찾기

다음을 듣고, 졸업식에 관해 언급되지 <u>않은</u> 것을 고르시오.

① 날짜 ② 장소 ③ 복장
④ 졸업 인원 ⑤ 특별 공연

W: Hello, fellow students. I'm Jia Park, the head of the graduation ceremony committee. As you know, the ceremony is 1) _____ _____, _____ _____ at 10 a.m. It'll be held in the school gym. Graduating students 2) _____ _____ _____ on that day. The school music band will 3) _____ _____ _____ _____. Further notice will be given early next week. Thank you.

09 화제 파악

다음을 듣고, 무엇에 관한 설명인지 고르시오.

① 김밥 ② 커피 ③ 핫도그
④ 컵라면 ⑤ 샌드위치

M: This is enjoyed by many people. You can eat this 1) _____ _____ _____ when you're busy. It comes in different tastes and sizes. You usually 2) _____ _____ _____ _____. These days, many convenience stores provide small tables for customers to eat this. To make this, you 3) _____ _____ _____, put in the soup powder, and pour in some boiled water. Then, you simply cover the lid and wait for about three minutes. Now, you are ready to enjoy this.

10 어색한 대화 찾기 🇬🇧

다음을 듣고, 두 사람의 대화가 <u>어색한</u> 것을 고르시오.

① ② ③ ④ ⑤

① W: Is everything okay? You look tired.
   M: I couldn't sleep well last night because it was too hot.
② W: Do you want to play chess?
   M: Can we play later? I'm 1) _____ _____ _____ with my homework.
③ W: Could you 2) _____ _____ _____ _____ to school in your car?
   M: Sure. Let's walk to school together.
④ W: 3) _____ _____ _____ _____ the window?
   M: Not at all. We need some fresh air.
⑤ W: I think I 4) _____ _____ _____ _____ this time.
   M: I'm sure you can. You've studied so hard for it.

11 할 일 파악

대화를 듣고, 남자가 할 일로 가장 적절한 것을 고르시오.

① 책 반납하기   ② 병문안 가기
③ 인터넷 검색하기   ④ 과학 과제 하기
⑤ 스케이트보드 타기

W: Hi, Peter! Where are you going?

M: Hi, Julie. I'm heading to the library.

W: Oh, I see. What for?

M: My younger sister 1) _____ _____ _____ _____ _____. She broke her leg and she cannot go anywhere for a while.

W: What happened?

M: She 2) _____ _____ _____.

W: Oh, I hope it's not too serious. So, are you going to get some books for her?

M: No, I'm just going to 3) _____ _____ _____ _____ that she borrowed. 4) _____ _____ _____.

W: I see. I hope she gets well soon.

M: Thanks.

12 위치 찾기

다음 학교 건물 배치도를 보면서 대화를 듣고, 두 사람이 선택할 동아리 부스 구역을 고르시오.

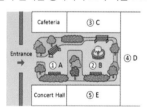

M: Minhee! Let's decide where to set up our club booth for the school festival.

W: Sure! Let's look at the map. *[pause]* How about Section B? It's in the garden.

M: Yeah, but I think it'll be 1) _____ _____ _____ _____.

W: Good point. Then, Section A is also not a good option. How about Section C? It's next to the cafeteria.

M: Let me see. It seems that all the booths in Section C are already taken. So, we have to choose from the two remaining options.

W: Well, Section D is 2) _____ _____ _____ _____ _____.

M: I agree. Then, we only have the one section left that's 3) _____ _____ _____ _____ _____.

W: Right. Many people can come to that area.

M: Good. Let's choose that section.

13 숫자 정보 파악

대화를 듣고, 두 사람이 영화를 보기로 한 시각을 고르시오.

① 1 p.m. ② 3 p.m. ③ 4 p.m.
④ 6 p.m. ⑤ 7 p.m.

*Focus on Sound   the evening

모음 앞의 the는 [디]로 발음된다.

W: Taemin! I'm so excited that the movie, *Space Adventure* is finally released!

M: I know. We have to watch it in 3D.

W: I agree. How about watching it together on Saturday?

M: Sounds good. Let me check the times on my phone. *[pause]* Saturday 1) _____ _____ _____ _____ _____ _____ looks good.

W: How about at 4 p.m.?

M: Oh, the tickets for the 4 p.m. movie 2) _____ _____ _____ _____ . Let's try 1 p.m.

W: But then, we won't have 3) _____ _____ _____ _____ . What about in *the evening?

M: Well... There's one at 6 p.m., but it's not in 3D. Do you still want to watch it?

W: No. Are there any other options?

M: 4) _____ _____ _____ _____ _____ , and it's in 3D.

W: Okay, let's watch that one.

14 한 일 파악

대화를 듣고, 남자가 어제 한 일로 가장 적절한 것을 고르시오.

① 쿠키 굽기 ② 생일 파티 하기
③ 생일 카드 쓰기 ④ 컵케이크 만들기
⑤ 할머니 뵈러 가기

W: Nick, how was your mom's birthday party last Friday?

M: It went well. She especially loved the 1) _____ _____ _____ _____ _____ .

W: Oh, you made them?

M: Yeah. I followed my grandmother's recipe.

W: Wow! Anything left? I 2) _____ _____ _____ _____ .

M: Sorry, we ate all the cupcakes over the weekend. But I 3) _____ _____ _____ . I can give you some of the cookies if you want.

W: That would be awesome!

M: Okay. See you after school.

15 목적 파악

다음을 듣고, 방송의 목적으로 가장 적절한 것을 고르시오.

① 특별 티켓을 홍보하려고
② 습득된 분실물을 알리려고
③ 웹사이트 주소를 안내하려고
④ 탑승 안전 수칙을 설명하려고
⑤ 운영 시간 변경을 공지하려고

M: Good afternoon, everyone. I hope everyone is having a good time at our amusement park, Fantasy Land. To help you save time waiting in line, we're 1) _____ _____ _____ _____ called Express Rider. With this ticket, you can go to the front of the line 2) _____ _____ _____ . The tickets are 10 dollars each. You can use this ticket five times on any ride. If you're interested, you can 3) _____ _____ _____ _____ _____ _____ or on our website. If you have any questions, please contact our customer service at 1800−3121. Thank you.

16 숫자 정보 파악

대화를 듣고, 여자가 지불할 금액을 고르시오.

① $20   ② $30   ③ $40
④ $50   ⑤ $70

M: Hi! Do you need any help?

W: Hi. I like this T-shirt. How much is it?

M: It's 20 dollars, and there's a special promotion. If you buy one, you 1) _____ _____ _____ _____ _____ .

W: Two for 20 dollars? 2) _____ _____ _____ _____ ! I'll get these two T-shirts.

M: Good choice! 3) _____ _____ _____ _____ . Is there anything else you need?

W: Yes. I'm also looking for a skirt. *[pause]* Um... How much is this?

M: 4) _____ _____ _____ .

W: Good. I'll buy this skirt as well.

M: Okay. Let me help you pay at the counter.

17 마지막 말에 이어질 응답 찾기 🇬🇧

대화를 듣고, 여자의 마지막 말에 대한 남자의 응답으로 가장 적절한 것을 고르시오.

Man: _____

① No, I don't like history class.
② Sure. You can go shopping now.
③ Okay. Let's talk to her this afternoon.
④ Well, I'm not sure if we can take her class.
⑤ Of course! I knew they would make a great team.

*Focus on Sound   neighborhood

gh는 묵음이어서 [네이버후드]로 발음된다.

W: Darren, how's your project going so far?

M: You mean Ms. Green's social studies project?

W: Yes. I decided to make a *neighborhood map indicating the local shops.

M: That's awesome! I'm going to interview the owners of the local shops to hear about the 1) _____ _____ _____ .

W: Hey, I have an idea. Why don't we 2) _____ _____ _____ _____ ?

M: That's a good idea. But, wasn't it an individual project? I'm not sure if it's possible.

W: I think we should ask Ms. Green if we can 3) _____ _____ _____ _____ _____ .

M: Okay. Let's talk to her this afternoon.

18 마지막 말에 이어질 응답 찾기

대화를 듣고, 남자의 마지막 말에 대한 여자의 응답으로 가장 적절한 것을 고르시오.

Woman: _____

① I'm sorry, but I can't make it to lunch.
② My friend is a famous Chinese chef.
③ I don't feel like eating noodles today.
④ Sounds great. I'll make a reservation.
⑤ I'm going on a business trip to Vietnam.

[Cell phone rings.]

M: Hi, Honey. How was your day?

W: It was a long day. Why don't we ¹⁾ _____ _____ ?

M: Sure. How about Chinese or Vietnamese?

W: Um... We had Chinese food last week. I ²⁾ _____ _____ _____ Vietnamese.

M: Okay. Let's ³⁾ _____ _____ _____ _____ .

W: Yeah, I really want to have some noodles and spring rolls.

M: I like them, too. Let's try the new Vietnamese restaurant that just opened down the street.

W: <u>Sounds great. I'll make a reservation.</u>

---

19 마지막 말에 이어질 응답 찾기

대화를 듣고, 남자의 마지막 말에 대한 여자의 응답으로 가장 적절한 것을 고르시오.

Woman: _____

① I think I should gain some weight.
② Sure. I'd love to play with you guys!
③ You need to control your diet to stay healthy.
④ No, thank you. I don't like to exercise in the morning.
⑤ I recommend that you start playing badminton every day.

W: Hi, Mark! You look great!

M: Thanks. I'm exercising a lot these days.

W: Good for you. I also have to ¹⁾ _____ _____ _____ to stay healthy. What kind of exercises do you do?

M: I play badminton in the school gym every day after all my classes.

W: Wow! Who do you play with?

M: I play with Alice and Jake. We're ²⁾ _____ _____ _____ _____ _____ .

W: Cool! I want to play badminton, too.

M: Really? Do you ³⁾ _____ _____ _____ _____ ? We're actually looking for another player.

W: <u>Sure. I'd love to play with you guys!</u>

---

20 상황에 적절한 말 찾기

다음 상황 설명을 듣고, Mr. Lee가 Mina에게 할 말로 가장 적절한 것을 고르시오.

Mr. Lee: Mina, _____

① isn't this theater too cold?
② you should believe in yourself.
③ you could have practiced more.
④ did you do your music homework?
⑤ I didn't know you joined this contest.

W: Mr. Lee is a high school music teacher. He is coaching one of his students, Mina for the local singing contest. Mina ¹⁾ _____ _____ _____ for more than two months. On the day of the contest, Mr. Lee finds out that Mina is ²⁾ _____ _____ _____ while waiting for her turn. So, Mr. Lee would like to tell her that she ³⁾ _____ _____ _____ _____ . In this situation, what would Mr. Lee most likely say to Mina?

능률 중학영어듣기
모의고사 22회
Level 3

실전모의고사 01회

정답 및 해설 pp. 10~15

점수: /20

보통속도 듣기 빠르게 듣기

01 대화를 듣고, 두 사람이 구입할 생일 카드를 고르시오.

①   ②   ③

④   ⑤

02 대화를 듣고, 두 사람이 보고 있는 온라인 상점에 관해 언급되지 <u>않은</u> 것을 고르시오.

① 제품 종류 　　　② 제품 품질
③ 배송료 　　　　④ 고객 후기
⑤ 수익금 사용처

03 대화를 듣고, 남자가 여자에게 전화한 목적으로 가장 적절한 것을 고르시오.

① 방 정리를 부탁하려고
② 만날 장소를 정하려고
③ 부엌 청소를 부탁하려고
④ 저녁 식사 준비를 부탁하려고
⑤ 지갑을 집에 두고 왔는지 확인하려고

04 대화를 듣고, 여자가 식당을 예약한 시각을 고르시오.

① 2:00 p.m.　② 2:30 p.m.　③ 3:00 p.m.
④ 3:30 p.m.　⑤ 5:30 p.m.

05 대화를 듣고, 남자의 심정으로 가장 적절한 것을 고르시오.

① angry　　② lonely　　③ worried
④ confident　⑤ satisfied

06 다음 그림의 상황에 가장 적절한 대화를 고르시오.

①　　　②　　　③　　　④　　　⑤

07 대화를 듣고, 여자가 남자에게 부탁한 일로 가장 적절한 것을 고르시오.

① 선거 후보로 출마하기
② 비디오카메라 고쳐주기
③ 토론 동아리에 가입하기
④ 선거 운동 동영상 만들어주기
⑤ 동아리 홍보 동영상 제작 도와주기

고난도
08 다음을 듣고, Kids' Playpit Resort에 관해 언급되지 <u>않은</u> 것을 고르시오.

① 개장일 　　　　② 객실 요금 할인
③ 수영장 이용 수칙　④ 부대시설 이용료
⑤ 예약 방법

09 다음을 듣고, 무엇에 관한 설명인지 고르시오.

① 드럼　　② 피아노　　③ 탬버린
④ 아코디언　⑤ 바이올린

10 다음을 듣고, 두 사람의 대화가 <u>어색한</u> 것을 고르시오.

①　　　②　　　③　　　④　　　⑤

11 대화를 듣고, 두 사람이 대화 직후에 할 일로 가장 적절한 것을 고르시오.

① 택시 타기 　　　② 집으로 돌아가기
③ 정비사 부르기　　④ 친구에게 전화하기
⑤ 공연장까지 걸어가기

12 다음 테이블 배치도를 보면서 대화를 듣고, 두 사람이 선택할 테이블을 고르시오.

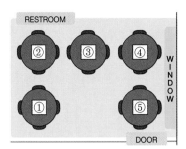

13 대화를 듣고, 가족 여행을 떠나기로 한 날짜를 고르시오.

① 3월 12일　② 3월 13일　③ 3월 19일
④ 3월 20일　⑤ 3월 26일

14 대화를 듣고, 남자가 오전에 한 일로 가장 적절한 것을 고르시오.

① 설거지하기
② TV 시청하기
③ 아침 식사 준비하기
④ 세탁소에 세탁물 맡기기
⑤ 제과점에서 샌드위치 사기

15 다음을 듣고, 방송의 목적으로 가장 적절한 것을 고르시오.

① 이재민 돕기를 독려하려고
② 태풍의 위험성을 경고하려고
③ 태풍 대피 요령을 안내하려고
④ 태풍 발생 원인을 설명하려고
⑤ 노숙자의 어려운 상황을 알리려고

16 대화를 듣고, 여자가 지불할 금액을 고르시오.

① $4　② $5　③ $6　④ $7　⑤ $8

17 대화를 듣고, 남자의 마지막 말에 대한 여자의 응답으로 가장 적절한 것을 고르시오.

Woman: _____

① I'm sure we have similar taste.
② Actually, they're not really my thing.
③ I agree. He's one of the best comedians.
④ Children should not watch scary movies.
⑤ Why don't we go to a movie together another day?

[18 - 19] 대화를 듣고, 여자의 마지막 말에 대한 남자의 응답으로 가장 적절한 것을 고르시오.

18 Man: _____

① I don't agree with you.
② I prefer the yellow ones.
③ I think that's a great idea.
④ I'm very sorry to bother you.
⑤ No, thanks. I don't need any.

19 Man: _____

① I'll go to Canada to learn English.
② You, too. I hope your paper is good.
③ Sorry, but I can't come to class tomorrow.
④ I'd like to join another internship program.
⑤ Thank you. I won't forget to hand in the paper.

20 다음 상황 설명을 듣고, Ben이 뒤에 있는 사람에게 할 말로 가장 적절한 것을 고르시오.

Ben: _____

① Thank you for waiting.
② Do you need some milk?
③ Don't worry. I don't mind.
④ Could you please hold my place?
⑤ I'm sorry. This is the end of the line.

Dictation Test 01

01 그림 정보 파악

대화를 듣고, 두 사람이 구입할 생일 카드를 고르시오.

① ② ③

④ ⑤

W: I hope Miranda will like our present.

M: Don't worry. I'm sure she will. It's her favorite perfume.

W: Yeah. Now we just need to choose a birthday card for her.

M: How about this? It 1) _____ _____ _____ _____ _____ with "Happy Birthday" written on it.

W: That's a little boring. I 2) _____ _____ _____ _____.

M: Then what about this one with a birthday cake on it? It says, "Happy Birthday," too.

W: Well... It's not bad, but I prefer this one with a picture of 3) _____ _____ _____ _____ _____. What do you think?

M: Yeah. That's a good choice.

02 언급되지 않은 내용 찾기

대화를 듣고, 두 사람이 보고 있는 온라인 상점에 관해 언급되지 않은 것을 고르시오.

① 제품 종류　　② 제품 품질

③ 배송료　　　④ 고객 후기

⑤ 수익금 사용처

W: What are you doing, Henry?

M: I'm shopping for pants. Would you help me choose some?

W: Sure. Oh, these look nice. But I think the 1) _____ _____ _____ _____ _____. I know some other online shops with good prices. Do you want me to recommend some?

M: Oh, thanks, but I want to buy from this site.

W: Why? Is there any special reason?

M: The quality of their products is good, and they 2) _____ _____ _____. And more importantly, some of their profits go toward helping the environment.

W: What do you mean?

M: When I buy from this site, they plant a tree.

W: Oh, that's wonderful. You can buy clothes and 3) _____ _____ _____ at the same time. You're a wise consumer.

목적 파악

대화를 듣고, 남자가 여자에게 전화한 목적으로 가장 적절한 것을 고르시오.

① 방 정리를 부탁하려고
② 만날 장소를 정하려고
③ 부엌 청소를 부탁하려고
④ 저녁 식사 준비를 부탁하려고
⑤ 지갑을 집에 두고 왔는지 확인하려고

[Phone rings.]

W: Hello?

M: Hello, Kelly. It's Nick.

W: Hi. Where are you?

M: I'm at work. Did you 1) _____ _____ _____ _____ _____ at home?

W: No. Did you leave it here?

M: I thought I took it, but I 2) _____ _____ _____ _____ . Can you see if it's in my room?

W: Sure. Wait a second. *[pause]* I don't think it's here.

M: Can you 3) _____ _____ _____ _____ , too?

W: Oh! I found it! Don't worry.

M: Okay, thanks! See you at home.

---

04 숫자 정보 파악 🇬🇧

대화를 듣고, 여자가 식당을 예약한 시각을 고르시오.

① 2:00 p.m.　② 2:30 p.m.　③ 3:00 p.m.
④ 3:30 p.m.　⑤ 5:30 p.m.

[Phone rings.]

M: Akura Restaurant. May I help you?

W: I'd like to make a reservation for two people this Sunday. I'd like a private room.

M: 1) _____ _____ _____ _____ _____ ?

W: Three p.m.

M: I'm sorry. We don't serve 2) _____ _____ _____ _____ .

W: Oh, I see. Then how about 2:00 p.m.?

M: Yes, that time's available. But we 3) _____ _____ _____ _____ . Is that okay with you?

W: Yes. And we can still sit and have lunch until 3:00, right?

M: Of course you can.

W: Great. That would be fine then.

대화를 듣고, 남자의 심정으로 가장 적절한 것을 고르시오.

① angry   ② lonely   ③ worried
④ confident   ⑤ satisfied

＊Focus on Sound   pretty

[t]는 모음 사이에서 약화되어 [프리티]가 아닌 [프리리]로 발음된다.

W: Jeremy, what's the matter? You look uncomfortable.

M: On my way home from school, a man 1) _____ _____ _____ _____ on the subway.

W: Are you all right?

M: Well, my foot really hurts now. And the man 2) _____ _____ _____!

W: Wow, that's ＊pretty rude.

M: And when he stepped on me, I dropped my smartphone. It hasn't been working since.

W: It sounds like you've 3) _____ _____ _____ _____.

M: I just wish people would 4) _____ _____ _____!

---

06 그림 상황에 적절한 대화 찾기

다음 그림의 상황에 가장 적절한 대화를 고르시오.

①   ②   ③   ④   ⑤

① W: Can I 1) _____ _____ _____ _____ _____?

M: I need to check your ID card first.

② W: They look quite heavy. Can I help you?

M: Yes, please. Thank you so much.

③ W: I read your article, and it was great.

M: Thank you. I worked really hard on it.

④ W: 2) _____ _____ _____ _____ _____ science fiction books?

M: You can find them in Section C.

⑤ W: 3) _____ _____ _____ _____ some of your books.

M: No problem. Let me go get them.

07 부탁한 일 파악

대화를 듣고, 여자가 남자에게 부탁한 일로 가장 적절한 것을 고르시오.

① 선거 후보로 출마하기
② 비디오카메라 고쳐주기
③ 토론 동아리에 가입하기
④ 선거 운동 동영상 만들어주기
⑤ 동아리 홍보 동영상 제작 도와주기

W: Hey, do you have a minute?
M: Yeah, what's up?
W: I 1) _____ _____ _____ _____ _____ _____ for the student president campaign last year, and I think you did a great job.
M: Oh, thanks.
W: Do you think you can 2) _____ _____ _____ _____ _____?
M: What do you need to make a video for?
W: It's for my debate club. We're 3) _____ _____ _____.
M: Hmm... I think I'll be able to help you next week. Is that okay with you?
W: Yes, it is. Thank you so much.

---

08 언급되지 않은 내용 찾기 🇬🇧

다음을 듣고, Kids' Playpit Resort에 관해 언급되지 않은 것을 고르시오.

① 개장일 　　　　② 객실 요금 할인
③ 수영장 이용 수칙　④ 부대시설 이용료
⑤ 예약 방법

M: Do you want to enjoy an exciting time with your kids? Then come to the Kids' Playpit Resort. We just opened on May 6. We're 1) _____ _____ _____ _____ _____ _____ for this month. Each room has a private pool, so you and your kids can 2) _____ _____ _____ at any time of the day. You can also swim in the bigger pool outside and enjoy the giant waterslide. Plus, we 3) _____ _____ _____ _____ located on the first floor of the main building. And if you stay at our resort, you can enjoy all of our facilities for free. 4) _____ _____ _____ _____, call 1600-2000 or visit our website, www.kidsplaypitresort.com. Thank you.

---

09 화제 파악

다음을 듣고, 무엇에 관한 설명인지 고르시오.

① 드럼　　② 피아노　　③ 탬버린
④ 아코디언　⑤ 바이올린

★Focus on Sound with it

자음의 끝과 모음의 처음이 만나면 연음되어 [위드 잇]이 아닌 [위딧]으로 발음된다.

W: I like to play this musical instrument. It comes in many different shapes and sizes. 1) _____ _____ _____ _____. Some are black and 2) _____ _____ _____ _____. Each key makes a different note, and 12 of these notes in a row make an octave. I play it 3) _____ _____ _____ _____ with my fingers and pushing the pedals with my feet. If I practice hard enough, I'll be able to make beautiful music *with it.

다음을 듣고, 두 사람의 대화가 <u>어색한</u> 것을 고르시오.

①   ②   ③   ④   ⑤

① M: Can you take my dog for a walk?

   W: Sorry, I don't have any time.

② M: 1) _____ _____ _____ _____ tomorrow?

   W: I was waiting in the library.

③ M: Why are you carrying an umbrella?

   W: It was raining this morning.

④ M: Let's play basketball after school.

   W: I'm sorry, but I have to 2) _____ _____ _____ _____ .

⑤ M: I was wondering if you could 3) _____ _____ _____ _____ _____ .

   W: Sure, here it is.

11 할 일 파악

대화를 듣고, 두 사람이 대화 직후에 할 일로 가장 적절한 것을 고르시오.

① 택시 타기   ② 집으로 돌아가기
③ 정비사 부르기   ④ 친구에게 전화하기
⑤ 공연장까지 걸어가기

M: There's something wrong with my car. I can't start the engine.

W: Oh, what should we do? We have only 30 minutes to get to the concert.

M: I'm sorry. I 1) _____ _____ _____ _____ _____ .

W: That's okay. Let's find another way. How about calling John and asking him to drive us to the concert hall? His house is close by.

M: He won't be able to. He 2) _____ _____ _____ _____ _____ yesterday.

W: Should we call a taxi?

M: Let's 3) _____ _____ _____ _____ , and then call a taxi. We can't just leave the car here.

W: You're right.

12 위치 찾기 🇬🇧

다음 테이블 배치도를 보면서 대화를 듣고, 두 사람이 선택할 테이블을 고르시오.

W: Jay, where do you want to sit?

M: Hmm, table 2 looks good. It's in the corner, so it will be quiet.

W: But it's ⁱ⁾ _____ _____ _____ _____ _____ . It might smell.

M: That's true. How about Table 5? We can sit beside the window.

W: But it's ²⁾ _____ _____ _____ _____ . It will be too cold and noisy.

M: Okay, then let's sit at Table 4.

W: It's not too close to the restroom. And it's ³⁾ _____ _____ _____ , so we can enjoy the view.

M: Perfect!

---

13 세부 정보 파악

대화를 듣고, 가족 여행을 떠나기로 한 날짜를 고르시오.

① 3월 12일   ② 3월 13일   ③ 3월 19일
④ 3월 20일   ⑤ 3월 26일

★ Focus on Sound   did you

[d]가 뒤의 반모음 [j]를 만나면 동화되어 [디드유]가 아닌 [디쥬]로 발음된다.

W: Honey, when should we go on our family picnic?

M: Do you have any dates in mind?

W: How about March 12 or March 19? They're both Saturdays.

M: I ¹⁾ _____ _____ _____ _____ _____ , remember? I'll be at a workshop with my coworkers, and I'll be back the next day.

W: Oh, right. Then can we ²⁾ _____ _____ _____ _____ ?

M: *Did you forget? Jamie's school talent show is that day.

W: You're right. Then what about the ³⁾ _____ _____ _____ _____ _____ ? We're free that day, aren't we?

M: That would be okay.

---

14 한 일 파악

대화를 듣고, 남자가 오전에 한 일로 가장 적절한 것을 고르시오.

① 설거지하기
② TV 시청하기
③ 아침 식사 준비하기
④ 세탁소에 세탁물 맡기기
⑤ 제과점에서 샌드위치 사기

W: David, have you washed the dishes yet?

M: Not yet. I was busy this morning. I just got back from the bakery. I went to ¹⁾ _____ _____ _____ _____ _____ .

W: But why were you gone for so long? It takes only ten minutes to go there.

M: I also ²⁾ _____ _____ _____ _____ .

W: Okay. Then do you have any plans in the afternoon?

M: No, I'll just watch TV.

W: Then why don't you ³⁾ _____ _____ _____ first?

M: No problem.

15 목적 파악

다음을 듣고, 방송의 목적으로 가장 적절한 것을 고르시오.

① 이재민 돕기를 독려하려고
② 태풍의 위험성을 경고하려고
③ 태풍 대피 요령을 안내하려고
④ 태풍 발생 원인을 설명하려고
⑤ 노숙자의 어려운 상황을 알리려고

M: Good afternoon, everyone. As you know, last Tuesday, a typhoon struck a nearby island. Sadly, about 200 people were killed. Many others escaped safely, but now they need your help. The typhoon left them homeless, and they 1) _____ _____ _____ _____ _____. You can help them 2) _____ _____ _____ _____ such as clothes or blankets. You can also donate money. They are your neighbors and are waiting for your help, so please 3) _____ _____ _____ _____.

16 숫자 정보 파악

대화를 듣고, 여자가 지불할 금액을 고르시오.
① $4   ② $5   ③ $6   ④ $7   ⑤ $8

M: What would you like to have?
W: I'd like a bacon sandwich. How much is it?
M: It's $4, but we 1) _____ _____ _____ _____. What about fried chicken?
W: Hmm... I don't like chicken. I'll take a cheeseburger. Is that $4, too?
M: Yes, it is. Would you like 2) _____ _____ _____? Sodas are $1, and coffees are $2.
W: Yes, I'd like a soda and 3) _____ _____ _____ _____ _____ _____. Here's my credit card.
M: Okay. I'll call this number when your order is ready.
W: Thank you.

17 마지막 말에 이어질 응답 찾기

대화를 듣고, 남자의 마지막 말에 대한 여자의 응답으로 가장 적절한 것을 고르시오.

Woman: _____
① I'm sure we have similar taste.
② Actually, they're not really my thing.
③ I agree. He's one of the best comedians.
④ Children should not watch scary movies.
⑤ Why don't we go to a movie together another day?

W: 1) _____ _____ _____ the movie today?
M: Well, it was a bit violent.
W: Oh, don't you like action movies?
M: I enjoyed watching them before, but these days they 2) _____ _____ _____ _____. Do you like them?
W: Sure. I like action movies 3) _____ _____ _____ _____ _____. I'm sorry you didn't enjoy it.
M: It's okay. I didn't know you liked action movies so much. What about comedies? I like them the best.
W: Actually, they're not really my thing.

18 마지막 말에 이어질 응답 찾기

대화를 듣고, 여자의 마지막 말에 대한 남자의 응답으로 가장 적절한 것을 고르시오.

Man: _____

① I don't agree with you.
② I prefer the yellow ones.
③ I think that's a great idea.
④ I'm very sorry to bother you.
⑤ No, thanks. I don't need any.

M: What are these?

W: They're color charts. I'm trying to 1) _____ _____ _____ for the new curtains. I don't know 2) _____ _____ _____ _____ _____.

M: The curtains for our living room? I like the way they look.

W: No, they're for my room.

M: Oh, okay. How about a bright color, then?

W: I like that idea. I'm trying to 3) _____ _____ _____ _____. Which do you like better?

M: I prefer the yellow ones.

19 마지막 말에 이어질 응답 찾기

대화를 듣고, 여자의 마지막 말에 대한 남자의 응답으로 가장 적절한 것을 고르시오.

Man: _____

① I'll go to Canada to learn English.
② You, too. I hope your paper is good.
③ Sorry, but I can't come to class tomorrow.
④ I'd like to join another internship program.
⑤ Thank you. I won't forget to hand in the paper.

M: Hello, Ms. White. I have something to tell you.

W: What's the matter, Sam?

M: It's about the paper you just assigned. I 1) _____ _____ _____ _____.

W: What's the problem?

M: I just 2) _____ _____ _____ _____ _____ _____.

W: Congratulations! How long is it?

M: It lasts for six weeks.

W: In that case, I will 3) _____ _____ _____ until the end of June.

M: Thank you. I won't forget to hand in the paper.

20 상황에 적절한 말 찾기

다음 상황 설명을 듣고, Ben이 뒤에 있는 사람에게 할 말로 가장 적절한 것을 고르시오.

Ben: _____

① Thank you for waiting.
② Do you need some milk?
③ Don't worry. I don't mind.
④ Could you please hold my place?
⑤ I'm sorry. This is the end of the line.

W: Ben is at the supermarket getting groceries. He is 1) _____ _____ _____ to pay at the counter. It is taking a long time because so many people are in the supermarket. Soon, he realizes he 2) _____ _____ _____ _____. He wants to go and get some, but he doesn't want to 3) _____ _____ _____ _____ _____ of the line. In this situation, what would Ben most likely say to the person behind him?

실전모의고사   02회

01 대화를 듣고, 여자가 주문할 티셔츠를 고르시오.

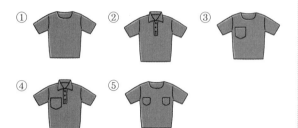

02 대화를 듣고, 호텔 이용에 관해 언급되지 <u>않은</u> 것을 고르시오.

① 식당 위치   ② 룸서비스 이용 시간
③ 국제 전화 이용 방법   ④ 세탁 서비스 이용 방법
⑤ 체크아웃 시간

03 대화를 듣고, 남자의 마지막 말에 담긴 의도로 가장 적절한 것을 고르시오.

① 감사   ② 격려   ③ 허락
④ 변명   ⑤ 축하

04 대화를 듣고, 두 사람이 만나기로 한 시각을 고르시오.

① 5:00 p.m.   ② 6:00 p.m.   ③ 7:00 p.m.
④ 8:00 p.m.   ⑤ 9:00 p.m.

05 대화를 듣고, 여자의 심정으로 가장 적절한 것을 고르시오.

① bored   ② nervous   ③ jealous
④ satisfied   ⑤ disappointed

06 다음 그림의 상황에 가장 적절한 대화를 고르시오.

①   ②   ③   ④   ⑤

07 대화를 듣고, 여자가 남자에게 부탁한 일로 가장 적절한 것을 고르시오.

① 책 반납하기
② 숙제 대신 제출하기
③ 서점 위치 알려 주기
④ 인터넷으로 자료 찾기
⑤ 도서관에서 책 빌려다 주기

08 다음을 듣고, Famous Singer에 관해 언급되지 <u>않은</u> 것을 고르시오.

① 참가 자격   ② 장르 제한
③ 참가자 나이 제한   ④ 우승자 상금
⑤ 참가 방법

09 다음을 듣고, 무엇에 관한 설명인지 고르시오.

① 오토바이   ② 전기 자전거
③ 스케이트보드   ④ 전동 킥보드
⑤ 인라인스케이트

10 다음을 듣고, 두 사람의 대화가 <u>어색한</u> 것을 고르시오.

①   ②   ③   ④   ⑤

11 대화를 듣고, 남자가 토요일에 할 일로 가장 적절한 것을 고르시오.

① 외식하기   ② 영화 보기
③ 박물관 가기   ④ 그림 그리기
⑤ 축구 경기 시청하기

12 다음 지도를 보면서 대화를 듣고, 두 사람이 머물 호텔을 고르시오.

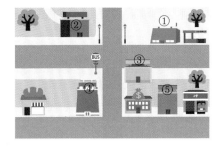

13 대화를 듣고, 두 사람이 만나기로 한 요일을 고르시오.

① 화요일   ② 수요일   ③ 목요일
④ 금요일   ⑤ 토요일

14 대화를 듣고, 남자가 주말에 한 일로 가장 적절한 것을 고르시오.

① 여행하기   ② 등산 가기
③ 병문안 가기   ④ 바닷가 가기
⑤ 여동생 돌보기

15 다음을 듣고, 방송의 목적으로 가장 적절한 것을 고르시오.

① 경기 취소를 공지하려고
② 매표소 위치를 안내하려고
③ 표 교환 방법을 설명하려고
④ 홈페이지 주소를 알려 주려고
⑤ 폭우에 대비할 것을 당부하려고

16 대화를 듣고, 여자가 지불할 금액을 고르시오.

① $4   ② $5   ③ $6   ④ $7   ⑤ $8

17 대화를 듣고, 여자의 마지막 말에 대한 남자의 응답으로 가장 적절한 것을 고르시오.

Man: _____

① I never liked those tigers.
② They should protect the animals.
③ I actually don't know anything about them.
④ Tigers are very good at hunting other animals.
⑤ Yeah, I recently read an interesting book about tigers.

[18-19] 대화를 듣고, 남자의 마지막 말에 대한 여자의 응답으로 가장 적절한 것을 고르시오.

18 Woman: _____

① I'm sure you'll be a good singer.
② I'm thinking to join another club.
③ I hope you can find a good singer.
④ I didn't know you were interested in singing.
⑤ Of course. I've been practicing my whole life for this moment!

19 Woman: _____

① No, but I'd like to.
② Yes, I think so, too.
③ No, I like fantasy movies better.
④ The book is based on a real person.
⑤ No, I'm busy studying for final exams tonight.

20 다음 상황 설명을 듣고, Roy가 Erin에게 할 말로 가장 적절한 것을 고르시오.

Roy: _____

① Haste makes waste.
② Better late than never.
③ Slow and steady wins the race.
④ The early bird catches the worm.
⑤ You can't judge a book by its cover.

Dictation Test 02

정답 및 해설 pp. 15~20

보통 속도 듣기   빠르게 듣기

01 그림 정보 파악

대화를 듣고, 여자가 주문할 티셔츠를 고르시오.

① ② ③ ④ ⑤

M: Have you decided on a class uniform for sports day?

W: Not yet. I don't know 1) _____ _____ _____ _____.
   Can you help?

M: Sure. What are the choices?

W: Well, this T-shirt comes with or without a collar. Which is better?

M: I like the one that 2) _____ _____ _____. It looks neat.

W: Okay. Then how about a pocket? Isn't it cuter 3) _____
   _____ _____ _____?

M: Yes, I think so. It looks much better than the one without a pocket.

W: All right. Thanks for your help. I'll order that style.

02 언급되지 않은 내용 찾기

대화를 듣고, 호텔 이용에 관해 언급되지 않은
것을 고르시오.

① 식당 위치
② 룸서비스 이용 시간
③ 국제 전화 이용 방법
④ 세탁 서비스 이용 방법
⑤ 체크아웃 시간

M: Welcome to the Atlantic Hotel.

W: Thanks. My name is Mandi Erickson. I'd like to check in, please.

M: All right. Here's your room key. If you're hungry, we have
   a restaurant 1) _____ _____ _____ _____.

W: Okay. Do you have room service?

M: Yes. Food can be 2) _____ _____ _____ _____ until
   midnight.

W: That's good. Can I 3) _____ _____ _____ from my
   room?

M: Yes, you can. Just dial "9" first.

W: Excellent. And I have one more question. What time do
   I 4) _____ _____ _____ _____?

M: You must leave your room by 11:00 a.m. tomorrow.

03 의도 파악 🇬🇧

대화를 듣고, 남자의 마지막 말에 담긴 의도로 가장 적절한 것을 고르시오.

① 감사   ② 격려   ③ 허락
④ 변명   ⑤ 축하

M: Let's ski down the mountain.

W: No way! I don't think I can do it.

M: Come on. This slope is not that steep.

W: I'm worried. I feel like 1) _____ _____ _____ _____ _____.

M: Don't be nervous. You'll be fine.

W: I think I'm too scared to move.

M: 2) _____ _____ _____ _____. And look straight ahead. Don't look down.

W: Okay, okay.

M: Good! Now move just a little, and you'll start skiing down the slope. 3) _____ _____ _____ _____.

04 숫자 정보 파악

대화를 듣고, 두 사람이 만나기로 한 시각을 고르시오.

① 5:00 p.m.   ② 6:00 p.m.   ③ 7:00 p.m.
④ 8:00 p.m.   ⑤ 9:00 p.m.

[Cell phone rings.]

M: Hello, Susan.

W: Hi, Patrick. Do you want to see the play *Hamlet* tonight?

M: That sounds great. What time does it start?

W: It 1) _____ _____ _____ p.m.

M: Okay. How about shopping at the mall before we go?

W: Do you have something to buy?

M: Yes. My mom 2) _____ _____ _____ _____ a few things.

W: I see. Shall we meet at the mall at 7:00?

M: No, we'll need more time. How about meeting 3) _____ _____ _____ _____ _____?

W: Okay, see you then.

05 심정 추론

대화를 듣고, 여자의 심정으로 가장 적절한 것을 고르시오.

① bored   ② nervous   ③ jealous
④ satisfied   ⑤ disappointed

W: Excuse me. Can you help me?

M: Sure. Are you trying to find your seat?

W: That's right. I can't 1) _____ _____ _____ _____ _____ _____ . This is my favorite band in the world.

M: That's terrific. Can I see your ticket?

W: Of course. Here you are.

M: Hmm… You're 2) _____ _____ _____ _____ . Your seat is up there.

W: Up there? You're kidding.

M: Nope. Walk up these stairs and then go about ten rows back.

W: I didn't realize I was so 3) _____ _____ _____ _____ _____ .

M: You'll still have a good view of the stage from there. Enjoy the Show!

06 그림 상황에 적절한 대화 찾기

다음 그림의 상황에 가장 적절한 대화를 고르시오.

①   ②   ③   ④   ⑤

① W: Oh no. I can't start my car!
  M: Just 1) _____ _____ _____ _____ _____ .

② W: I can't find a single parking spot.
  M: Let's check the other sections.

③ W: I don't remember 2) _____ _____ _____ _____ .
  M: I think it was in Section C.

④ W: I need to 3) _____ _____ _____ _____ . It's at the repair shop.
  M: I'll go with you.

⑤ W: Oh! 4) _____ _____ _____ _____ . Let's park here.
  M: Look at the sign. We can't park here.

62

07 부탁한 일 파악

대화를 듣고, 여자가 남자에게 부탁한 일로 가장 적절한 것을 고르시오.

① 책 반납하기
② 숙제 대신 제출하기
③ 서점 위치 알려 주기
④ 인터넷으로 자료 찾기
⑤ 도서관에서 책 빌려다 주기

W: Dave, I stayed up too late last night.
M: Why? Were you reading an interesting book?
W: No, I have history homework due tomorrow, so I was [1)] _____ _____ _____ _____ _____.
M: Did you finish it?
W: No, I have to [2)] _____ _____ _____ _____.
M: You should get some sleep after you finish it.
W: Yeah. But I also have science homework the day after tomorrow. I haven't even started it yet.
M: Oh, that's terrible. Is there anything that I can help you with?
W: Yes. Can you [3)] _____ _____ _____ from the library for me? I really need it for my homework.
M: Sure.

08 언급되지 않은 내용 찾기

다음을 듣고, Famous Singer에 관해 언급되지 않은 것을 고르시오.

① 참가 자격   ② 장르 제한
③ 참가자 나이 제한   ④ 우승자 상금
⑤ 참가 방법

M: Hello. If you love singing, this announcement is for you. Famous Singer is looking for people who want to be famous singers. To participate in this audition, you need to [1)] _____ _____ _____ _____. It can be any genre. [2)] _____ _____ _____ _____ _____ for participants either. If you win the contest, we'll give you an opportunity to [3)] _____ _____ _____ _____ and have a concert. Visit our website and sign up with your demo video.

09 화제 파악

다음을 듣고, 무엇에 관한 설명인지 고르시오.

① 오토바이   ② 전기 자전거
③ 스케이트보드   ④ 전동 킥보드
⑤ 인라인스케이트

W: This is enjoyed by many people these days. It is a vehicle that [1)] _____ _____ _____ _____, but it has handlebars. It is [2)] _____ _____ _____. You ride it in a standing position and it can move quite quickly. Anyone can drive one as long as they [3)] _____ _____ _____ _____. But it can be dangerous, so you need to drive slowly and carefully when there are people nearby.

다음을 듣고, 두 사람의 대화가 <u>어색한</u> 것을 고르시오.

① ② ③ ④ ⑤

① M: Is it okay if I have some more juice?

   W: Sure. 1) _____ _____.

② M: What are you doing these days?

   W: I just opened a café on Fifth Avenue.

③ M: It looks like it's going to rain.

   W: Maybe we 2) _____ _____ _____ _____.

④ M: Would you like to have dinner with me tomorrow?

   W: Sure. 3) _____ _____ _____ _____ _____?

⑤ M: I'm 4) _____ _____ _____ _____ tonight.

   W: No, I went to the park instead.

---

11 할 일 파악

대화를 듣고, 남자가 토요일에 할 일로 가장 적절한 것을 고르시오.

① 외식하기　　　② 영화 보기

③ 박물관 가기　　④ 그림 그리기

⑤ 축구 경기 시청하기

★Focus on Sound　Saturday

[t]가 강모음과 약모음 사이에서 약화되어 [새터데이]가 아닌 [새러데이]로 발음된다.

W: Tomorrow's *Saturday. Do you know what I want to do?

M: Let me guess. 1) _____ _____ _____ _____ and then watch a movie?

W: No. There are several paintings by Van Gogh at the City Museum this week.

M: Oh, really? You want to go there?

W: Yes, and I'd like you to come with me.

M: That sounds okay, but I'm planning to 2) _____ _____ _____ _____ between Spain and Germany tomorrow afternoon.

W: What time is the game?

M: It starts at 2:30.

W: Okay. Then we can 3) _____ _____ _____ _____ another day.

M: All right.

12 위치 찾기 🇬🇧

다음 지도를 보면서 대화를 듣고, 두 사람이 머물 호텔을 고르시오.

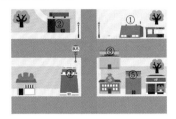

★ Focus on Sound bus stop

똑같은 발음의 자음이 겹치면 앞 자음 소리가 탈락하여 [버쓰 스탑]이 아닌 [버쓰탑]으로 발음된다.

M: Which hotel shall we stay at?

W: Well, the Flowers Hotel is 1) _____ _____ _____ _____ _____.

M: I know, but there's no elevator in that hotel. It will be 2) _____ _____ _____ _____ _____.

W: Then how about the Main Street Hotel? There's a *bus stop near it.

M: But we might need to withdraw some money from the bank. How about the Smithson Hotel? It's next to the bank.

W: Yeah, but there's a fire station next door. It will be too loud. What do you think of the Sweet Dreams Hotel? It's 3) _____ _____ _____ _____ _____ _____, and there's a bakery and a bus stop nearby.

M: That's good.

---

13 세부 정보 파악

대화를 듣고, 두 사람이 만나기로 한 요일을 고르시오.

① 화요일   ② 수요일   ③ 목요일
④ 금요일   ⑤ 토요일

★ Focus on Sound study

[s] 뒤에 [t]가 오면 된소리가 되어 [스터디]가 아닌 [스떠디]로 발음된다.

M: I think we have to meet one more time to finish our project.

W: I agree. When should we meet?

M: We have to 1) _____ _____ _____ _____ _____. But I have plans tomorrow. How about 2) _____ _____ _____ _____?

W: On Wednesday? I'm sorry, I can't. I 3) _____ _____ _____ _____ this Thursday, so I have to *study for it.

M: Then we can 4) _____ _____ _____ _____ _____. I'm free then, too.

W: Okay. See you then.

---

14 한 일 파악

대화를 듣고, 남자가 주말에 한 일로 가장 적절한 것을 고르시오.

① 여행하기   ② 등산 가기
③ 병문안 가기   ④ 바닷가 가기
⑤ 여동생 돌보기

★ Focus on Sound didn't you

[t]가 반모음 [j]를 만나면 동화되어 [디든트 유]가 아닌 [디든츄]로 발음된다.

W: Did you 1) _____ _____ _____ _____ last weekend?

M: Trip? What trip?

W: *Didn't you say that you would go to the beach on Sunday?

M: Oh, yes. But it was canceled. I actually ended up 2) _____ _____ _____ _____.

W: Why? What happened?

M: My dad 3) _____ _____ _____ _____ _____ _____ and spent the weekend in the hospital. And my mom had to take care of him.

W: That's too bad. Is he okay now?

M: Yeah. He's better now.

다음을 듣고, 방송의 목적으로 가장 적절한 것을 고르시오.

① 경기 취소를 공지하려고
② 매표소 위치를 안내하려고
③ 표 교환 방법을 설명하려고
④ 홈페이지 주소를 알려 주려고
⑤ 폭우에 대비할 것을 당부하려고

M: Ladies and gentlemen, please pay attention to the following announcement. Because of the heavy rainfall, today's 1) _____ _____ _____ _____ _____. We sincerely 2) _____ _____ _____ _____ _____. If you want to exchange today's ticket for a ticket to the next game, please visit the ticket office. Or you can 3) _____ _____ _____ _____ instead. I'd also like to let you know that tickets and information are always available on our website. You can visit our homepage at www.topbaseball.com.

대화를 듣고, 여자가 지불할 금액을 고르시오.

① $4 ② $5 ③ $6 ④ $7 ⑤ $8

M: May I 1) _____ _____ _____?
W: Yes, I want a regular latte and an orange muffin. How much will that be?
M: A regular latte is $4, and an orange muffin is $2. But if you buy a latte, you get the muffin 2) _____ _____.
W: That's great! And could you put whipped cream on my latte, please?
M: Okay. 3) _____ _____ _____ _____.
W: That's fine.

대화를 듣고, 여자의 마지막 말에 대한 남자의 응답으로 가장 적절한 것을 고르시오.

Man: _____
① I never liked those tigers.
② They should protect the animals.
③ I actually don't know anything about them.
④ Tigers are very good at hunting other animals.
⑤ Yeah, I recently read an interesting book about tigers.

M: Hey, Sarah. What are you doing?
W: I'm surfing the Internet. I have to write an essay about an animal for homework.
M: Oh. 1) _____ _____ _____ _____ _____?
W: I'll write about tigers. Do you know any facts about them?
M: Well, tigers mainly live in Asia. They live alone in the jungle and 2) _____ _____ _____ _____ _____. Their black stripes make them hard to see.
W: Wow, I didn't know you 3) _____ _____ _____ _____ _____.
M: Yeah, I recently read an interesting book about tigers.

18 마지막 말에 이어질 응답 찾기

대화를 듣고, 남자의 마지막 말에 대한 여자의 응답으로 가장 적절한 것을 고르시오.

Woman: _____

① I'm sure you'll be a good singer.
② I'm thinking to join another club.
③ I hope you can find a good singer.
④ I didn't know you were interested in singing.
⑤ Of course. I've been practicing my whole life for this moment!

W: I heard that your band is looking for a new singer.
M: That's right. Are you 1) _____ _____ _____ _____ _____?
W: Yes. Can I have more information?
M: Sure. We're 2) _____ _____ _____ _____ for our lead singer.
W: Okay. When is the audition?
M: It's on March 13.
W: I see. And where will it be held?
M: It'll be held in our practice room. Are you going to 3) _____ _____ _____ _____?
W: Of course. I've been practicing my whole life for this moment!

---

19 마지막 말에 이어질 응답 찾기 🇬🇧

대화를 듣고, 남자의 마지막 말에 대한 여자의 응답으로 가장 적절한 것을 고르시오.

Woman: _____

① No, but I'd like to.
② Yes, I think so, too.
③ No, I like fantasy movies better.
④ The book is based on a real person.
⑤ No, I'm busy studying for final exams tonight.

M: So, what did you think of the movie?
W: Wow, I loved it. I really 1) _____ _____ _____ _____. What about you?
M: I enjoyed it too, but I think the book was better than the film.
W: Is the movie quite different from the book?
M: Not so much. But they 2) _____ _____ _____ _____ _____.
W: How interesting! My brother said the same thing.
M: It's true. 3) _____ _____ _____ _____ _____ _____?
W: No, but I'd like to.

---

20 상황에 적절한 말 찾기

다음 상황 설명을 듣고, Roy가 Erin에게 할 말로 가장 적절한 것을 고르시오.

Roy: _____

① Haste makes waste.
② Better late than never.
③ Slow and steady wins the race.
④ The early bird catches the worm.
⑤ You can't judge a book by its cover.

W: Roy and Erin both enjoy seeing musicals. They were excited when they heard the news that their favorite musical, *Aida*, would 1) _____ _____ _____. And as soon as the 2) _____ _____ _____ _____, Roy bought one. But Erin forgot. She tried to buy one 3) _____ _____ _____ _____, but the tickets were sold out. So she couldn't get a ticket. In this situation, what would Roy most likely say to Erin?

실전모의고사 03 회

정답 및 해설 pp. 20~24

점수: /20

보통속도듣기

빠르게듣기

---

01 대화를 듣고, 여자가 원하는 헤어스타일을 고르시오.

①   ②   ③

④   ⑤

고난도

02 대화를 듣고, T Smart Watch에 관해 언급되지 <u>않은</u> 것을 고르시오.

① 무게   ② 기능
③ 내구성   ④ 화면 크기
⑤ 배터리 지속 시간

03 대화를 듣고, 남자가 Judy에게 전화한 목적으로 가장 적절한 것을 고르시오.

① 공책을 빌리려고
② 공책을 돌려받으려고
③ 모임 시간을 변경하려고
④ 모임 장소를 물어보려고
⑤ 함께 공부하자고 제안하려고

04 대화를 듣고, 두 사람이 만나기로 한 시각을 고르시오.

① 6:00 p.m.   ② 6:30 p.m.   ③ 7:00 p.m.
④ 7:30 p.m.   ⑤ 8:00 p.m.

05 대화를 듣고, 두 사람이 대화하는 장소로 가장 적절한 곳을 고르시오.

① 은행   ② 헬스장
③ 수선소   ④ 옷 가게
⑤ 분실물 보관소

06 다음 그림의 상황에 가장 적절한 대화를 고르시오.

①   ②   ③   ④   ⑤

07 대화를 듣고, 여자가 남자에게 부탁한 일로 가장 적절한 것을 고르시오.

① 책 구입해 주기
② 선물용 책 골라 주기
③ 책 입고 시 알려 주기
④ 책을 집으로 배송해 주기
⑤ 다른 매장에서 책 구해 주기

고난도

08 다음을 듣고, 졸업식에 관해 언급되지 <u>않은</u> 것을 고르시오.

① 연설자   ② 날짜
③ 온라인 대체 이유   ④ 시작 시각
⑤ 복장

09 다음을 듣고, 무엇에 관한 설명인지 고르시오.

① 입추   ② 추석   ③ 설날
④ 동지   ⑤ 정월 대보름

10 다음을 듣고, 두 사람의 대화가 <u>어색한</u> 것을 고르시오.

①   ②   ③   ④   ⑤

11 대화를 듣고, 두 사람이 할 일로 가장 적절한 것을 고르시오.

① 방 크기 재기   ② 책장 정리하기
③ 시내 쇼핑하기   ④ 중고 서점에 책 팔기
⑤ 가구 가격 비교하기

12 다음 극장 좌석표를 보면서 대화를 듣고, 두 사람이 선택한 구역을 고르시오.

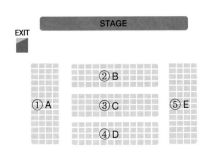

13 대화를 듣고, 남자의 현재 몸무게를 고르시오.

① 70kg   ② 72kg   ③ 74kg
④ 80kg   ⑤ 88kg

14 대화를 듣고, 남자가 일요일에 한 일로 가장 적절한 것을 고르시오.

① 집 청소하기   ② 시험공부하기
③ 축구 경기하기   ④ 가족 여행하기
⑤ 부모님 찾아뵙기

고난도

15 다음을 듣고, 방송의 목적으로 가장 적절한 것을 고르시오.

① 지진의 원인을 설명하려고
② 지진 피해 상황을 알리려고
③ 지진 발생 시 대처 요령을 안내하려고
④ 지진 피해 지역 방문의 위험성을 경고하려고
⑤ 난민을 돕기 위한 국제 기구 설립을 촉구하려고

16 대화를 듣고, 여자가 지불할 금액을 고르시오.

① $10   ② $12   ③ $18
④ $20   ⑤ $22

17 대화를 듣고, 남자의 마지막 말에 대한 여자의 응답으로 가장 적절한 것을 고르시오.

Woman: _____

① Can you help her swim?
② I want to go swimming with her.
③ Good. Let's go to the sports store.
④ I didn't know she was interested in fashion.
⑤ We should wear a swimming cap when swimming.

[18-19] 대화를 듣고, 여자의 마지막 말에 대한 남자의 응답으로 가장 적절한 것을 고르시오.

18 Man: _____

① See you around.
② I really enjoyed it, too.
③ How about four o'clock?
④ Tomorrow would be fine.
⑤ Let's meet at three o'clock, then.

19 Man: _____

① You can pay by credit card.
② No, I'm not ready to order yet.
③ Would you please come this way?
④ Sure, I'll bring you the menu right away.
⑤ Our restaurant usually closes at 10:00 p.m.

20 다음 상황 설명을 듣고, Claire가 Jimmy에게 할 말로 가장 적절한 것을 고르시오.

Claire: _____

① You should see your teacher more often.
② You should not go to bed too late at night.
③ You need to eat healthier and drink less coffee.
④ If I were you, I would not sleep during classes.
⑤ Why don't you talk to your parents about your problems?

Dictation Test 03

 보통속도 듣기 빠르게 듣기

01 그림 정보 파악

대화를 듣고, 여자가 원하는 헤어스타일을 고르시오.

M: Do you have any style in mind?

W: No. Could you recommend something?

M: Sure. Why don't you try this style?

W: You mean this short hairstyle? No way.

M: Why not? It seems pretty cute.

W: Well, I think I 1) _____ _____ _____ _____ _____.

M: I see. How about this one, then? You'd 2) _____ _____ _____ _____ _____.

W: Oh, that looks good.

M: Will you 3) _____ _____ _____, too? I think black hair would look good on you.

W: No, I like my brown hair.

02 언급되지 않은 내용 찾기

대화를 듣고, T Smart Watch에 관해 언급되지 않은 것을 고르시오.

① 무게   ② 기능
③ 내구성   ④ 화면 크기
⑤ 배터리 지속 시간

M: Kelly, you have a T Smart Watch, don't you?

W: Yes, why?

M: I'm thinking of buying one. Is it 1) _____ _____ _____ while exercising? I want to wear it when I swim and play basketball.

W: Not at all. It's just 30 g, so it never bothers me. And it's rather helpful for 2) _____ _____ _____ _____ _____. I think that's the best feature.

M: Good. What is its LCD made of? I'm afraid a ball could hit it and break it.

W: You don't need to worry about that. It is very strong.

M: That is good. And what other features do you like?

W: Its GPS is useful when I need to 3) _____ _____.

M: It sounds even more helpful than I thought. I think I'll have to buy one. By the way, how long does it 4) _____ _____ _____ _____?

W: It lasts about three days.

03 목적 파악

대화를 듣고, 남자가 Judy에게 전화한 목적으로 가장 적절한 것을 고르시오.

① 공책을 빌리려고
② 공책을 돌려받으려고
③ 모임 시간을 변경하려고
④ 모임 장소를 물어보려고
⑤ 함께 공부하자고 제안하려고

[Cell phone rings.]

W: Hello?

M: Hi, Judy. Will you 1) _____ _____ _____ _____ _____ ?

W: Sorry, this is not Judy. I'm her mom.

M: Oh, I'm so sorry, Ms. Jackson. This is Tom.

W: It's okay, Tom. Judy is busy at the moment, so I answered. Do you want to 2) _____ _____ _____ ?

M: Yes, please. Could you 3) _____ _____ _____ _____ _____ _____ if she comes to our study meeting today?

W: Sure. I'll tell her.

M: Thank you, bye.

04 숫자 정보 파악

대화를 듣고, 두 사람이 만나기로 한 시각을 고르시오.

① 6:00 p.m. ② 6:30 p.m. ③ 7:00 p.m.
④ 7:30 p.m. ⑤ 8:00 p.m.

W: The concert starts at 8:00 p.m., doesn't it?

M: Yes. Shall we meet at the concert hall?

W: 1) _____ _____ _____ _____ first?

M: Sounds great. What do you want to eat?

W: I'd like to go to a Japanese restaurant.

M: That's a good idea. I'll pick you up in front of your house at 7:00.

W: 2) _____ _____ _____ _____ ? We won't have enough time for dinner.

M: You're right. When would be good, then?

W: 3) _____ _____ _____ instead?

M: That sounds good.

05 장소 추론

대화를 듣고, 두 사람이 대화하는 장소로 가장 적절한 곳을 고르시오.

① 은행   ② 헬스장
③ 수선소   ④ 옷 가게
⑤ 분실물 보관소

M: Excuse me.

W: Yes, can I help you?

M: Yes. I'd like to 1) _____ _____ _____ .

W: Okay. Is there something wrong with them?

M: Well, they were a gift, but they're too tight.

W: I see. Would you like to 2) _____ _____ _____ _____ _____ _____ ?

M: Yes, please. Can you get me a medium?

W: Sure. I'll get them now so that you can 3) _____ _____ _____ _____ .

M: Thank you.

다음 그림의 상황에 가장 적절한 대화를 고르시오.

① ② ③ ④ ⑤

① W: Would you like someone to help you?

　M: That's okay. I already purchased tickets for the concert.

② W: May I ¹⁾ _____ _____ _____ _____ _____ ?

　M: I'm fine. I'm just trying to get another soda.

③ W: Can I help you with anything?

　M: Do you know ²⁾ _____ _____ _____ _____ _____ ?

④ W: Do you need any help?

　M: I'm trying to buy a ticket to Hongdae, but I don't know ³⁾ _____ _____ _____ _____ _____ .

⑤ W: How can I help you today?

　M: ⁴⁾ _____ _____ _____ _____ to Myeongdong station, please.

대화를 듣고, 여자가 남자에게 부탁한 일로 가장 적절한 것을 고르시오.

① 책 구입해 주기
② 선물용 책 골라 주기
③ 책 입고 시 알려 주기
④ 책을 집으로 배송해 주기
⑤ 다른 매장에서 책 구해 주기

M: May I help you?

W: Yes, I'm looking for a book for my son's birthday.

M: Do you have anything in mind?

W: Do you have a book called *One Summer Night*?

M: Oh, I'm sorry, but that book ¹⁾ _____ _____ _____ . In fact, none of the other bookstores in town have any copies either. More copies will arrive in a few days.

W: Okay. Then ²⁾ _____ _____ _____ _____ when they arrive, please?

M: Of course. We'll call you as soon as we ³⁾ _____ _____ .

W: Thanks. Here is my phone number.

다음을 듣고, 졸업식에 관해 언급되지 <u>않은</u> 것을 고르시오.

① 연설자 　　② 날짜
③ 온라인 대체 이유 　④ 시작 시각
⑤ 복장

M: Hello, students. This is Principal Barton. We're holding a graduation ceremony on February 16. We were supposed to have it in the school auditorium. But 1) _____ _____ _____ _____, the school committee has decided to have it online instead. I'd like to share with you some details about the ceremony. It'll 2) _____ _____ _____ a.m. So you need to log in to the school website before then. I want everyone to 3) _____ _____ _____ and look nice. People who are supposed to sing for the ceremony should come to the school studio by 8:00 a.m. Thank you for listening.

다음을 듣고, 무엇에 관한 설명인지 고르시오.

① 입춘 　　② 추석 　　③ 설날
④ 동지 　　⑤ 정월 대보름

W: This is a special traditional holiday Koreans celebrate. It is in December, and it has the shortest day and the 1) _____ _____ _____ _____ _____. It starts to get cold around this day, and Koreans believe this day is the 2) _____ _____ _____ _____. Families make red bean soup and eat it together, wishing each other good health and 3) _____ _____ _____ _____ _____.

다음을 듣고, 두 사람의 대화가 <u>어색한</u> 것을 고르시오.

① 　　② 　　③ 　　④ 　　⑤

① M: 1) _____ _____ _____ _____ your new job?
　W: It couldn't be better.
② M: Can you make it by 7:00 p.m.?
　W: It 2) _____ _____ _____ _____ _____.
③ M: What are you going to do during your vacation?
　W: I'm going to go backpacking.
④ M: How long have you been attending this school?
　W: For two years now.
⑤ M: I've been very busy, and I feel too tired now.
　W: You should drink more fluids and 3) _____ _____ _____ _____.

11 할 일 파악

대화를 듣고, 두 사람이 할 일로 가장 적절한 것을 고르시오.

① 방 크기 재기
② 책장 정리하기
③ 시내 쇼핑하기
④ 중고 서점에 책 팔기
⑤ 가구 가격 비교하기

W: What are you doing, honey?

M: I'm shopping online for a bookshelf. I want to get Jenny a new one. She has so many books that there isn't 1) _____ _____ _____ _____.

W: I agree. How about going to a shop and buying one?

M: We could, but we don't really have time to go downtown. Also, this online shop sells second-hand furniture, and 2) _____ _____ _____ _____.

W: I see. Do you have anything in mind?

M: This one looks good. What do you think about it?

W: It's made of steel, so it looks strong. But I think it's too big to fit in her room.

M: Do you? Why don't we 3) _____ _____ _____ _____?

W: Yes, we should definitely do that first.

12 위치 찾기

다음 극장 좌석표를 보면서 대화를 듣고, 두 사람이 선택한 구역을 고르시오.

```
         STAGE
EXIT

           ②B
①A    ③C         ⑤E
           ④D
```

W: Okay, where should we sit in the theater?

M: Hmm... The cheaper seats are in Sections A and E.

W: Yeah, but the 1) _____ _____ _____ _____.

M: True. Let's try and get seats in Section B.

W: It's too close to the stage and too expensive. What about Section D? The view will be good, and it's 2) _____ _____ _____ Section B.

M: But it's 3) _____ _____ _____ _____ _____. Let's sit in Section C.

W: Okay, fine. I'll buy the tickets.

M: I can't wait to see this musical.

W: Me neither. I've been waiting to see it for a long time.

13 숫자 정보 파악

대화를 듣고, 남자의 현재 몸무게를 고르시오.

① 70kg   ② 72kg   ③ 74kg
④ 80kg   ⑤ 88kg

W: You look quite different, Harry. What happened?
M: Well, I've 1) _____ _____ _____ _____ _____.
W: How did you do that?
M: I 2) _____ _____ _____. Over the last six *months, I swam and walked a lot almost every day.
W: Wonderful! How much weight did you lose?
M: Try to guess.
W: You seem to have lost about 10 kg.
M: 3) _____ _____ _____. When I started to exercise, I was 80 kg, and I've lost 8 kg.
W: Wow, you lost 8 kg in six months? That's great.

14 한 일 파악

대화를 듣고, 남자가 일요일에 한 일로 가장 적절한 것을 고르시오.

① 집 청소하기   ② 시험공부하기
③ 축구 경기하기   ④ 가족 여행하기
⑤ 부모님 찾아뵙기

M: Hi, Sally. What did you do last weekend?
W: Good morning, Tom. I just 1) _____ _____. How was your soccer game on Sunday?
M: Oh, I 2) _____ _____ _____ last weekend.
W: How come? You never miss a game.
M: It was my mother's birthday, so I 3) _____ _____ _____ and spent the day with them.
W: Oh, did you 4) _____ _____ _____ _____ _____ _____?
M: I did. She liked my *present.
W: That's good. What did you buy for her?
M: I got her a scarf.

15 목적 파악 🇬🇧

다음을 듣고, 방송의 목적으로 가장 적절한 것을 고르시오.

① 지진의 원인을 설명하려고
② 지진 피해 상황을 알리려고
③ 지진 발생 시 대처 요령을 안내하려고
④ 지진 피해 지역 방문의 위험성을 경고하려고
⑤ 난민을 돕기 위한 국제 기구 설립을 촉구하려고

M: Kolkata was 1) _____ _____ _____ _____ _____ last night. Many people felt the earth shake in the middle of the night. It was a 7-magnitude earthquake. Hundreds of people 2) _____ _____ _____ _____. Buildings and houses fell down, and roads were destroyed. Some aftershocks are anticipated as thousands of people without homes 3) _____ _____ _____ _____.

16 숫자 정보 파악

대화를 듣고, 여자가 지불할 금액을 고르시오.

① $10   ② $12   ③ $18
④ $20   ⑤ $22

W: Excuse me. I'd like to pay my bill.

M: Okay. How was your meal?

W: The pasta and salad were excellent.

M: Great. Here's your check. [1)] _____ _____ _____ _____.

W: Twenty dollars? Okay.

M: Do you [2)] _____ _____ _____ _____?

W: Yes, I do.

M: In that case, you [3)] _____ _____ _____ _____.

W: Oh, that's good. Here it is.

17 마지막 말에 이어질 응답 찾기

대화를 듣고, 남자의 마지막 말에 대한 여자의 응답으로 가장 적절한 것을 고르시오.

Woman: _____

① Can you help her swim?
② I want to go swimming with her.
③ Good. Let's go to the sports store.
④ I didn't know she was interested in fashion.
⑤ We should wear a swimming cap when swimming.

W: What will you buy for your sister?

M: I don't know. Do you have any suggestions?

W: Hmm. I think clothes or shoes are common presents.

M: Yeah, but she doesn't need those things. You should check out my sister's closet. It's [1)] _____ _____ _____ _____. And she has enough shoes.

W: Then how about a ring? It would be expensive, though.

M: Yes, that would be [2)] _____ _____ _____.

W: Well, what is she interested in these days?

M: Oh! She's started taking a swimming class! And she said that she [3)] _____ _____ _____ _____ _____.

W: Good. Let's go to the sports store.

18 마지막 말에 이어질 응답 찾기

대화를 듣고, 여자의 마지막 말에 대한 남자의 응답으로 가장 적절한 것을 고르시오.

Man: _____

① See you around.
② I really enjoyed it, too.
③ How about four o'clock?
④ Tomorrow would be fine.
⑤ Let's meet at three o'clock, then.

W: Would you like to see a movie at five today?

M: At five? Do you have a 1) _____ _____ _____ _____ _____ ?

W: Yes, there's a comedy I want to see. I'll 2) _____ _____ _____.

M: Sounds great! We can meet after I do some shopping.

W: Okay, how about meeting at three o'clock?

M: Well, I don't think I can finish shopping by then.

W: Okay. So 3) _____ _____ _____ _____ _____ for you?

M: How about four o'clock?

19 마지막 말에 이어질 응답 찾기 🇬🇧

대화를 듣고, 여자의 마지막 말에 대한 남자의 응답으로 가장 적절한 것을 고르시오.

Man: _____

① You can pay by credit card.
② No, I'm not ready to order yet.
③ Would you please come this way?
④ Sure, I'll bring you the menu right away.
⑤ Our restaurant usually closes at 10:00 p.m.

M: Good evening. Do you 1) _____ _____ _____ ?

W: No, I don't. I'd like a table for two, please.

M: I'm afraid that there aren't any seats right now. We're almost always 2) _____ _____ _____ _____ _____, so we recommend that you make a reservation in advance.

W: Hmm. How long do I have to wait?

M: I can't be sure, but you will have to wait for 3) _____ _____ _____ _____.

W: Then I'll wait here. 4) _____ _____ _____ _____ ?

M: Sure, I'll bring you the menu right away.

20 상황에 적절한 말 찾기 🇬🇧

다음 상황 설명을 듣고, Claire가 Jimmy에게 할 말로 가장 적절한 것을 고르시오.

Claire: _____

① You should see your teacher more often.
② You should not go to bed too late at night.
③ You need to eat healthier and drink less coffee.
④ If I were you, I would not sleep during classes.
⑤ Why don't you talk to your parents about your problems?

W: Jimmy is starting to 1) _____ _____ _____ _____ _____. Recently, he hasn't been able to fall asleep at night. It is becoming a big problem because he 2) _____ _____ _____ during class, and this is affecting his grades as well. Jimmy's friend Claire finds out that he eats a lot of fast food and drinks too much coffee. She thinks that this combination 3) _____ _____ _____ _____ _____ _____.

In this situation, what would Claire most likely say to Jimmy?

Word Test

Ⓐ 다음 영어의 우리말 뜻을 쓰시오.

01 apologize _____

02 besides _____

03 cancellation _____

04 midnight _____

05 homeless _____

06 lack _____

07 coworker _____

08 nearby _____

09 lively _____

10 offer _____

11 participant _____

12 recently _____

13 product _____

14 opportunity _____

15 prefer _____

16 shake _____

17 uncomfortable _____

18 sudden _____

19 recommend _____

20 stair _____

21 withdraw _____

22 beyond _____

23 pick _____

24 feature _____

25 auditorium _____

26 mainly _____

27 profit _____

28 quality _____

29 supply _____

30 gather _____

31 specific _____

32 environment _____

33 destroy _____

34 sign up _____

35 participate in _____

36 make a reservation _____

37 as soon as _____

38 hand in _____

39 give ~ a hand _____

40 have ~ in mind _____

B 다음 우리말 뜻에 맞는 영어를 쓰시오.

01 가파른

02 교장

03 선적; 배송

04 무례한

05 섬

06 제한

07 전통의

08 능력

09 기부[기증]하다

10 소비자

11 예산

12 수행하다; 공연하다

13 배경

14 지진

15 충전

16 시설, 설비

17 서두름

18 수리 기사, 정비사

19 영향을 미치다

20 꾸준한

21 식료품

22 세부 사항

23 배달하다

24 위원회

25 판단하다

26 담요

27 지구; 땅

28 깨닫다

29 똑바로

30 교환하다

31 사냥하다

32 향수

33 낭비, 허비

34 졸업식

35 무료로

36 주문을 받다

37 줄을 서다

38 출장을 가다

39 심호흡하다

40 ~에 접속하다

실전모의고사 04회

정답 및 해설 pp. 25~30

점수: /20

보통 속도 듣기   빠르게 듣기

01 대화를 듣고, 여자가 구입할 스카프를 고르시오.

①   ②   ③

④   ⑤

02 대화를 듣고, 남자의 마지막 말에 담긴 의도로 가장 적절한 것을 고르시오.

① 항의   ② 요구   ③ 반대
④ 거절   ⑤ 동의

03 대화를 듣고, 여자가 남자에게 전화한 목적으로 가장 적절한 것을 고르시오.

① 자동차 수리를 맡기려고
② 자동차 사고를 신고하려고
③ 데리러 오기를 부탁하려고
④ 정비소의 위치를 물어보려고
⑤ 자동차 보험에 관해 문의하려고

04 대화를 듣고, 여자가 책을 반납할 요일을 고르시오.

① 일요일   ② 월요일   ③ 화요일
④ 수요일   ⑤ 목요일

05 대화를 듣고, 남자의 심정으로 가장 적절한 것을 고르시오.

① jealous   ② excited   ③ relaxed
④ nervous   ⑤ embarrassed

06 다음 그림의 상황에 가장 적절한 대화를 고르시오.

①   ②   ③   ④   ⑤

07 대화를 듣고, 남자가 여자에게 부탁한 일로 가장 적절한 것을 고르시오.

① 공연 표 예매하기
② 공연 표 환불하기
③ 수업 시간 조정하기
④ 공연장에 데려다주기
⑤ 공연 표 매진 여부 알아보기

08 다음을 듣고, Science Camp에 관해 언급되지 않은 것을 고르시오.

① 날짜와 장소   ② 캠프 운영진 정보
③ 등록비   ④ 프로그램 활동
⑤ 캠프 등록 방법

09 다음을 듣고, 어떤 직업에 관한 설명인지 고르시오.

① 교통 경찰   ② 건축 설계사
③ 트럭 운전사   ④ 자동차 정비사
⑤ 자동차 디자이너

10 다음을 듣고, 두 사람의 대화가 어색한 것을 고르시오.

①   ②   ③   ④   ⑤

11 대화를 듣고, 남자가 한국에서 제일 먼저 할 일로 가장 적절한 것을 고르시오.

① 고궁에 가기　　　　② 쇼핑하기
③ 직장 구하기　　　　④ 친척 방문하기
⑤ 친구들 만나기

12 다음 표를 보면서 대화를 듣고, 내용과 일치하지 <u>않</u>는 것을 고르시오.

Reservation		
①	When	Friday, February 22
②	What Time	6:30 p.m.
③	How Many People	Two
④	Who	The Smiths
⑤	Phone Number	014-555-5309

13 대화를 듣고, 여자가 Alice를 만나기로 한 시각을 고르시오.

① 4:00 p.m.　② 4:30 p.m.　③ 5:00 p.m.
④ 5:30 p.m.　⑤ 6:00 p.m.

14 대화를 듣고, 남자가 주말에 한 일로 가장 적절한 것을 고르시오.

① 휴식하기　　　　② 하이킹하기
③ 농구 연습하기　　④ 친구 집 방문하기
⑤ 농구 경기 관람하기

15 다음을 듣고, 방송의 목적으로 가장 적절한 것을 고르시오.

① 차량 이동 주차를 요청하려고
② 주차장 폐쇄 일정을 안내하려고
③ 깨끗한 주차장 이용을 당부하려고
④ 주차장 청소 계획 변경을 알리려고
⑤ 불법 주차 차량의 견인 조치를 예고하려고

고난도
16 대화를 듣고, 남자가 지불할 금액을 고르시오.

① $240　　② $250　　③ $270
④ $300　　⑤ $330

17 대화를 듣고, 여자의 마지막 말에 대한 남자의 응답으로 가장 적절한 것을 고르시오.

Man: _____

① Hmm... I'd like some shoes.
② I hope they love my presents.
③ Christmas is my favorite holiday.
④ I want to watch a movie on Christmas Day.
⑤ The snow last Christmas was the best present ever!

[18-19] 대화를 듣고, 남자의 마지막 말에 대한 여자의 응답으로 가장 적절한 것을 고르시오.

18 Woman: _____

① I'd like to have this photo.
② Hang it in the living room.
③ I don't think it should be there.
④ The photo was sent to an art museum.
⑤ How about hanging it in your bedroom?

19 Woman: _____

① I need clean towels, too.
② Do you need room service?
③ I'll send the repairman right away.
④ What kind of room would you like?
⑤ Would you like something to drink with that?

20 다음 상황 설명을 듣고, 선생님이 진수에게 할 말로 가장 적절한 것을 고르시오.

Teacher: _____

① You missed the chance to sing.
② You should have practiced more.
③ I thought you were a good singer.
④ I have to tell you that I'm disappointed.
⑤ You will do great! Just relax and have fun.

Dictation Test 04

01 그림 정보 파악

대화를 듣고, 여자가 구입할 스카프를 고르시오.

① ② ③

④ ⑤

M: Hey, what are you doing?

W: I'm shopping online. This store is 1) _____ _____ _____ _____.

M: What are you going to buy?

W: How about this scarf?

M: It looks good, but do they only have designs with stripes?

W: No. There are a few other styles though, including plain and polka-dotted.

M: 2) _____ _____ _____, and I don't really like polka dots.

W: Me, neither. Then how about this one 3) _____ _____ _____ _____ on it?

M: That's nice.

W: I like this one the most. I'll buy it.

02 의도 파악

대화를 듣고, 남자의 마지막 말에 담긴 의도로 가장 적절한 것을 고르시오.

① 항의   ② 요구   ③ 반대
④ 거절   ⑤ 동의

M: You look angry, Samantha. Is something wrong?

W: That man is 1) _____ _____ _____ on his cell phone. I can't stand it.

M: Yes, it's very annoying. I can hear every word of his conversation.

W: I think cell phone users 2) _____ _____ _____ _____. These days, you can hear people talking loudly on their phones in all kinds of public places. You hear them in the theater, on the subway, and even in the library.

M: I 3) _____ _____ _____.

03 목적 파악

대화를 듣고, 여자가 남자에게 전화한 목적으로 가장 적절한 것을 고르시오.

① 자동차 수리를 맡기려고
② 자동차 사고를 신고하려고
③ 데리러 오기를 부탁하려고
④ 정비소의 위치를 물어보려고
⑤ 자동차 보험에 관해 문의하려고

[Cell phone rings.]

M: Hello?

W: Hi, Dad. It's Fiona.

M: I was about to call you. Where are you? You told me that you would be home an hour ago.

W: I know. I'm sorry, but ¹⁾ _____ _____ _____ _____ on the way home. So I'm at a service center right now.

M: Oh, that's too bad. Are you okay?

W: I'm fine.

M: What's wrong with the car?

W: I don't know, but they said it would ²⁾ _____ _____ _____ to fix it. Would you mind coming here to ³⁾ _____ _____ _____ _____ home?

M: Of course not. I'll be there soon. Which service center are you at?

04 세부 정보 파악

대화를 듣고, 여자가 책을 반납할 요일을 고르시오.

① 일요일　　② 월요일　　③ 화요일
④ 수요일　　⑤ 목요일

W: I'd like to ¹⁾ _____ _____ _____ _____.

M: Sure. Three books in total. Please ²⁾ _____ _____ _____ _____ _____.

W: Seven days? So they're due next Friday?

M: No. Today is Thursday. So, please return them by next Thursday.

W: I see.

M: Oh, I'm sorry. I made a mistake. Since these are new releases, you'll have to return them in four days.

W: Okay. I'll ³⁾ _____ _____ _____ _____.

M: All right.

심정 추론 🇬🇧

대화를 듣고, 남자의 심정으로 가장 적절한 것을 고르시오.

① jealous   ② excited   ③ relaxed
④ nervous   ⑤ embarrassed

W: Did you get your plane tickets?

M: Yes. I bought them on the Internet. Now I'm 1) _____ _____ _____ _____.

W: So when are you going exactly?

M: Ten days from now. I can't wait. It's going to 2) _____ _____ _____ _____.

W: Which countries are you planning to visit?

M: I'm going to visit England, France, and Italy. I'll be gone for a month.

W: I envy you. A month in Europe. What a great summer vacation!

M: Yeah, I've been planning this trip for a long time. Now all I want to do is 3) _____ _____.

---

06 그림 상황에 적절한 대화 찾기

다음 그림의 상황에 가장 적절한 대화를 고르시오.

①   ②   ③   ④   ⑤

① W: I'd like you to 1) _____ _____ _____ _____ from my dress.

   M: Okay. You can pick it up this Saturday.

② W: Would you go to the mall with me? I need a new dress.

   M: Sure. When do you want to go?

③ W: 2) _____ _____ _____ _____ in this dress?

   M: You look great!

④ W: Oh no! I spilled coffee on my dress!

   M: Don't worry. You can 3) _____ _____ _____.

⑤ W: I'd like to buy this dress.

   M: I'm sorry, ma'am. That one is 4) _____ _____ _____.

---

07 부탁한 일 파악

대화를 듣고, 남자가 여자에게 부탁한 일로 가장 적절한 것을 고르시오.

① 공연 표 예매하기
② 공연 표 환불하기
③ 수업 시간 조정하기
④ 공연장에 데려다주기
⑤ 공연 표 매진 여부 알아보기

M: Hey, Katie. I have a favor to ask, if you're not busy.

W: I'm not busy. What is it?

M: Justin Gilmore 1) _____ _____ _____ _____ in town.

W: Wow! You have been waiting for him to come, haven't you?

M: Yes, I have. But I have a problem.

W: What is it?

M: The 2) _____ _____ _____ _____ at three this afternoon, but I will be in class then. Could you try to 3) _____ _____ _____ _____?

W: Sure, I'll try. But they will sell out quickly, so I might not be able to get one.

M: I know.

다음을 듣고, Science Camp에 관해 언급되지 않은 것을 고르시오.

① 날짜와 장소　　② 캠프 운영진 정보
③ 등록비　　④ 프로그램 활동
⑤ 캠프 등록 방법

★Focus on Sound meeting

[t]는 모음 사이에서 약화되어 [미팅]이 아닌 [미링]으로 발음된다.

W: As the program director of Science Camp, I have an important announcement to make. This year's Science Camp will be held at Montgomery School from July 16 1) _____ _____ _____ . The camp is free! There is, however, a $20 fee 2) _____ _____ _____ _____ . Activities at the camp will include watching movies, playing games, doing science experiments, and ★meeting scientists from different fields. To 3) _____ _____ _____ _____ _____ _____ , please register at www.esfsci.com.

09 화제 파악

다음을 듣고, 어떤 직업에 관한 설명인지 고르시오.

① 교통 경찰　　② 건축 설계사
③ 트럭 운전사　　④ 자동차 정비사
⑤ 자동차 디자이너

M: People with this job 1) _____ _____ _____ _____ , such as cars and trucks. When a car breaks down, they find out what the problem is. Then they 2) _____ _____ _____ _____ _____ to fix it. Sometimes they also 3) _____ _____ _____ . To get this job, you need to know a lot about vehicles and machines. You also need to have a professional license.

10 어색한 대화 찾기

다음을 듣고, 두 사람의 대화가 어색한 것을 고르시오.

① ② ③ ④ ⑤

① M: Where have you been?
　 W: I was reading a book at the library.
② M: Have you seen my sunglasses?
　 W: I think they're on your desk.
③ M: I bought this shirt, but it has a hole in it.
　 W: I'm sorry. Let me 1) _____ _____ _____ _____ .
④ M: You didn't 2) _____ _____ _____ _____ , did you?
　 W: We don't have any milk in the refrigerator.
⑤ M: I think the red dress 3) _____ _____ _____ the white one.
　 W: I like the red dress, too.

11 할 일 파악

대화를 듣고, 남자가 한국에서 제일 먼저 할 일로 가장 적절한 것을 고르시오.

① 고궁에 가기   ② 쇼핑하기
③ 직장 구하기   ④ 친척 방문하기
⑤ 친구들 만나기

W: Do you have any plans for this vacation?

M: Yes! I'm going to travel to Korea!

W: Sounds exciting! When do you leave?

M: I'm [1] _____ _____ _____, and I'll be there for two weeks.

W: Wow! What are you going to do there?

M: I want to [2] _____ _____ _____ in Seoul. And I'll go shopping at Dongdaemun Market.

W: You also have a lot of friends in Korea, don't you?

M: Yes. I want to see them too. Actually, that's what I'll [3] _____ _____ _____ _____.

W: It sounds like you'll be very busy.

M: I will. I can't wait!

---

12 내용 일치 파악 🇬🇧

다음 표를 보면서 대화를 듣고, 내용과 일치하지 않는 것을 고르시오.

Reservation		
①	When	Friday, February 22
②	What Time	6:30 p.m.
③	How Many People	Two
④	Who	The Smiths
⑤	Phone Number	014-555-5309

*Focus on Sound　last

미국식은 a를 [애]로 발음하여 [래스트], 영국식은 [아]로 발음하여 [라스트]로 발음된다.

[Phone rings.]

W: Leonardo Restaurant. How can I help you?

M: I'd like to make a dinner reservation [1] _____ _____, _____ _____.

W: Sure. What time would you like to come?

M: How about 6:30?

W: Sorry, we don't have any free tables at that time. [2] _____ _____ _____ _____?

M: That's fine.

W: [3] _____ _____ _____ will there be in your party?

M: Just my wife and I. Our *last name is Smith.

W: And may I [4] _____ _____ _____ _____, please?

M: It's 014-555-5309.

W: All right. We'll see you this Friday.

13 숫자 정보 파악

대화를 듣고, 여자가 Alice를 만나기로 한 시각을 고르시오.

① 4:00 p.m.   ② 4:30 p.m.   ③ 5:00 p.m.
④ 5:30 p.m.   ⑤ 6:00 p.m.

W: What time is it?

M: Um, it's 4:30 p.m.

W: Oh! 1) _____ _____ _____ _____ now. It was so great to talk with you.

M: You're leaving already? We were in the middle of a conversation!

W: I have to meet Alice 2) _____ _____ _____.

M: Can you call her and push back your meeting time? We still have more to talk about.

W: Sorry, but I can't. 3) _____ _____ _____ _____ to a concert with her.

M: I see. Well, have a good time. And say hello to her for me.

W: Okay, I will.

14 한 일 파악

대화를 듣고, 남자가 주말에 한 일로 가장 적절한 것을 고르시오.

① 휴식하기   ② 하이킹하기
③ 농구 연습하기   ④ 친구 집 방문하기
⑤ 농구 경기 관람하기

W: Hi, Nick. How was your weekend?

M: Hi, Christie. It was pretty relaxing.

W: Didn't you go to a basketball game with Dan?

M: Unfortunately, Dan 1) _____ _____ _____, so he stayed home.

W: Then you didn't go?

M: No, I gave the tickets to my brother. And then 2) _____ _____ _____.

W: Really? By yourself?

M: That's right. The weather wasn't great, but I 3) _____ _____ _____.

W: That sounds great. Anyway, I'd love to go to a basketball game sometime. Let's go together.

M: Sure.

15 목적 파악

다음을 듣고, 방송의 목적으로 가장 적절한 것을 고르시오.

① 차량 이동 주차를 요청하려고
② 주차장 폐쇄 일정을 안내하려고
③ 깨끗한 주차장 이용을 당부하려고
④ 주차장 청소 계획 변경을 알리려고
⑤ 불법 주차 차량의 견인 조치를 예고하려고

W: Hello, Happy Town residents! I'm Lena from the management office. I have an announcement. As I have mentioned several times before, our apartment building is planning to 1) _____ _____ _____ _____ this week. And residents have been asked to move their cars. However, many cars are still parked in the parking lot, so we are 2) _____ _____ _____ _____. Furthermore, if you keep your car in the lot, it could get damaged. Today, we're cleaning the first basement level. So once again, I ask you to please 3) _____ _____ _____ to the second basement level or to another place. Thank you for your cooperation.

---

16 숫자 정보 파악

대화를 듣고, 남자가 지불할 금액을 고르시오.

① $240   ② $250   ③ $270
④ $300   ⑤ $330

W: Good afternoon. Can I help you?
M: Yes, I'd like to 1) _____ _____ _____. What are your prices?
W: It's 2) _____ _____ _____ for a medium-sized car. If you want to rent a van, it's $100 a day.
M: I'll take a medium-sized car 3) _____ _____ _____, please. And I need a car seat for my baby.
W: Okay. Then you will have to 4) _____ _____ _____ _____ per day.
M: All right. I'd like to pay by credit card.
W: No problem.

---

17 마지막 말에 이어질 응답 찾기

대화를 듣고, 여자의 마지막 말에 대한 남자의 응답으로 가장 적절한 것을 고르시오.

Man: _____

① Hmm... I'd like some shoes.
② I hope they love my presents.
③ Christmas is my favorite holiday.
④ I want to watch a movie on Christmas Day.
⑤ The snow last Christmas was the best present ever!

W: Have you bought Christmas gifts for your family yet?
M: Yes. And I can't wait to 1) _____ _____ _____ _____.
W: What did you get?
M: Well, I bought a tie for my father and a scarf for my mother. And I'm giving a T-shirt to my sister.
W: What did you buy for your brother, Tommy?
M: I 2) _____ _____ _____ _____ for him.
W: Oh, you're so nice! By the way, 3) _____ _____ _____ _____ for Christmas?
M: Hmm... I'd like some shoes.

18 마지막 말에 이어질 응답 찾기

대화를 듣고, 남자의 마지막 말에 대한 여자의 응답으로 가장 적절한 것을 고르시오.

Woman: _____

① I'd like to have this photo.
② Hang it in the living room.
③ I don't think it should be there.
④ The photo was sent to an art museum.
⑤ How about hanging it in your bedroom?

★Focus on Sound   true

[t]와 [r]이 연달아 나와 [트루]가 아닌 [츄루]로 발음된다.

W: That photo looks great! Did you take it?
M: My friend Eva took it. She's so talented. Her photographs have been in magazines.
W: You should 1) _____ _____ _____ in the living room. Then everyone can see it.
M: Our family portrait is already hanging in the living room. If we hang too many pictures in the same place, it 2) _____ _____ _____.
W: There aren't any photos in the kitchen.
M: That's *true. But the kitchen wall has a clock hanging on it. Hmm... Do you 3) _____ _____ _____ _____?
W: How about hanging it in your bedroom?

19 마지막 말에 이어질 응답 찾기 🇬🇧

대화를 듣고, 남자의 마지막 말에 대한 여자의 응답으로 가장 적절한 것을 고르시오.

Woman: _____

① I need clean towels, too.
② Do you need room service?
③ I'll send the repairman right away.
④ What kind of room would you like?
⑤ Would you like something to drink with that?

[Phone rings.]
W: Clayton Hotel reception desk. How may I help you?
M: 1) _____ _____ _____ I have a problem. The shower in my bathroom only has cold water.
W: I'm sorry about that, sir. We can 2) _____ _____ _____ by this afternoon.
M: This afternoon? I just came back from a long jog. And I 3) _____ _____ _____ _____ to take a shower.
W: I understand, sir. Which room are you staying in?
M: Room 403.
W: I'll send the repairman right away.

20 상황에 적절한 말 찾기

다음 상황 설명을 듣고, 선생님이 진수에게 할 말로 가장 적절한 것을 고르시오.

Teacher: _____

① You missed the chance to sing.
② You should have practiced more.
③ I thought you were a good singer.
④ I have to tell you that I'm disappointed.
⑤ You will do great! Just relax and have fun.

M: Jinsu is a senior at Mirae High School. His teacher asked him to 1) _____ _____ _____ _____ _____ because Jinsu is a very good singer. Jinsu practices singing every night because he 2) _____ _____ in front of many people. On the day of the ceremony, Jinsu feels worried and 3) _____ _____ _____ _____. Jinsu's teacher sees him and walks over to him. In this situation, what would his teacher most likely say to Jinsu?

실전모의고사 05 회

정답 및 해설 pp.30~34

점수: /20

보통속도 듣기   빠르게 듣기

01 대화를 듣고, 여자가 만들 초대장을 고르시오.

고난도

02 대화를 듣고, Hope Goods에 관해 언급되지 <u>않은</u> 것을 고르시오.

① 설립 목적   ② 설립 연도   ③ 자선 행사
④ 기부 품목   ⑤ 기부금 사용처

03 대화를 듣고, 여자의 마지막 말에 담긴 의도로 가장 적절한 것을 고르시오.

① 거절   ② 충고   ③ 위로
④ 칭찬   ⑤ 허락

04 대화를 듣고, 두 사람이 만나기로 한 시각을 고르시오.

① 2:00 p.m.   ② 2:30 p.m.   ③ 3:00 p.m.
④ 3:30 p.m.   ⑤ 4:00 p.m.

05 다음 그림의 상황에 가장 적절한 대화를 고르시오.

①   ②   ③   ④   ⑤

06 대화를 듣고, 두 사람이 대화하는 장소로 가장 적절한 곳을 고르시오.

① 공항   ② 호텔   ③ 경찰서
④ 쇼핑몰   ⑤ 기차역

07 대화를 듣고, 남자가 여자에게 부탁한 일로 가장 적절한 것을 고르시오.

① 약 사다 주기   ② 병원에 데려가기
③ 수프 만들어 주기   ④ 외식할 식당 예약하기
⑤ 매운 음식 만들어 주기

고난도

08 다음을 듣고, 아동 비만의 원인으로 언급되지 <u>않은</u> 것을 고르시오.

① 유전적 요인
② 신체 활동 시간 감소
③ 스트레스
④ 수면 부족
⑤ 건강에 좋지 않은 식습관

09 다음을 듣고, 무엇에 관한 설명인지 고르시오.

① 월드컵   ② 올림픽
③ 엑스포   ④ 프리미어리그
⑤ 세계 야구 클래식

10 다음을 듣고, 두 사람의 대화가 <u>어색한</u> 것을 고르시오.

①   ②   ③   ④   ⑤

11 대화를 듣고, 두 사람이 공원에 가기 전에 먼저 할 일로 가장 적절한 것을 고르시오.

① 간식 사기   ② 건전지 사기
③ 자동차 주유하기   ④ 전화기 충전하기
⑤ 일기 예보 확인하기

12 대화를 듣고, 두 사람이 만나기로 한 시각을 고르시오.

① 1:00 p.m.   ② 1:30 p.m.   ③ 2:00 p.m.
④ 2:30 p.m.   ⑤ 3:00 p.m.

13 다음 지도를 보면서 대화를 듣고, 여자가 가려고 하는 장소를 고르시오.

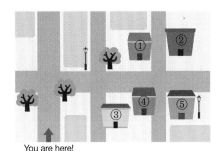

You are here!

14 대화를 듣고, 남자가 주말에 한 일로 가장 적절한 것을 고르시오.

① 미술관 관람하기   ② 벚꽃 축제 참가하기
③ 백악관 방문하기   ④ 공항 라운지 방문하기
⑤ 백악관 투어 예약하기

15 다음을 듣고, 방송의 목적으로 가장 적절한 것을 고르시오.

① 병가 사용을 권장하려고
② 사무실 청결 유지를 요청하려고
③ 감기와 독감의 차이를 설명하려고
④ 독감 예방 주사 접종을 권고하려고
⑤ 독감 유행에 따른 주의점을 당부하려고

16 대화를 듣고, 여자가 받을 거스름돈을 고르시오.

① $2   ② $4   ③ $6   ④ $8   ⑤ $10

17 대화를 듣고, 남자의 마지막 말에 대한 여자의 응답으로 가장 적절한 것을 고르시오.

Woman: _____

① I hope to go fishing again.
② I like to hike with my family.
③ I want to go to summer camp this vacation.
④ It would be much better if the weather was good.
⑤ I really enjoyed hiking, but I liked rock climbing even more.

[18 - 19] 대화를 듣고, 여자의 마지막 말에 대한 남자의 응답으로 가장 적절한 것을 고르시오.

18 Man: _____

① I can't wait to go.
② Thank you for inviting me.
③ The food was really delicious.
④ I have plans with my own family that day.
⑤ I can't eat these because I'm allergic to eggs.

19 Man: _____

① I work five days a week.
② I'm going to work hard.
③ I'd like to work for a bank.
④ I've worked as a reporter before.
⑤ Congratulations on your graduation!

20 다음 상황 설명을 듣고, Jenny가 친구들에게 할 말로 가장 적절한 것을 고르시오.

Jenny: _____

① I'm so excited to go camping.
② I think we should wait until next weekend.
③ This is the best camping trip I've ever been on.
④ It's difficult to go to a different mountain from here.
⑤ I'm sorry, but I don't want to be in charge of transportation.

Dictation Test 05

정답 및 해설 pp. 30~34

01 그림 정보 파악

대화를 듣고, 여자가 만들 초대장을 고르시오.

①
②
③
④
⑤ welcome

M: Wow, are you making the invitations for your dinner party? They look amazing.

W: Do you think so? I've been working on them for a while, but I'm not sure.

M: I like the card with the 1) _____ _____ _____ _____.

W: I drew a whole cake with a candle at first, but I changed it to 2) _____ _____ _____ _____.

M: The strawberry on this cake is so cute.

W: Where do you think I should put "welcome"?

M: 3) _____ _____ _____ _____ would be good.

W: Good idea. That's where I'll put it.

02 언급되지 않은 내용 찾기

대화를 듣고, Hope Goods에 관해 언급되지 않은 것을 고르시오.

① 설립 목적   ② 설립 연도   ③ 자선 행사
④ 기부 품목   ⑤ 기부금 사용처

W: What are you doing, Jaemin?

M: I'm gathering my old clothes to throw them away. I don't wear them anymore.

W: Why don't you donate them to Hope Goods?

M: Hope Goods? What's that?

W: It's a charity that 1) _____ _____ _____. It was founded in 2020.

M: Oh, I'd like to help them. What items can I donate besides clothes?

W: I heard 2) _____ _____ _____ _____.

M: How about food?

W: I don't think they accept food, but they do use money from donations to provide refugees with 3) _____ _____ _____ _____ _____.

M: I see. I'll donate some money too, then.

W: Good idea. I will as well.

03 의도 파악 🇬🇧

대화를 듣고, 여자의 마지막 말에 담긴 의도로 가장 적절한 것을 고르시오.

① 거절 ② 충고 ③ 위로
④ 칭찬 ⑤ 허락

W: It looks like it's going to snow.

M: Yes, clouds are suddenly gathering. 1) _____ _____ _____.

W: Hey, look! It's snowing already.

M: Oh no. I don't like driving in the snow.

W: The 2) _____ _____ _____ _____. Maybe we should stop for a second and put snow chains on the tires.

M: Well, I'm afraid I don't have them with me. I didn't know it would snow today.

W: Are you serious? You 3) _____ _____ _____ _____ _____ in the winter. You know that it's better to be safe than sorry.

04 숫자 정보 파악

대화를 듣고, 두 사람이 만나기로 한 시각을 고르시오.

① 2:00 p.m. ② 2:30 p.m. ③ 3:00 p.m.
④ 3:30 p.m. ⑤ 4:00 p.m.

W: I'm going to get a birthday gift for my mother tomorrow. Do you want to come with me?

M: Sure, that sounds like fun. When are you going?

W: Let's meet at the mall tomorrow after school. How about at 3:00 p.m.?

M: No, I can't meet you then. I 1) _____ _____ _____ _____ _____.

W: Oh, really? How long does practice last?

M: We usually finish 2) _____ _____ _____ _____.

W: Okay, then let's meet 3) _____ _____ _____ _____ at 3:30.

M: Great! See you then!

다음 그림의 상황에 가장 적절한 대화를 고르시오.

① ② ③ ④ ⑤

① W: I'd like to learn photography.

　M: There are some good classes at our school.

② W: This camera looks expensive. How much is it?

　M: It's $500, but we have some cheaper models, too.

③ W: 1) _____ _____ _____ _____ _____ going to Paris?

　M: That sounds great.

④ W: Can you 2) _____ _____ _____ _____ with the Eiffel Tower?

　M: Sure. Give me your camera.

⑤ W: Do you think you can 3) _____ _____ _____? I can't turn it on.

　M: I'm afraid I can't do that right now.

대화를 듣고, 두 사람이 대화하는 장소로 가장 적절한 곳을 고르시오.

① 공항　　　② 호텔　　　③ 경찰서
④ 쇼핑몰　　⑤ 기차역

M: What can I do for you?

W: I've just arrived here, but I can't find my bag.

M: 1) _____ _____ _____ _____ _____ ?

W: It was Flight 303 from Los Angeles.

M: All right. Can you 2) _____ _____ _____ _____ ?

W: It's dark brown. It's about half a meter tall. And it's made of a tough fabric.

M: Does it 3) _____ _____ _____ _____ on it?

W: Yes. I wrote my name on it, Susan Brown.

M: I see. Wait right here. I'll see if I can find it.

대화를 듣고, 남자가 여자에게 부탁한 일로 가장 적절한 것을 고르시오.

① 약 사다 주기　　　② 병원에 데려가기
③ 수프 만들어 주기　④ 외식할 식당 예약하기
⑤ 매운 음식 만들어 주기

M: Mom, what are you making for dinner?

W: I'm making spicy cold noodles. Your dad wants something spicy.

M: Oh. Can I have something else?

W: Why? What's wrong?

M: Well, I'm not feeling very well. I think I have a cold. So I want 1) _____ _____ _____ _____ .

W: Really? Is it bad? 2) _____ _____ _____ _____ ?

M: No, it's not that bad. Can you just 3) _____ _____ _____ _____ ?

W: Of course. Go wait in your room. I'll call you when it's done.

다음을 듣고, 아동 비만의 원인으로 언급되지 않은 것을 고르시오.

① 유전적 요인
② 신체 활동 시간 감소
③ 스트레스
④ 수면 부족
⑤ 건강에 좋지 않은 식습관

★ Focus on Sound overweight

gh는 묵음으로 [오버ㄹ웨이트]로 발음된다.

W: Did you read the story about *overweight children in the newspaper? The number of overweight children is growing. They make up 14% of all overweight people. What [1)] _____ _____ _____ _____? There are many causes. Some researchers say that genetic factors lead to child obesity. But most importantly, children [2)] _____ _____ _____ _____ _____ _____ because of computer games and studying. That's a serious problem. [3)] _____ _____ _____ can be another cause. Also, some children [4)] _____ _____ _____ _____.

---

09 화제 파악

다음을 듣고, 무엇에 관한 설명인지 고르시오.

① 월드컵   ② 올림픽
③ 엑스포   ④ 프리미어리그
⑤ 세계 야구 클래식

★ Focus on Sound honor

[h]는 묵음으로 [아너]로 발음된다.

M: This is one of the world's [1)] _____ _____ _____. It is held every four years. It [2)] _____ _____ _____ _____. In 1988, it was held in Seoul. Many athletes think it is an *honor to [3)] _____ _____ _____. The winners of each event get either a gold, silver, or bronze medal. People all around the world look forward to this.

---

10 어색한 대화 찾기

다음을 듣고, 두 사람의 대화가 어색한 것을 고르시오.

①   ②   ③   ④   ⑤

★ Focus on Sound must be

[t]는 자음 앞에서 거의 발음되지 않아 [머스트비]가 아닌 [머스비]로 발음된다.

① M: I worked on my science project all night.
   W: You *must be so tired.
② M: [1)] _____ _____ _____ _____ ice skating tomorrow.
   W: That sounds interesting. Can I join you?
③ M: [2)] _____ _____ _____ _____ _____ your dog?
   W: Once or twice a day.
④ M: Can you tell me [3)] _____ _____ _____ _____ City Hall?
   W: Oh, you can take the subway, line 2.
⑤ M: [4)] _____ _____ _____ _____ _____ tomorrow?
   W: Every Tuesday and Thursday.

11 할 일 파악

대화를 듣고, 두 사람이 공원에 가기 전에 먼저 할 일로 가장 적절한 것을 고르시오.

① 간식 사기
② 건전지 사기
③ 자동차 주유하기
④ 전화기 충전하기
⑤ 일기 예보 확인하기

W: It's such a lovely day, isn't it?

M: Yes, it is. Why don't we go to the park and enjoy the weather?

W: That sounds like a great idea.

M: Okay. Let's 1) _____ _____ _____.

W: Sure! Pictures are the best way to record memories.

M: You're right. But we need to 2) _____ _____ _____ _____ _____ first.

W: Why? Do you want to buy some snacks?

M: No. My phone battery is almost dead, so I 3) _____ _____ _____ _____.

W: Okay. We can stop at the convenience store next to the park.

12 숫자 정보 파악

대화를 듣고, 두 사람이 만나기로 한 시각을 고르시오.

① 1:00 p.m.
② 1:30 p.m.
③ 2:00 p.m.
④ 2:30 p.m.
⑤ 3:00 p.m.

M: What time shall we meet?

W: How about 2:00 p.m.?

M: No, 1) _____ _____ _____.

W: How long does it take to get to the theater?

M: I'm not very sure, but it'll 2) _____ _____ _____ _____ _____. And we have to arrive 30 minutes before the play starts.

W: I didn't consider that. 3) _____ _____ _____ ?

M: At three o'clock.

W: Then when would be good?

M: How about 4) _____ _____ _____ _____ _____ ? We can take our time, then.

W: That's perfect!

13 위치 찾기

다음 지도를 보면서 대화를 듣고, 여자가 가려고 하는 장소를 고르시오.

You are here!

W: Excuse me, are there any bakeries in this area?

M: Yes, there's one.

W: Oh, good. Is it far from here?

M: No, it's 1) _____ _____ _____ _____ _____ . But you can also get there on foot.

W: Could you 2) _____ _____ _____ ?

M: Sure. 3) _____ _____ _____ _____ _____ and turn right.

W: One block and turn right. And then?

M: Walk two blocks and 4) _____ _____ _____ _____ _____ . You'll see it on your left.

W: Thank you very much.

14 한 일 파악

대화를 듣고, 남자가 주말에 한 일로 가장 적절한 것을 고르시오.

① 미술관 관람하기   ② 벚꽃 축제 참가하기
③ 백악관 방문하기   ④ 공항 라운지 방문하기
⑤ 백악관 투어 예약하기

W: Hey, John. How was your trip to Washington, D.C. last weekend?

M: It was so much fun! I really enjoyed visiting the National Gallery of Art.

W: That's nice.

M: And the cherry blossom festival was held nearby. So more tourists came to Washington, D.C. than usual.

W: Did you 1) _____ _____ _____ _____ , too?

M: Unfortunately, I couldn't. I 2) _____ _____ _____ _____ to go.

W: How about the White House?

M: I was 3) _____ _____ _____ _____ right before I went to the airport. But I was not allowed to go inside.

W: Why?

M: I 4) _____ _____ _____ .

W: Sorry to hear that.

15 목적 파악

다음을 듣고, 방송의 목적으로 가장 적절한 것을 고르시오.

① 병가 사용을 권장하려고
② 사무실 청결 유지를 요청하려고
③ 감기와 독감의 차이를 설명하려고
④ 독감 예방 주사 접종을 권고하려고
⑤ 독감 유행에 따른 주의점을 당부하려고

Focus on Sound symptom

자음 3개가 겹쳐 나와 중간 자음인 [p]가 약화되어 [심프텀]이 아닌 [심텀]으로 발음된다.

W: May I have your attention, please? These days, many people in our city are 1) _____ _____ _____. In a crowded office like ours, this can be a real problem. The early *symptoms include a 2) _____ _____ _____ _____. Later, you'll get a stomachache and start sneezing. If you think you may be getting the flu, please 3) _____ _____ _____ _____. Also, be sure to wash your hands frequently and to 4) _____ _____ _____ when sneezing or coughing. Thanks, and have a great day.

16 숫자 정보 파악

대화를 듣고, 여자가 받을 거스름돈을 고르시오.

① $2　　② $4　　③ $6
④ $8　　⑤ $10

M: Hi, Kate. Here's your ticket for the concert.

W: Oh, thanks for getting it for me. How much did it cost?

M: The total was $16. So 1) _____ _____ _____.

W: All right. Here's $10.

M: Hold on a minute. Uh-oh... I 2) _____ _____ _____ _____ for you right now. Can I give it to you later?

W: Sure. You can 3) _____ _____ _____ anytime. Anyway, we'd better hurry up. The concert starts in 10 minutes.

17 마지막 말에 이어질 응답 찾기

대화를 듣고, 남자의 마지막 말에 대한 여자의 응답으로 가장 적절한 것을 고르시오.

Woman: _____

① I hope to go fishing again.
② I like to hike with my family.
③ I want to go to summer camp this vacation.
④ It would be much better if the weather was good.
⑤ I really enjoyed hiking, but I liked rock climbing even more.

M: Hey, Lily. 1) _____ _____ _____ _____ _____ _____?

W: Hi! I had a great time. We did so many interesting things.

M: I'm glad you enjoyed it. What kinds of things did you do?

W: Well, we went swimming and 2) _____ _____ _____ _____. We also went hiking and rock climbing.

M: Wow, it sounds like a lot of fun. So which part 3) _____ _____ _____ _____ _____?

W: I really enjoyed hiking, but I liked rock climbing even more.

18 마지막 말에 이어질 응답 찾기

대화를 듣고, 여자의 마지막 말에 대한 남자의 응답으로 가장 적절한 것을 고르시오.

Man: _____

① I can't wait to go.
② Thank you for inviting me.
③ The food was really delicious.
④ I have plans with my own family that day.
⑤ I can't eat these because I'm allergic to eggs.

W: It's almost the end of the year.
M: Yes. Time flies. How are you going to spend New Year's Eve?
W: I'm going to 1) _____ _____ _____ _____ _____.
   I'll make some mandoo.
M: Mandoo?
W: Yes, they're a kind of Asian dumpling. 2) _____ _____ _____ _____ _____?
M: No, I haven't.
W: They're very delicious. Would you 3) _____ _____ _____ _____?
M: Thanks, but I can't.
W: Why not?
M: I have plans with my own family that day.

19 마지막 말에 이어질 응답 찾기 🇬🇧

대화를 듣고, 여자의 마지막 말에 대한 남자의 응답으로 가장 적절한 것을 고르시오.

Man: _____

① I work five days a week.
② I'm going to work hard.
③ I'd like to work for a bank.
④ I've worked as a reporter before.
⑤ Congratulations on your graduation!

M: I can't believe our graduation is just two months away.
W: Me neither. Time flies.
M: What are you going to 1) _____ _____ _____?
W: I'll be going to graduate school. How about you?
M: I'm getting ready to 2) _____ _____ _____ at several companies.
W: What kind of company do you 3) _____ _____ _____ _____?
M: I'd like to work for a bank.

20 상황에 적절한 말 찾기 🇬🇧

다음 상황 설명을 듣고, Jenny가 친구들에게 할 말로 가장 적절한 것을 고르시오.

Jenny: _____

① I'm so excited to go camping.
② I think we should wait until next weekend.
③ This is the best camping trip I've ever been on.
④ It's difficult to go to a different mountain from here.
⑤ I'm sorry, but I don't want to be in charge of transportation.

M: Jenny and her friends are planning for a camping trip this weekend. Everyone 1) _____ _____ _____ _____ to do. Harry is 2) _____ _____ _____ _____, and Lindsey will bring the camping equipment. Jenny will take care of the rest. Jenny 3) _____ _____ _____ _____, and it says that it will rain the whole weekend. She thinks it might be best to 4) _____ _____ _____ _____ _____. In this situation, what would Jenny most likely say to her friends?

정답 및 해설 pp. 34~39

점수: /20

보통속도듣기

빠르게듣기

01 대화를 듣고, 여자가 구입할 티셔츠를 고르시오.

02 대화를 듣고, 캠핑 준비물로 언급되지 <u>않은</u> 것을 고르시오.

① 침낭   ② 손전등   ③ 간식
④ 모자   ⑤ 자외선 차단제

03 대화를 듣고, 남자가 여자에게 전화한 목적으로 가장 적절한 것을 고르시오.

① 주문하려고   ② 교환하려고
③ 항의하려고   ④ 사과하려고
⑤ 취소하려고

고난도
04 대화를 듣고, 두 사람이 만나기로 한 시각을 고르시오.

① 7:00 a.m.   ② 8:00 a.m.   ③ 9:00 a.m.
④ 10:00 a.m. ⑤ 11:00 a.m.

05 대화를 듣고, 두 사람이 대화하는 장소로 가장 적절한 곳을 고르시오.

① 동물원   ② 공연장   ③ 미술관
④ 식료품점   ⑤ 동물 병원

06 다음 그림의 상황에 가장 적절한 대화를 고르시오.

①   ②   ③   ④   ⑤

07 대화를 듣고, 남자가 여자에게 부탁한 일로 가장 적절한 것을 고르시오.

① 의자 옮기기   ② 의자 고치기
③ 전구 교체하기   ④ 새 전구 사 오기
⑤ 의자 잡아 주기

고난도
08 다음을 듣고, Caldecott Award에 관해 언급되지 <u>않은</u> 것을 고르시오.

① 최초 시상 연도   ② 최초 수상 작품
③ 이름의 기원   ④ 상의 종류
⑤ 수상 작품 수

09 다음을 듣고, 어떤 직업에 관한 설명인지 고르시오.

① 프로 게이머
② 웹 디자이너
③ 컴퓨터 프로그래머
④ 컴퓨터 시스템 분석가
⑤ 컴퓨터 게임 시나리오 작가

10 다음을 듣고, 두 사람의 대화가 <u>어색한</u> 것을 고르시오.

①   ②   ③   ④   ⑤

11 대화를 듣고, 남자가 대화 직후에 할 일로 가장 적절한 것을 고르시오.

① 야구 연습하기
② 야구 경기 관람하기
③ 야구 경기 표 예매하기
④ 야구팀 팬클럽 가입하기
⑤ 야구 선수 정보 검색하기

12 다음 표를 보면서 대화를 듣고, 내용과 일치하지 <u>않</u>는 것을 고르시오.

	Checkup	
①	Name	Alex Kim
②	Age	26
③	Taking Medicine Regularly	Yes ☐ No ☑
④	Basic Examination	Weight ☑ Vision ☑ Hearing ☑
⑤	Extra Examination	Allergy test ☑

13 대화를 듣고, 두 사람이 만나기로 한 요일을 고르시오.

① 월요일 ② 화요일 ③ 수요일
④ 목요일 ⑤ 금요일

14 대화를 듣고, 남자가 주말에 한 일로 가장 적절한 것을 고르시오.

① 등산 가기 ② 산책하기
③ 병문안 가기 ④ 출장 준비하기
⑤ 동호회 모임 참가하기

15 다음을 듣고, 방송의 목적으로 가장 적절한 것을 고르시오.

① 엘리베이터 운행 중단을 알리려고
② 엘리베이터 운행 재개를 알리려고
③ 엘리베이터 이용 안전 수칙을 설명하려고
④ 엘리베이터 고장 시 대처 방법을 안내하려고
⑤ 에너지 절약을 위해 엘리베이터 이용 자제를 당부하려고

16 대화를 듣고, 여자가 지불할 금액을 고르시오.

① $80 ② $82 ③ $84
④ $102 ⑤ $104

17 대화를 듣고, 여자의 마지막 말에 대한 남자의 응답으로 가장 적절한 것을 고르시오.

Man: _____

① I hope your dream comes true.
② I should show you my paintings.
③ You should paint pictures more often.
④ You can be a great painter like Picasso.
⑤ Why don't you try to paint your students?

[18 - 19] 대화를 듣고, 남자의 마지막 말에 대한 여자의 응답으로 가장 적절한 것을 고르시오.

18 Woman: _____

① I think I saw somebody suspicious.
② I don't know where to get a bicycle.
③ I'll call you when I find your bicycle.
④ I don't know where I put my bicycle.
⑤ You should go ask for help at the police station.

19 Woman: _____

① Can I apply for the position?
② We're looking for a talented designer.
③ Congratulations, you passed the test.
④ I think you might be the right person for us.
⑤ I'm sorry, but we don't need a reporter right now.

20 다음 상황 설명을 듣고, Amy가 남자에게 할 말로 가장 적절한 것을 고르시오.

Amy: _____

① I'm sorry to hear that.
② I think you've made a mistake.
③ I'd like to help you, but I'm new here, too.
④ I'm afraid there aren't any bus stops near here.
⑤ Sorry, I thought you were somebody I knew.

Dictation Test 06

정답 및 해설 pp. 34~39

01 그림 정보 파악

대화를 듣고, 여자가 구입할 티셔츠를 고르시오.

W: I'm sad to be leaving Paris so soon. I need to 1) _____ _____ _____ before we leave.

M: What will you buy?

W: Well, I always collect T-shirts when I visit different cities.

M: I see. What about this one? It's white and has the Eiffel Tower 2) _____ _____ _____.

W: I like the Eiffel Tower, but 3) _____ _____ _____.

M: Then what about this one that reads, "I LOVE PARIS"?

W: It's not bad, but it's very similar to the one I bought in New York. Oh! Look at this. It has an upside-down Eiffel Tower, and it says, "PARIS LOVES ME." I'll get this one.

M: Wow. That's nice.

02 언급되지 않은 내용 찾기

대화를 듣고, 캠핑 준비물로 언급되지 않은 것을 고르시오.

① 침낭   ② 손전등   ③ 간식
④ 모자   ⑤ 자외선 차단제

M: Are you ready to go camping?

W: Yes, I'm almost ready. I 1) _____ _____ _____ _____ and a lantern.

M: Did you pack snacks?

W: Yes, I 2) _____ _____ _____ _____ and some water in my bag.

M: What about a tent?

W: I don't need to bring one. Mine is too old, so I asked Megan to bring hers instead.

M: Good! And 3) _____ _____ _____ _____ and sunglasses. It's so sunny outside.

W: Don't worry, Dad. I packed them, too.

03 목적 파악

대화를 듣고, 남자가 여자에게 전화한 목적으로 가장 적절한 것을 고르시오.

① 주문하려고
② 교환하려고
③ 항의하려고
④ 사과하려고
⑤ 취소하려고

[Phone rings.]

W: Thanks for calling Speedy Pizza. How can I help you?

M: Hi. My name is Sam Smith. I 1) _____ _____ _____ an hour ago.

W: Is there a problem with the pizza?

M: Yes, there's a problem. It 2) _____ _____ _____ .

W: I'm so sorry. May I have your address?

M: 7374 North Avenue.

W: Please hold. *[pause]* The system says 3) _____ _____ _____ _____ half an hour ago. I can't say for sure what's happened, but I'll 4) _____ _____ _____ _____ . Is that okay?

M: All right. I'll wait.

04 숫자 정보 파악 🇬🇧

대화를 듣고, 두 사람이 만나기로 한 시각을 고르시오.

① 7:00 a.m. ② 8:00 a.m. ③ 9:00 a.m.
④ 10:00 a.m. ⑤ 11:00 a.m.

★ Focus on Sound **need to**

[d]는 자음 앞에서 거의 발음되지 않아 [니드 투]가 아닌 [니투]로 발음된다.

W: I'm excited about this trip. What time does our flight leave tomorrow?

M: At ten in the morning.

W: Then what time shall we meet? How about 1) _____ _____ _____ _____ _____ ?

M: I think that's a little too late. We *need to be ready to board 2) _____ _____ _____ _____ _____ _____ .

W: You're right. At 8:00, then?

M: Do you have anything to buy before the trip? If you do, we'd 3) _____ _____ _____ _____ to shop.

W: I don't need anything. How about you?

M: Me neither. Then two hours 4) _____ _____ _____ .

W: All right. See you then.

대화를 듣고, 두 사람이 대화하는 장소로 가장 적절한 곳을 고르시오.

① 동물원   ② 공연장   ③ 미술관
④ 식료품점   ⑤ 동물 병원

W: One adult and two student tickets, please.

M: Okay. Here are three tickets.

W: Thanks. Can we see the baby bear today?

M: I'm sorry, but you can't. He's been sick for a few days.

W: That's too bad. Then could you tell me [1) _____ _____ _____ _____ ?

M: Sure. Keep walking straight and turn left [2) _____ _____ _____ _____ _____ .

W: Great. Where can I get some food for the deer?

M: Sorry, but you [3) _____ _____ _____ .

다음 그림의 상황에 가장 적절한 대화를 고르시오.

① ② ③ ④ ⑤

① W: Where should we [1) _____ _____ _____ ?
   M: There's an empty spot over there.
② W: There's no crosswalk nearby.
   M: Let's walk one more block.
③ W: I'm giving you a [2) _____ _____ _____ .
   M: I understand, officer.
④ W: I'd like to [3) _____ _____ _____ _____ .
   M: Okay, what seems to be the problem?
⑤ W: We're [4) _____ _____ _____ _____ _____ .
   I'm afraid we'll be late.
   M: Don't worry. We still have time.

대화를 듣고, 남자가 여자에게 부탁한 일로 가장 적절한 것을 고르시오.

① 의자 옮기기   ② 의자 고치기
③ 전구 교체하기   ④ 새 전구 사 오기
⑤ 의자 잡아 주기

W: Hey, where are you taking that chair?

M: Oh, I have to [1) _____ _____ _____ _____ in the bedroom. One of them burned out.

W: I can [2) _____ _____ _____ _____ .

M: Oh, no thanks.

W: Okay. Do you need any help changing the bulb?

M: No, I can do it myself. It will take only a few minutes.

W: All right. Just be careful.

M: Hey, honey? Can you come over here and [3) _____ _____ _____ ?

W: Sure. I don't want you to fall down.

다음을 듣고, Caldecott Award에 관해 언급
되지 <u>않은</u> 것을 고르시오.

① 최초 시상 연도   ② 최초 수상 작품
③ 이름의 기원   ④ 상의 종류
⑤ 수상 작품 수

M: Have you ever heard of the Caldecott Award? 1) _____ _____ _____ _____, it has been awarded to the best American picture book for children. It 2) _____ _____ _____ _____ Randolph Caldecott, who is called the father of picture books. It is one of the most famous children's book awards. Only one book wins the Caldecott Medal each year, but 3) _____ _____ _____ _____ _____ receive Caldecott honors for their outstanding illustrations.

다음을 듣고, 어떤 직업에 관한 설명인지 고르시오.

① 프로 게이머
② 웹 디자이너
③ 컴퓨터 프로그래머
④ 컴퓨터 시스템 분석가
⑤ 컴퓨터 게임 시나리오 작가

W: People who have this job are creative. They help 1) _____ _____ _____ _____ by writing stories and creating characters for them. They work with programmers, game designers, and directors. 2) _____ _____ _____, they need to have a lot of knowledge about computer games and understand computer coding. Plus, they should understand 3) _____ _____ _____ _____ _____ people like and want.

다음을 듣고, 두 사람의 대화가 <u>어색한</u> 것을 고르시오.

①   ②   ③   ④   ⑤

① M: I'm going to the grocery store.
   W: Can you get me some oranges?
② M: I 1) _____ _____ _____ _____ _____.
   W: Don't worry. Your turn is next.
③ M: 2) _____ _____ _____ _____ your new school?
   W: Everything is good.
④ M: How far is it to Seoul Station?
   W: It's six stops from here.
⑤ M: Sorry, there are 3) _____ _____ _____ _____ right now.
   W: Then I'm okay with a double room.

11 할 일 파악 🇬🇧

대화를 듣고, 남자가 대화 직후에 할 일로 가장 적절한 것을 고르시오.

① 야구 연습하기
② 야구 경기 관람하기
③ 야구 경기 표 예매하기
④ 야구팀 팬클럽 가입하기
⑤ 야구 선수 정보 검색하기

M: Where are you going?

W: I'm going home. I just finished watching a baseball game at the stadium.

M: How was the game?

W: It was very exciting.

M: Did your team 1) _____ _____ _____?

W: Yes! But the winner wasn't decided until the very end. Thanks to David Park's home run, my team won.

M: 2) _____ _____ _____ _____ _____. Is he a new player?

W: Yes, but he is very good. You can 3) _____ _____ _____ about him online.

M: Really? I'll 4) _____ _____ _____ right now with my cell phone.

12 내용 일치 파악

다음 표를 보면서 대화를 듣고, 내용과 일치하지 않는 것을 고르시오.

Checkup		
① Name	Alex Kim	
② Age	26	
③ Taking Medicine Regularly	Yes☐ No☑	
④ Basic Examination	Weight☑ Vision☑ Hearing☑	
⑤ Extra Examination	Allergy test☑	

M: I'd like to 1) _____ _____ _____ _____.

W: Okay. Before the examination, I need some basic information. May I have your name and age?

M: Alex Kim. I'm 26 years old.

W: Are you 2) _____ _____ _____ _____?

M: No.

W: I see. A doctor will check your 3) _____, _____, _____. Are you wearing contact lenses?

M: Yes. Do I have to take them out?

W: Yes, you do. Do you need anything else checked?

M: No, I don't.

W: Okay. Please wait here for a moment.

13 세부 정보 파악

대화를 듣고, 두 사람이 만나기로 한 요일을 고르시오.

① 월요일   ② 화요일   ③ 수요일
④ 목요일   ⑤ 금요일

W: Hey, Max. We need to change our plans for the museum.

M: Why? Are you busy on Monday?

W: No. But I checked and the museum ¹⁾ _____ _____ _____ _____.

M: Ah, okay. What about going on Tuesday, then?

W: Sorry, but I've already ²⁾ _____ _____ _____ _____. What about on Wednesday or Thursday?

M: I have a test on Friday, so I ³⁾ _____ _____ _____ _____ _____.

W: Then let's go on Wednesday.

M: That works for me.

W: Perfect!

---

14 한 일 파악

대화를 듣고, 남자가 주말에 한 일로 가장 적절한 것을 고르시오.

① 등산 가기   ② 산책하기
③ 병문안 가기   ④ 출장 준비하기
⑤ 동호회 모임 참가하기

W: Hey, Jason! How was your weekend? You said you were going to ¹⁾ _____ _____ _____, right?

M: Yes, but I didn't go hiking. ²⁾ _____ _____ _____.

W: Canceled? How come?

M: One of the members of my hiking club was badly hurt.

W: What happened?

M: She was hit by a truck. She was ³⁾ _____ _____ _____ _____ _____ from a business trip.

W: That's terrible. I hope she is okay. So what did you do last weekend?

M: I ⁴⁾ _____ _____ _____ to enjoy the weather.

W: That sounds fun. The weather is so nice these days.

M: Definitely!

---

15 목적 파악

다음을 듣고, 방송의 목적으로 가장 적절한 것을 고르시오.

① 엘리베이터 운행 중단을 알리려고
② 엘리베이터 운행 재개를 알리려고
③ 엘리베이터 이용 안전 수칙을 설명하려고
④ 엘리베이터 고장 시 대처 방법을 안내하려고
⑤ 에너지 절약을 위해 엘리베이터 이용 자제를 당부하려고

M: Attention, residents. All the elevators in the building ¹⁾ _____ _____ _____. We hope to have them running again soon, but we have decided to keep them ²⁾ _____ _____ _____ _____ _____ _____. We have been having many problems with the elevators lately, so we need to find out ³⁾ _____ _____ _____ _____ and fix it. When they are running again, we'll let you know. Hopefully, it ⁴⁾ _____ _____ _____. We're really sorry for this inconvenience and thank you for your cooperation.

16 숫자 정보 파악

대화를 듣고, 여자가 지불할 금액을 고르시오.

① $80   ② $82   ③ $84
④ $102   ⑤ $104

M: Do you see anything you like, ma'am?

W: Yes. I like these shoes.

M: Good choice. 1) _____ _____ _____ now.

W: Oh, good. I'll take them. How much are they?

M: They were $100. But they're on sale for 20% off.

W: Okay. And I also want an 2) _____ _____ _____ _____.

M: Here you are. The shoelaces are $4, but they are on sale 3) _____ _____ _____.

W: That's good. I'll take them.

17 마지막 말에 이어질 응답 찾기

대화를 듣고, 여자의 마지막 말에 대한 남자의 응답으로 가장 적절한 것을 고르시오.

Man: _____

① I hope your dream comes true.
② I should show you my paintings.
③ You should paint pictures more often.
④ You can be a great painter like Picasso.
⑤ Why don't you try to paint your students?

M: Hi, Clara! Where are you going?

W: Oh, hi! I'm going to an exhibition.

M: What exhibition?

W: It's a Picasso exhibition. Some of his greatest paintings 1) _____ _____ _____ _____.

M: Wow, sounds cool! Do you know how to paint?

W: Yes, I do. I 2) _____ _____ _____ _____.

M: Nice! Do you want to be a painter?

W: No, I want to 3) _____ _____ _____ _____. I also like teaching children.

M: I hope your dream comes true.

108

18 마지막 말에 이어질 응답 찾기

대화를 듣고, 남자의 마지막 말에 대한 여자의 응답으로 가장 적절한 것을 고르시오.

Woman: _____

① I think I saw somebody suspicious.
② I don't know where to get a bicycle.
③ I'll call you when I find your bicycle.
④ I don't know where I put my bicycle.
⑤ You should go ask for help at the police station.

M: Excuse me, ma'am. Can you help me with something?

W: I can try. What do you need?

M: I left my bicycle here, but I can't find it now. Somebody
   1) _____ _____ _____ _____.

W: That's too bad. How can I help?

M: Well, have you 2) _____ _____ _____?

W: I'm afraid not. I'm sorry.

M: I don't really 3) _____ _____ _____ _____.

W: You should go ask for help at the police station.

19 마지막 말에 이어질 응답 찾기 🇬🇧

대화를 듣고, 남자의 마지막 말에 대한 여자의 응답으로 가장 적절한 것을 고르시오.

Woman: _____

① Can I apply for the position?
② We're looking for a talented designer.
③ Congratulations, you passed the test.
④ I think you might be the right person for us.
⑤ I'm sorry, but we don't need a reporter right now.

M: Hey, Martha, long time no see. How are you doing these days?

W: I'm quite busy at work, but everything is okay.

M: I heard that your company is 1) _____ _____ _____
   _____ _____ _____.

W: Yes, we are. Are you interested in joining us?

M: Yes. What kind of person are you looking for?

W: We want someone 2) _____ _____ _____ _____
   _____ in this field. Do you have any?

M: Yes. I worked for a fashion magazine for three years. And
   I 3) _____ _____ _____ _____ for my reporting last
   year.

W: I think you might be the right person for us.

20 상황에 적절한 말 찾기 🇬🇧

다음 상황 설명을 듣고, Amy가 남자에게 할 말로 가장 적절한 것을 고르시오.

Amy: _____

① I'm sorry to hear that.
② I think you've made a mistake.
③ I'd like to help you, but I'm new here, too.
④ I'm afraid there aren't any bus stops near here.
⑤ Sorry, I thought you were somebody I knew.

W: Amy is on the subway going downtown. Amy sees a boy
   1) _____ _____ _____ _____. After a while, Amy thinks she
   2) _____ _____ _____ _____. She thinks his name
   is Tim, a friend from elementary school. Amy feels so sure that she
   walks over and 3) _____ _____ _____ _____. When
   he turns around, Amy realizes that he is not Tim. In this situation,
   what would Amy most likely say to the boy?

Word Test

A 다음 영어의 우리말 뜻을 쓰시오.

01 remove

02 portrait

03 outstanding

04 award

05 found

06 professional

07 damage

08 include

09 examination

10 pack

11 immediately

12 competition

13 palace

14 hang

15 provide

16 athlete

17 stomachache

18 task

19 area

20 upside-down

21 frequently

22 material

23 creative

24 allow

25 describe

26 repairman

27 crosswalk

28 stadium

29 register

30 messy

31 by oneself

32 on display

33 come true

34 give directions

35 shut down

36 stop by

37 break down

38 be in charge of

39 lead to

40 be named after

B 다음 우리말 뜻에 맞는 영어를 쓰시오.

01	직물, 천	_____	21	비행; 항공편	_____
02	실험	_____	22	비만	_____
03	사슴	_____	23	지식	_____
04	유전의	_____	24	차량, 탈것	_____
05	협조	_____	25	구멍	_____
06	청동의	_____	26	기념품	_____
07	고대의	_____	27	동향, 추세	_____
08	장비	_____	28	증상	_____
09	청력	_____	29	요인	_____
10	불편	_____	30	부러워하다	_____
11	기억, 추억	_____	31	서 있다; 참다	_____
12	붐비는, 혼잡한	_____	32	재능이 있는	_____
13	공공의	_____	33	초대(장)	_____
14	비슷한	_____	34	교통 체증	_____
15	들판; 분야	_____	35	일기 예보	_____
16	얼룩	_____	36	한 조각의	_____
17	배려심 있는	_____	37	(TV 등을) 켜다	_____
18	지원하다, 신청하다	_____	38	실수하다	_____
19	관광객	_____	39	~을 고대하다	_____
20	연장, 도구	_____	40	체중이 늘다	_____

01 대화를 듣고, 여자가 찾는 공책을 고르시오.

02 대화를 듣고, 여자가 해변에 가져갈 물건으로 언급되지 <u>않은</u> 것을 고르시오.

① 수영복   ② 수건   ③ 파라솔
④ 물안경   ⑤ 선글라스

03 대화를 듣고, 남자가 여자에게 전화한 목적으로 가장 적절한 것을 고르시오.

① 택배 배달을 예고하려고
② 택배 배달 지연을 알리려고
③ 택배 분실 사고를 신고하려고
④ 택배 물건 이동을 부탁하려고
⑤ 택배 수령지 주소를 확인하려고

고난도
04 대화를 듣고, 남자가 받을 거스름돈을 고르시오.

① $7.50   ② $9.00   ③ $10.00
④ $11.00   ⑤ $12.50

05 다음 그림의 상황에 가장 적절한 대화를 고르시오.

①   ②   ③   ④   ⑤

06 대화를 듣고, 두 사람이 대화하는 장소로 가장 적절한 곳을 고르시오.

① 주유소   ② 우체국   ③ 정비소
④ 주차장   ⑤ 경찰서

07 대화를 듣고, 여자가 남자에게 부탁한 일로 가장 적절한 것을 고르시오.

① 약 사다주기   ② 병원에 데려다주기
③ 휴일 함께 보내기   ④ 필기한 것 빌려주기
⑤ 영어 숙제 도와주기

08 다음을 듣고, 선거 공약으로 언급되지 <u>않은</u> 것을 고르시오.

① 교복 없는 날 제정
② 건강한 식단 제안
③ 체육 수업 시수 확보
④ 깨끗한 교실 유지
⑤ 학급 의견함 설치

09 다음을 듣고, 무엇에 관한 설명인지 고르시오.

① 풀   ② 자석   ③ 종이
④ 지구본   ⑤ 플라스틱

10 다음을 듣고, 두 사람의 대화가 <u>어색한</u> 것을 고르시오.

①   ②   ③   ④   ⑤

11 대화를 듣고, 두 사람이 미술관에 가기 전에 할 일로 가장 적절한 것을 고르시오.

① 그림 구입하기
② 교통편 알아보기
③ 작품 정보 조사하기
④ 미술관 위치 확인하기
⑤ 입장권 할인 앱 내려받기

12 대화를 듣고, 남자가 선택한 수업의 시작 시각을 고르시오.

① 2 p.m.　　② 3 p.m.　　③ 4 p.m.
④ 5 p.m.　　⑤ 6 p.m.

13 다음 경기장 좌석 배치도를 보면서 대화를 듣고, 두 사람이 선택할 구역을 고르시오.

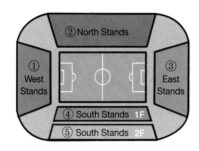

14 대화를 듣고, 여자가 여름 방학에 한 일로 가장 적절한 것을 고르시오.

① 수영하기　　② 낚시하기
③ 하이킹하기　　④ 보트 강습 받기
⑤ 호수 사진 찍기

15 다음을 듣고, 방송의 목적으로 가장 적절한 것을 고르시오.

① 야생 동물 대처법을 안내하려고
② 야생 동물 출몰 소식을 전하려고
③ 동물 구조대의 역할을 설명하려고
④ 라디오 방송 시간 변경을 공지하려고
⑤ 야생 동물 보호 구역 지정을 요청하려고

고난도
16 대화를 듣고, 여자가 구입할 디지털카메라의 가격을 고르시오.

① $70　　② $100　　③ $170
④ $270　　⑤ $300

17 대화를 듣고, 남자의 마지막 말에 대한 여자의 응답으로 가장 적절한 것을 고르시오.

Woman: _____

① I just arrived here.
② I'd like to get a perm.
③ The sooner, the better.
④ Please tell me when it's my turn.
⑤ I'd like you to recommend a good color for me.

[18 - 19] 대화를 듣고, 여자의 마지막 말에 대한 남자의 응답으로 가장 적절한 것을 고르시오.

18 Man: _____

① It's Thursday, April 15.
② It's just three blocks away.
③ It costs $40 for a dozen roses.
④ It's about a quarter after three.
⑤ The train doesn't stop at this station.

고난도
19 Man: _____

① I'm glad that you came to an agreement.
② You're right. The more workers, the better.
③ But remember, you should respect others' opinions.
④ If there are many people on a team, some don't do any work.
⑤ I think the team is better when there are only three members.

20 다음 상황 설명을 듣고, Lisa가 고객 센터에 전화해서 할 말로 가장 적절한 것을 고르시오.

Lisa: _____

① I can't order the books I want.
② I haven't received my order yet.
③ I wrote the wrong delivery address.
④ The items were delivered incorrectly.
⑤ The goods were damaged during delivery.

Dictation Test 07

정답 및 해설　pp. 39~44

01 　그림 정보 파악

대화를 듣고, 여자가 찾는 공책을 고르시오.

[Cell phone rings.]

M: Hello, Cindy. What's wrong?

W: Dad, I forgot my notebook. Could you bring it to school? It's on my desk.

M: Okay, but there are several notebooks on your desk. Do you want the 1) _____ _____ _____ _____ _____ on its cover?

W: No, that isn't the one. Is there a red one?

M: Yes, there are two red notebooks. 2) _____ _____ _____ _____ on it, and the other has a sunflower.

W: I 3) _____ _____ _____ _____. Thanks, Dad. I'll wait for you in front of the school gate at 11:00.

02 　언급되지 않은 내용 찾기

대화를 듣고, 여자가 해변에 가져갈 물건으로 언급되지 <u>않은</u> 것을 고르시오.

① 수영복　　② 수건　　③ 파라솔
④ 물안경　　⑤ 선글라스

M: Honey, where are you?

W: I'm in the bedroom.

M: Oh, there you are. Are you 1) _____ _____ _____ _____ _____?

W: Yes, I'm packing everything I need. I've got 2) _____ _____ _____ _____ _____ right here.

M: What's that over there?

W: It's our beach umbrella. Oops, I almost forgot something!

M: What? Do you want to bring a book to read?

W: No. I 3) _____ _____ _____. Can you get them for me? They're in the bathroom.

M: Sure. I'll be right back.

03 목적 파악

대화를 듣고, 남자가 여자에게 전화한 목적으로 가장 적절한 것을 고르시오.

① 택배 배달을 예고하려고
② 택배 배달 지연을 알리려고
③ 택배 분실 사고를 신고하려고
④ 택배 물건 이동을 부탁하려고
⑤ 택배 수령지 주소를 확인하려고

[Cell phone rings.]

W: Hello?

M: Hello, is this Ms. White?

W: Yes, this is she. Who's speaking?

M: My name is Matt. I'm a delivery driver. I'll be 1) _____ _____ _____ around 5:00 p.m. today. Will you be home?

W: Oh, I don't think so. I probably won't 2) _____ _____ _____ _____ _____. Can you just leave it at the security guard's office?

M: Sure. It's quite heavy, so get some help when you 3) _____ _____ _____.

W: Okay, I will. Thank you so much.

04 숫자 정보 파악

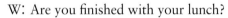

대화를 듣고, 남자가 받을 거스름돈을 고르시오.

① $7.50   ② $9.00   ③ $10.00
④ $11.00   ⑤ $12.50

W: Are you finished with your lunch?

M: Yes, thank you. I'd like to pay now.

W: Sure. Let's see... You had the fried rice and 1) _____ _____ _____ _____, right?

M: Yes, that's right.

W: Okay. The rice is $5, and the coffee is 2) _____ _____ _____.

M: Do I need to 3) _____ _____ _____ _____?

W: No, there's no restaurant tax here.

M: All right. 4) _____ _____ _____ _____.

W: Thank you. I'll be back in a minute with your change.

05 그림 상황에 적절한 대화 찾기

다음 그림의 상황에 가장 적절한 대화를 고르시오.

①   ②   ③   ④   ⑤

① W: How does this ticket machine work?
   M: 1) _____ _____ _____ on the wall.

② W: I'm afraid I took the wrong train.
   M: Where are you going?

③ W: 2) _____ _____ _____ _____ to Portland, please.
   M: That will be $95.

④ W: Excuse me, but we've been waiting in line. You 3) _____ _____ _____ _____ _____.
   M: Sorry, I didn't see you.

⑤ W: Where's Platform B?
   M: Platform A is right downstairs, and Platform B is 4) _____ _____ _____.

06 장소 추론 🇬🇧

대화를 듣고, 두 사람이 대화하는 장소로 가장 적절한 곳을 고르시오.

① 주유소　　② 우체국　　③ 정비소
④ 주차장　　⑤ 경찰서

W: Excuse me. Can somebody help me?

M: Sure. What seems to be the problem?

W: Well, I was jogging in the park this morning. When I came back to my car, somebody 1) _____ _____ _____ _____.

M: Are you sure it was stolen?

W: Yes. The window 2) _____ _____ _____ with a rock.

M: Oh, I see. You'll need to fill out this form, then.

W: Okay.

M: We'll try to 3) _____ _____ _____. Hopefully, we can get your purse back.

W: I hope so. I had a lot of money in it.

07 부탁한 일 파악

대화를 듣고, 여자가 남자에게 부탁한 일로 가장 적절한 것을 고르시오.

① 약 사다주기　　　② 병원에 데려다주기
③ 휴일 함께 보내기　④ 필기한 것 빌려주기
⑤ 영어 숙제 도와주기

M: Where were you this morning?

W: I wasn't feeling well, so I stayed home.

M: Oh. Do you want me to 1) _____ _____ _____ _____ _____ _____?

W: No, thanks. 2) _____ _____ _____ now.

M: That's good to hear.

W: By the way, how was English class?

M: It was good. We learned some important expressions, so I took notes.

W: Really? 3) _____ _____ _____ _____?

M: Sure. I'll tell you about our homework for the holidays, too.

다음을 듣고, 선거 공약으로 언급되지 않은 것을 고르시오.

① 교복 없는 날 제정
② 건강한 식단 제안
③ 체육 수업 시수 확보
④ 깨끗한 교실 유지
⑤ 학급 의견함 설치

W: Hello, everyone! I'm Anna Smith, and I am 1) _____ _____ _____ _____. As class president, I would improve the following things: First, I'd 2) _____ _____ _____ _____ _____. On this day, you would be free to wear whatever you wanted. Second, I'd 3) _____ _____ _____ _____ for the school cafeteria. Third, I'd ask to have gym classes more than once a week. Lastly, I would 4) _____ _____ _____ _____. These are only some of the great things I could do. If elected, I'll make our school better and always consider your great ideas! I'm Anna Smith, and I need your vote!

다음을 듣고, 무엇에 관한 설명인지 고르시오.

① 풀   ② 자석   ③ 종이
④ 지구본   ⑤ 플라스틱

M: This is a thing that can 1) _____ _____ _____ _____ toward itself. It can't pull things like paper or plastic. It has 2) _____ _____, _____ _____. The opposite poles pull toward each other, and the same poles 3) _____ _____ _____ _____. This is used in a lot of everyday products, including fans and refrigerators.

다음을 듣고, 두 사람의 대화가 어색한 것을 고르시오.

①   ②   ③   ④   ⑤

① M: What is the 1) _____ _____ _____ _____ _____?
　 W: It's one week from today.
② M: Which skirt do you think looks better?
　 W: I think you look great.
③ M: Did you 2) _____ _____ _____ _____ _____?
　 W: Yes, they're in my bag.
④ M: May I ask you a question?
　 W: Sure. What do you want to know?
⑤ M: How did you 3) _____ _____ _____ _____ yesterday?
　 W: My mother drove me.

11 할 일 파악

대화를 듣고, 두 사람이 미술관에 가기 전에 할 일로 가장 적절한 것을 고르시오.

① 그림 구입하기
② 교통편 알아보기
③ 작품 정보 조사하기
④ 미술관 위치 확인하기
⑤ 입장권 할인 앱 내려받기

W: Do you have any free time this Sunday?

M: Yes, I do. Why?

W: Would you like to 1) _____ _____ _____ _____ at the City Gallery with me?

M: Sure, that sounds great.

W: How about going there in the afternoon?

M: All right, but let's 2) _____ _____ _____ about the paintings before we go. It'll *help us understand the exhibition better.

W: Okay, but I heard 3) _____ _____ _____ that the gallery made for visitors. It 4) _____ _____ _____ _____ _____ about the artwork and the artists.

M: Wow, that's great! Let's download it then.

12 숫자 정보 파악

대화를 듣고, 남자가 선택한 수업의 시작 시각을 고르시오.

① 2 p.m.   ② 3 p.m.   ③ 4 p.m.
④ 5 p.m.   ⑤ 6 p.m.

W: Hello, how can I help you?

M: I 1) _____ _____ _____ _____ a one-day tennis lesson for my child.

W: How old is your child?

M: He's seven.

W: How about two o'clock? There are some kids his age in that class.

M: Well, later would be a 2) _____ _____ _____ _____ .

W: Let's see. [pause] We have lessons scheduled at 3, 4, and 5 p.m.

M: Let's 3) _____ _____ _____ to be safe.

W: Okay. We'll look forward to seeing him then.

13 위치 찾기

다음 경기장 좌석 배치도를 보면서 대화를 듣고, 두 사람이 선택할 구역을 고르시오.

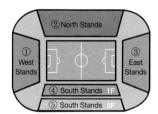

M: I'm buying tickets for the soccer game this Saturday. Where do you want to sit?

W: How about in the west stands? The 1) _____ _____ _____ _____ . It would be noisy but fun!

M: Tickets for the west stands are already sold out.

W: That's too bad.

M: The east stands are for the away supporters. How about sitting there?

W: Well, maybe. But if we 2) _____ _____ _____ , we can see the whole field.

M: Good idea. Hmm... I think we'd be too hot in the south stands 3) _____ _____ _____ _____ . How about in the north stands?

W: Okay! The view will be perfect!

---

14 한 일 파악

대화를 듣고, 여자가 여름 방학에 한 일로 가장 적절한 것을 고르시오.

① 수영하기   ② 낚시하기
③ 하이킹하기   ④ 보트 강습 받기
⑤ 호수 사진 찍기

M: Tania, how was your summer vacation?

W: It was great. I 1) _____ _____ _____ _____ _____ at Steamboat Lake.

M: What did you do there?

W: 2) _____ _____ _____ and enjoyed the beautiful lake views.

M: Sounds great. I want to go there sometime.

W: You should. You'll love it.

M: Is there anything else fun to do at the lake?

W: You can swim or go hiking.

M: Wow. 3) _____ _____ _____ _____ sounds fun.

---

15 목적 파악

다음을 듣고, 방송의 목적으로 가장 적절한 것을 고르시오.

① 야생 동물 대처법을 안내하려고
② 야생 동물 출몰 소식을 전하려고
③ 동물 구조대의 역할을 설명하려고
④ 라디오 방송 시간 변경을 공지하려고
⑤ 야생 동물 보호 구역 지정을 요청하려고

W: I'm sorry for interrupting the radio broadcast. 1) _____ _____ _____ _____ . A group of wild boars has come down from the mountains and is in the park near the town hall. Currently, the 1–1–9 rescue team is conducting an operation to 2) _____ _____ _____ _____ . For your safety, please don't go near this area. 3) _____ _____ until the situation is resolved. Thank you for your cooperation. We will give you another update as soon as we have news.

16 숫자 정보 파악

대화를 듣고, 여자가 구입할 디지털카메라의 가격을 고르시오.

① $70 ② $100 ③ $170
④ $270 ⑤ $300

M: Hey, Kate. Let's go to an amusement park together tomorrow.

W: I can't. I 1)_____ _____ _____ _____ to buy a digital camera.

M: Oh, I see. Digital cameras cost a lot of money. I paid $300 for mine.

W: Yes, I know. So far, I 2)_____ _____ _____.

M: That's all? You'll need a lot more than that.

W: Well, after getting paid for my part-time job, I'll 3)_____ _____ _____. That will be $170.

M: How much more will you need for the camera you want?

W: I'll just need to 4)_____ _____ _____.

M: I see. Well, good luck with that.

17 마지막 말에 이어질 응답 찾기

대화를 듣고, 남자의 마지막 말에 대한 여자의 응답으로 가장 적절한 것을 고르시오.

Woman: _____

① I just arrived here.
② I'd like to get a perm.
③ The sooner, the better.
④ Please tell me when it's my turn.
⑤ I'd like you to recommend a good color for me.

M: Hello. How can I help you?

W: I'd like to 1)_____ _____ _____ _____.

M: All right. Have you had your hair done here before?

W: Yes, Gina usually does it for me.

M: Okay, but I'm afraid Gina is 2)_____ _____ _____ _____. You'll have to wait until all the people with appointments are finished.

W: Really? How long will I 3)_____ _____ _____?

M: I don't know exactly. How about making a reservation and coming back later?

W: Okay, that would be fine.

M: When would you 4)_____ _____ _____ _____?

W: The sooner, the better.

18 마지막 말에 이어질 응답 찾기

대화를 듣고, 여자의 마지막 말에 대한 남자의 응답으로 가장 적절한 것을 고르시오.

Man: _____

① It's Thursday, April 15.
② It's just three blocks away.
③ It costs $40 for a dozen roses.
④ It's about a quarter after three.
⑤ The train doesn't stop at this station.

W: Excuse me.
M: Oh, hello. Can I help you?
W: Yes, I hope so. My family just 1) _____ _____ _____ last week.
M: I see. Well, welcome to the neighborhood.
W: Thank you. Anyway, I'm trying to 2) _____ _____ _____ to buy some flowers for my mother's birthday.
M: Flowers? Let's see... I think there's a flower shop at Westlake Mall.
W: Great. 3) _____ _____ _____ _____ from here?
M: It's just three blocks away.

19 마지막 말에 이어질 응답 찾기

대화를 듣고, 여자의 마지막 말에 대한 남자의 응답으로 가장 적절한 것을 고르시오.

Man: _____

① I'm glad that you came to an agreement.
② You're right. The more workers, the better.
③ But remember, you should respect others' opinions.
④ If there are many people on a team, some don't do any work.
⑤ I think the team is better when there are only three members.

M: Have you guys decided what to do for the school festival this year?
W: No, we haven't. We just can't seem to 1) _____ _____ _____ .
M: What seems to be the problem?
W: I'm not sure. Last year, there were only three of us. But this year, we have ten members on the festival planning team.
M: You didn't have this problem last year?
W: No. Last year, it was easy to 2) _____ _____ _____ _____ . But this time, each of us has a different opinion, so we 3) _____ _____ _____ _____ .
M: I think the team is better when there are only three members.

20 상황에 적절한 말 찾기

다음 상황 설명을 듣고, Lisa가 고객 센터에 전화해서 할 말로 가장 적절한 것을 고르시오.

Lisa: _____

① I can't order the books I want.
② I haven't received my order yet.
③ I wrote the wrong delivery address.
④ The items were delivered incorrectly.
⑤ The goods were damaged during delivery.

M: Lisa ordered some books online. When she checked the order, it said that the 1) _____ _____ _____ within two days at the latest. However, after three days, the 2) _____ _____ _____ _____ _____ . On top of that, she hasn't received any notice about the delay. So she's going to 3) _____ _____ _____ and complain. In this situation, what would Lisa most likely say?

실전모의고사 **08**회

보통속도듣기   빠르게듣기

01 대화를 듣고, 여자가 구입할 선물을 고르시오.

①   ②   ③

④   ⑤

02 대화를 듣고, 여자가 남자에게 부탁한 일로 가장 적절한 것을 고르시오.

① 휴대전화 빌려주기
② 새 휴대전화 골라주기
③ 과제 자료 조사 도와주기
④ 휴대전화 매장 위치 알려주기
⑤ 새 휴대전화 사용법 설명해주기

03 다음 그림의 상황에 가장 적절한 대화를 고르시오.

①   ②   ③   ④   ⑤

04 대화를 듣고, 남자가 치과에 방문할 요일을 고르시오.

① 월요일   ② 화요일   ③ 수요일
④ 목요일   ⑤ 금요일

05 대화를 듣고, 비행에 관해 언급되지 <u>않은</u> 것을 고르시오.

① 목적지   ② 기내식
③ 출발 시각   ④ 비행시간
⑤ 도착 시각

06 대화를 듣고, 두 사람이 대화하는 장소로 가장 적절한 곳을 고르시오.

① 카페   ② 서점   ③ 도서관
④ 인쇄소   ⑤ 컴퓨터 가게

07 다음을 듣고, 두 사람의 대화가 <u>어색한</u> 것을 고르시오.

①   ②   ③   ④   ⑤

08 대화를 듣고, 남자가 여자에게 부탁한 일로 가장 적절한 것을 고르시오.

① 병문안 가기   ② 약 사다주기
③ 음식 주문하기   ④ 병원에 데려다주기
⑤ 약국에 데려다주기

09 다음을 듣고, 무엇에 관한 방송인지 고르시오.

① 학생회장 소개   ② 학교 행사 공지
③ 벌점 제도 안내   ④ 등교 시간 준수 당부
⑤ 학교 연간 일정 공지

고난도
10 대화를 듣고, 여자가 지불할 금액을 고르시오.

① $10.00   ② $11.00   ③ $12.00
④ $13.20   ⑤ $22.00

11 대화를 듣고, 두 사람이 할 일로 가장 적절한 것을 고르시오.

① 내기하기   ② 테니스 연습하기
③ 남자의 집에 가기   ④ 테니스 시합하기
⑤ 점심 먹으러 가기

12 다음을 듣고, 할인 행사에 관해 언급되지 <u>않은</u> 것을 고르시오.

① 기간　　　② 할인 품목　　③ 사은품
④ 장소　　　⑤ 할인 쿠폰

13 다음 아파트 배치도를 보면서 대화를 듣고, 두 사람이 선택할 집을 고르시오.

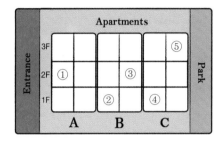

14 다음을 듣고, 무엇에 관한 설명인지 고르시오.

① 썰매　　　② 스키　　　③ 스케이트
④ 스노보드　⑤ 아이스하키

15 대화를 듣고, 여자가 대화 직후에 할 일로 가장 적절한 것을 고르시오.

① 신발 교환하기
② 바닥 청소하기
③ 신발 수선 맡기기
④ 병원 진료 예약하기
⑤ 고객 서비스 데스크 방문하기

16 대화를 듣고, 변경된 회의 일정을 고르시오.

① 월요일 오후 1시　　② 화요일 오전 11시
③ 수요일 오전 11시　　④ 목요일 오전 11시
⑤ 금요일 오후 1시

17 대화를 듣고, 여자의 마지막 말에 대한 남자의 응답으로 가장 적절한 것을 고르시오.

Man: _____

① Okay. Let's go out for dinner.
② Could you pick me up at the department store?
③ I have something to buy at the department store.
④ No, that's where everyone meets. It's too crowded.
⑤ I'm sorry. I forgot to make a reservation for the restaurant.

[18 - 19] 대화를 듣고, 남자의 마지막 말에 대한 여자의 응답으로 가장 적절한 것을 고르시오.

18 Woman: _____

① I want to be a football player.
② I don't think it's going to rain.
③ I'll go to the stadium with my family.
④ I think he's the best player on the team.
⑤ I like baseball more than any other sport.

고난도
19 Woman: _____

① We don't have time to play games.
② Why don't we just do it next week?
③ Sure, I trust you to choose a good gift.
④ No, Dad doesn't like computer games.
⑤ Okay, I'll let you know when I'm done.

20 다음 상황 설명을 듣고, Ted가 매장 관리자에게 할 말로 가장 적절한 것을 고르시오.

Ted: _____

① I want to buy the yogurt.
② I'm here to meet the store manager.
③ Excuse me, where can I find the milk?
④ I'm here to apply for the part-time job.
⑤ This milk has passed its expiration date.

Dictation Test 08

보통속도듣기 빠르게듣기

정답 및 해설 pp. 44~48

01 그림 정보 파악

대화를 듣고, 여자가 구입할 선물을 고르시오.

①   ②   ③

④ 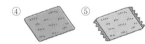 ⑤

M: Hello, how may I help you?

W: I'd like to 1) _____ _____ _____ _____.

M: I see. Do you have anything in mind?

W: Well, I don't know. Can you recommend something?

M: How about a teapot? They're popular as gifts.

W: I'm not sure. My friend 2) _____ _____ _____ _____.

M: I see. Then what about a lamp or a rug?

W: Either would be good. But I think a 3) _____ _____ _____ _____.

M: How about this? Rugs with tassels 4) _____ _____ _____ are popular these days.

W: It's pretty. I'll take it.

M: Okay. I hope your friend likes it.

02 부탁한 일 파악

대화를 듣고, 여자가 남자에게 부탁한 일로 가장 적절한 것을 고르시오.

① 휴대전화 빌려주기
② 새 휴대전화 골라주기
③ 과제 자료 조사 도와주기
④ 휴대전화 매장 위치 알려주기
⑤ 새 휴대전화 사용법 설명해주기

M: Did you buy a new cell phone yesterday?

W: I went to the store, but I didn't buy one.

M: Why? Didn't you find anything you liked?

W: That was the problem. There were too many new cell phones, and I didn't know 1) _____ _____ _____.

M: Yes, there are lots of new models these days. I 2) _____ _____ _____ _____ before buying a new cell phone last week.

W: Oh, did you buy a new one?

M: Yes, I did. I like it.

W: If you don't mind, can you 3) _____ _____ _____ _____?

M: Sure, I'd love to.

03 그림 상황에 적절한 대화 찾기

다음 그림의 상황에 가장 적절한 대화를 고르시오.

① ② ③ ④ ⑤

① M: What is your height and weight?

W: I am 170 cm tall, and I weigh 60 kg.

② M: I need to 1) _____ _____ _____ to Jeju.

W: What is in the package?

③ M: Did you pack your bags yourself?

W: Yes, I did.

④ M: I didn't know you were coming here this evening.

W: I always 2) _____ _____ _____ _____.

⑤ M: Would you like 3) _____ _____ _____ _____ _____ _____?

W: A window seat, please.

---

04 세부 정보 파악 🇬🇧

대화를 듣고, 남자가 치과에 방문할 요일을 고르시오.

① 월요일 ② 화요일 ③ 수요일
④ 목요일 ⑤ 금요일

★ Focus on Sound appointment

자음 3개가 겹쳐 나와 중간 자음인 [t]가 약화되어 [어포인트먼트]가 아닌 [어포인먼트]로 발음된다.

[Phone rings.]

W: Kim's Dental Clinic. May I help you?

M: Hi, I'd like to make an *appointment 1) _____ _____ _____ _____.

W: Okay, when would you like to come in?

M: Do you 2) _____ _____ _____ on Tuesday?

W: Sorry, the dentist will be doing volunteer work on that day. How about Wednesday?

M: I'm afraid I can't. What is 3) _____ _____ _____ that I can make an appointment on? I want to see him as soon as possible.

W: That would be Friday.

M: Okay, that works for me.

05

대화를 듣고, 비행에 관해 언급되지 <u>않은</u> 것을 고르시오.

① 목적지   ② 기내식 메뉴
③ 출발 시각   ④ 비행시간
⑤ 도착 시각

★Focus on Sound can't

미국식은 a를 [애]로 발음하여 [캔트], 영국식은 [아]로 발음하여 [칸트]로 발음된다.

M: Have you finished packing yet, Liz?

W: Yes, I have. I *can't wait to visit our son in Seattle. Does our flight leave at 8:30 tomorrow morning?

M: No, it 1) _____ _____ _____. Don't forget to set the alarm. We should arrive at the airport at least two hours before the flight.

W: Okay. And the trip takes about six hours, right?

M: No, it doesn't take that long. It 2) _____ _____ _____ _____.

W: Oh, I see. So we'll arrive in Seattle at about 12:30.

M: Actually, because of the time change, it'll 3) _____ _____ _____.

---

06 장소 추론

대화를 듣고, 두 사람이 대화하는 장소로 가장 적절한 곳을 고르시오.

① 카페   ② 서점   ③ 도서관
④ 인쇄소   ⑤ 컴퓨터 가게

★Focus on Sound have it

자음의 끝과 모음의 처음이 만나면 연음되어 [해브 잇]이 아닌 [해빗]으로 발음된다.

M: Hello. May I help you?

W: Yes, I'm looking for Peter Underwood's newest novel.

M: Do you mean *The Last Door*?

W: Yes, that's the name of it. I've looked everywhere, but I can't find it.

M: 1) _____ _____ _____ _____ _____ to see if we *have it.

W: Thank you.

M: Well, we 2) _____ _____ _____ _____. It's in the New Books section.

W: Oh, I didn't look there.

M: The only problem is that it's a little damaged. But I can 3) _____ _____ _____ _____.

07

다음을 듣고, 두 사람의 대화가 <u>어색한</u> 것을 고르시오.

①   ②   ③   ④   ⑤

---

① W: I went to London during the vacation.
    M: 1) _____ _____ _____ _____?

② W: Have you seen my blue sweater?
    M: I saw a nice blue sweater at the department store.

③ W: It's raining hard, and I don't have an umbrella.
    M: You can take mine.

④ W: I'm going to compete in a singing contest this evening.
    M: I'll 2) _____ _____ _____ _____ for you.

⑤ W: Let's turn on the heater. It's too cold.
    M: It's 3) _____ _____ _____ _____.

08 부탁한 일 파악

대화를 듣고, 남자가 여자에게 부탁한 일로 가장 적절한 것을 고르시오.

① 병문안 가기
② 약 사다주기
③ 음식 주문하기
④ 병원에 데려다주기
⑤ 약국에 데려다주기

W: Are you okay? You don't look so good.

M: I have a stomachache. I think I ate something bad.

W: Uh-oh. You 1) _____ _____ _____ _____. I'll take you.

M: Thanks, but it's 2) _____ _____ _____.

W: Is there anything I can do for you?

M: Can you 3) _____ _____ _____ _____ _____ instead? I'd like to get some medicine.

W: Sure. No problem.

09 주제 파악

다음을 듣고, 무엇에 관한 방송인지 고르시오.

① 학생회장 소개
② 학교 행사 공지
③ 벌점 제도 안내
④ 등교 시간 준수 당부
⑤ 학교 연간 일정 공지

M: May I have your attention? This is Jim Carter, the student president. I just wanted to remind you that all students 1) _____ _____ _____ _____ by 8 a.m. Unfortunately, more and more students have been arriving late these days. This is a problem, as it 2) _____ _____ and interrupts teachers' lessons. Please make an effort to 3) _____ _____ _____ _____ and be in your classroom before the start of the school day. Thank you.

10 숫자 정보 파악

대화를 듣고, 여자가 지불할 금액을 고르시오.

① $10.00
② $11.00
③ $12.00
④ $13.20
⑤ $22.00

W: How was your meal?

M: Perfect! I'm sure I'll return to this restaurant again.

W: Yes, I enjoyed it, too. Oh, here's the bill. Do you want to 1) _____ _____?

M: Sure, let's do that.

W: Let me see. 2) _____ _____ _____ _____, and yours was $12.

M: Yes, and there's also a 10% tax.

W: Okay, so I'll pay 3) _____ _____ _____ _____ _____.

할 일 파악

대화를 듣고, 두 사람이 할 일로 가장 적절한 것을 고르시오.
① 내기하기   ② 테니스 연습하기
③ 남자의 집에 가기   ④ 테니스 시합하기
⑤ 점심 먹으러 가기

M: Yes! Forty to fifteen. One more point, and I win.

W: 1) _____ _____ _____ _____ _____ .

M: Of course it is. Here's the ball!

W: Oh no! I missed it completely!

M: I win! Don't forget that the loser 2) _____ _____ _____ .

W: Okay. I didn't know you could play tennis so well.

M: I practiced a bit for today.

W: Let's go. 3) _____ _____ _____ _____ _____ .

---

12 언급되지 않은 내용 찾기

다음을 듣고, 할인 행사에 관해 언급되지 <u>않은</u> 것을 고르시오.
① 기간   ② 할인 품목   ③ 사은품
④ 장소   ⑤ 할인 쿠폰

W: Hello, customers. I'm Maggie Grace, the owner of Maggie's Coffee. I'd like to announce a special holiday offer from December 25th to the 28th. During this time, you can get our special holiday drinks 1) _____ _____ _____ . In addition, customers who order a holiday drink will 2) _____ _____ _____ _____ . This special offer is 3) _____ _____ _____ _____ _____ across the country. Come with your friends and family and enjoy our holiday drinks.

13 위치 찾기 🏴󠁧󠁢󠁥󠁮󠁧󠁿

다음 아파트 배치도를 보면서 대화를 듣고, 두 사람이 선택할 집을 고르시오.

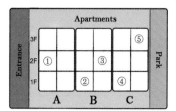

W: Honey, let's talk about the apartments we checked out. What did you think about them?

M: I liked the one in building A. I think the size is perfect for us.

W: Yes, it is. But I think it would be too noisy there because it's 1) _____ _____ _____ .

M: That's true. We shouldn't choose an apartment 2) _____ _____ _____ _____ either, because it would be noisy too.

W: I agree. How about the apartments 3) _____ _____ _____ ?

M: They are too big for us. We don't need three rooms.

W: Then there is only one choice left.

M: Yes. I think it's good. It's 4) _____ _____ _____ , so it will be easy to exercise.

14 화제 파악

다음을 듣고, 무엇에 관한 설명인지 고르시오.

① 썰매　　② 스키　　③ 스케이트
④ 스노보드　⑤ 아이스하키

M: This is a popular winter sport. It started in northern Europe, which 1) _____ _____ _____ _____ _____ . People do this on snowy mountains. They wear special boots and put them on special boards. They 2) _____ _____ to balance and change direction. People can 3) _____ _____ _____ _____ _____ slowly or quickly. This sport is an important part of the Winter Olympics.

15 할 일 파악

대화를 듣고, 여자가 대화 직후에 할 일로 가장 적절한 것을 고르시오.

① 신발 교환하기
② 바닥 청소하기
③ 신발 수선 맡기기
④ 병원 진료 예약하기
⑤ 고객 서비스 데스크 방문하기

M: Hello, may I help you?

W: Yes, I bought these shoes yesterday. But 1) _____ _____ _____ _____ _____ this morning.

M: Oh, really? What happened?

W: I was just walking down the hall. There must have been something wrong with the shoe. I'm pretty upset.

M: I'm really sorry. Do you want to 2) _____ _____ _____ ?

W: No, I just want to 3) _____ _____ _____ _____ .

M: In that case, please go to the top floor and ask for Ms. Langley 4) _____ _____ _____ _____ _____ . She can help you.

W: I see. I'll do that, then.

16 세부 정보 파악

대화를 듣고, 변경된 회의 일정을 고르시오.

① 월요일 오후 1시
② 화요일 오전 11시
③ 수요일 오전 11시
④ 목요일 오전 11시
⑤ 금요일 오후 1시

[Cell phone rings.]

W: Hello?

M: Hi, Sharon. This is Bob.

W: Hi, Bob. What's up?

M: I'm calling to let you know about the 1) _____ _____ _____ _____ _____.

W: Oh, really? Isn't it 2) _____ _____ _____ _____ a.m.?

M: It was. But the meeting has been 3) _____ _____ _____ _____ because of the annual conference.

W: Okay. Has the time changed as well?

M: No, it hasn't.

17 마지막 말에 이어질 응답 찾기

대화를 듣고, 여자의 마지막 말에 대한 남자의 응답으로 가장 적절한 것을 고르시오.

Man: _____

① Okay. Let's go out for dinner.
② Could you pick me up at the department store?
③ I have something to buy at the department store.
④ No, that's where everyone meets. It's too crowded.
⑤ I'm sorry. I forgot to make a reservation for the restaurant.

M: Do you remember that we're 1) _____ _____ _____ for dinner?

W: Of course. It is 2) _____ _____, right?

M: Right. But can we meet at 6:00 instead? I have to drop by the library before we meet.

W: Sure. No problem.

M: Great. Where shall we meet?

W: Why don't we meet 3) _____ _____ _____ _____ _____ _____? It is near the restaurant.

M: No, that's where everyone meets. It's too crowded.

18 [마지막 말에 이어질 응답 찾기] 🏴󠁧󠁢󠁥󠁮󠁧󠁿

대화를 듣고, 남자의 마지막 말에 대한 여자의 응답으로 가장 적절한 것을 고르시오.

Woman: _____

① I want to be a football player.
② I don't think it's going to rain.
③ I'll go to the stadium with my family.
④ I think he's the best player on the team.
⑤ I like baseball more than any other sport.

M: Hi, Sandy. Are you getting excited about tonight's football game?
W: Yes. I think our team has a 1) _____ _____ _____ _____.
M: I think so, too. The team has really been playing well lately.
W: I 2) _____ _____ _____ _____ them play. So where are you watching tonight's game?
M: 3) _____ _____ _____ with some friends. How about you?
W: I'll go to the stadium with my family.

19 [마지막 말에 이어질 응답 찾기]

대화를 듣고, 남자의 마지막 말에 대한 여자의 응답으로 가장 적절한 것을 고르시오.

Woman: _____

① We don't have time to play games.
② Why don't we just do it next week?
③ Sure, I trust you to choose a good gift.
④ No, Dad doesn't like computer games.
⑤ Okay, I'll let you know when I'm done.

M: Hey, Nancy. Do you remember what tomorrow is?
W: Of course I do. It's Dad's birthday.
M: That's right. And we 1) _____ _____ _____ _____ yet.
W: I know. Let's go to the mall 2) _____ _____ _____ _____ _____.
M: Well, I could go right now by myself.
W: No, I want to 3) _____ _____ _____.
M: All right. Well, I'll be in my room playing computer games.
W: Okay, I'll let you know when I'm done.

20 [상황에 적절한 말 찾기]

다음 상황 설명을 듣고, Ted가 매장 관리자에게 할 말로 가장 적절한 것을 고르시오.

Ted: _____

① I want to buy the yogurt.
② I'm here to meet the store manager.
③ Excuse me, where can I find the milk?
④ I'm here to apply for the part-time job.
⑤ This milk has passed its expiration date.

W: Ted goes to the supermarket to 1) _____ _____ _____. He buys vegetables, fish, cheese, and milk. He comes back home and puts all of it in the kitchen. When he puts the milk in the refrigerator, he sees that the 2) _____ _____ _____ _____ _____. So he goes back to the store and 3) _____ _____ _____ _____ _____ _____. In this situation, what would Ted most likely say to the store manager?

01 대화를 듣고, 남자가 구입할 케이크를 고르시오.

① ② ③

④ ⑤

02 대화를 듣고, 가수에 관해 언급되지 <u>않은</u> 것을 고르시오.

① 외모   ② 출연작   ③ 대표곡
④ 노래 실력   ⑤ 수상 경력

03 대화를 듣고, 여자가 남자에게 전화한 목적으로 가장 적절한 것을 고르시오.

① 호텔 예약을 변경하려고
② 호텔 위치를 문의하려고
③ 객실을 추가로 예약하려고
④ 호텔 예약 날짜를 확인하려고
⑤ 호텔 객실 크기를 문의하려고

04 대화를 듣고, 두 사람이 만나기로 한 시각을 고르시오.

① 10 a.m.   ② 12 p.m.   ③ 1 p.m.
④ 2 p.m.   ⑤ 3 p.m.

05 대화를 듣고, 남자의 심정으로 가장 적절한 것을 고르시오.

① lonely   ② relaxed   ③ pleased
④ regretful   ⑤ worried

06 다음 그림의 상황에 가장 적절한 대화를 고르시오.

① ② ③ ④ ⑤

07 대화를 듣고, 여자가 남자에게 부탁한 일로 가장 적절한 것을 고르시오.

① 책 가져다주기
② 함께 식사하기
③ Jane에게 전화하기
④ 저녁 재료 사다 주기
⑤ Jane의 집에 데려다주기

고난도
08 다음을 듣고, 야영지에 관해 언급되지 <u>않은</u> 것을 고르시오.

① 위치   ② 운영 시기   ③ 수용 인원
④ 즐길 거리   ⑤ 예약 방법

09 다음을 듣고, 어떤 장소에 관한 설명인지 고르시오.

① 호텔   ② 공항   ③ 쇼핑몰
④ 기차역   ⑤ 버스 터미널

10 다음을 듣고, 두 사람의 대화가 <u>어색한</u> 것을 고르시오.

① ② ③ ④ ⑤

11 대화를 듣고, 남자가 대화 직후에 할 일로 가장 적절한 것을 고르시오.

① 청소하기   ② 커튼 달기
③ 조명 달기   ④ 벽지 바꾸기
⑤ 가구 배치하기

12 다음 메모를 보면서 대화를 듣고, 내용과 일치하지 <u>않는</u> 것을 고르시오.

> **Help Wanted: Oakville High School**
> ① Part-time cafeteria worker
> ② Duties: serving food & cleaning
> ③ Must have worked in a restaurant or cafeteria before
> ④ Experience working in a school is not required
> ⑤ Hours: 11 a.m. to 3 p.m., Tuesdays and Thursdays

고난도
13 대화를 듣고, 두 사람이 만나기로 한 요일을 고르시오.

① 월요일   ② 화요일   ③ 수요일
④ 목요일   ⑤ 금요일

14 대화를 듣고, 여자가 어제 한 일로 가장 적절한 것을 고르시오.

① 영화 보기   ② 방 청소하기
③ 태블릿 사기   ④ 침구 정리하기
⑤ 영상 통화하기

고난도
15 다음을 듣고, 연설의 목적으로 가장 적절한 것을 고르시오.

① 투표 지지를 부탁하려고
② 세금 인상을 공지하려고
③ 도시 정비 계획을 발표하려고
④ 도시 보안 강화 필요성을 알리려고
⑤ 자전거 도로 공사 일정을 안내하려고

16 대화를 듣고, 여자가 지불할 금액을 고르시오.

① $4.00   ② $4.80   ③ $5.00
④ $9.00   ⑤ $9.80

17 대화를 듣고, 남자의 마지막 말에 대한 여자의 응답으로 가장 적절한 것을 고르시오.

Woman: _____

① I went there last year.
② Yes, it was a really good trip.
③ I really want to go to Europe.
④ This year I'm going to visit Italy.
⑤ I don't want to go there anymore.

[18 - 19] 대화를 듣고, 여자의 마지막 말에 대한 남자의 응답으로 가장 적절한 것을 고르시오.

18 Man: _____

① Better late than never.
② I see, but that's no excuse.
③ When did you fall asleep last night?
④ You'd better set a couple of alarm clocks.
⑤ How about taking the subway next time?

19 Man: _____

① Yeah, that would be perfect.
② We have two options left then.
③ How about mixing two colors?
④ Then we should buy yellow paint.
⑤ I really like all of the bright colors.

20 다음 상황 설명을 듣고, Julie가 남자에게 할 말로 가장 적절한 것을 고르시오.

Julie: _____

① How can I get to the park?
② Excuse me, is this your map?
③ Can I help you find something?
④ Have you ever been to America?
⑤ How many stops are there before the airport?

Dictation Test 09

정답 및 해설　pp. 48~53

01 그림 정보 파악

대화를 듣고, 남자가 구입할 케이크를 고르시오.

① ② ③

④ ⑤

W: Good morning, Sally's Bakery. How may I help you?

M: Hi, I'd like to 1) _____ _____ _____ _____ for my mom.

W: If you want something special, how about a double-layer cake? It looks more impressive than a single-layer cake.

M: Really? Then I'll 2) _____ _____ _____ _____ _____.

W: You can also choose the shape of the cake.

M: What shapes are there?

W: It can be made in a variety of shapes, including round, square, and heart-shaped.

M: Then please 3) _____ _____ _____ _____.

W: Okay.

02 언급되지 않은 내용 찾기

대화를 듣고, 가수에 관해 언급되지 <u>않은</u> 것을 고르시오.

① 외모 　② 출연작 　③ 대표곡
④ 노래 실력 　⑤ 수상 경력

M: What are you watching?

W: It's a singing competition for people who were once famous.

M: Oh, I think I know that handsome guy. But I can't remember his name.

W: His name is Steve Owens.

M: Hasn't he been in movies before?

W: Yes, he was 1) _____ _____ _____ _____ *First Love*, and it was a complete failure.

M: But 2) _____ _____ _____, doesn't he?

W: Yes, he sings very well. He even 3) _____ _____ _____ for one of his songs.

03 목적 파악

대화를 듣고, 여자가 남자에게 전화한 목적으로
가장 적절한 것을 고르시오.

① 호텔 예약을 변경하려고
② 호텔 위치를 문의하려고
③ 객실을 추가로 예약하려고
④ 호텔 예약 날짜를 확인하려고
⑤ 호텔 객실 크기를 문의하려고

* Focus on Sound   right

gh는 묵음으로 [라이트]로 발음된다.

[Phone rings.]

M: Hello, this is the Flower Hotel. How may I help you?

W: Hi. My name is Karen Smith. I 1) _____ _____ _____ .

M: Yes, you booked a twin room for two people on September 16. Is that *right?

W: Yes. But I want to 2) _____ _____ _____ _____ _____ .

M: In that case, you'd need to 3) _____ _____ _____ _____ _____ . But the bigger rooms are all booked on that day.

W: Really? Then can I 4) _____ _____ _____ _____ _____ ?

M: Yes, we have one available for that day.

W: That's great.

04 숫자 정보 파악

대화를 듣고, 두 사람이 만나기로 한 시각을 고
르시오.

① 10 a.m.   ② 12 p.m.   ③ 1 p.m.
④ 2 p.m.   ⑤ 3 p.m.

M: When are we going to do our history project?

W: How about 10:00 a.m. tomorrow? We don't have school.

M: I can't. I'm supposed to attend a special lecture at that time.

W: What time does the lecture end?

M: It 1) _____ _____ _____ .

W: Then why don't we meet after lunch, at 1:00 p.m.?

M: Okay. I'm 2) _____ _____ _____ p.m.

W: Oh, I have something scheduled at 3:00 p.m., though. So we have to finish our work before then.

M: I see. Well, we should be able to 3) _____ _____ _____ _____ _____ .

W: I think so too.

05 심정 추론 🇬🇧

대화를 듣고, 남자의 심정으로 가장 적절한 것을
고르시오.

① lonely   ② relaxed   ③ pleased
④ regretful   ⑤ worried

M: Honey, has Brenda called? It's 1) _____ _____ _____ .

W: She said she'd be back from her friend's house by 8:30.

M: But it is already 8:45.

W: Honey, she's only 15 minutes late.

M: Yes, but she's 2) _____ _____ _____ _____ _____ . She calls us whenever she's late.

W: Relax. She's probably just riding her bicycle home.

M: I think 3) _____ _____ _____ _____ to wait for her.

06 그림 상황에 적절한 대화 찾기 🇬🇧

다음 그림의 상황에 가장 적절한 대화를 고르시오.

① ② ③ ④ ⑤

① M: Can I buy these crackers?

W: Sorry, but they 1) _____ _____ _____ _____.

② M: Where is the restroom?

W: You can 2) _____ _____ _____ _____ _____.

③ M: How much is this ice cream?

W: It is $4.

④ M: I don't think this is my order. I ordered a muffin and an Americano.

W: I'm sorry. I'll get you the right order.

⑤ M: I want to take a coffee-making class.

W: If you'd like to take the class, please 3) _____ _____ _____ _____.

07 부탁한 일 파악

대화를 듣고, 여자가 남자에게 부탁한 일로 가장 적절한 것을 고르시오.

① 책 가져다주기
② 함께 식사하기
③ Jane에게 전화하기
④ 저녁 재료 사다 주기
⑤ Jane의 집에 데려다주기

W: Where are you going, Johnny?

M: Mom asked me to 1) _____ _____ _____ _____ _____.

W: Really? Which supermarket are you going to?

M: I'm going to the Quality Mart on Fourth Avenue.

W: Then you will 2) _____ _____ _____ _____.
Could you 3) _____ _____ _____ _____ on your way home?

M: Okay. Call Jane and let her know.

W: Thank you. 4) _____ _____ _____ right now.

08 언급되지 않은 내용 찾기

다음을 듣고, 야영지에 관해 언급되지 <u>않은</u> 것을 고르시오.

① 위치   ② 운영 시기   ③ 수용 인원
④ 즐길 거리   ⑤ 예약 방법

W: Are you looking for a unique experience this winter? How about spending a day in the mountain snow? We are ready to provide you with the perfect campground and some unforgettable memories. 1) _____ _____ _____ about an hour away from the city, and we are open from December to February. You can 2) _____ _____ _____ _____ in the mountains, and there are hiking trails lit with lamps at night. You can also use the public campfire area. Space is limited, so hurry up and make a reservation! Please 3) _____ _____ _____ _____ _____ .

09 화제 파악

다음을 듣고, 어떤 장소에 관한 설명인지 고르시오.

① 호텔   ② 공항   ③ 쇼핑몰
④ 기차역   ⑤ 버스 터미널

∗ Focus on Sound   country

[t]와 [r]이 연달아 나와 [컨트리]가 아닌 [컨츄리]로 발음된다.

M: This is a place that is 1) _____ _____ _____ _____ . They go there when they want to 2) _____ _____ _____ to a place that is far away. From this place, they fly to various cities and ∗countries. It may have stores, restaurants, or even fitness centers. Some people go to this place 3) _____ _____ _____ who are coming from somewhere else.

10 어색한 대화 찾기

다음을 듣고, 두 사람의 대화가 <u>어색한</u> 것을 고르시오.

①   ②   ③   ④   ⑤

① W: Let's go to that new restaurant tomorrow.
    M: I'd love to. What time shall we meet?
② W: I lost my sister's jacket.
    M: You 1) _____ _____ _____ _____ _____ .
③ W: Did you do well on the math test?
    M: No. My score was 2) _____ _____ _____ _____ .
④ W: How did you get here so quickly?
    M: I 3) _____ _____ _____ .
⑤ W: Why didn't you call me last night?
    M: I 4) _____ _____ _____ _____ because it wasn't working.

11 할 일 파악

대화를 듣고, 남자가 대화 직후에 할 일로 가장 적절한 것을 고르시오.

① 청소하기　　　② 커튼 달기
③ 조명 달기　　　④ 벽지 바꾸기
⑤ 가구 배치하기

W: It's amazing. The house looks completely different.

M: Simply 1) _____ _____ _____ improved it a lot.

W: I think so, too. What is the next step?

M: First, I'll hang the curtains and 2) _____ _____ _____.
Then I'll hang the lights on the ceiling.

W: Actually, can we 3) _____ _____ _____ _____ first?
I want to see the whole house without furniture.

M: Okay.

12 내용 일치 파악

다음 메모를 보면서 대화를 듣고, 내용과 일치하지 <u>않는</u> 것을 고르시오.

Help Wanted: Oakville High School

① Part-time cafeteria worker
② Duties: serving food & cleaning
③ Must have worked in a restaurant or cafeteria before
④ Experience working in a school is not required
⑤ Hours: 11 a.m. to 3 p.m., Tuesdays and Thursdays

[Phone rings.]

M: Oakville High School. How can I help you?

W: Hi. I'm 1) _____ _____ _____ _____ _____.

M: Okay. You'd be working in the cafeteria, 2) _____ _____ _____ and cleaning up. Have you ever worked at a restaurant?

W: Yes. I worked at Chang's Restaurant last summer.

M: Great. We need someone who 3) _____ _____ _____ _____ _____. How about in a school?

W: Actually, I haven't.

M: That's okay. You don't necessarily need that experience. Can you 4) _____ _____ _____ _____ _____ from 11:00 a.m. to 3:00 p.m.?

W: Yes, I'm available every day except Tuesdays and Thursdays.

M: Excellent. Can you come to the school for an interview tomorrow?

W: Sure, that sounds great.

13 세부 정보 파악

대화를 듣고, 두 사람이 만나기로 한 요일을 고르시오.

① 월요일　　② 화요일　　③ 수요일
④ 목요일　　⑤ 금요일

M: What are you doing tomorrow?

W: I'm going to the Greenville Theater to 1) _____ _____ _____.

M: Which movie?

W: *The Truth.*

M: That sounds fun. I want to see that movie.

W: Why don't you go with me? Tickets are 30% off 2) _____ _____ _____ _____.

M: I want to, but I can't. I have to work tomorrow.

W: What about 3) _____ _____ _____ _____? We can still get the discount then.

M: Sounds great! I'd love to.

---

14 한 일 파악 🇬🇧

대화를 듣고, 여자가 어제 한 일로 가장 적절한 것을 고르시오.

① 영화 보기　　② 방 청소하기
③ 태블릿 사기　　④ 침구 정리하기
⑤ 영상 통화하기

W: Have you seen my tablet?

M: No, I haven't. Did you look in your room?

W: I've looked all over the house, including my room, but I can't find it.

M: 1) _____ _____ _____ _____ you used it?

W: I made a video call on it last night. I didn't use it today.

M: Where did you 2) _____ _____ _____ _____?

W: In my bedroom.

M: You should 3) _____ _____ _____ again.

W: Okay. I'll look again. *[pause]*

M: Did you find it?

W: Yes, I did. I couldn't see it because it was under the bed.

---

15 목적 파악

다음을 듣고, 연설의 목적으로 가장 적절한 것을 고르시오.

① 투표 지지를 부탁하려고
② 세금 인상을 공지하려고
③ 도시 정비 계획을 발표하려고
④ 도시 보안 강화 필요성을 알리려고
⑤ 자전거 도로 공사 일정을 안내하려고

W: Good afternoon, everyone. I'm honored and grateful to be in front of you today. As you all know, 1) _____ _____ _____ _____ _____. Once again, I would like to 2) _____ _____ _____ _____. As your representative, I've worked hard to improve our community. I had a bike path built along the stream. I also helped fund a new public library. And I have made the city safer by reducing crime. Most importantly, I did all of this without raising taxes. In the future, I will do even more 3) _____ _____ _____ _____. With your help, we can build a better future together.

16 숫자 정보 파악

대화를 듣고, 여자가 지불할 금액을 고르시오.

① $4.00   ② $4.80   ③ $5.00
④ $9.00   ⑤ $9.80

M: May I help you?

W: Yes, please. I'd like to buy these apples.

M: Okay. Let's see. Six apples? That 1) _____ _____ _____.

W: Actually, there are only five apples.

M: Oh, I'm sorry. I 2) _____ _____ _____. In that case, it's $4.

W: All right.

M: Would you like anything else? Our oranges are good today.

W: Yes, they look fresh. How much are they?

M: 3) _____ _____ _____.

W: Okay, I'll 4) _____ _____ _____, too.

17 마지막 말에 이어질 응답 찾기

대화를 듣고, 남자의 마지막 말에 대한 여자의 응답으로 가장 적절한 것을 고르시오.

Woman: _____

① I went there last year.
② Yes, it was a really good trip.
③ I really want to go to Europe.
④ This year I'm going to visit Italy.
⑤ I don't want to go there anymore.

W: I'm so excited. 1) _____ _____ _____ _____ _____.

M: That's right. What are you going to do this year?

W: I'm going to 2) _____ _____ _____ to Europe.

M: That's great. Didn't you go to Germany last year?

W: Yes, and I went to Switzerland, Austria, and France as well.

M: Wow, you 3) _____ _____ _____ _____. So, how about this year?

W: This year I'm going to visit Italy.

18 마지막 말에 이어질 응답 찾기

대화를 듣고, 여자의 마지막 말에 대한 남자의 응답으로 가장 적절한 것을 고르시오.

Man: _____

① Better late than never.
② I see, but that's no excuse.
③ When did you fall asleep last night?
④ You'd better set a couple of alarm clocks.
⑤ How about taking the subway next time?

M: Laura, do you know what time it is?

W: I'm sorry for being late, Mr. Stewart.

M: Yesterday, you said you were late because of a 1) _____ _____ _____. Did you get up late again today?

W: No, I got up early today.

M: Then 2) _____ _____ _____ _____?

W: Well, I left home early today, but I 3) _____ _____ _____ _____ _____ and missed my stop.

M: I see, but that's no excuse.

19 마지막 말에 이어질 응답 찾기 🇬🇧

대화를 듣고, 여자의 마지막 말에 대한 남자의 응답으로 가장 적절한 것을 고르시오.

Man: _____

① Yeah, that would be perfect.
② We have two options left then.
③ How about mixing two colors?
④ Then we should buy yellow paint.
⑤ I really like all of the bright colors.

W: Honey, we need to paint the kitchen walls. I'm 1) _____ _____ _____ _____.

M: Oh, that's what I was thinking. I never liked that brown.

W: How about painting the kitchen blue? It will look clean.

M: I think it would 2) _____ _____ _____ _____.

W: What about yellow or green?

M: Well, yellow is too bright. But green 3) _____ _____ _____ _____.

W: I agree. I've heard that it 4) _____ _____ _____ _____.

M: Yeah, that would be perfect.

20 상황에 적절한 말 찾기

다음 상황 설명을 듣고, Julie가 남자에게 할 말로 가장 적절한 것을 고르시오.

Julie: _____

① How can I get to the park?
② Excuse me, is this your map?
③ Can I help you find something?
④ Have you ever been to America?
⑤ How many stops are there before the airport?

M: It's Sunday morning, and Julie is 1) _____ _____ _____ _____. Many people are enjoying the nice weather. Julie sees a man sitting alone in the park. When she gets close to him, she notices that he is a tourist. He is looking at a map and 2) _____ _____ _____. Julie thinks he might be lost, so she 3) _____ _____ _____ _____ _____. In this situation, what would Julie most likely say to him?

Word Test

A 다음 영어의 우리말 뜻을 쓰시오.

01 purse		21 pharmacy	
02 rescue		22 grateful	
03 delivery		23 score	
04 expression		24 option	
05 alone		25 resolve	
06 relax		26 consider	
07 height		27 opposite	
08 disrupt		28 reduce	
09 broadcast		29 capture	
10 currently		30 probably	
11 opinion		31 receive	
12 require		32 aisle	
13 election		33 due date	
14 vote		34 breaking news	
15 conference		35 expiration date	
16 improve		36 pass by	
17 instruction		37 get ready for	
18 interrupt		38 push back	
19 notice		39 be free to-v	
20 available		40 make a decision	

B 다음 우리말 뜻에 맞는 영어를 쓰시오.

01 지연 _____

02 범죄 _____

03 세금 _____

04 재료 _____

05 섞다 _____

06 연례의 _____

07 경관; 시야 _____

08 가구 _____

09 천장 _____

10 집들이 _____

11 언젠가 _____

12 부정확하게 _____

13 무게, 체중 _____

14 의무; 직무 _____

15 이웃 _____

16 식료품 _____

17 존경하다, 존중하다 _____

18 승강장 _____

19 바라건대 _____

20 한정된, 제한된 _____

21 패자 _____

22 경쟁하다; 참가하다 _____

23 정리하다, 배치하다 _____

24 맞다, 환영하다 _____

25 잊지 못할 _____

26 훔치다 _____

27 발뒤꿈치; 신발의 굽 _____

28 자국, 흔적; 산길 _____

29 약속, 예약 _____

30 ~에 싫증이 나다 _____

31 ~에 동의하다 _____

32 줄을 서서 기다리다 _____

33 시계의 알람을 맞추다 _____

34 ~을 작성하다[기입하다] _____

35 ~에 출마하다 _____

36 미끄러져 내려가다 _____

37 필기하다 _____

38 전액 환불받다 _____

39 (아무리) 늦어도 _____

40 머리를 하다 _____

실전모의고사 10회

01 대화를 듣고, 여자가 입양할 개를 고르시오.

① ② ③

④ ⑤

02 대화를 듣고, 핼러윈 케이크에 관해 언급되지 <u>않은</u> 것을 고르시오.

① 모양　　　② 크기　　　③ 재료
④ 구입처　　⑤ 가격

03 대화를 듣고, 남자가 여자에게 전화한 목적으로 가장 적절한 것을 고르시오.

① 책을 주문하려고
② 인터뷰를 요청하려고
③ 팬클럽에 가입하려고
④ 공부 모임 날짜를 정하려고
⑤ 영어 과제에 대해 물어보려고

04 대화를 듣고, 여자가 탑승할 기차의 출발 시각을 고르시오.

① 5:15 p.m.　② 5:30 p.m.　③ 5:40 p.m.
④ 6:30 p.m.　⑤ 6:40 p.m.

05 대화를 듣고, 두 사람이 대화하는 장소로 가장 적절한 곳을 고르시오.

① 카페　　　② 식당　　　③ 약국
④ 도서관　　⑤ 식료품점

06 다음 그림의 상황에 가장 적절한 대화를 고르시오.

① ② ③ ④ ⑤

07 대화를 듣고, 남자가 여자에게 부탁한 일로 가장 적절한 것을 고르시오.

① 방 정리하기
② 수학 공부 도와주기
③ 노트 필기 보여주기
④ 시험 시간표 알려주기
⑤ 공부 방법에 대해 조언해주기

08 다음을 듣고, Top Circus에 관해 언급되지 <u>않은</u> 것을 고르시오.

① 공연 시간　② 공연 장소　③ 특별 출연자
④ 입장료　　⑤ 공연 요일

고난도
09 다음을 듣고, 어떤 직업에 관한 설명인지 고르시오.

① 화가　　　② 과학자　　③ 수학자
④ 조각가　　⑤ 건축가

10 다음을 듣고, 두 사람의 대화가 <u>어색한</u> 것을 고르시오.

① ② ③ ④ ⑤

11 대화를 듣고, 두 사람이 대화 직후에 할 일로 가장 적절한 것을 고르시오.

① 집에 가기　　　　② 간식 먹기
③ 바이킹 타기　　　④ 친구 기다리기
⑤ 롤러코스터 타기

12 다음 지도를 보면서 대화를 듣고, 남자가 가려고 하는 장소를 고르시오.

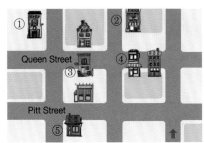

13 대화를 듣고, 여자가 등록할 수업의 시작 시각을 고르시오.

① 3:30 p.m. ② 4:00 p.m. ③ 5:00 p.m.
④ 6:00 p.m. ⑤ 7:00 p.m.

14 대화를 듣고, 남자가 토요일에 한 일로 가장 적절한 것을 고르시오.

① 독서하기   ② 역사 과제하기
③ 가족 여행 가기   ④ 전시회 관람하기
⑤ 이집트 자료 조사하기

15 다음을 듣고, 방송의 목적으로 가장 적절한 것을 고르시오.

① 특가 항공권을 홍보하려고
② 비행기 탑승 시작을 알리려고
③ 공항 내 편의 시설을 안내하려고
④ 비행기 탑승 시각 변경을 공지하려고
⑤ 비행기 탑승 안전 수칙을 설명하려고

16 대화를 듣고, 남자가 지불할 금액을 고르시오.

① $40   ② $54   ③ $60
④ $90   ⑤ $100

17 대화를 듣고, 여자의 마지막 말에 대한 남자의 응답으로 가장 적절한 것을 고르시오.

Man: _____

① Yes, let's ask for the manager.
② We shouldn't have gotten the steak.
③ Yes, I think we should order the soup.
④ Yes, let's come here again and get ice cream.
⑤ I'm sorry we spent so much money on a bad meal.

[18 - 19] 대화를 듣고, 남자의 마지막 말에 대한 여자의 응답으로 가장 적절한 것을 고르시오.

18 Woman: _____

① You can try again next time.
② There are two pages missing.
③ That's great! I'm so proud of you.
④ I can't believe they picked my essay!
⑤ I don't understand why you put it there.

고난도
19 Woman: _____

① Actually, I prefer regular books.
② Can I borrow your book for a few days?
③ I think you should get a new desktop PC.
④ What are the benefits of reading e-books?
⑤ Thank you for recommending this book to me.

20 다음 상황 설명을 듣고, Jake가 두 학생에게 할 말로 가장 적절한 것을 고르시오.

Jake: _____

① Do you want to help me?
② Would you mind being quiet?
③ Did you do well on your test?
④ Is there anything you want me to pick up?
⑤ You're not allowed to listen to music in the library.

01 그림 정보 파악

대화를 듣고, 여자가 입양할 개를 고르시오.

①   ②   ③

④   ⑤

M: Welcome to our dog shelter. How can I help you?

W: I'd like to 1) _____ _____ _____.

M: Do you have any preferences?

W: Yes. I hope it's not too big. I have small children at home.

M: Then what about this dog? It is really gentle and would get along well with children.

W: I think it's too small. I 2) _____ _____ _____ _____ that can play in our backyard.

M: Then this dog is perfect. It's neither too big nor too small. 3) _____ _____ _____ _____, but that won't be a problem if you keep it outside.

W: I agree. And I like its long fur.

02 언급되지 않은 내용 찾기

대화를 듣고, 핼러윈 케이크에 관해 언급되지 않은 것을 고르시오.

① 모양   ② 크기   ③ 재료
④ 구입처   ⑤ 가격

W: Hey, what's that?

M: It's a Halloween cake.

W: Is it a 1) _____ _____? It's so cool.

M: Yeah. I especially like this hat part. It 2) _____ _____ _____ _____.

W: Where did you buy it?

M: I got it at the new cake shop that opened on Main Street. 3) _____ _____ _____ _____ because of their grand opening sale.

W: Really? I should go buy one, too.

M: Hurry up. There were only a few left.

03 목적 파악

대화를 듣고, 남자가 여자에게 전화한 목적으로 가장 적절한 것을 고르시오.

① 책을 주문하려고
② 인터뷰를 요청하려고
③ 팬클럽에 가입하려고
④ 공부 모임 날짜를 정하려고
⑤ 영어 과제에 대해 물어보려고

[Phone rings.]

W: Hello?

M: Hello, may I speak to Mary O'Donnell, please?

W: This is Mary O'Donnell. Who is this?

M: You don't know me, but my name is Michael. I'm a student at East Hill High School.

W: Hello, Michael. What can I do for you?

M: Well, I'm a 1) _____ _____ _____ _____ _____.
I think you're a great writer.

W: Thank you very much.

M: I was wondering 2) _____ _____ _____ _____
_____ next week.

W: Interview me? What for?

M: 3) _____ _____ _____ I'm writing for my English class.

W: Sure. That would be fine.

04 숫자 정보 파악 🏴󠁧󠁢󠁥󠁮󠁧󠁿

대화를 듣고, 여자가 탑승할 기차의 출발 시각을 고르시오.

① 5:15 p.m. ② 5:30 p.m. ③ 5:40 p.m.
④ 6:30 p.m. ⑤ 6:40 p.m.

★Focus on Sound train

[t]와 [r]이 연달아 나와 [트레인]이 아닌 [츄레인]으로 발음된다.

M: Good afternoon. How can I help you?

W: Hi, I'd like to buy a *train ticket to Seoul.

M: Okay. Which train would you like to take?

W: I'm not sure. But I need to 1) _____ _____ _____
tonight.

M: Okay. There's a train that 2) _____ _____ _____.

W: What time does it arrive in Seoul?

M: It 3) _____ _____ _____ _____, so it should arrive at 6:30.

W: Oh, that's perfect. I'll take one ticket, please.

M: All right. That will be $15.

05 장소 추론 🇬🇧

대화를 듣고, 두 사람이 대화하는 장소로 가장 적절한 곳을 고르시오.

① 카페 ② 식당 ③ 약국
④ 도서관 ⑤ 식료품점

M: Is something wrong with me?

W: You just 1) _____ _____ _____ _____. You need to stay home and rest for a day.

M: All right. Should I take any medicine?

W: Yes. 2) _____ _____ _____ _____ _____ each day for the next three days.

M: Okay. What do you recommend I eat?

W: You should eat fruit and drink lots of water every day.

M: All right. I will.

W: Also, try not to talk too much. It will 3) _____ _____ _____ _____ _____.

M: Okay. Thank you.

06 그림 상황에 적절한 대화 찾기

다음 그림의 상황에 가장 적절한 대화를 고르시오.

① ② ③ ④ ⑤

★**Focus on Sound**   선택의문문

선택의문문에서 or 앞은 올리고, 뒤는 내린다.

① W: How may I help you?

   M: I'd like to buy a fan.

② W: I feel cold. Could you 1) _____ _____ _____ _____?

   M: Sure. I'll get you a blanket, too.

③ W: What season 2) _____ _____ _____ _____?

   M: I like summer the most.

④ W: 3) _____ _____ _____ if I turned on the fan?

   M: No, of course not.

⑤ W: *Which should we buy, a fan or an air conditioner?

   M: I'd prefer a fan.

07 부탁한 일 파악

대화를 듣고, 남자가 여자에게 부탁한 일로 가장 적절한 것을 고르시오.

① 방 정리하기
② 수학 공부 도와주기
③ 노트 필기 보여주기
④ 시험 시간표 알려주기
⑤ 공부 방법에 대해 조언해주기

W: Why do you have 1) _____ _____ _____ _____?

M: I have finals next week, but 2) _____ _____ _____ _____.

W: What subject is the most difficult for you? I'll help you.

M: Most subjects are fine, but math is the problem. Can you 3) _____ _____ _____ _____?

W: Sure. Do you want to study at your house now?

M: How about at your house? My room is dirty.

W: Okay. Let's go.

08 언급되지 않은 내용 찾기

다음을 듣고, Top Circus에 관해 언급되지 않은 것을 고르시오.

① 공연 시간 ② 공연 장소 ③ 특별 출연자
④ 입장료 ⑤ 공연 요일

M: Ladies and gentlemen, boys and girls... it's Top Circus time again in Central Park! Come to the circus and be captivated by the most fantastic sights you've ever seen! This year, we 1) _____ _____ _____ _____ who has never been seen before in the Top Circus. Meet Peter, the legendary acrobat! Bring your family and friends and be prepared to be thrilled. Enjoy a day at the circus 2) _____ _____ _____. The show will run 3) _____ _____ _____ _____, this Saturday and Sunday. Don't miss this opportunity. We hope to see you soon!

---

09 화제 파악

다음을 듣고, 어떤 직업에 관한 설명인지 고르시오.

① 화가 ② 과학자 ③ 수학자
④ 조각가 ⑤ 건축가

W: People who have this job practice the science and art of 1) _____ _____. They design all kinds of things like homes, apartments, and office buildings. They need to be good at math and drawing. They also need to 2) _____ _____ _____ _____. They make sure buildings look attractive, but they also make sure that they're 3) _____ _____ _____. They design each building for a specific purpose. They can produce a work of art, but it must also be functional.

---

10 어색한 대화 찾기

다음을 듣고, 두 사람의 대화가 어색한 것을 고르시오.

① ② ③ ④ ⑤

① M: I wonder when the school festival will begin.
  W: It will 1) _____ _____ _____ _____.
② M: Do you have any free time?
  W: Sorry, I'm pretty busy.
③ M: 2) _____ _____ _____ _____ _____ to the gym?
  W: More than twice a week.
④ M: Can you tell me about the book?
  W: It's about the life of an artist. It's very interesting.
⑤ M: The math test was really easy, wasn't it?
  W: Yes, 3) _____ _____ _____.

11 할 일 파악

대화를 듣고, 두 사람이 대화 직후에 할 일로 가장 적절한 것을 고르시오.

① 집에 가기 ② 간식 먹기
③ 바이킹 타기 ④ 친구 기다리기
⑤ 롤러코스터 타기

M: It's been a great day at the amusement park so far.

W: It sure has.

M: I especially liked the Viking. What are we 1) _____ _____ _____ _____?

W: We haven't ridden the roller coaster yet.

M: That's right. Let's 2) _____ _____ _____.

W: Oh, the line looks pretty long. Maybe we should eat first. I'm getting hungry.

M: Okay. Let's 3) _____ _____ _____.

W: Sounds good. Then we can ride the roller coaster.

12 위치 찾기

다음 지도를 보면서 대화를 듣고, 남자가 가려고 하는 장소를 고르시오.

You are here!

M: Excuse me, do you know a restaurant called Joe's Place?

W: Yes. It's famous around here.

M: Can you tell me 1) _____ _____ _____ _____?

W: Sure. Walk down to Queen Street and turn left. Then 2) _____ _____ _____ _____. It's on your left.

M: Turn left on Queen Street and go one block?

W: Oh, sorry. I got confused. You should go two blocks on Queen Street, and then 3) _____ _____ _____ _____. You can't miss it.

M: Thank you.

13 숫자 정보 파악

대화를 듣고, 여자가 등록할 수업의 시작 시각을 고르시오.

① 3:30 p.m. ② 4:00 p.m. ③ 5:00 p.m.
④ 6:00 p.m. ⑤ 7:00 p.m.

M: Hello, how may I help you?

W: I'd like to 1)_____ _____ _____ _____ _____.

M: Okay. We have a class beginning at four o'clock.

W: I get out of school at 3:30, so I'm not sure if I could make it.

M: We have another class that starts at five o'clock.

W: Are there any later classes?

M: Actually, 2)_____ _____ _____ _____ from 4:00 p.m. to 7:00 p.m.

W: Then I'll take the last one, the 3)_____ _____ _____.

M: Okay. Please fill out this form.

14 한 일 파악

대화를 듣고, 남자가 토요일에 한 일로 가장 적절한 것을 고르시오.

① 독서하기   ② 역사 과제하기
③ 가족 여행 가기   ④ 전시회 관람하기
⑤ 이집트 자료 조사하기

W: James, what are you doing?

M: I'm 1)_____ _____ _____ _____ _____.

W: Are you interested in Egypt?

M: Yes. I like Egyptian history and culture, so I often 2)_____ _____ _____ about Egypt.

W: Then I have some good news for you.

M: What is it?

W: I heard that the King Tut Exhibition is on display.

M: At the National Museum? I already 3)_____ _____ _____ last Saturday.

W: That's too bad. If you hadn't seen it, I was going to ask you to go with me.

15 목적 파악 🇬🇧

다음을 듣고, 방송의 목적으로 가장 적절한 것을 고르시오.

① 특가 항공권을 홍보하려고
② 비행기 탑승 시작을 알리려고
③ 공항 내 편의 시설을 안내하려고
④ 비행기 탑승 시각 변경을 공지하려고
⑤ 비행기 탑승 안전 수칙을 설명하려고

M: Good morning. This is an 1)_____ _____ _____ traveling on flight 123 to Jeju. Flight 123 2)_____ _____ _____ at gate 10. We are now inviting those passengers with express boarding tickets, and passengers with young children. Please have your 3)_____ _____ _____ _____ _____. We'd appreciate it if regular passengers would remain in their seats until pre-boarding has finished. 4)_____ _____ _____ _____ in about 10 minutes. Thank you.

16 숫자 정보 파악

대화를 듣고, 남자가 지불할 금액을 고르시오.

① $40   ② $54   ③ $60
④ $90   ⑤ $100

W: May I help you?

M: Yes, I'd like to buy a wallet.

W: How do you like this one? It's our 1) _____ _____.

M: How much is it?

W: It's $90.

M: That's a bit too expensive. Do you 2) _____ _____ _____ _____?

W: How about this brown one? It was $100, but 3) _____ _____ _____ now.

M: Okay, I'll take it.

17 마지막 말에 이어질 응답 찾기 🏴

대화를 듣고, 여자의 마지막 말에 대한 남자의 응답으로 가장 적절한 것을 고르시오.

Man: _____

① Yes, let's ask for the manager.
② We shouldn't have gotten the steak.
③ Yes, I think we should order the soup.
④ Yes, let's come here again and get ice cream.
⑤ I'm sorry we spent so much money on a bad meal.

M: So... what do you think?

W: To be honest, this is 1) _____ _____ _____ I've ever been to.

M: I agree. My soup was cold, and my steak was too tough.

W: And the waiter! He was so rude.

M: I know. He spilled water on me and didn't even apologize.

W: I wish we 2) _____ _____ _____.

M: I can't believe we have to pay $40 for our meal.

W: Do you think 3) _____ _____ _____?

M: Yes, let's ask for the manager.

18 마지막 말에 이어질 응답 찾기

대화를 듣고, 남자의 마지막 말에 대한 여자의 응답으로 가장 적절한 것을 고르시오.

Woman: _____

① You can try again next time.
② There are two pages missing.
③ That's great! I'm so proud of you.
④ I can't believe they picked my essay!
⑤ I don't understand why you put it there.

M: Look, Mom! It's the school newspaper!
W: Calm down. What's 1) _____ _____ _____ _____ ?
M: Look at the front page.
W: All right. There's an article about a new cafeteria.
M: No! Look below that.
W: Okay. Hey, that's a 2) _____ _____ _____ .
M: Yes, and the essay I wrote. They put it 3) _____ _____ _____ _____ !
W: That's great! I'm so proud of you.

---

19 마지막 말에 이어질 응답 찾기

대화를 듣고, 남자의 마지막 말에 대한 여자의 응답으로 가장 적절한 것을 고르시오.

Woman: _____

① Actually, I prefer regular books.
② Can I borrow your book for a few days?
③ I think you should get a new desktop PC.
④ What are the benefits of reading e-books?
⑤ Thank you for recommending this book to me.

W: Wow, you've got an e-reader! It looks nice!
M: Yes. I got a compact one, so I 1) _____ _____ _____ .
W: It seems convenient.
M: Yes, it is. I 2) _____ _____ _____ _____ all the time. I can read e-books while I ride the bus or subway, and I can even use it for schoolwork.
W: Does it have any other benefits?
M: Well, when I don't understand something I read, I can 3) _____ _____ _____ _____ _____ . It's really useful. I'd recommend getting one for yourself.
W: Actually, I prefer regular books.

---

20 상황에 적절한 말 찾기

다음 상황 설명을 듣고, Jake가 두 학생에게 할 말로 가장 적절한 것을 고르시오.

Jake: _____

① Do you want to help me?
② Would you mind being quiet?
③ Did you do well on your test?
④ Is there anything you want me to pick up?
⑤ You're not allowed to listen to music in the library.

W: Jake is a high school student. One Sunday afternoon, he went to a public library near his home to 1) _____ _____ _____ _____ _____ . The library was quiet, so he was able to concentrate well. Then, about an hour later, two students came into the library and sat at the table next to him. They 2) _____ _____ _____ . It became hard for Jake to 3) _____ _____ _____ _____ _____ . Jake stared at them, but they kept talking. In this situation, what would Jake most likely say to them?

실전모의고사 11 회

정답 및 해설   pp. 58~62

점수: /20

01 대화를 듣고, 남자가 그린 그림을 고르시오.

① ② ③

④ ⑤

02 대화를 듣고, 남자가 여자에게 부탁한 일로 가장 적절한 것을 고르시오.

① 음식 주문하기   ② 친구 초대하기
③ 식당 예약하기   ④ 바비큐 준비하기
⑤ 파티 용품 사기

03 다음 그림의 상황에 가장 적절한 대화를 고르시오.

① ② ③ ④ ⑤

04 대화를 듣고, 두 사람이 시험을 치를 요일을 고르시오.

① 월요일   ② 화요일   ③ 목요일
④ 금요일   ⑤ 토요일

05 대화를 듣고, 미술관에서 지켜야 할 사항으로 언급되지 않은 것을 고르시오.

① 휴대전화 전원 끄기   ② 음식 반입하지 않기
③ 껌 씹지 않기   ④ 실내에서 뛰지 않기
⑤ 미술품 촬영하지 않기

06 대화를 듣고, 두 사람이 대화하는 장소로 가장 적절한 곳을 고르시오.

① 식당   ② 공항   ③ 비행기
④ 영화관   ⑤ 가구점

07 다음을 듣고, 두 사람의 대화가 어색한 것을 고르시오.

① ② ③ ④ ⑤

08 대화를 듣고, 여자가 남자에게 부탁한 일로 가장 적절한 것을 고르시오.

① 준비 시간 주기
② 대본 가져다주기
③ 의상 교체해주기
④ 대본 연습 같이 하기
⑤ 감독에게 재촬영 요청하기

09 다음을 듣고, 무엇에 관한 방송인지 고르시오.

① 날씨 예보   ② 정전 안내
③ 행사 홍보   ④ 홍수 피해 보고
⑤ 폭풍 시 안전 수칙 설명

10 대화를 듣고, 남자가 지불할 금액을 고르시오.

① $630   ② $700   ③ $770
④ $900   ⑤ $1,000

11 대화를 듣고, 남자가 대화 직후에 할 일로 가장 적절한 것을 고르시오.

① 숙제하기   ② 서점 방문하기
③ 역사 시험공부하기   ④ 빌린 책 복사하기
⑤ 인터넷으로 책 구입하기

12 다음을 듣고, 슬라임에 관해 언급되지 않은 것을 고르시오.

① 재료   ② 비용   ③ 구입처
④ 제작 방법   ⑤ 제작 소요 시간

고난도

13 다음 표를 보면서 대화를 듣고, 내용과 일치하지 않는 것을 고르시오.

	You're Invited to a Dinner Party!	
①	For Whom	Danny and Lisa
②	Why	To celebrate their daughter's first birthday
③	Where	The Golden Fish Restaurant on Fourth Street
④	When	Sunday, April 27
⑤	What Time	From 5 p.m. to 8 p.m.

14 다음을 듣고, 무엇에 관한 설명인지 고르시오.

① 탁구   ② 테니스   ③ 배구
④ 축구   ⑤ 농구

15 대화를 듣고, 여자가 대화 직후에 할 일로 가장 적절한 것을 고르시오.

① 은행에 가기   ② 세탁실에 가기
③ 프런트에 가기   ④ 세탁기 수리하기
⑤ 다른 숙소로 옮기기

고난도

16 대화를 듣고, 오늘의 날짜를 고르시오.

① 7월 5일   ② 7월 7일   ③ 7월 10일
④ 7월 14일   ⑤ 7월 15일

고난도

17 대화를 듣고, 남자의 마지막 말에 대한 여자의 응답으로 가장 적절한 것을 고르시오.

Woman: _____

① It won't take that long.
② You can take more time.
③ You should prepare for it.
④ I'm afraid it'll cost too much.
⑤ Sure. Give us a few minutes to prepare.

[18 - 19] 대화를 듣고, 여자의 마지막 말에 대한 남자의 응답으로 가장 적절한 것을 고르시오.

18 Man: _____

① Don't take it too hard.
② They're due next Friday.
③ The total is eight dollars.
④ Sure, that's not a problem.
⑤ You should have returned them earlier.

19 Man: _____

① It was the best movie ever!
② I hope you enjoy the movie.
③ Where is the nearest theater?
④ That's just around the corner.
⑤ Let's go to the movie together.

20 다음 상황 설명을 듣고, Carol이 남동생에게 할 말로 가장 적절한 것을 고르시오.

Carol: _____

① I ordered a new camera already.
② Thank you for finding my camera.
③ Why are you talking to me about this now?
④ Please ask me first if you want to borrow something.
⑤ I didn't want to come back from my vacation today.

Dictation Test

정답 및 해설 pp. 58~62

01 그림 정보 파악

대화를 듣고, 남자가 그린 그림을 고르시오.

① ② ③

④ ⑤

W: Wow. This wall is decorated beautifully.

M: Isn't it cool? Each of my classmates drew one dinosaur.

W: Which one did you draw?

M: The one I drew is near that big tree.

W: You mean the 1) _____ _____ _____?

M: No, it's 2) _____ _____ _____ _____.

W: Which one is it, the one with a long neck or 3) _____ _____ _____ _____ _____?

M: Neither of them. Mine is the one with the bony plates along its back.

W: Oh, that one. It's nice!

02 부탁한 일 파악

대화를 듣고, 남자가 여자에게 부탁한 일로 가장 적절한 것을 고르시오.

① 음식 주문하기 ② 친구 초대하기
③ 식당 예약하기 ④ 바비큐 준비하기
⑤ 파티 용품 사기

M: Christmas is just around the corner. What should we do for dinner?

W: We can 1) _____ _____ _____ at home.

M: Yeah, but we always do that. How about 2) _____ _____ _____?

W: What about having a party at a fancy restaurant?

M: That sounds great! We can invite our friends and have fun together.

W: But won't the popular restaurants 3) _____ _____ _____ _____?

M: They might be. Can you 4) _____ _____ _____ _____ to find out?

W: Sure, I'll do that right now.

03 그림 상황에 적절한 대화 찾기

다음 그림의 상황에 가장 적절한 대화를 고르시오.

① ② ③ ④ ⑤

① W: I'd like to 1)＿＿＿ ＿＿＿ ＿＿＿ ＿＿＿.

　M: Sure. How much would you like to exchange?

② W: I would like to 2)＿＿＿ ＿＿＿ ＿＿＿ ＿＿＿.

　M: Please fill out this form and give it back to me with your ID.

③ W: It seems a little big to me. Is it the right size?

　M: Yes. It's supposed to fit that way.

④ W: It's 8,000 won in ＊total, right?

　M: Yes, that's right. Here's your change.

⑤ W: Excuse me. 3)＿＿＿ ＿＿＿ ＿＿＿ ＿＿＿ ＿＿＿ the bank?

　M: Go that way. It's at the end of the street.

04 세부 정보 파악

대화를 듣고, 두 사람이 시험을 치를 요일을 고르시오.

① 월요일　② 화요일　③ 목요일
④ 금요일　⑤ 토요일

M: Are you ready for the exam? I'm afraid I don't have much time to study.

W: Didn't you hear? All 1)＿＿＿ ＿＿＿ ＿＿＿ ＿＿＿.

M: Really? I didn't know that. Why?

W: Because it's our school's 50th anniversary. So the teacher 2)＿＿＿ ＿＿＿ ＿＿＿ for one day.

M: 3)＿＿＿ ＿＿＿ ＿＿＿. That means we 4)＿＿＿ ＿＿＿ ＿＿＿ ＿＿＿ ＿＿＿. I think that's enough time.

W: I agree. I'm going to the library this Saturday. Why don't you study with me?

M: Okay. That sounds good.

05 언급되지 않은 내용 찾기 🇬🇧

대화를 듣고, 미술관에서 지켜야 할 사항으로 언급되지 <u>않은</u> 것을 고르시오.

① 휴대전화 전원 끄기 ② 음식 반입하지 않기
③ 껌 씹지 않기 ④ 실내에서 뛰지 않기
⑤ 미술품 촬영하지 않기

M: Welcome to the Baltimore Museum of Art. May I see your ticket?

W: Here you are.

M: Thank you. Before you enter, please 1) _____ _____ _____ _____.

W: Oh, thank you for reminding me.

M: Also, you 2) _____ _____ _____ _____ or drinks inside. Chewing gum isn't allowed, either.

W: All right. Can I 3) _____ _____ _____ _____ _____ ?

M: I'm sorry, but you can't.

W: Really? That's disappointing.

M: There's a gift shop in the lobby. You 4) _____ _____ _____ of the artwork there.

W: Okay. That'll work for me.

---

06 장소 추론

대화를 듣고, 두 사람이 대화하는 장소로 가장 적절한 곳을 고르시오.

① 식당 ② 공항 ③ 비행기
④ 영화관 ⑤ 가구점

M: Excuse me. Could you ask the person behind me to 1) _____ _____ _____ _____ ?

W: I will. Sorry for the inconvenience.

M: Thank you. By the way, what time is it in Beijing?

W: The 2) _____ _____ _____ _____ in the morning.

M: What's the time difference?

W: They are nine hours behind us.

M: Oh, I see. Thanks. Could I also ask you to 3) _____ _____ _____ _____ _____ ?

W: Sure. Just a second.

---

07 어색한 대화 찾기

다음을 듣고, 두 사람의 대화가 <u>어색한</u> 것을 고르시오.

① ② ③ ④ ⑤

① M: 1) _____ _____ _____ _____ tomorrow?

W: Let's meet in front of the library.

② M: 2) _____ _____ _____ _____ _____ the game?

W: It was very exciting.

③ M: I'm worried about the English Speech Contest.

W: Don't worry. You'll do well.

④ M: Do you remember that you borrowed my history notebook last week?

W: Yes. I'll 3) _____ _____ _____ to you tomorrow.

⑤ M: Who is that tall woman with the long hair?

W: I don't know where she was yesterday.

대화를 듣고, 여자가 남자에게 부탁한 일로 가장 적절한 것을 고르시오.

① 준비 시간 주기
② 대본 가져다주기
③ 의상 교체해주기
④ 대본 연습 같이 하기
⑤ 감독에게 재촬영 요청하기

M: That was good acting, Ms. Banks. Get some rest before shooting the next scene.

W: Actually, I don't think it was very good. I should have been more emotional.

M: It seemed okay to me. Should I ask the director to 1) _____ _____ _____ _____ ?

W: Yes. But before you do that, let me take some time to prepare.

M: Do you want to practice? I can 2) _____ _____ _____ _____ .

W: No, thanks. I just 3) _____ _____ _____ _____ to really get into character.

M: Okay.

09 주제 파악

다음을 듣고, 무엇에 관한 방송인지 고르시오.

① 날씨 예보
② 정전 안내
③ 행사 홍보
④ 홍수 피해 보고
⑤ 폭풍 시 안전 수칙 설명

M: This is Jake Brown 1) _____ _____ _____ _____ . Well, the sunny days are over, so don't make any plans outdoors this week. As you can see on this satellite image, a 2) _____ _____ _____ . It is expected to bring heavy rain and winds tonight. The rain will continue all week, so please be extra careful. Tomorrow morning, the temperature will drop to 15°C. So I hope you wear a warm jacket and 3) _____ _____ _____ _____ _____ when you go out. Thank you.

10 숫자 정보 파악

대화를 듣고, 남자가 지불할 금액을 고르시오.

① $630
② $700
③ $770
④ $900
⑤ $1,000

W: So, what do you think of this tour package?

M: I like it, 1) _____ _____ _____ _____ . It seems a little expensive.

W: Well, that's because it provides excellent hotels and activities. But I can also recommend a cheaper one with less expensive hotels.

M: How much is the cheaper one?

W: The prices 2) _____ _____ _____ _____ _____ . It depends on the dates you choose.

M: How about leaving on May 10?

W: It's not high season, so that 3) _____ _____ _____ .

M: Oh, that sounds reasonable. I'll take it.

11 [할 일 파악]

대화를 듣고, 남자가 대화 직후에 할 일로 가장 적절한 것을 고르시오.

① 숙제하기
② 서점 방문하기
③ 역사 시험공부하기
④ 빌린 책 복사하기
⑤ 인터넷으로 책 구입하기

M: I'm 1) _____ _____ _____ _____ .

W: Did you buy the book you were looking for?

M: No, it was sold out.

W: Oh, let me look for it on the Internet. What was the name of it?

M: *The Josun Dynasty.*

W: Okay. Let me 2) _____ _____ _____ .

M: Sure. Do they have it?

W: Yes, I found it. And they 3) _____ _____ _____ _____ .

M: How long will it take to get here if I order it now? I need it this weekend for my homework.

W: It says this Friday.

M: That's great. I'll 4) _____ _____ _____ right now.

12 [언급되지 않은 내용 찾기]

다음을 듣고, 슬라임에 관해 언급되지 <u>않은</u> 것을 고르시오.

① 재료
② 비용
③ 구입처
④ 제작 방법
⑤ 제작 소요 시간

W: Would you like to make homemade slime? 1) _____ _____ _____ _____ glue, baking soda, and water. It's pretty simple, and 2) _____ _____ _____ _____ . Before you begin, put on gloves so that the slime doesn't touch your skin directly. Then start by 3) _____ _____ _____ _____ _____ into a bowl and stirring it. Next, add the baking soda and stir the mixture again. After mixing it well, rub it with your hands. It will be sticky at first, but keep rubbing it until it is no longer sticky. It will 4) _____ _____ _____ _____ . Then you're finished! Have fun playing with it!

13 내용 일치 파악

다음 표를 보면서 대화를 듣고, 내용과 일치하지 않는 것을 고르시오.

	You're Invited to a Dinner Party!	
①	For Whom	Danny and Lisa
②	Why	To celebrate their daughter's first birthday
③	Where	The Golden Fish Restaurant on Fourth Street
④	When	Sunday, April 27
⑤	What Time	From 5 p.m. to 8 p.m.

W: Hey, Jason. Do you want to go to a party with me?

M: What kind of party?

W: My cousin Kate 1) _____ _____ _____ _____ _____, so my Aunt Lisa and Uncle Danny are having a party.

M: That's great. Is it at their house?

W: No. It's 2) _____ _____ _____ _____ on Fourth Street.

M: The Golden Fish?

W: That's right. The party is 3) _____ _____ _____ from 5:00 to 8:00 p.m. Can you come?

M: April 27? Is that a Sunday? I 4) _____ _____ _____ on Sundays.

W: No, it's a Saturday.

M: In that case, I'd love to go.

14 화제 파악

다음을 듣고, 무엇에 관한 설명인지 고르시오.

① 탁구　　② 테니스　　③ 배구
④ 축구　　⑤ 농구

M: This is a popular sport that requires a net and a ball. The ball is about the 1) _____ _____ _____ _____ _____.
The game is played by two teams. Sometimes, it is played inside with 2) _____ _____ _____ _____ _____.
Other times, it is 3) _____ _____ _____ _____ with two people on each team. One player serves the ball over the net. Then the two teams hit the ball back and forth. They 4) _____ _____ _____ _____ _____. If the ball touches the ground, the other team gets a point.

15 할 일 파악

대화를 듣고, 여자가 대화 직후에 할 일로 가장 적절한 것을 고르시오.

① 은행에 가기　　② 세탁실에 가기
③ 프런트에 가기　　④ 세탁기 수리하기
⑤ 다른 숙소로 옮기기

M: Where are you going?

W: I'm going down to the front desk. I have a question.

M: What do you need to know?

W: I want to ask if the hostel has a laundry service.

M: Oh, they 1) _____ _____ _____ _____ on this floor. I saw it earlier.

W: Oh, good. Where is it?

M: There's a laundry room just around the corner. But you'll need to 2) _____ _____ _____.

W: I'm afraid I don't have any coins right now.

M: Well, I'm sure they can 3) _____ _____ _____ at the front desk.

W: Yes, you're right. I'll go there first.

---

16 세부 정보 파악

대화를 듣고, 오늘의 날짜를 고르시오.

① 7월 5일　　② 7월 7일　　③ 7월 10일
④ 7월 14일　　⑤ 7월 15일

M: What do we need?

W: We have to buy some eggs and spinach.

M: Here are the eggs. Let's get these. They're on sale.

W: Make sure to 1) _____ _____ _____ _____ first. Stores often put older items on sale.

M: They're good until July 14.

W: Okay. That means we 2) _____ _____ _____ _____ _____ them.

M: No. Actually, 3) _____ _____ _____.

W: Oh, you're right. I got confused. Let's get them.

---

17 마지막 말에 이어질 응답 찾기

대화를 듣고, 남자의 마지막 말에 대한 여자의 응답으로 가장 적절한 것을 고르시오.

Woman: _____

① It won't take that long.
② You can take more time.
③ You should prepare for it.
④ I'm afraid it'll cost too much.
⑤ Sure. Give us a few minutes to prepare.

W: How long has it been hurting?

M: It started to hurt at dinner last night. Then I 1) _____ _____ _____ when I brushed my teeth this morning.

W: Open your mouth and let me take a look. *[pause]* Hmm...

M: Is it serious?

W: It's not good news, I'm afraid. You 2) _____ _____ _____.

M: Really? What should I do?

W: First, you need fillings. I 3) _____ _____ _____, since they will last the longest.

M: Okay, can you 4) _____ _____ _____ _____?

W: Sure. Give us a few minutes to prepare.

18 마지막 말에 이어질 응답 찾기

대화를 듣고, 여자의 마지막 말에 대한 남자의 응답으로 가장 적절한 것을 고르시오.

Man: _____

① Don't take it too hard.
② They're due next Friday.
③ The total is eight dollars.
④ Sure, that's not a problem.
⑤ You should have returned them earlier.

M: Can I help you?

W: I'd like to 1) _____ _____ , please.

M: Sure. How many do you have?

W: There are six. Is that okay?

M: Actually, you can check out only five books at a time.

W: Oh, okay. I'll 2) _____ _____ _____ _____ , then.

M: All right. Can I see your student ID?

W: Here you are. When do I 3) _____ _____ _____ them?

M: They're due next Friday.

19 마지막 말에 이어질 응답 찾기

대화를 듣고, 여자의 마지막 말에 대한 남자의 응답으로 가장 적절한 것을 고르시오.

Man: _____

① It was the best movie ever!
② I hope you enjoy the movie.
③ Where is the nearest theater?
④ That's just around the corner.
⑤ Let's go to the movie together.

M: Can you tell me about your new movie?

W: It's a science fiction film. It's 1) _____ _____ _____ _____ _____ .

M: Sounds interesting. What was the most difficult part of directing it?

W: Creating the war scenes was hard. We 2) _____ _____ _____ _____ _____ .

M: I see. When can we see your movie in theaters?

W: 3) _____ _____ _____ in November.

M: That's just around the corner.

20 상황에 적절한 말 찾기

다음 상황 설명을 듣고, Carol이 남동생에게 할 말로 가장 적절한 것을 고르시오.

Carol: _____

① I ordered a new camera already.
② Thank you for finding my camera.
③ Why are you talking to me about this now?
④ Please ask me first if you want to borrow something.
⑤ I didn't want to come back from my vacation today.

W: Carol bought a new camera a few weeks ago. She is going to go on a vacation this weekend, so she's packing everything she needs for it. While she is packing, she notices that her 1) _____ _____ _____ _____ . She looks everywhere and finds it 2) _____ _____ _____ _____ _____ . He apologizes and says that he was going to return it right after he used it. She is angry because he 3) _____ _____ _____ _____ _____ her things. In this situation, what would Carol most likely say to her brother?

실전모의고사 회

정답 및 해설 pp. 62~67

점수: /20

01 대화를 듣고, 여자가 그린 그림을 고르시오.

02 대화를 듣고, 기숙사에 관해 언급되지 <u>않은</u> 것을 고르시오.

① 룸메이트 수   ② 방 크기
③ 비용   ④ 구내식당 음식
⑤ 강의실과의 거리

03 대화를 듣고, 남자가 여자에게 전화한 목적으로 가장 적절한 것을 고르시오.

① 컴퓨터를 빌리려고
② 약속 시각을 변경하려고
③ 모임 일정을 알려 주려고
④ 컴퓨터 수리를 부탁하려고
⑤ 숙제를 도와달라고 부탁하려고

04 대화를 듣고, 남자가 예약한 진료 시각을 고르시오.

① 10:00 a.m. ② 10:30 a.m. ③ 11:00 a.m.
④ 11:30 a.m. ⑤ 12:00 p.m.

05 대화를 듣고, 두 사람이 대화하는 장소로 가장 적절한 곳을 고르시오.

① 서점   ② 백화점
③ 영어 교실   ④ 버스 정류장
⑤ 분실물 보관소

06 다음 그림의 상황에 가장 적절한 대화를 고르시오.

①   ②   ③   ④   ⑤

07 대화를 듣고, 남자가 여자에게 부탁한 일로 가장 적절한 것을 고르시오.

① 친구 도와주기   ② 공연장에 데려다주기
③ 공연 녹화해주기   ④ 공연장 자리 맡아주기
⑤ 함께 과학 실험실에 가기

08 다음을 듣고, 패키지여행에 관해 언급되지 <u>않은</u> 것을 고르시오.

① 방문 국가   ② 여행 기간   ③ 호텔 위치
④ 불포함 항목 ⑤ 여행사 위치

09 다음을 듣고, 어떤 직업에 관한 설명인지 고르시오.

① 의사   ② 과학자   ③ 교육 연구원
④ 운동선수   ⑤ 우주 비행사

10 다음을 듣고, 두 사람의 대화가 <u>어색한</u> 것을 고르시오.

①   ②   ③   ④   ⑤

11 대화를 듣고, 여자가 크리스마스 준비를 위해 먼저 할 일로 가장 적절한 것을 고르시오.

① 쇼핑하기   ② 카드 쓰기
③ 쿠키 굽기   ④ 트리 장식하기
⑤ 선물 목록 작성하기

12 다음 정원 그림을 보면서 대화를 듣고, 두 사람이 개집을 놓을 곳을 고르시오.

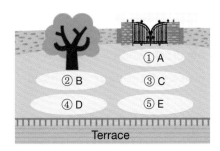

① A
② B
③ C
④ D
⑤ E
Terrace

고난도
13 대화를 듣고, 남자의 경주가 시작하는 시각을 고르시오.

① 1:00 p.m. ② 2:00 p.m. ③ 2:30 p.m.
④ 3:00 p.m. ⑤ 4:00 p.m.

14 대화를 듣고, 여자가 어제 한 일로 가장 적절한 것을 고르시오.

① 쇼핑하기 ② 숙제하기
③ 한복 체험하기 ④ 미국 여행하기
⑤ 한국 음식 먹기

15 다음을 듣고, 방송의 목적으로 가장 적절한 것을 고르시오.

① 학교 행사를 알리려고
② 학교 도서관을 소개하려고
③ 독서 동아리를 홍보하려고
④ 자원봉사자 모집을 공고하려고
⑤ 도서관 이용 수칙을 안내하려고

16 대화를 듣고, 여자가 지불할 금액을 고르시오.

① $10 ② $12 ③ $14
④ $20 ⑤ $22

17 대화를 듣고, 여자의 마지막 말에 대한 남자의 응답으로 가장 적절한 것을 고르시오.

Man: _____

① I can't wait to meet you.
② Say hello to your parents for me.
③ I wish I could attend the meeting.
④ I was wondering if you could come.
⑤ I'm leaving for a camping trip next Friday.

[18 - 19] 대화를 듣고, 남자의 마지막 말에 대한 여자의 응답으로 가장 적절한 것을 고르시오.

고난도
18 Woman: _____

① Great. I'll get the tools to fix it.
② We don't need an air conditioner.
③ Let's go to the electronics store now.
④ Okay. I don't care how much it costs.
⑤ Okay. But let's buy a new one if it breaks again.

19 Woman: _____

① I'm happy that you enjoyed it.
② I can use it with my computer.
③ That's all right. Forget about it.
④ I hope your dog gets well soon.
⑤ Be sure to return it by the due date.

20 다음 상황 설명을 듣고, Jen이 Anderson에게 할 말로 가장 적절한 것을 고르시오.

Jen: _____

① I'm glad to hear you got the part!
② I'll give you a role in my next play.
③ You'll get a part at the next audition.
④ You should always look directly at the audience.
⑤ You need to be more relaxed and breathe naturally.

Dictation Test 12

정답 및 해설 pp. 62~67

보통속도 듣기 빠르게 듣기

01 그림 정보 파악

대화를 듣고, 여자가 그린 그림을 고르시오.

①   ②   ③

④   ⑤

M: That's a nice painting. Who's the artist?

W: I painted it myself. It's my dream house.

M: This is your dream house? I thought you liked 1) _____ _____ _____ _____.

W: Actually, I want to 2) _____ _____ _____ _____ _____ someday.

M: Like the house in this painting? That's cool.

W: Yes. The best thing about this house is the window on the front. I want sunlight to come in 3) _____ _____ _____ _____.

M: It's very nice. I think anyone would be happy living there.

02 언급되지 않은 내용 찾기

대화를 듣고, 기숙사에 관해 언급되지 <u>않은</u> 것을 고르시오.

① 룸메이트 수   ② 방 크기
③ 비용   ④ 구내식당 음식
⑤ 강의실과의 거리

W: Hi, Alex. How's college?

M: It's great. I just moved into a new dormitory.

W: Really? What was wrong with the old one?

M: I had to share a room with three people. But now I 1) _____ _____ _____ _____.

W: That's good.

M: The rooms are bigger in the new dormitory, too.

W: Are they? How about the food?

M: It has 2) _____ _____ _____ _____ _____.

W: Wow, lucky you.

M: And best of all, it's 3) _____ _____ _____ _____ than my old dormitory.

03 목적 파악

대화를 듣고, 남자가 여자에게 전화한 목적으로 가장 적절한 것을 고르시오.

① 컴퓨터를 빌리려고
② 약속 시각을 변경하려고
③ 모임 일정을 알려 주려고
④ 컴퓨터 수리를 부탁하려고
⑤ 숙제를 도와달라고 부탁하려고

★ Focus on Sound   about to

똑같은 발음의 자음이 겹치면 앞 자음 소리가 탈락하여 [어바우트 투]가 아닌 [어바우투]로 발음된다.

[Cell phone rings.]

W: Hello?

M: Hi, Alison.

W: Hi, Walter. What's going on?

M: I was doing my homework on my computer, and it 1) _____ _____ _____. I don't know what's wrong. Could you help me?

W: Oh, I'm *about to go to a drama club meeting. Is it urgent?

M: Yes, I need to finish this homework today. So I was wondering if you could 2) _____ _____ _____ _____ _____.

W: I see. I'll come over to your place 3) _____ _____ _____ _____.

M: Okay. I'll see you then.

04 숫자 정보 파악

대화를 듣고, 남자가 예약한 진료 시각을 고르시오.

① 10:00 a.m. ② 10:30 a.m. ③ 11:00 a.m.
④ 11:30 a.m. ⑤ 12:00 p.m.

[Phone rings.]

W: Hello, Dr. Baker's office.

M: Hi. I'm having a problem. My eyes are very red and dry these days.

W: Have you been here before?

M: Yes. 1) _____ _____ _____ by Dr. Baker before.

W: Okay. When would you like to see him?

M: Well, I just need him to 2) _____ _____ _____ _____.

W: Okay, but you still need to 3) _____ _____ _____ _____.

M: I understand. May I come tomorrow morning at 11:00?

W: Sorry, but he's 4) _____ _____ _____ at 11:00. Can you come at 11:30?

M: Okay, that's fine.

05 장소 추론

대화를 듣고, 두 사람이 대화하는 장소로 가장 적절한 곳을 고르시오.

① 서점
② 백화점
③ 영어 교실
④ 버스 정류장
⑤ 분실물 보관소

W: Hi. Can I help you with something?

M: Yes. I was riding Bus 35 this morning, and I 1) _____ _____ _____ _____.

W: I see. Where did you get on the bus?

M: I got on at City Hall and got off three stops later.

W: Do you remember 2) _____ _____ _____ _____ _____?

M: I'm not sure exactly, but I guess it was around 8:00 a.m.

W: Okay. Can you 3) _____ _____ _____ _____?

M: It's a small, black shopping bag. And there's a new English dictionary inside.

W: All right. Wait a moment while I 4) _____ _____ _____ if it's here.

06 그림 상황에 적절한 대화 찾기 🇬🇧

다음 그림의 상황에 가장 적절한 대화를 고르시오.

① ② ③ ④ ⑤

① M: I ordered this jacket from an online shopping mall.

　　W: It 1) _____ _____ _____ _____ on you.

② M: May I help you?

　　W: No, I'm 2) _____ _____ _____.

③ M: I'd like to return this jacket.

　　W: Oh, is there anything wrong with it?

④ M: It's a bit small. Do you have this in a larger size?

　　W: Yes. 3) _____ _____ _____ _____ for you.

⑤ M: I like this color.

　　W: Yes, and it 4) _____ _____ _____.

07 부탁한 일 파악

대화를 듣고, 남자가 여자에게 부탁한 일로 가장 적절한 것을 고르시오.

① 친구 도와주기
② 공연장에 데려다주기
③ 공연 녹화해주기
④ 공연장 자리 맡아주기
⑤ 함께 과학 실험실에 가기

*Focus on Sound 20(twenty)

nt가 강모음과 약모음 사이에 오면 [t]가 [n]에 동화되어 [투엔티]가 아닌 [투에니]로 발음된다.

W: Eddie, where are you going? Aren't you going to see the school band? The concert hall is that way.

M: I am, but I have to 1) _____ _____ _____ _____ _____ first.

W: Why? The show will start in *20 minutes.

M: Yeah, but Dana just called, and she needs some help. It will 2) _____ _____ _____ _____ _____.

W: Okay, but hurry. There won't be any seats left.

M: Could you 3) _____ _____ _____ _____ _____ _____ for Dana and me? We'll hurry.

W: I'm not sure if I can, but I'll try!

다음을 듣고, 패키지여행에 관해 언급되지 <u>않은</u> 것을 고르시오.

① 방문 국가　② 여행 기간　③ 호텔 위치
④ 불포함 항목　⑤ 여행사 위치

W: Are you looking for something to do this winter vacation? 1) _____ _____ _____ beautiful Mexico? Global Travel has the perfect package tour for you. You can spend five days and four nights in a luxury hotel just 2) _____ _____ _____ _____ _____. The package includes trips to local markets and villages with a professional guide. Airplane tickets, however, 3) _____ _____ _____ _____. For prices and more information, call Global Travel today.

다음을 듣고, 어떤 직업에 관한 설명인지 고르시오.

① 의사　② 과학자　③ 교육 연구원
④ 운동선수　⑤ 우주 비행사

M: People who have this job 1) _____ _____ _____ _____. Before they can travel into space, they have to go through a lot of mental and physical preparation. For example, they have to get used to 2) _____ _____ _____. Before a mission, they also have to do a lot of research. They read lots of books, conduct experiments, and 3) _____ _____ _____ _____. When they get to space, they carry out many special tasks to study things like asteroids and other planets.

다음을 듣고, 두 사람의 대화가 <u>어색한</u> 것을 고르시오.

①　　②　　③　　④　　⑤

① W: You should exercise more often.
　 M: I know, but I've been too busy.
② W: 1) _____ _____ _____ does this book have?
　 M: It's one of our best-selling books.
③ W: Why don't we 2) _____ _____ _____ tomorrow?
　 M: I don't think that would be a good idea. It's going to rain all day.
④ W: 3) _____ _____ _____ some more ice cream?
　 M: Yes, but just a little bit.
⑤ W: How about going to the park?
　 M: No, 4) _____ _____ _____ _____ _____ at home.

대화를 듣고, 여자가 크리스마스 준비를 위해 먼저 할 일로 가장 적절한 것을 고르시오.

① 쇼핑하기　　　② 카드 쓰기
③ 쿠키 굽기　　　④ 트리 장식하기
⑤ 선물 목록 작성하기

M: Are you okay, Julia?

W: Yes, but it's almost Christmas! I have so many things to do.

M: What kinds of things? Are you going to 1) _____ _____ _____ _____ for your apartment?

W: Yes, of course. I also need to buy some 2) _____ _____ _____ to decorate it. But first, I'm going to 3) _____ _____ _____ of all the gifts I need to buy.

M: Okay. I hope you bake some of your delicious gingerbread men cookies, too!

W: I will, but not today.

다음 정원 그림을 보면서 대화를 듣고, 두 사람이 개집을 놓을 곳을 고르시오.

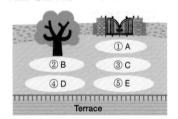

M: Where shall we put the doghouse?

W: How about at the back of the yard 1) _____ _____ _____ _____? Our dog can bark if a stranger comes.

M: That's too far away. I want to watch the dog from the terrace.

W: Well, how about 2) _____ _____ _____ _____ _____ _____ then?

M: That's too close. Our dog might be noisy.

W: So how about on the left, 3) _____ _____ _____?

M: That's perfect. It's not too far, and our dog can relax under the shade of the tree.

W: Great! Let's put it there.

13 숫자 정보 파악

대화를 듣고, 남자의 경주가 시작하는 시각을 고르시오.

① 1:00 p.m. ② 2:00 p.m. ③ 2:30 p.m.
④ 3:00 p.m. ⑤ 4:00 p.m.

W: Your race starts in a few hours, right? How do you feel?

M: I'm nervous.

W: I'm sure you'll do well.

M: Thank you. I think it would help if I could see you [1) _____ _____ _____ at the track.

W: I'm afraid I can't go to your race. I have an important meeting at 2:00 p.m. I won't be able to [2) _____ _____ _____ _____ _____ _____.

M: How long will the meeting last?

W: It won't take long. I expect it to [3) _____ _____ _____ _____ _____.

M: Then you can come! The first race starts at 1:00, but the 1,000 meter race I'm running in starts [4) _____ _____ _____.

14 한 일 파악

대화를 듣고, 여자가 어제 한 일로 가장 적절한 것을 고르시오.

① 쇼핑하기   ② 숙제하기
③ 한복 체험하기   ④ 미국 여행하기
⑤ 한국 음식 먹기

M: Hi, Jane. [1) _____ _____ _____ _____ for the last couple of days?

W: I've been busy since my friend Kate came from America.

M: What did you do with her?

W: Well, we did a lot of things, like [2) _____, _____, _____ _____ Korean food.

M: Does your friend like it here?

W: Of course. Yesterday, we [3) _____ _____ _____ _____ _____, and she loved it.

M: Nice! It must have been a great experience for her.

15 목적 파악

다음을 듣고, 방송의 목적으로 가장 적절한 것을 고르시오.

① 학교 행사를 알리려고
② 학교 도서관을 소개하려고
③ 독서 동아리를 홍보하려고
④ 자원봉사자 모집을 공고하려고
⑤ 도서관 이용 수칙을 안내하려고

W: Hello, students! This is your librarian, Emily Brown. We have been [1) _____ _____ _____ for the past three days, but we still need more help. I'd like to encourage you to [2) _____ _____ _____ _____. In the school library, volunteers help by putting returned books back on the shelves, helping students find books, and cleaning up. If you'd like to volunteer, come to the library and [3) _____ _____ _____ _____ _____.
I promise this will be a good experience for you. Thank you.

대화를 듣고, 여자가 지불할 금액을 고르시오.

① $10   ② $12   ③ $14
④ $20   ⑤ $22

W: What cute souvenirs! How much are those dolls?

M: These dolls? They're $5 each, ma'am.

W: No, not those big ones. The little ones over there.

M: Oh, I see. Those are 1) _____ _____ .

W: Okay. I like those T-shirts over there, too.

M: They are very popular. They 2) _____ _____ _____
_____ _____ : white, blue, and green.

W: How much do they cost?

M: They're 3) _____ _____ .

W: Okay. I'll take 4) _____ _____ _____ _____
_____ and a blue T-shirt.

M: Certainly. I'll put them in a bag for you.

---

17 마지막 말에 이어질 응답 찾기

대화를 듣고, 여자의 마지막 말에 대한 남자의 응답으로 가장 적절한 것을 고르시오.

Man: _____

① I can't wait to meet you.
② Say hello to your parents for me.
③ I wish I could attend the meeting.
④ I was wondering if you could come.
⑤ I'm leaving for a camping trip next Friday.

[Cell phone rings.]

M: Hi, Sue. What's up?

W: Hi, Shawn. Nothing much. I just 1) _____ _____ _____
_____ . We haven't seen each other in a while. We should meet soon.

M: I agree.

W: Are you 2) _____ _____ _____ _____ _____
next Friday?

M: No, 3) _____ _____ _____ _____ .

W: Why not?

M: I'm leaving for a camping trip next Friday.

18 마지막 말에 이어질 응답 찾기 🇬🇧

대화를 듣고, 남자의 마지막 말에 대한 여자의 응답으로 가장 적절한 것을 고르시오.

Woman: _____

① Great. I'll get the tools to fix it.
② We don't need an air conditioner.
③ Let's go to the electronics store now.
④ Okay. I don't care how much it costs.
⑤ Okay. But let's buy a new one if it breaks again.

M: Is the air conditioner broken?
W: Yes, the repairman said it didn't look good.
M: Can he fix it?
W: He can, but it's too old. Even after he fixes it, 1) _____ _____ _____ _____.
M: Then what should we do?
W: I think it's better to 2) _____ _____ _____ _____.
M: But buying a new air conditioner 3) _____ _____ _____.
W: That's true. The repairman said it wouldn't cost much to fix it.
M: Well, how about 4) _____ _____ _____ _____?
W: Okay. But let's buy a new one if it breaks again.

---

19 마지막 말에 이어질 응답 찾기

대화를 듣고, 남자의 마지막 말에 대한 여자의 응답으로 가장 적절한 것을 고르시오.

Woman: _____

① I'm happy that you enjoyed it.
② I can use it with my computer.
③ That's all right. Forget about it.
④ I hope your dog gets well soon.
⑤ Be sure to return it by the due date.

M: Sohee, do you remember that game 1) _____ _____ _____ _____?
W: Yes, I do. Did you enjoy it?
M: To be honest, I never played it.
W: Really? Why not?
M: I left it on the sofa, and 2) _____ _____ _____ _____.
W: You're kidding. 3) _____ _____ _____?
M: No, it isn't. I'm really sorry.
W: That's all right. Forget about it.

---

20 상황에 적절한 말 찾기

다음 상황 설명을 듣고, Jen이 Anderson에게 할 말로 가장 적절한 것을 고르시오.

Jen: _____

① I'm glad to hear you got the part!
② I'll give you a role in my next play.
③ You'll get a part at the next audition.
④ You should always look directly at the audience.
⑤ You need to be more relaxed and breathe naturally.

M: Anderson is an actor. He goes to many auditions for musicals, but he 1) _____ _____ _____ _____. He doesn't know why he keeps failing. He thinks there must be some reason. One of his friends, Jen, has performed in many musicals. He 2) _____ _____ _____ _____. He sings a song in front of her, and Jen sees the problem. Anderson 3) _____ _____ _____, so he doesn't breathe naturally. In this situation, what would Jen most likely say to Anderson?

Word Test

A 다음 영어의 우리말 뜻을 쓰시오.

01 purpose		21 librarian	
02 encourage		22 drawer	
03 drop		23 separately	
04 directly		24 explore	
05 shelter		25 share	
06 laundry		26 postpone	
07 asteroid		27 ornament	
08 urgent		28 mental	
09 stir		29 pour	
10 captivate		30 spill	
11 rub		31 bank account	
12 activity		32 washing machine	
13 shoot		33 to be honest	
14 audience		34 take time	
15 purchase		35 stare at	
16 local		36 except for	
17 compact		37 go through	
18 approach		38 be about to-v	
19 professional		39 carry out	
20 disappointing		40 get used to v-ing	

B 다음 우리말 뜻에 맞는 영어를 쓰시오.

01 끈적거리는 _____

02 육체적인 _____

03 위성 _____

04 상상력 _____

05 처방전 _____

06 과목 _____

07 승객 _____

08 짖다 _____

09 감정적인 _____

10 접착제, 풀 _____

11 큰 소리로, 시끄럽게 _____

12 사전 _____

13 전설적인 _____

14 자연스럽게 _____

15 대하다; 치료하다 _____

16 역할 _____

17 축하하다 _____

18 그늘 _____

19 왕조 _____

20 관광 _____

21 사라지다 _____

22 호흡하다 _____

23 유용한 _____

24 탑승하다 _____

25 중력 _____

26 장식하다 _____

27 무례한 _____

28 대본 _____

29 집중하다 _____

30 폭풍 _____

31 기숙사 _____

32 동전 _____

33 입양하다 _____

34 공연하다, 연기하다 _____

35 편리한 _____

36 ~에 달려 있다 _____

37 ~에 관심이 있다 _____

38 ~을 응원하다 _____

39 ~와 잘 지내다 _____

40 목록을 작성하다 _____

실전모의고사 13 회

정답 및 해설 pp. 68~72

점수: /20

01 대화를 듣고, 남자가 구입할 시계를 고르시오.

① ② ③ ④ ⑤

02 대화를 듣고, 영어 실력 향상 방안으로 언급되지 않은 것을 고르시오.

① 영어 신문 읽기
② 미국 드라마 시청하기
③ 영어 일기 쓰기
④ 영어 캠프 참가하기
⑤ 영어로 온라인 채팅하기

03 대화를 듣고, 남자가 여자에게 전화한 목적으로 가장 적절한 것을 고르시오.

① 어디 있는지 물어보려고
② 수학 숙제를 물어보려고
③ 친구의 전화번호를 물어보려고
④ 영화를 같이 보자고 제안하려고
⑤ 노트 필기를 보여 달라고 부탁하려고

04 대화를 듣고, 두 사람이 보기로 한 공연의 시작 시각을 고르시오.

① 1:30 p.m. ② 2:00 p.m. ③ 3:00 p.m.
④ 7:00 p.m. ⑤ 8:00 p.m.

05 대화를 듣고, 남자의 심정으로 가장 적절한 것을 고르시오.

① worried ② hopeful ③ grateful
④ curious ⑤ disappointed

06 다음 그림의 상황에 가장 적절한 대화를 고르시오.

① ② ③ ④ ⑤

07 대화를 듣고, 여자가 남자에게 부탁한 일로 가장 적절한 것을 고르시오.

① 음식 만들어주기
② 버스 노선 알려주기
③ 저녁 식사에 초대해주기
④ 지하철역 위치 알려주기
⑤ 버스 정류장까지 데려다주기

08 다음을 듣고, Jim Stewart에 관해 언급되지 않은 것을 고르시오.

① 나이   ② 대학 전공   ③ 경력
④ 담당 과목   ⑤ 담당 학년

09 다음을 듣고, 어떤 장소에 관한 설명인지 고르시오.

① 공원   ② 동물원   ③ 농장
④ 동물 병원   ⑤ 유기견 보호소

10 다음을 듣고, 두 사람의 대화가 어색한 것을 고르시오.

① ② ③ ④ ⑤

11 대화를 듣고, 여자가 오후에 할 일로 가장 적절한 것을 고르시오.

① 이사하기   ② 정원 가꾸기
③ 집 계약하기   ④ 꽃 사러 가기
⑤ 아이 방 꾸미기

12 다음 표를 보면서 대화를 듣고, 내용과 일치하지 <u>않</u>는 것을 고르시오.

Hotel Reservation		
①	Room Type	Double
②	Date	August 19 – 21
③	Name	Gillian Thompson
④	View	Mountain view
⑤	Total Price	$600

13 대화를 듣고, 남자가 치과를 방문하기로 한 시각을 고르시오.

① 9 a.m.   ② 1 p.m.   ③ 3 p.m.
④ 5 p.m.   ⑤ 9 p.m.

14 대화를 듣고, 남자가 어제 한 일로 가장 적절한 것을 고르시오.

① 거리 걷기   ② 여행 짐 꾸리기
③ 파티 즐기기   ④ 관광지 방문하기
⑤ 여행 계획 세우기

15 다음을 듣고, 방송의 목적으로 가장 적절한 것을 고르시오.

① 학교 시설을 소개하려고
② 학교 규칙을 설명하려고
③ 학교 동아리를 홍보하려고
④ 점심 메뉴 변경을 공지하려고
⑤ 학교 식당 공사에 대해 알리려고

고난도
16 대화를 듣고, 남자가 받을 거스름돈을 고르시오.

① $1   ② $2   ③ $3   ④ $4   ⑤ $5

17 대화를 듣고, 남자의 마지막 말에 대한 여자의 응답으로 가장 적절한 것을 고르시오.

Woman: _____

① I don't know where it is.
② I have a favor to ask of you.
③ The tickets are so expensive.
④ Sorry, but I don't like that musical.
⑤ That sounds wonderful. What time does it begin?

[18-19] 대화를 듣고, 여자의 마지막 말에 대한 남자의 응답으로 가장 적절한 것을 고르시오.

18 Man: _____

① It's five stops from here.
② You should get on another bus.
③ Where did you get on this bus?
④ I wouldn't go there if I were you.
⑤ You should turn left at the corner.

고난도
19 Man: _____

① Of course. Practice makes perfect.
② Basketball players are usually very tall.
③ I don't think he is the right person for MVP.
④ Tall players have many benefits in basketball.
⑤ Absolutely! We should never judge a book by its cover.

20 다음 상황 설명을 듣고, Douglas가 Eva에게 할 말로 가장 적절한 것을 고르시오.

Douglas: _____

① Are you feeling any better?
② Did you do well on the exam?
③ I'd like to join your study group.
④ I will send you an email next week.
⑤ Would you mind lending me your notes?

Dictation Test 13

정답 및 해설 pp. 68~72

01 [그림 정보 파악]

대화를 듣고, 남자가 구입할 시계를 고르시오.

W: Hello, how can I help you?

M: Hi, I'm looking for a watch for myself.

W: I see. This model is popular these days. We have two types, round and square.

M: The 1) _____ _____ _____ _____ to me.

W: What kind of watch strap do you prefer, metal or leather?

M: I usually prefer metal, but the 2) _____ _____ _____ on this design.

W: Then how about this one with striped leather?

M: Well... I don't like to stand out, so I'll take this one 3) _____ _____ _____.

W: Good choice. It will look good on you.

02 [언급되지 않은 내용 찾기]

대화를 듣고, 영어 실력 향상 방안으로 언급되지 않은 것을 고르시오.

① 영어 신문 읽기
② 미국 드라마 시청하기
③ 영어 일기 쓰기
④ 영어 캠프 참가하기
⑤ 영어로 온라인 채팅하기

＊Focus on Sound foreign

[g]는 묵음이어서 [포린]으로 발음된다.

M: Juha, your English has greatly improved.

W: Thanks for saying that.

M: What do you do to 1) _____ _____ _____?

W: I read English newspapers every day.

M: Wow. Do you watch TV programs in English, too?

W: Yes. I 2) _____ _____ _____ _____. They were hard to understand at first, but now I can understand them without subtitles.

M: Great! What else do you do?

W: I 3) _____ _____ _____ _____ and chat online in English with my ＊foreign friends.

M: Those are some good ideas.

03 목적 파악

대화를 듣고, 남자가 여자에게 전화한 목적으로 가장 적절한 것을 고르시오.

① 어디 있는지 물어보려고
② 수학 숙제를 물어보려고
③ 친구의 전화번호를 물어보려고
④ 영화를 같이 보자고 제안하려고
⑤ 노트 필기를 보여 달라고 부탁하려고

[Cell phone rings.]

W: Hey, John. What's up?

M: Hey! Where are you? Are you out?

W: Yes, I'm 1) _____ _____ _____ _____ with my sister.

M: I see. Anyway, I'm calling because I forgot to 2) _____ _____ _____ _____ _____ again. What was it?

W: Actually, I wrote it down, but I don't remember exactly now. 3) _____ _____ _____ _____ _____ Max?

M: Okay, I will.

W: Sorry for 4) _____ _____ _____ _____.

M: No problem! Have fun!

04 숫자 정보 파악 🇬🇧

대화를 듣고, 두 사람이 보기로 한 공연의 시작 시각을 고르시오.

① 1:30 p.m.   ② 2:00 p.m.   ③ 3:00 p.m.
④ 7:00 p.m.   ⑤ 8:00 p.m.

W: There's going to be a classical music concert on Saturday.

M: I know, but I don't think I can go. It starts at 7:00 p.m., but I have to 1) _____ _____ _____ _____ at the airport at 8:00.

W: Why don't you go to the afternoon performance?

M: 2) _____ _____ _____ _____ ?

W: Yes, at 2:00. That's when I'm going.

M: Great! We can go together.

W: Good. Then 3) _____ _____ _____ _____ at the subway station.

M: Sounds good to me.

05 심정 추론 🇬🇧

대화를 듣고, 남자의 심정으로 가장 적절한 것을 고르시오.

① worried   ② hopeful   ③ grateful
④ curious   ⑤ disappointed

★ Focus on Sound   speak

[s] 뒤에 [p]가 오면 된소리가 되어 [스피크]가 아닌 [스삐크]로 발음된다.

[Cell phone rings.]

M: Hello?

W: Hello, can I *speak to Mr. Brown?

M: This is he. Who's calling, please?

W: Hi, I'm calling to tell you that I 1) _____ _____ _____ on the street.

M: Oh, great! How did you 2) _____ _____ _____ ?

W: It was on a business card in your wallet.

M: Oh, I don't know how to thank you.

W: How do you want to 3) _____ _____ _____ ?

M: If you can tell me where you are, I'll come meet you. I want to 4) _____ _____ _____ _____.

06 그림 상황에 적절한 대화 찾기

다음 그림의 상황에 가장 적절한 대화를 고르시오.

① ② ③ ④ ⑤

① W: Do you have any questions?

  M: Yes. Can you tell me which one is the latest model?

② W: Hello. What can I do for you today?

  M: Can you take a look at my finger? I think it's broken.

③ W: Do you need any help?

  M: I'd like to return this and 1) _____ _____ _____.

④ W: How can I get to the service center?

  M: Go straight one block, and it's 2) _____ _____ _____ _____.

⑤ W: How can I help you today?

  M: My phone's screen is broken. I'd like to 3) _____ _____ _____.

07 부탁한 일 파악

대화를 듣고, 여자가 남자에게 부탁한 일로 가장 적절한 것을 고르시오.

① 음식 만들어주기
② 버스 노선 알려주기
③ 저녁 식사에 초대해주기
④ 지하철역 위치 알려주기
⑤ 버스 정류장까지 데려다주기

W: Dinner was so nice. But it's getting late, so I'll probably 1) _____ _____ _____.

M: How did you get here?

W: I took the subway, but I 2) _____ _____ _____. It took quite a long time.

M: Oh, but there's a bus that 3) _____ _____ _____ _____.

W: Really? Which bus is it?

M: It's the 142 bus. The bus stop is near Standard Bank.

W: I don't know where that is. Can you 4) _____ _____ _____ _____ _____ _____?

M: Sure. It's getting dark. Let's go.

08 언급되지 않은 내용 찾기

다음을 듣고, Jim Stewart에 관해 언급되지 않은 것을 고르시오.

① 나이　　② 대학 전공　③ 경력
④ 담당 과목　⑤ 담당 학년

W: Good morning, everyone. Thank you all for coming. I called this meeting to 1) _____ _____ _____ _____, Jim Stewart. He graduated from university with a 2) _____ _____ _____ _____. He has worked as an English teacher in several schools and community centers over the past decade. He will be teaching English at our school. He will also 3) _____ _____ _____ _____. I'm excited to have him join our staff. Please welcome him!

09 화제 파악

다음을 듣고, 어떤 장소에 관한 설명인지 고르시오.

① 공원　　② 동물원　　③ 농장
④ 동물 병원　⑤ 유기견 보호소

M: This is a place where 1) _____ _____ _____ and shown to the public. This place gives people the chance to observe animals that they might not see anywhere else. In this place, the animals are kept in houses. Cages and fences 2) _____ _____ _____ _____ _____. The fences also keep people from getting too close to the animals. The animals in this place are 3) _____ _____ _____ _____. The experts try to make the animals' houses look like natural habitats. A vet often 4) _____ _____ _____ of the animals and treats them immediately if they get hurt or sick.

10 어색한 대화 찾기

다음을 듣고, 두 사람의 대화가 어색한 것을 고르시오.

①　　②　　③　　④　　⑤

① M: The music is too loud.
　 W: Oh, sorry. I'll 1) _____ _____ _____ _____.
② M: How have you been doing?
　 W: I've been pretty busy.
③ M: It's the worst movie I've ever seen.
　 W: What makes you say that?
④ M: Which restaurant 2) _____ _____ _____ _____?
　 W: The new French restaurant next to the bank.
⑤ M: 3) _____ _____ _____ _____ _____ from school?
　 W: The library is open every day.

대화를 듣고, 여자가 오후에 할 일로 가장 적절한 것을 고르시오.

① 이사하기　　　② 정원 가꾸기
③ 집 계약하기　　④ 꽃 사러 가기
⑤ 아이 방 꾸미기

M: Sandy! I heard you bought a new house. When are you moving?

W: Actually, I already have. I 1) _____ _____ _____.

M: Really? So what's it like?

W: It has three bedrooms — one for my husband and me, and two for my kids. Now my kids have their own rooms.

M: Your boys 2) _____ _____ _____ _____ _____.

W: They are. And it has a big kitchen. I love it!

M: Good for you. Do you have your own garden?

W: Yes! It's not very big, but it's beautiful. I'm planning to 3) _____ _____ _____ _____ and plant some flowers this afternoon.

M: That sounds like a good idea.

다음 표를 보면서 대화를 듣고, 내용과 일치하지 <u>않는</u> 것을 고르시오.

Hotel Reservation		
①	Room Type	Double
②	Date	August 19 – 21
③	Name	Gillian Thompson
④	View	Mountain view
⑤	Total Price	$600

＊Focus on Sound　would you

[d]가 뒤의 반모음 [j]를 만나면 동화되어 [우드유]가 아닌 [우쥬]로 발음된다.

[Phone rings.]

M: Hello, this is Holiday Hotel.

W: Hi, I'd like to 1) _____ _____ _____ with a double bed for next weekend. That's August 19 through the 21.

M: Sure. Can I get your name?

W: It's Gillian Thompson.

M: ＊Would you like a room 2) _____ _____ _____ _____ or an ocean view?

W: Well, either would be fine.

M: Okay. Let me check. We have 3) _____ _____ _____ per night. It's a room with an ocean view.

W: That's good.

M: Okay. You've reserved a 4) _____ _____ _____ _____.

W: Thank you very much.

13 숫자 정보 파악

대화를 듣고, 남자가 치과를 방문하기로 한 시각을 고르시오.

① 9 a.m. ② 1 p.m. ③ 3 p.m.
④ 5 p.m. ⑤ 9 p.m.

[Phone rings.]

W: Good morning. ABC Dental Clinic.

M: Hi, this is Harry Kane. I'd like to make an appointment.

W: Okay. How about tomorrow morning at nine o'clock?

M: It's 1) _____ _____ _____ _____, so is it possible to come in today?

W: What's the matter?

M: I broke my tooth playing soccer.

W: Then how about 2) _____ _____ _____ _____?

M: Can't it be 3) _____ _____ _____? It hurts quite a bit.

W: 4) _____ _____ _____ _____ with you? That's the best I can do.

M: That's good. Thank you very much.

W: My pleasure. See you then.

14 한 일 파악

대화를 듣고, 남자가 어제 한 일로 가장 적절한 것을 고르시오.

① 거리 걷기   ② 여행 짐 꾸리기
③ 파티 즐기기   ④ 관광지 방문하기
⑤ 여행 계획 세우기

W: Hey, how was your trip to New York?

M: It was so much fun. I can't wait to go traveling again.

W: 1) _____ _____ _____ _____ _____ _____?

M: For two weeks.

W: Which place did you like the most?

M: I liked all of the 2) _____ _____ _____, but I also liked just walking around the streets.

W: I want to walk in New York, too.

M: The best day of all was yesterday. My friend Mark 3) _____ _____ _____ _____ for me.

W: Wow, that must have been great.

15 목적 파악

다음을 듣고, 방송의 목적으로 가장 적절한 것을 고르시오.

① 학교 시설을 소개하려고
② 학교 규칙을 설명하려고
③ 학교 동아리를 홍보하려고
④ 점심 메뉴 변경을 공지하려고
⑤ 학교 식당 공사에 대해 알리려고

W: Hello, students! This is your principal speaking. As I have announced before, the 1) _____ _____ _____ _____ today. The construction is expected to 2) _____ _____ _____ _____ _____ until next Friday. During this period, please 3) _____ _____ _____ _____ _____ _____. If you do have to walk past the construction area, please be careful. I apologize in advance for the construction noise. I ask for your patience and understanding. Thank you.

16 숫자 정보 파악

대화를 듣고, 남자가 받을 거스름돈을 고르시오.

① $1　② $2　③ $3　④ $4　⑤ $5

M: I'd like to ¹⁾ _____ _____ _____ .

W: Okay. Let's see. *[pause]* You've got five books.

M: Yes. How much will it be?

W: They're $2 each.

M: So it's ²⁾ _____ _____ _____ ?

W: Oh, wait. Two of them ³⁾ _____ _____ _____ . New releases are $3 each.

M: I see. Here's $15.

W: And here's your change. Don't forget to ⁴⁾ _____ _____ _____ _____ _____ .

17 마지막 말에 이어질 응답 찾기

대화를 듣고, 남자의 마지막 말에 대한 여자의 응답으로 가장 적절한 것을 고르시오.

Woman: _____

① I don't know where it is.

② I have a favor to ask of you.

③ The tickets are so expensive.

④ Sorry, but I don't like that musical.

⑤ That sounds wonderful. What time does it begin?

M: Have you been to the new theater downtown?

W: Not yet, but I heard a great musical is playing there.

M: That's right, *Wicked*! The original cast is performing. Are you ¹⁾ _____ _____ _____ it?

W: Yes, I am. But I ²⁾ _____ _____ _____ _____ a ticket.

M: You know what? I have two tickets for it.

W: Really? Where did you get them?

M: My older sister gave them to me. Would you like to ³⁾ _____ _____ _____ ?

W: That sounds wonderful. What time does it begin?

18 마지막 말에 이어질 응답 찾기 🇬🇧

대화를 듣고, 여자의 마지막 말에 대한 남자의 응답으로 가장 적절한 것을 고르시오.

Man: _____

① It's five stops from here.
② You should get on another bus.
③ Where did you get on this bus?
④ I wouldn't go there if I were you.
⑤ You should turn left at the corner.

W: Excuse me. Can I ask you a question?
M: Sure. What is it?
W: I'm new here, and I'm worried I'm 1) _____ _____ _____ _____.
M: Where are you going?
W: I'm going to the Plaza Hotel.
M: Oh, you're on the right bus. We'll 2) _____ _____ _____ _____ _____ _____.
W: Oh, that's good. 3) _____ _____ _____ do I need to go?
M: It's five stops from here.

---

19 마지막 말에 이어질 응답 찾기

대화를 듣고, 여자의 마지막 말에 대한 남자의 응답으로 가장 적절한 것을 고르시오.

Man: _____

① Of course. Practice makes perfect.
② Basketball players are usually very tall.
③ I don't think he is the right person for MVP.
④ Tall players have many benefits in basketball.
⑤ Absolutely! We should never judge a book by its cover.

W: What did you think about Sports Day last week?
M: I really liked it.
W: It was exciting, wasn't it?
M: It was. I 1) _____ _____ _____ _____ _____, especially the basketball game.
W: Me too. The game was very exciting. And Ted was the MVP! I didn't know that he was 2) _____ _____ _____ _____.
M: Neither did I. I thought only tall people were good at basketball.
W: I know! 3) _____ _____ _____ _____ _____, he played great!
M: Absolutely! We should never judge a book by its cover.

---

20 상황에 적절한 말 찾기

다음 상황 설명을 듣고, Douglas가 Eva에게 할 말로 가장 적절한 것을 고르시오.

Douglas: _____

① Are you feeling any better?
② Did you do well on the exam?
③ I'd like to join your study group.
④ I will send you an email next week.
⑤ Would you mind lending me your notes?

M: Douglas missed his class because he was ill. Eva, his classmate, calls him to find out 1) _____ _____ _____ _____ _____. She lets him know what he 2) _____ _____ _____. Then she tells him that the teacher talked about some important topics that will be on the exam next week. Douglas wants to 3) _____ _____ _____ _____ _____.
In this situation, what would Douglas most likely say to Eva?

실전모의고사 14 회

정답 및 해설 pp. 72~77

점수: /20

보통 속도 듣기   빠르게 듣기

01 대화를 듣고, 여자가 만든 열쇠고리를 고르시오.

02 대화를 듣고, 남자의 역할로 언급되지 <u>않은</u> 것을 고르시오.

① 음식 조리   ② 식재료 확인

③ 요리사 관리   ④ 손님 응대

⑤ 주방 청결 관리

03 대화를 듣고, 남자의 마지막 말에 담긴 의도로 가장 적절한 것을 고르시오.

① 초대   ② 추천   ③ 동의

④ 허락   ⑤ 축하

04 대화를 듣고, 여자가 탈 버스의 출발 시각을 고르시오.

① 1:00 p.m.   ② 1:30 p.m.   ③ 2:00 p.m.

④ 2:30 p.m.   ⑤ 3:00 p.m.

05 대화를 듣고, 남자의 심정으로 가장 적절한 것을 고르시오.

① lonely   ② excited   ③ scared

④ surprised   ⑤ disappointed

06 다음 그림의 상황에 가장 적절한 대화를 고르시오.

①   ②   ③   ④   ⑤

07 대화를 듣고, 여자가 남자에게 부탁한 일로 가장 적절한 것을 고르시오.

① 저녁 준비하기   ② 회의 참석하기

③ 식당 예약하기   ④ 냉장고 정리하기

⑤ 음식 배달 주문하기

08 다음을 듣고, 타지마할에 관해 언급되지 <u>않은</u> 것을 고르시오.

① 위치   ② 건축 시기   ③ 건축 목적

④ 색   ⑤ 자재

09 다음을 듣고, 무엇에 관한 설명인지 고르시오.

① 에어컨   ② 체온계   ③ 히터

④ 텔레비전   ⑤ 리모컨

10 다음을 듣고, 두 사람의 대화가 <u>어색한</u> 것을 고르시오.

①   ②   ③   ④   ⑤

11 대화를 듣고, 남자가 대화 직후에 할 일로 가장 적절한 것을 고르시오.

① 옷 쇼핑하기

② 친구 만나러 가기

③ 낡은 옷 정리하기

④ 전자레인지 고치기

⑤ 중고품 교환 시장에 가기

12 다음 갤러리 안내도를 보면서 대화를 듣고, 두 사람이 초상화를 전시할 구역을 고르시오.

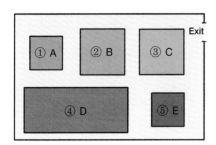

13 대화를 듣고, 두 사람이 만나기로 한 시각을 고르시오.

① 6:00 p.m.　② 6:30 p.m.　③ 7:00 p.m.
④ 7:30 p.m.　⑤ 8:00 p.m.

14 대화를 듣고, 남자가 어제 한 일로 가장 적절한 것을 고르시오.

① 영화 보기　　　② 영화 예매하기
③ 원작 소설 읽기　④ 친구와 약속 정하기
⑤ 영화 평론 찾아보기

15 다음을 듣고, 방송의 목적으로 가장 적절한 것을 고르시오.

① 새 학기 시작을 알리려고
② 행사 장소 변경을 공지하려고
③ 체육관 시설에 대해 안내하려고
④ 새로 오신 선생님을 소개하려고
⑤ 학교 동아리 회원 모집을 홍보하려고

고난도
16 대화를 듣고, 여자가 지불할 금액을 고르시오.

① $70　　② $75　　③ $80
④ $85　　⑤ $90

고난도
17 대화를 듣고, 여자의 마지막 말에 대한 남자의 응답으로 가장 적절한 것을 고르시오.

Man: _____

① How long did that take?
② How much do you weigh now?
③ You should pay attention to your diet.
④ Be careful. It's not healthy to be too thin.
⑤ Eating too much fat is not good for your health.

[18-19] 대화를 듣고, 남자의 마지막 말에 대한 여자의 응답으로 가장 적절한 것을 고르시오.

18 Woman: _____

① You need to rest.
② Let me check your temperature.
③ Drink as much water as possible.
④ If it gets worse, go to the hospital.
⑤ Three times a day, after every meal.

19 Woman: _____

① Here's your change.
② It's on the kitchen table.
③ I didn't enjoy it very much.
④ I like coffee better than tea.
⑤ No, thanks. Coffee is enough.

고난도
20 다음 상황 설명을 듣고, Kevin이 점원에게 할 말로 가장 적절한 것을 고르시오.

Kevin: _____

① I want a full refund.
② Do you have any other sizes?
③ I'm afraid there's a mistake on the receipt.
④ Didn't you like the birthday gift I got you?
⑤ When are you having your birthday party?

Dictation Test 14

01 그림 정보 파악

대화를 듣고, 여자가 만든 열쇠고리를 고르시오.

M: Sue, what's on your bag? It's cute.

W: Oh, I went to a leather workshop yesterday. I 1) _____ _____ _____ _____ there.

M: Did you make it yourself? That's cool.

W: Yes. It was really hard to make.

M: Really? Does it take a lot of time?

W: Yes, I spent all my time making a face, so I 2) _____ _____ _____ _____.

M: It looks fine 3) _____ _____ _____ _____. Did you choose the design yourself?

W: Yes. At first, I thought about making a rabbit, but I 4) _____ _____ _____ _____.

M: Great choice.

02 언급되지 않은 내용 찾기

대화를 듣고, 남자의 역할로 언급되지 <u>않은</u> 것을 고르시오.

① 음식 조리   ② 식재료 확인
③ 요리사 관리   ④ 손님 응대
⑤ 주방 청결 관리

W: Hello, everyone. Today, I have a special guest, Samuel Anderson.

M: Hi. Thank you for inviting me.

W: Can you tell us what it's like to be a chef?

M: Sure. As a chef, I don't just make food for our customers. Every morning, I 1) _____ _____ _____ _____ that will be used in our dishes. I also 2) _____ _____ _____.

W: Wow, you're 3) _____ _____ _____ so many things! Are there any other things that you do?

M: The kitchen should always be clean, so I check every corner of it every day.

W: So you're more 4) _____ _____ _____ _____.

03 의도 파악

대화를 듣고, 남자의 마지막 말에 담긴 의도로 가장 적절한 것을 고르시오.

① 초대   ② 추천   ③ 동의
④ 허락   ⑤ 축하

W: My family is planning to take a trip this summer.

M: Oh, really? Where are you going?

W: We haven't decided yet. We 1) _____ _____ _____ _____ _____, but it's not easy to decide.

M: Well, 2) _____ _____ _____ _____, I would go to Jeju Island. It's a UNESCO World Heritage Site.

W: Oh, that's one of our choices. Have you been there?

M: Yes, I went there last summer, and it was fantastic. The scenery was beautiful, and there were 3) _____ _____ _____ _____ _____ and eat.

04 숫자 정보 파악

대화를 듣고, 여자가 탈 버스의 출발 시각을 고르시오.

① 1:00 p.m.   ② 1:30 p.m.   ③ 2:00 p.m.
④ 2:30 p.m.   ⑤ 3:00 p.m.

M: How may I help you?

W: I'd like to buy a bus ticket to Yongin. Which bus leaves the soonest?

M: Hmm... There is a bus that 1) _____ _____ _____ _____, but it is a regular one. There are also express buses to Yongin.

W: What is the difference between the two buses?

M: To get to Yongin, it takes 2) _____ _____ _____ _____ _____ and only 30 minutes on the express bus.

W: What time does the express bus leave?

M: It leaves at three o'clock.

W: That is too late. I'll just 3) _____ _____ _____ _____.

M: Okay.

05 심정 추론

대화를 듣고, 남자의 심정으로 가장 적절한 것을 고르시오.

① lonely   ② excited   ③ scared
④ surprised   ⑤ disappointed

W: How are you feeling, Tom?

M: I'm okay. I'm just a little tired.

W: You'll feel better soon. The 1) _____ _____ _____ _____.

M: That's great. When can I go home? I want to play badminton.

W: Well, I think you need to stay at the hospital and receive treatment for a week or so.

M: Oh, I 2) _____ _____ _____ in a month. I need to practice. I can't waste time staying in bed.

W: I understand, but I 3) _____ _____ - _____ _____ _____ for some time. We need to watch your progress carefully, even though the operation was successful.

다음 그림의 상황에 가장 적절한 대화를 고르시오.

①   ②   ③   ④   ⑤

① W: This coffee is very hot, so please be careful.

    M: Thanks. I will be.

② W: How long do I have to wait for my coffee?

    M: It'll 1) _____ _____ _____ _____ _____.

③ W: This isn't 2) _____ _____ _____.

    M: I'm sorry. I think that was my mistake.

④ W: I found a good place for coffee.

    M: Yeah? Let's go check it out.

⑤ W: I'm so sorry. Are you all right?

    M: I'm fine. Don't worry, it will 3) _____ _____ _____

       _____ _____.

---

07 부탁한 일 파악

대화를 듣고, 여자가 남자에게 부탁한 일로 가장 적절한 것을 고르시오.

① 저녁 준비하기   ② 회의 참석하기

③ 식당 예약하기   ④ 냉장고 정리하기

⑤ 음식 배달 주문하기

[Cell phone rings.]

M: Hi, Mom.

W: Oh, Andy. I'm sorry, but I'll be a little late from work. I 1) _____

    _____ _____ _____.

M: How late?

W: It depends on when the meeting ends. It will be over by eight o'clock at the latest.

M: Eight o'clock? That's so late.

W: I'm sorry. I think you'll have to 2) _____ _____ _____.

M: It's okay, Mom.

W: There is a phone number for a pizza restaurant on the fridge. Order something and 3) _____ _____ _____.

M: All right, Mom.

08 언급되지 않은 내용 찾기

다음을 듣고, 타지마할에 관해 언급되지 않은 것을 고르시오.

① 위치　　② 건축 시기　　③ 건축 목적

④ 색　　　⑤ 자재

M: Welcome to the Taj Mahal. The Taj Mahal is the most famous building in India. It 1) ＿＿＿＿＿ ＿＿＿＿＿ ＿＿＿＿＿ the city of Agra. It was built in the 17th century by the emperor Shah Jahan. He built the structure 2) ＿＿＿＿＿ ＿＿＿＿＿ ＿＿＿＿＿ ＿＿＿＿＿ for his beloved wife after her death. The Taj Mahal is one of the most beautiful buildings in the world. It is known for 3) ＿＿＿＿＿ ＿＿＿＿＿ ＿＿＿＿＿ ＿＿＿＿＿. Now, follow me and enjoy the beauty of the Taj Mahal.

09 화제 파악

다음을 듣고, 무엇에 관한 설명인지 고르시오.

① 에어컨　　② 체온계　　③ 히터

④ 텔레비전　⑤ 리모컨

W: This is a very useful product. It comes in a variety of shapes and sizes, but it is simple to use. We can turn it on and off by pressing a button. People use this 1) ＿＿＿＿＿ ＿＿＿＿＿ ＿＿＿＿＿ ＿＿＿＿＿. When the weather is hot, it 2) ＿＿＿＿＿ ＿＿＿＿＿ ＿＿＿＿＿ ＿＿＿＿＿. We also use it on rainy days because it can dry the air, too. It works by 3) ＿＿＿＿＿ ＿＿＿＿＿ ＿＿＿＿＿ ＿＿＿＿＿ from the indoor air and transferring the unwanted heat and humidity outside. In this way, the temperature inside the house 4) ＿＿＿＿＿ ＿＿＿＿＿ ＿＿＿＿＿.

10 어색한 대화 찾기

다음을 듣고, 두 사람의 대화가 어색한 것을 고르시오.

①　　②　　③　　④　　⑤

① M: Are you going to 1) ＿＿＿＿＿ ＿＿＿＿＿ ＿＿＿＿＿ ＿＿＿＿＿?

　W: No, I won't. I'm in the drama club already.

② M: Did Jimin 2) ＿＿＿＿＿ ＿＿＿＿＿ ＿＿＿＿＿ ＿＿＿＿＿?

　W: Yes, she is still doing it.

③ M: Would you like to join us?

　W: I'd like to, but I have a lot of things to do.

④ M: 3) ＿＿＿＿＿ ＿＿＿＿＿ ＿＿＿＿＿ will it take?

　W: About 30 minutes. I'm working as fast as I can.

⑤ M: Where should I send this package?

　W: To my office, please. The address is 22 Elm Street, Springfield, Ohio.

11 할 일 파악 🏴󠁧󠁢

대화를 듣고, 남자가 대화 직후에 할 일로 가장 적절한 것을 고르시오.

① 옷 쇼핑하기
② 친구 만나러 가기
③ 낡은 옷 정리하기
④ 전자레인지 고치기
⑤ 중고품 교환 시장에 가기

W: Where are you going?

M: I'm going to a swap meet. People can trade things there. I have some old clothes I don't need anymore. I'm 1) _____ _____ _____ for a used microwave oven. Mine broke.

W: Oh, is that why you're carrying those clothes?

M: Yes. Have you ever been to a swap meet?

W: No, I haven't.

M: Why don't you go with me?

W: I'd like to go, but I'm going to 2) _____ _____ _____.

M: Oh, I see. Maybe you can come next time. It is held on Saturdays in front of the police station.

W: Sounds good. But before I go, 3) _____ _____ _____ _____ I can trade there.

12 위치 찾기 🏴󠁧󠁢

다음 갤러리 안내도를 보면서 대화를 듣고, 두 사람이 초상화를 전시할 구역을 고르시오.

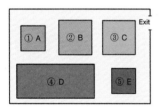

★**Focus on Sound** either

[이더]나 [아이더] 둘 다로 발음할 수 있다.

W: Let's prepare for our art exhibition. Which section would be best for the portraits?

M: I think Section D would be good. It's 1) _____ _____ _____.

W: Hmm. Maybe the 2) _____ _____ _____ there. We have more of them.

M: You're right. Well, Section A and E are too small. What about Section C?

W: Well, *either Section B or C would be okay. They are the same size. Which do you think is better?

M: I would prefer to put them in the section 3) _____ _____ _____ _____.

W: Good! We'll put them there!

13 숫자 정보 파악

대화를 듣고, 두 사람이 만나기로 한 시각을 고르시오.

① 6:00 p.m. ② 6:30 p.m. ③ 7:00 p.m.
④ 7:30 p.m. ⑤ 8:00 p.m.

[Cell phone rings.]

W: Hello?

M: Hey, Lisa. Are you free this evening?

W: Yeah, what's going on?

M: My brother is coming back from a trip. Why don't we go to the airport to 1) _____ _____ _____ ?

W: Okay. When shall we meet?

M: 2) _____ _____ _____ ? His flight arrives at 8:00 p.m., but 3) _____ _____ _____ _____ to get to the airport from here.

W: Isn't that too tight? Why don't we meet 4) _____ _____ _____ ?

M: Great! See you at your house.

W: Okay.

---

14 한 일 파악

대화를 듣고, 남자가 어제 한 일로 가장 적절한 것을 고르시오.

① 영화 보기   ② 영화 예매하기
③ 원작 소설 읽기   ④ 친구와 약속 정하기
⑤ 영화 평론 찾아보기

M: Hey, Jane. I've been looking for you.

W: Why?

M: Didn't you say you were interested in the movie *Blast Off*?

W: Yes, 1) _____ _____ _____ _____ _____ .

M: I heard it will be released on Friday.

W: Really? I should check for tickets, then... *[pause]* Oh no!

M: What's wrong?

W: There are 2) _____ _____ _____ .

M: Don't worry. I 3) _____ _____ _____ for us yesterday.

W: What a friend! I can't wait for Friday.

---

15 목적 파악

다음을 듣고, 방송의 목적으로 가장 적절한 것을 고르시오.

① 새 학기 시작을 알리려고
② 행사 장소 변경을 공지하려고
③ 체육관 시설에 대해 안내하려고
④ 새로 오신 선생님을 소개하려고
⑤ 학교 동아리 회원 모집을 홍보하려고

M: Hello. A new school year is here. I'm happy to announce that we have a variety of club activities this year. Each club 1) _____ _____ _____ now. If you want to see photos of each club's activities, you can come to the gym and check them out. Our school will actively 2) _____ _____ _____ and give awards at the end of the year. We hope that many of you will be participating. Come by the gym to 3) _____ _____ _____ _____ _____ , and don't forget to apply for any that interest you.

16 [숫자 정보 파악]

대화를 듣고, 여자가 지불할 금액을 고르시오.

① $70 ② $75 ③ $80
④ $85 ⑤ $90

[Phone rings.]

M: Hello, this is Mega Seafood Buffet. How can I help you?

W: I'd like to ¹⁾ _____ _____ _____ _____ for next Sunday under the name Betty Summers.

M: Sure. For how many people?

W: Two adults and two children. And I'd like to know ²⁾ _____ _____ _____ _____ _____ .

M: Of course. On weekdays, it's $20 for adults and $10 for children under 13. On weekends, we ³⁾ _____ _____ _____ _____ _____ . Are your children under 13?

W: Just my daughter.

M: Okay, then that'll be ⁴⁾ _____ _____ _____ _____ _____ . Thanks a lot. See you then.

17 [마지막 말에 이어질 응답 찾기]

대화를 듣고, 여자의 마지막 말에 대한 남자의 응답으로 가장 적절한 것을 고르시오.

Man: _____

① How long did that take?
② How much do you weigh now?
③ You should pay attention to your diet.
④ Be careful. It's not healthy to be too thin.
⑤ Eating too much fat is not good for your health.

✱ Focus on Sound weighed

gh는 묵음이어서 [웨이드]로 발음된다.

M: Hi, Carol. ¹⁾ _____ _____ _____ _____ ?

W: Good, I guess. I've lost five kilograms already.

M: Really? That was quick!

W: Yes. Just two months ago, I ✱weighed 60 kilograms.

M: That's wonderful. But you don't need to ²⁾ _____ _____ _____ _____ . You look good now.

W: Well, thanks, but summer is coming. So I ³⁾ _____ _____ _____ _____ _____ _____ .

M: Be careful. It's not healthy to be too thin.

194

18 마지막 말에 이어질 응답 찾기

대화를 듣고, 남자의 마지막 말에 대한 여자의 응답으로 가장 적절한 것을 고르시오.

Woman: _____

① You need to rest.
② Let me check your temperature.
③ Drink as much water as possible.
④ If it gets worse, go to the hospital.
⑤ Three times a day, after every meal.

W: Hello. How can I help you?
M: Hello. I think I've 1) _____ _____ _____.
W: Let's see. Hmm, you have a 39-degree fever.
M: And I 2) _____ _____ _____ and a runny nose.
W: Anything else?
M: I have a cough, too.
W: Here you are. 3) _____ _____ _____.
M: 4) _____ _____ _____ _____ _____ it?
W: <u>Three times a day, after every meal.</u>

19 마지막 말에 이어질 응답 찾기 🏴

대화를 듣고, 남자의 마지막 말에 대한 여자의 응답으로 가장 적절한 것을 고르시오.

Woman: _____

① Here's your change.
② It's on the kitchen table.
③ I didn't enjoy it very much.
④ I like coffee better than tea.
⑤ No, thanks. Coffee is enough.

W: Thanks for inviting me for lunch. The spaghetti was very delicious.
M: I'm 1) _____ _____ _____ _____. Do you want some coffee for dessert?
W: That sounds good. Thanks.
M: 2) _____ _____ _____ _____ your coffee?
W: With cream and sugar, please.
M: 3) _____ _____ _____ _____ _____ with your coffee?
W: <u>No, thanks. Coffee is enough.</u>

20 상황에 적절한 말 찾기

다음 상황 설명을 듣고, Kevin이 점원에게 할 말로 가장 적절한 것을 고르시오.

Kevin: _____

① I want a full refund.
② Do you have any other sizes?
③ I'm afraid there's a mistake on the receipt.
④ Didn't you like the birthday gift I got you?
⑤ When are you having your birthday party?

W: Tomorrow is a special day for Kevin's mother. It is her birthday. Kevin wants to 1) _____ _____ _____ _____, so he goes to the mall to shop. He buys many things, including a birthday cake, some flowers, and balloons for decorations. When he pays, it's 2) _____ _____ _____ _____ _____. So he checks his receipt and realizes that the 3) _____ _____ _____. In this situation, what would Kevin most likely say to the clerk?

01 대화를 듣고, 여자가 구입할 음료를 고르시오.

02 대화를 듣고, 남자가 건강을 되찾기 위해 한 일로 언급되지 <u>않은</u> 것을 고르시오.

① 긍정적으로 생각하기
② 충분히 자기
③ 채소 많이 먹기
④ 물 충분히 마시기
⑤ 규칙적으로 운동하기

03 대화를 듣고, 여자가 남자에게 전화한 목적으로 가장 적절한 것을 고르시오.

① 약속을 취소하려고
② 작별 인사를 하려고
③ 만날 시간을 정하려고
④ 공부를 함께 하자고 제안하려고
⑤ 공항에 데려다 달라고 부탁하려고

04 대화를 듣고, 남자가 예약할 비행기의 출발 시각을 고르시오.

① 1 p.m.   ② 2 p.m.   ③ 3 p.m.
④ 4 p.m.   ⑤ 5 p.m.

05 대화를 듣고, 남자의 심정으로 가장 적절한 것을 고르시오.

① lonely   ② curious   ③ bored
④ frightened   ⑤ disappointed

06 다음 그림의 상황에 가장 적절한 대화를 고르시오.

① ② ③ ④ ⑤

07 대화를 듣고, 여자가 남자에게 부탁한 일로 가장 적절한 것을 고르시오.

① 프린터 추천하기
② 드라이버 빌려주기
③ 컴퓨터 가르쳐주기
④ 드라이버 재설치하기
⑤ 전자 제품 판매점에 함께 가기

08 다음을 듣고, J.K. Rowling에 관해 언급되지 <u>않은</u> 것을 고르시오.

① 출생지   ② 대표작   ③ 주요 독자층
④ 수상 경력   ⑤ 책 판매 부수

고난도
09 다음을 듣고, 무엇에 관한 설명인지 고르시오.

① 커피콩   ② 코코넛   ③ 카카오
④ 사탕수수   ⑤ 파인애플

10 다음을 듣고, 두 사람의 대화가 <u>어색한</u> 것을 고르시오.

① ② ③ ④ ⑤

11 대화를 듣고, 남자가 일요일에 할 일로 가장 적절한 것을 고르시오.

① 캠핑 가기   ② 영화 보기
③ 아버지 돕기   ④ 졸업 여행 가기
⑤ 자동차 정비소 가기

12 다음 표를 보면서 대화를 듣고, 내용과 일치하지 <u>않</u>는 것을 고르시오.

Train Ticket		
①	Destination	Daegu
②	Departure Time	8:15 p.m.
③	Arrival Time	10:00 p.m.
④	Fare	₩15,000
⑤	Platform	3

13 대화를 듣고, 여자가 구입할 콘서트 티켓의 날짜를 고르시오.

① 11월 10일　　② 11월 11일
③ 11월 12일　　④ 11월 13일
⑤ 11월 14일

14 대화를 듣고, 남자가 지난주에 한 일로 가장 적절한 것을 고르시오.

① 발표 준비하기
② 발명품 만들기
③ 발명품 고안하기
④ 보고서 작성하기
⑤ 과학 경진 대회 참가하기

15 다음을 듣고, 방송의 목적으로 가장 적절한 것을 고르시오.

① 우회 도로를 안내하려고
② 도로 정체 상황을 알리려고
③ 탑승 안전 수칙을 설명하려고
④ 도로 공사 계획을 공지하려고
⑤ 안전 운전의 중요성을 강조하려고

16 대화를 듣고, 여자가 지불할 금액을 고르시오.

① $35　　② $40　　③ $50
④ $70　　⑤ $100

17 대화를 듣고, 남자의 마지막 말에 대한 여자의 응답으로 가장 적절한 것을 고르시오.

Woman: _____

① I'd like to reach the top.
② I've never been there before.
③ I prefer mountains to the sea.
④ Okay. Thanks for your concern.
⑤ It's not difficult to hike with a walking stick.

[18 - 19] 대화를 듣고, 여자의 마지막 말에 대한 남자의 응답으로 가장 적절한 것을 고르시오.

고난도
18 Man: _____

① I always try my best to help my patients.
② Patients should follow their doctors' advice.
③ I think being a doctor would be the best job.
④ Salary is not that important in choosing a job.
⑤ I feel proud of myself when my patients get better.

19 Man: _____

① I graduated three months ago.
② I majored in computer science.
③ I went to school for four years.
④ I'd like to work for your company.
⑤ My grades were better than average.

고난도
20 다음 상황 설명을 듣고, Dan이 Mira에게 할 말로 가장 적절한 것을 고르시오.

Dan: _____

① Easy come, easy go.
② Where there's smoke, there's fire.
③ It is no use crying over spilt milk.
④ Mistakes are often the best teachers.
⑤ Bad workers always blame their tools.

Dictation Test 15

보통속도 듣기 빠르게 듣기

01 그림 정보 파악 🏴󠁧󠁢󠁥󠁮󠁧󠁿

대화를 듣고, 여자가 구입할 음료를 고르시오.

①   ②   ③

④   ⑤

M: Next, please.

W: It's so cold that I 1) _____ _____ _____ _____. Do you have any recommendations?

M: How about vanilla milk? It's a popular drink here in our café.

W: That would be great.

M: What size would you like? We have small or large.

W: 2) _____ _____ _____ _____ _____, please.

M: Is that for here or to go?

W: I will have it here.

M: If you drink it here, you will get a mug 3) _____ _____ _____ _____ _____. Is that okay?

W: Sure.

02 언급되지 않은 내용 찾기

대화를 듣고, 남자가 건강을 되찾기 위해 한 일로 언급되지 않은 것을 고르시오.

① 긍정적으로 생각하기
② 충분히 자기
③ 채소 많이 먹기
④ 물 충분히 마시기
⑤ 규칙적으로 운동하기

W: Hi, Nick. I heard you've been sick, but you look amazing now.

M: Thank you. I 1) _____ _____ three months ago, but I'm fine now.

W: You look so energetic! What's your secret?

M: I don't have any great secrets. Since the surgery, I've tried to think positively about everything, and I 2) _____ _____ _____ every night.

W: That's all?

M: Well, I'm also trying to 3) _____ _____ _____ _____ _____.

W: That sounds important.

M: It is. And 4) _____ _____ has also helped.

W: Oh, I see.

03 목적 파악

대화를 듣고, 여자가 남자에게 전화한 목적으로 가장 적절한 것을 고르시오.

① 약속을 취소하려고
② 작별 인사를 하려고
③ 만날 시간을 정하려고
④ 공부를 함께 하자고 제안하려고
⑤ 공항에 데려다 달라고 부탁하려고

[Phone rings.]

M: Hello?

W: Hi, Charles. It's Betty.

M: Hi, Betty. How's it going?

W: Well, I have a problem. My cousin from Korea is coming to visit.

M: That's great. What's the problem?

W: Her flight arrives on Tuesday night. I have to ¹⁾ _____ _____ _____ at the airport.

M: Tuesday night? We ²⁾ _____ _____ _____ _____ for our history test on Tuesday night.

W: I know. But ³⁾ _____ _____ _____ _____ . I'm sorry.

M: That's okay. We can reschedule.

W: Thanks for understanding.

04 숫자 정보 파악

대화를 듣고, 남자가 예약할 비행기의 출발 시각을 고르시오.

① 1 p.m.   ② 2 p.m.   ③ 3 p.m.
④ 4 p.m.   ⑤ 5 p.m.

[Cell phone rings.]

W: Go Travel Agency. How can I help you?

M: I'm going to Busan on Friday and need to ¹⁾ _____ _____ _____ .

W: Will that be one-way or round trip?

M: Round trip, please.

W: There are 1:00 p.m., 2:00 p.m., and 5:00 p.m. departures. Will any of these times work for you?

M: Isn't there a ²⁾ _____ _____ _____ _____ _____ ?

W: I'm afraid there isn't.

M: All right, then, ³⁾ _____ _____ _____ _____ _____ .

W: Okay.

05 심정 추론 🇬🇧

대화를 듣고, 남자의 심정으로 가장 적절한 것을 고르시오.

① lonely   ② curious   ③ bored
④ frightened   ⑤ disappointed

W: You don't look well. What's wrong?

M: Something happened while I was driving.

W: Really? What?

M: A taxi ¹⁾ _____ _____ _____ _____ _____ _____. I barely managed to stop in time. I thought we were going to crash into each other. My heart is ²⁾ _____ _____ _____ right now.

W: It's okay. Calm down. Anyway, it was fortunate that you were able to ³⁾ _____ _____ _____ _____ _____. Just sit down and relax for a few minutes.

M: Yeah. My hands ⁴⁾ _____ _____ _____.

---

06 그림 상황에 적절한 대화 찾기

다음 그림의 상황에 가장 적절한 대화를 고르시오.

① ② ③ ④ ⑤

① W: ¹⁾ _____ _____ _____ _____ _____ _____ this book for?

M: It can be checked out for a week.

② W: ²⁾ _____ _____ _____ _____ _____?

M: I'm going to the library.

③ W: What kind of music do you like?

M: I love hip-hop.

④ W: Can I help you?

M: Yes, ³⁾ _____ _____ _____ Blue Band's new CD.

⑤ W: Could you ⁴⁾ _____ _____ _____ _____, please?

M: Oh, okay. I'm sorry.

---

07 부탁한 일 파악 🇬🇧

대화를 듣고, 여자가 남자에게 부탁한 일로 가장 적절한 것을 고르시오.

① 프린터 추천하기
② 드라이버 빌려주기
③ 컴퓨터 가르쳐주기
④ 드라이버 재설치하기
⑤ 전자 제품 판매점에 함께 가기

W: Can you give me a hand with this printer? ¹⁾ _____ _____ _____.

M: What's wrong with it?

W: Even if I turn the power off and on, I ²⁾ _____ _____ _____ _____ _____.

M: I know what the problem is. I've had this happen before.

W: How can I fix it?

M: You need to ³⁾ _____ _____ _____.

W: I don't know how to do that. Can you do it for me?

M: Sure. It's not that hard.

다음을 듣고, J.K. Rowling에 관해 언급되지 않은 것을 고르시오.

① 출생지　　② 대표작　　③ 주요 독자층
④ 수상 경력　　⑤ 책 판매 부수

W: I'm going to talk today about the famous fantasy novelist, J.K. Rowling. She 1) _____ _____ _____ Yate, England, on July 31, 1965. She was a bookworm, and she wrote her first work when she was six years old. She 2) _____ _____ _____ the Harry Potter series of books. This series has been widely read and has a huge fan base, 3) _____ _____ _____. Harry Potter books are now published in 80 languages and have sold over 500 million copies worldwide. Due to the popularity of the books, Rowling 4) _____ _____ _____ _____ _____.

다음을 듣고, 무엇에 관한 설명인지 고르시오.

① 커피콩　　② 코코넛　　③ 카카오
④ 사탕수수　　⑤ 파인애플

M: This 1) _____ _____ _____ in tropical regions of America and Africa. With it, we can 2) _____ _____ _____ enjoyed by people all over the world. Its history began in Central America. The Maya lived in the area a long time ago and first used this to 3) _____ _____ _____ _____. When Europeans discovered America in the 15th century, they brought it to Europe. It was made into treats by mixing milk and sugar with its powder, which was the 4) _____ _____ _____ _____. Since then, it has been loved by many Europeans.

다음을 듣고, 두 사람의 대화가 <u>어색한</u> 것을 고르시오.

①　　②　　③　　④　　⑤

① M: How often does the bus leave for New York?
　 W: It leaves 1) _____ _____ _____.
② M: Take these pills three times a day and come back in three days.
　 W: I will. Thank you so much.
③ M: I 2) _____ _____ _____ _____ after lunch.
　 W: Lunch was great. Thank you.
④ M: 3) _____ _____ _____ taking our picture?
　 W: Not at all.
⑤ M: How about doing our homework together?
　 W: Okay. When should we meet?

11 할 일 파악

대화를 듣고, 남자가 일요일에 할 일로 가장 적절한 것을 고르시오.

① 캠핑 가기   ② 영화 보기
③ 아버지 돕기   ④ 졸업 여행 가기
⑤ 자동차 정비소 가기

★Focus on Sound   graduate

동사일 때는 [그래쥬에이트]로 발음되고, 명사일 때는 [그래쥬엇]으로 발음된다.

W: Hey, Jason. What are your 1) _____ _____ _____ _____?

M: I'm pretty busy. I'm going camping on Saturday.

W: Camping? Who are you going with?

M: My whole family. It's a party for my older sister. She just *graduated from high school.

W: I see. Well, 2) _____ _____ _____?

M: I promised my father I'd 3) _____ _____ _____ _____ _____ that day.

W: Well, I wanted to watch a movie with you, but it seems like you're quite busy.

M: Sorry, maybe we can watch one next week.

---

12 내용 일치 파악

다음 표를 보면서 대화를 듣고, 내용과 일치하지 <u>않는</u> 것을 고르시오.

Train Ticket		
①	Destination	Daegu
②	Departure Time	8:15 p.m.
③	Arrival Time	10:00 p.m.
④	Fare	₩15,000
⑤	Platform	3

W: How can I help you?

M: I'd like to buy a ticket for Daegu.

W: All right. What time would you like to leave?

M: Actually, I need to leave 1) _____ _____ _____ _____.

W: Okay, it's 8:30 now. That means a train left five minutes ago. And the next train 2) _____ _____ _____ p.m.

M: I see. And when does it arrive in Daegu?

W: It 3) _____ _____ _____ p.m.

M: I guess that would be okay. I'll take one ticket, please. 4) _____ _____ _____ _____ _____?

W: It's 15,000 won.

M: Okay, here you are. Which platform does the train leave from?

W: It will depart from Platform 3.

13 세부 정보 파악

대화를 듣고, 여자가 구입할 콘서트 티켓의 날짜를 고르시오.

① 11월 10일 ② 11월 11일
③ 11월 12일 ④ 11월 13일
⑤ 11월 14일

[Phone rings.]

M: Hello?

W: Hello. Do you 1) _____ _____ _____ _____ for Saturday's concert?

M: Do you mean the one on November 10?

W: Yes.

M: I'm sorry, but the tickets for that concert 2) _____ _____ _____.

W: Oh dear. That's too bad.

M: How about Sunday? There are quite a few seats left for the show on November 11.

W: That might be okay. Are there tickets left for any other days?

M: If you don't mind going to a concert during the week, there are tickets available for 3) _____ _____ _____ _____ _____.

W: That's good. Then I'll reserve two 4) _____ _____ _____, _____ _____.

M: Okay.

14 한 일 파악

대화를 듣고, 남자가 지난주에 한 일로 가장 적절한 것을 고르시오.

① 발표 준비하기
② 발명품 만들기
③ 발명품 고안하기
④ 보고서 작성하기
⑤ 과학 경진 대회 참가하기

W: Tony, will you take part in the science contest next week?

M: Of course. I've prepared for almost a month for that day.

W: Wow, a month?

M: Yes. In the first week, I 1) _____ _____ _____ _____, and in the second week, I created it.

W: Then what did you do last week?

M: I 2) _____ _____ _____ last week.

W: Great. You're so prepared.

M: All I have to do is 3) _____ _____ _____ _____ this week.

W: I'm sure you'll do well.

M: I hope so.

15 목적 파악

다음을 듣고, 방송의 목적으로 가장 적절한 것을 고르시오.

① 우회 도로를 안내하려고
② 도로 정체 상황을 알리려고
③ 탑승 안전 수칙을 설명하려고
④ 도로 공사 계획을 공지하려고
⑤ 안전 운전의 중요성을 강조하려고

W: Good evening. Here is the traffic report. If you're on the roads listening to this, you already know that 1) _____ _____ _____ than usual. There was a traffic accident on Hudson Street around 6:00 p.m. today. 2) _____ _____ _____ _____, vehicles have come to a halt. It is expected that this problem will 3) _____ _____ _____ _____ to resolve. After that, the traffic will clear up. This has been Ellen Burrell with your traffic update. Thank you.

16 숫자 정보 파악

대화를 듣고, 여자가 지불할 금액을 고르시오.

① $35   ② $40   ③ $50
④ $70   ⑤ $100

M: Can I help you?
W: I'd like to buy a new shirt. What do you recommend?
M: What about this green one?
W: I like it. How much does it cost?
M: It was $70, but 1) _____ _____ _____ today.
W: Oh, really?
M: Yes, today is the 2) _____ _____ _____ _____ _____. You're lucky.
W: Okay. 3) _____ _____ _____ _____, so I'll take two. I'll give one to my sister.
M: Okay. Wait a minute, please.

17 마지막 말에 이어질 응답 찾기

대화를 듣고, 남자의 마지막 말에 대한 여자의 응답으로 가장 적절한 것을 고르시오.

Woman: _____

① I'd like to reach the top.
② I've never been there before.
③ I prefer mountains to the sea.
④ Okay. Thanks for your concern.
⑤ It's not difficult to hike with a walking stick.

M: Hi, Cara. What are you doing?
W: Oh, hi. I'm 1) _____ _____ _____. I'm going hiking.
M: You're going hiking at this time of year? It's so cold outside.
W: Don't worry. The exercise keeps me warm, so I don't really feel the cold.
M: Still, I think you need to be careful. It's 2) _____ _____ _____ _____ _____.
W: That's true. Do you have any suggestions?
M: Why don't you 3) _____ _____ _____ just in case?
W: Okay. Thanks for your concern.

18 마지막 말에 이어질 응답 찾기

대화를 듣고, 여자의 마지막 말에 대한 남자의 응답으로 가장 적절한 것을 고르시오.

Man: _____

① I always try my best to help my patients.
② Patients should follow their doctors' advice.
③ I think being a doctor would be the best job.
④ Salary is not that important in choosing a job.
⑤ I feel proud of myself when my patients get better.

W: Today, we're going to talk about your career.
M: Okay, good.
W: Your job 1) _____ _____ _____, Mr. Stevens. What is the most difficult part about it?
M: Well, I often 2) _____ _____ _____ _____ _____. But nervousness can cause mistakes, so I try to relax.
W: I see. What kind of operations do you perform?
M: I usually treat people who have heart disease.
W: When do you feel your job 3) _____ _____ _____?
M: I feel proud of myself when my patients get better.

---

19 마지막 말에 이어질 응답 찾기 🇬🇧

대화를 듣고, 여자의 마지막 말에 대한 남자의 응답으로 가장 적절한 것을 고르시오.

Man: _____

① I graduated three months ago.
② I majored in computer science.
③ I went to school for four years.
④ I'd like to work for your company.
⑤ My grades were better than average.

W: Thank you for coming to this job interview today. Can you 1) _____ _____ _____?
M: Hi. I'm Hunter Clinton. I'm 27 years old, and I'm from London.
W: All right. Do you have any experience in this kind of work?
M: I 2) _____ _____ _____ _____ for ABC Bank.
W: Good. Did you enjoy your experience there?
M: Yes. It was interesting to apply what I learned in university to a real job.
W: I see. What did you 3) _____ _____ _____?
M: I majored in computer science.

---

20 상황에 적절한 말 찾기

다음 상황 설명을 듣고, Dan이 Mira에게 할 말로 가장 적절한 것을 고르시오.

Dan: _____

① Easy come, easy go.
② Where there's smoke, there's fire.
③ It is no use crying over spilt milk.
④ Mistakes are often the best teachers.
⑤ Bad workers always blame their tools.

M: Dan and Mira are in the same Spanish class. Mira is 1) _____ _____ _____ _____ _____. Dan asks Mira why she doesn't say anything. Mira says it's because she has to speak Spanish during class but she doesn't speak well. She's 2) _____ _____ _____ _____ and being laughed at. Dan thinks she should just try. He also wants to tell her that it's fun to share ideas in Spanish and that 3) _____ _____ _____ _____ _____. In this situation, what would Dan most likely say to Mira?

Word Test

A 다음 영어의 우리말 뜻을 쓰시오.

01 novelist

02 period

03 original

04 nervousness

05 avoid

06 concern

07 discover

08 continue

09 escape

10 actively

11 decade

12 surgery

13 birth

14 construction

15 reserve

16 energetic

17 support

18 invention

19 regularly

20 observe

21 emergency

22 crash

23 departure

24 extra

25 staff

26 career

27 publish

28 progress

29 blame

30 in person

31 care for

32 due to

33 calm down

34 turn in

35 throw a party

36 prepare for

37 can't afford to-v

38 in advance

39 get worse

40 look good on

B 다음 우리말 뜻에 맞는 영어를 쓰시오.

01 출구 _____

02 10억 _____

03 외국의 _____

04 습기 _____

05 ~에 닿다[도달하다] _____

06 급행의 _____

07 가죽 _____

08 학위 _____

09 인기 _____

10 온도 _____

11 성공적인 _____

12 두통 _____

13 대하다; 치료하다 _____

14 영수증 _____

15 낮추다, 내리다 _____

16 보람이 있는 _____

17 100년, 세기 _____

18 수의사 _____

19 등급; 성적 _____

20 급여, 월급 _____

21 긍정적으로 _____

22 경치 _____

23 황제 _____

24 문학 _____

25 인내, 인내심 _____

26 금속 _____

27 전문가 _____

28 100만 _____

29 차이 _____

30 (상점의) 점원 _____

31 평균 _____

32 제안 _____

33 만약을 위해서 _____

34 ~을 전공하다 _____

35 ~을 생각해 내다 _____

36 ~을 졸업하다 _____

37 ~로 알려져 있다 _____

38 일기를 쓰다 _____

39 (소리를) 줄이다 _____

40 가능한 한 빨리 _____

실전모의고사 16회

보통속도 듣기

빠르게 듣기

01 대화를 듣고, 남자가 구입할 여권 지갑을 고르시오.

고난도
02 대화를 듣고, 남자가 이사 갈 집에 관해 언급되지 않은 것을 고르시오.

① 위치   ② 방 개수   ③ 연식
④ 가격   ⑤ 색

03 대화를 듣고, 여자가 남자에게 전화한 목적으로 가장 적절한 것을 고르시오.

① 진료 예약을 하려고
② 실수에 대해 사과하려고
③ 소음에 대해 항의하려고
④ 잃어버린 고양이를 찾으려고
⑤ 개를 돌봐 달라고 부탁하려고

04 대화를 듣고, 두 사람이 만나기로 한 시각을 고르시오.

① 1 p.m.   ② 4 p.m.   ③ 5 p.m.
④ 6 p.m.   ⑤ 7 p.m.

05 대화를 듣고, 두 사람이 대화하는 장소로 가장 적절한 곳을 고르시오.

① 서점   ② 호텔   ③ 박물관
④ 도서관   ⑤ 컴퓨터실

06 다음 그림의 상황에 가장 적절한 대화를 고르시오.

①   ②   ③   ④   ⑤

07 대화를 듣고, 여자가 남자에게 부탁한 일로 가장 적절한 것을 고르시오.

① 차 빌려주기   ② 가방 들어주기
③ 우편물 챙기기   ④ 택시에 짐 실어주기
⑤ 역까지 데려다주기

08 다음을 듣고, Frida Kahlo에 관해 언급되지 않은 것을 고르시오.

① 출생지   ② 가족 관계
③ 화가가 된 계기   ④ 수상 경력
⑤ 작품 소재

09 다음을 듣고, 어떤 직업에 관한 설명인지 고르시오.

① 교사   ② 정원사   ③ 주방장
④ 청소부   ⑤ 마트 점원

10 다음을 듣고, 두 사람의 대화가 어색한 것을 고르시오.

①   ②   ③   ④   ⑤

11 대화를 듣고, 남자가 대화 직후에 할 일로 가장 적절한 것을 고르시오.

① 청소하기   ② 꽃 사기
③ 케이크 만들기   ④ 축하 카드 쓰기
⑤ 저녁 식사 준비하기

12 다음 스터디룸 배치도를 보면서 대화를 듣고, 여자가 선택할 스터디룸을 고르시오.

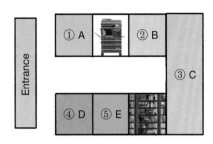

13 대화를 듣고, 두 사람이 탑승할 버스의 출발 시각을 고르시오.

① 1:00 p.m.　② 1:30 p.m.　③ 2:00 p.m.
④ 2:30 p.m.　⑤ 3:00 p.m.

14 대화를 듣고, 여자가 주말에 한 일로 가장 적절한 것을 고르시오.

① 대청소하기　　② 집에서 쉬기
③ 병문안 가기　　④ 가족 모임 하기
⑤ 봄맞이 여행 가기

15 다음을 듣고, 방송의 목적으로 가장 적절한 것을 고르시오.

① 지진 발생 소식을 알리려고
② 응급 처치 방법을 설명하려고
③ 도로 교통법 준수를 당부하려고
④ 지진 발생 위험에 대해 경고하려고
⑤ 지진 발생 시 안전 수칙을 설명하려고

16 대화를 듣고, 남자가 지불할 금액을 고르시오.

① $15　② $21　③ $24　④ $30　⑤ $42

17 대화를 듣고, 여자의 마지막 말에 대한 남자의 응답으로 가장 적절한 것을 고르시오.

Man: _____

① It won't be easy to get degree.
② I decided to go abroad three years ago.
③ It will take about 14 hours to get there.
④ It will take me three years to get my degree.
⑤ I'm planning to study English before I leave.

[18 - 19] 대화를 듣고, 남자의 마지막 말에 대한 여자의 응답으로 가장 적절한 것을 고르시오.

18 Woman: _____

① Don't forget to lock the door.
② I wish I could take a few days off.
③ We should go visit her in the hospital.
④ Thank goodness. I'm glad to hear that.
⑤ You should be more careful in the future.

19 Woman: _____

① In a couple of days.
② The sooner, the better.
③ I'll take the brown one.
④ Sorry for keeping you waiting.
⑤ I just bought it three weeks ago.

고난도
20 다음 상황 설명을 듣고, Tim이 자신에게 할 말로 가장 적절한 것을 고르시오.

Tim: _____

① I need to learn from failure and keep trying.
② It is difficult to motivate myself day after day.
③ I should think long and hard about my future.
④ Working together is better than working alone.
⑤ If I act like a leader, other people will follow me.

Dictation Test 16

정답 및 해설 pp. 82~87

01 그림 정보 파악

대화를 듣고, 남자가 구입할 여권 지갑을 고르시오.

W: Hello, how can I help you?

M: Hi. I'm 1) _____ _____ _____ _____ _____.

W: We have two types: 2) _____ _____ _____ _____ _____, and ones that hold only a passport.

M: I'd prefer one with a wallet.

W: Which design do you like best?

M: I think this 3) _____ _____ _____ _____. It is nicer than the striped patterns.

W: Good choice. It's new, and it's one of our best-selling items.

M: I'll take it.

02 언급되지 않은 내용 찾기

대화를 듣고, 남자가 이사 갈 집에 관해 언급되지 않은 것을 고르시오.

① 위치   ② 방 개수   ③ 연식
④ 가격   ⑤ 색

M: Guess what? My family is moving.

W: Oh, no! Are you going to change schools?

M: No. The house is just 1) _____ _____ _____ _____ where I live now.

W: That's good. But why are you moving?

M: Our old house is too small. This one has 2) _____ _____ _____ _____ _____.

W: That sounds great. Is it new?

M: No. It was 3) _____ _____ _____ _____. New houses are too expensive.

W: I know. My uncle just bought a new house. It 4) _____ _____ _____ _____ _____!

M: Wow! Anyway, you should take a look at it. It's the red house on the corner.

03 목적 파악 🇬🇧

대화를 듣고, 여자가 남자에게 전화한 목적으로 가장 적절한 것을 고르시오.

① 진료 예약을 하려고
② 실수에 대해 사과하려고
③ 소음에 대해 항의하려고
④ 잃어버린 고양이를 찾으려고
⑤ 개를 돌봐 달라고 부탁하려고

[Cell phone rings.]

M: Hello?

W: Hi, Thomas. It's your neighbor, Fiona.

M: Good morning, Fiona. How are you?

W: Not good. I 1) _____ _____ _____ _____.

M: Really? Are you feeling ill?

W: No. It was because of your dog. He 2) _____ _____ _____ _____.

M: Oh, I'm so sorry about that. I think there was a cat outside my window.

W: I understand, but it was very annoying. Could you please 3) _____ _____ _____ at night?

M: Yes. I'll make sure that he 4) _____ _____ _____ _____ _____ anymore.

W: Thank you, Thomas.

04 숫자 정보 파악

대화를 듣고, 두 사람이 만나기로 한 시각을 고르시오.

① 1 p.m.　　② 4 p.m.　　③ 5 p.m.
④ 6 p.m.　　⑤ 7 p.m.

M: Hey, would you like to 1) _____ _____ _____ _____ tonight?

W: Well, let me check my schedule.

M: Is it a busy day today?

W: Yes. I 2) _____ _____ _____ _____ _____ and there is a group meeting at 5 p.m.

M: What time is your meeting over?

W: It should only take about an hour or so.

M: Then 3) _____ _____ _____ _____ _____. Would that work for you?

W: Yes, I think so. I'll see you then.

05 장소 추론

대화를 듣고, 두 사람이 대화하는 장소로 가장 적절한 곳을 고르시오.

① 서점　　② 호텔　　③ 박물관

④ 도서관　　⑤ 컴퓨터실

M: Can I help you find something?

W: Yes, please. I'm 1) _____ _____ _____ _____ for my mid-term exam.

M: All right. What's the name of the book?

W: It's called *The History of Southern France.*

M: Okay. Do you know the 2) _____ _____ _____ _____?

W: No, that's the problem.

M: That's all right. I can 3) _____ _____ _____ on the computer.

W: Great. I really appreciate your help.

M: Sorry, but that book 4) _____ _____ _____ _____ _____. It'll be returned this Thursday.

W: All right. I'll come back then.

---

06 그림 상황에 적절한 대화 찾기

다음 그림의 상황에 가장 적절한 대화를 고르시오.

① ② ③ ④ ⑤

① W: 1) _____ _____ _____ _____ _____ tomorrow?

M: The news says it will rain.

② W: I think I left my bag at the library.

M: You should go back and get it.

③ W: Did you 2) _____ _____ _____?

M: Not yet. I'll return them after class.

④ W: I love your raincoat. Where did you buy it?

M: My parents bought it for me.

⑤ W: Oh, I 3) _____ _____ _____ _____ _____. I need to buy one.

M: Why don't you share mine?

대화를 듣고, 여자가 남자에게 부탁한 일로 가장 적절한 것을 고르시오.

① 차 빌려주기   ② 가방 들어주기
③ 우편물 챙기기   ④ 택시에 짐 실어주기
⑤ 역까지 데려다주기

M: Hey, Minju. That's a big bag! Where are you going?

W: Hi, Mike. I'm going to my parents' house. I 1) _____ _____ _____ for a week.

M: Where do your parents live?

W: They live in Busan. I will take the KTX to get there.

M: Oh, I'm going downtown now. Do you want me to 2) _____ _____ _____ _____ to the station?

W: Thanks, but I already called a taxi. But Mike, can you 3) _____ _____ _____ _____?

M: Sure, what is it?

W: Could you 4) _____ _____ _____ while I'm away? I heard there are many thieves targeting empty houses these days.

M: Okay. No problem.

다음을 듣고, Frida Kahlo에 관해 언급되지 않은 것을 고르시오.

① 출생지   ② 가족 관계
③ 화가가 된 계기   ④ 수상 경력
⑤ 작품 소재

W: Now, I'd like to talk about the famous Mexican artist, Frida Kahlo. She 1) _____ _____ _____ _____ and grew up with her parents and six sisters. At first, she studied medicine, but she changed her career path 2) _____ _____ _____ _____ _____ _____ at age 18. She often painted 3) _____ _____ _____. She wanted to show people her suffering.

다음을 듣고, 어떤 직업에 관한 설명인지 고르시오.

① 교사   ② 정원사   ③ 주방장
④ 청소부   ⑤ 마트 점원

M: People who have this job work in 1) _____ _____ _____ _____ _____. They are responsible for everything about the food. They buy ingredients, create menus, and 2) _____ _____ _____. They also manage the operation of the kitchen. They make sure that the 3) _____ _____ _____ _____. To get this job, you need experience working in a restaurant. It also helps to get a professional education 4) _____ _____ _____ _____.

다음을 듣고, 두 사람의 대화가 어색한 것을 고르시오.

① ② ③ ④ ⑤

① M: Can I help you?

W: No, thanks. I'm 1) _____ _____ _____.

② M: Could you 2) _____ _____ _____ _____ _____, please?

W: Yes. This soup is a little bit salty.

③ M: Do you know where the nearest bank is?

W: Yes. It's next to the red building over there.

④ M: You look tired. Didn't you get enough sleep?

W: No. I 3) _____ _____ _____ watching movies.

⑤ M: Do you have any thoughts about our summer vacation?

W: How about going camping?

---

11 할 일 파악

대화를 듣고, 남자가 대화 직후에 할 일로 가장 적절한 것을 고르시오.

① 청소하기　　② 꽃 사기
③ 케이크 만들기　　④ 축하 카드 쓰기
⑤ 저녁 식사 준비하기

★Focus on Sound cleaned the

비슷한 자음이 겹쳐서 나오면 앞의 자음이 탈락하여 [클린드 더]가 아닌 [클린더]로 발음된다.

M: Today's my wife's birthday. So I'm 1) _____ _____ _____ _____ _____ tonight.

W: Have you finished preparing for it?

M: Almost. I've ★cleaned the house and 2) _____ _____ _____ that she likes.

W: How about a cake?

M: It's in the oven. I'm 3) _____ _____ _____ _____.

W: Wow, you're working really hard.

M: Yes, I am. Now I need to 4) _____ _____ _____.

W: What are you going to make?

M: I'm going to make a pepperoni pizza. It's one of her favorites.

---

12 위치 찾기

다음 스터디룸 배치도를 보면서 대화를 듣고, 여자가 선택할 스터디룸을 고르시오.

W: Hi. Can we use the study room now?

M: Sure. How many people are there?

W: Three.

M: Okay. Please check this chart and choose one of the available rooms.

W: I don't want the room 1) _____ _____ _____. I used it before, and it was a bit noisy. Can we use Room C?

M: Sorry, that room is for groups of more than eight people. How about the room near the bookshelves? You can 2) _____ _____ _____ _____.

W: Well... Actually, I'd prefer to use the room 3) _____ _____ _____ _____. I need to copy some material.

M: Okay. Please fill out this form.

13 숫자 정보 파악

대화를 듣고, 두 사람이 탑승할 버스의 출발 시각을 고르시오.

① 1:00 p.m. ② 1:30 p.m. ③ 2:00 p.m.
④ 2:30 p.m. ⑤ 3:00 p.m.

W: This highway rest stop is great.

M: Yeah. I think there are more stores here than at my local shopping mall.

W: Let's take a look at what we can buy.

M: We only have time for a quick look around. Our 1) _____ _____ _____ _____ _____ _____ .

W: What time is it now?

M: It's 1:30 p.m. Let's 2) _____ _____ _____ _____ first and look around while eating.

W: That's a good idea.

M: There are so many shops I want to see. I hope the bus leaves 3) _____ _____ _____ .

W: That's what I was about to say.

14 한 일 파악 🇬🇧

대화를 듣고, 여자가 주말에 한 일로 가장 적절한 것을 고르시오.

① 대청소하기   ② 집에서 쉬기
③ 병문안 가기   ④ 가족 모임 하기
⑤ 봄맞이 여행 가기

M: How was your weekend?

W: It was very productive. I got a lot done.

M: What did you do? Didn't you say 1) _____ _____ _____ _____ _____ ?

W: It was canceled because 2) _____ _____ _____ _____ .

M: Too bad. You were looking forward to it, weren't you?

W: Yeah, but I did chores instead.

M: That's good. Did you 3) _____ _____ _____ _____ ?

W: Yes. I cleaned everything from top to bottom.

M: I'm sure you did a great job.

15 목적 파악

다음을 듣고, 방송의 목적으로 가장 적절한 것을 고르시오.

① 지진 발생 소식을 알리려고
② 응급 처치 방법을 설명하려고
③ 도로 교통법 준수를 당부하려고
④ 지진 발생 위험에 대해 경고하려고
⑤ 지진 발생 시 안전 수칙을 설명하려고

W: Every day, we hear about terrible disasters happening around the world. It's best to be prepared for anything. If an earthquake hits and you are indoors, 1) _____ _____ _____ _____ . Instead, hide under a desk or stand in a doorway. If you are outside, 2) _____ _____ _____ _____ _____ _____ and trees. And if you're driving, 3) _____ _____ _____ to the side of the road and don't leave your car. Remember, knowing what to do in an emergency could save your life.

16 숫자 정보 파악 🏴󠁧󠁢

대화를 듣고, 남자가 지불할 금액을 고르시오.

① $15 ② $21 ③ $24 ④ $30 ⑤ $42

M: I'd like one ticket for the amusement park, please.

W: That's $30. If you have a membership card, you can 1) _____
_____ _____.

M: I don't have one.

W: We also 2) _____ _____ _____ _____. If you are
a student, we can give you 20% off.

M: No, I'm not a student either. I think I'll have to 3) _____
_____ _____.

W: Well, you can 4) _____ _____ _____ _____ if you
wait until after 4 p.m. to buy it.

M: Okay, I'll do that.

---

17 마지막 말에 이어질 응답 찾기

대화를 듣고, 여자의 마지막 말에 대한 남자의
응답으로 가장 적절한 것을 고르시오.

Man: _____

① It won't be easy to get degree.

② I decided to go abroad three years ago.

③ It will take about 14 hours to get there.

④ It will take me three years to get my
degree.

⑤ I'm planning to study English before
I leave.

W: What are your plans for next year, Jinsu?

M: I'm going to go to the U.S.A. I 1) _____ _____
_____.

W: Really? Wow, that's great. What are you going to study?

M: Computer science. I want to become a programmer.

W: How interesting! When do you leave?

M: School starts in September, but I'm 2) _____ _____
_____ to find an apartment.

W: An apartment? 3) _____ _____ _____ _____
_____ on staying there?

M: It will take me three years to get my degree.

18 마지막 말에 이어질 응답 찾기

대화를 듣고, 남자의 마지막 말에 대한 여자의 응답으로 가장 적절한 것을 고르시오.

Woman: _____

① Don't forget to lock the door.
② I wish I could take a few days off.
③ We should go visit her in the hospital.
④ Thank goodness. I'm glad to hear that.
⑤ You should be more careful in the future.

M: How was work today, honey?

W: I was a little busy, but it wasn't bad.

M: Good.

W: By the way, I $^{1)}$ _____ _____ _____ _____ on my way home. Was there a fire in the neighborhood?

M: Yes, Ms. Baker's house caught fire.

W: Really? $^{2)}$ _____ _____ _____ _____ _____?

M: Fortunately, it wasn't. The fire trucks arrived quickly, so $^{3)}$ _____ _____ _____.

W: Thank goodness. I'm glad to hear that.

---

19 마지막 말에 이어질 응답 찾기 🇬🇧

대화를 듣고, 남자의 마지막 말에 대한 여자의 응답으로 가장 적절한 것을 고르시오.

Woman: _____

① In a couple of days.
② The sooner, the better.
③ I'll take the brown one.
④ Sorry for keeping you waiting.
⑤ I just bought it three weeks ago.

W: Hi. May I help you?

M: Yes. I bought this smartphone about five months ago, and I need to $^{1)}$ _____ _____ _____.

W: Sure. For one year, all repairs are free. What's the problem?

M: It suddenly stopped working, and I don't know why.

W: Okay. Please leave it here, and $^{2)}$ _____ _____ _____ _____ what's wrong.

M: Thanks. When can I $^{3)}$ _____ _____ _____ _____?

W: In a couple of days.

---

20 상황에 적절한 말 찾기

다음 상황 설명을 듣고, Tim이 자신에게 할 말로 가장 적절한 것을 고르시오.

Tim: _____

① I need to learn from failure and keep trying.
② It is difficult to motivate myself day after day.
③ I should think long and hard about my future.
④ Working together is better than working alone.
⑤ If I act like a leader, other people will follow me.

M: Tim has worked hard $^{1)}$ _____ _____ _____ _____ _____ over the past three months. He took an online course, and he solved problems for an hour every day. On weekends, he read books on computer science. That's why $^{2)}$ _____ _____ _____ _____ the competition. However, what happened was unexpected. He was $^{3)}$ _____ _____ _____ _____ _____. He was very disappointed but $^{4)}$ _____ _____ _____ _____. In this situation, what would Tim most likely say to himself?

정답 및 해설 pp. 87~92

점수: /20

보통속도 듣기
빠르게 듣기

01 대화를 듣고, 두 사람이 구입할 담요를 고르시오.

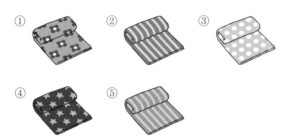

02 대화를 듣고, Nancy Bailey에 관해 언급되지 않은 것을 고르시오.

① 학교   ② 전공   ③ 나이
④ 경력   ⑤ 성격

03 대화를 듣고, 남자가 여자에게 전화한 목적으로 가장 적절한 것을 고르시오.

① 음식을 주문하려고
② 식당 위치를 물어보려고
③ 식당 예약을 변경하려고
④ 일자리에 대해 문의하려고
⑤ 음식 배달 상황을 확인하려고

04 대화를 듣고, 두 사람이 만나기로 한 시각을 고르시오.

① 1:00 p.m.   ② 2:00 p.m.   ③ 3:00 p.m.
④ 4:00 p.m.   ⑤ 5:00 p.m.

05 대화를 듣고, 여자의 심정으로 가장 적절한 것을 고르시오.

① proud   ② excited   ③ jealous
④ surprised   ⑤ worried

06 다음 그림의 상황에 가장 적절한 대화를 고르시오.

①   ②   ③   ④   ⑤

07 대화를 듣고, 여자가 남자에게 부탁한 일로 가장 적절한 것을 고르시오.

① 배역 바꾸기   ② 연극 표 팔기
③ 연기 연습 돕기   ④ 연극 보러 오기
⑤ 축제에 함께 가기

08 다음을 듣고, 견학에 관해 언급되지 않은 것을 고르시오.

① 장소   ② 집합 시각   ③ 복장
④ 이동 방법   ⑤ 준비물

고난도
09 다음을 듣고, 무엇에 관한 설명인지 고르시오.

① 편지   ② 신문   ③ 잡지
④ 포스터   ⑤ 팸플릿

10 다음을 듣고, 두 사람의 대화가 어색한 것을 고르시오.

①   ②   ③   ④   ⑤

11 대화를 듣고, 여자가 대화 직후에 할 일로 가장 적절한 것을 고르시오.

① 병원에 가기   ② 주소 알려 주기
③ 응급처치하기   ④ 아버지 눕혀 드리기
⑤ 도움 요청하기

12 다음 비행기 좌석 배치도를 보면서 대화를 듣고, 남자가 선택할 좌석을 고르시오.

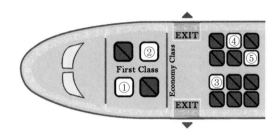

13 대화를 듣고, 남자가 이용할 셔틀버스의 출발 시각을 고르시오.

① 1:00 p.m.   ② 2:00 p.m.   ③ 3:00 p.m.
④ 4:00 p.m.   ⑤ 6:00 p.m.

14 대화를 듣고, 여자가 어제 한 일로 가장 적절한 것을 고르시오.

① 토마토 심기   ② 가족 여행 가기
③ 토마토 수확하기   ④ 토마토 모종 사기
⑤ 농산물 시장에 가기

15 다음을 듣고, 방송의 목적으로 가장 적절한 것을 고르시오.

① 특별 행사를 홍보하려고
② 새 웹 사이트를 광고하려고
③ 수영 대회 개최를 알리려고
④ 매장 운영 시간을 알리려고
⑤ 행사 장소 변경을 공지하려고

고난도
16 대화를 듣고, 여자가 지불할 금액을 고르시오.

① $70   ② $100   ③ $140
④ $170   ⑤ $200

17 대화를 듣고, 남자의 마지막 말에 대한 여자의 응답으로 가장 적절한 것을 고르시오.

Woman: _____

① I'd better stay home.
② That shirt looks good, too.
③ I'm pretty good at painting.
④ No, I can't pick you up there.
⑤ Sure. How about this blue one?

[18 - 19] 대화를 듣고, 여자의 마지막 말에 대한 남자의 응답으로 가장 적절한 것을 고르시오.

18 Man: _____

① Sorry, I'm busy right now.
② I'd like to pay by credit card.
③ I don't like that place. It's so crowded.
④ Tomorrow at seven o'clock would be fine.
⑤ How about the Mexican restaurant downtown?

19 Man: _____

① I don't think it's their fault.
② I don't understand you at all.
③ Just complaining cannot be helpful.
④ You're right. It won't happen again.
⑤ I was busy because there were so many customers.

20 다음 상황 설명을 듣고, Jessica가 남자에게 할 말로 가장 적절한 것을 고르시오.

Jessica: _____

① Do you like hip-hop?
② What is the title of this song?
③ Could you turn the music down?
④ Is there an empty seat around here?
⑤ Where did you buy your headphones?

Dictation Test 17

01 그림 정보 파악

대화를 듣고, 두 사람이 구입할 담요를 고르시오.

W: Winter's coming, Jacob. You need a warmer blanket for your bed.

M: Okay, Mom. There are some blankets over there. Let's pick one out together.

W: All right. I like this one, but I guess you don't like flowers.

M: That's right. I don't. I 1) _____ _____ _____ _____, though.

W: Yes, but it's too thin. It won't keep you warm. How about this one instead?

M: I don't like those circles. I 2) _____ _____ _____.

W: Let me feel it. All right, I think 3) _____ _____ _____.

M: Great. Let's get this one, then.

02 언급되지 않은 내용 찾기

대화를 듣고, Nancy Bailey에 관해 언급되지 않은 것을 고르시오.

① 학교   ② 전공   ③ 나이
④ 경력   ⑤ 성격

M: Hey, Laura. Have you finished all the interviews yet?

W: Yes, I just finished them.

M: Were there any good candidates?

W: Yes, there's one named Nancy Bailey. She 1) _____ _____ _____ _____ _____ as me.

M: What did she major in?

W: Journalism. She also has 2) _____ _____ _____ _____ _____.

M: Do you think she will fit in with our company?

W: Yes. She's 3) _____ _____ _____. Her personality would fit in well with our company's culture.

M: That's great.

03 목적 파악 🇬🇧

대화를 듣고, 남자가 여자에게 전화한 목적으로 가장 적절한 것을 고르시오.

① 음식을 주문하려고
② 식당 위치를 물어보려고
③ 식당 예약을 변경하려고
④ 일자리에 대해 문의하려고
⑤ 음식 배달 상황을 확인하려고

★ **Focus on Sound** advertisement

미국식 영어에서는 [애드버ㄹ타이즈먼트]로 발음되지만, 영국식 영어에서는 [어드버티스먼트]로 발음된다.

[Phone rings.]

W: Thanks for calling Pizza World. How can I help you?

M: Hi. My name is Patrick, and I saw your *advertisement for a part-time worker. Are you still 1) _____ _____ _____ ?

W: Yes. We 2) _____ _____ _____ _____ _____ .

M: What are the working hours?

W: Four hours each weekday, starting at 5:00 p.m.

M: Oh, that sounds fine. And can you tell me 3) _____ _____ _____ _____ _____ ?

W: You'll be getting ten dollars an hour. If you're interested, 4) _____ _____ _____ _____ tomorrow?

M: Okay. I'll see you then.

---

04 숫자 정보 파악

대화를 듣고, 두 사람이 만나기로 한 시각을 고르시오.

① 1:00 p.m.   ② 2:00 p.m.   ③ 3:00 p.m.
④ 4:00 p.m.   ⑤ 5:00 p.m.

W: My ankle hurts so much. I can't go any further.

M: What? Come on. It will 1) _____ _____ _____ _____ _____ to get to the top.

W: Sorry, but I'm finished. I can't take another step.

M: Okay. Why don't you go wait in that shelter over there?

W: Good idea. You can finish the hike on your own.

M: You don't mind? It will be a couple of hours.

W: I'll be fine. I'll see you 2) _____ _____ _____ .

M: Okay. It's 3:00 p.m. now, so I'll 3) _____ _____ _____ _____ _____ .

W: Okay.

---

05 심정 추론

대화를 듣고, 여자의 심정으로 가장 적절한 것을 고르시오.

① proud   ② excited   ③ jealous
④ surprised   ⑤ worried

W: I can't find my keys.

M: Do you remember where you had them last?

W: Oh no. I think I 1) _____ _____ _____ _____ _____ in my car this morning. I can't believe it. What should I do?

M: Don't you have another key?

W: I have one at my house. But my house key is 2) _____ _____ _____ _____ as well.

M: Why don't you call a locksmith? They can send someone quickly.

W: But I'm 3) _____ _____ _____ _____ my daughter at her kindergarten in 20 minutes. I don't have time to wait for a locksmith.

06 그림 상황에 적절한 대화 찾기 🇬🇧

다음 그림의 상황에 가장 적절한 대화를 고르시오.

REFUND

①   ②   ③   ④   ⑤

① M: Excuse me, I'm looking for a white shirt.

    W: They're over there by the sweaters.

② M: Can I pay with a credit card?

    W: Sorry, we 1) _____ _____ _____ .

③ M: There is a hole in this shirt.

    W: Oh, sorry about that. Would you like to 2) _____ _____

    _____ _____ _____ _____ ?

④ M: Where is the nearest bank? I want to 3) _____ _____

    _____ .

    W: You can use the ATM over there.

⑤ M: How much is it?

    W: It's $30. Do you want to 4) _____ _____ _____

    _____ _____ ?

07 부탁한 일 파악

대화를 듣고, 여자가 남자에게 부탁한 일로 가장 적절한 것을 고르시오.

① 배역 바꾸기   ② 연극 표 팔기

③ 연기 연습 돕기   ④ 연극 보러 오기

⑤ 축제에 함께 가기

M: Hi, Amber. What's wrong?

W: Our club is performing a play at the school festival.

M: That's great. So what's the problem? Didn't you 1) _____

    _____ _____ _____ ?

W: Actually, I'll play the main character in the play.

M: Good for you. Congratulations.

W: Thanks. But 2) _____ _____ _____ _____

    _____ .

M: Is it a difficult role?

W: It's not that kind of problem. 3) _____ _____ _____ for

    our play have been sold.

M: Don't worry. People will start buying them soon.

W: Do you really think so? Maybe you could 4) _____ _____

    _____ _____ _____ ?

M: Sure. I'd be happy to.

언급되지 않은 내용 찾기

다음을 듣고, 견학에 관해 언급되지 <u>않은</u> 것을 고르시오.

① 장소   ② 집합 시각   ③ 복장
④ 이동 방법   ⑤ 준비물

W: Attention, students! Tomorrow we will go to the Modern Art Museum for a field trip. You must 1) _____ _____ _____ _____ by 9:00 a.m. Could you try to be on time, please? You don't have to wear your uniforms tomorrow. You 2) _____ _____ _____ . You should bring a small notebook and some pens. You 3) _____ _____ _____ _____ _____ too. We will return to the school by 4:00 p.m. I hope you all have a great time tomorrow.

---

09 **화제 파악** 🇬🇧

다음을 듣고, 무엇에 관한 설명인지 고르시오.

① 편지   ② 신문   ③ 잡지
④ 포스터   ⑤ 팸플릿

M: These are 1) _____ _____ . They are often printed on high-quality paper. They typically 2) _____ _____ , _____ , _____ _____ . Each one has its own characteristics: some are filled with light reading material, while others are more specialized. They 3) _____ _____ _____ , usually every week or every month. They can be purchased at bookstores or delivered to your home. They can also be found in libraries or on the Internet.

---

10 **어색한 대화 찾기**

다음을 듣고, 두 사람의 대화가 <u>어색한</u> 것을 고르시오.

①   ②   ③   ④   ⑤

① W: I 1) _____ _____ _____ about these pants.
   M: Can I ask what the problem is?
② W: Have you ever played soccer?
   M: No, I don't like sports.
③ W: Did you call me last night?
   M: Yes, but your phone 2) _____ _____ _____ .
④ W: Can you tell me about the movie?
   M: It's about the life of Picasso, and it's very interesting.
⑤ W: Where should I put the garbage?
   M: 3) _____ _____ _____ , I think.

11 할 일 파악

대화를 듣고, 여자가 대화 직후에 할 일로 가장 적절한 것을 고르시오.

① 병원에 가기 ② 주소 알려 주기
③ 응급처치하기 ④ 아버지 눕혀 드리기
⑤ 도움 요청하기

[Phone rings.]

M: Hello, 119. What's your emergency?

W: My dad 1) _____ _____ _____ _____ . I think he broke his leg.

M: What's your address?

W: It's 1123 Main Street.

M: Okay. I'm 2) _____ _____ _____ now. But please stay on the line.

W: Please hurry. He doesn't look good. He can't move.

M: The ambulance is on the way. Is he able to lie down?

W: I guess so.

M: Then 3) _____ _____ _____ and tell him not to move. Help will be there soon.

W: Okay.

12 위치 찾기

다음 비행기 좌석 배치도를 보면서 대화를 듣고, 남자가 선택할 좌석을 고르시오.

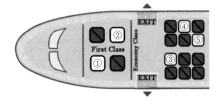

W: How may I help you, sir?

M: I'd like to book a flight to New York for March 30. Are there 1) _____ _____ _____ ?

W: Yes, there are several open seats. Do you want first-class or economy?

M: Economy class. It's a short flight, so I don't think it's 2) _____ _____ _____ _____ .

W: Okay. And would you like a window seat or 3) _____ _____ _____ ?

M: Aisle seat, please. Is there a seat 4) _____ _____ _____ ?

W: Yes. It's $500.

M: Okay, I'll take it.

13 숫자 정보 파악

대화를 듣고, 남자가 이용할 셔틀버스의 출발 시각을 고르시오.

① 1:00 p.m. ② 2:00 p.m. ③ 3:00 p.m.
④ 4:00 p.m. ⑤ 6:00 p.m.

[Phone rings.]

W: Hello, Beachside Hotel.

M: Hi. I'd like to make a reservation for January 13.

W: Okay. Would you like a room with a twin bed?

M: Yes, please. When is check-in time?

W: You can check in 1) _____ _____ _____ _____ p.m.

M: Good. What is the best way to get to the hotel from the airport?

W: We 2) _____ _____ _____ _____ _____ . What time is your flight arriving?

M: It'll arrive at 1:00 p.m.

W: Our shuttle bus 3) _____ _____ _____ _____ at 2:00, 4:00, and 6:00 p.m.

M: Good. The 4) _____ _____ _____ would be perfect.

---

14 한 일 파악

대화를 듣고, 여자가 어제 한 일로 가장 적절한 것을 고르시오.

① 토마토 심기   ② 가족 여행 가기
③ 토마토 수확하기   ④ 토마토 모종 사기
⑤ 농산물 시장에 가기

W: Hi, Jake. I have some tomatoes for you.

M: Oh, I like tomatoes. Thank you. Where did you get them?

W: I grew them myself.

M: Really? You 1) _____ _____ _____ _____ ?

W: No. My family 2) _____ _____ _____ _____ _____ in the countryside.

M: That's great.

W: Yeah, I planted those tomatoes last spring and 3) _____ _____ _____ _____ yesterday.

M: Great. Thank you for sharing them with me.

---

15 목적 파악

다음을 듣고, 방송의 목적으로 가장 적절한 것을 고르시오.

① 특별 행사를 홍보하려고
② 새 웹 사이트를 광고하려고
③ 수영 대회 개최를 알리려고
④ 매장 운영 시간을 알리려고
⑤ 행사 장소 변경을 공지하려고

W: Hello, everyone! May I have your attention, please? I'd like to 1) _____ _____ _____ _____ on all our summer products. We're 2) _____ _____ _____ _____ on all beach items, including swimsuits, flip-flops, beach towels, and sunblock. But this 3) _____ _____ _____ _____ _____ today only! All our prices will return to normal tomorrow. Be sure to take advantage of these great deals, which are available online as well!

16 숫자 정보 파악

대화를 듣고, 여자가 지불할 금액을 고르시오.

① $70   ② $100   ③ $140
④ $170   ⑤ $200

M: Hello. How can I help you?

W: I need two tickets to *Dr. Jekyll and Mr. Hyde* next week.

M: Okay. ¹⁾ _____ _____ _____.

W: I have a theater membership. Do I get a discount?

M: Yes, you do. If you show me your membership card, you will ²⁾ _____ _____ _____ _____.

W: That's great. Here's my membership card.

M: Okay. The ³⁾ _____ _____ _____, but this is your new total after the 30% discount.

17 마지막 말에 이어질 응답 찾기

대화를 듣고, 남자의 마지막 말에 대한 여자의 응답으로 가장 적절한 것을 고르시오.

Woman: _____

① I'd better stay home.
② That shirt looks good, too.
③ I'm pretty good at painting.
④ No, I can't pick you up there.
⑤ Sure. How about this blue one?

M: ¹⁾ _____? I'm going to a party tonight.

W: Let me see... Your shirt and pants look very nice.

M: Thanks. And I'm going to wear this jacket.

W: That's a good choice. Are you going to wear a tie?

M: Yes. I was trying to decide between these two.

W: To be honest, I don't think ²⁾ _____ _____ _____ _____ _____.

M: Really? Choosing a tie is always difficult. Can you ³⁾ _____ _____ _____ for me?

W: Sure. How about this blue one?

18 마지막 말에 이어질 응답 찾기

대화를 듣고, 여자의 마지막 말에 대한 남자의 응답으로 가장 적절한 것을 고르시오.

Man: _____

① Sorry, I'm busy right now.
② I'd like to pay by credit card.
③ I don't like that place. It's so crowded.
④ Tomorrow at seven o'clock would be fine.
⑤ How about the Mexican restaurant downtown?

W: I'm home!
M: You look happy. Did 1) _____ _____ _____ ?
W: Yes. My project at work is finished, and the boss loved it. I'm so glad.
M: Good for you! I'm 2) _____ _____ _____ _____ .
   Why don't we go out for dinner to celebrate?
W: That sounds good. Do you 3) _____ _____ _____
   _____ _____ ?
M: How about the Mexican restaurant downtown?

---

19 마지막 말에 이어질 응답 찾기 🇬🇧

대화를 듣고, 여자의 마지막 말에 대한 남자의 응답으로 가장 적절한 것을 고르시오.

Man: _____

① I don't think it's their fault.
② I don't understand you at all.
③ Just complaining cannot be helpful.
④ You're right. It won't happen again.
⑤ I was busy because there were so many customers.

★ **Focus on Sound**   polite to

똑같은 발음의 자음이 겹치면 앞 자음 소리가 탈락하여 [폴라이트 투]가 아닌 [폴라이투]로 발음된다.

W: Hi, Drake. Please take a seat.
M: Thank you, Ms. Jones.
W: I wanted to talk to you about some 1) _____ _____
   _____ _____ _____ .
M: Oh! What were they about?
W: Well, a few customers this week said that 2) _____ _____
   _____ to them.
M: Oh, sorry. Please let me explain. I 3) _____ _____ _____
   _____ this week, so some customers may have noticed. But I'll
   be more careful next time.
W: I see. But 4) _____ _____ _____ _____ _____ ,
   you must always be *polite to our customers.
M: You're right. It won't happen again.

---

20 상황에 적절한 말 찾기

다음 상황 설명을 듣고, Jessica가 남자에게 할 말로 가장 적절한 것을 고르시오.

Jessica: _____

① Do you like hip-hop?
② What is the title of this song?
③ Could you turn the music down?
④ Is there an empty seat around here?
⑤ Where did you buy your headphones?

M: Jessica is a high school student. She has midterms tomorrow, so
   she is 1) _____ _____ _____ _____ _____ .
   The man sitting next to Jessica is listening to music. The sound
   from his headphones is 2) _____ _____ _____ Jessica
   can't concentrate. The library is full, and there are 3) _____
   _____ _____ _____ . In this situation, what would
   Jessica most likely say to the man next to her?

실전모의고사  회

정답 및 해설 pp.92~96

점수: /20

보통 속도 듣기 빠르게 듣기

01 대화를 듣고, 여자가 구입할 보석함을 고르시오.

① ② ③
④ ⑤

02 대화를 듣고, 발표 능력 향상을 위한 방안으로 언급되지 않은 것을 고르시오.

① 긴장 풀기
② 불안감 극복하기
③ 많이 연습하기
④ 거울 앞에서 연습하기
⑤ 메모 카드 만들기

03 대화를 듣고, 남자의 마지막 말에 담긴 의도로 가장 적절한 것을 고르시오.

① 동의   ② 제안   ③ 거절
④ 수락   ⑤ 충고

04 대화를 듣고, 두 사람이 만나기로 한 시각을 고르시오.

① 11:00 a.m.   ② 12:00 p.m.   ③ 1:00 p.m.
④ 2:00 p.m.   ⑤ 3:00 p.m.

05 대화를 듣고, 두 사람이 대화하는 장소로 가장 적절한 곳을 고르시오.

① 약국   ② 호텔   ③ 교실
④ 동물원   ⑤ 동물 병원

06 다음 그림의 상황에 가장 적절한 대화를 고르시오.

① ② ③ ④ ⑤

07 대화를 듣고, 여자가 남자에게 부탁한 일로 가장 적절한 것을 고르시오.

① 공책 빌려주기
② 숙제 제출해주기
③ 함께 일본 방문하기
④ 학교 프로그램에 지원하기
⑤ 교수님께 결석 사유 말씀드려주기

고난도
08 다음을 듣고, 청소년 기자에 관해 언급되지 않은 것을 고르시오.

① 저작물 종류   ② 지원 자격   ③ 활동 내용
④ 혜택   ⑤ 지원 방법

09 다음을 듣고, 무엇에 관한 내용인지 고르시오.

① 집안 청소 방법   ② 혹한 대비 방법
③ 에너지 절약 방법   ④ 환경 보호 방법
⑤ 냉장고 고르는 방법

10 다음을 듣고, 두 사람의 대화가 어색한 것을 고르시오.

① ② ③ ④ ⑤

11 대화를 듣고, 여자가 대화 직후에 할 일로 가장 적절한 것을 고르시오.

① 빨래하기 　　　② 개 목욕시키기
③ 설거지하기 　　④ 저녁 식사 준비하기
⑤ 집 청소하기

12 다음 공원 지도를 보면서 대화를 듣고, 두 사람이 선택할 피크닉 장소를 고르시오.

13 대화를 듣고, 현재 시각을 고르시오.

① 3:00 　　② 3:10 　　③ 3:15
④ 3:45 　　⑤ 4:00

14 대화를 듣고, 남자가 어제 한 일로 가장 적절한 것을 고르시오.

① 체육 숙제하기 　　　② 체육복 챙기기
③ 체육복 세탁하기 　　④ 체육복 빌리기
⑤ 집에서 운동하기

고난도
15 다음을 듣고, 방송의 목적으로 가장 적절한 것을 고르시오.

① 채소 섭취를 장려하려고
② 신임 영양사를 소개하려고
③ 급식 메뉴 변경을 알리려고
④ 채소의 영양소를 설명하려고
⑤ 급식 품질 개선을 촉구하려고

16 대화를 듣고, 여자가 지불할 금액을 고르시오.

① $200 　　② $300 　　③ $450
④ $700 　　⑤ $900

17 대화를 듣고, 여자의 마지막 말에 대한 남자의 응답으로 가장 적절한 것을 고르시오.

Man: _____

① Don't be late again.
② What grade did you get?
③ I'm so happy to hear that!
④ I'm sorry. I forgot to tell you.
⑤ I can't believe I missed the test!

[18-19] 대화를 듣고, 남자의 마지막 말에 대한 여자의 응답으로 가장 적절한 것을 고르시오.

18 Woman: _____

① I don't agree with you.
② It's very nice of you to say so.
③ Never mind. Everything is okay.
④ Don't give up. You can do better.
⑤ I wish you good luck with the contest.

19 Woman: _____

① I can't wait to go there.
② Three weeks is not so long.
③ I'll leave for Dubai at 6 a.m.
④ The plane ticket is expensive.
⑤ It takes about 10 hours by plane.

20 다음 상황 설명을 듣고, Walter가 점원에게 할 말로 가장 적절한 것을 고르시오.

Walter: _____

① Can I get a refund?
② I think I have a coupon for this store.
③ I don't want these two shirts anymore.
④ I think there's a mistake with the price.
⑤ Which is better, the blue one or the yellow one?

Dictation Test 18

보통 속도 듣기 빠르게 듣기

01 [그림 정보 파악]

대화를 듣고, 여자가 구입할 보석함을 고르시오.

①   ②   ③

④   ⑤

M: Are you looking for a gift for Lucy?

W: Yes. What do you think of 1) _____ _____ _____?

M: They're nice. She likes cute things.

W: Some of them play music. Which do you think is better, 2) _____ _____ _____ _____?

M: I think the ones that play music are better.

W: I agree. And look what happens when you 3) _____ _____ _____.

M: Wow! A ballerina is spinning to the music.

W: This one has a unicorn, and that one has a mermaid.

M: I think 4) _____ _____ _____ _____ _____ is the cutest.

W: I agree. I'll buy it.

02 [언급되지 않은 내용 찾기]

대화를 듣고, 발표 능력 향상을 위한 방안으로 언급되지 않은 것을 고르시오.

① 긴장 풀기
② 불안감 극복하기
③ 많이 연습하기
④ 거울 앞에서 연습하기
⑤ 메모 카드 만들기

W: What's wrong, Gary?

M: Nothing. I just have to give a speech at school tomorrow.

W: Oh, that's great. I love giving speeches.

M: How can you be that confident?

W: Well, it's important to relax. You should try to 1) _____ _____ _____. And you need to practice a lot. I always 2) _____ _____ _____ _____ before an actual speech.

M: I see. But what if I forget what to say during a speech?

W: You should write everything down 3) _____ _____ _____ _____. Make sure they are easy to read. You can use colored pencils to highlight the main points.

M: That's a good idea! Thank you for the tips.

W: You're welcome. 4) _____ _____ _____ _____, the more relaxed you will feel.

03 의도 파악

대화를 듣고, 남자의 마지막 말에 담긴 의도로 가장 적절한 것을 고르시오.

① 동의　②제안　③거절

④ 수락　⑤충고

M: What can I do for you today?

W: I want to try a new hairstyle. I think a perm would look nice.

M: Yes, I think a 1) _____ _____ _____ _____. Are you a student?

W: Yes, I go to Seoul Middle School. Why?

M: We're offering a special price on perms. Students can 2) _____ _____ _____ just by showing their student ID.

W: That's great! But I 3) _____ _____ _____ _____ a few days ago. Is there any way you can still give me the discount?

M: Sorry, but without the ID, we 4) _____ _____ _____ _____ _____.

04 숫자 정보 파악 🇬🇧

대화를 듣고, 두 사람이 만나기로 한 시각을 고르시오.

① 11:00 a.m.　② 12:00 p.m.　③ 1:00 p.m.

④ 2:00 p.m.　⑤ 3:00 p.m.

W: What is our schedule today?

M: Our first stop will be at the Royal Gardens. We'll be 1) _____ _____ _____ _____ p.m.

W: Are we staying that long? It's 11:00 a.m. now.

M: We'll have about two hours to stroll around the gardens.

W: What will we do after that?

M: We'll have lunch 2) _____ _____ _____ _____ p.m.

W: What's for lunch?

M: We'll have traditional local food. I'm sure you'll like it.

W: I'm looking forward to it.

M: We've now arrived at our first destination. Explore the garden, and we'll 3) _____ _____ _____ _____ _____ _____.

W: Okay. See you then.

대화를 듣고, 두 사람이 대화하는 장소로 가장 적절한 곳을 고르시오.

① 약국   ② 호텔   ③ 교실
④ 동물원   ⑤ 동물 병원

* Focus on Sound   **used to**

'~하곤 했다'의 의미인 경우 [유스투]로 발음된다.

M: May I help you?

W: Yes. I think my cat is sick, and I don't know why. She doesn't eat much and 1) _____ _____ _____ _____. She *used to be very active.

M: I see. Let me check her. *[pause]*

W: How is she?

M: Well, I think she's 2) _____ _____ _____ _____ _____ _____. But I need to take a closer look at her. Can you leave her for a day?

W: Sure. I hope she'll be okay.

M: We'll 3) _____ _____ _____ _____ _____. Don't worry too much.

---

06 그림 상황에 적절한 대화 찾기

다음 그림의 상황에 가장 적절한 대화를 고르시오.

①   ②   ③   ④   ⑤

① W: Have you done your homework?
   M: Yes, 1) _____ _____ _____ it.

② W: Where is your ball?
   M: I think I forgot it. I 2) _____ _____ _____ at school.

③ W: You shouldn't play soccer near the window.
   M: Sorry. I 3) _____ _____ _____ _____ from now on.

④ W: It's cold outside. You should wear a jacket.
   M: Okay. Where is it?

⑤ W: Could you 4) _____ _____ _____ the window?
   M: Sure! Can I use this cloth?

대화를 듣고, 여자가 남자에게 부탁한 일로 가장 적절한 것을 고르시오.

① 공책 빌려주기
② 숙제 제출해주기
③ 함께 일본 방문하기
④ 학교 프로그램에 지원하기
⑤ 교수님께 결석 사유 말씀드려주기

M: Hi, Jenny. You look happy. Did something good happen?

W: Yes. I was 1) _____ _____ _____ _____ _____

_____.

M: Wow, congratulations.

W: Thanks. I'm going to Japan next week to take part in the first leadership workshop.

M: That's great! I guess 2) _____ _____ _____ _____

_____, though.

W: Yes, that's right. I've already talked to the professor about it. Could I 3) _____ _____ _____ after I come back from Japan?

M: Sure, no problem.

다음을 듣고, 청소년 기자에 관해 언급되지 <u>않은</u> 것을 고르시오.

① 저작물 종류 ② 지원 자격 ③ 활동 내용
④ 혜택 ⑤ 지원 방법

W: Do you like 1) _____, _____, _____ _____

_____? Whatever it is, we'd love for you to share your emotions and experiences with us. Apply to be a youth reporter for *Teen News*. 2) _____ _____ _____ _____ of 10 and 18 can apply. As a youth reporter, you can 3) _____ _____

_____ _____ to our website. You decide what to write because it's your content. We're on hand to 4) _____ _____

_____ and offer support as you upload your work. Not only can your friends and family read your posts, but they can also leave you messages on your blog. Apply to become a youth reporter today!

다음을 듣고, 무엇에 관한 내용인지 고르시오.

① 집안 청소 방법 ② 혹한 대비 방법
③ 에너지 절약 방법 ④ 환경 보호 방법
⑤ 냉장고 고르는 방법

M: Everyone agrees that we need to reduce energy waste. But what can you do? You can start by always 1) _____ _____

_____ _____ when you leave a room. Also, if you're cold during the winter, don't turn up the heat. Instead, 2) _____

_____ _____ _____ _____ _____ _____.

When you're looking for something to eat, don't think about it with the refrigerator door open. 3) _____ _____ _____

before you open the door. All of these little things can add up to big savings over time.

10 어색한 대화 찾기

다음을 듣고, 두 사람의 대화가 <u>어색한</u> 것을 고르시오.

①   ②   ③   ④   ⑤

① M: I'm planning to go rock climbing this Sunday.

   W: 1) _____ _____ _____ .

② M: I'm sad that I lost the match.

   W: Cheer up! You can try again next month.

③ M: 2) _____ _____ _____ ?

   W: I've been to China before.

④ M: I'd like to 3) _____ _____ _____ .

   W: Certainly. Can you fill out this application form?

⑤ M: 4) _____ _____ _____ _____ _____ to get to the hotel?

   W: It will take an hour and a half.

11 할 일 파악

대화를 듣고, 여자가 대화 직후에 할 일로 가장 적절한 것을 고르시오.

① 빨래하기   ② 개 목욕시키기
③ 설거지하기   ④ 저녁 식사 준비하기
⑤ 집 청소하기

M: What time will Mom and Dad be back home?

W: They said around eight o'clock.

M: Hmm... They'll be very tired from the trip. Why don't we clean up the house and 1) _____ _____ before they arrive?

W: That's a great idea. They'll be pleased.

M: Right. While I 2) _____ _____ _____ _____ , why don't you cook?

W: Okay. I'll 3) _____ _____ _____ _____ .

M: Good, they'll love it. Let's get started.

12 위치 찾기

다음 공원 지도를 보면서 대화를 듣고, 두 사람이 선택할 피크닉 장소를 고르시오.

W: Where shall we have our picnic?

M: How about under that tree? There's shade, so we 1) _____ _____ _____ .

W: I think we might get too cold. I want to sit in the sun. How about sitting 2) _____ _____ _____ _____ ?

M: There are too many people there. I 3) _____ _____ _____ _____ _____ during our picnic.

W: Hmm... I want to sit on the bench, but it's 4) _____ _____ .

M: Then how about sitting next to the ice cream truck? We can easily move to the bench when the people sitting there get up.

W: Sounds great!

13 숫자 정보 파악 🇬🇧

대화를 듣고, 현재 시각을 고르시오.

① 3:00   ② 3:10   ③ 3:15
④ 3:45   ⑤ 4:00

M: Hello, Michelle. I need to 1) _____ _____ _____ .

W: I'm sorry, but he's in a meeting right now.

M: When did it start?

W: At 3:00. But it 2) _____ _____ _____ _____ .

M: What time do you think it will be finished?

W: The meeting is scheduled to end at 4:00.

M: Okay. I guess I just need to 3) _____ _____ _____ _____ .

W: Yes. You can sit here. Do you want anything to drink?

M: No thanks.

---

14 한 일 파악

대화를 듣고, 남자가 어제 한 일로 가장 적절한 것을 고르시오.

① 체육 숙제하기   ② 체육복 챙기기
③ 체육복 세탁하기   ④ 체육복 빌리기
⑤ 집에서 운동하기

M: What's our next class?

W: It's P.E.

M: Oh no! I 1) _____ _____ _____ at home.

W: Didn't you know we had P.E. today?

M: I did. But I washed my gym clothes yesterday, and I 2) _____ _____ _____ _____ _____ to school.

W: You should 3) _____ _____ _____ _____ from one of your friends.

M: Good idea. If I'm late, please tell the teacher why.

W: Okay.

---

15 목적 파악

다음을 듣고, 방송의 목적으로 가장 적절한 것을 고르시오.

① 채소 섭취를 장려하려고
② 신임 영양사를 소개하려고
③ 급식 메뉴 변경을 알리려고
④ 채소의 영양소를 설명하려고
⑤ 급식 품질 개선을 촉구하려고

W: Hello, students. This is Dr. Phillips, the school nutritionist. These days, students tend to eat everything in their school lunches 1) _____ _____ _____ _____ . Vegetables are vital foods that must be included in our daily diet. They are an important source of vitamin and minerals, so a diet rich in vegetables is important 2) _____ _____ _____ _____ _____ . Our school provides students with daily lunches that contain essential nutrients. Therefore, students 3) _____ _____ _____ _____ _____ included in the school lunch. Thank you.

대화를 듣고, 여자가 지불할 금액을 고르시오.

① $200   ② $300   ③ $450
④ $700   ⑤ $900

W: I'd like to purchase a plane ticket to Tokyo on March 7.

M: One-way or return?

W: Return, please. I'd like to 1) _____ _____ _____.

M: Okay. Would you like to fly first-class, business, or economy?

W: How much is it for business class?

M: 2) _____ _____ _____.

W: That's more than I expected. How much for economy class?

M: That would be 3) _____ _____ _____ of a business-class ticket.

W: Great, I'll 4) _____ _____ _____ _____.

17 마지막 말에 이어질 응답 찾기

대화를 듣고, 여자의 마지막 말에 대한 남자의 응답으로 가장 적절한 것을 고르시오.

Man: _____

① Don't be late again.
② What grade did you get?
③ I'm so happy to hear that!
④ I'm sorry. I forgot to tell you.
⑤ I can't believe I missed the test!

M: Hey, Lucy. Are you ready for our big history test?

W: Not yet. I've still 1) _____ _____ _____ _____.

M: Me, too! I don't think I'll be ready by tomorrow. This is terrible.

W: What do you mean? Didn't you hear the news?

M: News? What news?

W: The teacher announced that the test has been 2) _____ _____ _____ _____.

M: Are you sure?

W: Yes. It was 3) _____ _____ _____ _____ _____ yesterday.

M: I'm so happy to hear that!

18 마지막 말에 이어질 응답 찾기

대화를 듣고, 남자의 마지막 말에 대한 여자의 응답으로 가장 적절한 것을 고르시오.

Woman: _____

① I don't agree with you.
② It's very nice of you to say so.
③ Never mind. Everything is okay.
④ Don't give up. You can do better.
⑤ I wish you good luck with the contest.

M: You look so happy. What's up?
W: Do you remember when I was preparing for the cooking contest?
M: Yes! Did you win?
W: Yeah. I [1)] _____ _____ _____.
M: Congratulations! What did you make for the contest?
W: I cooked fish in a honey sauce. I [2)] _____ _____ _____ for the sauce myself!
M: It [3)] _____ _____ _____ that you won. You're a great cook!
W: It's very nice of you to say so.

19 마지막 말에 이어질 응답 찾기

대화를 듣고, 남자의 마지막 말에 대한 여자의 응답으로 가장 적절한 것을 고르시오.

Woman: _____

① I can't wait to go there.
② Three weeks is not so long.
③ I'll leave for Dubai at 6 a.m.
④ The plane ticket is expensive.
⑤ It takes about 10 hours by plane.

M: Why are you reading a travel guide? Are you planning a trip?
W: Yes, I'm going to visit Dubai [1)] _____ _____ _____ _____ _____.
M: Wow. You'll be there for a long time. Have you [2)] _____ _____ _____ _____ yet?
W: Not yet. That's why I'm reading the travel guide.
M: I see. [3)] _____ _____ _____ _____ _____ to get there?
W: It takes about 10 hours by plane.

20 상황에 적절한 말 찾기

다음 상황 설명을 듣고, Walter가 점원에게 할 말로 가장 적절한 것을 고르시오.

Walter: _____

① Can I get a refund?
② I think I have a coupon for this store.
③ I don't want these two shirts anymore.
④ I think there's a mistake with the price.
⑤ Which is better, the blue one or the yellow one?

M: Walter is shopping for new clothes. He sees a nice sweater on sale as part of a "buy one, get one free" promotion. The sweater is $50, and he thinks [1)] _____ _____ _____ _____ is a great deal. He takes a blue one and a yellow one up to the counter. The clerk scans his items, and Walter [2)] _____ _____ _____ on the cash register's monitor. He thinks there [3)] _____ _____ _____ _____ with the register. In this situation, what would Walter most likely say to the clerk?

Word Test

Ⓐ 다음 영어의 우리말 뜻을 쓰시오.

01 anxiety _____

02 characteristic _____

03 terrible _____

04 attached _____

05 essential _____

06 fault _____

07 reunion _____

08 target _____

09 jewelry _____

10 author _____

11 access _____

12 entrance _____

13 create _____

14 thin _____

15 contain _____

16 candidate _____

17 global _____

18 annoying _____

19 garbage _____

20 appear _____

21 countryside _____

22 indoors _____

23 accept _____

24 typically _____

25 vital _____

26 thought _____

27 suffering _____

28 specialized _____

29 eliminate _____

30 overcome _____

31 personality _____

32 depart from _____

33 on time _____

34 come by _____

35 give a speech _____

36 take a seat _____

37 take advantage of _____

38 be filled with _____

39 come down with _____

40 from top to bottom _____

B 다음 우리말 뜻에 맞는 영어를 쓰시오.

01 인출하다 _____

02 예상 밖의 _____

03 조리법 _____

04 교수 _____

05 교육 _____

06 현금 _____

07 두꺼운 _____

08 생산적인 _____

09 ~의 가치가 있는 _____

10 자신감 있는 _____

11 실망한 _____

12 실패 _____

13 열정적인 _____

14 체크무늬의 _____

15 동기를 부여하다 _____

16 재앙 _____

17 영양사 _____

18 집안일 _____

19 불평, 항의 _____

20 (복장이) 편안하게 _____

21 발목 _____

22 주소 _____

23 수확 _____

24 보통의; 정상 _____

25 예의 바른, 정중한 _____

26 잠그다 _____

27 도둑 _____

28 평일 _____

29 유치원 _____

30 예행연습을 하다 _____

31 광고 _____

32 복사기 _____

33 소방차 _____

34 ~을 자랑스러워하다 _____

35 포기하다 _____

36 ~하는 경향이 있다 _____

37 둘러보다 _____

38 늦게까지 깨어 있다 _____

39 (차를) 길가에 대다 _____

40 ~에 책임이 있다 _____

01 대화를 듣고, 남자가 만든 표를 고르시오.

02 대화를 듣고, 캠프장에 관해 언급되지 <u>않은</u> 것을 고르시오.

① 텐트 설치 위치
② 불 사용 위치
③ 화장실 위치
④ 소등 시각
⑤ 야생 동물 발견 시 신고 방법

03 대화를 듣고, 남자의 마지막 말에 담긴 의도로 가장 적절한 것을 고르시오.

① 초대   ② 거절   ③ 부탁
④ 염려   ⑤ 동의

04 대화를 듣고, 두 사람이 만나기로 한 시각을 고르시오.

① 4:00 p.m.   ② 4:30 p.m.   ③ 5:00 p.m.
④ 5:30 p.m.   ⑤ 6:00 p.m.

05 대화를 듣고, 두 사람이 대화하는 장소로 가장 적절한 곳을 고르시오.

① 공항   ② 서점   ③ 우체국
④ 주유소   ⑤ 여행 안내소

06 다음 그림의 상황에 가장 적절한 대화를 고르시오.

①   ②   ③   ④   ⑤

07 대화를 듣고, 남자가 여자에게 부탁한 일로 가장 적절한 것을 고르시오.

① 과학 숙제 도와주기
② 노트북 컴퓨터 고쳐주기
③ 노트북 컴퓨터 빌려주기
④ 컴퓨터 수리점에 데려다주기
⑤ 노트북 컴퓨터 배터리 충전하기

08 다음을 듣고, 정원 관리 시 고려 사항에 관해 언급되지 않은 것을 고르시오.

① 위치   ② 토질   ③ 소요 시간
④ 식물 배치   ⑤ 정원 크기

09 다음을 듣고, 무엇에 관한 설명인지 고르시오.

① 오븐   ② 인터폰   ③ 소화기
④ 가스레인지   ⑤ 스프링클러

10 다음을 듣고, 두 사람의 대화가 <u>어색한</u> 것을 고르시오.

①   ②   ③   ④   ⑤

11 대화를 듣고, 남자가 이번 주말에 할 일로 가장 적절한 것을 고르시오.

① 휴식 취하기   ② 시험공부하기
③ 할머니 댁 방문하기   ④ 현장 학습 가기
⑤ 동아리 모임 참석하기

12 다음 배치도를 보면서 대화를 듣고, 두 사람이 선택할 구역을 고르시오.

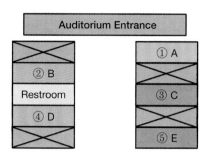

13 대화를 듣고, 오늘 날짜를 고르시오.

① 5월 8일　　② 5월 9일　　③ 5월 10일
④ 5월 14일　　⑤ 5월 15일

14 대화를 듣고, 여자가 겨울 방학에 한 일로 가장 적절한 것을 고르시오.

① 아이 돌보기
② 친척들과 놀기
③ 독서 감상문 쓰기
④ 부족한 과목 공부하기
⑤ 도서관에서 자원봉사하기

15 다음을 듣고, 방송의 목적으로 가장 적절한 것을 고르시오.

① 휴교를 공지하려고
② 폭설 피해 상황을 알리려고
③ 방학 기간 연장을 발표하려고
④ 폭설에 대비할 것을 당부하려고
⑤ 폭설 시 안전 수칙을 설명하려고

16 대화를 듣고, 여자가 지불할 금액을 고르시오.

① $320　　② $360　　③ $390
④ $420　　⑤ $450

17 대화를 듣고, 남자의 마지막 말에 대한 여자의 응답으로 가장 적절한 것을 고르시오.

Woman: _____

① Yes, it's a very good place.
② I want to go there someday.
③ It's cheaper if you take a train.
④ It takes two hours to get there.
⑤ I recommend that you go to Bulguksa.

[18 - 19] 대화를 듣고, 여자의 마지막 말에 대한 남자의 응답으로 가장 적절한 것을 고르시오.

18 Man: _____

① I wish I were older.
② Do you have a ticket?
③ You can go without me.
④ Then can I ride it alone?
⑤ I didn't know that you don't like roller coasters.

19 Man: _____

① I hope she can get a new job.
② Maybe you can visit her again, instead.
③ That would be nice, but I don't have much time.
④ I'm looking forward to visiting the museum.
⑤ Right. I'm glad she found a job, but I really wanted to see her.

20 다음 상황 설명을 듣고, Jake가 직원에게 할 말로 가장 적절한 것을 고르시오.

Jake: _____

① I want to get a refund.
② I'd like to cancel my order.
③ This jacket is too big for me.
④ Could I exchange this jacket for a large?
⑤ What color would you recommend for me?

01 그림 정보 파악

대화를 듣고, 남자가 만든 표를 고르시오.

M: Jisun, would you like to come to a play? It's a performance by our drama club.

W: Sure, I'd love to.

M: I'll be 1) _____ _____ _____ . Here is a ticket. You can see the name of the play at the top. It's *Romeo and Juliet*.

W: This ticket looks great.

M: Really? Actually, 2) _____ _____ _____ _____ .

W: I like the 3) _____ _____ _____ _____ _____ .

M: It's the symbol of our club. It represents joy. We want the audience to feel joyful while watching our plays.

W: It's very nice. When is the play?

M: The date is 4) _____ _____ _____ of the rose, and the place is under it.

W: Oh, I see it now! I'll definitely come.

02 언급되지 않은 내용 찾기

대화를 듣고, 캠프장에 관해 언급되지 <u>않은</u> 것을 고르시오.

① 텐트 설치 위치
② 불 사용 위치
③ 화장실 위치
④ 소등 시각
⑤ 야생 동물 발견 시 신고 방법

M: Hi. Can I help you?

W: We need a place to stay for the night.

M: Just one night?

W: Yes, we'll be leaving in the morning.

M: Okay. You can 1) _____ _____ _____ _____ over there.

W: Where? In front of that big tree?

M: No, next to that picnic table. You can 2) _____ _____ _____ by those rocks.

W: Great. Is there a bathroom nearby?

M: Yes. It's just down that road.

W: Oh, I see it. Thank you.

M: No problem. Please 3) _____ _____ _____ _____ _____ before midnight and don't make a lot of noise. Lastly, 4) _____ _____ _____ _____ .

W: All right. We won't.

03 의도 파악

대화를 듣고, 남자의 마지막 말에 담긴 의도로 가장 적절한 것을 고르시오.

① 초대　　② 거절　　③ 부탁
④ 염려　　⑤ 동의

W: Hi, Jihun. You look worried. What's the matter?

M: My brother is coming from the US to visit Korea. I told him that I'd 1) _____ _____ _____ at the airport, but I don't think I can.

W: Oh, you've got something to do?

M: Yes, I 2) _____ _____ _____ _____ _____.

W: When is he arriving?

M: At 4:00 p.m. this Saturday.

W: Saturday? Well, I 3) _____ _____ _____ _____ for Saturday yet.

M: Oh, really? Then 4) _____ _____ _____ _____ _____ pick him up for me.

04 숫자 정보 파악

대화를 듣고, 두 사람이 만나기로 한 시각을 고르시오.

① 4:00 p.m.　② 4:30 p.m.　③ 5:00 p.m.
④ 5:30 p.m.　⑤ 6:00 p.m.

M: Monday is Parents' Day.

W: I know. Why don't we buy a nice gift for Mom and Dad?

M: That's a good idea. Let's go to the mall and 1) _____ _____ _____ _____ today.

W: Okay. How about meeting after school at 4:00 p.m.?

M: Hmm… Can we 2) _____ _____ _____? I have a piano lesson at 4:30.

W: Sure. When does it finish?

M: It 3) _____ _____ _____.

W: And I guess it would 4) _____ _____ _____ _____ to get to the mall from there.

M: Right.

W: Okay. I'll see you then at the mall.

M: See you.

05 장소 추론 🇬🇧

대화를 듣고, 두 사람이 대화하는 장소로 가장 적절한 곳을 고르시오.

① 공항 ② 서점 ③ 우체국
④ 주유소 ⑤ 여행 안내소

M: Hello. What can I do for you?

W: I'd like to 1) _____ _____ _____.

M: Okay. What's in it?

W: Just some books. I'm sending them to a friend in Australia.

M: How would you like to send it?

W: If I 2) _____ _____ _____ _____ _____, when will it arrive?

M: It will get there 3) _____ _____ _____.

W: Okay, then I'll send it by regular mail.

M: Let's see... It's 2 kg. That 4) _____ _____ _____.

W: All right. Here you are.

06 그림 상황에 적절한 대화 찾기 🇬🇧

다음 그림의 상황에 가장 적절한 대화를 고르시오.

① ② ③ ④ ⑤

*Focus on Sound receipt

p는 묵음이어서 [리씨트]로 발음된다.

① W: Your camera is really good. Where did you get it?

M: I 1) _____ _____ _____ an online shopping mall.

② W: Wow! This picture is really amazing.

M: Yes. It was painted by Picasso.

③ W: I'd like to 2) _____ _____ _____. I don't like it.

M: Sure. Could you show me the *receipt?

④ W: You're 3) _____ _____ _____ _____ _____ here.

M: Oh, I'm sorry. I didn't know that.

⑤ W: Could you 4) _____ _____ _____ _____?

M: Here it is.

07 부탁한 일 파악

대화를 듣고, 남자가 여자에게 부탁한 일로 가장 적절한 것을 고르시오.

① 과학 숙제 도와주기
② 노트북 컴퓨터 고쳐주기
③ 노트북 컴퓨터 빌려주기
④ 컴퓨터 수리점에 데려다주기
⑤ 노트북 컴퓨터 배터리 충전하기

★ Focus on Sound   assignment

[g]가 묵음이어서 [어싸인먼트]로 발음된다.

M: Oh no!

W: What's the matter, Henry?

M: My laptop suddenly stopped.

W: Do you think it's because of a virus or because the battery is low?

M: I don't know. 1) _____ _____ _____ this morning, so it shouldn't be because of the battery. I need to 2) _____ _____ _____ _____ _____ _____.

W: Yes, you should.

M: But I need a laptop for a class presentation this afternoon. 3) _____ _____ _____ _____?

W: Sure. I don't need it this afternoon.

M: Thank you very much.

W: But I need it tonight to do my science ★assignment.

M: Okay. I'll 4) _____ _____ _____ as soon as I finish my presentation.

08 언급되지 않은 내용 찾기

다음을 듣고, 정원 관리 시 고려 사항에 관해 언급되지 않은 것을 고르시오.

① 위치   ② 토질   ③ 소요 시간
④ 식물 배치   ⑤ 정원 크기

W: When starting a garden, the most important thing to determine is the location. Ideally, the garden should be placed in the area where it will 1) _____ _____ _____ _____. It is also important to 2) _____ _____ _____ _____ of the area. Drawing up a plan is another way to help increase the potential of the garden. The tallest plants should be planted in the north of the garden to 3) _____ _____ _____ _____.
The size of the garden is also important. If there's not much space, containers are another option for growing plants.

09 화제 파악 🏴

다음을 듣고, 무엇에 관한 설명인지 고르시오.

① 오븐   ② 인터폰   ③ 소화기
④ 가스레인지   ⑤ 스프링클러

M: This device is now found in almost every building. In fact, in many countries, all public buildings are required to 1) _____ _____ _____ _____. It can be seen in areas such as hallways or offices. Sometimes it is kept in a glass safety box. It can contain gas, liquid, foam, or powder. It is usually red. Many people learn how to use it 2) _____ _____ _____. It is used to 3) _____ _____ _____ _____.

10 어색한 대화 찾기

다음을 듣고, 두 사람의 대화가 <u>어색한</u> 것을 고르시오.

①   ②   ③   ④   ⑤

① M: How's the weather?

     W: It looks like it's going to rain.

② M: What does Sam 1) _____ _____?

     W: He likes to play golf.

③ M: That was the worst movie I've ever seen.

     W: You 2) _____ _____ _____ _____.

④ M: How many brothers and sisters do you have?

     W: I'm an only child.

⑤ M: What would you do if you 3) _____ _____ _____?

     W: I would buy a nice car.

11 할 일 파악

대화를 듣고, 남자가 이번 주말에 할 일로 가장 적절한 것을 고르시오.

① 휴식 취하기   ② 시험공부하기
③ 할머니 댁 방문하기   ④ 현장 학습 가기
⑤ 동아리 모임 참석하기

W: Hi, Arnold. Are you going to the science club meeting this weekend?

M: Yes, I am. I'm the club president, so I have to be there. But it's not this weekend.

W: Oh, really? 1) _____ _____ _____ _____?

M: Yes, we're having it on Monday instead. Several members are 2) _____ _____ _____ _____ _____ this weekend.

W: I see. Are you going on the field trip?

M: No. I'll be 3) _____ _____ _____ _____ _____ instead. How about you?

W: I have to 4) _____ _____ _____. I have a big test next week.

M: Oh, I'm sorry to hear that.

12 위치 찾기

다음 배치도를 보면서 대화를 듣고, 두 사람이 선택할 구역을 고르시오.

W: Look at this map. There are five zones available. Which zone do you think would be best for us?

M: We will be selling popcorn and beverages, so I don't want the zone 1) _____ _____ _____ _____.

W: Me neither. How about Zone E?

M: I don't think it's good. It is 2) _____ _____ _____ _____ where the movies will be shown. People going to a movie are likely to want popcorn and drinks.

W: Yes, so the zone next to the 3) _____ _____ _____ _____ would be best.

M: That's what I think too.

13 세부 정보 파악

대화를 듣고, 오늘 날짜를 고르시오.

① 5월 8일　② 5월 9일　③ 5월 10일
④ 5월 14일　⑤ 5월 15일

W: Hey, Jinho. Have you moved into your new house yet?

M: Not yet. We'll move in next week.

W: Which day next week?

M: Tuesday.

W: Tuesday? Is that 1) _____ _____ ?

M: No, that's Monday. We're 2) _____ _____ _____ _____ .

W: Oh, that's right. So there are 3) _____ _____ _____ _____ before you move. Have you packed everything?

M: No, I'll 4) _____ _____ _____ _____ .

W: Let me know if there's anything I can help you with.

14 한 일 파악

대화를 듣고, 여자가 겨울 방학에 한 일로 가장 적절한 것을 고르시오.

① 아이 돌보기
② 친척들과 놀기
③ 독서 감상문 쓰기
④ 부족한 과목 공부하기
⑤ 도서관에서 자원봉사하기

M: Hey, Judy. How was your winter vacation?

W: It was great. I spent it with a lot of kids.

M: What kids? Did you 1) _____ _____ _____ _____ ?

W: No.

M: Hmm... Did you 2) _____ _____ _____ _____ ?

W: No.

M: Then what did you do? Don't keep me guessing.

W: I 3) _____ _____ _____ _____ to help with the reading program.

M: What did they have you do?

W: I 4) _____ _____ _____ _____ and listened to children describe the books they read.

15 목적 파악

다음을 듣고, 방송의 목적으로 가장 적절한 것을 고르시오.

① 휴교를 공지하려고
② 폭설 피해 상황을 알리려고
③ 방학 기간 연장을 발표하려고
④ 폭설에 대비할 것을 당부하려고
⑤ 폭설 시 안전 수칙을 설명하려고

W: This is a notice for all local students. As you know, due to the severe weather, we have decided to close 1) _____ _____ _____ _____ _____ . Temperatures have dropped to –25°C. And with nearly a meter of snow on the streets, travel has become impossible. For these reasons, we have decided that it would be safer for 2) _____ _____ _____ _____ _____ rather than go to school. The number of class hours will be adjusted by shortening the vacation period. The 3) _____ _____ _____ _____ until further notice. Please listen for updates notices and take care.

16 숫자 정보 파악 🇬🇧

대화를 듣고, 여자가 지불할 금액을 고르시오.

① $320   ② $360   ③ $390
④ $420   ⑤ $450

[Phone rings.]

M: Hello, how may I help you?

W: I'd like to 1) _____ _____ _____ .

M: Okay. What is your name and reservation number?

W: It's Ruby Robinson, and my reservation number is 15366.

M: Let me check. You reserved a sports sedan 2) _____ _____ _____ . It's $80 a day.

W: Yes. And I also asked for a child seat.

M: That's right. It's 3) _____ _____ _____ . If you download the coupon from our website, you can 4) _____ _____ _____ _____ on the total.

W: Okay, I will.

M: Don't forget to bring your driver's license when you pick up the car.

W: Thanks.

17 마지막 말에 이어질 응답 찾기 🇬🇧

대화를 듣고, 남자의 마지막 말에 대한 여자의 응답으로 가장 적절한 것을 고르시오.

Woman: _____

① Yes, it's a very good place.
② I want to go there someday.
③ It's cheaper if you take a train.
④ It takes two hours to get there.
⑤ I recommend that you go to Bulguksa.

W: Martin, I heard you're going to Gyeongju.

M: Yes. I'm going there 1) _____ _____ _____ _____ .

W: When are you going?

M: I'm going there by KTX this weekend. I want to look around the city before I come back.

W: Great. 2) _____ _____ _____ _____ _____ in Gyeongju.

M: Oh, have you been there?

W: Yes, I've taken the train to Gyeongju many times. My grandparents live there.

M: Really? Can you recommend 3) _____ _____ _____ _____ _____ ?

W: I recommend that you go to Bulguksa.

18 마지막 말에 이어질 응답 찾기

대화를 듣고, 여자의 마지막 말에 대한 남자의 응답으로 가장 적절한 것을 고르시오.

Man: _____

① I wish I were older.
② Do you have a ticket?
③ You can go without me.
④ Then can I ride it alone?
⑤ I didn't know that you don't like roller coasters.

M: Mom, can Jimmy and I ride the roller coaster?
W: Sure. But I won't come with you. I don't like roller coasters.
M: That's okay. We 1) _____ _____ _____ _____ .
W: All right. Where is it?
M: Right over there.
W: Oh, honey. Did you read that sign?
M: No. Oh, it says that 2) _____ _____ _____ _____ _____ this roller coaster.
W: Right. You're old enough, but Jimmy 3) _____ _____ _____ .
M: Then can I ride it alone?

19 마지막 말에 이어질 응답 찾기

대화를 듣고, 여자의 마지막 말에 대한 남자의 응답으로 가장 적절한 것을 고르시오.

Man: _____

① I hope she can get a new job.
② Maybe you can visit her again, instead.
③ That would be nice, but I don't have much time.
④ I'm looking forward to visiting the museum.
⑤ Right. I'm glad she found a job, but I really wanted to see her.

W: Hi, Brad. Is something wrong?
M: Yes. I just got an email from my friend in Spain.
W: Oh. Didn't you visit her last summer?
M: Yes. It was a wonderful trip. She 1) _____ _____ _____ _____ _____ next month.
W: But she's not coming?
M: No, she's not. She was just 2) _____ _____ _____ at a museum, and it starts next week.
W: I see. So she can't 3) _____ _____ _____ yet.
M: Right. I'm glad she found a job, but I really wanted to see her.

20 상황에 적절한 말 찾기

다음 상황 설명을 듣고, Jake가 직원에게 할 말로 가장 적절한 것을 고르시오.

Jake: _____

① I want to get a refund.
② I'd like to cancel my order.
③ This jacket is too big for me.
④ Could I exchange this jacket for a large?
⑤ What color would you recommend for me?

M: Jake needed a jacket for his school trip next month. He found a nice one on an online shopping mall. The color and style were exactly what he was looking for. He decided to buy it. He usually wears medium-sized jackets, so he 1) _____ _____ . Two days later, he got the jacket. He tried it on, but it was 2) _____ _____ _____ for him. He thinks that a larger jacket would fit him. He wants to return it and 3) _____ _____ _____ . In this situation, what would Jake most likely say to the customer service employee?

01 대화를 듣고, 여자가 구입할 아이스크림을 고르시오.

①   ②   ③

④   ⑤

02 대화를 듣고, 축구 경기에 관해 언급되지 <u>않은</u> 것을 고르시오.

① 경기 날짜   ② 출전 팀
③ 우승 팀   ④ 최종 스코어
⑤ 결승골을 넣은 선수

03 대화를 듣고, 남자가 여자에게 전화한 목적으로 가장 적절한 것을 고르시오.

① 신문에 광고를 내려고
② 신문 구독을 신청하려고
③ 신문 구독 중단을 요청하려고
④ 신문 배달 문제를 해결하려고
⑤ 신문 배달 아르바이트를 하려고

04 대화를 듣고, 두 사람이 탑승하려는 기차의 출발 시각을 고르시오.

① 1:00 p.m. ② 2:00 p.m. ③ 4:00 p.m.
④ 5:00 p.m. ⑤ 9:00 p.m.

05 대화를 듣고, 남자의 심정으로 가장 적절한 것을 고르시오.

① bored   ② pleased   ③ satisfied
④ hopeful   ⑤ regretful

06 다음 그림의 상황에 가장 적절한 대화를 고르시오.

①   ②   ③   ④   ⑤

07 대화를 듣고, 남자가 여자에게 요청한 일로 가장 적절한 것을 고르시오.

① 환불해 주기
② 주문 취소하기
③ 상품 재고 확인하기
④ 배송 날짜 변경하기
⑤ 구입한 물건 교환해 주기

08 다음을 듣고, Hannah Park에 관해 언급되지 <u>않은</u> 것을 고르시오.

① 나이   ② 출생지
③ 재학 중인 학교   ④ 첫 출연 작품
⑤ 구사 가능 언어 수

09 다음을 듣고, 무엇에 관한 설명인지 고르시오.

① 설날   ② 단오   ③ 추석
④ 현충일   ⑤ 성탄절

10 다음을 듣고, 두 사람의 대화가 <u>어색한</u> 것을 고르시오.

①   ②   ③   ④   ⑤

11 대화를 듣고, 남자가 대화 직후에 할 일로 가장 적절한 것을 고르시오.

① 축구하기   ② 전화하기
③ 샤워하기   ④ 저녁 먹기
⑤ 배터리 충전하기

12 다음 표를 보면서 대화를 듣고, 내용과 일치하지 <u>않</u>는 것을 고르시오.

Job Application		
①	Name	Jason Han
②	Age	20
③	Experience	Yes ☐ / No ☑
④	Driver's License	Yes ☑ / No ☐
⑤	Available Hours	Weekdays after 6:00 p.m.

13 대화를 듣고, 남자가 여자의 집을 방문할 요일을 고르시오.

① 월요일　　② 화요일　　③ 수요일
④ 목요일　　⑤ 금요일

14 대화를 듣고, 남자가 어제 한 일로 가장 적절한 것을 고르시오.

① 만화방에 가기　　② 휴식 취하기
③ 서점 구경하기　　④ 병원 방문하기
⑤ 만화책 정리하기

15 다음을 듣고, 방송의 목적으로 가장 적절한 것을 고르시오.

① 지난 수업 내용을 요약하려고
② 새로운 소셜 미디어를 홍보하려고
③ 소셜 미디어의 이점을 설명하려고
④ 소셜 미디어의 부작용을 알리려고
⑤ 사이버 폭력의 해결책을 제안하려고

16 대화를 듣고, 남자가 지불할 금액을 고르시오.

① $30　　② $40　　③ $45
④ $55　　⑤ $60

17 대화를 듣고, 여자의 마지막 말에 대한 남자의 응답으로 가장 적절한 것을 고르시오.

Man: _____

① You can just visit the community center.
② If you are interested, why don't you join us?
③ You need to speak English fluently to teach them.
④ Teaching is much more difficult than I thought.
⑤ Once a week. But we'll increase the number of times during the vacation.

[18 - 19] 대화를 듣고, 남자의 마지막 말에 대한 여자의 응답으로 가장 적절한 것을 고르시오.

18 Woman: _____

① Don't worry. I'm a safe driver.
② In that case, let's take the subway.
③ That's right, but today is Saturday.
④ We don't have time to listen to the radio.
⑤ I told you we should have taken the subway.

19 Woman: _____

① Okay, I'm willing to give it a try.
② I didn't know you worked there.
③ It must be difficult having two jobs.
④ I'm sorry, but I didn't hear the news.
⑤ Oh, then it will be helpful for your career, too.

20 다음 상황 설명을 듣고, Katie가 남자에게 할 말로 가장 적절한 것을 고르시오.

Katie: _____

① Where did you buy your ticket?
② Did you buy popcorn and a soda?
③ This room is too dark to see the ticket.
④ Do you want to watch a movie tonight?
⑤ Excuse me. I think you're sitting in my seat.

고난도 Dictation Test 02

정답 및 해설 pp. 102~106

01 그림 정보 파악

대화를 듣고, 여자가 구입할 아이스크림을 고르시오.

W: Hi, I'd like to buy some ice cream.

M: Sure! We have many different varieties of ice cream here.

W: Great! I'll take a double scoop of vanilla and one scoop of strawberry.

M: I'm sorry, but strawberry is ¹⁾ _____ _____ _____ _____ _____ _____.

W: Oh, that's too bad. I really like strawberry. I'll just ²⁾ _____ _____ _____ _____ _____ _____ then.

M: Would you like a cup or a cone?

W: A cup, please.

M: Would you like any toppings?

W: Yes, I'd like ³⁾ _____ _____ _____ _____, please.

M: Okay. Please wait for a moment.

02 언급되지 않은 내용 찾기

대화를 듣고, 축구 경기에 관해 언급되지 않은 것을 고르시오.

① 경기 날짜   ② 출전 팀
③ 우승 팀   ④ 최종 스코어
⑤ 결승골을 넣은 선수

W: Did you go to the soccer game yesterday?

M: Yes. It was great.

W: ¹⁾ _____ _____ _____ ?

M: Brazil and Germany.

W: Wow! Who won?

M: Brazil ²⁾ _____ _____ _____ _____ _____ 2 to 1.

W: Was it an exciting game?

M: Yes, the game was really tight. The ³⁾ _____ _____ _____ until the end of the game.

W: What happened at the end?

M: Anthony ⁴⁾ _____ _____ _____ five minutes before the end of the game. It was dramatic.

W: Wow, I wish I could have seen it.

03 목적 파악

대화를 듣고, 남자가 여자에게 전화한 목적으로 가장 적절한 것을 고르시오.

① 신문에 광고를 내려고
② 신문 구독을 신청하려고
③ 신문 구독 중단을 요청하려고
④ 신문 배달 문제를 해결하려고
⑤ 신문 배달 아르바이트를 하려고

[Phone rings.]

W: Thank you for calling the Daily News. How can I help you?

M: Hi. I subscribe to your newspaper, but I 1) _____ _____ _____ _____ yet.

W: Oh, let me check. Can I 2) _____ _____ _____ _____ _____, please?

M: My name is Ben James, and I live on Grand Avenue in Westville.

W: Oh, there's a new delivery person in charge of the Westville area, and I guess he 3) _____ _____ _____. I'm very sorry.

M: Actually, this isn't the first time. It happened last week as well.

W: I apologize for the mistake. I'll 4) _____ _____ _____ _____ to your house immediately, and I'll make sure that it doesn't happen again.

M: Okay. Thank you.

04 숫자 정보 파악

대화를 듣고, 두 사람이 탑승하려는 기차의 출발 시각을 고르시오.

① 1:00 p.m.　② 2:00 p.m.　③ 4:00 p.m.
④ 5:00 p.m.　⑤ 9:00 p.m.

＊Focus on Sound　skip

[s] 뒤에 [k]가 오면 된소리가 되어 [스킵]이 아닌 [스낍]으로 발음된다.

W: I got my class schedule today. Did you get yours?

M: Yes, here it is. Let's plan our trip.

W: Okay. I don't have a class after one o'clock on Friday. How about you?

M: My last class on Friday 1) _____ _____ _____ p.m.

W: That's too late. We wouldn't arrive in Jeongdongjin until 9:00 p.m.

M: Let's look at the train schedule first.

W: Okay. There are trains from Seoul 2) _____ _____ _____ starting at 2:00 p.m.

M: If I ＊skip my last class, we can take the train 3) _____ _____ _____ p.m.

W: Is that okay?

M: Yes. I can miss class if I 4) _____ _____ _____ _____ _____.

W: Okay. I'll buy the tickets tomorrow then.

대화를 듣고, 남자의 심정으로 가장 적절한 것을 고르시오.

① bored ② pleased ③ satisfied
④ hopeful ⑤ regretful

W: Hi, Eric. You said you needed a new scarf. Why don't we go shopping tomorrow?

M: I'd really love to, but I can't.

W: Do you have something to do?

M: No. Actually, I [1)] _____ _____ _____ _____ on food, so I don't have any money now.

W: You spent all your money on food?

M: Yes. I think I should have been [2)] _____ _____ _____. Next time, I'll be more [3)] _____ _____ _____ _____ _____.

W: Yeah, you never know when you'll need it.

---

06 그림 상황에 적절한 대화 찾기

다음 그림의 상황에 가장 적절한 대화를 고르시오.

① ② ③ ④ ⑤

① W: Why did you bring your umbrella on a sunny day?
   M: The forecast said it would rain.

② W: The snow [1)] _____ _____ _____ _____. Be careful.
   M: Okay, I will.

③ W: Look at the dark clouds in the sky.
   M: There is a [2)] _____ _____ _____ _____.

④ W: There is barely a cloud in the sky.
   M: Yes, it's a good day to [3)] _____ _____ _____.

⑤ W: Do you see that cloud of smoke rising from that house?
   M: It might be on fire!

---

07 요청한 일 파악

대화를 듣고, 남자가 여자에게 요청한 일로 가장 적절한 것을 고르시오.

① 환불해 주기
② 주문 취소하기
③ 상품 재고 확인하기
④ 배송 날짜 변경하기
⑤ 구입한 물건 교환해 주기

[Phone rings.]

W: Ace Car Parts, how can I help you?

M: Hi. I ordered seat covers for my car from your website last week.

W: All right. Were they [1)] _____ _____ _____?

M: Yes, they arrived yesterday. But they [2)] _____ _____ _____ _____ _____.

W: Really? Did we send you the wrong ones?

M: No, I just [3)] _____ _____ _____ _____ _____. I need smaller ones.

W: I see. How about the color and style? Are those okay?

M: Yes, those are fine.

W: Okay. Just send back the wrong seat covers, and I'll [4)] _____ _____ _____ _____ to you.

다음을 듣고, Hannah Park에 관해 언급되지 않은 것을 고르시오.

① 나이
② 출생지
③ 재학 중인 학교
④ 첫 출연 작품
⑤ 구사 가능 언어 수

W: Today, we're going to interview Hannah Park. She's the young actress who starred in this summer's biggest movie, *Panda Attack*. 1) _____ _____ _____ _____, Ms. Park has appeared in many TV shows and commercials. But *Panda Attack* is only her second movie. She 2) _____ _____ _____ _____ _____, but she grew up here in Los Angeles. She is currently attending Stanford University and can 3) _____ _____ _____. Ladies and gentlemen, please welcome Hannah Park.

---

09 화제 파악

다음을 듣고, 무엇에 관한 설명인지 고르시오.

① 설날
② 단오
③ 추석
④ 현충일
⑤ 성탄절

M: This is one of the most 1) _____ _____ _____ in Korea. Across the country, people travel back to their hometowns to 2) _____ _____ _____ and honor their ancestors. Family members visit the tombs of their ancestors and hold a memorial service to pay their respects. They share food and eat traditional dishes, such as rice cakes. People also make wishes and stay up to 3) _____ _____ _____ _____ in the night sky. This holiday is celebrated on the 4) _____ _____ _____ _____ _____ _____.

---

10 어색한 대화 찾기

다음을 듣고, 두 사람의 대화가 어색한 것을 고르시오.

① ② ③ ④ ⑤

① M: Please 1) _____ _____ _____ _____ your family.
　 W: There are four people in my family.
② M: How much did you 2) _____ _____ _____?
　 W: I didn't pay anything. It was free.
③ M: Will you bring that phone over here?
　 W: In a minute. I need to finish this first.
④ M: I have a fever. What should I do?
　 W: Why don't you 3) _____ _____ _____ before it gets worse?
⑤ M: Are you going to play games on the computer tonight?
　 W: No, I'm 4) _____ _____ _____ _____ some friends.

11 할 일 파악

대화를 듣고, 남자가 대화 직후에 할 일로 가장 적절한 것을 고르시오.

① 축구하기   ② 전화하기
③ 샤워하기   ④ 저녁 먹기
⑤ 배터리 충전하기

M: Mom, I'm home.

W: Hi, Paul. Why are you so late today?

M: I 1) _____ _____ _____ _____ _____ after school.

W: Why didn't you call me? Dinner was ready an hour ago, and we've been waiting for you.

M: Sorry, Mom. 2) _____ _____ _____ _____ _____ .

W: Bring an extra battery from now on. Anyway, you must be very hungry. Let's have dinner.

M: Sure. But I think I 3) _____ _____ _____ _____ first. I was sweating a lot. I'll be as quick as I can.

W: Okay.

12 내용 일치 파악 🇬🇧

다음 표를 보면서 대화를 듣고, 내용과 일치하지 <u>않는</u> 것을 고르시오.

Job Application		
①	Name	Jason Han
②	Age	20
③	Experience	Yes ☐ / No ☑
④	Driver's License	Yes ☑ / No ☐
⑤	Available Hours	Weekdays after 6:00 p.m.

[Phone rings.]

W: Hello. Can I help you?

M: Yes, my name is Jason Han. I called earlier about the job.

W: Oh, that's right. How old are you, Jason?

M: 1) _____ _____ _____ _____ _____ .

W: All right. Do you 2) _____ _____ _____ working in an animal hospital?

M: No, I don't. But I have two dogs, and I really love animals.

W: That's good. Can you drive?

M: Well, I don't have a car. But I 3) _____ _____ _____ _____ _____ .

W: All right. Can you work on weekends?

M: No. I'm 4) _____ _____ _____ _____ after 6:00 p.m.

W: I see. Let me talk to the manager, and we'll give you a call back.

13 세부 정보 파악

대화를 듣고, 남자가 여자의 집을 방문할 요일을 고르시오.

① 월요일 ② 화요일 ③ 수요일
④ 목요일 ⑤ 금요일

M: Seyeon, I heard that you got a new dog.

W: Yes, he's a cute little puppy. Would you like to [1) _____ _____ _____ _____ _____] after school this week?

M: I'd love to. What day is good for you?

W: Any day [2) _____ _____ _____ _____]. That's when I go swimming.

M: I see. I have to visit my grandparents this Friday, so I can't come then. And we have to go to Nate's birthday party this Tuesday.

W: Oh, the party [3) _____ _____ _____], not Tuesday.

M: You're right. Then we only have one day when we're both free.

W: Okay. See you then.

14 한 일 파악 🇬🇧

대화를 듣고, 남자가 어제 한 일로 가장 적절한 것을 고르시오.

① 만화방에 가기 ② 휴식 취하기
③ 서점 구경하기 ④ 병원 방문하기
⑤ 만화책 정리하기

W: Hey, Alex. Is everything okay with you? You look like [1) _____ _____ _____ _____].

M: Yeah. I do need rest.

W: Why are you so tired?

M: I [2) _____ _____ _____ _____] yesterday and donated some to charity.

W: Really? You've collected hundreds of comic books.

M: Right. And I [3) _____ _____ _____ _____] of my favorite ones.

W: It must have been hard work.

M: Yeah, [4) _____ _____ _____ _____] hundreds of books.

15 목적 파악

다음을 듣고, 방송의 목적으로 가장 적절한 것을 고르시오.

① 지난 수업 내용을 요약하려고
② 새로운 소셜 미디어를 홍보하려고
③ 소셜 미디어의 이점을 설명하려고
④ 소셜 미디어의 부작용을 알리려고
⑤ 사이버 폭력의 해결책을 제안하려고

W: As I discussed in a previous lesson, social media connects people all around the world. But the [1) _____ _____ _____ _____ _____] are getting worse. According to research, the usage of social media is gradually increasing among teens. More time spent on social media can [2) _____ _____ _____], depression, and exposure to content that is not age appropriate. [3) _____ _____ _____ _____] cannot be ignored. If you find that social media is hurting your life, take a break from it.

16 숫자 정보 파악

대화를 듣고, 남자가 지불할 금액을 고르시오.

① $30   ② $40   ③ $45
④ $55   ⑤ $60

＊Focus on Sound   second one

단어가 nd로 끝날 때는 끝소리 [d]가 탈락되어 [세컨 원]으로 발음된다.

M: Hi. I'm here to buy a gift for my son. It's his birthday next week.

W: We have thousands of computer games for sale. Do you know which game he wants?

M: He likes sports games. Could you recommend some?

W: This basketball game and that soccer game are [1) _____ _____ _____ _____ _____ .

M: How much are they?

W: They are [2) _____ _____ .

M: Well, I'd like to buy both of them, but $60 is [3) _____ _____ _____ .

W: Oh, we have a special sale this week. If you buy two, you [4) _____ _____ _____ the ＊second one.

M: That's excellent. I'll take both, then.

17 마지막 말에 이어질 응답 찾기

대화를 듣고, 여자의 마지막 말에 대한 남자의 응답으로 가장 적절한 것을 고르시오.

Man: _____

① You can just visit the community center.
② If you are interested, why don't you join us?
③ You need to speak English fluently to teach them.
④ Teaching is much more difficult than I thought.
⑤ Once a week. But we'll increase the number of times during the vacation.

M: What are you going to do during winter vacation?

W: I don't know yet. How about you?

M: I'm a member of a volunteering club, so I'll [1) _____ _____ _____ _____ .

W: Oh, really? What kind of work do you usually do?

M: We often go to the community center [2) _____ _____ _____ _____ . Sometimes we teach elderly people who want to learn English.

W: Wow, sounds great! [3) _____ _____ _____ _____ _____ them?

M: Once a week. But we'll increase the number of times during the vacation.

18 마지막 말에 이어질 응답 찾기 🏴󠁧󠁢󠁥󠁮󠁧󠁿

대화를 듣고, 남자의 마지막 말에 대한 여자의 응답으로 가장 적절한 것을 고르시오.

Woman: _____

① Don't worry. I'm a safe driver.
② In that case, let's take the subway.
③ That's right, but today is Saturday.
④ We don't have time to listen to the radio.
⑤ I told you we should have taken the subway.

W: Are you ready to leave?
M: Yes, but I think we should take the subway.
W: Why? It's 1) _____ _____ _____ _____ to the station. My car is right over there. I'll drive.
M: I know. But I'm worried there will 2) _____ _____ _____ _____ _____.
W: It's Saturday. There's not much traffic on Saturday mornings.
M: But I was just listening to the radio. 3) _____ _____ _____ _____ _____ downtown. I don't think we can get to the theater before the movie starts.
W: In that case, let's take the subway.

---

19 마지막 말에 이어질 응답 찾기

대화를 듣고, 남자의 마지막 말에 대한 여자의 응답으로 가장 적절한 것을 고르시오.

Woman: _____

① Okay, I'm willing to give it a try.
② I didn't know you worked there.
③ It must be difficult having two jobs.
④ I'm sorry, but I didn't hear the news.
⑤ Oh, then it will be helpful for your career, too.

W: Hello, Jinsu. Why are you smiling?
M: Hi, Bora! I just found out that I've been 1) _____ _____ _____ _____ _____ for ABC's teen magazine. I worked really hard to 2) _____ _____ _____, so I'm really pleased.
W: What exactly will you be doing?
M: I'll be writing about what happens at my school. The articles will be published in the magazine.
W: Wow. That's great.
M: Yes, it will 3) _____ _____ _____ _____. Actually, I want to 4) _____ _____ _____ _____ one day.
W: Oh, then it will be helpful for your career, too.

---

20 상황에 적절한 말 찾기

다음 상황 설명을 듣고, Katie가 남자에게 할 말로 가장 적절한 것을 고르시오.

Katie: _____

① Where did you buy your ticket?
② Did you buy popcorn and a soda?
③ This room is too dark to see the ticket.
④ Do you want to watch a movie tonight?
⑤ Excuse me. I think you're sitting in my seat.

M: Katie is going to watch a movie. It is a movie that she has wanted to watch for a long time. She 1) _____ _____ _____ _____ _____. She buys some popcorn and a soda to enjoy while watching the movie. She 2) _____ _____ _____ _____ on the ticket and enters the dark auditorium. She looks for her seat. Soon she finds it, but there is already a 3) _____ _____ _____. She checks her ticket again, and it's the correct seat. In this situation, what would Katie most likely say to the man?

Word Test 고난도 실전모의고사 01~02회

A 다음 영어의 우리말 뜻을 쓰시오.

01 adjust

02 amazing

03 beverage

04 determine

05 allowance

06 connect

07 drop

08 organize

09 assignment

10 completely

11 discuss

12 confirm

13 employee

14 block

15 container

16 severe

17 usage

18 previous

19 submit

20 definitely

21 joy

22 skip

23 tomb

24 location

25 gradually

26 barely

27 subscribe

28 appropriate

29 careful

30 cinema

31 shorten

32 further

33 set ~ up

34 put out

35 hang out with

36 run out

37 make a noise

38 give it a try

39 draw up a plan

40 pay one's respect

B 다음 우리말 뜻에 맞는 영어를 쓰시오.

01	땀을 흘리다	21	우울증
02	잠재력	22	미끄러운
03	북쪽	23	무시하다
04	액체	24	불가능한
05	이상적으로	25	여배우
06	언어	26	묶다; 동점을 이루다
07	공연	27	경험
08	조상	28	강당, 객석
09	자선 단체	29	출판하다; 게재하다[싣다]
10	극적인	30	기회; 가능성
11	먹이를 주다	31	노출
12	상징	32	중독
13	갑자기	33	유창하게
14	증가시키다	34	야생 동물
15	토양, 흙	35	부작용
16	십 대	36	득점하다, 골을 넣다
17	예측, 예보	37	복권에 당첨되다
18	장비, 기구	38	휴가를 내다
19	지친, 기진맥진한	39	~로 이어지다
20	친척	40	~에 따르면

지은이

NE능률 영어교육연구소

NE능률 영어교육연구소는 혁신적이며 효율적인 영어 교재를 개발하고
영어 학습의 질을 한 단계 높이고자 노력하는 NE능률의 연구조직입니다.

능률 중학영어 듣기 모의고사 22회 〈Level 3〉

펴 낸 이	주민홍
펴 낸 곳	서울특별시 마포구 월드컵북로 396(상암동) 누리꿈스퀘어 비즈니스타워 10층
	㈜NE능률 (우편번호 03925)
펴 낸 날	2023년 1월 5일 개정판 제1쇄 발행
	2024년 9월 15일 제7쇄
전 화	02 2014 7114
팩 스	02 3142 0356
홈 페 이 지	www.neungyule.com
등 록 번 호	제1-68호
I S B N	979-11-253-4039-3 53740
정 가	15,000원

NE 능률

고객센터

교재 내용 문의 : contact.nebooks.co.kr (별도의 가입 절차 없이 작성 가능)

제품 구매, 교환, 불량, 반품 문의 : 02-2014-7114

☎ 전화문의는 본사 업무시간 중에만 가능합니다.

NE능률 교재 MAP

아래 교재 MAP을 참고하여 본인의 현재 혹은 목표 수준에 따라 교재를 선택하세요.
NE능률 교재들과 함께 영어실력을 쑥쑥~ 올려보세요!
MP3 등 교재 부가 학습 서비스 및 자세한 교재 정보는 www.nebooks.co.kr 에서 확인하세요.

듣기
말하기
쓰기

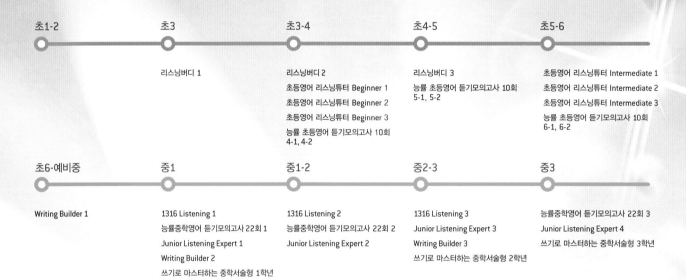

초1-2	초3	초3-4	초4-5	초5-6
	리스닝버디 1	리스닝버디 2 초등영어 리스닝튜터 Beginner 1 초등영어 리스닝튜터 Beginner 2 초등영어 리스닝튜터 Beginner 3 능률 초등영어 듣기모의고사 10회 4-1, 4-2	리스닝버디 3 능률 초등영어 듣기모의고사 10회 5-1, 5-2	초등영어 리스닝튜터 Intermediate 1 초등영어 리스닝튜터 Intermediate 2 초등영어 리스닝튜터 Intermediate 3 능률 초등영어 듣기모의고사 10회 6-1, 6-2

초6-예비중	중1	중1-2	중2-3	중3
Writing Builder 1	1316 Listening 1 능률중학영어 듣기모의고사 22회 1 Junior Listening Expert 1 Writing Builder 2 쓰기로 마스터하는 중학서술형 1학년	1316 Listening 2 능률중학영어 듣기모의고사 22회 2 Junior Listening Expert 2	1316 Listening 3 Junior Listening Expert 3 Writing Builder 3 쓰기로 마스터하는 중학서술형 2학년	능률중학영어 듣기모의고사 22회 3 Junior Listening Expert 4 쓰기로 마스터하는 중학서술형 3학년

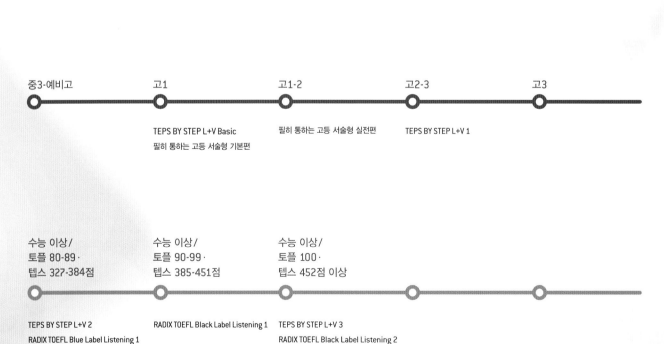

중3-예비고	고1	고1-2	고2-3	고3
	TEPS BY STEP L+V Basic 필히 통하는 고등 서술형 기본편	필히 통하는 고등 서술형 실전편	TEPS BY STEP L+V 1	

수능 이상/ 토플 80-89 · 텝스 327-384점	수능 이상/ 토플 90-99 · 텝스 385-451점	수능 이상/ 토플 100 · 텝스 452점 이상		
TEPS BY STEP L+V 2 RADIX TOEFL Blue Label Listening 1 RADIX TOEFL Blue Label Listening 2	RADIX TOEFL Black Label Listening 1	TEPS BY STEP L+V 3 RADIX TOEFL Black Label Listening 2		

전국 16개 시·도 교육청 주관 **영어듣기평가 실전대비서**

능률 중학영어 듣기 모의고사

22회

정답 및 해설

LEVEL
3

NE 능률

능률 중학영어 듣기 모의고사

22회

정답 및 해설

LEVEL
3

기출문제 01회

pp. 26~27

01 ④	02 ⑤	03 ③	04 ④	05 ②
06 ⑤	07 ②	08 ④	09 ②	10 ①
11 ②	12 ①	13 ④	14 ③	15 ④
16 ③	17 ③	18 ⑤	19 ②	20 ①

01 ④

남: 안녕하세요, 부인. 뭘 도와드릴까요?
여: 안녕하세요, 쿠션을 사고 싶은데요.
남: 알겠습니다. 이것들이 저희가 가지고 있는 제품입니다. 정사각형과 하트 모양이 있어요.
여: 아, 이 하트 모양들이 마음에 들어요. 이들 중 하나를 살게요.
남: 알겠습니다. 그리고 무늬가 없는 것과 줄무늬인 것 두 가지 스타일이 있어요.
여: 음, 줄무늬인 게 더 좋아요.
남: 알겠습니다. 그것들 중 하나에는 'LOVE' 글자가 있어요.
여: 없는 게 더 좋아요. 이걸로 할게요.
남: 알겠습니다.

해설 여자는 하트 모양 중에 줄무늬이고 'LOVE' 글자가 없는 쿠션을 구입하기로 했다.

어휘 plain [plein] 명백한; *무늬가 없는 striped [straipt] 줄무늬의

02 ⑤

여: 여보, 세계 음식 축제에 관한 이 포스터 좀 봐요.
남: 아, 5월 초에 열리는 연례 축제네요, 맞죠?
여: 네. 올해는 서울 그랜드 호텔에서 열릴 거예요. 그러니까 우리가 갈 수 있어요.
남: 잘됐네요. 아이들을 위한 특별 프로그램이 있나요?
여: 아, 여기 요리 프로그램이 있다고 되어 있어요.
남: 멋지네요. 우리 아이들이 아주 좋아할 거예요.
여: 네. 그리고 다음 주말까지 구매하면 입장권이 한 장에 겨우 8달러밖에 하지 않아요.
남: 좋아요! 오늘 삽시다!

해설 개최 시기(매년 5월 초), 행사 장소(서울 그랜드 호텔), 프로그램(아이들을 위한 요리 프로그램), 참가비(다음 주말까지 구매 시 8달러)에 관해서는 언급되었으나, 기념품은 언급되지 않았다.

어휘 annual [ǽnjuəl] 매년의, 연례의 early [ə́ːrli] 초기의

03 ③

[전화벨이 울린다.]
남: 안녕하세요, 24 Design Office입니다.
여: 안녕하세요, Top 중학교인데요. 이메일로 보내 주신 포스터 받았어요.
남: 네. 어떠세요?
여: 좋긴 한데요, 약간 변경을 했으면 해요.
남: 네. 뭔지 알려 주세요.
여: 포스터 제목 색상이 충분히 밝지 않은 것 같아요. 읽기가 어려워요.
남: 무슨 뜻인지 알겠어요.
여: 노란색이 더 나을 것 같다는 생각이에요.
남: 동의해요. 제목 색상을 회색에서 노란색으로 바꿀게요.
여: 고맙습니다.

해설 여자는 남자가 보내 준 포스터의 제목 색상이 밝지 않아서 노란색으로 변경하면 좋겠다고 했다.

어휘 slight [slait] 약간의 change [tʃeindʒ] 변화, 변경

04 ④

여: 안녕하세요, 이 선생님. 시간 좀 있으세요?
남: 물론이지. 무슨 일이니?
여: 제 과제물에 대해 의견을 주실 수 있나요?
남: 그래. 하지만 교사 회의에 가는 길이란다. 내일 오후 3시에 다시 오겠니?
여: 그때는 방과 후 수업이 있어요. 오후 5시에 시간 괜찮으세요?
남: 어디 보자. [잠시 후] 그때는 다른 학생을 만날 예정이야. 오후 4시에 오겠니?
여: 네. 감사합니다. 그때 뵐게요.

해설 여자가 내일 오후 5시에 시간이 괜찮은지 묻자, 남자는 그때 다른 학생을 만날 예정이니 오후 4시에 오라고 했다.

어휘 feedback [fíːdbæk] 피드백, 의견 essay [ései] 수필; *과제물

05 ②

남: 여기 있습니다. 식사 맛있게 하세요.
여: 음… 잠시만요, 이건 제가 주문한 게 아닌데요.
남: 정말요? 확인해 볼게요. [잠시 후] 오, 이런!
여: 무슨 일이죠?
남: 정말 죄송합니다. 요리사가 틀린 음식을 만든 것 같아요.
여: 정말인가요? 이미 20분 넘게 기다렸는걸요.
남: 오늘 정말 바빠서요. 정말 죄송합니다.
여: 그럼, 또 오래 기다려야 하나요?
남: 15분 더 걸릴 것 같습니다.
여: 말도 안 돼요!

해설 20분 넘게 기다렸으나 주문한 것과 다른 음식을 받아 더 기다려야

하는 상황이므로, 여자는 속상할(upset) 것이다.
① 자랑스러운 ③ 겁먹은 ④ 안도하는 ⑤ 고마워하는

어휘 meal [miːl] 식사

06 ⑤

① 남: 좋은 아침입니다, 어떻게 도와드릴까요?
여: 피자를 주문하고 싶어요.
② 남: 저 책들을 제자리에 놓아 주시겠어요?
여: 네. 즉시 그렇게 할게요.
③ 남: 물건을 교환하시겠어요, 아니면 환불받으시겠어요?
여: 반품하고 싶어요.
④ 남: 이 가방들은 정말 무거워요.
여: 나르는 거 도와드릴게요.
⑤ 남: 주문하신 거 여기 있습니다. 좋은 하루 보내세요.
여: 고맙습니다. 당신도요.

해설 카페에게 점원이 여자가 주문한 음식을 내어주고 있는 상황이다.

어휘 correct [kərékt] 적절한, 옳은 right away 곧바로, 즉시
exchange [ikstʃéindʒ] 교환하다 get a refund 환불받다

07 ②

남: 얘. 뭐 하고 있니?
여: 어버이의 날이라서 엄마 아빠를 위해 요리하고 있어.
남: 좋아하시겠다. 나도 뭔가를 하고 싶은데.
여: 음, 나는 세탁이랑 화장실 청소도 할 계획이야. 그것들 중 하나 할래?
남: 응. 내가 어느 걸 하면 될까?
여: 내가 화장실을 청소하는 동안 세탁을 해 줄래?
남: 그래. 물론이지.

해설 여자는 자신이 화장실을 청소하는 동안 남자에게 세탁을 해 달라고 부탁했다.

어휘 do the laundry 세탁하다

08 ④

여: 안녕하세요, 급우 여러분. 오늘 우리는 인기 소설 〈Miracle〉의 작가 Andy Cooper에 대해서 알아보겠습니다. 그는 1969년 워싱턴에서 태어났습니다. 가난한 가정에서 자랐습니다. 하지만 책에서 희망과 기쁨을 찾았답니다. 그의 취미는 책을 읽고 요약하는 것이었습니다. 그는 19살이었을 때, 내셔널 북 어워드의 최연소 수상자가 되었습니다. 현재 그는 20세기 최고의 작가로 여겨집니다.

해설 출생 년도(1969년), 성장 환경(가난한 가정에서 자람), 취미 생활(책 읽고 요약하기), 수상 경력(내셔널 북 어워드 수상)에 관해서는 언급되었으나, 대학 전공은 언급되지 않았다.

어휘 novel [nάːvl] 소설 summarize [sΛ́məràiz] 요약하다

09 ②

남: 이것은 팀 스포츠입니다. 이것은 세계에서 가장 인기 있는 스포츠 중 하나입니다. 두 팀이 함께 경기합니다. 그들은 대개 넓은 잔디 경기장에서 경기합니다. 선수들은 공을 차서 서로에게 패스합니다. 그들 대부분은 손으로 공을 만질 수 없습니다. 한 팀의 선수 11명 중 오직 한 선수만이 손으로 공을 만질 수 있습니다. 득점하기 위해서 선수들은 공을 차거나 헤딩해서 큰 골대에 넣습니다.

해설 한 팀에 11명의 선수들이 경기하며, 공을 차거나 헤딩해서 골대에 넣어 득점하는 스포츠는 축구이다.

어휘 grass [græs] 풀, 잔디 field [fiːld] 들판; *경기장 kick [kik] 차다 score [skɔːr] 득점하다 head [hed] 머리; *헤딩하다 net [net] 그물[망]; *골대

10 ①

① 남: 너는 어떤 종류의 차를 가장 좋아해?
여: 그들은 여러 종류의 차를 판매해.
② 남: 대구까지 가는 데 얼마나 걸리니?
여: 기차로 두 시간 정도 걸려.
③ 남: 이번 주말에 가장 친한 친구를 만나는 게 기대돼.
여: 그 애를 만나다니 분명 기쁘겠구나.
④ 남: 우리 10시에 만날 수 있을까?
여: 난 안 될 것 같아. 수영 강습이 있어.
⑤ 남: 내가 시험에서 낙제하다니 믿을 수가 없어.
여: 기운 내! 다음에는 훨씬 더 잘할 거야.

해설 어떤 종류의 차를 가장 좋아하는지 물었으므로, 좋아하는 차를 구체적으로 말하는 응답이 이어져야 자연스럽다.

어휘 can't wait to-v ~하는 게 기다려지다[기대되다] fail [feil] 실패하다; *낙제하다

11 ②

남: 여보, 내일 캠핑 가서 정말 신이 나요.
여: 나도요. 텐트랑 침낭 챙겼나요?
남: 네, 챙겼어요.
여: 좋아요. 캠핑 의자랑 탁자는요?
남: 이미 차에 넣었죠.
여: 좋아요. 아직 우리가 필요한 가장 중요한 걸 챙겨야 해요, 바비큐용 고기 말이에요!
남: 맞아요. 고기 사러 갑시다.
여: 지금 내가 혼자 할게요. 당신은 이미 많이 했잖아요.
남: 좋아요. 고마워요.

해설 바비큐용 고기를 사러 가자는 남자의 말에 여자는 자신이 혼자 하겠다고 했다.

어휘 pack [pæk] 꾸리다, 챙기다 sleeping bag 침낭

12 ①

여: 안녕하세요, 뭘 도와드릴까요?
남: 안녕하세요, 제 3살 딸을 위한 아이스크림 케이크를 찾고 있어요.
여: 네. 그 나이 아이들을 위한 이 강아지 모양과 새끼 고양이 모양 케이크가 있어요.
남: 그 애는 고양이를 정말 좋아하니까, 새끼 고양이 케이크로 할게요.
여: 알겠습니다. 초콜릿과 딸기 두 가지 맛으로 나와요.
남: 그 애는 딸기보다 초콜릿을 더 좋아해요. 그러니 초콜릿 케이크로 할게요.
여: 네. 케이크에 메시지를 원하시나요?
남: 아뇨, 괜찮습니다.
여: 알겠습니다. 준비해 드릴게요.

[해설] 남자는 새끼 고양이 모양의 초콜릿 맛 케이크에 메시지는 원하지 않는다고 했다.

[어휘] flavor [fléivər] 맛 prefer A to B B보다 A를 더 좋아하다

13 ④

[휴대전화가 울린다.]
남: 안녕, Sarah.
여: 안녕, Andy. 나 내일 아이스스케이트 타러 갈까 생각 중이었어. 나랑 같이 갈래?
남: 재미있겠다. 언제 가니?
여: 오전 10시로 생각 중이야. 그때 시간 되니?
남: 안 될 것 같아. 여동생 과제를 도와주기로 약속했거든. 오후 1시는 어때?
여: 그 시간에 Emily랑 점심 먹을 거야. 오후 5시 괜찮니?
남: 응. 학교 앞에서 그때 봐.

[해설] 오전 10시에는 남자가 여동생 과제를 도와줘야 하고 오후 1시에는 여자가 점심 약속이 있어서, 두 사람은 오후 5시에 만나기로 했다.

[어휘] promise [prάmis] 약속하다

14 ③

여: 안녕, Dan. 잘 지내니?
남: 안녕, Stacy. 학교 사진 대회에 대해서 들었니?
여: 응. 며칠 전에 그에 관한 포스터 봤어. 난 참가할 거야.
남: 그럴 거라고 생각했어. 사진 촬영 시작했니?
여: 아니 아직. 카메라 화면이 깨져서 못 해.
남: 아, 이런! 수리 중이니?
여: 응. 어제 수리점에 카메라를 맡겼어.
남: 빨리 고쳐서 네가 사진 촬영을 시작할 수 있으면 좋겠다.

[해설] 여자는 카메라 화면이 깨져서 어제 수리점에 맡겼다고 했다.

[어휘] a couple of 둘의, 몇의 enter [éntər] 들어가다; *참가하다 screen [skri:n] 화면 fix [fiks] 고치다 repair shop 수리점

15 ④

남: 안녕하세요! 학생회의 Teo입니다. 이번 주 금요일은 우정의 날입니다. 특별 행사가 있을 예정인데요. 그것에 참여하려면, 친구에게 감사 편지나 사과 편지를 쓰세요. 그런 다음 점심시간 전에 학생회 사무실로 오세요. 거기서 장미 한 송이를 가져가서 편지와 함께 친구에게 주면 됩니다. 감사합니다.

[해설] 우정의 날 특별 행사에 참여하려면 어떻게 해야 하는지 알려 주고 있다.

[어휘] student council 학생회 friendship [fréndʃip] 우정 take part in ~에 참여[참가]하다 apology [əpάlədʒi] 사과

16 ③

여: Blue 수영장에 오신 걸 환영합니다. 어떻게 도와드릴까요?
남: 안녕하세요. 저와 제 아들을 수영 수업에 등록하고 싶어요.
여: 알겠습니다. 아드님이 몇 살이죠?
남: 8살이에요.
여: 그렇군요. 성인 수업은 70달러이고 어린이 수업은 40달러예요.
남: 알겠습니다. 함께 등록하면 할인이 있나요?
여: 네. 총액에서 5달러 할인받으실 거예요.
남: 좋네요. 그럼 저희 둘 다 수업에 등록할게요. 여기 제 신용 카드요.

[해설] 성인 수업 70달러에 어린이 수업 40달러로 총 110달러인데 함께 등록하여 5달러 할인받으므로, 105달러를 지불할 것이다.

[어휘] sign up ~ for ~을 …에 등록시키다 off [ɔ:f] 할인하여 total [tóutl] 총액, 합계

17 ③

남: Nancy, 의사 선생님께서 네 발목이 그렇게 나쁘지 않다고 말씀하셔서 다행이야.
여: 저도요. 아빠.
남: 내가 가서 차를 가져오는 동안 여기 남아 있지 그러니?
여: 아, 그러니까 저더러 여기 있으라고요?
남: 그래. 그게 너한테 좋을 거야.
여: 음, 차까지 걸어가도 괜찮은데요.
남: 넌 걷는 건 피하려고 해야 해. 내가 몇 분이면 돌아올 거야.
여: 알겠어요. 오실 때까지 여기서 기다릴게요.

[해설] 남자는 차를 가져오는 동안 여자가 그 자리에서 기다리길 계속해서 권유하고 있으므로, 이를 받아들이는 응답이 가장 적절하다.
① 좋아요. 차까지 함께 걸어가요.
② 네. 함께 산책하고 싶어요.
④ 좋은 생각이에요. 제가 우리를 태울 택시를 부를게요.
⑤ 물론이죠. 차를 가지고 바로 돌아올게요.

[어휘] relieved [rilí:vd] 안도하는, 다행으로 여기는 ankle [ǽŋkl] 발목 mind [maind] 꺼리다 avoid [əvɔ́id] 피하다 [문제] pick up ~을 태우다

18 ⑤

여: Tom, 어떤 방과 후 수업을 등록했니?
남: 테니스 수업. 너는?
여: 나도 그거 들을 거야!
남: 잘됐다! 자기 라켓을 가져와야 한다는 거 봤니?
여: 응. 그래서 어제 온라인으로 하나 주문했어.
남: 어떤 웹 사이트에서? 나도 하나 사야 하거든.
여: 기억이 안 나. 내 전화기에서 링크를 찾아볼게. *[잠시 후]* 아, 찾았다.
남: 잘됐다. 지금 나한테 보내 줘.

[해설] 남자는 여자에게 테니스 라켓을 주문한 웹 사이트가 어딘지 물었고 여자가 전화기에서 웹 사이트 링크를 찾았으므로, 그 링크를 보내 달라는 응답이 가장 적절하다.
　① 고마워. 하지만 나는 이미 괜찮은 걸 갖고 있어.
　② 걱정하지 마. 여기 내 집 주소야.
　③ 아니 아직. 나는 아직 더 연습해야 해.
　④ 좋아. 내일 다시 올게.

[어휘] racket [rǽkit] (테니스 등의) 라켓 link [liŋk] 관련성; *링크

19 ②

여: Toby, 이 기사에서 그러는데 요즘 십 대들이 책을 많이 안 읽는대.
남: 그건 놀라운 일도 아니지. 나는 올해 초에 책을 더 많이 읽으려고 노력했는데, 그러지 못했어.
여: 나는 몇 달 전에 독서회에 가입한 이후로 더 많이 읽을 수 있었어.
남: 정말?
여: 응. 그건 책에 대한 감상을 다른 사람들과 나누게 되기 때문에 책 읽는 걸 재밌게 만들어.
남: 흥미로운데! 나도 가입하고 싶어.
여: 누구든 가입할 수 있어. 우리는 매주 수요일 오후 3시에 도서관에서 만나.
남: 좋아. 그때 거기로 갈게.

[해설] 여자는 독서회 가입에 관심을 보이는 남자에게 모임 시간과 장소를 알려 주었으므로, 모임에 가겠다는 응답이 가장 적절하다.
　① 물론이지. 금요일에 봐.
　③ 미안해. 너는 그 동아리에 가입할 수 없어.
　④ 응. 나는 음악 동아리에 관심이 있어.
　⑤ 아니. 도서관은 수요일에 안 열어.

[어휘] article [ɑ́ːrtikl] 글, 기사 teenager [tíːnèidʒər] 십 대 surprising [sərpráiziŋ] 놀라운 share [ʃɛər] 나누다, 공유하다

20 ①

남: Ryan은 중학생입니다. 오늘 그는 영어 시험 때문에 학교 도서관에서 공부하고 있습니다. 너무 더워서, 사서 Amy 선생님은 에어컨을 켭니다. 몇 시간 후에, Ryan은 정말 춥습니다. 그래서 Amy 선생님에게 잠깐 에어컨을 정지시킬 수 있는지 여쭤보고 싶습니다. 이런 상황에서, Ryan은 Amy 선생님에게 뭐라고 말하겠습니까?
Ryan: Amy 선생님, 잠시 에어컨을 꺼 주실 수 있나요?

[해설] Ryan은 너무 추워서 사서 선생님께 잠시 에어컨을 정지시킬 수 있는지 묻고 싶다고 했다.
　② 도서관이 너무 시끄러운 것 같아 걱정이에요.
　③ 언제 에어컨을 청소하셨나요?
　④ 이 과학책을 복사해도 괜찮나요?
　⑤ 에어컨이 고장 난 것 같아요.

[어휘] librarian [laibrɛ́ːəriən] 사서 turn on ~을 켜다 air conditioner 에어컨 [문제] turn off ~을 끄다 for a while 잠시 동안 noisy [nɔ́izi] 시끄러운 copy [kɑ́pi] 복사하다

Dictation Test 01

pp. 28~35

01　1) these heart-shaped ones 2) prefer a striped one
　　3) the one without it

02　1) held in early May 2) special programs for kids
　　3) only 8 dollars each

03　1) make a slight change 2) hard to read
　　3) change the color

04　1) give me feedback 2) come back at 3 p.m.
　　3) come at 4 p.m.

05　1) made the wrong thing 2) wait a long time again
　　3) take another 15 minutes

06　1) I'd like to order 2) exchange the items
　　3) Here's your order

07　1) want to do something 2) cleaning the bathroom
　　3) do the laundry

08　1) was born in 2) reading and summarizing books
　　3) the youngest winner

09　1) big grass field 2) by kicking it
　　3) with their hands 4) into a large net

10　1) How long does it take 2) can't wait to see
　　3) failed the test

11　1) packed the tent 2) put them in the car
　　3) go shopping for the meat

12　1) go for a kitten cake 2) come in two flavors
　　3) prefers chocolate to strawberry

13　1) thinking of going ice skating 2) Are you free
　　3) Is 5 p.m. okay

14 1) going to enter it 2) getting it fixed
   3) to the repair shop
15 1) thank-you or apology letter
   2) come to the student council office
   3) pick up a rose
16 1) 70 dollars 2) 40 dollars 3) sign up together
   4) get 5 dollars off
17 1) Why don't you stay here 2) don't mind walking
   3) I'll be back
18 1) bring your own racket 2) ordered one online
   3) Let me find the link
19 1) joined a book club 2) makes reading books fun
   3) meet every Wednesday
20 1) turns on the air conditioner 2) feels really cold
   3) stop the air conditioner

기출문제 02회

pp. 36~37

01 ③	02 ②	03 ⑤	04 ⑤	05 ③
06 ①	07 ①	08 ④	09 ④	10 ③
11 ①	12 ⑤	13 ⑤	14 ①	15 ①
16 ④	17 ③	18 ④	19 ②	20 ②

01 ③

남: 안녕하세요, 도와드릴까요?

여: 안녕하세요. 제 7살 아들을 위한 자전거를 찾고 있어요.

남: 네. 바구니가 있는 자전거를 원하시나요, 아니면 없는 자전거를 원하시나요?

여: 음… 바구니가 있는 자전거가 더 편리할 것 같아요.

남: 좋습니다. 그러면 이것들 중 하나를 선택하시면 됩니다. 줄무늬가 있는 것과 없는 게 있어요. 이것들 모두 인기 있습니다.

여: 모두 멋져 보이지만, 줄무늬인 게 더 좋을 것 같네요.

남: 좋은 선택이에요! 자, 뒤에 보조 바퀴가 있는 게 필요하신가요?

여: 네. 이제 막 자전거 타는 법을 배우기 시작했거든요. 그러니까 보조 바퀴가 있는 걸로 할게요.

남: 네. 아드님이 이 자전거를 마음에 들어 하면 좋겠네요.

[해설] 여자는 바구니와 보조 바퀴가 있는 줄무늬 자전거를 구입하기로 했다.

[어휘] basket [bǽskit] 바구니 convenient [kənvíːnjənt] 편리한 training wheel 보조 바퀴

02 ②

남: 얘, Laura. 너 전에 Calming Soap 써 봤지, 그렇지?

여: 응, 늘 그걸 사용해. 왜?

남: Irene의 생일 선물로 비누를 좀 사 줄까 생각 중이거든.

여: 좋은 생각이야. 그건 진정 효과로 유명해.

남: 정말? Irene이 딱 그런 걸 원한다고 말했거든.

여: 그렇다면 그 애가 아주 좋아할 거야. 가게에 가면 다양한 향기를 찾을 수 있어. 모든 비누가 향이 정말 좋은데, 라벤더가 내가 가장 좋아하는 거야.

남: 알려 줘서 고마워. 얼마인지 아니?

여: 응. 개당 7달러인데, 정말 그만한 가치가 있어.

남: 아, 그렇구나. 각기 다른 모양으로 나오니?

여: 물론이지. 고를 수 있는 많은 종류의 모양이 있어.

남: 알았어, 고마워.

[해설] 효과(진정 효과), 향기(다양한 향기), 가격(개당 7달러), 모양(많은 종류의 모양)에 관해서는 언급되었으나, 무게는 언급되지 않았다.

[어휘] be well known for ~로 잘 알려져 있다 scent [sent] 향기 totally [tóutəli] 완전히 worth [wəːrθ] 가치가 있는

03 ⑤

[전화벨이 울린다.]

여: 안녕하세요. Gentlemen Shoes Company입니다.

남: 안녕하세요, 온라인으로 검은색 신발 한 켤레를 주문했는데요, 흰색 신발을 대신 받았어요. 제가 주문한 검은색 신발을 보내 주시겠어요?

여: 아, 정말요? 주문 번호가 어떻게 되나요?

남: 확인해 볼게요. [잠시 후] AB213이에요.

여: [타이핑 소리] 아, 배송 착오가 있었던 것 같아요. 불편을 드려 정말 죄송합니다. 가능한 한 빨리 흰색 신발을 수거하고 검은색 신발 한 켤레를 새로 보내 드리겠습니다.

남: 네. 이번에는 맞는 걸로 보내 주세요.

여: 물론입니다! 그리고 이후 주문에 쓰실 수 있는 20퍼센트 할인 쿠폰도 보내 드릴게요. 다시 한번 사과드립니다.

남: 괜찮아요. 쿠폰 고맙습니다.

[해설] 남자는 주문한 신발이 잘못 배송되어 다시 보내 줄 것을 요청했다.

[어휘] delivery [dilívəri] 배달, 배송 inconvenience [ìnkənvíːnjəns] 불편 collect [kəlékt] 모으다; *찾으러 가다 as soon as possible 가능한 한 빨리 apologize [əpɑ́lədʒàiz] 사과하다

04 ⑤

여: 안녕하세요, 커뮤니티 센터에 오신 걸 환영합니다. 어떻게 도와드릴까요?

남: 안녕하세요! 힙합 댄스 강좌를 개설한다고 하던데요. 등록 가능한가요?

여: 네, 가능해요. 금요일에 수업이 두 개 있어요. A반은 오후 3시에 시작하고, B반은 오후 6시에 시작해요. 둘 다 두 시간 동안 하고요.

남: 음… 저는 오후 5시까지 일하기 때문에 A반은 못 들어요.

여: 그렇다면 한 가지 선택권밖에 없는 듯하네요. 등록하시겠어요?

남: 네, 오후 6시에 시작하는 B반으로 선택할게요.

여: 좋습니다. 이 양식을 작성해 주세요.

남: 알겠습니다.

[해설] 남자는 오후 5시까지 일하기 때문에 6시에 시작하는 B반 수업을 선택했다.

[어휘] offer [ɔ́ːfər] 제공하다; *(강좌를) 개설하다 available [əvéiləbl] 이용 가능한 register [rédʒistər] 등록하다 fill out ~을 작성하다

05 ③

남: 안녕, Olivia. 무슨 일이니?

여: 내가 학생회 구성원으로 선발되었어.

남: 와! 잘됐다!

여: 하지만 학생회에 아무도 몰라서 불안해. 전에 이런 걸 해 본 적이 전혀 없거든.

남: 괜찮아. 넌 잘 할 거고 새로운 친구들을 사귈 거야.

여: 다른 구성원들과 잘 지내지 못하면 어쩌지?

남: 괜찮을 거야. 너는 영리하고 재미있고 친절하잖아. 자신감을 가져!

여: 난 모르겠어. 여전히 걱정돼.

[해설] 여자는 학생회 구성원으로 선발되어 잘 할 수 있을지 걱정하고 (concerned) 있다.
① 지루한 ② 신이 난 ④ 안도하는 ⑤ 만족하는

[어휘] select [silékt] 선발하다 nervous [nə́ːrvəs] 불안한, 초조한 get along with ~와 잘 지내다 confident [kánfidənt] 자신감 있는

06 ①

① 남: 도움이 필요한가요?
　여: 저 책이 필요한데요, 닿질 않네요.

② 남: 저 대신 표를 예매해 줄 수 있나요?
　여: 물론이죠. 몇 장이나 필요하신가요?

③ 남: 서점에 언제 올 수 있나요?
　여: 음, 10분 후에 그곳에 도착할 수 있을 것 같아요.

④ 남: 뭐 하고 있나요?
　여: 딸을 위해 책장을 만들고 있어요.

⑤ 남: 이제 수영 시작하자.
　여: 잠깐! 스트레칭 먼저 해야 해.

[해설] 책장 앞에서 여자가 손이 닿지 않는 곳의 책을 꺼내려 하고 있는 상황이다.

[어휘] reach [riːtʃ] 이르다, 닿다 bookshelf [búkʃèlf] 책장

07 ①

[휴대전화가 울린다.]

여: 여보, 식당에 벌써 도착했나요?

남: 거의 다 왔어요. 당신은요?

여: 미안한데요, 약간 늦을 것 같아요.

남: 괜찮아요. 서두를 필요 없어요. 예약을 변경하길 원하나요?

여: 아뇨. 먼저 식사를 주문해 줄래요? 정말 배고파요.

남: 그래요. 뭘 먹을래요?

여: 소고기 구이랑 구운 감자요.

남: 좋아요. 그밖에 다른 건요?

여: 아뇨, 그게 다예요. 곧 봐요.

[해설] 여자는 식당에 늦을 것 같아 식사를 먼저 주문해 달라고 부탁했다.

[어휘] slightly [sláitli] 약간, 조금 roast [roust] 구운

08 ④

여: 안녕하세요, 급우 여러분. 졸업식 위원회 책임자 박지아입니다. 아시다시피, 졸업식이 다음 주 금요일, 2월 8일 오전 10시에 있습니다. 졸업식은 학교 체육관에서 열릴 것입니다. 졸업하는 학생들은 그날 교복을 입어야 합니다. 학교 밴드가 특별 공연을 할 예정입니다. 추가 공지는 다음 주 초에 있을 예정입니다. 고맙습니다.

[해설] 날짜(2월 8일), 장소(학교 체육관), 복장(졸업자는 교복 착용), 특별 공연(학교 밴드의 공연)에 관해서는 언급되었으나, 졸업 인원은 언급되지 않았다.

[어휘] head [hed] 머리; *책임자 graduation ceremony 졸업식 committee [kəmíti] 위원회 performance [pərfɔ́ːrməns] 공연 further [fə́ːrðər] 더 이상의, 추가의 notice [nóutis] 공지

09 ④

남: 이것은 많은 사람들이 즐깁니다. 바쁠 때는 이것을 식사로 먹을 수 있습니다. 이것은 각기 다른 맛과 크기로 나옵니다. 주로 이것은 젓가락으로 먹습니다. 요즘 많은 편의점에서는 손님이 이것을 먹을 수 있도록 작은 탁자를 제공합니다. 이것을 만들려면, 뚜껑을 열고, 수프 가루를 넣고, 끓인 물을 붓습니다. 그러고 나서 뚜껑을 닫고 3분 정도 기다리기만 하면 됩니다. 이제 이것을 즐길 준비가 되었습니다.

[해설] 뚜껑을 열고 수프 가루와 끓인 물을 부어 먹는 음식은 컵라면이다.

[어휘] chopstick [tʃápstik] 젓가락 convenience store 편의점 lid [lid] 뚜껑 powder [páudər] 가루 boiled [bɔild] 끓인

10 ③

① 여: 괜찮니? 너 피곤해 보여.

남: 어젯밤에 너무 더워서 잘 못 잤어.
② 여: 체스 둘래?
　　남: 나중에 해도 될까? 숙제 때문에 좀 바빠.
③ 여: 차로 학교에 데려다주실 수 있나요?
　　남: 물론이지. 같이 학교까지 걸어가자.
④ 여: 창문 열어도 될까요?
　　남: 물론이죠. 신선한 공기가 좀 필요해요.
⑤ 여: 내가 이번에는 시험에 합격할 수 있을 것 같아.
　　남: 분명 합격할 수 있을 거야. 그걸 위해서 정말 열심히 공부했잖아.

[해설] 차로 학교에 데려다줄 수 있는지 물었는데, 긍정의 대답과 함께 같이 걸어가자는 응답은 어색하다.

[어휘] kind of 약간, 조금 pass the exam 시험에 합격하다

11 ①

여: 안녕, Peter! 어디 가니?
남: 안녕, Julie! 도서관에 가는 중이야.
여: 아, 그렇구나. 왜?
남: 내 여동생이 나한테 부탁을 했어. 다리가 부러져서 한동안 아무 데도 못 가거든.
여: 무슨 일이 있었는데?
남: 스케이트보드를 타다 넘어졌어.
여: 아, 너무 심각한 게 아니면 좋겠다. 그래서 그 애를 위해서 책을 좀 갖다 주려고?
남: 아니, 단지 그 애가 빌린 과학책을 반납할 거야. 기한이 오늘까지거든.
여: 그렇구나. 그 애가 금방 회복하길 바랄게.
남: 고마워.

[해설] 남자는 다리를 다친 여동생이 빌린 책을 반납하러 도서관에 가는 길이라고 했다.

[어휘] head to ~로 향하다 ask ~ for a favor ~에게 부탁하다 fall [fɔːl] 넘어지다 (fall-fell-fallen) return [ritə́ːrn] 반납하다 borrow [bárou] 빌리다 due [djuː] (기한이) ~까지인 get well 회복하다

12 ⑤

남: 민희야! 학교 축제 동아리 부스를 어디에 설치할지 결정하자.
여: 그래! 지도를 보자. [잠시 후] B 구역은 어때? 정원에 있어.
남: 응, 하지만 야외는 조금 추울 것 같아.
여: 좋은 지적이네. 그렇다면 A 구역도 좋은 선택이 아니네. C 구역은? 학교 식당 옆이야.
남: 어디 보자. C 구역의 모든 부스가 이미 선택된 것 같아. 그러니 우리는 남아 있는 두 선택지 중에 골라야 해.
여: 음, D 구역은 출입구에서 너무 멀어.
남: 동의해. 그러면 콘서트홀 옆에 있는 한 구역만 남았네.
여: 응. 많은 사람들이 그 구역에 올 거야.

남: 좋아. 그 구역으로 선택하자.

[해설] A 구역과 B 구역은 야외라 추워서 제외하고, C 구역은 남은 부스 자리가 없어서 선택할 수 없고, D 구역은 출입구에서 멀어서 제외하기로 했고, 남은 구역은 콘서트홀 옆에 있는 E 구역이다.

[어휘] set up ~을 설치하다 remaining [riméiniŋ] 남아 있는 entrance [éntrəns] 출입구

13 ⑤

여: 태민아! 영화 〈Space Adventure〉가 드디어 개봉해서 너무 신이 나!
남: 그래. 그건 3D로 봐야지.
여: 동의해. 토요일에 같이 보는 게 어때?
남: 좋아. 내가 전화기로 시간을 확인해 볼게. [잠시 후] 토요일 오후 1시나 4시가 좋아 보여.
여: 오후 4시 어때?
남: 아, 오후 4시 영화표는 이미 매진됐네. 오후 1시로 해 보자.
여: 그런데 그러면 점심 먹을 시간이 충분하지 않을 거야. 저녁은 어때?
남: 음… 저녁 6시에 하나 있는데, 3D가 아니야. 그래도 보고 싶어?
여: 아니. 다른 선택지가 있니?
남: 오후 7시에 하나 있고, 3D야.
여: 좋아, 그걸 보자.

[해설] 두 사람은 오후 7시에 하는 3D 영화를 보기로 했다.

[어휘] release [rilíːs] 풀어주다; *개봉하다 sold out 매진된

14 ①

여: Nick, 지난 금요일에 어머니 생신 파티는 어땠어?
남: 좋았어. 내가 어머니를 위해 만든 컵케이크를 특히 좋아하셨어.
여: 아, 너가 만들었다고?
남: 응. 할머니의 요리법을 따라 했지.
여: 와! 남아 있는 게 있니? 좀 맛보고 싶어.
남: 미안한데, 우리가 주말에 다 먹었어. 하지만 내가 어제 쿠키를 구웠어. 원한다면 쿠키를 좀 줄 수 있어.
여: 그럼 정말 좋지!
남: 그래. 방과 후에 보자.

[해설] 남자는 어제 쿠키를 구웠다며 여자가 원한다면 좀 줄 수 있다고 했다.

[어휘] taste [teist] 맛보다 awesome [ɔ́ːsəm] 기막히게 좋은

15 ①

남: 좋은 오후입니다, 여러분. 모두 저희 놀이공원 Fantasy Land에서 좋은 시간 보내고 계시길 바랍니다. 저희는 여러분이 줄 서서 기다리는 시간을 절약하는 데 도움이 되기 위해서, Express Rider라고 하는 특별 티켓을 판매하고 있습니다. 이 티켓이 있으면, 전혀 기

다리지 않고 줄 앞으로 갈 수 있습니다. 티켓은 장당 10달러입니다. 이 티켓은 어떤 놀이기구든 다섯 번 사용할 수 있습니다. 관심 있다면, 매표소나 웹사이트에서 구입할 수 있습니다. 궁금한 점이 있으면, 고객 센터 1800-3121로 연락 주세요. 감사합니다.

[해설] 기다리지 않고 놀이기구를 이용할 수 있는 특별 티켓을 판매하고 있음을 알리고 있다.

[어휘] amusement park 놀이공원 purchase [pə́ːrtʃəs] 구입하다 ticket office 매표소

16 ④

남: 안녕하십니까! 도움이 필요하세요?
여: 안녕하세요. 이 티셔츠가 마음에 드는데요. 얼마인가요?
남: 20달러인데요, 특별 판촉이 있어요. 하나 사시면, 하나는 공짜입니다.
여: 20달러에 두 장이라고요? 정말 좋은 가격이네요! 이 티셔츠 두 장 살게요.
남: 좋은 선택입니다! 그러면 20달러가 됩니다. 다른 필요하신 게 있나요?
여: 네. 치마도 찾고 있어요. [잠시 후] 음… 이건 얼마예요?
남: 30달러입니다.
여: 좋네요. 이 치마도 살게요.
남: 알겠습니다. 계산대에서 계산 도와드릴게요.

[해설] 티셔츠 두 장이 20달러이고 치마가 30달러이므로, 여자가 지불할 금액은 50달러이다.

[어휘] promotion [prəmóuʃən] 홍보, 판촉 as well 역시, 또한 counter [káuntər] 계산대

17 ③

여: Darren, 지금까지 과제는 어떻게 되어 가?
남: Green 선생님의 사회 과제 말이니?
여: 응. 난 지역 상점들을 보여 주는 인근 지도를 만들기로 결정했어.
남: 멋지다! 난 상점들의 역사에 대해 듣기 위해 지역 상점 주인들을 인터뷰할 거야.
여: 얘, 내가 아이디어가 있어. 우리 과제를 같이 하는 게 어때?
남: 좋은 생각이야. 하지만 그건 개인 과제 아니었니? 가능한지 모르겠어.
여: 팀으로 해도 되는지 Green 선생님께 여쭤봐야 할 것 같아.
남: 좋아. 오늘 오후에 선생님께 말씀드리자.

[해설] 여자는 남자에게 팀으로 과제를 하자고 제안하며 그게 가능한지 선생님께 여쭤보자고 했으므로, 오후에 말씀드리자는 응답이 가장 적절하다.
① 아니, 나는 역사 수업을 좋아하지 않아.
② 물론이야. 넌 지금 쇼핑하러 가도 돼.
④ 글쎄, 우리가 그 선생님의 수업을 들을 수 있을지 모르겠어.
⑤ 물론이지! 그들이 좋은 팀을 이룰 거라는 걸 난 알고 있었어.

[어휘] neighborhood [néibərhùd] 근처, 인근, 이웃 indicate [índikèit] 나타내다, 보여 주다 individual [ìndivídʒuəl] 개인의

18 ④

[휴대전화가 울린다.]
남: 안녕, 여보. 하루 잘 보냈어요?
여: 긴 하루였어요. 오늘 밤 외식하는 게 어때요?
남: 그래요. 중국 음식이나 베트남 음식 어때요?
여: 음… 우리 지난주에 중국 음식을 먹었잖아요. 난 베트남 음식을 먹고 싶어요.
남: 좋아요. 당신의 선택대로 해요.
여: 그래요, 난 국수와 스프링롤이 정말 먹고 싶어요.
남: 나도 그게 좋아요. 저 길 아래 이제 막 개업한 새로운 베트남 음식점에서 먹어 봅시다.
여: 좋은 생각이에요. 내가 예약할게요.

[해설] 남자가 저녁을 먹으러 갈 식당을 제안했으므로, 이를 수락하며 예약하겠다고 말하는 응답이 가장 적절하다.
① 미안하지만, 점심 때 맞춰서 못 가겠어요.
② 내 친구가 유명한 중국 음식 요리사예요.
③ 오늘은 국수를 먹고 싶지 않아요.
⑤ 난 베트남으로 출장을 갈 거예요.

[어휘] eat out 외식하다 feel like v-ing ~하고 싶다 noodle [núːdl] 국수 [문제] make it (어느 장소에 시간 맞춰) 도착하다 business trip 출장

19 ②

여: 안녕, Mark! 너 아주 좋아 보여!
남: 고마워. 요즘 운동을 많이 하고 있거든.
여: 좋네. 나도 건강하게 지내려면 운동을 시작해야 하는데. 넌 어떤 종류의 운동을 하니?
남: 수업이 다 끝나고 매일 학교 체육관에서 배드민턴 쳐.
여: 와! 누구랑 치니?
남: Alice랑 Jake랑 쳐. 아주 즐거운 시간을 보내고 있지.
여: 멋지다! 나도 배드민턴 치고 싶다.
남: 정말? 우리랑 같이 할래? 실은 우리가 칠 사람을 한 명 더 찾고 있거든.
여: 물론이야. 너희들이랑 치고 싶어!

[해설] 배드민턴에 관심을 보이는 여자에게 남자가 함께 하자고 제안했으므로, 이를 수락하는 응답이 가장 적절하다.
① 난 체중을 좀 늘려야 할 것 같아.
③ 넌 건강하게 지내려면 식습관을 조절할 필요가 있어.
④ 아니, 괜찮아. 난 아침에 운동하는 걸 좋아하지 않아.
⑤ 매일 배드민턴 치기를 시작하길 추천해.

[어휘] work out 운동하다 [문제] gain weight 체중을 늘리다 control [kəntróul] 통제하다; *조절하다 diet [dáiət] 식습관

20 ②

여: 이 선생님은 고등학교 음악 교사입니다. 그는 지역 노래 대회를 위해 미나라는 학생을 지도하고 있습니다. 미나는 두 달 넘게 열심히 연습해 오고 있습니다. 대회 당일, 이 선생님은 미나가 자신의 차례를 기다리며 무척 불안해하고 있다는 것을 알게 됩니다. 그래서 이 선생님은 그녀에게 스스로를 믿어야 한다고 말하고 싶습니다. 이런 상황에서, 이 선생님은 미나에게 뭐라고 말하겠습니까?

이 선생님: 미나야, 넌 스스로를 믿어야 해.

해설 이 선생님은 불안해하는 미나에게 스스로를 믿어야 한다고 말하고 싶다고 했다.
① 이 극장은 너무 춥지 않니?
③ 넌 더 연습할 수 있었는데.
④ 너 음악 과제 했니?
⑤ 난 네가 이 대회에 참가하는지 몰랐어.

어휘 coach [koutʃ] 코치하다, 지도하다 contest [kántest] 대회, 시합 turn [təːrn] 돌다; *차례 trust [trʌst] 믿다, 신뢰하다 [문제] believe in ~을 믿다

Dictation Test 02
pp. 38~45

01 1) bicycle with a basket
    2) striped one would be better
    3) with training wheels

02 1) its relaxing effects 2) smell really nice
    3) seven dollars each 4) many kinds of shapes

03 1) ordered a pair of black shoes
    2) there was a delivery mistake
    3) send me the correct ones

04 1) Are they available 2) work until 5
    3) starts at 6

05 1) I'm nervous 2) make some new friends
    3) can't get along with 4) I'm still worried

06 1) can't reach it 2) can be there 3) need to stretch

07 1) be slightly late 2) change our reservation
    3) order our meals

08 1) next Friday, February 8th
    2) should wear school uniforms
    3) give a special performance

09 1) as a meal 2) eat this with chopsticks
    3) open the lid

10 1) kind of busy 2) give me a ride
    3) Do you mind opening 4) can pass the exam

11 1) asked me for a favor 2) fell while skateboarding
    3) return the science book 4) It's due today

12 1) a little cold outside 2) too far from the entrance
    3) next to the concert hall

13 1) at 1 p.m. or 4 p.m. 2) are sold out already
    3) enough time for lunch 4) There's one at 7 p.m.

14 1) cupcakes I made for her 2) want to taste some
    3) baked cookies yesterday

15 1) selling a special ticket 2) without any waiting
    3) purchase them at our ticket office

16 1) can get one for free 2) What a great deal
    3) That'll be 20 dollars 4) It's 30 dollars

17 1) history of their shops
    2) put our projects together 3) work on it as a team

18 1) eat out tonight 2) feel like eating
    3) go with your choice

19 1) start working out 2) having a lot of fun
    3) want to join us

20 1) has practiced hard 2) feeling very nervous
    3) has to trust herself

실전모의고사 01 회
pp. 48~49

01 ⑤	02 ④	03 ⑤	04 ①	05 ①
06 ②	07 ⑤	08 ③	09 ②	10 ②
11 ③	12 ④	13 ④	14 ⑤	15 ①
16 ④	17 ②	18 ②	19 ⑤	20 ④

01 ⑤

여: Miranda가 우리 선물을 좋아하면 좋겠어.
남: 걱정하지 마. 그럴 거라고 확신해. 그게 그 애가 가장 좋아하는 향수잖아.
여: 그래. 이제 그 애를 위한 생일 카드를 고르기만 하면 돼.
남: 이건 어때? 단순한 흰색 배경 위에 "생일 축하해"라고 쓰여 있어.
여: 그건 조금 따분해. 난 좀 더 경쾌한 걸 원해.
남: 그러면 생일 케이크가 있는 이건 어때? 이것도 "생일 축하해"라고 쓰여 있어.
여: 음… 나쁘지는 않은데, 난 케이크와 풍선 세 개 그림이 있는 이게 더 좋아. 넌 어떻게 생각해?

남: 그래. 좋은 선택이야.

두 사람은 케이크와 풍선 세 개 그림이 있는 생일 카드를 구입하기로 했다.

어휘 perfume [pə́ːrfjùːm] 향수 background [bǽkgràund] 배경 lively [láivli] 경쾌한 prefer [prifə́ːr] 더 좋아하다 balloon [bəlúːn] 풍선 choice [tʃɔis] 선택

02 ④

여: Henry, 뭐 하고 있니?
남: 바지를 쇼핑하고 있어. 내가 고르는 걸 도와줄래?
여: 그래. 오, 이거 좋아 보여. 그런데 가격이 조금 높은 것 같아. 내가 가격이 괜찮은 다른 온라인 상점을 몇 군데 알거든. 좀 추천해 줄까?
남: 아, 고맙지만, 난 이 사이트에서 사고 싶어.
여: 왜? 어떤 특별한 이유가 있니?
남: 제품의 질이 좋고 무료로 배송해 주거든. 그리고 더 중요한 것은, 수익금의 일부가 환경을 돕는 데 쓰인다는 거야.
여: 그게 무슨 뜻이야?
남: 내가 이 사이트에서 구매를 하면, 그들이 나무를 심어.
여: 오, 멋지다. 너는 옷을 구매하는 동시에 환경을 돕는 거네. 너는 현명한 소비자야.

해설 제품 종류(바지), 제품 품질(질이 좋음), 배송료(무료), 수익금 사용처(수익금의 일부가 나무 심는 데 사용됨)에 관해서는 언급되었으나, 고객 후기는 언급되지 않았다.

어휘 a bit 약간 recommend [rèkəménd] 추천하다 quality [kwáləti] 질 product [prɑ́dəkt] 상품, 제품 offer [ɔ́ːfər] 제공하다 shipping [ʃípiŋ] 선적; *배송 profit [prɑ́fit] 이익 go toward ~에 쓰이다 environment [inváiərənmənt] 환경 plant [plænt] 식물; *심다 wise [waiz] 현명한 consumer [kənsúːmər] 소비자

03 ⑤

[전화벨이 울린다.]
여: 여보세요?
남: 여보세요, Kelly. 나 Nick이야.
여: 안녕. 너 어디야?
남: 회사야. 혹시 집에서 내 지갑 봤니?
여: 아니. 지갑을 여기에 뒀어?
남: 가져온 줄 알았는데, 어디서도 못 찾겠어. 그게 내 방에 있는지 좀 봐 줄 수 있니?
여: 물론이지. 잠깐만 기다려. *[잠시 후]* 여기 없는 것 같아.
남: 부엌 식탁도 확인해 줄래?
여: 아! 찾았다! 걱정하지 마.
남: 알았어, 고마워! 집에서 보자.

해설 남자는 여자에게 집에 지갑이 있는지 확인해 달라고 했다.

어휘 be at work 근무 중이다; *직장에 있다 wallet [wɑ́lit] 지갑

04 ①

[전화벨이 울린다.]
남: Akura 식당입니다. 도와드릴까요?
여: 이번 주 일요일에 두 명 자리를 예약하고 싶어요. 개별룸으로 원해요.
남: 몇 시에 원하시나요?
여: 오후 3시요.
남: 죄송합니다. 저희는 3시부터 5시 30분까지 식사를 제공하지 않습니다.
여: 아, 그렇군요. 그러면 오후 2시는요?
남: 네, 그때는 이용 가능합니다. 그런데 저희가 주문받는 것을 2시 30분에 잠시 중단합니다. 괜찮으신가요?
여: 네. 그리고 3시까지는 계속 앉아서 점심 식사를 할 수 있는 거죠, 그렇죠?
남: 물론 그러실 수 있습니다.
여: 좋아요. 그러면 괜찮겠네요.

해설 여자는 처음에 오후 3시에 식당을 예약하려고 했으나 음식을 제공하지 않는 시간이라 2시에 예약하기로 했다.

어휘 make a reservation 예약하다 private [práivit] 개인의, 개별의 serve [səːrv] (음식을) 제공하다 available [əvéiləbl] 이용 가능한 take an order 주문을 받다

05 ①

여: Jeremy, 무슨 일 있니? 너 불편해 보여.
남: 학교에서 집으로 오는 길에, 어떤 남자가 지하철에서 내 발을 밟았어.
여: 괜찮아?
남: 음, 지금 발이 정말 아파. 그리고 심지어 그 남자는 사과도 하지 않았어!
여: 와, 그거 상당히 무례하네.
남: 그리고 그 남자가 내 발을 밟았을 때, 내 스마트폰을 떨어뜨렸어. 그때 이후로 작동하지 않아.
여: 힘든 하루를 보낸 것 같구나.
남: 난 그저 사람들이 더 남을 배려하면 좋겠어!

해설 남자는 어떤 사람이 자신의 발을 밟고 사과도 하지 않은 데다, 그때 스마트폰이 떨어져 작동하지 않으므로 화가 났을(angry) 것이다.
② 외로운 ③ 걱정스러운 ④ 자신만만한 ⑤ 만족스러운

어휘 uncomfortable [ʌnkʌ́mfərtəbl] 불편한 step on ~을 밟다 hurt [həːrt] 아프다 apologize [əpɑ́lədʒàiz] 사과하다 pretty [príti] 꽤, 상당히 rude [ruːd] 무례한 drop [drɑp] 떨어뜨리다 since [sins] 그때 이후로 rough [rʌf] 거친; *힘든, 고된 considerate [kənsídərət] 사려 깊은, (남을) 배려하는

06 ②

① 여: 이 책들을 대출할 수 있을까요?
　남: 먼저 신분증을 확인해야 합니다.
② 여: 그것들이 꽤 무거워 보이네요. 도와드릴까요?
　남: 네, 부탁드려요. 정말 고맙습니다.
③ 여: 네 글을 읽었는데, 훌륭했어.
　남: 고마워. 그것에 정말 공들였거든.
④ 여: 공상 과학 소설책은 어디에서 찾을 수 있나요?
　남: C 구역에서 찾을 수 있습니다.
⑤ 여: 네 책 몇 권을 빌리고 싶어.
　남: 문제없어. 내가 가서 가져올게.

[해설] 책을 많이 들고 있어 무거워 보이는 남자에게 여자가 손을 내밀어 도와주려 하고 있는 상황이다.

[어휘] check out (책 등을) 대출하다 ID [àidíː] 신분증(= identification) article [áːrtikl] 글, 기사 science fiction 공상 과학 소설 section [sékʃən] 구역

07 ⑤

여: 얘, 잠깐 시간 있니?
남: 응, 무슨 일이야?
여: 작년 학생회장 선거 운동을 위해 네가 만든 동영상을 봤는데, 아주 잘 만든 것 같아.
남: 아, 고마워.
여: 내가 동영상 만드는 것 좀 도와줄 수 있니?
남: 무엇 때문에 동영상을 만들어야 하는데?
여: 내 토론 동아리를 위한 거야. 우리가 신입 회원을 모집하고 있거든.
남: 음… 다음 주에 도와줄 수 있을 것 같아. 괜찮니?
여: 응, 그래. 정말 고마워.

[해설] 여자는 동아리 신입 회원 모집을 위한 동영상 만드는 것을 도와달라고 부탁했다.

[어휘] student president 학생회장 campaign [kæmpéin] (정치적·사회적) 운동, 캠페인 debate [dibéit] 토론 recruit [rikrúːt] 모집하다

08 ③

남: 아이들과 함께 신나는 시간을 보내고 싶으신가요? 그렇다면 Kids' Playpit Resort로 오세요. 저희 리조트는 5월 6일에 막 개장했습니다. 이달 동안 객실 가격의 50% 할인을 제공하고 있습니다. 각 객실에는 개별 수영장이 있어서, 여러분과 아이들은 하루 언제든 개별적으로 수영을 즐기실 수 있습니다. 실외의 더 큰 수영장에서도 수영하실 수 있으며, 대형 워터 슬라이드를 즐기실 수 있습니다. 여기에 더하여, 본관 1층에는 큰 체육관이 위치해 있습니다. 그리고 저희 리조트에 묵으시면, 모든 시설을 무료로 즐기실 수 있습니다. 예약하시려면, 1600-2000으로 전화하시거나 저희 웹 사이트 www.

kidsplaypitresort.com을 방문해 주세요. 감사합니다.

[해설] 개장일(5월 6일), 객실 요금 할인(이달에 50% 할인), 부대시설 이용료(투숙 시 무료), 예약 방법(전화 예약 또는 웹 사이트 방문)에 관해서는 언급되었으나, 수영장 이용 수칙은 언급되지 않았다.

[어휘] privately [práivitli] 개별적으로, 사적으로 waterslide [wɔ́ːtərslàid] 워터 슬라이드 gym [dʒim] 체육관 located [lóukeited] ~에 위치한 main building 본관 stay [stei] 묵다 facility [fəsíləti] 시설, 설비 for free 무료로

09 ②

여: 나는 이 악기를 연주하는 것을 좋아합니다. 그것은 여러 다른 모양과 크기로 나옵니다. 그것은 88개의 건반을 가지고 있습니다. 일부는 검은색이고 나머지는 흰색입니다. 각각의 건반은 각기 다른 음을 내고, 이 중 잇단 12개의 음이 한 옥타브를 만듭니다. 나는 손가락으로 건반을 누르고 발로 페달을 밟아 그것을 연주합니다. 내가 충분히 열심히 연습하면, 그것으로 아름다운 음악을 만들 수 있을 것입니다.

[해설] 검은색과 흰색의 88개 건반이 있고 손가락으로 건반을 눌러서 연주하는 악기는 피아노이다.

[어휘] musical instrument 악기 key [kiː] 열쇠; *(피아노의) 건반 note [nout] 메모; *음, 음표 in a row 잇달아[연이어] octave [áktiv] 옥타브 pedal [pédəl] 페달

10 ②

① 남: 내 개를 산책시켜 줄 수 있니?
　여: 미안해, 나는 시간이 전혀 없어.
② 남: 우리 내일 어디서 만날까?
　여: 나는 도서관에서 기다리고 있었어.
③ 남: 너 왜 우산을 들고 있니?
　여: 오늘 아침에 비가 오고 있었어.
④ 남: 방과 후에 농구하자.
　여: 미안하지만, 난 치과에 가야 해.
⑤ 남: 네가 나한테 휴대전화를 빌려줄 수 있는지 궁금해하고 있었어.
　여: 그래, 여기 있어.

[해설] 내일 어디서 만나겠냐는 질문에 도서관에서 기다리고 있었다는 대답은 어색하다.

[어휘] take ~ for a walk ~을 산책시키다 go to the dentist 치과에 가다 wonder [wʌ́ndər] 궁금해하다 lend [lend] 빌려주다

11 ③

남: 차에 뭔가 잘못된 게 있어요. 시동을 걸 수가 없네요.
여: 아, 우리 어떻게 해야 하죠? 콘서트에 가려면 30분밖에 남지 않았

어요.

남: 미안해요. 엔진을 점검했어야 했는데요.

여: 괜찮아요. 다른 방법을 찾아봐요. John에게 전화해서 공연장까지 우리를 태워달라고 하는 건 어때요? 그의 집이 이 근처잖아요.

남: 그는 그럴 수 없을 거예요. 어제 출장을 갔거든요.

여: 택시를 부를까요?

남: 우선 정비사를 부르고, 그다음에 택시를 부릅시다. 차를 여기에 그냥 두고 갈 수는 없죠.

여: 당신 말이 맞아요.

해설 두 사람은 차에 시동이 안 걸려서 먼저 정비사를 부른 다음 택시를 타고 공연장에 가기로 했다.

어휘 start the engine 차의 시동을 걸다 should have p.p. ~했어야 했는데 (하지 못했다) close by 바로 곁에 go on a business trip 출장을 가다 mechanic [məkǽnik] 수리 기사, 정비사

12 ④

여: Jay, 넌 어디에 앉고 싶어?

남: 음, 2번 테이블이 좋아 보여. 구석에 있어서 조용할 거야.

여: 하지만 화장실과 너무 가까워. 냄새가 날지도 몰라.

남: 맞아. 5번 테이블은 어때? 우린 창 옆에 앉을 수 있어.

여: 하지만 문 옆이야. 너무 춥고 시끄러울 거야.

남: 알았어, 그러면 4번 테이블에 앉자.

여: 화장실과 그렇게 가깝지 않네. 그리고 창 옆이어서 경치를 즐길 수 있어.

남: 완벽해!

해설 두 사람은 화장실과 너무 가깝지 않고 문 옆도 아니면서 경치를 볼 수 있는 창 옆 테이블을 골랐다.

어휘 corner [kɔ́ːrnər] 구석, 모퉁이 restroom [réstruːm] 화장실 beside [bisáid] ~ 옆에

13 ④

여: 여보, 우리 가족 여행을 언제 가야 할까요?

남: 생각하고 있는 날짜라도 있나요?

여: 3월 12일이나 3월 19일 어때요? 둘 다 토요일이에요.

남: 내가 12일에는 계획이 있잖아요, 기억하죠? 동료들과 워크숍을 갔다가, 다음 날 돌아올 거예요.

여: 아, 맞아요. 그럼 19일에는 갈 수 있어요?

남: 잊었어요? Jamie의 학교 장기 자랑이 그날이잖아요.

여: 당신 말이 맞아요. 그럼 장기 자랑 다음 날은 어때요? 우리 그날은 다른 계획 없잖아요, 그렇죠?

남: 그게 좋겠어요.

해설 Jamie의 학교 장기 자랑이 있는 3월 19일의 다음 날인 3월 20일에 가족 여행을 떠나기로 했다.

어휘 have ~ in mind ~을 염두에 두다, ~을 생각하다 workshop

[wə́ːrkʃàp] (회사 등의) 워크숍, 연수회 coworker [kóuwə̀ːrkər] 동료 talent show 장기 자랑 free [friː] 한가한, 다른 계획이 없는

14 ⑤

여: David, 설거지 했니?

남: 아직. 난 오늘 아침에 바빴어. 제과점에서 이제 막 돌아왔어. 아침으로 먹을 샌드위치를 좀 사러 갔었거든.

여: 그런데 왜 그렇게 오랫동안 가 있었니? 거기 가는 데 10분밖에 걸리지 않잖아.

남: 세탁물도 찾았어.

여: 그래. 그럼 오후에는 무슨 계획이라도 있니?

남: 아니, 그냥 TV 볼 거야.

여: 그럼 설거지를 먼저 하지 그러니?

남: 문제없어.

해설 남자는 아침에 제과점에 가서 샌드위치를 사고 세탁물을 찾았다고 했다.

어휘 wash[do] the dishes 설거지하다 pick up ~을 찾아오다 laundry [lɔ́ːndri] 세탁물

15 ①

남: 안녕하십니까, 여러분. 아시다시피, 지난 화요일에 태풍이 인근 섬을 덮쳤습니다. 안타깝게도, 약 200명이 사망했습니다. 다른 많은 사람들은 안전하게 대피했지만, 지금 그들은 여러분의 도움이 필요합니다. 태풍은 사람들이 집을 잃게 했고, 그들은 식량과 기초 보급품이 부족합니다. 여러분은 옷이나 담요 같은 작은 것들을 보냄으로써 그들을 도울 수 있습니다. 돈을 기부할 수도 있습니다. 그들은 여러분의 이웃이며, 여러분의 도움을 기다리고 있으니, 부디 그들을 도와주세요.

해설 남자는 인근 섬이 태풍 피해를 입은 소식을 전하며 이재민을 도울 것을 독려하고 있다.

어휘 typhoon [táiːfun] 태풍 strike [straik] 치다; *덮치다 (strike-struck-struck) nearby [nìərbái] 인근의 island [áilənd] 섬 escape [iskéip] 벗어나다 homeless [hóumlis] 집 없는 lack [læk] 부족하다 supply [səplái] 보급품 blanket [blǽŋkit] 담요 donate [dóuneit] 기부[기증]하다 give ~ a hand ~을 돕다

16 ④

남: 무엇을 드시겠어요?

여: 베이컨 샌드위치 주세요. 얼마예요?

남: 4달러인데, 베이컨이 다 떨어졌어요. 프라이드 치킨은 어떠세요?

여: 음… 제가 닭고기를 좋아하지 않아요. 치즈 버거로 할게요. 그것도 4달러인가요?

남: 네, 그렇습니다. 마실 것을 원하시나요? 탄산음료는 1달러이고, 커

피는 2달러입니다.

여: 네, 탄산음료 한 잔과 커피 한 잔 포장해 주세요. 여기 제 신용카드입니다.

남: 네. 주문하신 것이 준비되면 이 번호로 부르겠습니다.

여: 고맙습니다.

[해설] 여자는 치즈 버거($4), 탄산음료($1), 커피($2)를 주문했으므로, 총 7달러를 지불할 것이다.

[어휘] run out of ~을 다 써 버리다

17 ②

여: 오늘 영화 어땠어?

남: 음, 약간 폭력적이었어.

여: 아, 너 액션 영화 안 좋아하니?

남: 전에는 액션 영화 보는 걸 즐겼는데, 요즘에는 더 이상 나의 흥미를 끌지 않아. 너는 액션 영화 좋아하니?

여: 물론이지. 다른 어떤 종류보다도 액션 영화를 더 좋아해. 재미있지 않았다니 유감이야.

남: 괜찮아. 네가 액션 영화를 그렇게 많이 좋아하는지 몰랐어. 코미디는 어때? 나는 코미디를 가장 좋아해.

여: 실은, 내 취향이 아니야.

[해설] 남자는 액션 영화를 가장 좋아한다는 여자에게 코미디는 어떤지 물었으므로, 코미디에 대한 취향을 말하는 응답이 가장 적절하다.
① 나는 우리가 비슷한 취향을 가지고 있다고 확신해.
③ 동의해. 그는 최고의 코미디언 중 한 명이지.
④ 어린이는 무서운 영화를 보면 안 돼.
⑤ 우리 다른 날 영화를 함께 보러 가는 게 어때?

[어휘] violent [váiələnt] 폭력적인 no longer 더 이상 ~ 아니다 interest [íntərəst] ~의 흥미를 끌다 [문제] similar [símələr] 비슷한 taste [teist] 맛; *취향 not really one's thing ~의 취향이 아니다 scary [skéri] 무서운

18 ②

남: 이것들은 뭐예요?

여: 색상표예요. 새 커튼의 색을 결정하려 하고 있어요. 어느 색이 더 나을지 모르겠어요.

남: 우리 거실 커튼이요? 나는 그대로가 좋아요.

여: 아니요, 내 방에 할 거예요.

남: 아, 그래요. 그럼 밝은 색 어때요?

여: 좋은 생각이에요. 난 이 두 개 중에 고르려고 하거든요. 어느 게 더 마음에 드나요?

남: 나는 노란 게 더 좋아요.

[해설] 여자는 남자에게 두 가지 색 중 어느 것이 더 마음에 드는지 물었으므로, 하나를 선택해서 말하는 응답이 가장 적절하다.
① 나는 당신 말에 동의하지 않아요.

③ 좋은 생각 같아요.
④ 귀찮게 해서 정말 미안해요.
⑤ 괜찮아요. 나는 아무것도 필요하지 않아요.

[어휘] chart [tʃɑːrt] 차트, 표 decide on ~을 결정하다 bright [brait] 밝은 [문제] bother [bɑ́ðər] 괴롭히다, 귀찮게 하다

19 ⑤

남: 안녕하세요, White 선생님. 말씀드릴 것이 있어요.

여: 무슨 일이니, Sam?

남: 방금 선생님께서 내 주신 과제에 관한 거예요. 저는 마감 기한을 맞출 수 없어요.

여: 무슨 문제가 있니?

남: 제가 방금 인턴십 프로그램에 합격했거든요.

여: 축하해! 그게 얼마 동안이니?

남: 6주 동안이에요.

여: 그렇다면 6월 말까지 네 마감 기한을 연장해 주마.

남: 감사해요. 과제 제출하는 걸 잊지 않을게요.

[해설] 여자는 인턴십 프로그램에 참여해야 하는 남자에게 과제 마감 기한을 연장해 주겠다고 했으므로, 감사의 뜻을 나타내는 응답이 가장 적절하다.
① 저는 영어를 배우러 캐나다에 갈 거예요.
② 너도. 네 보고서가 훌륭하길 바랄게.
③ 죄송하지만, 저는 내일 수업에 올 수 없어요.
④ 저는 다른 인턴십 프로그램에 참여하고 싶어요.

[어휘] paper [péipər] 종이; *과제, 리포트 assign [əsáin] (일·책임 등을) 맡기다 deadline [dédlàin] 마감 기한 get accepted 합격하다 in that case 그런 경우에는, 그렇다면 extend [iksténd] 연장하다 [문제] hand in ~을 제출하다

20 ④

여: Ben은 식료품을 사느라 슈퍼마켓에 있습니다. 그는 계산을 하려고 계산대에 줄을 서 있습니다. 매우 많은 사람들이 슈퍼마켓에 있어서 시간이 오래 걸리고 있습니다. 곧, 그는 우유를 사는 걸 잊었다는 것을 깨닫습니다. 그는 가서 가져오고 싶지만, 줄 맨 끝으로 돌아가고 싶지는 않습니다. 이런 상황에서, Ben은 뒤에 있는 사람에게 뭐라고 말하겠습니까?

Ben: 제 자리를 맡아 주시겠어요?

[해설] Ben은 슈퍼마켓에서 계산대에 줄을 서 있던 중에 사야 하는 물건을 가지러 가야 하는데 줄 맨 끝으로 돌아가고 싶지는 않은 상황이므로, 자리를 맡아 달라고 부탁하는 말이 가장 적절하다.
① 기다려 주셔서 감사합니다.
② 우유가 좀 필요하신가요?
③ 걱정하지 마세요. 저는 괜찮아요.
⑤ 미안합니다. 이게 줄의 끝이에요.

[어휘] grocery [gróusəri] 식료품 stand in line 줄을 서다 realize

[ríːəlàiz] 깨닫다 [문제] hold [hould] 유지하다, 지키다 place [pleis] 장소; *자리

Dictation Test 01

01 1) has a simple white background
2) want something more lively
3) a cake and three balloons

02 1) price is a bit high 2) offer free shipping
3) help the environment

03 1) happen to see my wallet
2) can't find it anywhere 3) check the kitchen table

04 1) What time would you like 2) from 3:00 to 5:30
3) stop taking orders at 2:30

05 1) stepped on my foot 2) didn't even apologize
3) had a rough day 4) be more considerate

06 1) check out these books 2) Where can I find
3) I'd like to borrow

07 1) watched the video you made
2) help me make a video
3) recruiting new members

08 1) offering 50% off our room prices
2) enjoy swimming privately 3) have a large gym
4) To make a reservation

09 1) It has 88 keys 2) the others are white
3) by pushing the keys

10 1) Where should we meet 2) go to the dentist
3) lend me your cell phone

11 1) should have checked the engine
2) went on a business trip 3) call a mechanic first

12 1) too close to the restroom 2) next to the door
3) beside the window

13 1) have plans on the 12th 2) go on the 19th
3) day after the talent show

14 1) get some sandwiches for breakfast
2) picked up the laundry 3) do the dishes

15 1) lack food and basic supplies
2) by sending small things 3) give them a hand

16 1) ran out of bacon 2) anything to drink
3) a cup of coffee to go

17 1) How did you like 2) no longer interest me
3) more than any other kind

18 1) decide on a color 2) which color would be better
3) choose between these two

19 1) can't make the deadline
2) got accepted into an internship program
3) extend your deadline

20 1) standing in line 2) forgot to get milk
3) go back to the end

실전모의고사 02회

01 ④	02 ④	03 ②	04 ②	05 ⑤
06 ⑤	07 ⑤	08 ④	09 ④	10 ⑤
11 ⑤	12 ④	13 ③	14 ⑤	15 ①
16 ②	17 ⑤	18 ⑤	19 ①	20 ④

01 ④

남: 운동회 때 입을 반 단체복 정했어?
여: 아직. 어떤 스타일을 선택해야 할지 모르겠어. 도와줄래?
남: 물론이지. 선택 사항들이 뭔데?
여: 음, 이 티셔츠는 깃이 있는 것과 없는 것이 있어. 어떤 게 더 나아?
남: 깃이 있는 게 좋아. 단정해 보여.
여: 좋아. 그럼 주머니는 어때? 큰 주머니가 있는 게 더 귀엽지 않아?
남: 응, 그런 것 같아. 주머니가 없는 것보다 훨씬 더 좋아 보여.
여: 알았어. 도와줘서 고마워. 그 스타일로 주문해야지.

해설 여자는 깃과 큰 주머니가 있는 티셔츠를 주문할 것이라고 했다.

어휘 collar [kálər] 칼라, 깃 neat [niːt] 단정한 order [ɔ́ːrdər] 주문하다

02 ④

남: Atlantic 호텔에 오신 걸 환영합니다.
여: 고맙습니다. 제 이름은 Mandi Erickson이에요. 체크인하고 싶은데요.
남: 알겠습니다. 여기 객실 열쇠입니다. 배가 고프시면, 1층에 식당이 있습니다.
여: 네. 룸서비스가 있나요?
남: 네. 자정까지 객실로 음식을 배달시키실 수 있습니다.
여: 좋아요. 방에서 국제 전화를 걸 수 있나요?
남: 네, 가능합니다. 먼저 '9번' 버튼만 누르시면 됩니다.

정답 및 해설 15

여: 좋네요. 그리고 질문이 하나 더 있어요. 몇 시에 체크아웃해야 하나요?

남: 내일 오전 11시까지 방을 비워 주셔야 합니다.

[해설] 식당의 위치(1층), 룸서비스 이용 시간(자정까지), 국제 전화 이용 방법(9번 버튼 누르기), 체크아웃 시간(오전 11시까지)에 관해서는 언급되었으나, 세탁 서비스 이용 방법은 언급되지 않았다.

[어휘] deliver [dilívər] 배달하다 midnight [mídnàit] 자정 international call 국제 전화

03 ②

남: 스키를 타고 산을 내려가자.

여: 말도 안 돼! 난 할 수 없을 것 같아.

남: 어서. 이 경사는 그리 가파르지 않아.

여: 난 걱정돼. 넘어질 것 같아.

남: 불안해하지 마. 괜찮을 거야.

여: 나 너무 겁이 나서 못 움직일 것 같아.

남: 심호흡을 해. 그리고 똑바로 앞을 봐. 밑을 보지 말고.

여: 응, 알겠어.

남: 좋아! 이제 조금만 움직여 봐, 그러면 스키를 타고 경사를 내려가기 시작할 거야. 넌 할 수 있어.

[해설] 남자는 스키를 타기 무서워하는 여자가 스키를 탈 수 있도록 격려하고 있다.

[어휘] slope [sloup] 경사지, 경사면 steep [sti:p] 가파른 fall down 넘어지다 scared [skɛərd] 겁에 질린 take a deep breath 심호흡하다 straight [streit] 똑바로 ahead [əhéd] 앞으로

04 ②

[휴대전화가 울린다.]

남: 여보세요, Susan.

여: 안녕, Patrick. 너 오늘 밤에 연극 〈햄릿〉 볼래?

남: 좋아. 몇 시에 시작해?

여: 저녁 8시에 시작해.

남: 좋아. 가기 전에 쇼핑몰에서 쇼핑을 하면 어떨까?

여: 뭐 살 게 있어?

남: 응. 엄마가 내게 몇 가지를 사다 달라고 하셨어.

여: 그렇구나. 7시에 쇼핑몰에서 만날까?

남: 아니, 시간이 더 필요할 거야. 연극 두 시간 전에 만나는 게 어때?

여: 좋아, 그때 보자.

[해설] 연극 시작 시각이 8시인데, 두 사람은 쇼핑몰에 들르기 위해 그보다 두 시간 전에 만나기로 했다.

[어휘] play [plei] 놀다; *연극 mall [mɔːl] 쇼핑몰

05 ⑤

여: 실례합니다. 저 좀 도와주시겠어요?

남: 물론이죠. 좌석을 찾으려고 하시나요?

여: 맞아요. 콘서트가 빨리 시작하면 좋겠어요. 제가 세상에서 가장 좋아하는 밴드거든요.

남: 아주 잘됐네요. 표를 볼 수 있을까요?

여: 네. 여기 있어요.

남: 음… 잘못된 곳에 계시네요. 고객님의 좌석은 저 위예요.

여: 저 위요? 농담이시죠.

남: 그럴 리가요. 이 계단으로 올라가셔서 10줄 정도 뒤로 가세요.

여: 무대에서 그렇게 먼지 몰랐어요.

남: 거기서도 무대는 잘 보일 거예요. 즐거운 관람 되세요!

[해설] 여자는 자신의 좌석이 무대에서 멀다는 것을 알고 실망했을 (disappointed) 것이다.
① 지루해하는 ② 초조한 ③ 질투하는 ④ 만족스러운

[어휘] seat [si:t] 좌석 terrific [tərífik] 아주 좋은, 훌륭한 kid [kid] 농담하다 stair [stɛər] 계단 row [rou] 열, 줄 stage [steidʒ] 무대

06 ⑤

① 여: 이런. 내 차에 시동을 걸 수가 없어!
　남: 좀 진정하고 다시 해 봐.

② 여: 주차할 자리를 하나도 찾을 수가 없어.
　남: 다른 구역을 확인해 보자.

③ 여: 내 차를 어디에 주차했는지 기억이 안 나.
　남: C 구역이었던 것 같아.

④ 여: 난 내 차를 가지러 가야 해. 수리소에 있거든.
　남: 내가 같이 갈게.

⑤ 여: 아! 여기 빈 자리가 있어. 여기에 주차하자.
　남: 표지판을 봐. 우리는 여기에 주차할 수 없어.

[해설] 두 사람은 차 안에서 장애인 전용 주차 구역 표시를 바라보고 있는 상황이다.

[어휘] calm down 진정하다 empty [émpti] 비어 있는 spot [spɑt] 자리, 장소 sign [sain] 표지판

07 ⑤

여: Dave, 나 어젯밤에 너무 늦게까지 깨어 있었어.

남: 왜? 재미있는 책을 읽고 있었니?

여: 아니, 내일까지가 기한인 역사 숙제가 있어서, 밤새 그것을 하고 있었거든.

남: 끝냈어?

여: 아니, 정보를 좀 더 찾아야 해.

남: 그거 끝내고 나면 잠을 좀 자야겠네.

여: 그래. 하지만 모레는 과학 숙제도 있어. 그건 아직 시작도 못 했어.

남: 아, 그거 심하네. 내가 도울 수 있는 게 있을까?

여: 응. 날 위해 도서관에서 책을 한 권 빌려다 줄래? 숙제에 그게 정말 필요하거든.

남: 물론이야.

해설 여자는 숙제하는 데 필요한 책을 도서관에서 빌려다 달라고 부탁했다.

어휘 stay up 안 자다[깨어 있다] history [hístəri] 역사 due [du:] ~까지가 기한인 work on ~을 작업하다 information [infərméiʃən] 정보 terrible [térəbl] 끔찍한, 심한

08 ④

남: 안녕하세요. 노래하는 것을 좋아하신다면, 이 공고는 여러분을 위한 것입니다. Famous Singer는 유명 가수가 되고자 하는 사람들을 찾고 있습니다. 이 오디션에 참가하기 위해서는, 자신의 노래가 있어야 합니다. 어느 장르든 가능합니다. 참가자 나이 제한도 없습니다. 대회에서 우승하면, 여러분의 앨범을 발매하고 공연을 할 수 있는 기회를 드릴 것입니다. 저희 웹 사이트를 방문하셔서 데모 영상과 함께 등록해 주십시오.

해설 참가 자격(자신의 노래가 있어야 함), 장르 제한(없음), 참가자 나이 제한(없음), 참가 방법(웹 사이트에 데모 영상과 함께 등록)에 관해서는 언급되었으나, 우승자 상금은 언급되지 않았다.

어휘 announcement [ənáunsmənt] 공고, 발표 participate in ~에 참가하다 audition [ɔːdíʃən] 오디션 genre [ʒáːnrə] 장르 limit [límit] 제한 participant [paːrtísəpənt] 참가자 contest [kántest] 대회, 시합 opportunity [ɑ̀pərtjúːnəti] 기회 release [rilíːs] 공개[발표]하다, (앨범 등을) 발매하다 sign up 등록하다

09 ④

여: 이것은 요즘 많은 사람들이 즐기는 것입니다. 스케이트보드처럼 생긴 탈것이지만, 핸들이 있습니다. 그것은 전기로 동력이 공급됩니다. 서 있는 자세로 타며, 꽤 빠르게 이동할 수 있습니다. 운전면허가 있기만 하면 누구든 운전할 수 있습니다. 하지만 위험할 수 있기 때문에, 근처에 사람들이 있을 때는 천천히 조심히 운전해야 합니다.

해설 스케이트보드처럼 생겼는데 핸들이 있고, 전기로 움직이며, 서 있는 자세로 타는 것은 전동 킥보드이다.

어휘 vehicle [víːikəl] 탈것 handlebar [hǽndəlbàːr] (자전거·오토바이 등의) 핸들 power [páuər] 동력을 공급하다 electricity [ilektrísəti] 전기 position [pəzíʃən] 위치; *자세 as long as ~하기만 하면 driver's license 운전면허

10 ⑤

① 남: 주스 좀 더 마셔도 되나요?
　여: 물론이야. 마음껏 마셔.
② 남: 요즘 뭐 하고 지내?
　여: 5번가에 카페를 막 열었어.
③ 남: 비가 올 것 같아.
　여: 아무래도 우리 소풍을 취소해야겠어.
④ 남: 내일 나랑 같이 저녁 먹을래?
　여: 그래. 몇 시에 만날까?
⑤ 남: 나는 오늘 밤에 영화 보러 갈 거야.
　여: 아니, 대신에 나는 공원에 갔어.

해설 오늘 밤 영화를 보러 갈 거라고 계획을 말하는데, 공원에 갔었다며 지난 일을 말하는 것은 어색하다.

어휘 Help yourself. 마음껏 드세요. avenue [ǽvənùː] 거리, ~ 가 cancel [kǽnsəl] 취소하다 instead [instéd] 대신에

11 ⑤

여: 내일은 토요일이야. 내가 뭐 하고 싶은지 알아?

남: 내가 맞혀 볼게. 저녁에 외식하고 나서 영화 보는 거?

여: 아니. 이번 주에 시립 박물관에서 반 고흐의 몇몇 그림들이 전시되고 있어.

남: 아, 정말? 거기에 가고 싶니?

여: 응, 그리고 네가 나와 같이 가면 좋겠어.

남: 그것도 괜찮지만, 난 내일 오후에 스페인과 독일의 축구 경기를 볼 계획이야.

여: 경기가 몇 시야?

남: 2시 30분에 시작해.

여: 그래. 그럼 우리 그림은 다른 날 가서 봐야겠다.

남: 알겠어.

해설 남자는 토요일에 스페인과 독일의 축구 경기를 볼 계획이라고 했다.

어휘 several [sévərəl] 몇몇의 match [mætʃ] 경기, 시합

12 ④

남: 우리 어느 호텔에 머물까?

여: 글쎄, Flowers 호텔이 지하철역에서 가까워.

남: 나도 알지만, 그 호텔에는 엘리베이터가 없어. 짐 옮기는 것이 힘들 거야.

여: 그럼 Main Street 호텔은 어때? 그 근처에 버스 정류장이 있어.

남: 하지만 우리가 은행에서 돈을 좀 인출해야 할 수도 있어. Smithson 호텔은 어때? 은행 옆에 있어.

여: 맞아, 하지만 옆 건물에 소방서가 있어. 너무 시끄러울 거야. Sweet Dreams 호텔은 어떻게 생각해? 은행에서 길 건너편에 있고, 인근에 제과점과 버스 정류장이 있어.

남: 그거 좋네.

해설 두 사람은 은행에서 길 건너편에 위치하고 제과점과 버스 정류장이 가까이에 있는 호텔에 머물기로 했다.

어휘 baggage [bǽgidʒ] 짐 withdraw [wiðdrɔ́ː] 빼다; *(돈을) 인출하다 next door 옆 집[건물]에

어휘 pay attention to ~에 주목하다 heavy rainfall 폭우 sincerely [sinsíərli] 진심으로 sudden [sʌ́dən] 갑작스러운 cancellation [kæ̀nsəléiʃən] 취소 exchange [ikstʃéindʒ] 교환하다 ticket office 매표소 receive a full refund 전액 환불받다

13 ③

남: 과제를 끝마치려면 우리가 한 번 더 만나야 할 것 같아.
여: 동의해. 언제 만날까?
남: 우리는 이번 주 금요일에 그걸 제출해야 해. 그런데 나는 내일 계획이 있어. 모레는 어때?
여: 수요일에? 미안한데, 난 안 돼. 이번 주 목요일에 수학 시험이 있어서, 그걸 공부해야 하거든.
남: 그럼 우리 시험 끝나고 만나면 되겠다. 그땐 나도 시간 있어.
여: 좋아. 그때 보자.

해설 두 사람은 목요일에 여자가 수학 시험을 본 후에 만나서 함께 과제를 끝마치기로 했다.

어휘 project [prɑ́dʒekt] 과제, 연구 프로젝트

14 ⑤

여: 지난 주말에 가족 여행 즐거웠니?
남: 여행? 무슨 여행?
여: 일요일에 바닷가에 간다고 하지 않았어?
남: 아, 그랬지. 그런데 취소됐어. 사실 난 결국 내 여동생을 돌보게 됐어.
여: 왜? 무슨 일이 있었는데?
남: 아빠가 등산을 하다가 다리를 다치셔서 병원에서 주말을 보내셨거든. 그리고 엄마는 아빠를 돌봐드려야 했어.
여: 정말 안됐다. 지금은 괜찮으셔?
남: 응. 지금은 나아지셨어.

해설 남자는 주말에 부모님이 병원에 계셔서 여동생을 돌봤다고 했다.

어휘 actually [ǽktʃuəli] 실제로, 사실은 end up v-ing 결국 ~하다 look after ~을 돌보다

15 ①

남: 신사 숙녀 여러분, 다음 소식에 주목해 주시기 바랍니다. 폭우로 인하여 오늘 야구 경기가 취소되었습니다. 이 갑작스러운 취소에 대해 진심으로 사과드립니다. 오늘의 표를 다음 경기 표로 교환하길 원하시면, 매표소를 방문하시기 바랍니다. 아니면 대신 전액 환불을 받으실 수 있습니다. 표와 정보는 저희 웹 사이트에서 언제든 이용하실 수 있다는 것 또한 알려 드립니다. 저희 홈페이지 www.topbaseball.com을 방문하시면 됩니다.

해설 폭우로 인해 오늘 야구 경기가 취소되었음을 알리고 있다.

16 ②

남: 주문하시겠어요?
여: 네, 보통 크기 라테 한 잔이랑 오렌지 머핀 하나 주세요. 얼마죠?
남: 보통 크기 라테는 4달러이고, 오렌지 머핀은 2달러입니다. 하지만 라테를 한 잔 사시면, 머핀이 무료예요.
여: 잘됐네요! 그리고 라테에 휘핑크림을 올려 주시겠어요?
남: 알겠습니다. 그건 추가 1달러입니다.
여: 좋아요.

해설 라테($4)를 사면 머핀은 무료이고 휘핑크림($1)을 추가했으므로, 여자는 총 5달러를 지불해야 한다.

어휘 regular [régjələr] 규칙적인; *(크기가) 보통의 muffin [mʌ́fin] 머핀 extra [ékstrə] 추가로

17 ⑤

남: 얘, Sarah. 뭐 하고 있니?
여: 인터넷 서핑을 하고 있어. 숙제로 동물에 관한 글을 써야 하거든.
남: 아. 어떤 동물을 골랐니?
여: 호랑이에 대해서 쓸 거야. 호랑이에 대해 아는 사실이 있니?
남: 음, 호랑이는 주로 아시아에 살아. 밀림에서 혼자 살고, 먹이로 다른 동물들을 사냥해. 검은 줄무늬는 그들이 눈에 잘 안 띄게 해 주지.
여: 와, 네가 동물에 그렇게 관심이 있는 줄 몰랐어.
남: 응, 내가 최근에 호랑이에 관한 흥미로운 책을 읽었거든.

해설 여자는 남자가 호랑이에 대해 잘 알고 동물에 관심이 많은 것에 놀랐으므로, 호랑이에 관심을 갖게 된 계기나 이유를 말하는 응답이 가장 적절하다.
① 나는 그 호랑이들을 좋아한 적이 없어.
② 그들은 동물을 보호해야 해.
③ 나는 사실 그것들에 관해 아무것도 몰라.
④ 호랑이는 다른 동물 사냥에 아주 능숙해.

어휘 surf the Internet 인터넷 서핑을 하다 essay [ései] 과제물, 글 pick [pik] 고르다 fact [fækt] 사실 mainly [méinli] 주로, 대부분 hunt [hʌnt] 사냥하다 stripe [straip] 줄무늬 [문제] protect [prətékt] 보호하다 recently [ríːsəntli] 최근에

18 ⑤

여: 너희 밴드에서 새로운 가수를 찾고 있다고 들었어.
남: 맞아. 너 우리 밴드에 가입하는 것에 관심 있니?
여: 응. 정보를 더 얻을 수 있을까?

남: 물론이지. 우리는 리드 싱어를 뽑으려고 공개 오디션을 계획하고 있어.

여: 그렇구나. 오디션이 언제니?

남: 3월 13일이야.

여: 알겠어. 그리고 어디서 열리니?

남: 우리 연습실에서 열릴 거야. 너 오디션에 참가할 거니?

여: 물론이지. 나는 이 순간을 위해 평생을 연습해 왔어!

해설 남자는 밴드 가입에 관심이 있다는 여자에게 리드 싱어를 뽑는 오디션에 참가할지 물었으므로, 참가 여부를 말하는 응답이 가장 적절하다.
① 나는 네가 훌륭한 가수가 될 거라 확신해.
② 나는 다른 동아리에 가입할 생각이야.
③ 네가 좋은 가수를 찾길 바라.
④ 나는 네가 노래 부르기에 관심 있는 줄 몰랐어.

어휘 join [dʒɔin] 가입하다 open [óupən] 열린; *공개된 practice [prǽktis] 연습; 연습하다 [문제] whole [houl] 전체의 moment [móumənt] 순간

19 ①

남: 자, 영화는 어땠니?

여: 와, 정말 마음에 들었어. 난 액션 장면이 정말 좋았어. 넌 어때?

남: 나도 재미있게 보긴 했는데, 책이 영화보다 더 나았던 것 같아.

여: 영화가 책과 많이 다르니?

남: 그렇게 많이는 아니야. 하지만 몇몇 중요한 등장인물들을 없앴어.

여: 흥미롭다! 내 남동생도 같은 말을 했어.

남: 사실이야. 너 그 책 읽어 봤니?

여: 아니, 하지만 그러고 싶어.

해설 남자는 여자에게 영화의 원작인 책을 읽어 봤는지 물었으므로, 그 여부를 말하는 응답이 가장 적절하다.
② 응, 나도 그렇게 생각해.
③ 아니, 나는 판타지 영화를 더 좋아해.
④ 그 책은 실존 인물에 바탕을 둔 거야.
⑤ 아니, 나는 오늘 밤에 기말시험공부를 하느라 바빠.

어휘 scene [si:n] 장면 film [film] 영화 cut out (글 등에서) ~을 삭제하다[빼다] character [kǽriktər] 등장인물 [문제] fantasy movie 판타지 영화 be based on ~에 바탕을 두다 real [ríːəl] 실제의

20 ④

여: Roy와 Erin은 둘 다 뮤지컬 보는 것을 즐깁니다. 그들은 가장 좋아하는 뮤지컬인 〈아이다〉가 곧 공연될 거라는 소식을 듣고 신이 났습니다. 그리고 표가 판매되자마자, Roy는 표를 샀습니다. 하지만 Erin은 잊어버렸습니다. 그녀는 며칠 뒤에 표를 사려고 했지만, 표는 매진되었습니다. 그래서 그녀는 표를 구하지 못했습니다. 이런 상황에서, Roy는 Erin에게 뭐라고 말하겠습니까?

Roy: 일찍 일어나는 새가 벌레를 잡지.

해설 Roy는 판매가 시작되자마자 표를 샀지만 Erin은 뒤늦게 사려다 표가 매진되어 구하지 못했으므로, 부지런함의 이점을 뜻하는 말이 가장 적절하다.
① 서두르면 일을 망쳐.
② 늦어도 안 하는 것보다 낫지.
③ 천천히 하지만 꾸준히 하는 자가 이기는 법이야.
⑤ 겉모습만 보고 판단하면 안 돼.

어휘 perform [pərfɔ́ːrm] 수행하다; *공연하다 as soon as ~하자마자 go on sale 판매[시판]되다 sold out 매진된 [문제] haste [heist] 서두름 waste [weist] 낭비, 허비 steady [stédi] 꾸준한 race [reis] 경주 judge [dʒʌdʒ] 판단하다

Dictation Test 02
pp. 60~67

01   1) what style to choose 2) has a collar
3) with the big pocket

02   1) on the first floor 2) delivered to your room
3) make international calls 4) need to check out

03   1) I'm going to fall down 2) Take a deep breath
3) You can do it

04   1) starts at 8:00 2) asked me to buy
3) two hours before the play

05   1) wait for the concert to start
2) in the wrong place 3) far away from the stage

06   1) calm down and try again
2) where I parked my car 3) go pick up my car
4) Here's an empty spot

07   1) working on it all night
2) find some more information 3) borrow a book

08   1) have your own song 2) There is no age limit
3) release your own album

09   1) looks like a skateboard 2) powered by electricity
3) have a driver's license

10   1) Help yourself 2) should cancel our picnic
3) What time shall we meet 4) going to the movies

11   1) Go out for dinner 2) watch the soccer match
3) go see the paintings

12   1) close to the subway station
2) hard to move our baggage
3) across the street from the bank

13   1) hand it in this Friday 2) the day after tomorrow
3) have a math test 4) meet after the test

14	1) enjoy your family trip 2) looking after my sister
	3) hurt his leg while hiking
15	1) baseball game has been canceled
	2) apologize for this sudden cancellation
	3) receive a full refund
16	1) take your order 2) for free
	3) That's a dollar extra
17	1) Which animal did you pick
	2) hunt other animals for food
	3) were so interested in animals
18	1) interested in joining our band
	2) planning an open audition
	3) participate in the audition
19	1) liked the action scenes
	2) cut out some important characters
	3) Have you read the book
20	1) be performed soon 2) tickets went on sale
	3) a few days later

실전모의고사 03회

pp. 68~69

01 ④	02 ④	03 ②	04 ②	05 ④
06 ④	07 ③	08 ①	09 ④	10 ②
11 ①	12 ③	13 ②	14 ⑤	15 ②
16 ③	17 ③	18 ③	19 ④	20 ③

01 ④

남: 염두에 두신 스타일이 있나요?
여: 아뇨. 뭔가 추천해 주실 수 있나요?
남: 물론이죠. 이 스타일을 시도해 보는 건 어떠세요?
여: 이 짧은 헤어스타일 말씀이세요? 안 돼요.
남: 왜요? 꽤 귀여워 보이는데요.
여: 음, 저는 긴 머리가 더 잘 어울리는 것 같아요.
남: 알겠어요. 그럼 이 스타일은 어떠세요? 손님은 파마머리가 잘 어울리실 거예요.
여: 오, 그거 좋아 보이네요.
남: 머리 염색도 하실 건가요? 검은색 머리가 잘 어울리실 것 같아요.
여: 아니에요, 저는 제 갈색 머리가 좋아요.

해설 여자는 길고 파마한 헤어스타일에 자신의 갈색 머리 그대로가 좋다

고 했다.

어휘 have ~ in mind ~을 염두에 두다, ~을 생각하다 try [trai] 시도하다 seem [siːm] ~처럼 보이다 perm [pəːrm] 파마 dye [dai] 염색하다

02 ④

남: Kelly, 너 T 스마트 워치 있지, 그렇지 않니?
여: 응, 왜?
남: 하나 살까 생각 중이야. 운동할 때 무겁거나 불편하니? 수영하고 농구할 때 착용하고 싶거든.
여: 전혀. 겨우 30g이라, 절대 신경 쓰이지 않아. 그리고 오히려 내가 얼마나 운동하는지 기록하는 데 도움이 돼. 그게 가장 좋은 기능인 것 같아.
남: 좋네. LCD는 뭘로 만들어졌니? 공이 쳐서 고장 낼까 봐 걱정이야.
여: 그건 걱정할 필요 없어. 아주 튼튼해.
남: 좋네. 그리고 어떤 다른 기능이 마음에 들어?
여: 위치를 알아야 할 때 GPS가 유용해.
남: 내가 생각한 것보다 훨씬 더 도움이 되는 것 같아. 하나 사야 할 것 같네. 그런데 한 번 충전하면 얼마나 오래 지속되니?
여: 3일 정도 지속돼.

해설 무게(30g), 기능(운동 기록, GPS), 내구성(튼튼함), 배터리 지속 시간(3일 정도)에 관해서는 언급되었으나, 화면 크기는 언급되지 않았다.

어휘 uncomfortable [ʌnkʌ́mfərtəbl] 불편한 rather [rǽðər] 오히려 feature [fíːtʃər] 기능 LCD [elsiːdiː] 액정 화면(liquid crystal display) hit [hit] 치다 GPS [dʒiːpiːes] 전 지구 위치 파악 시스템(global positioning system) get directions 위치를 알다 last [læst] 지속되다 charge [tʃɑːrdʒ] 충전

03 ②

[휴대전화가 울린다.]
여: 여보세요?
남: 안녕, Judy. 우리 공부 모임에 올 거니?
여: 미안하지만, 난 Judy가 아니란다. 그 애 엄마야.
남: 아, 정말 죄송해요, Jackson 아주머니. 저 Tom이에요.
여: 괜찮아, Tom. 지금 Judy가 바빠서 내가 받았어. 메시지를 남기겠니?
남: 네, 부탁드릴게요. 오늘 저희 공부 모임에 오면, 제 공책을 가져오라고 그 애에게 전해 주시겠어요?
여: 그래. 말해 줄게.
남: 감사합니다, 안녕히 계세요.

해설 남자는 여자에게 오늘 공부 모임에 오면 자신의 공책을 가져오라고 Judy에게 말해 달라고 했다.

어휘 at the moment 바로 지금 leave a message 메시지를 남기다

04 ②

여: 콘서트가 8시에 시작하지, 그렇지 않니?
남: 응. 우리 콘서트홀에서 만날까?
여: 먼저 저녁을 먹는 게 어때?
남: 좋아. 뭐 먹고 싶어?
여: 나는 일본 음식점에 가고 싶어.
남: 그거 좋은 생각이다. 7시에 너희 집 앞으로 데리러 갈게.
여: 너무 늦지 않아? 저녁 먹을 시간이 충분하지 않을 거야.
남: 네 말이 맞아. 그럼 언제가 좋을까?
여: 대신 6시 30분은 어때?
남: 좋아.

[해설] 7시에 만나면 콘서트 시작 전에 저녁 먹을 시간이 충분하지 않아서 6시 30분에 만나기로 했다.

[어휘] pick ~ up ~을 태우러 가다 in front of ~의 앞에

05 ④

남: 실례합니다.
여: 네, 도와드릴까요?
남: 네. 이 바지를 반품하고 싶어요.
여: 알겠습니다. 바지에 무슨 문제라도 있나요?
남: 음, 선물이었는데, 너무 꽉 껴요.
여: 알겠습니다. 다른 치수로 교환하시겠어요?
남: 네, 그렇게 해 주세요. 중간 치수로 주시겠어요?
여: 네. 여기서 그걸 입어 보실 수 있도록 지금 가져올게요.
남: 감사합니다.

[해설] 남자는 선물로 받은 바지를 다른 치수로 교환을 요청하고 있으므로, 두 사람이 대화하는 장소로 가장 적절한 곳은 옷 가게이다.

[어휘] return [ritə́:rn] 돌려주다, 반납하다 tight [tait] (옷이) 꽉 끼는

06 ④

① 여: 도와줄 사람을 원하시나요?
   남: 괜찮아요. 이미 콘서트 표를 샀습니다.
② 여: 기계 사용하는 것을 도와드릴까요?
   남: 괜찮습니다. 그냥 탄산음료를 하나 더 사려는 중이에요.
③ 여: 뭘 좀 도와드릴까요?
   남: 지하철역이 어디에 있는지 아시나요?
④ 여: 도움이 필요하신가요?
   남: 홍대로 가는 표를 사려고 하는데, 이 기계를 어떻게 사용하는지 모르겠어요.
⑤ 여: 오늘은 무엇을 도와드릴까요?
   남: 명동역으로 가는 표를 주세요.

[해설] 티켓 자판기 앞에서 어리둥절해하는 남자를 여자가 도와주려 하고 있는 상황이다.

[어휘] purchase [pə́:rtʃəs] 사다, 구입하다 machine [məʃíːn] 기계
soda [sóudə] 탄산음료

07 ③

남: 도와드릴까요?
여: 네, 아들의 생일 선물로 줄 책을 찾고 있어요.
남: 생각하신 게 있나요?
여: 〈One Summer Night〉이라는 책이 있나요?
남: 아, 죄송하지만 그 책은 품절되었어요. 사실, 동네에 다른 서점들에도 그 책은 전혀 없습니다. 며칠 있으면 책이 더 도착할 거예요.
여: 알겠습니다. 그럼 책이 도착하면 제게 전화해 주실 수 있나요?
남: 물론입니다. 저희가 책을 더 받는 대로 전화를 드리겠습니다.
여: 고맙습니다. 여기 제 전화번호입니다.

[해설] 여자는 사려는 책이 품절되었고 며칠 뒤 더 입고될 거라는 남자의 말에 책이 도착하면 전화 달라고 부탁했다.

[어휘] none [nʌn] 아무(것)도 ~ 않다 copy [kápi] 복사; *(책·신문 등의) 한 부[권]

08 ①

남: 안녕하세요, 학생 여러분. Barton 교장입니다. 2월 16일에 졸업식을 개최합니다. 우리는 학교 강당에서 졸업식을 하기로 되어 있었습니다. 하지만 바이러스 때문에, 학교 위원회는 온라인에서 대신 하기로 결정했습니다. 졸업식에 관한 몇 가지 세부 사항을 공유하려고 합니다. 졸업식은 오전 9시에 시작할 것입니다. 그러므로 그 전에 학교 웹 사이트에 접속해야 합니다. 모두 교복을 입고 단정해 보이기를 바랍니다. 졸업식 때 노래를 부르기로 되어 있는 사람들은 오전 8시까지 학교 스튜디오로 와야 합니다. 경청해 주셔서 고맙습니다.

[해설] 날짜(2월 16일), 온라인 대체 이유(바이러스), 시작 시각(오전 9시), 복장(교복 착용)에 관해서는 언급되었으나, 연설자는 언급되지 않았다.

[어휘] principal [prínsəpəl] 교장 graduation ceremony 졸업식 be supposed to-v ~하기로 되어 있다 auditorium [ɔ̀:ditɔ́:riəm] 강당 committee [kəmíti] 위원회 decide [disáid] 결정하다 detail [ditéil] 세부 사항 log in to ~에 접속하다 school uniform 교복

09 ④

여: 이것은 한국인들이 기념하는 특별한 전통 명절입니다. 이것은 12월에 있으며, 일 년 중 낮이 가장 짧고 밤이 가장 깁니다. 이날쯤 추워지기 시작하며, 한국인들은 이날이 겨울의 시작이라 믿습니다. 가정에서는 팥죽을 만들어 함께 먹으며, 서로에게 건강과 다가오는 해의 행운을 빌어 줍니다.

[해설] 연중 낮이 가장 짧고 밤이 가장 긴 날로, 팥죽을 먹으며 건강과 행운을 비는 한국 명절은 동지이다.

어휘 traditional [trədíʃənəl] 전통의 celebrate [séləbrèit] 기념하다 day [dei] 날, 하루; *낮 red bean 팥 luck [lʌk] 행운 coming [kʌ́miŋ] 다가오는

10 ②

① 남: 새 직장 어때?
　여: 더할 나위 없이 좋아.
② 남: 오후 7시까지 할 수 있겠니?
　여: 내가 생각했던 것보다 오래 걸렸어.
③ 남: 방학 동안 무엇을 할 거니?
　여: 배낭여행을 갈 거야.
④ 남: 이 학교에 다닌 지 얼마나 됐니?
　여: 이제 2년이 됐어.
⑤ 남: 난 아주 바빴고, 지금 너무 피곤해.
　여: 넌 마실 것을 더 마시고 많이 쉬어야 해.

해설 7시까지 할 수 있겠냐는 질문에 생각보다 오래 걸렸다며 과거의 일을 말하는 것은 어색하다.

어휘 vacation [vekéiʃn] 방학, 휴가 go backpacking 배낭여행을 가다 attend [əténd] 참석하다; *(~에) 다니다 fluid [flúːid] 액체; *수분, 마실 것 plenty of 많은

11 ①

여: 여보, 뭐 하고 있어요?
남: 온라인으로 책장 쇼핑하고 있어요. Jenny에게 새것을 사 주고 싶어서요. 책이 정말 많아서 공간이 넉넉하지 않아요.
여: 맞아요. 상점에 가서 사는 게 어때요?
남: 그럴 수도 있지만, 시내에 갈 시간이 정말 없어요. 그리고 이 온라인 상점은 중고 가구를 파는데, 가격이 적당해요.
여: 알았어요. 염두에 둔 게 있나요?
남: 이게 좋아 보여요. 어떻게 생각해요?
여: 강철로 만들어져서 튼튼해 보여요. 하지만 그건 너무 커서 그 애 방에 맞지 않을 것 같아요.
남: 그래요? 그 애 방 크기를 확인해 보는 게 어때요?
여: 네, 분명 그걸 먼저 해야 해요.

해설 두 사람은 온라인 상점에서 사려는 책장이 커 보여서 방 크기를 먼저 확인해 보기로 했다.

어휘 bookshelf [búkʃèlf] 책장 space [speis] 우주; *공간 downtown [dàuntáun] 시내에[로] second-hand [sékəndhǽnd] 중고의 furniture [fɔ́ːrnitʃər] 가구 reasonable [ríːzənəbl] 합리적인; *(가격이) 적정한 steel [stiːl] 강철 fit [fit] (어느 장소에 들어가기에) 맞다 definitely [défənitli] 분명히, 틀림없이

12 ③

여: 자, 우리 극장에서 어디에 앉아야 할까?
남: 음… 더 저렴한 좌석은 A와 E 구역에 있어.
여: 그래, 하지만 거기서는 잘 안 보여.
남: 맞아. B 구역에 있는 좌석을 사보자.
여: 거긴 무대에 너무 가깝고 너무 비싸. D 구역은 어때? 잘 보일 거고, B 구역보다 훨씬 더 저렴해.
남: 하지만 거긴 무대에서 너무 멀어. C 구역에 앉자.
여: 그래, 좋아. 내가 표를 살게.
남: 빨리 이 뮤지컬을 보고 싶어.
여: 나도. 그걸 보려고 오랫동안 기다려 왔어.

해설 두 사람은 무대가 잘 보이면서 무대에 너무 가깝거나 멀지 않은 C 구역의 표를 사기로 했다.

어휘 theater [θíːətər] 극장 cheaper [tʃíːpər] 더 싼 (cheap의 비교급) view [vjuː] 시야 can't wait to-v 빨리 ~하고 싶다

13 ②

여: Harry, 너 아주 달라 보여. 무슨 일 있었니?
남: 음, 살을 많이 뺐어.
여: 어떻게 한 거니?
남: 아주 열심히 운동했어. 지난 6개월 동안, 거의 매일 수영을 하고 많이 걸었어.
여: 멋져! 얼마나 뺐니?
남: 맞혀 봐.
여: 10kg 정도 빠진 것 같아 보여.
남: 꽤 비슷해. 운동을 시작했을 때 80kg이었는데, 8kg을 뺐어.
여: 와, 6개월 만에 8kg을 뺐단 말이야? 대단하다.

해설 남자는 6개월 전 80kg이었고 운동을 하면서 8kg을 뺐다고 했으므로, 현재 몸무게는 72kg이다.

어휘 lose weight 살을 빼다 close [klous] 가까운; *비슷한

14 ⑤

남: 안녕, Sally. 지난 주말에 뭐 했니?
여: 안녕, Tom. 그냥 집에 있었어. 일요일에 축구 경기는 어땠어?
남: 아, 지난 주말에는 축구 안 했어.
여: 왜? 넌 경기에 절대 빠지지 않잖아.
남: 어머니 생신이어서 부모님을 찾아뵙고 같이 하루를 보냈어.
여: 오, 어머니께 뭔가를 사 드렸니?
남: 응. 어머니께서 내 선물을 좋아하셨어.
여: 잘됐다. 어머니께 무엇을 사 드렸어?
남: 스카프를 사 드렸어.

해설 남자는 일요일이 어머니 생신이어서 부모님을 찾아뵙고 함께 시간을 보냈다고 했다.

어휘 How come? 왜[어째서]? miss [mis] 놓치다; *빠지다, 가지 못하다

15 ②

남: 어젯밤 강력한 지진이 콜카타를 강타했습니다. 많은 사람들이 한밤 중에 땅이 흔들리는 것을 느꼈습니다. 진도 7의 지진이었습니다. 수백 명의 사람들이 사망하거나 부상을 입었습니다. 건물과 집이 무너지고 도로가 파손되었습니다. 몇 차례의 여진이 예상되는 가운데, 집을 잃은 수천 명의 사람들이 국제 원조를 기다리고 있습니다.

해설 어젯밤 발생한 지진으로 인한 피해 상황에 대해 말하고 있다.

어휘 earthquake [ə́ːrθkwèik] 지진 earth [əːrθ] 지구; *땅 shake [ʃeik] 흔들리다 magnitude [mǽgnətùːd] (지진의) 규모, 진도 hundreds of 수백의 hurt [həːrt] 부상을 입다 destroy [distrɔ́i] 파괴하다 aftershock [ǽftərʃɑ̀ːk] (큰 지진 후의) 여진 anticipate [æntísəpèit] 예상하다 thousands of 수천의 international aid 국제 원조

16 ③

여: 실례합니다. 계산할게요.
남: 네. 식사는 어떠셨나요?
여: 파스타와 샐러드가 훌륭했어요.
남: 다행이네요. 여기 계산서가 있습니다. 총 20달러입니다.
여: 20달러요? 알겠어요.
남: 회원 카드가 있으신가요?
여: 네, 있어요.
남: 그렇다면 10% 할인을 받으실 수 있습니다.
여: 아, 그거 좋네요. 여기 있습니다.

해설 식사 비용 총 20달러에서 회원 카드로 10% 할인이 된다고 했으므로, 여자가 지불할 금액은 18달러이다.

어휘 pay one's bill 돈을 내다[치르다] meal [miːl] 식사 excellent [éksələnt] 훌륭한, 매우 좋은 check [tʃek] 확인; *계산서 discount [diskáunt] 할인

17 ③

여: 너희 누나에게 뭐 사 줄 거야?
남: 모르겠어. 제안할 만한 게 있니?
여: 음. 옷이나 신발이 일반적인 선물인 것 같은데.
남: 응, 그런데 우리 누나는 그런 것들이 필요 없어. 네가 우리 누나 옷장을 한번 봐야 해. 새 옷들로 가득 차 있어. 그리고 신발도 충분해.
여: 그러면 반지는 어때? 비싸긴 하겠지만 말이야.
남: 응, 그건 내 예산을 넘을 것 같아.
여: 음, 요즘 누나가 무엇에 관심이 있니?
남: 아! 수영 강습을 받기 시작했어! 그리고 누나는 새 수영모가 필요하

다고 했어.
여: 잘됐다. 스포츠 매장에 가자.

해설 남자는 누나에게 줄 선물을 여자와 상의하고 있는데 누나가 수영모가 필요하다고 말했다고 했으므로, 스포츠 매장에 가자는 응답이 가장 적절하다.
① 그녀가 수영하는 걸 도와줄 수 있니?
② 그녀와 수영하러 가고 싶어.
④ 그녀가 패션에 관심이 있는지 몰랐어.
⑤ 우리는 수영할 때 수영모를 써야 해.

어휘 suggestion [səʤéstʃən] 제안 common [kámən] 일반적인, 평범한 check out ~을 확인하다 closet [klázit] 옷장 though [ðou] 그러나, 하지만 beyond [bijánd] ~의 범위를 넘어서 budget [búʤit] 예산

18 ③

여: 오늘 5시에 영화 볼래?
남: 5시? 생각해 둔 특정 영화가 있니?
여: 응, 보고 싶은 코미디가 있어. 내가 표를 예매할게.
남: 좋아! 내가 쇼핑을 좀 한 다음에 만나면 되겠다.
여: 그래, 3시 정각에 만나는 게 어때?
남: 글쎄, 내가 그때까지 쇼핑을 마칠 수 있을 것 같지 않아.
여: 알았어. 그럼 너는 언제가 좋겠어?
남: 4시 정각은 어때?

해설 남자가 3시까지 쇼핑을 마칠 수 없을 것 같다고 하자 여자는 언제 만나면 좋을지 물었으므로, 3시 이후로 가능한 시각을 말하는 응답이 가장 적절하다.
① 또 보자.
② 나도 정말 즐거웠어.
④ 내일이 괜찮을 것 같아.
⑤ 그럼 3시 정각에 만나자.

어휘 specific [spisífik] 특정한 book [buk] 책; *예약하다

19 ④

남: 안녕하세요. 예약하셨습니까?
여: 아니요, 안 했어요. 두 사람 자리 주세요.
남: 죄송하지만, 지금 당장은 자리가 없습니다. 주말에는 거의 항상 예약이 꽉 차기 때문에, 미리 예약하실 것을 권해 드립니다.
여: 음. 얼마나 기다려야 하나요?
남: 확신할 수는 없지만, 최소한 15분은 기다리셔야 할 겁니다.
여: 그럼 여기서 기다릴게요. 먼저 주문해도 되나요?
남: 그럼요, 바로 메뉴를 갖다드릴게요.

해설 여자는 식당에서 자리가 나기를 기다리겠다며 주문을 먼저 해도 되는지 물었으므로, 메뉴를 갖다주겠다는 응답이 가장 적절하다.
① 신용카드로 지불하실 수 있습니다.

② 아니요, 아직 주문할 준비가 안 됐어요.

③ 이쪽으로 오시겠어요?

⑤ 저희 식당은 보통 밤 10시에 문을 닫습니다.

[어휘] have[make] a reservation 예약하다 fully [fúli] 완전히
in advance 미리 at least 최소한, 적어도 [문제] credit card
신용카드

20 ③

여: Jimmy는 자신의 건강에 대해 걱정하기 시작합니다. 최근에 그는
밤에 잠을 잘 수가 없습니다. 수업 시간에 깨어 있는 데 어려움을 겪
고 있으며 이는 그의 성적에도 영향을 미치기 때문에, 그것은 큰 문
제가 되고 있습니다. Jimmy의 친구 Claire는 그가 패스트푸드를
많이 먹고 커피를 너무 많이 마신다는 것을 알게 됩니다. 그녀는 이
러한 조합이 그가 잠을 잘 자는 능력에 영향을 미친다고 생각합니
다. 이런 상황에서, Claire는 Jimmy에게 뭐라고 말하겠습니까?

Claire: 너는 더 건강하게 먹고 커피를 덜 마셔야 해.

[해설] Claire는 Jimmy가 패스트푸드를 많이 먹고 커피를 너무 많이 마셔
서 숙면을 취하지 못한다고 생각하므로, 더 건강한 식사를 하고 커피
를 줄이라는 말이 가장 적절하다.

① 너는 네 선생님을 더 자주 봬야 해.

② 너는 밤에 너무 늦게 자면 안 돼.

④ 내가 너라면, 수업 중에 자지 않을 텐데.

⑤ 네 문제에 대해 부모님께 말씀드리는 게 어때?

[어휘] fall asleep 잠들다 struggle to-v ~하려고 애쓰다, ~하는 데 어
려움을 겪다 stay awake 자지 않고 깨어 있다 affect [əfékt] 영
향을 미치다 grade [greid] 성적 as well ~도, 역시 find out
~을 알아내다 combination [kàmbənéiʃən] 결합, 조합 ability
[əbíləti] 능력

Dictation Test 03

pp. 70~77

01 1) look better with long hair
    2) look good with a perm 3) dye your hair

02 1) heavy or uncomfortable
    2) recording how much I exercise
    3) get directions 4) last with one charge

03 1) come to our study meeting 2) leave a message
    3) tell her to bring my notes

04 1) How about eating dinner
    2) Isn't that too late 3) How about 6:30

05 1) return these pants
    2) exchange them for a different size
    3) try them on here

06 1) help you with the machine
    2) where the subway station is
    3) how to use this machine 4) I'd like a ticket

07 1) is sold out 2) can you call me
    3) get more copies

08 1) because of the virus 2) start at 9:00
    3) wear school uniforms

09 1) longest night of the year
    2) beginning of the winter
    3) luck for the coming year

10 1) How do you like 2) took longer than I thought
    3) get plenty of rest

11 1) enough space for them
    2) its prices are reasonable 3) check her room size

12 1) view is bad from there 2) still cheaper than
    3) too far from the stage

13 1) lost a lot of weight 2) exercised very hard
    3) That's quite close

14 1) stayed home 2) didn't play soccer
    3) visited my parents
    4) buy something for your mother

15 1) hit by a powerful earthquake
    2) were killed or hurt 3) wait for international aid

16 1) Twenty dollars in total
    2) have a membership card 3) get a 10% discount

17 1) full of new clothes 2) beyond my budget
    3) needed a new swimming cap

18 1) specific movie in mind 2) book the tickets
    3) when would be a good time

19 1) have a reservation
    2) fully booked on the weekend
    3) at least 15 minutes 4) Can I order first

20 1) get worried about his health
    2) struggles to stay awake
    3) affects his ability to sleep well

Word Test 01~03

pp. 78~79

A

01 사과하다
02 ~ 외에
03 취소
04 자정
05 집 없는
06 부족하다
07 동료
08 인근의
09 경쾌한
10 제공하다
11 참가자
12 최근에
13 상품, 제품
14 기회
15 더 좋아하다
16 흔들리다
17 불편한
18 갑작스러운
19 추천하다
20 계단
21 빼다; (돈을) 인출하다
22 ~의 범위를 넘어서
23 고르다
24 기능
25 강당
26 주로, 대부분
27 이익
28 질
29 보급품
30 모으다
31 특정한
32 환경
33 파괴하다
34 등록하다
35 ~에 참가하다
36 예약하다
37 ~하자마자
38 ~을 제출하다
39 ~을 돕다
40 ~을 염두에 두다, ~을 생각하다

B

01 steep
02 principal
03 shipping
04 rude
05 island
06 limit
07 traditional
08 ability
09 donate
10 consumer
11 budget
12 perform
13 background
14 earthquake
15 charge
16 facility
17 haste
18 mechanic
19 affect
20 steady
21 grocery
22 detail
23 deliver
24 committee
25 judge
26 blanket
27 earth
28 realize
29 straight
30 exchange
31 hunt
32 perfume
33 waste
34 graduation ceremony
35 for free
36 take an order
37 stand in line
38 go on a business trip
39 take a deep breath
40 log in to

실전모의고사 04회

pp. 80~81

01 ⑤	02 ⑤	03 ③	04 ②	05 ②
06 ①	07 ①	08 ②	09 ④	10 ④
11 ⑤	12 ②	13 ③	14 ②	15 ①
16 ③	17 ①	18 ⑤	19 ③	20 ⑤

01 ⑤

남: 얘, 뭐 하고 있어?
여: 온라인으로 쇼핑하고 있어. 이 매장은 재고 정리 세일을 하고 있거든.
남: 뭘 살 거야?
여: 이 스카프 어때?
남: 좋아 보이기는 한데, 줄무늬가 있는 디자인만 있어?
여: 아니. 무늬가 없는 것과 물방울무늬가 있는 것을 포함해서 몇 가지 다른 스타일이 있어.
남: 무늬가 없는 것은 밋밋하고, 나는 물방울무늬는 별로 좋아하지 않아.
여: 나도. 그럼 작은 꽃무늬가 있는 이것은 어때?
남: 그거 좋네.
여: 나는 이게 가장 좋아. 그걸 사야겠어.

해설 여자는 작은 꽃무늬가 있는 스카프를 사기로 했다.

어휘 clearance sale 재고 정리 세일 including [ínklú:diŋ] ~을 포함하여 plain [plein] 무늬가 없는; *무지의 직물 polka dot 물방울무늬

02 ⑤

남: Samantha, 너 화난 것 같아. 무슨 일이니?
여: 저 남자가 휴대전화로 너무 크게 말하고 있어. 참을 수가 없어.
남: 맞아, 정말 짜증 나. 그가 대화하는 모든 말이 들려.
여: 휴대전화 사용자들은 좀 더 배려심이 있어야 한다고 생각해. 요즘, 사람들이 공공장소 곳곳에서 전화로 크게 이야기하는 걸 들을 수 있어. 극장에서도, 지하철에서도, 심지어 도서관에서도 들리잖아.
남: 전적으로 동의해.

해설 여자가 공공장소에서 휴대전화로 크게 말하는 사람들이 남을 배려하는 마음을 가져야 한다고 하자, 남자는 그에 동의하고 있다.

어휘 loudly [láudli] 큰 소리로 stand [stænd] 서 있다; *참다 annoying [ənɔ́iiŋ] 짜증스러운 conversation [kànvərséiʃən] 대화 thoughtful [θɔ́:tfəl] 배려심 있는 public [pʌ́blik] 공공의

03 ③

[휴대전화가 울린다.]
남: 여보세요?

여: 여보세요, 아빠. Fiona에요.

남: 너에게 전화하려던 참이었어. 너 어디에 있니? 네가 한 시간 전에 집에 올 거라고 했잖아.

여: 알아요. 죄송해요, 하지만 집에 가는 길에 제 차가 고장 났어요. 그래서 지금 정비소에 있어요.

남: 아, 그거 참 안됐구나. 너는 괜찮니?

여: 괜찮아요.

남: 차에 무슨 문제가 있는 거니?

여: 모르겠지만, 차를 고치는 데 시간이 좀 걸릴 거라고 했어요. 여기로 오셔서 저를 집까지 태워 주시겠어요?

남: 물론이지. 금방 거기로 갈게. 어느 정비소에 있니?

[해설] 여자는 남자에게 차가 고장 나서 정비소에 있다며 자신을 데리러 오기를 부탁했다.

[어휘] be about to-v 막 ~하려고 하다 break down 고장 나다 on the way home 집에 오는[가는] 길에 service center (자동차·전기 제품 등의) 수리소, 정비소 give ~ a ride ~을 태워 주다

04 ②

여: 이 책들을 빌리고 싶은데요.

남: 네. 총 세 권이네요. 7일 이내에 반납해 주세요.

여: 7일이요? 그러면 다음 주 금요일까지인가요?

남: 아뇨. 오늘은 목요일입니다. 그러니 다음 주 목요일까지 반납해 주세요.

여: 알겠습니다.

남: 아, 죄송합니다. 제가 실수했네요. 이건 신작이라서, 4일 후에 반납하셔야 할 겁니다.

여: 알겠습니다. 월요일에 반납할게요.

남: 알겠습니다.

[해설] 여자가 빌린 책은 신작이라 반납 기한이 4일 후라고 해서, 다음 주 월요일에 책을 반납하겠다고 했다.

[어휘] check out (책 등을) 대출하다 make a mistake 실수하다 since [sins] ~ 이래; *~이므로 new release 신간

05 ②

여: 너 항공권은 샀니?

남: 응. 인터넷으로 샀어. 이제 여행 짐을 싸고 있어.

여: 그래서 정확히 언제 가니?

남: 지금부터 10일 후에. 빨리 가고 싶어. 정말 재미있을 거야.

여: 넌 어떤 나라들을 갈 계획이야?

남: 영국, 프랑스, 그리고 이탈리아를 갈 거야. 한 달간 가 있을 거야.

여: 부럽다. 유럽에서 한 달이라니. 정말 멋진 여름휴가야!

남: 응, 난 이 여행을 오랫동안 계획해 왔어. 이제 내가 원하는 것은 거기에 가는 것뿐이야.

[해설] 남자는 오랫동안 계획해 온 유럽 여행을 빨리 가고 싶다고 했으므로 신이 날(excited) 것이다.

① 질투하는 ③ 느긋한 ④ 초조한 ⑤ 당황한

[어휘] pack [pæk] (짐 등을) 싸다, 챙기다 exactly [igzǽktli] 정확히 country [kʌ́ntri] 국가, 나라 envy [énvi] 부러워하다

06 ①

① 여: 제 원피스에서 얼룩을 제거해 주시면 좋겠어요.

남: 알겠습니다. 이번 주 토요일에 찾으러 오시면 됩니다.

② 여: 나랑 쇼핑몰에 갈래? 새 원피스가 필요해.

남: 물론이야. 언제 가고 싶어?

③ 여: 나 이 원피스 입은 거 어때?

남: 정말 좋아 보여!

④ 여: 이런! 내 원피스에 커피를 쏟았어!

남: 걱정하지 마. 씻어내면 돼.

⑤ 여: 이 원피스를 사고 싶어요.

남: 죄송합니다, 부인. 그건 비매품입니다.

[해설] 세탁소에서 여자는 남자에게 얼룩이 묻은 옷을 보여 주고 있는 상황이다.

[어휘] remove [rimúːv] 제거하다 stain [stein] 얼룩 spill [spil] (액체 등을) 쏟다, 엎지르다 wash ~ off ~을 씻어내다 not for sale 비매품

07 ①

남: 얘, Katie. 부탁할 게 있는데, 네가 바쁘지 않다면 말이야.

여: 나 바쁘지 않아. 뭔데?

남: Justin Gilmore가 시내에서 공연을 해.

여: 와! 너 그가 오기를 기다려 왔잖아, 그렇지 않니?

남: 응. 하지만 문제가 있어.

여: 그게 뭔데?

남: 오늘 오후 3시에 표가 판매되는데, 그때 나는 수업 중일 거야. 네가 나 대신 한 장 사 줄 수 있니?

여: 물론이야, 해 볼게. 하지만 빠르게 매진될 거라, 사지 못할지도 몰라.

남: 알아.

[해설] 남자는 기다려 온 가수의 공연 표가 판매될 시간에 수업 중일 자신을 대신하여 여자에게 표를 사 달라고 부탁했다.

[어휘] sell out 다 팔리다, 매진되다

08 ②

여: Science Camp의 프로그램 책임자로서, 중요한 공고를 할 것이 있습니다. 올해의 Science Camp는 7월 16일부터 7월 30일까지 Montgomery 학교에서 열릴 예정입니다. 캠프는 무료입니다! 그러나 재료와 준비물을 위한 20달러의 등록비는 있습니다. 캠프에서의 활동은 영화 감상, 게임, 과학 실험, 그리고 다양한 분야에 있는 과학자들과의 만남을 포함하고 있습니다. 캠프 참가자로 지원하려면,

www.esfsci.com에서 등록하세요.

[해설] 날짜와 장소(7월 16일부터 7월 30일까지 Montgomery 학교에서), 등록비(기본 무료이나 재료비 20달러 있음), 프로그램 활동(영화 감상, 게임, 과학 실험, 과학자들과의 만남), 캠프 등록 방법(www. esfsci.com에서 등록)에 관해서는 언급되었으나, 캠프 운영진 정보는 언급되지 않았다.

[어휘] director [diréktər] 책임자 fee [fi:] 요금, 가입비 material [mətí:riəl] 재료 supply [səplái] 공급; *준비물 activity [æktívəti] 활동 include [inklú:d] 포함하다 experiment [ikspérəmənt] 실험 field [fi:ld] 들판; *분야 apply [əplái] 지원하다, 신청하다 register [rédʒistər] 등록하다

09 ④

남: 이 직업을 가진 사람들은 자동차와 트럭 같은 차량을 수리하고 관리합니다. 자동차가 고장 나면, 그들은 문제가 무엇인지 알아냅니다. 그리고 나서 연장과 특수 기계를 사용하여 그것을 수리합니다. 때때로 그들은 새로운 부품을 설치하기도 합니다. 이 직업을 갖기 위해서는, 차량과 기계에 관해 많이 알아야 합니다. 또한 전문 면허가 있어야 합니다.

[해설] 전문적으로 차량을 수리하고 관리하는 일을 하는 직업은 자동차 정비사이다.

[어휘] fix [fiks] 고치다, 수리하다 maintain [meintéin] (점검·보수하여) 유지하다, 관리하다 vehicle [ví:ikl] 차량, 탈것 tool [tu:l] 연장, 도구 install [instɔ́:l] 설치하다 professional [prəféʃənəl] 전문적인 license [láisəns] 허가(증), 면허(증)

10 ④

① 남: 너 어디에 있었니?
  여: 도서관에서 책을 읽고 있었어.
② 남: 내 선글라스 봤니?
  여: 네 책상 위에 있는 것 같아.
③ 남: 제가 이 셔츠를 샀는데, 구멍이 있어요.
  여: 죄송합니다. 새것으로 드리겠습니다.
④ 남: 우유 사는 거 잊지 않았지, 그렇지?
  여: 우리 냉장고에 우유가 하나도 없어.
⑤ 남: 나는 흰 원피스보다 빨간 원피스가 더 나은 것 같아.
  여: 나도 빨간 원피스가 마음에 들어.

[해설] 우유 사는 것을 잊지 않았는지 묻는데, 냉장고에 우유가 없다는 응답은 어색하다.

[어휘] hole [houl] 구멍 forget to-v ~할 것을 잊다 refrigerator [rifrídʒərèitər] 냉장고

11 ⑤

여: 이번 방학에 무슨 계획이라도 있니?
남: 응! 한국으로 여행을 갈 거야!
여: 신나겠다! 언제 떠나?
남: 이번 주말에 떠날 거야. 그리고 거기서 2주 동안 있을 거야.
여: 와! 거기서 뭐 할 거니?
남: 서울에 있는 고궁에 가고 싶어. 그리고 동대문 시장에 쇼핑하러 갈 거야.
여: 너 한국에 친구도 많잖아, 그렇지 않니?
남: 응. 그들도 보고 싶어. 사실, 그게 다른 어떤 것보다 먼저 할 일이야.
여: 너 아주 바쁘겠구나.
남: 그럴 거야. 너무 기대돼!

[해설] 남자는 한국에서 고궁 방문과 쇼핑보다 먼저 할 일이 친구들을 만나는 일이라고 했다.

[어휘] palace [pǽlis] 궁궐

12 ②

[전화벨이 울린다.]
여: Leonardo 음식점입니다. 무엇을 도와드릴까요?
남: 2월 22일 금요일에 저녁 식사 예약을 하고 싶은데요.
여: 네. 몇 시에 오길 원하시나요?
남: 6시 30분이 어떨까 하는데요?
여: 죄송하지만, 그 시간에는 빈 테이블이 없습니다. 7시는 어떠세요?
남: 좋아요.
여: 일행이 몇 분이 될까요?
남: 제 아내와 저뿐이에요. 저희 성은 Smith입니다.
여: 그리고 손님의 전화번호를 알려 주시겠어요?
남: 014-555-5309입니다.
여: 알겠습니다. 금요일에 뵙겠습니다.

[해설] 6시 30분에는 빈 테이블이 없어서 7시로 예약을 했다.

예약		
①	언제	2월 22일 금요일
②	시각	저녁 6:30
③	인원	2
④	누구	Smith 부부
⑤	전화번호	014-555-5309

[어휘] free [fri:] 자유로운; *비어 있는 party [pá:rti] 파티; *일행, 단체 last name 성(姓)

13 ③

여: 몇 시야?
남: 음, 오후 4시 30분이야.
여: 아! 나 지금 가야 해. 너와 이야기 나눠서 정말 좋았어.
남: 벌써 간다고? 우리 한참 대화 중이었잖아!

여: 30분 후에 Alice를 만나야 해.

남: 그 애에게 전화해서 너희가 만나는 시간을 미룰 수 있니? 우리 이야기할 게 아직 더 있잖아.

여: 미안하지만, 안 돼. 그 애와 콘서트에 가기로 되어 있거든.

남: 그렇구나. 음, 즐거운 시간 보내. 그리고 그 애에게 내 안부 전해 줘.

여: 응, 그럴게.

해설 현재 시각은 4시 30분이고 여자는 30분 후에 Alice를 만나야 한다고 했으므로, 만나기로 한 시각은 5시이다.

어휘 push back (시간·날짜를 뒤로) 미루다 have a good time 즐거운 시간을 보내다 say hello to ~에게 안부를 전하다

14 ②

여: 안녕, Nick. 주말 어떻게 보냈어?

남: 안녕, Christie. 꽤 여유로웠어.

여: Dan이랑 농구 경기 보러 안 갔어?

남: 유감스럽게도, Dan이 몸이 좋지 않아서, 그 앤 집에 있었어.

여: 그러면 너도 안 갔니?

남: 응, 그 표들을 남동생에게 줬어. 그리고 난 하이킹을 갔어.

여: 정말? 혼자서?

남: 응. 날씨가 좋진 않았지만, 정말 즐겁게 보냈어.

여: 잘됐네. 그나저나 언젠가 농구 경기를 보러 가고 싶어. 같이 가자.

남: 좋아.

해설 남자는 주말에 함께 농구 경기를 보기로 했던 친구가 아파서, 혼자 하이킹을 갔다고 했다.

어휘 relaxing [riléksiŋ] 마음을 느긋하게 해 주는, 여유로운 unfortunately [ʌnfɔ́ːrtʃənətli] 불행하게도, 유감스럽게도 go hiking 하이킹을 가다 by oneself 혼자서 enjoy oneself 즐기다, 즐겁게 보내다

15 ①

여: 안녕하세요, Happy Town 주민 여러분! 관리 사무실의 Lena입니다. 공지가 있습니다. 이전에 여러 번 언급했듯이, 우리 아파트는 이번 주에 주차장을 청소할 계획입니다. 그리고 주민들께 차를 이동해 주실 것을 요청드렸습니다. 하지만 많은 차들이 여전히 주차장에 주차되어 있어서, 주차장 청소에 어려움을 겪고 있습니다. 더욱이, 주차장에 차를 두시면, 차가 훼손될 수 있습니다. 오늘은 지하 1층을 청소합니다. 그러니 다시 한번, 지하 2층이나 다른 장소로 차를 이동해 주시기를 요청드립니다. 협조 감사합니다.

해설 아파트 주차장 청소를 위해 주민들에게 차를 이동 주차해 달라고 말하고 있다.

어휘 resident [rézidənt] 주민 management office 관리 사무실 mention [ménʃən] 언급하다 parking lot 주차장 have difficulty v-ing ~하는 데 어려움을 겪다 furthermore [fə́ːrðərmɔ̀ːr] 더욱이 damage [dǽmidʒ] 훼손하다 basement level 지하층 cooperation [kouàpəréiʃən] 협조

16 ③

여: 안녕하세요. 도와드릴까요?

남: 네, 차를 빌리고 싶어요. 가격이 얼마인가요?

여: 중형차는 하루에 80달러입니다. 승합차를 빌리기 원하시면, 하루에 100달러입니다.

남: 중형차를 3일간 빌리는 걸로 할게요. 그리고 아기를 위한 카시트가 하나 필요해요.

여: 네. 그러면 하루에 10달러씩 추가로 내셔야 할 거예요.

남: 알겠습니다. 신용카드로 지불할게요.

여: 문제없습니다.

해설 중형차의 1일 대여료는 80달러이고 카시트가 하루에 10달러이므로, 3일간의 총 대여료는 270달러($80x3＋$10x3)이다.

어휘 rent [rent] 빌리다 van [væn] 밴, 승합차 extra [ékstrə] 추가의 per [pər] ~ 당

17 ①

여: 가족들에게 줄 크리스마스 선물을 벌써 샀니?

남: 응. 그리고 빨리 그 선물들을 주고 싶어.

여: 뭘 샀는데?

남: 음, 아빠를 위해서는 넥타이, 엄마를 위해서는 스카프를 샀어. 그리고 누나에겐 티셔츠를 줄 거야.

여: 네 남동생 Tommy를 위해서는 뭘 샀니?

남: 그 애를 위해서는 장난감 차를 샀어.

여: 아, 너 정말 착하구나! 그런데 너는 크리스마스에 뭘 받고 싶어?

남: 음… 나는 신발이 좋겠어.

해설 여자는 남자에게 크리스마스에 뭘 받고 싶은지 물었으므로, 받고 싶은 선물을 말하는 응답이 가장 적절하다.
② 그들이 내 선물을 마음에 들어 하면 좋겠어.
③ 크리스마스는 내가 가장 좋아하는 휴일이야.
④ 나는 크리스마스에 영화를 보고 싶어.
⑤ 작년 크리스마스의 눈은 여태껏 최고의 선물이었어!

어휘 yet [jet] (의문문에서) 이미, 벌써 [문제] holiday [hɔ́lədei] 공휴일, 휴일

18 ⑤

여: 저 사진 멋져 보여! 네가 찍었니?

남: 내 친구 Eva가 찍었어. 그 애는 정말 재능이 있어. 그 애의 사진들은 잡지에 실렸어.

여: 그 사진을 거실에 걸어야겠어. 그럼 모든 사람이 그걸 볼 수 있잖아.

남: 우리 가족사진이 이미 거실에 걸려 있어. 같은 장소에 사진을 너무 많이 걸면, 지저분해 보일 거야.

여: 부엌에는 아무 사진도 없잖아.

남: 맞아. 하지만 부엌 벽에는 시계가 걸려 있어. 음… 어떤 다른 제안이 있니?

여: 네 침실에 거는 게 어때?

[해설] 남자는 여자에게 사진을 어디에 걸지 다른 제안이 있느냐고 물었으므로, 앞에서 언급한 거실과 부엌을 제외하고 사진을 걸만한 위치를 말하는 응답이 가장 적절하다.
① 난 이 사진을 갖고 싶어.
② 거실에 그것을 걸으렴.
③ 그건 거기에 있으면 안 될 것 같아.
④ 그 사진은 미술관으로 보냈어.

[어휘] talented [tǽləntid] 재능이 있는 hang [hæŋ] 걸다, 걸리다 portrait [pɔ́ːrtrit] 초상화; *인물 사진 messy [mési] 지저분한

19 ③

[전화벨이 울린다.]
여: Clayton 호텔 프런트입니다. 무엇을 도와드릴까요?
남: 문제가 있어서 전화했어요. 욕실 샤워기에서 차가운 물만 나오네요.
여: 그렇다니 죄송합니다, 고객님. 오늘 오후까지 수리해 드릴 수 있습니다.
남: 오늘 오후요? 제가 조깅을 오래 하고 막 돌아왔거든요. 그래서 샤워를 하려면 뜨거운 물이 즉시 필요해요.
여: 알겠습니다, 고객님. 어느 객실에 묵고 계신가요?
남: 403호 객실이요.
여: 수리 기사를 곧바로 보내 드리겠습니다.

[해설] 남자는 욕실에 뜨거운 물이 나오지 않는데 지금 샤워를 해야 한다고 했으므로, 수리 기사를 바로 보내겠다는 응답이 가장 적절하다.
① 깨끗한 수건도 필요해요.
② 룸서비스가 필요하세요?
④ 어떤 방을 원하세요?
⑤ 함께 드실 음료를 원하세요?

[어휘] reception desk (호텔의) 접수처, 프런트 immediately [imíːdiətli] 즉시 [문제] repairman [ripɛ́ərmæ̀n] 수리 기사 right away 곧바로

20 ⑤

남: 진수는 미래 고등학교의 졸업반입니다. 진수는 노래를 아주 잘하기 때문에, 선생님이 그에게 졸업식에서 노래를 불러 달라고 요청했습니다. 진수는 많은 사람들 앞에서는 불안해지기 때문에, 매일 밤 노래 부르는 것을 연습합니다. 졸업식이 있는 날, 진수는 걱정이 되고 다리에 힘이 없습니다. 진수의 선생님은 그를 보고 그에게 걸어갑니다. 이런 상황에서, 그의 선생님은 진수에게 뭐라고 말하겠습니까?

선생님: 넌 잘할 거야! 그저 긴장을 풀고 즐기렴.

[해설] 진수가 졸업식 날 노래 공연 때문에 걱정하고 있으므로, 격려의 말이 가장 적절하다.
① 너는 노래할 기회를 놓쳤구나.
② 너는 연습을 더 했어야 했어.
③ 나는 네가 노래를 잘한다고 생각했어.

④ 네게 실망했다고 말할 수밖에 없구나.

[어휘] senior [síːnjər] 연장자; *(학교의) 최상급생, 졸업반 anxious [ǽŋkʃəs] 걱정하는, 불안해하는 weak [wiːk] 약한, 힘이 없는

Dictation Test 04

pp. 82~89

01 1) having a clearance sale 2) Plain is boring
3) with the little flowers

02 1) talking too loudly 2) should be more thoughtful
3) couldn't agree more

03 1) my car broke down 2) take some time
3) give me a ride

04 1) check out these books
2) return them within seven days
3) return them on Monday

05 1) packing for the trip 2) be so much fun
3) get there

06 1) remove a stain 2) How do I look 3) wash it off
4) not for sale

07 1) is having a concert 2) tickets go on sale
3) get one for me

08 1) through July 30 2) for materials and supplies
3) apply to be a camp participant

09 1) fix and maintain vehicles
2) use tools and special machines
3) install new parts

10 1) get you a new one 2) forget to buy milk
3) looks better than

11 1) leaving this weekend 2) visit old palaces
3) do before anything else

12 1) for Friday, February 22
2) How about seven o'clock 3) How many people
4) have your phone number

13 1) I've got to go 2) in 30 minutes
3) I'm supposed to go

14 1) wasn't feeling well 2) I went hiking
3) really enjoyed myself

15 1) clean the parking lot
2) having difficulty cleaning it 3) move your car

16 1) rent a car 2) $80 a day 3) for three days
4) pay an extra $10

17 1) give the presents to them 2) got a toy car
    3) what do you want
18 1) hang the photo 2) will look messy
    3) have any other suggestions
19 1) I'm calling because 2) get it fixed
    3) need hot water immediately
20 1) sing at the graduation ceremony 2) gets anxious
    3) his legs feel weak

실전모의고사 05회

01 ⑤	02 ③	03 ②	04 ④	05 ④
06 ①	07 ③	08 ③	09 ②	10 ⑤
11 ④	12 ①	13 ⑤	14 ①	15 ⑤
16 ①	17 ⑤	18 ④	19 ③	20 ②

01 ⑤

남: 와, 네 저녁 파티 초대장을 만들고 있는 거야? 멋져 보여.
여: 그렇게 생각하니? 한동안 이걸 하고 있었는데, 잘 모르겠어.
남: 난 가운데 케이크가 있는 카드가 마음에 들어.
여: 처음에는 초가 있는 케이크 하나를 통째로 그렸는데, 케이크 한 조각으로 바꿨어.
남: 이 케이크 위에 있는 딸기가 정말 귀여워.
여: 'Welcome'을 어디에 넣어야 할 것 같아?
남: 케이크 바로 위가 좋겠어.
여: 좋은 생각이야. 거기에 넣을래.

해설 여자는 초대장에 딸기가 있는 케이크 한 조각을 그렸고, 그 바로 위에 'Welcome'을 써넣기로 했다.

어휘 invitation 초대(장) for a while 한동안 a piece of 한 조각의

02 ③

여: 재민아, 뭐 하고 있니?
남: 오래된 옷을 버리려고 모으고 있어. 더 이상 안 입거든.
여: 그것들을 Hope Goods에 기부하지 그래?
남: Hope Goods? 그게 뭔데?
여: 전쟁 난민들을 돕는 자선 단체야. 2020년에 설립되었어.
남: 아, 그들을 돕고 싶어. 옷 이외에 어떤 물품들을 기부할 수 있니?

여: 담요도 필요하다고 들었어.
남: 음식은?
여: 음식은 받지 않는 것 같은데, 그들은 기부금을 사용해서 난민들에게 통조림 식품이나 병에 든 생수를 제공해.
남: 그렇구나. 그러면 돈도 좀 기부할래.
여: 좋은 생각이야. 나도 해야겠다.

해설 설립 목적(전쟁 난민 돕기), 설립 연도(2020년), 기부 품목(옷, 담요), 기부금 사용처(난민에게 식량과 물 제공)에 관해서는 언급되었으나, 자선 행사는 언급되지 않았다.

어휘 gather [ɡǽðər] 모으다, 모이다 throw ~ away ~을 버리다 charity [tʃǽrəti] 자선 단체 war [wɔːr] 전쟁 refugee [rèfjudʒíː] 난민 found [faund] 설립하다 besides [bisáidz] ~ 외에 donation [dounéiʃən] 기부(금), 기증(물) provide [prəváid] 제공하다 canned food 통조림 식품 bottled water 병에 든 생수

03 ②

여: 눈이 올 것 같아.
남: 그래, 구름이 갑자기 모이고 있어. 서두르는 것이 좋겠어.
여: 어머, 봐! 벌써 눈이 오고 있어.
남: 오, 이런. 눈 올 때 운전하는 거 싫은데.
여: 눈이 점점 더 많이 오고 있어. 아무래도 잠깐 멈춰서 타이어에 스노 체인을 채워야겠어.
남: 음, 유감이지만 내게 스노 체인이 없어. 오늘 눈이 올 줄 몰랐거든.
여: 정말이야? 겨울에는 항상 스노 체인을 가지고 다녀야 해. 후회하는 것보다 안전한 게 낫다는 거 알잖아.

해설 여자는 겨울에 눈이 올 것을 대비해 항상 스노 체인을 가지고 다녀야 한다고 충고하고 있다.

어휘 suddenly [sʌ́dənli] 갑자기 heavy [hévi] 무거운; *(양·정도 등이 보통보다) 많은, 심한 snow chains 스노 체인(눈길을 달릴 수 있도록 자동차 바퀴에 감는 체인)

04 ④

여: 내일 엄마 생신 선물을 살 거야. 나랑 같이 갈래?
남: 그래, 재미있겠다. 언제 갈 거니?
여: 내일 방과 후에 쇼핑몰에서 만나자. 오후 3시 어때?
남: 안 돼, 그때는 못 만나. 2시에 밴드 연습이 있어.
여: 아, 정말? 연습이 얼마나 걸리니?
남: 보통 한 시간 정도 후에 끝나.
여: 그래, 그럼 너 밴드 연습 끝나고 3시 30분에 만나자.
남: 좋아! 그때 보자!

해설 남자의 밴드 연습이 2시에 시작해서 한 시간 정도 후에 끝나서, 두 사람은 3시 30분에 만나기로 했다.

어휘 practice [prǽktis] 연습

05 ④

① 여: 사진술을 배우고 싶어요.
　남: 우리 학교에 몇몇 괜찮은 강좌가 있어요.
② 여: 이 카메라는 비싸 보여요. 얼마예요?
　남: 500달러인데, 더 저렴한 모델들도 좀 있어요.
③ 여: 파리에 가는 거 어떻게 생각해?
　남: 그거 좋은데.
④ 여: 에펠탑과 함께 저희 사진 좀 찍어 주시겠어요?
　남: 물론이죠. 카메라 주세요.
⑤ 여: 제 카메라를 고칠 수 있을 것 같으세요? 그걸 켤 수가 없어요.
　남: 지금 바로는 못할 것 같습니다.

[해설] 에펠탑 앞에서 여자는 남자에게 자신과 일행의 사진 촬영을 부탁하는 상황이다.

[어휘] photography [fətɑ́grəfi] 사진술　expensive [ikspénsiv] 비싼　turn on (TV 등을) 켜다

06 ①

남: 무엇을 도와드릴까요?
여: 제가 이곳에 막 도착했는데, 제 가방을 찾을 수가 없어요.
남: 어떤 항공편을 타셨죠?
여: 로스앤젤레스에서 온 303편이에요.
남: 알겠습니다. 잃어버린 가방을 설명해 주시겠어요?
여: 짙은 갈색이에요. 높이가 50센티미터 정도고요. 그리고 견고한 천으로 만들어졌어요.
남: 거기에 이름표가 있나요?
여: 네. 거기에 제 이름 Susan Brown을 적었어요.
남: 알겠습니다. 여기서 기다리세요. 찾을 수 있는지 확인해 볼게요.

[해설] 여자는 항공편을 이용해서 막 도착한 후 가방을 찾고 있으므로, 두 사람이 대화하는 장소로 가장 적절한 곳은 공항이다.

[어휘] flight [flait] 비행; *항공편　describe [diskráib] 묘사하다, 설명하다　missing [mísiŋ] 없어진　be made of ~로 만들어지다　tough [tʌf] 질긴, 견고한　fabric [fǽbrik] 직물, 천　name tag 이름표

07 ③

남: 엄마, 저녁으로 무엇을 만들고 계세요?
여: 매콤한 냉면을 만들고 있어. 아빠가 뭔가 매운 걸 원하시는구나.
남: 저는 다른 거 먹어도 되나요?
여: 왜? 무슨 일이니?
남: 음, 전 몸이 별로 좋지 않아요. 감기에 걸린 것 같아요. 그래서 부드럽고 따뜻한 걸 먹고 싶어요.
여: 정말? 심하니? 약 필요하니?
남: 아니요, 그렇게 심하진 않아요. 그냥 수프 좀 만들어 주실 수 있으세요?
여: 물론이지. 네 방에 가서 기다리렴. 다 되면 부를게.

[해설] 남자는 감기에 걸린 것 같다며 여자에게 수프를 만들어 달라고 부탁했다.

[어휘] spicy [spáisi] 양념 맛이 강한, 매콤한　cold noodle 냉면　have a cold 감기에 걸리다　medicine [médisn] 약

08 ③

여: 신문에서 비만 아동에 관한 기사를 읽었습니까? 비만 아동 수가 증가하고 있습니다. 비만인 사람들 전체의 14%를 차지합니다. 무엇이 아이들의 체중을 증가하게 만들까요? 많은 원인들이 있습니다. 몇몇 연구자들은 유전적 요인이 아동 비만으로 이어진다고 말합니다. 하지만 가장 중요하게는, 컴퓨터 게임과 공부 때문에 아이들은 밖에서 놀 시간이 없습니다. 그건 심각한 문제입니다. 수면 부족이 또 다른 원인이 될 수 있습니다. 또한, 어떤 아이들은 건강한 식사를 하지 않습니다.

[해설] 아동 비만의 원인으로 스트레스는 언급되지 않았다.

[어휘] overweight [òuvərwéit] 과체중의, 비만의　make up ~을 차지하다　gain weight 체중이 늘다　cause [kɔːz] 원인　researcher [risə́ːrtʃər] 연구자　genetic [dʒənétik] 유전의　factor [fǽktər] 요인　lead to ~로 이어지다　obesity [oubíːsəti] 비만　serious [síriəs] 심각한　lack [læk] 부족

09 ②

남: 이것은 세계에서 가장 유명한 스포츠 대회 중 하나입니다. 이것은 4년마다 개최됩니다. 이것은 고대 그리스에서 유래했습니다. 1988년에는 이것이 서울에서 개최되었습니다. 많은 운동선수들이 이것에 참가하는 것을 영광으로 생각합니다. 각 경기의 우승자는 금메달, 은메달, 또는 동메달을 받습니다. 전 세계 사람들이 이것을 고대합니다.

[해설] 4년마다 개최되는 국제 스포츠 대회로 고대 그리스에서 유래했으며, 우승자에게 금메달, 은메달, 동메달을 수여하는 것은 올림픽이다.

[어휘] competition [kàmpətíʃn] 대회, 시합　hold [hould] 개최하다 (hold-held-held)　originate [ərídʒineit] 유래하다　ancient [éinʃənt] 고대의　athlete [ǽθliːt] 운동선수　honor [áːnər] 영광　event [ivént] 사건; *경기　winner [wínər] 우승자　bronze [brɑnz] 청동의　look forward to ~을 고대하다

10 ⑤

① 남: 나 밤새 과학 과제를 했어.
　여: 너 정말 피곤하겠다.
② 남: 내일 스케이트를 타러 갈까 생각 중이야.
　여: 재미있겠다. 나도 너랑 함께 가도 돼?

③ 남: 네 개에게 얼마나 자주 먹이를 주니?
　여: 하루에 한두 번.
④ 남: 시청에 어떻게 가는지 말씀해 주시겠어요?
　여: 아, 지하철 2호선을 타시면 됩니다.
⑤ 남: 내일 언제 만날까?
　여: 매주 화요일과 목요일에.

[해설] 내일 언제 만나겠냐는 질문에 매주 화요일과 목요일이라는 대답은 어색하다.

[어휘] feed [fi:d] 먹이를 주다

11 ④

여: 정말 멋진 날이다, 안 그래?
남: 그래, 맞아. 공원에 가서 날씨를 만끽하는 게 어때?
여: 좋은 생각이야.
남: 좋아. 사진을 좀 찍자.
여: 그래! 사진이 추억을 기록하는 가장 좋은 방법이지.
남: 네 말이 맞아. 하지만 우리는 먼저 편의점에 들러야 해.
여: 왜? 간식을 좀 사려고?
남: 아니. 내 전화기 배터리가 거의 다 돼서, 충전해야 해.
여: 알겠어. 공원 옆에 있는 편의점에 들르면 돼.

[해설] 전화기 배터리가 거의 다 돼서 공원에 가기 전에 편의점에서 충전하기로 했다.

[어휘] record [rikɔ́:rd] 기록하다 memory [méməri] 기억, 추억 stop by ~에 들르다 convenience store 편의점 dead [ded] 죽은; *(전지 등이) 다 된 charge [tʃɑːrdʒ] 충전하다

12 ①

남: 우리 몇 시에 만날까?
여: 오후 2시 어때?
남: 아니, 그건 너무 늦어.
여: 극장에 가는 데 얼마나 걸리니?
남: 그리 확실하진 않지만, 적어도 한 시간은 걸릴 거야. 그리고 우리는 연극이 시작하기 30분 전에 도착해야 해.
여: 내가 그걸 고려하지 않았네. 연극이 언제 시작해?
남: 3시 정각에.
여: 그럼 언제가 좋을까?
남: 연극 두 시간 전 어때? 그러면 천천히 할 수 있어.
여: 완벽해!

[해설] 두 사람은 연극이 시작하는 3시보다 두 시간 전인 1시에 만나기로 했다.

[어휘] consider [kənsídər] 고려하다 take one's time 천천히 하다

13 ⑤

여: 실례합니다만, 이 지역에 제과점이 있나요?
남: 네, 하나 있어요.
여: 아, 잘됐네요. 여기서 먼가요?
남: 아뇨, 버스로 한 정거장 떨어져 있어요. 하지만 거기까지 걸어갈 수도 있어요.
여: 길을 알려 주시겠어요?
남: 네. 한 블록 직진해서 오른쪽으로 도세요.
여: 한 블록 가서 우회전이요. 그러고 나서요?
남: 두 블록 걸어가서 모퉁이에서 오른쪽으로 도세요. 왼편에 보일 거예요.
여: 정말 감사해요.

[해설] 제과점은 현재 위치에서 한 블록 직진해서 오른쪽으로 돈 후, 두 블록 걸어가서 오른쪽으로 돌면 왼편에 있다고 했다.

[어휘] area [ériə] 지역 away [əwéi] 떨어져 give directions 길을 알려 주다

14 ①

여: 얘, John. 지난 주말에 워싱턴 D.C. 여행은 어땠어?
남: 아주 재미있었어! 난 국립 미술관을 관람하는 것이 정말 즐거웠어.
여: 좋았겠다.
남: 그리고 근처에서 벚꽃 축제가 열렸어. 그래서 평소보다 더 많은 관광객들이 워싱턴 D.C.에 왔어.
여: 너도 그 축제에 갔었니?
남: 아쉽지만 못 갔어. 갈만한 충분한 시간이 없었거든.
여: 백악관은 어땠어?
남: 공항 가기 바로 전에 그곳에 가려고 계획하고 있었어. 하지만 나는 안에 들어가는 게 허가되지 않았어.
여: 왜?
남: 예약이 필요했어.
여: 안됐다.

[해설] 남자는 워싱턴 D.C.에서 미술관 관람이 정말 즐거웠다고 말했다.

[어휘] cherry blossom 벚꽃 festival [féstivəl] 축제 tourist [túːərist] 관광객 allow [əláu] 허락[허가]하다

15 ⑤

여: 주목해 주시겠습니까? 요즘 우리 시의 많은 사람들이 독감에 걸리고 있습니다. 우리와 같이 혼잡한 사무실에서, 이는 정말 문제가 될 수 있습니다. 초기 증상에는 두통과 콧물이 포함됩니다. 나중에는 배가 아프고 재채기를 시작할 것입니다. 만약 여러분이 독감에 걸린 것 같다고 생각되시면, 관리자에게 즉각 말씀해 주시기 바랍니다. 또한, 반드시 손을 자주 씻고, 재채기나 기침을 할 때는 입을 가리세요. 감사합니다. 좋은 하루 보내세요.

[해설] 독감이 유행하고 있어 사무실에서 주의해야 할 점들에 관해 말하고 있다.

[어휘] attention [əténʃən] 주의, 주목 catch the flu 독감에 걸리다 crowded [kráudid] 붐비는, 혼잡한 symptom [símptəm] 증상 runny nose 콧물 stomachache [stáməkèik] 복통 sneeze [sniːz] 재채기하다 supervisor [súːpərvàizər] 감독관, 관리자 frequently [fríːkwəntli] 자주 cough [kɔːf] 기침하다

16 ①

남: 안녕, Kate. 네 콘서트 표 여기 있어.
여: 오, 나 대신 구매해 줘서 고마워. 얼마였니?
남: 총 16달러였어. 그러니까 각자 8달러씩이야.
여: 알았어. 여기 10달러야.
남: 잠깐 기다려. 어… 지금 당장은 너에게 줄 잔돈이 없어. 내가 나중에 줘도 될까?
여: 물론이지. 아무 때나 돌려줘도 돼. 어쨌든 우리 서두르는 게 좋겠어. 10분 후면 콘서트가 시작해.

[해설] 표 가격이 8달러인데 여자가 남자에게 10달러를 줬으므로, 여자가 받을 거스름돈은 2달러이다.

[어휘] hold on (명령문 형태로 쓰여) 기다려[멈춰] change [tʃeindʒ] 잔돈 pay ~ back ~에게 (빌린 돈을) 갚다[돌려주다]

17 ⑤

남: 얘, Lily. 여름 캠프는 어땠어?
여: 안녕! 정말 즐거웠어. 우리는 재미있는 것들을 정말 많이 했어.
남: 네가 즐거웠다니 기뻐. 어떤 것들을 했니?
여: 음, 수영하러 가고 호수에 낚시하러 갔어. 그리고 하이킹과 암벽 등반을 하러 갔어.
남: 와, 정말 재미있을 것 같아. 그래서 어느 부분이 가장 좋았어?
여: 하이킹도 정말 좋았지만, 암벽 등반이 훨씬 더 좋았어.

[해설] 남자는 여자가 여름 캠프에서 한 일들 중에서 어떤 것이 가장 좋았는지 물었으므로, 좋았던 활동을 구체적으로 말하는 응답이 가장 적절하다.
① 또 낚시하러 가고 싶어.
② 나는 가족과 하이킹하는 걸 좋아해.
③ 나는 이번 방학에 여름 캠프를 가고 싶어.
④ 날씨가 좋았다면 훨씬 더 좋았을 텐데.

[어휘] rock climbing 암벽 등반 [문제] go fishing 낚시하러 가다

18 ④

여: 연말이 다가오고 있어.
남: 그래. 시간이 정말 빨리 흘러. 새해 전날을 어떻게 보낼 거니?
여: 가족과 함께 저녁을 먹을 거야. 만두를 좀 만들려고.

남: 만두?
여: 응, 그건 아시아 덤플링의 한 종류야. 먹어 본 적 있니?
남: 아니, 없어.
여: 정말 맛있어. 우리랑 함께 할래?
남: 고맙지만, 안 돼.
여: 왜?
남: 그날 우리 가족과 계획이 있어.

[해설] 여자는 남자가 새해 전날 함께 만두를 만들어 먹자는 제안을 거절하자 그 이유를 물었으므로, 다른 계획이 있다는 응답이 가장 적절하다.
① 빨리 가고 싶어.
② 나를 초대해 줘서 고마워.
③ 음식이 정말 맛있었어.
⑤ 나는 달걀에 알레르기가 있어서 이걸 먹을 수 없어.

[어휘] dumpling [dʌ́mpliŋ] 덤플링 [문제] can't wait to-v 빨리 ~하고 싶다 allergic to ~에 알레르기가 있는

19 ③

남: 우리 졸업이 이제 두 달밖에 안 남았다니 믿기지 않아.
여: 나도 안 믿겨. 시간이 정말 빨리 간다.
남: 졸업 후에 넌 뭐 할 거야?
여: 대학원에 갈 거야. 너는?
남: 나는 몇몇 회사에 지원하려고 준비하고 있어.
여: 너는 어떤 회사에서 일하고 싶니?
남: 나는 은행에서 일하고 싶어.

[해설] 어떤 회사에서 일하고 싶은지 물었으므로, 회사나 직종을 구체적으로 말하는 응답이 가장 적절하다.
① 나는 일주일에 5일 근무해.
② 나는 열심히 일할 거야.
④ 나는 전에 기자로 일했어.
⑤ 졸업을 축하해!

[어휘] graduation [græ̀dʒəwéiʃən] 졸업 graduate school 대학원 apply for ~에 지원하다 several [sévərəl] 몇몇 company [kʌ́mpəni] 회사

20 ②

남: Jenny와 친구들은 이번 주말에 캠핑 여행을 계획하고 있습니다. 모두 각기 다른 할 일들이 있습니다. Harry는 음식을 담당하고, Lindsey는 캠핑 장비를 가져오기로 합니다. Jenny는 나머지를 챙길 예정입니다. Jenny가 일기 예보를 확인하는데, 주말 내내 비가 올 것이라고 합니다. 그녀는 캠핑 여행을 미루는 것이 최선일지도 모른다고 생각합니다. 이런 상황에서, Jenny는 친구들에게 뭐라고 말하겠습니까?
Jenny: 우리 다음 주말까지 기다려야 할 것 같아.

[해설] 이번 주말 내내 비 예보가 있으므로 캠핑을 가지 말고 다음 주말까지 기다려 보자는 말이 가장 적절하다.

① 캠핑을 가게 되어 너무 신이 나.
③ 이건 내가 갔던 최고의 캠핑 여행이야.
④ 여기서 다른 산에 가는 것은 어려워.
⑤ 미안하지만, 난 차량을 담당하고 싶지 않아.

어휘 task [tæsk] 일, 과업 be in charge of ~을 담당하다
equipment [ikwípmənt] 장비 weather report 일기 예보
put off ~을 미루다 [문제] transportation [trænspərtéiʃən]
수송, 차량

Dictation Test 05

pp. 92~99

01 1) cake in the middle 2) a piece of cake
    3) Right above the cake

02 1) helps war refugees
    2) they also need blankets
    3) canned food and bottled water

03 1) We'd better hurry 2) snow is getting heavier
    3) should always carry snow chains

04 1) have band practice at 2:00 2) in about an hour
    3) after your band practice

05 1) What do you think about 2) take a picture of us
    3) fix my camera

06 1) What flight were you on
    2) describe the missing bag
    3) have a name tag

07 1) something soft and warm
    2) Do you need medicine
    3) make me some soup

08 1) makes children gain weight
    2) don't have time to play outside
    3) Lack of sleep 4) don't eat healthy meals

09 1) most famous sporting competitions
    2) originated in ancient Greece
    3) participate in this

10 1) I'm thinking about going
    2) How often do you feed 3) how to get to
    4) When would you like to meet

11 1) take some pictures
    2) stop by the convenience store
    3) need to charge it

12 1) that's too late 2) take at least an hour
    3) When does the play start
    4) two hours before the play

13 1) one stop away by bus 2) give me directions
    3) Go straight for one block
    4) turn right at the corner

14 1) go to that festival 2) didn't have enough time
    3) planning to go there 4) needed a reservation

15 1) catching the flu 2) headache and runny nose
    3) tell your supervisor immediately
    4) cover your mouth

16 1) that's $8 each 2) don't have any change
    3) pay me back

17 1) How was your summer camp
    2) fishing in the lake 3) did you like the most

18 1) have dinner with my family
    2) Have you ever tried one 3) like to join us

19 1) do after graduation 2) apply for jobs
    3) want to work for

20 1) has a different task 2) in charge of food
    3) checks the weather report
    4) put off the camping trip

실전모의고사 06회

pp. 100~101

01 ⑤	02 ⑤	03 ③	04 ②	05 ①
06 ⑤	07 ⑤	08 ②	09 ⑤	10 ②
11 ⑤	12 ⑤	13 ③	14 ②	15 ①
16 ②	17 ①	18 ⑤	19 ④	20 ⑤

01 ⑤

여: 이렇게 금방 파리를 떠나다니 슬퍼. 떠나기 전에 기념품을 사야겠어.
남: 뭘 살 거야?
여: 음, 난 각기 다른 도시들을 방문할 때 늘 티셔츠를 모아.
남: 그렇구나. 이건 어때? 흰색이고 에펠탑이 프린트되어 있어.
여: 에펠탑은 마음에 들지만, 너무 단순해.
남: 그럼 'I LOVE PARIS'라고 쓰인 이건 어때?
여: 나쁘지는 않지만, 그건 내가 뉴욕에서 산 것과 아주 비슷해. 아! 이걸 봐. 거꾸로 된 에펠탑이 있고, 'PARIS LOVES ME'라고 쓰여 있어. 나 이걸로 살래.
남: 와. 그거 멋지네.

해설 여자는 거꾸로 된 에펠탑이 있고 'PARIS LOVES ME'라고 쓰인 티

셔츠를 사기로 했다.

어휘 souvenir [sùːvəníər] 기념품 similar [símələr] 비슷한
upside-down [ʌ̀psɑiddáun] 거꾸로의, 뒤집힌

02 ⑤

남: 캠핑 갈 준비가 됐니?
여: 네, 거의 다 준비됐어요. 침낭과 손전등을 챙겼어요.
남: 간식은 챙겼니?
여: 네, 가방 안에 초콜릿 바랑 물을 좀 넣었어요.
남: 텐트는?
여: 텐트는 가져갈 필요가 없어요. 제 것이 너무 낡아서, 대신 Megan
에게 그 애의 것을 가져다 달라고 부탁했어요.
남: 잘됐구나! 그리고 모자와 선글라스 잊지 마. 밖에 아주 햇살이 내리
쬔단다.
여: 걱정하지 마세요, 아빠. 그것들도 챙겼어요.

해설 캠핑 준비물로 자외선 차단제는 언급되지 않았다.

어휘 sleeping bag 침낭 lantern [lǽntərn] 손전등, 랜턴

03 ③

[전화벨이 울린다.]
여: Speedy Pizza에 전화 주셔서 감사합니다. 무엇을 도와드릴까요?
남: 안녕하세요. 제 이름은 Sam Smith인데요. 한 시간 전에 피자를
주문했어요.
여: 피자에 문제가 있나요?
남: 네, 문제가 있어요. 피자가 아직 도착하지 않았어요.
여: 정말 죄송합니다. 주소 좀 알려 주시겠어요?
남: North가 7374번지예요.
여: 잠시만요. [잠시 후] 시스템에 따르면 저희 운전 기사가 30분 전에
여기서 떠났어요. 무슨 일이 일어난 건지 확실히 말씀드릴 수는 없
지만, 바로 다시 전화드릴게요. 괜찮으신가요?
남: 좋아요. 기다릴게요.

해설 남자는 한 시간 전에 주문한 피자가 아직 도착하지 않았다고 말했다.

어휘 order [ɔ́ːrdər] 주문하다 arrive [əráiv] 도착하다 address
[ǽdres] 주소 for sure 확실히 happen [hǽpən] 일어나다, 발
생하다

04 ②

여: 나는 이번 여행에 신이 나. 우리 비행기가 내일 몇 시에 떠나지?
남: 오전 10시에.
여: 그러면 우리 몇 시에 만날까? 공항에서 9시에 어때?
남: 좀 너무 늦는 것 같아. 비행기가 떠나기 2시간 전에 우린 탑승할 준
비가 되어 있어야 해.
여: 맞는 말이야. 그러면 8시에?

남: 여행 전에 뭐 살 거 있니? 그렇다면, 쇼핑하는 데 한 시간 정도는 필
요할 거야.
여: 나는 아무것도 안 필요해. 너는?
남: 나도 없어. 그러면 2시간이면 적합하겠다.
여: 좋아. 그때 보자.

해설 비행기 출발 시각이 오전 10시이고 두 사람은 그보다 2시간 전에 만
나기로 했다.

어휘 board [bɔːrd] (배·비행기 등에) 타다, 탑승하다 good enough
적합한, 만족스러운

05 ①

여: 성인 입장권 한 장이랑 학생 입장권 두 장 주세요.
남: 네. 여기 표 세 장 있습니다.
여: 고맙습니다. 오늘 새끼 곰을 볼 수 있나요?
남: 죄송하지만, 볼 수 없습니다. 며칠째 아프거든요.
여: 유감이네요. 그러면 사슴이 어디 있는지 알려 주시겠어요?
남: 네. 쭉 걷다가 기린이 보이면 왼쪽으로 도세요.
여: 알겠습니다. 사슴에게 줄 먹이를 어디에서 살 수 있죠?
남: 죄송하지만, 사슴에게 먹이를 주시면 안 됩니다.

해설 입장권을 사고 동물 구경에 관해 이야기하고 있으므로, 두 사람이 대
화하는 장소로 가장 적절한 곳은 동물원이다.

어휘 adult [ədʌ́lt] 성인 a few 약간, 몇몇 deer [diər] 사슴 (복수형
deer)

06 ⑤

① 여: 우리 차를 어디에 주차해야 할까?
   남: 저쪽에 빈자리가 하나 있어.
② 여: 근처에 횡단보도가 없어.
   남: 한 블록 더 걸어가자.
③ 여: 속도위반으로 딱지를 떼겠습니다.
   남: 알겠습니다, 경찰관님.
④ 여: 제 차 수리를 맡기고 싶습니다.
   남: 네, 뭐가 문제인 것 같나요?
⑤ 여: 우리 교통 체증에 갇혔어. 늦을까 봐 걱정돼.
   남: 걱정하지 마. 아직 시간 있어.

해설 교통 체증으로 꽉 막혀 있는 도로 위 차 안에서 대화를 나누는 상황
이다.

어휘 crosswalk [krɔ́ːswɔ̀ːk] 횡단보도 ticket [tíkit] 표; *(교통 위반)
딱지 speeding [spíːdiŋ] (차량의) 속도위반 officer [ɔ́ːfisər] 장
교; *경찰관 stuck [stʌk] 갇힌 traffic jam 교통 체증

07 ⑤

여: 저기, 그 의자를 어디로 가져가는 거예요?

남: 아, 침실 전구를 교체해야 해서요. 전구 중 한 개가 고장 났어요.

여: 의자 옮기는 거 도와줄게요.

남: 아, 고맙지만 괜찮아요.

여: 그래요. 전구 교체하는 데 도움 필요해요?

남: 아뇨, 혼자 할 수 있어요. 몇 분이면 될 거예요.

여: 좋아요. 조심해요.

남: 저기, 여보? 여기 와서 의자를 잡아 줄 수 있어요?

여: 물론이죠. 당신이 떨어지는 건 원치 않아요.

해설 남자는 여자에게 전구를 교체하는 동안 의자를 잡아 달라고 부탁했다.

어휘 light bulb 전구 burn out (가열되어) 고장이 나다 fall down 떨어지다

08 ②

남: 칼데콧 상에 대해 들어 본 적이 있나요? 1939년 이래로 매년, 그것은 최고의 미국 아동 그림책에 수여되어 왔습니다. 그것은 그림책의 아버지라 불리는 영국 삽화가 Randolph Caldecott의 이름을 따서 지어졌습니다. 그것은 가장 유명한 아동 도서 상 중 하나입니다. 매년 오직 한 권의 책이 칼데콧 메달을 수상하며, 그다음 5권까지는 뛰어난 삽화에 대한 칼데콧 명예상을 받습니다.

해설 최초 시상 연도(1939년), 이름의 기원(영국 삽화가 Randolph Caldecott의 이름을 따서 지음), 상의 종류(칼데콧 메달과 칼데콧 명예상), 수상 작품 수(메달은 1권, 명예상은 5권까지)에 관해서는 언급되었으나, 최초 수상 작품은 언급되지 않았다.

어휘 award [əwɔ́:rd] 상; 수여하다 be named after ~의 이름을 따서 짓다 illustrator [íləstrèitər] 삽화가 receive [risíːv] 받다 outstanding [àutstǽndiŋ] 뛰어난 illustration [ìləstréiʃən] 삽화

09 ⑤

여: 이 직업을 가진 사람들은 창의적입니다. 그들은 이야기를 쓰고 그것들을 위한 캐릭터를 만들어 냄으로써 재미있는 컴퓨터 게임을 만드는 것을 돕습니다. 그들은 프로그래머, 게임 설계자, 그리고 감독과 함께 일합니다. 이야기를 쓰기 위해서, 그들은 컴퓨터 게임에 관한 많은 지식을 가지고 있어야 하며 컴퓨터 코딩을 이해해야 합니다. 덧붙여, 사람들이 좋아하고 원하는 게임 유형에 관한 동향도 알아야 합니다.

해설 컴퓨터 게임의 이야기를 쓰고 캐릭터를 만들어 내는 사람은 컴퓨터 게임 시나리오 작가이다.

어휘 creative [kriéitiv] 창의적인 create [kriéit] 창조하다, 만들어 내다 director [diréktər] 감독 knowledge [nálidʒ] 지식 trend [trend] 동향, 추세

10 ②

① 남: 나 식료품점에 가는 길이야.

　여: 오렌지 좀 사다 줄래?

② 남: 겨울 방학이 너무 기대돼.

　여: 걱정하지 마. 다음이 네 차례야.

③ 남: 새 학교는 어때?

　여: 모든 게 좋아.

④ 남: 서울역까지 얼마나 머니?

　여: 여기서 여섯 정거장이야.

⑤ 남: 죄송하지만, 지금은 이용 가능한 1인실이 없습니다.

　여: 그럼 2인실도 괜찮습니다.

해설 겨울 방학이 기대된다는 말에 다음이 네 차례라는 응답은 어색하다.

어휘 grocery store 식료품점 winter break 겨울 방학 available [əvéiləbl] 이용 가능한

11 ⑤

남: 어디 가는 중이니?

여: 집에 가는 중이야. 이제 막 경기장에서 야구 경기 관람을 마쳤어.

남: 경기는 어땠어?

여: 정말 흥미진진했어.

남: 네가 응원하는 팀이 이겼니?

여: 응! 하지만 맨 마지막이 되어서야 승자가 결정났어. David Park의 홈런 덕분에 우리 팀이 이겼어.

남: 그 사람에 대해 들어 본 적 없는데. 신인 선수니?

여: 응, 하지만 정말 잘해. 온라인에서 그 선수에 대해 더 알아낼 수 있을 거야.

남: 정말? 휴대전화로 지금 바로 한번 봐야겠다.

해설 남자는 여자가 칭찬한 신인 야구 선수에 대해 지금 바로 휴대전화로 찾아보겠다고 했다.

어휘 stadium [stéidiəm] 경기장 take a look 한번 보다

12 ⑤

남: 건강 검진을 받고 싶습니다.

여: 알겠습니다. 검사 전에, 기본 정보가 필요해요. 이름과 나이를 알려 주시겠어요?

남: Alex Kim입니다. 26세이고요.

여: 정기적으로 약을 복용하고 계신 것이 있나요?

남: 아니요.

여: 알겠습니다. 의사 선생님이 체중, 시력, 청력을 체크하실 거예요. 콘택트렌즈를 끼고 계시나요?

남: 네. 빼야 하나요?

여: 네. 다른 검사가 필요하신가요?

남: 아니요.

여: 알겠습니다. 잠시만 여기서 기다려 주세요.

해설 남자는 체중, 시력, 청력 외에 다른 검사는 원하지 않는다고 했다.

	검진	
①	이름	Alex Kim
②	나이	26
③	정기적인 약 복용	예 □ 아니오 ☑
④	기본 검사	체중 ☑ 시력 ☑ 청력 ☑
⑤	추가 검사	알레르기 검사 ☑

어휘 medical checkup 건강 검진 examination [igzæmənéiʃən] 조사, 검사 basic [béisik] 기초의, 기본의 regularly [régjələrli] 규칙적으로, 정기적으로 check [tʃek] 확인하다 weight [weit] 무게, 체중 vision [víʒən] 시력 hearing [híːəriŋ] 청력 contact lens 콘택트렌즈

13 ③

여: 얘, Max. 우리 박물관에 가는 계획을 바꿔야 해.
남: 왜? 월요일에 바쁘니?
여: 아니. 하지만 내가 확인해 봤는데, 박물관이 월요일에 문을 닫아.
남: 아, 알았어. 그럼 화요일에 가는 건 어때?
여: 미안하지만, 난 화요일에 이미 계획을 잡았어. 수요일이나 목요일은 어때?
남: 난 금요일에 시험이 있어서, 목요일에는 공부해야 해.
여: 그럼 수요일에 가자.
남: 나한텐 그게 좋겠어.
여: 완벽해!

해설 여자가 수요일이나 목요일에 박물관에 가자고 하자, 남자는 목요일에 시험공부를 해야 해서 수요일이 좋다고 했다.

어휘 work for ~에게 가능하다[좋다]

14 ②

여: 얘, Jason! 주말 어떻게 보냈어? 등산 갈 거라고 했잖아, 맞지?
남: 응, 하지만 등산은 안 갔어. 취소됐어.
여: 취소됐어? 왜?
남: 등산 동호회 회원 중 한 명이 심하게 다쳤거든.
여: 무슨 일이었는데?
남: 트럭에 치었어. 출장에서 집으로 돌아가는 길이었어.
여: 끔찍하다. 그녀가 괜찮으면 좋겠어. 그럼 지난 주말에 뭐 했니?
남: 날씨를 만끽하려고 산책했어.
여: 재밌었겠다. 요즘 날씨가 정말 좋지.
남: 정말 그래!

해설 남자는 주말에 계획했던 등산이 취소돼서, 산책을 갔다고 했다.

어휘 climb a mountain 등산하다 How come? 왜[어째서]? badly [bǽdli] 심하게 hit [hit] 치다 (hit-hit-hit) business trip 출장

15 ①

남: 주민 여러분, 주목해 주시기 바랍니다. 건물 내 모든 엘리베이터가 작동을 멈췄습니다. 곧 다시 운행하면 좋겠지만, 저희는 잠시 엘리베이터를 정지시키기로 결정했습니다. 최근에 엘리베이터에 문제가 많았기 때문에, 문제점이 무엇인지 알아내서 바로잡아야 합니다. 다시 운행하게 되면, 알려 드리겠습니다. 바라건대 오래 걸리지 않을 겁니다. 이렇게 불편을 끼쳐 드려 정말 죄송하고, 여러분의 협조 감사합니다.

해설 엘리베이터의 문제점을 확인하고 바로잡기 위해 운행을 잠시 중단하겠다고 말하고 있다.

어휘 shut down (기계를) 정지시키다 lately [léitli] 최근에 fix [fiks] 수리하다, 바로잡다 inconvenience [ìnkənvíːnjəns] 불편

16 ②

남: 마음에 드시는 게 있습니까, 손님?
여: 네. 이 신발이 마음에 드네요.
남: 잘 선택하셨어요. 그 신발은 지금 할인 중이에요.
여: 오, 좋아요. 그걸로 할게요. 얼마죠?
남: 100달러였어요. 하지만 20% 할인 중이에요.
여: 그렇군요. 그리고 추가로 신발끈도 주세요.
남: 여기 있습니다. 신발끈은 4달러인데, 50% 할인 중이에요.
여: 좋네요. 그걸 살게요.

해설 100달러인 신발을 20% 할인받으면 80달러, 4달러인 신발끈을 50% 할인받으면 2달러이므로, 여자는 총 82달러를 지불해야 한다.

어휘 shoelace [ʃúːlèis] 신발끈

17 ①

남: 안녕, Clara! 어디 가니?
여: 어, 안녕! 전시회에 가는 중이야.
남: 무슨 전시회?
여: 피카소 전시회야. 그의 엄청난 그림들 일부가 전시될 거야.
남: 와, 멋지다! 너 그림 그릴 줄 아니?
여: 응. 난 그림 그리는 거 무척 좋아해.
남: 멋지구나! 너 화가가 되고 싶니?
여: 아니, 미술 선생님이 되고 싶어. 난 아이들을 가르치는 것도 좋아하거든.
남: 네 꿈이 이루어지길 바랄게.

해설 여자는 그림 그리는 것과 아이들을 가르치는 것을 좋아해서 미술 선생님이 되고 싶다고 했으므로, 꿈이 이루어지길 바란다는 응답이 가장 적절하다.
② 너한테 내 그림을 보여 줄게.
③ 너는 그림을 더 자주 그려야 해.
④ 너는 피카소처럼 훌륭한 화가가 될 수 있어.
⑤ 학생들을 그려 보지 그래?

어휘 exhibition [èksəbíʃən] 전시회 on display 전시된 painter [péintər] 도장공; *화가 [문제] come true 실현되다, 이루어지다

18 ⑤

남: 실례합니다, 부인. 저 좀 도와주실 수 있으세요?

여: 그럴게요. 뭔데요?

남: 여기에 제 자전거를 뒀는데, 지금 찾을 수가 없어요. 누군가 훔쳐간 게 틀림없어요.

여: 유감이네요. 제가 어떻게 도울 수 있을까요?

남: 음, 누구든 의심스러운 사람을 보셨나요?

여: 아니요. 유감입니다.

남: 전 정말 무엇을 해야 할지 모르겠어요.

여: 경찰서에 가서 도움을 요청하셔야 해요.

해설 자전거를 도난당한 남자가 어떻게 해야 할지 모르겠다고 했으므로, 대처 방법을 조언하는 응답이 가장 적절하다.
① 제가 의심스러운 사람을 본 것 같아요.
② 자전거를 어디서 사야 할지 모르겠어요.
③ 자전거를 찾으면 전화할게요.
④ 제 자전거를 어디에 뒀는지 모르겠어요.

어휘 steal [stiːl] 훔치다 (steal-stole-stolen) suspicious [səspíʃəs] 의심스러운 [문제] ask for ~을 요청하다

19 ④

남: 얘, Martha, 오랜만이야. 요즘 어떻게 지내?

여: 직장에서 꽤 바쁘지만, 모든 게 좋아.

남: 너희 회사에서 새 패션 기자를 찾고 있다고 들었어.

여: 응, 그래. 우리와 함께 할 의향이 있니?

남: 응. 어떤 사람을 찾고 있니?

여: 이 분야에 경험이 많은 사람을 원해. 너 경험이 좀 있니?

남: 응. 패션 잡지사에서 3년간 일했어. 그리고 작년에 내 보도로 상을 받았어.

여: 넌 우리에게 딱 맞는 사람인 것 같아.

해설 여자의 회사에서 경험 많은 패션 기자를 찾고 있는데 남자가 자신의 잡지사 근무와 수상 경력을 말했으므로, 적임자일 것 같다는 응답이 가장 적절하다.
① 내가 그 자리에 지원해도 될까?
② 우리는 재능 있는 디자이너를 찾고 있어.
③ 축하해, 너는 시험에 합격했어.
⑤ 미안하지만, 우리는 지금 당장 기자를 필요로 하지 않아.

어휘 reporter [ripɔ́ːrtər] 기자 experience [ikspíəriəns] 경험 reporting [ripɔ́ːrtiŋ] 보도 [문제] position [pəzíʃən] 자세; *(일)자리, 직위 pass [pæs] 통과하다; *합격하다

20 ⑤

여: Amy는 시내로 가는 지하철에 있습니다. Amy는 낯익어 보이는 남자아이를 봅니다. 잠시 후, Amy는 그가 누구인지 기억한다고 생각합니다. 그녀는 이름이 Tim인 초등학교 친구라고 생각합니다. Amy는 아주 확실하다고 느껴서 그에게 다가가 인사를 합니다. 그가 돌아보자, Amy는 그가 Tim이 아니라는 걸 깨닫습니다. 이런 상황에서, Amy는 그 남자아이에게 뭐라고 말하겠습니까?

Amy: 죄송해요, 제가 아는 사람이라고 생각했어요.

해설 모르는 사람을 친구로 착각하고 인사했으므로, 그에 대해 사과를 하는 말이 가장 적절하다.
① 그 말을 들으니 유감이네요.
② 당신이 실수한 것 같아요.
③ 도와주고 싶지만, 저도 여기가 처음이에요.
④ 유감이지만, 이 근처에는 버스 정류장이 없어요.

어휘 familiar [fəmíljər] 낯익은 turn around 돌아보다 realize [ríːəlàiz] 깨닫다

Dictation Test 06

pp. 102~109

01 1) buy a souvenir 2) printed on it
3) it's too simple

02 1) packed a sleeping bag 2) put a chocolate bar
3) don't forget your cap

03 1) ordered a pizza 2) hasn't arrived yet
3) our driver left here 4) call you right back

04 1) at 9:00 at the airport
2) two hours before the flight leaves
3) need about one hour 4) is good enough

05 1) where the deer are
2) when you see the giraffes 3) can't feed them

06 1) park our car 2) ticket for speeding
3) have my car repaired 4) stuck in a traffic jam

07 1) change a light bulb 2) help you move it
3) hold the chair

08 1) Every year since 1939
2) was named after English illustrator
3) up to five other books

09 1) make interesting computer games
2) To write stories
3) trends about the types of games

10 1) can't wait for my winter break
2) How do you like 3) no single rooms available

11 1) win the game 2) I've never heard of him
   3) find out more 4) take a look

12 1) get a medical checkup
   2) taking any medicine regularly
   3) weight, vision, and hearing

13 1) is closed on Monday 2) made plans on Tuesday
   3) have to study on Thursday

14 1) climb a mountain 2) It was canceled
   3) on her way back home 4) took a walk

15 1) have stopped working
   2) shut down for a little while
   3) what the problem is 4) won't take long

16 1) They're on sale 2) extra pair of shoelaces
   3) for 50% off

17 1) will be on display 2) love to paint pictures
   3) be an art teacher

18 1) must have stolen it 2) seen anybody suspicious
   3) know what to do

19 1) looking for a new fashion reporter
   2) with a lot of experience 3) was given an award

20 1) who looks familiar 2) remembers who he is
   3) says hello to him

37 고장 나다   38 ~을 담당하다
39 ~로 이어지다   40 ~의 이름을 따서 짓다

Ⓑ
01 fabric   02 experiment
03 deer   04 genetic
05 cooperation   06 bronze
07 ancient   08 equipment
09 hearing   10 inconvenience
11 memory   12 crowded
13 public   14 similar
15 field   16 stain
17 thoughtful   18 apply
19 tourist   20 tool
21 flight   22 obesity
23 knowledge   24 vehicle
25 hole   26 souvenir
27 trend   28 symptom
29 factor   30 envy
31 stand   32 talented
33 invitation   34 traffic jam
35 weather report   36 a piece of
37 turn on   38 make a mistake
39 look forward to   40 gain weight

Word Test 04~06

pp. 110~111

Ⓐ
01 제거하다   02 초상화; 인물 사진
03 뛰어난   04 상; 수여하다
05 설립하다   06 전문적인
07 훼손하다   08 포함하다
09 조사, 검사   10 (짐 등을) 싸다, 챙기다
11 즉시   12 대회, 시합
13 궁궐   14 걸다, 걸리다
15 제공하다   16 운동선수
17 복통   18 일, 과업
19 지역   20 거꾸로의, 뒤집힌
21 자주   22 재료
23 창의적인   24 허락[허가]하다
25 묘사하다, 설명하다   26 수리 기사
27 횡단보도   28 경기장
29 등록하다   30 지저분한
31 혼자서   32 전시된
33 실현되다, 이루어지다   34 길을 알려 주다
35 (기계를) 정지시키다   36 ~에 들르다

실전모의고사 07회

pp. 112~113

01 ②	02 ④	03 ①	04 ③	05 ④
06 ⑤	07 ④	08 ⑤	09 ②	10 ②
11 ③	12 ③	13 ②	14 ②	15 ②
16 ④	17 ③	18 ②	19 ⑤	20 ②

01 ②

[휴대전화가 울린다.]
남: 안녕, Cindy. 무슨 일이니?
여: 아빠, 제가 공책을 깜박했어요. 그걸 학교에 가져다주실 수 있어요? 제 책상 위에 있어요.
남: 그래, 근데 네 책상 위에 공책이 여러 권 있구나. 표지에 별이 있는 노란색 공책을 원하니?
여: 아니요, 그거 아니에요. 빨간 거 있어요?
남: 그래, 빨간색 공책이 두 권 있구나. 한 권에는 하트가 있고, 다른 한

권에는 해바라기가 있어.

여: 앞에 말씀하신 게 필요해요. 고마워요, 아빠. 11시에 학교 문 앞에서 기다릴게요.

해설 여자는 표지에 하트가 있는 빨간색 공책을 가져다 달라고 했다.

어휘 sunflower [sʌ́nflàuər] 해바라기 gate [ɡeit] 문

02 ④

남: 여보, 어디에 있어요?

여: 침실에 있어요.

남: 오, 거기 있군요. 해변에 갈 준비하고 있어요?

여: 네, 필요한 것들을 모두 챙기고 있어요. 내 수영복과 수건을 바로 여기에 챙겼어요.

남: 저기에 있는 건 뭐죠?

여: 우리 파라솔이에요. 이런, 깜빡 잊을 뻔한 게 있어요!

남: 뭐예요? 읽을 책을 가져갈 건가요?

여: 아뇨. 난 선글라스가 필요해요. 나에게 그걸 가져다줄래요? 욕실에 있어요.

남: 알았어요. 금방 돌아올게요.

해설 여자가 해변에 가져갈 물건으로 물안경은 언급되지 않았다.

어휘 get ready for ~에 대한 준비를 하다 swimsuit [swímsù:t] 수영복 beach umbrella 파라솔 bathroom [bǽθrù:m] 욕실

03 ①

[휴대전화가 울린다.]

여: 여보세요?

남: 여보세요, White 씨이신가요?

여: 네, 그렇습니다. 누구시죠?

남: 제 이름은 Matt입니다. 택배 기사입니다. 오늘 오후 5시쯤 택배를 배달하려고 해요. 집에 계실 건가요?

여: 아, 아닐 것 같아요. 아마 7시 넘어서야 집에 올 거예요. 그냥 경비실에 맡겨 주시겠어요?

남: 물론이죠. 꽤 무거우니, 찾아가실 때 도움을 좀 받으세요.

여: 네, 그럴게요. 정말 고맙습니다.

해설 남자는 여자의 집으로 오후 5시쯤 택배 배달을 갈 것이라고 했다.

어휘 delivery [dilívəri] 배달, 배송 package [pǽkidʒ] 소포 probably [prάbəbli] 아마 security guard's office 경비실

04 ③

여: 점심 식사는 다 하셨나요?

남: 네, 감사해요. 지금 계산을 하고 싶은데요.

여: 네. 어디 볼까요… 볶음밥과 커피 두 잔 드셨네요, 맞으시죠?

남: 네, 맞아요.

여: 알겠습니다. 밥은 5달러이고, 커피는 한 잔에 2달러 50센트입니다.

남: 세금으로 10% 더해야 하나요?

여: 아니요, 이곳엔 식당 세금이 없습니다.

남: 그렇군요. 여기 20달러짜리 지폐입니다.

여: 감사합니다. 거스름돈을 가지고 금방 돌아오겠습니다.

해설 볶음밥 가격 5달러와 한 잔에 2달러 50센트인 커피 두 잔의 가격을 합하면 10달러인데, 남자가 20달러를 냈으므로 거스름돈은 10달러이다.

어휘 fried rice 볶음밥 add [æd] 더하다 tax [tæks] 세금 bill [bil] 계산서; *지폐

05 ④

① 여: 이 티켓 발매기는 어떻게 작동하나요?
　남: 벽에 사용법 있어요.

② 여: 제가 기차를 잘못 탄 것 같아요.
　남: 어디로 가시나요?

③ 여: 포틀랜드행 표 두 장 주세요.
　남: 95달러입니다.

④ 여: 실례지만, 우리는 줄을 서서 기다리고 있었어요. 당신이 우리 앞에 끼어들었어요.
　남: 죄송합니다, 제가 못 봤네요.

⑤ 여: B 승강장이 어디예요?
　남: A 승강장이 바로 아래층이고 B 승강장은 그 옆이에요.

해설 매표소에서 여자가 앞에 선 남자에게 뭔가 말하자 남자는 겸연쩍어 하는 상황이다.

어휘 instruction [instrʌ́kʃən] 지시; *설명서, 사용법 wall [wɔ:l] 벽 wait in line 줄을 서서 기다리다 platform [plǽtfɔ:rm] 승강장

06 ⑤

여: 실례합니다. 누가 좀 도와주시겠어요?

남: 네. 무슨 문제인가요?

여: 음, 제가 오늘 아침에 공원에서 조깅을 하고 있었어요. 차에 돌아와 보니, 누군가가 제 지갑을 훔쳐갔어요.

남: 도난당한 게 확실한가요?

여: 네. 창문이 돌로 깨져 있었어요.

남: 아, 알겠습니다. 그러면 이 양식을 작성해 주셔야 해요.

여: 알겠습니다.

남: 도둑을 잡기 위해 노력할게요. 지갑을 되찾을 수 있으면 좋겠네요.

여: 그러면 좋겠어요. 그 안에 돈이 많이 있었거든요.

해설 여자는 차 안에 있던 지갑을 도난당한 것을 신고하고 남자가 도둑을 잡겠다고 했으므로, 두 사람이 대화하는 장소로 가장 적절한 곳은 경찰서이다.

어휘 steal [sti:l] 훔치다 (steal-stole-stolen) purse [pə:rs] 지갑 fill out ~을 작성하다[기입하다] hopefully [hóupfəli] 바라건대

07 ④

남: 너 오늘 아침에 어디에 있었어?
여: 몸이 좋지 않아서, 집에 있었어.
남: 아. 병원에 데려다줄까?
여: 고맙지만, 괜찮아. 지금은 훨씬 나아졌어.
남: 그렇다니 다행이야.
여: 그나저나, 영어 수업은 어땠어?
남: 좋았어. 몇몇 중요한 표현들을 배워서, 내가 필기했어.
여: 정말? 내가 그걸 빌릴 수 있을까?
남: 물론이야. 휴일에 해야 할 숙제에 대해서도 말해 줄게.

[해설] 여자는 몸이 좋지 않아 수업에 빠져서 남자에게 필기한 것을 빌려 달라고 부탁했다.

[어휘] expression [ikspréʃən] 표현 take notes 필기하다

08 ⑤

여: 안녕하세요, 여러분! 저는 Anna Smith이고, 학급 회장에 출마 중입니다. 학급 회장으로서, 저는 다음의 것들을 개선하겠습니다. 첫째, 교복 없는 날을 가질 것입니다. 이날에 여러분은 원하는 무엇이든 자유롭게 입을 것입니다. 둘째, 학교 식당에 더 건강한 식단을 제안하겠습니다. 셋째, 일주일에 한 번 이상 체육 수업을 하도록 요청하겠습니다. 마지막으로, 저는 우리 교실을 깨끗하게 유지하겠습니다. 이것들은 제가 할 수 있는 훌륭한 것들 중 일부일 뿐입니다. 만약 선출된다면, 저는 우리 학교를 더 좋게 만들고 항상 여러분의 훌륭한 아이디어를 고려하겠습니다! 저는 Anna Smith이고, 여러분의 표가 필요합니다!

[해설] 선거 공약으로 학급 의견함 설치는 언급되지 않았다.

[어휘] run for ~에 출마하다 president [prézidənt] 회장 improve [imprúːv] 개선하다, 개선되다 be free to-v 자유롭게 ~하다 suggest [sədʒést] 제안하다 elect [ilékt] 선출하다 consider [kənsídər] 고려하다 vote [vout] 표

09 ②

남: 이것은 특정 종류의 금속을 자신 쪽으로 끌어당길 수 있는 것입니다. 이것은 종이나 플라스틱 같은 것들은 끌어당길 수 없습니다. 이것은 극이라고 불리는 두 개의 끝을 가지고 있습니다. 반대의 극은 서로의 쪽으로 끌어당기고, 같은 극은 서로 밀어냅니다. 이것은 선풍기와 냉장고를 포함해서 많은 일상 제품에도 사용됩니다.

[해설] 양 끝에 극이 있어 반대의 극은 서로 끌어당기고 같은 극은 밀어내는 것은 자석이다.

[어휘] toward [tɔːrd] ~ 쪽으로 pole [poul] 극 opposite [ápəzit] 반대의 product [prádəkt] 제품

10 ②

① 남: 우리 보고서 기한이 언제까지야?
  여: 오늘부터 일주일 후야.
② 남: 어느 치마가 더 나아 보이는 것 같아?
  여: 너 멋져 보이는 것 같아.
③ 남: 내 책들 가져오는 거 기억했니?
  여: 응, 내 가방에 있어.
④ 남: 질문 하나 해도 될까요?
  여: 물론이죠. 무엇을 알고 싶나요?
⑤ 남: 어제 학교에 어떻게 갔니?
  여: 어머니가 차로 데려다주셨어.

[해설] 어느 치마가 더 나아 보이는지 물었는데, 멋져 보인다는 응답은 어색하다.

[어휘] due date 만기일, 기한 report [ripɔ́ːrt] 보도; *보고서 remember to-v ~할 것을 기억하다

11 ③

여: 이번 주 일요일에 한가한 시간 좀 있니?
남: 응, 있어. 왜?
여: 나랑 시립 미술관에서 새로 열리는 전시회에 갈래?
남: 그래, 재밌겠다.
여: 오후에 거기에 가는 게 어때?
남: 좋아, 하지만 가기 전에 그림들에 대해 조사를 좀 해 보자. 우리가 전시회를 더 잘 이해하는 데 도움이 될 거야.
여: 그래, 그런데 그 미술관에서 관람객을 위해 만든 앱이 있다고 들었어. 그것은 작품과 화가에 관한 많은 정보를 제공해.
남: 와, 굉장하다! 그럼 그걸 내려받자.

[해설] 전시회를 보러 가기 전에 작품들에 대해 조사하기 위해 관련 앱을 내려받기로 했다.

[어휘] do research 조사를 하다 artwork [áːrtwərk] 미술품 download [dáunlòud] 다운로드하다, 내려받다

12 ③

여: 안녕하세요, 무엇을 도와드릴까요?
남: 저희 아이를 위한 1일 테니스 수업 일정을 잡고 싶어요.
여: 아이가 몇 살인가요?
남: 일곱 살이에요.
여: 두 시 어떠세요? 그 반에 또래 아이들이 몇 명 있어요.
남: 음, 더 나중이 아이에게 더 잘 맞을 거예요.
여: 한번 볼게요. [잠시 후] 오후 3시, 4시, 그리고 5시에 수업이 잡혀 있어요.
남: 안전하게 4시로 하죠.
여: 좋아요. 그때 아이를 만나기를 고대할게요.

[해설] 여자는 3시에서 5시 사이의 수업을 제안했고, 남자는 4시로 하겠다고 했다.

[어휘] schedule [skédʒuːl] 일정을 잡다 fit [fit] 맞다; *맞는 것

13 ②

남: 이번 주 토요일 축구 경기 표를 살 거야. 어디에 앉고 싶니?
여: 웨스트석은 어때? 홈 팬들이 거기에 앉아. 시끄럽지만 재미있을 거야.
남: 웨스트석 표는 이미 매진됐어.
여: 정말 안타깝다.
남: 이스트석은 원정 팬들을 위한 곳이야. 거기 앉는 건 어때?
여: 음, 글쎄. 그런데 우리가 미드필드 근처에 앉으면, 경기장 전체를 볼 수 있어.
남: 좋은 생각이야. 음… 햇빛 때문에 사우스석에서는 너무 더울 것 같아. 노스석은 어때?
여: 좋아! 시야가 완벽할 거야!

[해설] 두 사람은 시야가 좋으면서 너무 덥지 않은 노스석을 선택했다.

[어휘] stand [stænd] 서다; *(경기장의) 관중석 supporter [səpɔ́ːrtər] 지지자; *(특정 스포츠팀의) 팬 sunlight [sʌ́nlàit] 햇빛 view [vjuː] 경관; *시야

14 ②

남: Tania, 여름 방학은 어땠어?
여: 아주 좋았어. 나는 방학 대부분을 Steamboat 호수에서 보냈어.
남: 거기서 뭐 했어?
여: 낚시하러 가고 아름다운 호수 경관을 즐겼어.
남: 좋았겠다. 나도 언젠가 거기에 가고 싶어.
여: 그래야지. 네가 정말 좋아할 거야.
남: 호수에서 할 수 있는 다른 재미있는 게 있니?
여: 수영하거나 하이킹을 갈 수 있어.
남: 와. 호수에서 수영하는 거 재미있겠다.

[해설] 여자는 호수에서 낚시하고 경관을 즐기며 여름 방학 대부분을 보냈다고 했다.

[어휘] sometime [sʌ́mtàim] 언젠가

15 ②

여: 라디오 방송을 방해해서 죄송합니다. 뉴스 속보입니다. 멧돼지 무리가 산에서 내려와 시청 근처 공원에 있습니다. 현재 1-1-9 구조대가 멧돼지 포획을 위한 작전을 수행 중입니다. 안전을 위해, 이 지역 근처에 가는 것을 삼가 주십시오. 상황이 해결될 때까지 안전하게 계십시오. 협조 감사합니다. 소식이 들어오는 대로 다시 전해 드리겠습니다.

[해설] 멧돼지 무리가 공원에 출몰하여 구조대가 포획 작전 수행 중임을 알리고 있다.

[어휘] interrupt [ìntərʌ́pt] 방해하다 broadcast [brɔ́ːdkæ̀st] 방송 breaking news 뉴스 속보 wild boar 멧돼지 town hall 읍사무소[시청] currently [kɔ́ːrəntli] 현재 rescue [réskjuː] 구조 conduct [kʌ́ndʌkt] (특정한 활동을) 하다; *수행하다 operation [ùpəréiʃən] 수술; *작전 capture [kǽptʃər] 포획하다 area [ɛ́əriə] 지역 resolve [rizálv] 해결하다

16 ④

남: 얘, Kate. 내일 같이 놀이공원에 가자.
여: 난 못 가. 디지털카메라를 사려면 돈을 모아야 해.
남: 아, 알았어. 디지털카메라는 돈이 많이 들지. 내 것에는 300달러를 지출했어.
여: 응, 알아. 지금까지 나는 70달러를 모았어.
남: 그게 다야? 그것보다 훨씬 더 많이 필요할 텐데.
여: 음, 아르바이트 임금을 받고 나면, 100달러가 더 생겨. 그러면 170달러가 될 거야.
남: 네가 원하는 카메라를 사려면 얼마가 더 필요하니?
여: 100달러만 더 벌면 돼.
남: 그렇구나. 그래, 행운을 빌어.

[해설] 여자가 지금까지 모은 돈 70달러와 아르바이트 임금 100달러 외에 추가로 100달러가 더 필요하다고 했으므로, 디지털카메라의 가격은 270달러이다.

[어휘] so far 지금까지 save [seiv] 구하다; *(돈을) 모으다, 저축하다 a lot 훨씬 part-time job 시간제 일, 아르바이트 earn [əːrn] (돈을) 벌다

17 ③

남: 안녕하세요. 무엇을 도와드릴까요?
여: 머리하고 싶어서요.
남: 알겠습니다. 여기서 전에 머리하신 적이 있나요?
여: 네, 보통 Gina님이 해 주시죠.
남: 알겠습니다, 하지만 지금은 Gina님이 예약이 다 찼어요. 예약한 사람들이 모두 끝날 때까지 기다리셔야 할 거예요.
여: 정말요? 얼마나 기다려야 하나요?
남: 정확히는 모르겠습니다. 예약을 하시고 나중에 다시 오시는 건 어떠세요?
여: 그래요, 그게 좋겠어요.
남: 언제 다시 오시길 원하시나요?
여: 빠를수록 좋아요.

[해설] 남자는 여자에게 머리하러 언제 다시 올 것인지 물었으므로, 방문을 희망하는 때에 관한 응답이 가장 적절하다.
① 저는 막 여기 도착했어요.
② 머리를 파마하고 싶어요.

④ 제 차례가 되면 얘기해 주세요.
⑤ 저한테 어울리는 색을 추천해 주시면 좋겠어요.

어휘 get one's hair done 머리하다 fully [fúli] 충분히, 완전히 appointment [əpɔ́intmənt] 약속, 예약 make a reservation 예약하다 [문제] perm [pəːrm] 파마 recommend [rèkəménd] 추천하다

18 ②

여: 실례합니다.
남: 아, 안녕하세요. 도와드릴까요?
여: 네, 그래 주시면 좋겠어요. 저희 가족이 지난주에 이 동네로 막 이사 왔거든요.
남: 그렇군요. 음, 이웃이 되신 걸 환영합니다.
여: 감사해요. 그나저나 어머니 생신에 드릴 꽃을 살 수 있는 곳을 찾으려고 하는 중이에요.
남: 꽃이요? 어디 보자… Westlake 쇼핑몰에 꽃 가게가 있는 것 같아요.
여: 잘됐네요. 여기서 얼마나 먼가요?
남: 겨우 세 블록 떨어져 있어요.

해설 여자는 꽃 가게가 얼마나 멀리 있는지 물었으므로, 거리에 관한 응답이 가장 적절하다.
① 4월 15일 목요일이에요.
③ 장미 12송이에 40달러예요.
④ 3시 15분 정도 됐어요.
⑤ 그 열차는 이 역에 정차하지 않아요.

어휘 neighborhood [néibərhùd] 이웃 [문제] dozen [dʌ́zn] 12개의 quarter [kwɔ́ːrtər] 4분의 1; *15분

19 ⑤

남: 너희들 올해 학교 축제에서 뭐 할지 결정했니?
여: 아니, 아직. 우리는 어느 것에도 합의가 되지 못하는 것 같아.
남: 문제가 뭔 것 같아?
여: 잘 모르겠어. 작년에 우리는 3명뿐이었어. 하지만 올해는 축제 기획 팀에 팀원 10명이 있어.
남: 작년에는 이런 문제가 없었니?
여: 응. 작년에는 합의를 보는 게 쉬웠어. 하지만 이번에는, 우리 각자가 의견이 달라서, 어떤 결정도 못 하고 있어.
남: 회원이 3명만 있을 때 팀이 더 나은 것 같구나.

해설 여자는 팀원이 3명이던 작년과 달리 올해는 10명이 합의하기 어렵다고 했으므로, 인원이 적을 때 팀 운영이 더 나은 것 같다는 응답이 가장 적절하다.
① 너희가 합의를 봤다니 기뻐.
② 네 말이 맞아. 일할 사람이 많을수록 더 좋지.
③ 하지만 기억해, 다른 사람의 의견을 존중해야 한다는 걸.
④ 팀에 사람이 많으면, 어떤 사람은 아무 일도 안 하지.

어휘 decide [disáid] 결정하다 agree on ~에 동의하다[합의가 되다] come to an agreement 합의를 보다 opinion [əpínjən] 의견 make a decision 결정하다 [문제] respect [rispékt] 존경하다, 존중하다

20 ②

여: Lisa는 온라인으로 책 몇 권을 샀습니다. 그녀가 주문을 확인했을 때, 배송이 늦어도 이틀 안에 도착할 것이라고 되어 있었습니다. 하지만, 사흘 후에 책은 아직도 배송되지 않았습니다. 게다가, 그녀는 지연에 대한 어떤 통지도 받지 못했습니다. 그래서 그녀는 고객 센터에 전화해서 항의하려고 합니다. 이런 상황에서, Lisa는 뭐라고 말하겠습니까?
Lisa: 제가 주문한 것을 아직 받지 못했어요.

해설 늦어도 이틀 안에 도착하기로 되어 있던 책이 사흘 후에도 배송되지 않았으므로, 배송 지연에 대해 항의하는 말이 가장 적절하다.
① 제가 원하는 책을 주문할 수가 없어요.
③ 배송지 주소를 잘못 썼어요.
④ 상품이 잘못 배송되었어요.
⑤ 배송 중에 상품이 훼손되었어요.

어휘 at the latest (아무리) 늦어도 receive [risíːv] 받다 notice [nóutis] 통지 delay [diléi] 지연 complain [kəmpléin] 항의하다 [문제] incorrectly [ìnkəréktli] 부정확하게 goods [gudz] 상품, 제품

Dictation Test 07

pp. 114~121

01 1) yellow one with a star 2) One has a heart
3) need the first one

02 1) getting ready for the beach
2) my swimsuit and my towel
3) need my sunglasses

03 1) delivering your package
2) be home until after 7:00 3) pick it up

04 1) two cups of coffee 2) $2.50 per cup
3) add 10% for tax 4) Here's a $20 bill

05 1) There are instructions 2) I'd like two tickets
3) cut in front of us 4) next to it

06 1) had stolen my purse 2) had been broken
3) catch the thief

07 1) take you to the doctor's office 2) I'm much better
3) Can I borrow them

08 1) running for class president
2) have a no uniform day
3) suggest a healthier menu
4) keep our classrooms clean

09 1) pull certain types of metal
2) two ends, called poles 3) push each other away

10 1) due date for our report
2) remember to bring my books 3) get to school

11 1) go to a new exhibition 2) do some research
3) there's an app 4) offers a lot of information

12 1) would like to schedule 2) better fit for him
3) make it 4:00

13 1) home supporters sit there 2) sit near midfield
3) because of the sunlight

14 1) spent most of my vacation 2) I went fishing
3) Swimming in the lake

15 1) This is breaking news 2) capture the wild boars
3) Stay safe

16 1) need to save money 2) have $70 saved
3) have $100 more 4) earn $100 more

17 1) get my hair done 2) fully booked right now
3) have to wait 4) like to come back

18 1) moved to this town 2) find a place
3) How far is it

19 1) agree on anything 2) come to an agreement
3) can't make any decisions

20 1) delivery would arrive
2) books still haven't been delivered
3) call the customer center

실전모의고사 08회

pp. 122~123

01 ⑤

남: 안녕하세요, 무엇을 도와드릴까요?

여: 집들이 선물을 사고 싶어요.

남: 그렇군요. 생각해 두신 게 있나요?

여: 글쎄요, 잘 모르겠어요. 뭔가 추천해 주시겠어요?

남: 찻주전자는 어떠세요? 선물로 인기 있어요.

여: 잘 모르겠어요. 제 친구는 차를 자주 마시지 않거든요.

남: 그렇군요. 그럼 등이나 러그는 어떠세요?

여: 둘 다 좋아요. 하지만 저는 러그가 더 좋을 것 같아요.

남: 이건 어떠세요? 양쪽에 술이 달린 러그가 요즘 인기 있어요.

여: 예쁘네요. 그걸 살게요.

남: 알겠습니다. 친구분이 좋아하시길 바랍니다.

해설 여자는 집들이 선물로 양쪽에 술이 달린 러그를 사기로 했다.

어휘 housewarming [háuswɔ̀ːrmiŋ] 집들이 teapot [tíːpɑ̀t] 찻주전자 tea [tiː] 차, 홍차 lamp [læmp] 램프, 등 tassel [tǽsl] (쿠션·옷 등에 장식으로 다는) 술

02 ②

남: 너 어제 새 휴대전화 샀어?

여: 매장에 갔는데, 안 샀어.

남: 왜? 맘에 드는 걸 아무것도 찾지 못했어?

여: 그게 문제였어. 새 휴대전화가 너무 많아서, 어떤 걸 고를지 모르겠더라.

남: 그래, 요즘 새로운 모델이 많아. 난 지난주에 새 휴대전화 사기 전에 조사를 많이 했어.

여: 아, 너 새것 샀어?

남: 응, 샀지. 마음에 들어.

여: 네가 괜찮다면, 내가 휴대전화 고르는 걸 도와줄 수 있니?

남: 물론이지, 그렇게.

해설 남자가 새 휴대전화를 사기 전에 조사를 많이 했다고 하자, 여자는 자신의 새 휴대전화 고르는 것을 도와달라고 부탁했다.

어휘 mind [maind] 마음; *언짢아하다

03 ②

① 남: 키와 체중이 어떻게 되세요?
여: 키는 170cm이고, 체중은 60kg입니다.
② 남: 이 상자를 제주로 보내야 해요.
여: 상자 안에 뭐가 있나요?
③ 남: 가방을 직접 샀나요?
여: 네.
④ 남: 당신이 오늘 저녁에 여기 올 줄 몰랐어요.
여: 저는 일요일에 항상 여기서 쇼핑을 해요.
⑤ 남: 창가 자리로 드릴까요, 아니면 통로 자리로 드릴까요?
여: 창가 자리로 주세요.

해설 우체국에서 남자가 상자를 우편으로 보내려고 하는 상황이다.

어휘 height [hait] 높이, 키 weight [weit] 무게, 체중 weigh [wei] 무게가 ~이다 mail [meil] (우편으로) 보내다 aisle [ail] 통로

04 ⑤

[전화벨이 울린다.]

여: Kim's 치과입니다. 도와드릴까요?

남: 안녕하세요, 치과 검진 예약을 하고 싶습니다.

여: 알겠습니다, 언제 오시겠어요?

남: 화요일에 비어 있는 시간이 있나요?

여: 죄송합니다, 의사 선생님이 그날 자원봉사를 하실 거예요. 수요일은 어떠세요?

남: 안 될 것 같아요. 제가 예약할 수 있는 가장 빠른 날이 언제인가요? 가능한 한 빨리 진료를 받고 싶습니다.

여: 금요일이 될 것 같아요.

남: 알겠습니다, 저도 좋습니다.

해설 여자가 검진 예약이 가능한 가장 빠른 날이 금요일이라고 하자, 남자도 좋다고 했다.

어휘 make an appointment 예약을 하다 dental checkup 치과 검진 opening [óupəniŋ] 구멍; *공석 dentist [déntist] 치과 의사 as soon as possible 가능한 한 빨리

05 ②

남: Liz, 벌써 짐 싸는 거 마쳤어요?

여: 네. 시애틀에 있는 우리 아들을 보러 가는 게 무척 기대돼요. 우리 항공편이 내일 아침 8시 30분에 출발하나요?

남: 아뇨, 7시 30분에 출발해요. 알람 맞추는 것을 잊지 말아요. 우린 적어도 비행 두 시간 전에는 공항에 도착해야 해요.

여: 알았어요. 그리고 가는 데 여섯 시간 정도 걸리는 거죠, 맞죠?

남: 아뇨, 그렇게 오래 걸리지 않아요. 다섯 시간 정도 걸려요.

여: 아, 그렇군요. 그러면 시애틀에 12시 30분 정도에 도착하겠네요.

남: 실제로는, 시차 때문에 11시 30분 정도일 거예요.

해설 목적지(시애틀), 출발 시각(아침 7시 30분), 비행시간(다섯 시간 정도), 도착 시각(11시 30분 정도)에 관해서는 언급되었으나, 기내식 메뉴는 언급되지 않았다.

어휘 set the alarm 시계의 알람을 맞추다

06 ②

남: 안녕하세요. 도와드릴까요?

여: 네, Peter Underwood의 최신 소설을 찾고 있어요.

남: 〈The Last Door〉 말씀하시는 건가요?

여: 네, 그게 제목이에요. 모든 곳을 찾아봤는데, 찾을 수가 없네요.

남: 그 책이 있는지 컴퓨터로 확인해 볼게요.

여: 감사합니다.

남: 음, 한 부가 남아 있네요. 신간 코너에 있어요.

여: 아, 제가 거기는 보지 않았어요.

남: 한 가지 문제가 있는데 책이 약간 하자가 있어요. 하지만 할인해 드릴 수 있어요.

해설 남자는 여자가 찾는 소설책 재고가 한 부 있는데 약간 하자가 있어 할인해 줄 수 있다고 했으므로, 두 사람이 대화하는 장소로 가장 적절한 곳은 서점이다.

어휘 novel [nάvəl] 소설 copy [kάpi] 사본; *부, 권 section [sékʃən] 부분, 구획 discount [dískaunt] 할인

07 ②

① 여: 난 휴가 동안 런던에 갔었어.

　　남: 여행 어땠니?

② 여: 내 파란색 스웨터 봤니?

　　남: 백화점에서 예쁜 파란색 스웨터를 봤어.

③ 여: 비가 많이 오는데, 난 우산이 없어.

　　남: 내 것을 써도 돼.

④ 여: 나 오늘 저녁에 노래 대회에 참가할 거야.

　　남: 네게 행운을 빌어 줄게.

⑤ 여: 히터를 켜자. 너무 추워.

　　남: 이미 켜져 있어.

해설 자신의 스웨터를 봤냐고 물었는데, 백화점에서 예쁜 스웨터를 봤다는 응답은 어색하다.

어휘 department store 백화점 compete [kəmpíːt] 경쟁하다; *참가하다 keep one's fingers crossed 행운을 빌다, 잘 되길 바라다 turn on ~을 켜다

08 ⑤

여: 너 괜찮니? 별로 안 좋아 보여.

남: 나 배가 아파. 뭔가 상한 걸 먹은 것 같아.

여: 이런. 너 진찰을 받아야겠다. 내가 데려다줄게.

남: 고맙지만, 그렇게 심각하지 않아.

여: 내가 뭐 해 줄 거 없어?

남: 대신 약국에 태워다 줄래? 약을 좀 사고 싶어.

여: 물론이지. 문제없어.

해설 남자는 복통이 심하지 않다며 여자에게 병원 대신 약국에 데려다 달라고 부탁했다.

어휘 stomachache [stʌ́məkèik] 복통 serious [síəriəs] 심각한 pharmacy [fάːrməsi] 약국 medicine [médisn] 약

09 ④

남: 주목해 주시겠습니다? 저는 학생회장 Jim Carter입니다. 모든 학

생들은 오전 8시까지 학교에 와야 한다는 것을 다시 한번 알려 드리고자 합니다. 유감스럽게도, 요즘 점점 더 많은 학생들이 늦게 도착하고 있습니다. 이는 수업에 방해가 되고 선생님의 수업을 중단시키기 때문에 문제가 됩니다. 학교 규칙을 준수하여 학교 수업 시작 전에 교실에 와 있도록 노력해 주십시오. 감사합니다.

[해설] 요즘 많은 학생들이 학교에 늦게 오고 있다며 오전 8시까지 등교할 것을 당부하고 있다.

[어휘] remind [rimáind] 상기시키다, 다시 한번 알려 주다 disrupt [disrʌ́pt] 방해하다, 지장을 주다 make an effort 노력하다, 애쓰다

10 ②

여: 식사 어땠어?
남: 완벽했어! 난 꼭 이 식당에 다시 올 거야.
여: 응, 나도 잘 먹었어. 아, 여기 계산서 있어. 개별적으로 낼까?
남: 그래, 그렇게 하자.
여: 어디 보자. 내 식사는 10달러였고, 네 것은 12달러였어.
남: 그래, 그리고 10% 세금도 있어.
여: 응, 그럼 난 10달러에 추가로 10% 세금을 내야겠네.

[해설] 여자의 식사는 10달러였고 10% 세금이 있다고 했으므로, 여자가 지불할 금액은 11달러이다.

[어휘] bill [bil] 계산서 separately [sépərətli] 따로따로, 개별적으로

11 ⑤

남: 좋아! 40 대 15. 1점 더 내면, 내가 이겨.
여: 경기는 아직 끝나지 않았어.
남: 물론 끝났지. 여기 공!
여: 이런! 완전히 놓쳤어!
남: 내가 이겼다! 진 사람이 점심값 낸다는 거 잊지 마.
여: 알았어. 네가 테니스를 그렇게 잘 칠 줄은 몰랐어.
남: 오늘을 위해 조금 연습했어.
여: 가자. 내가 좋은 곳을 알고 있어.

[해설] 남자는 테니스 시합에서 이기자 진 사람이 점심값 내기로 한 것을 상기시켰고, 여자가 좋은 곳을 안다며 가자고 했다.

[어휘] match [mætʃ] 경기, 시합 completely [kəmplíːtli] 완전히 loser [lúːzər] 패자 practice [prǽktis] 연습하다

12 ⑤

여: 안녕하세요, 고객 여러분. 〈Maggie's 커피〉의 주인인 Maggie Grace입니다. 저는 12월 25일부터 28일까지의 특별 홀리데이 할인을 알려 드리려고 합니다. 이 기간 동안, 여러분은 저희 특별 홀리데이 음료를 반값에 구매하실 수 있습니다. 게다가, 홀리데이 음료

를 주문하시는 고객분들은 무료 쿠키를 받으실 수 있습니다. 이 특별 할인은 전국 저희 모든 매장에서 이용하실 수 있습니다. 친구나 가족과 함께 오셔서 저희 홀리데이 음료를 즐기세요.

[해설] 기간(12월 25일부터 28일까지), 할인 품목(특별 홀리데이 음료), 사은품(무료 쿠키), 장소(전국 모든 매장)에 관해서는 언급되었으나, 할인 쿠폰은 언급되지 않았다.

[어휘] owner [óunər] 주인 half [hæf] 반 in addition 게다가 special offer 특별 할인 across the country 전국의

13 ⑤

여: 여보, 우리가 조사한 아파트들에 대해 이야기해요. 그것들이 어땠어요?
남: 나는 A동 아파트가 좋았어요. 크기가 우리에게 딱 맞는 것 같아요.
여: 네, 그래요. 하지만 거긴 출입구 근처라서 너무 시끄러울 것 같아요.
남: 사실이에요. 1층에 있는 아파트도 시끄러울 테니 고르지 말아야 해요.
여: 동의해요. B동 아파트는 어때요?
남: 우리에겐 너무 커요. 우린 방 세 개는 필요 없어요.
여: 그럼 선택할 수 있는 것이 하나만 남네요.
남: 네. 좋은 것 같아요. 공원과 가까워서, 운동하기 편할 거예요.

[해설] A동과 1층은 시끄럽고 B동은 너무 크다고 했으므로, C동의 3층을 선택할 것이다.

[어휘] check out ~을 확인하다[조사하다] entrance [éntrəns] (출)입구, 문

14 ②

남: 이것은 인기 있는 겨울 스포츠입니다. 이것은 북유럽에서 시작되었는데, 그곳은 눈이 많이 옵니다. 사람들은 눈 덮인 산에서 이것을 합니다. 사람들은 특수 부츠를 신고 그것을 특수 보드 위에 붙입니다. 사람들은 균형을 잡고 방향을 바꾸기 위해 막대를 사용합니다. 사람들은 이 눈 덮인 산을 천천히 또는 빠르게 미끄러져 내려갈 수 있습니다. 이 스포츠는 동계 올림픽의 중요한 부분입니다.

[해설] 특수 보드 위에 붙인 특수 부츠를 신고 막대를 사용하여 방향을 바꾸며 눈 덮인 산을 미끄러져 내려오는 스포츠는 스키다.

[어휘] northern [nɔ́ːrðərn] 북쪽에 위치한 snowy [snóui] 눈에 덮인 stick [stik] 막대 balance [bǽləns] 균형을 잡다 slide down 미끄러져 내려가다

15 ⑤

남: 안녕하세요, 도와드릴까요?
여: 네, 어제 이 신발을 샀는데요. 오늘 아침에 굽 하나가 망가졌어요.
남: 아, 정말요? 무슨 일이 있었죠?

여: 그냥 복도를 걷고 있었을 뿐이에요. 신발에 문제가 있었던 게 분명해요. 무척 당황스럽네요.

남: 정말 죄송합니다. 수선받길 원하시나요?

여: 아뇨, 그냥 전액 환불받고 싶어요.

남: 그런 경우라면, 맨 위층으로 가서서 고객 서비스 데스크에 있는 Langley 씨에게 요청하세요. 그녀가 당신을 도와줄 수 있을 거예요.

여: 알겠어요. 그럼 그렇게 할게요.

해설 여자가 신발을 구입한 지 하루 만에 굽이 망가져서 전액 환불을 원하자, 남자는 고객 서비스 데스크에 가서 요청하라고 했다.

어휘 heel [hi:l] 발뒤꿈치; *신발의 굽 hall [hɔ:l] 복도 must have p.p. ~이었음에 틀림없다 upset [ʌpsét] 속상한, 당황한 repair [ripέər] 수리하다 get a full refund 전액 환불받다

16 ④

[휴대전화가 울린다.]

여: 여보세요?

남: 안녕, Sharon. 나 Bob이야.

여: 안녕, Bob. 무슨 일이야?

남: 우리 회의 일정 변경을 알려 주려고 전화하는 거야.

여: 아, 정말? 화요일 오전 11시 아니야?

남: 그랬지. 그런데 연례 회의 때문에 그 회의가 이틀 뒤로 밀렸어.

여: 알았어. 시간도 변경되었니?

남: 아니.

해설 회의는 화요일 오전 11시에서 이틀 연기되고 시간은 변경되지 않았다고 했다.

어휘 push back (회의 등을) 뒤로 미루다 annual [ǽnjuəl] 연례의 conference [kάnfərəns] 회의, 학회 as well 또한, 역시, ~도

17 ④

남: 우리 만나서 저녁 먹기로 한 거 기억하지?

여: 물론이지. 5시 30분, 맞지?

남: 맞아. 그런데 우리 대신 6시에 만날 수 있을까? 만나기 전에 내가 도서관에 들러야 하거든.

여: 응. 괜찮아.

남: 좋아. 우리 어디서 만날까?

여: 백화점 앞에서 만나는 거 어때? 식당에서 가깝거든.

남: 아니, 거긴 모든 사람이 만나는 곳이야. 너무 붐벼.

해설 여자가 만날 장소를 제안했으므로, 그에 대한 수락이나 거절의 응답이 가장 적절하다.
① 좋아. 저녁 먹으러 나가자.
② 백화점으로 나를 데리러 올래?
③ 백화점에서 살 것이 있어.
⑤ 미안해. 식당 예약하는 걸 잊었어.

어휘 be supposed to-v ~하기로 되어 있다

18 ③

남: 안녕, Sandy. 오늘 밤 축구 경기 때문에 신이 나니?

여: 응. 내 생각엔 우리 팀이 이길 확률이 큰 것 같아.

남: 나도 그렇게 생각해. 팀이 최근에 정말 잘하고 있잖아.

여: 그들이 경기하는 걸 빨리 보고 싶어. 그래서 넌 오늘 밤 경기를 어디서 볼 거니?

남: 친구들하고 우리 집에서. 너는?

여: 나는 가족과 경기장에 갈 거야.

해설 축구 경기를 어디서 볼지 물었으므로, 장소에 관한 응답이 가장 적절하다.
① 나는 축구 선수가 되고 싶어.
② 비가 올 것 같지 않아.
④ 나는 그가 그 팀에서 최고의 선수라고 생각해.
⑤ 나는 다른 어떤 스포츠보다도 야구가 좋아.

어휘 have a good chance of v-ing ~할 가능성이 크다

19 ⑤

남: 얘, Nancy. 내일이 무슨 날인지 기억해?

여: 물론 기억하지. 아빠 생신이잖아.

남: 맞아. 그리고 우린 아직 아빠께 선물을 안 드렸잖아.

여: 알아. 내 숙제가 끝나면 쇼핑몰에 가자.

남: 음, 지금 나 혼자 갈 수 있는데.

여: 아니야, 나도 너랑 같이 가고 싶어.

남: 좋아. 그럼, 내 방에서 컴퓨터 게임을 하고 있을게.

여: 그래, 다 하면 알려 줄게.

해설 여자가 숙제를 마치면 쇼핑몰에 가자고 하자 남자는 방에서 기다리겠다고 했으므로, 다 하면 알려 주겠다는 응답이 가장 적절하다.
① 우린 게임할 시간이 없어.
② 우리 그건 그냥 다음 주에 하는 게 어떨까?
③ 그래, 난 네가 좋은 선물을 고르리라 믿어.
④ 아니야, 아빠는 컴퓨터 게임을 좋아하시지 않으셔.

어휘 by oneself 혼자 [문제] trust [trʌst] 신뢰하다

20 ⑤

여: Ted는 식료품을 사러 슈퍼마켓에 갑니다. 그는 채소, 생선, 치즈와 우유를 삽니다. 그는 집에 돌아와서 그 모든 것을 부엌에 놓습니다. 우유를 냉장고에 넣다가, 유통 기한이 이미 지난 것을 봅니다. 그래서 그는 가게로 돌아가서 그것을 매장 관리자에게 보여 줍니다. 이런 상황에서, Ted는 매장 관리자에게 뭐라고 말하겠습니까?

Ted: 이 우유는 유통 기한이 지났어요.

해설 매장에서 구입한 우유의 유통 기한이 지나 있음을 알리는 말이 가장 적절하다.
① 저는 그 요구르트를 사고 싶어요.

② 매장 관리자를 만나러 왔어요.
③ 실례합니다만, 우유는 어디에 있나요?
④ 시간제 일자리에 지원하러 왔어요.

어휘 grocery [gróusəri] 식료품 expiration date 유통 기한

18 1) good chance of winning 2) can't wait to see
   3) At my house
19 1) haven't gotten him a present
   2) when I finish my homework 3) go with you
20 1) buy some groceries
   2) expiration date has already passed
   3) shows it to the store manager

Dictation Test 08
pp. 124~131

01 1) buy a housewarming gift
   2) doesn't drink tea often 3) rug would be better
   4) on both sides
02 1) which to choose 2) did a lot of research
   3) help me choose one
03 1) mail this package 2) shop here on Sundays
   3) a window or an aisle seat
04 1) for my dental checkup 2) have any openings
   3) the earliest day
05 1) leaves at 7:30 2) takes about five hours
   3) be around 11:30
06 1) Let me check the computer
   2) have one copy left 3) give you a discount
07 1) How was your trip 2) keep my fingers crossed
   3) already been turned on
08 1) should see a doctor 2) not that serious
   3) drive me to the pharmacy
09 1) must be in school 2) disrupts classes
   3) follow the school rules
10 1) pay separately 2) My meal was $10
   3) ten dollars plus 10% tax
11 1) The match isn't over yet 2) pays for lunch
   3) I know a good place
12 1) at half price 2) get a free cookie
   3) available at all our shops
13 1) near the entrance 2) on the first floor
   3) in building B 4) near the park
14 1) has a lot of snow 2) use sticks
   3) slide down these snowy mountains
15 1) one of the heels broke 2) get them repaired
   3) get a full refund 4) at the customer service desk
16 1) change in our meeting schedule
   2) on Tuesday at 11 3) pushed back two days
17 1) supposed to meet 2) at 5:30
   3) in front of the department store

실전모의고사 09회
pp. 132~133

01 ④	02 ③	03 ①	04 ③	05 ⑤
06 ④	07 ①	08 ③	09 ②	10 ⑤
11 ③	12 ⑤	13 ③	14 ⑤	15 ①
16 ④	17 ④	18 ②	19 ①	20 ③

01 ④

여: 좋은 아침이에요, Sally's 제과점입니다. 무엇을 도와드릴까요?
남: 안녕하세요, 엄마를 위한 특별한 케이크를 주문하고 싶어요.
여: 뭔가 특별한 것을 원하신다면, 이층 케이크는 어떠세요? 단층 케이크보다 더 인상적이어 보이거든요.
남: 정말요? 그럼 이층 케이크로 할게요.
여: 케이크 모양도 선택하실 수 있어요.
남: 어떤 모양이 있나요?
여: 둥근 모양, 네모 모양, 하트 모양을 포함해서 여러 가지 모양으로 만들 수 있어요.
남: 그럼 하트 모양의 케이크를 만들어 주세요.
여: 알겠습니다.

해설 남자는 엄마를 위해 하트 모양의 이층 케이크를 주문했다.

어휘 layer [léiər] 층 impressive [imprésiv] 인상적인 a variety of 여러 가지의 including [inklú:diŋ] ~을 포함하여

02 ③

남: 뭐 보고 있니?
여: 이건 한때 유명했던 사람들을 위한 노래 경연 대회야.
남: 오, 나 저 잘생긴 남자를 아는 것 같아. 그런데 이름은 기억이 안 나네.
여: 그의 이름은 Steve Owens야.

남: 전에 영화에 출연한 적 있지 않아?

여: 응, 〈First Love〉라는 영화에 출연했었는데, 완전 실패작이었어.

남: 하지만 노래를 잘하잖아, 그렇지 않니?

여: 응, 노래를 아주 잘해. 심지어 그의 노래 중 하나로 상도 받았어.

해설 외모(잘생김), 출연작(First Love), 노래 실력(노래를 잘함), 수상 경력(그의 노래 중 하나로 상을 받음)에 관해서는 언급되었으나, 대표곡은 언급되지 않았다.

어휘 complete [kəmplíːt] 완전한 failure [féiljər] 실패(작) win an award 상을 타다

03 ①

[전화벨이 울린다.]

남: 여보세요, Flower 호텔입니다. 무엇을 도와드릴까요?

여: 안녕하세요. 제 이름은 Karen Smith입니다. 예약을 했는데요.

남: 네, 9월 16일로 두 분을 위한 트윈룸 하나를 예약하셨네요. 맞습니까?

여: 네. 그런데 네 명으로 바꾸고 싶어요.

남: 그렇다면, 더 큰 객실로 바꾸셔야 할 겁니다. 하지만 더 큰 객실들은 그날 예약이 다 찼습니다.

여: 정말요? 그럼 트윈룸을 하나 더 예약할 수 있나요?

남: 네, 그날 가능한 객실이 하나 있습니다.

여: 잘됐네요.

해설 여자는 예약한 호텔의 투숙 인원을 두 명에서 네 명으로 변경하고 싶다고 했다.

어휘 switch [switʃ] 바꾸다 reserve [rizə́ːrv] 예약하다

04 ③

남: 우리 역사 과제 언제 할 거야?

여: 내일 오전 10시 어때? 우리 학교 수업이 없잖아.

남: 안 돼. 나는 그 시간에 특강에 참석하기로 되어 있어.

여: 강의가 몇 시에 끝나?

남: 정오에 끝나.

여: 그럼 점심 먹고 오후 1시에 만나는 게 어때?

남: 좋아. 난 오후 1시에 한가해.

여: 아, 그런데 내가 오후 3시에 예정된 일이 있어. 그러니 우리는 그전에 과제를 끝내야 해.

남: 알겠어. 음, 우리는 2시간 안에 끝낼 수 있을 거야.

여: 나도 그렇게 생각해.

해설 두 사람은 역사 과제를 하기 위해 오후 1시에 만나 3시 전까지 끝내기로 했다.

어휘 attend [əténd] 참석하다, 출석하다 lecture [léktʃər] 강의 free [friː] 한가한

05 ⑤

남: 여보, Brenda가 전화했어요? 밖이 거의 어두워졌는데요.

여: 친구 집에 있다가 8시 30분까지 돌아오겠다고 했어요.

남: 하지만 이미 8시 45분이에요.

여: 여보, 겨우 15분 늦은 걸요.

남: 그래요, 하지만 휴대전화를 안 받아요. 늦을 때마다 우리에게 전화하잖아요.

여: 진정해요. 아마 이제 막 자전거를 타고 집에 오고 있을 거예요.

남: 내가 밖에 나가서 기다리는 게 나을 것 같아요.

해설 남자는 Brenda의 귀가가 늦어지고 휴대전화도 받지 않아 걱정스러울(worried) 것이다.
　① 외로운 ② 편안한 ③ 기쁜 ④ 후회하는

어휘 relax [rilǽks] 진정하다 had better ~하는 게 낫겠다

06 ④

① 남: 이 크래커 살 수 있나요?
　여: 죄송하지만, 그건 비매품입니다.
② 남: 화장실이 어디에 있나요?
　여: 오른쪽에 보일 거예요.
③ 남: 이 아이스크림 얼마예요?
　여: 4달러입니다.
④ 남: 이건 제가 주문한 게 아닌 것 같아요. 전 머핀과 아메리카노를 주문했어요.
　여: 죄송합니다. 주문하신 것에 맞게 갖다드릴게요.
⑤ 남: 커피 만들기 강좌를 듣고 싶습니다.
　여: 강좌를 들으시려면, 이 양식을 작성해 주세요.

해설 여자 점원이 남자가 주문한 것과 다른 음식을 주려고 한 상황이다.

어휘 cracker [krǽkər] 크래커, 과자 not for sale 비매품 restroom [réstruːm] 화장실

07 ①

여: Johnny, 어디 가니?

남: 엄마가 나에게 저녁 재료를 좀 사다 달라고 부탁하셨어.

여: 정말? 어느 슈퍼마켓에 가니?

남: 4번가에 있는 Quality Mart에 갈 거야.

여: 그럼 Jane의 집 옆을 지나가겠네. 집에 오는 길에 내 책을 가져다줄래?

남: 알았어. Jane에게 전화해서 알려 줘.

여: 고마워. 지금 바로 전화할게.

해설 여자는 남자에게 슈퍼마켓에 다녀오는 길에 Jane의 집에서 책을 가져다 달라고 부탁했다.

어휘 ingredient [ingríːdiənt] 재료 pass by ~ 옆을 지나가다

08 ③

여: 이번 겨울에 특별한 경험을 찾고 계시나요? 설산에서 하루를 보내시는 것은 어떤가요? 저희는 여러분에게 완벽한 야영지과 잊지 못할 추억을 제공할 준비가 되어 있습니다. 저희는 시내에서 약 1시간 거리에 위치해 있으며, 12월부터 2월까지 영업합니다. 여러분은 산에서 스키나 썰매 타기를 즐기실 수 있고, 밤에는 램프가 비추는 등산로가 있습니다. 여러분은 공용 캠프파이어장을 이용하실 수도 있습니다. 공간이 제한되어 있으니, 서둘러 예약하세요! 예약을 위해 저희 웹 사이트를 방문해 주세요.

해설 위치(시내에서 약 1시간 거리), 운영 시기(12월부터 2월), 즐길 거리(스키, 썰매, 등산, 캠프파이어), 예약 방법(웹 사이트 방문)에 관해서는 언급되었으나, 수용 인원은 언급되지 않았다.

어휘 unique [juníːk] 특별한 campground [kǽmpgràund] 야영지 unforgettable [ʌ̀nfərgétəbl] 잊지 못할 sled [sled] 썰매를 타다 trail [treil] 자국, 흔적; *산길 light [lait] (빛을) 비추다 (light-lit-lit) campfire [kǽmpfàiər] 캠프파이어, (야영장의) 모닥불 limited [límitid] 한정된, 제한된

09 ②

남: 이곳은 많은 이동객들이 방문하는 장소입니다. 그들은 멀리 있는 장소로 비행기를 타고 이동하길 원할 때 거기에 갑니다. 이곳에서 그들은 다양한 도시와 국가로 비행기를 타고 갑니다. 이곳에는 상점, 음식점, 심지어 헬스클럽이 있기도 합니다. 어떤 사람들은 다른 곳에서 오는 방문객을 맞기 위해서 이곳으로 옵니다.

해설 멀리 있는 도시나 다른 국가로 비행기를 타고 가거나 다른 곳에서 오는 방문객을 맞기 위해 가는 장소는 공항이다.

어휘 travel [trǽvl] 여행하다; *이동하다 for away 멀리 fitiness center 헬스클럽 greet [griːt] 맞다, 환영하다 visitor [vízitər] 방문객, 손님

10 ⑤

① 여: 내일 새로 생긴 그 음식점에 가자.
　 남: 나도 가고 싶어. 몇 시에 만날까?
② 여: 나 우리 언니의 재킷을 잃어버렸어.
　 남: 넌 언니에게 사과해야 해.
③ 여: 수학 시험 잘 봤니?
　 남: 아니. 예상한 것보다 점수가 더 나빴어.
④ 여: 어떻게 그렇게 빨리 여기에 도착했니?
　 남: 자전거를 타고 왔어.
⑤ 여: 왜 어젯밤에 나에게 전화하지 않았어?
　 남: 전화기가 작동을 안 해서 전화를 못 받았어.

해설 전화를 하지 않은 이유를 물었는데 전화를 받지 못한 이유를 말하는 것은 어색하다.

어휘 score [skɔːr] 점수 worse [wəːrs] 더 나쁜 (bad의 비교급) expect [ikspékt] 예상하다 ride [raid] 타다 (ride-rode-ridden)

11 ③

여: 굉장해. 집이 완전히 달라 보여.
남: 단지 벽지를 바꾼 것으로 많이 개선되었어.
여: 나도 그렇게 생각해. 다음 단계는 뭐야?
남: 먼저, 커튼을 달고 가구를 배치할 거야. 그런 다음 천장에 조명을 달 거야.
여: 실은, 먼저 조명을 달아도 될까? 가구 없는 집 전체를 보고 싶어.
남: 알았어.

해설 남자는 가구를 배치하기 전에 조명을 먼저 달아 달라는 여자의 요청을 수락했다.

어휘 completely [kəmplíːtli] 완전히 wallpaper [wɔ́ːlpèipər] 벽지 improve [imprúv] 개선하다, 개선되다 arrange [əréindʒ] 정리하다, 배치하다 furniture [fə́ːrnitʃər] 가구 ceiling [síːliŋ] 천장

12 ⑤

[전화벨이 울린다.]
남: Oakville 고등학교입니다. 무엇을 도와드릴까요?
여: 안녕하세요. 시간제 일자리 때문에 전화했는데요.
남: 네. 구내식당에서 음식을 나르고 청소하는 일을 하시게 될 겁니다. 음식점에서 일하신 적이 있나요?
여: 네. 전 지난여름에 Chang's 음식점에서 일했어요.
남: 좋아요. 저희는 그런 경험이 있는 사람이 필요해요. 학교에서 일하신 적은요?
여: 실은, 없어요.
남: 괜찮습니다. 그 경험이 반드시 필요한 건 아니니까요. 수요일과 금요일 오전 11시부터 오후 3시까지 일하실 수 있나요?
여: 네, 화요일과 목요일을 제외하고는 매일 시간이 돼요.
남: 좋아요. 면접을 위해 내일 학교로 오실 수 있나요?
여: 네, 좋습니다.

해설 수요일과 금요일에 일할 사람이 필요하다고 했다.

구인: Oakville 고등학교
① 구내식당 시간제 근로자
② 직무: 음식 서빙과 청소
③ 전에 음식점이나 구내식당에서 일했어야 함
④ 학교 근무 경험이 필요하지는 않음
⑤ 시간: 화요일과 목요일 오전 11시부터 오후 3시

어휘 cafeteria [kæ̀fətíəriə] 구내식당 not necessarily 반드시 ~하지 않다 available [əvéiləbl] 이용할 수 있는; *시간이 있는 except [iksépt] ~을 제외하고는 [문제] duty [dúːti] 의무; *직

무 require [rikwáiər] 필요하다

13 ③

남: 너 내일 뭐 할 거니?
여: 영화를 보러 Greenvill 극장에 갈 거야.
남: 어떤 영화?
여: 〈The Truth〉.
남: 그거 재미있겠다. 그 영화 보고 싶어.
여: 나랑 같이 갈래? 표가 화요일과 수요일마다 30% 할인돼.
남: 나도 가고 싶지만, 그럴 수 없어. 내일 일해야 하거든.
여: 모레는 어때? 그때도 여전히 할인을 받을 수 있어.
남: 좋아! 가고 싶어.

해설 영화표는 화요일과 수요일마다 할인되는데, 내일은 남자가 일 때문에 안 된다고 해서 두 사람은 모레 수요일에 만나기로 했다.

어휘 the day after tomorrow 모레

14 ⑤

여: 내 태블릿 봤어?
남: 아니. 네 방 들여다봤어?
여: 내 방을 포함해서 집 전체를 봤는데, 못 찾겠어.
남: 마지막으로 그걸 사용한 게 언제였어?
여: 어젯밤에 그걸로 영상 통화를 했어. 오늘은 사용하지 않았어.
남: 영상 통화를 어디서 했는데?
여: 내 방에서.
남: 네 방을 다시 확인해 봐. [잠시 후]
여: 알겠어. 다시 볼게.
남: 찾았어?
여: 응. 침대 밑에 있어서 못 봤어.

해설 여자는 어젯밤 방에서 영상 통화를 했다고 말했다.

어휘 video call 영상 통화, 화상 통화

15 ①

여: 안녕하세요, 여러분. 오늘 여러분 앞에 서게 되어 영광이고 감사합니다. 다들 아시다시피, 선거철이 다시 다가오고 있습니다. 다시 한번 여러분의 지지를 부탁드립니다. 여러분의 대표로서, 저는 우리 지역 사회를 개선하기 위해 열심히 일했습니다. 개울을 따라 자전거 도로를 짓게 했습니다. 또한 새 공공 도서관에 자금을 대는 것을 도왔습니다. 그리고 범죄를 줄임으로써 도시를 더 안전하게 만들어 왔습니다. 가장 중요한 것은, 제가 세금 인상 없이 이 모든 것을 해냈습니다. 앞으로 저는 우리 도시를 개선하기 위해 훨씬 더 많은 일을 할 것입니다. 여러분의 도움으로, 우리는 함께 더 나은 미래를 만들 수 있습니다.

해설 여자는 지역 사회 개선을 위해 한 일들을 이야기하며, 다가오는 선거철에 다시 한번 자신을 지지해 줄 것을 부탁했다.

어휘 honored [ánərd] 명예로운; *영광으로 생각하여 grateful [gréitfl] 고마워하는 election [ilékʃən] 선거 support [səpɔ́ːrt] 지지 representative [rèprizéntətiv] 대표(자) stream [striːm] 개울 fund [fʌnd] 자금[기금]; *자금[기금]을 대다 reduce [ridjúːs] 줄이다, 감소시키다 crime [kraim] 범죄 raise [reiz] 들어올리다; *인상하다

16 ④

남: 도와드릴까요?
여: 네. 이 사과들을 사고 싶어요.
남: 알겠습니다. 어디 볼까요. 사과 여섯 개요? 총 4달러 80센트입니다.
여: 실은, 사과가 5개뿐인데요.
남: 아, 죄송합니다. 제가 착각했습니다. 그렇다면 4달러입니다.
여: 네.
남: 다른 것 더 필요하신 것 있나요? 오늘 오렌지가 좋은데요.
여: 네, 신선해 보이네요. 얼마인가요?
남: 한 개에 1달러입니다.
여: 좋아요, 오렌지도 5개 살게요.

해설 사과 5개($4)와 오렌지 5개($1x5)를 샀으므로, 여자가 지불할 금액은 총 9달러이다.

어휘 come to (총계가) ~이 되다 make a mistake 실수하다

17 ④

여: 너무 신이 나. 이제 여름 휴가야.
남: 맞아. 너는 올해 뭘 할 거니?
여: 유럽으로 또 여행을 갈 거야.
남: 멋지다. 작년에 독일에 가지 않니?
여: 맞아, 그리고 스위스랑 오스트리아, 프랑스에도 갔어.
남: 와, 많은 곳을 갔구나. 그럼 올해는?
여: <u>올해는 이탈리아에 갈 거야.</u>

해설 여자가 작년에 이어 올해도 유럽 여행을 갈 거라고 하자 어느 곳에 갈 건지 물었으므로, 구체적인 유럽의 여행지를 말하는 응답이 가장 적절하다.
① 나는 작년에 그곳에 갔었어.
② 응, 정말 좋은 여행이었어.
③ 나는 정말 유럽에 가고 싶어.
⑤ 나는 더는 거기에 가고 싶지 않아.

어휘 take a trip 여행을 가다 as well ~도, 역시

18 ②

남: Laura, 지금이 몇 시인지 아니?

여: 늦어서 죄송합니다, Stewart 선생님.

남: 어제 넌 고장 난 알람 시계 때문에 지각했다고 말했었지. 오늘 또 늦게 일어났니?

여: 아니요, 오늘은 일찍 일어났어요.

남: 그럼 오늘은 이유가 뭐니?

여: 음, 오늘 집을 일찍 나섰는데, 지하철에서 잠이 들어서 역을 놓쳤어요.

남: <u>알겠다, 하지만 그건 이유가 되지 않아.</u>

해설 여자는 어제에 이어 오늘도 지각한 또 다른 이유를 설명하고 있으므로, 이유가 되지 않는다고 말하는 응답이 가장 적절하다.
① 늦더라도 안 하는 것보다는 낫지.
③ 어젯밤에 언제 잠들었니?
④ 알람 시계를 몇 개 맞춰 놓는 게 낫겠구나.
⑤ 다음번에는 지하철을 타는 게 어떠니?

어휘 broken [bróukən] 고장이 난 fall asleep 잠이 들다 stop [stap] 멈춤; *정거장, 역 [문제] no excuse 이유가 되지 않는, 변명의 여지가 없는

---

19 ①

여: 여보, 부엌 벽을 페인트칠해야겠어요. 이 색상에 싫증 났어요.

남: 아, 나도 그 생각을 하고 있었어요. 나는 저 갈색이 좋았던 적이 없네요.

여: 부엌을 파란색으로 페인트칠하는 게 어때요? 깨끗해 보일 거예요.

남: 약간 추운 느낌이 들 것 같아요.

여: 노란색이나 녹색은 어때요?

남: 글쎄요, 노란색은 너무 밝아요. 하지만 나는 녹색은 괜찮은 것 같아요.

여: 나도 그렇게 생각해요. 녹색이 사람들을 편안하게 느끼게 한다고 들었어요.

남: <u>네, 그게 딱 좋을 거예요.</u>

해설 녹색으로 페인트칠하는 게 좋겠다는 남자의 말에 여자도 동의했으므로, 합의를 나타내는 응답이 가장 적절하다.
② 그러면 우리는 두 가지 선택이 남네요.
③ 두 가지 색을 섞는 게 어때요?
④ 그러면 우리는 노란색 페인트를 사야 해요.
⑤ 나는 모든 밝은 색이 정말 좋아요.

어휘 be tired of ~에 싫증이 나다 bright [brait] 밝은 relaxed [rilǽkst] 편안한 [문제] option [ápʃən] 선택(권) mix [miks] 섞다

---

20 ③

남: 오늘은 일요일 아침이고, Julie는 공원에서 걸어다니고 있습니다. 많은 사람들이 화창한 날씨를 즐기고 있습니다. Julie는 공원에 홀로 앉아 있는 남자를 봅니다. 그녀는 그에게 가까이 갔을 때, 그가 관광객임을 알아챕니다. 그는 지도를 보고 있고 매우 혼란스러워 보

입니다. Julie는 그가 길을 잃었을지도 모른다고 생각해서, 그를 도와주고 싶습니다. 이런 상황에서, Julie는 그에게 뭐라고 말하겠습니까?

Julie: <u>뭔가 찾는 것을 도와드릴까요?</u>

해설 혼란스러운 표정으로 지도를 보고 있는 관광객을 발견하고 도와주려는 상황이므로, 도움이 필요한지 묻는 말이 가장 적절하다.
① 공원에 어떻게 가나요?
② 실례합니다만, 이것이 당신의 지도인가요?
④ 미국에 가 본 적이 있나요?
⑤ 공항까지 몇 정거장인가요?

어휘 alone [əlóun] 홀로 notice [nóutis] 알아차리다 confused [kənfjúːzd] 혼란스러워하는

Dictation Test ⓞ9

pp. 134~141

01 1) order a special cake
    2) go with a double-layer cake
    3) make a heart-shaped cake

02 1) in a movie called 2) he sings well
    3) won an award

03 1) made a reservation 2) change it to four people
    3) switch to a bigger room
    4) reserve one more twin room

04 1) ends at noon 2) free at 1:00
    3) finish it in two hours

05 1) almost dark outside
    2) not answering her cell phone
    3) I'd better go outside

06 1) are not for sale 2) find it on the right
    3) fill out this form

07 1) buy some ingredients for dinner
    2) pass by Jane's house 3) pick up my book
    4) I'll call her

08 1) We are located 2) enjoy skiing or sledding
    3) visit our website for reservations

09 1) visited by many travelers 2) travel by airplane
    3) to greet visitors

10 1) need to apologize to her
    2) worse than I expected 3) rode my bicycle
    4) couldn't answer the phone

11 1) changing the wallpaper
    2) arrange the furniture 3) hang the lights up

12 1) calling about the part-time job
   2) bringing out food 3) has that kind of experience
   4) work on Wednesdays and Fridays

13 1) watch a movie 2) on Tuesdays and Wednesdays
   3) the day after tomorrow

14 1) When was the last time 2) make the video call
   3) check your room

15 1) election time is coming again
   2) ask for your support 3) to improve our city

16 1) comes to $4.80 2) made a mistake
   3) One dollar each 4) take five oranges

17 1) It's time for summer vacation
   2) take another trip 3) went to many places

18 1) broken alarm clock 2) what's the reason today
   3) fell asleep on the subway

19 1) tired of this color 2) feel a little cold
   3) seems fine to me 4) makes people feel relaxed

20 1) walking in the park 2) looks very confused
   3) wants to help him out

B

01 delay
02 crime
03 tax
04 ingredient
05 mix
06 annual
07 view
08 furniture
09 ceiling
10 housewarming
11 sometime
12 incorrectly
13 weight
14 duty
15 neighborhood
16 grocery
17 respect
18 platform
19 hopefully
20 limited
21 loser
22 compete
23 arrange
24 greet
25 unforgettable
26 steal
27 heel
28 trail
29 appointment
30 be tired of
31 agree on
32 wait in line
33 set the alarm
34 fill out
35 run for
36 slide down
37 take notes
38 get a full refund
39 at the latest
40 get one's hair done

Word Test 07~09

A

01 지갑
02 구조
03 배달, 배송
04 표현
05 홀로
06 진정하다
07 높이, 키
08 방해하다, 지장을 주다
09 방송
10 현재
11 의견
12 필요하다
13 선거
14 표
15 회의, 학회
16 개선하다, 개선되다
17 지시; 설명서, 사용법
18 방해하다
19 통지; 알아차리다
20 이용할 수 있는; 시간이 있는
21 약국
22 고마워하는
23 점수
24 선택(권)
25 해결하다
26 고려하다
27 반대의
28 줄이다, 감소시키다
29 포획하다
30 아마
31 받다
32 통로
33 만기일, 기한
34 뉴스 속보
35 유통 기한
36 ~ 옆을 지나가다
37 ~에 대한 준비를 하다
38 (회의 등을) 뒤로 미루다
39 자유롭게 ~하다
40 결정하다

실전모의고사 10 회

pp. 144~145

01 ②	02 ②	03 ②	04 ②	05 ③
06 ④	07 ②	08 ①	09 ⑤	10 ⑤
11 ②	12 ③	13 ⑤	14 ④	15 ②
16 ③	17 ①	18 ③	19 ①	20 ②

01 ②

남: 저희 유기견 보호소에 오신 것을 환영합니다. 무엇을 도와드릴까요?

여: 개를 입양하고 싶어요.

남: 선호하시는 바가 있습니까?

여: 네. 너무 크지 않았으면 좋겠어요. 집에 어린아이들이 있거든요.

남: 그럼 이 개는 어떠세요? 정말 순하고 아이들과 아주 잘 지낼 겁니다.

여: 너무 작은 것 같아요. 저희 뒷마당에서 놀 수 있는 중간 크기의 개를 원해요.

남: 그렇다면 이 개가 딱 맞네요. 너무 크지도 너무 작지도 않아요. 털이 길지만, 밖에서 기르면 그건 문제가 되지 않을 거예요.

여: 동의해요. 게다가 저는 그 긴 털이 좋아요.

[해설] 여자는 털이 긴 중간 크기의 개를 입양하려고 한다.

[어휘] shelter [ʃéltər] 보호소 adopt [ədápt] 입양하다 preference [préfrəns] 선호 gentle [dʒéntl] 순한 get along with ~와 잘 지내다 backyard [bækjɑ:rd] 뒷마당 perfect [pə́:rfikt] 완벽한; *딱 맞는

02 ②

여: 얘, 그거 뭐야?
남: 핼러윈 케이크야.
여: 마녀 모양의 케이크야? 정말 멋지다.
남: 응. 특히 이 모자 부분이 마음에 들어. 블루베리로 만들어졌어.
여: 너 그거 어디서 샀어?
남: Main 가에 개업한 새로운 케이크 가게에서 샀어. 개점 할인 때문에 겨우 20달러였어.
여: 정말? 나도 하나 사러 가야겠어.
남: 서둘러. 몇 개밖에 안 남았어.

[해설] 모양(마녀 모양), 재료(블루베리), 구입처(Main 가의 새로운 케이크 가게), 가격(20달러)에 관해서는 언급되었으나, 크기는 언급되지 않았다.

[어휘] especially [ispéʃəli] 특히 grand opening 개점

03 ②

[전화벨이 울린다.]
여: 여보세요?
남: 여보세요, Mary O'Donnell 씨와 통화할 수 있을까요?
여: 제가 Mary O'Donnell입니다. 누구시죠?
남: 저를 모르시겠지만, 제 이름은 Michael입니다. East Hill 고등학교에 다니는 학생입니다.
여: Michael, 반가워요. 무슨 도움이 필요한가요?
남: 음, 저는 정말 선생님의 열렬한 팬이에요. 선생님이 훌륭한 작가라고 생각해요.
여: 정말 고마워요.
남: 다음 주에 제가 선생님을 인터뷰할 수 있을지 궁금합니다.
여: 저를 인터뷰 한다고요? 무엇을 위한 거죠?
남: 제 영어 수업 때문에 쓰고 있는 보고서를 위한 거예요.
여: 그래요. 좋을 것 같네요.

[해설] 남자는 영어 수업 보고서를 위해 여자에게 인터뷰를 요청했다.

[어휘] wonder [wʌ́ndər] 궁금하다

04 ②

남: 안녕하세요. 무엇을 도와드릴까요?

여: 안녕하세요, 서울로 가는 기차표를 사고 싶은데요.
남: 네. 어떤 기차를 타실 건가요?
여: 잘 모르겠어요. 하지만 오늘 저녁 6시 40분까지 도착해야 해요.
남: 알겠습니다. 5시 30분에 출발하는 기차가 있네요.
여: 그건 서울에 몇 시에 도착하나요?
남: 한 시간 정도 걸리니까, 6시 30분에 도착할 거예요.
여: 오, 딱 맞네요. 표 한 장 주세요.
남: 알겠습니다. 15달러입니다.

[해설] 여자는 5시 30분에 출발해서 6시 30분에 도착하는 기차표를 구매했다.

[어휘] take [teik] (시간이) 걸리다

05 ③

남: 저한테 무슨 문제가 있나요?
여: 심한 감기에 걸린 것뿐이에요. 하루 집에 머물면서 쉬시면 됩니다.
남: 알겠습니다. 약을 좀 먹어야 하나요?
여: 네. 앞으로 3일 동안 매일 이 알약 세 알을 드세요.
남: 알겠습니다. 뭘 먹는 걸 추천하세요?
여: 매일 과일을 먹고 물을 많이 마셔야 합니다.
남: 알겠습니다. 그럴게요.
여: 그리고 말을 너무 많이 하지 않도록 하세요. 그러면 목이 더 좋아질 거예요.
남: 네. 감사합니다.

[해설] 여자는 감기에 걸린 남자에게 약을 주며 복용법을 설명해 주었으므로, 두 사람이 대화하는 장소로 가장 적절한 곳은 약국이다.

[어휘] rest [rest] 쉬다 pill [pil] 알약 throat [θrout] 목

06 ④

① 여: 무엇을 도와드릴까요?
　남: 선풍기를 사려고요.
② 여: 나 추워요. 난방기 좀 켜 줄래요?
　남: 그래요. 담요도 가져다줄게요.
③ 여: 무슨 계절을 가장 좋아해요?
　남: 나는 여름이 가장 좋아요.
④ 여: 내가 선풍기를 켜도 될까요?
　남: 네, 물론이죠.
⑤ 여: 우리 어느 것을 사야 할까요, 선풍기 아니면 에어컨?
　남: 난 선풍기가 더 좋을 것 같아요.

[해설] 방 안에 선풍기가 멈춰 있고 여자와 남자 둘 다 더워서 땀을 흘리고 있는 상황이다.

[어휘] fan [fæn] 선풍기 blanket [blǽŋkit] 담요 air conditioner 에어컨

07 ②

여: 왜 그렇게 우울한 얼굴을 하고 있니?

남: 다음 주에 기말시험이 있는데 공부하기 어려워.

여: 너에게 가장 어려운 과목이 뭐야? 내가 도와줄게.

남: 대부분의 과목은 괜찮은데, 수학이 문제야. 나 수학 좀 도와줄래?

여: 물론이지. 지금 너희 집에서 공부할래?

남: 너희 집에서는 어때? 내 방은 더럽거든.

여: 좋아. 가자.

[해설] 남자는 다음 주에 기말시험이 있는데 수학 공부가 어렵다며 여자에게 도와달라고 부탁했다.

[어휘] a long face 우울한 얼굴 final [fáinəl] 기말시험 subject [sʌ́bdʒikt] 과목

08 ①

남: 신사 숙녀, 소년 소녀 여러분… 센트럴 파크에 다시 Top Circus의 시간이 왔습니다! 서커스에 오셔서 여러분이 이제껏 본 것 중 가장 환상적인 광경에 마음을 사로잡혀 보세요! 올해는 Top Circus에서 이전에 한 번도 본 적 없는 특별한 출연자를 모셨습니다. 전설적인 곡예사 Peter를 만나 보세요! 가족과 친구들을 데리고 와서 열광할 준비를 하십시오. 단돈 20달러로 서커스에서 하루를 즐기십시오. 공연은 이번 주 토요일과 일요일, 단 이틀 동안만 진행될 것입니다. 이 기회를 놓치지 마세요. 곧 뵙기를 바랍니다!

[해설] 공연 장소(센트럴 파크), 특별 출연자(전설적인 곡예사 Peter), 입장료(20달러), 공연 요일(토요일과 일요일)에 관해서는 언급되었으나, 공연 시간은 언급되지 않았다.

[어휘] captivate [kǽptəvèit] ~의 마음을 사로잡다 sight [sait] 광경 guest [gest] 손님; *특별 출연자 legendary [léʤəndèri] 전설적인 acrobat [ǽkrəbæ̀t] 곡예사 thrill [θril] 열광시키다 opportunity [ɑ̀pərtjú:nəti] 기회

09 ⑤

여: 이 직업을 가진 사람들은 건물 설계의 과학과 예술을 실천합니다. 그들은 주택, 아파트, 사무실 건물과 같은 모든 종류의 것을 설계합니다. 그들은 수학과 제도를 잘해야 합니다. 그들은 또한 뛰어난 상상력을 가져야 합니다. 그들은 건물이 매력적으로 보일 뿐만 아니라 안전하고 편한지 확인합니다. 그들은 각각의 건물을 특정한 목적을 위해 설계합니다. 그들은 예술 작품을 만들 수 있지만, 그것은 또한 실용적이어야 합니다.

[해설] 주택, 아파트, 사무실 건물과 같은 모든 종류의 건물을 설계하는 직업은 건축가이다.

[어휘] practice [prǽktis] 연습하다; *실천하다, 실행하다 drawing [drɔ́:iŋ] 그림 소묘; *제도 imagination [imæ̀ʤinéiʃən] 상상력 attractive [ətrǽktiv] 매력적인 comfortable [kʌ́mfərtəbl]

편(안)한 specific [spəsífik] 특정한 purpose [pə́:rpəs] 목적 produce [prədjú:s] 생산하다, 만들어 내다 functional [fʌ́ŋkʃənəl] 실용적인

10 ⑤

① 남: 학교 축제가 언제 시작할지 궁금해.
  여: 2주 후에 시작할 거야.

② 남: 시간 좀 있니?
  여: 미안하지만, 아주 바빠.

③ 남: 체육관에 얼마나 자주 가니?
  여: 일주일에 두 번 이상.

④ 남: 그 책에 대해 말해 줄 수 있니?
  여: 한 예술가의 인생에 관한 책이야. 아주 재미있어.

⑤ 남: 수학 시험이 정말 쉬웠어, 그렇지 않았니?
  여: 그래, 걱정 마.

[해설] 시험이 쉬웠다며 동조를 구하는 말에, 걱정하지 말라는 응답은 어색하다.

[어휘] pretty [príti] 예쁜; *아주, 매우 gym [ʤim] 체육관 take it easy (명령형으로 쓰여) 진정해, 걱정 마

11 ②

남: 지금까지 놀이공원에서 즐거운 하루였어.

여: 정말 그랬어.

남: 나는 특히 바이킹이 좋았어. 우리 다음엔 뭘 탈까?

여: 우리는 아직 롤러코스터를 안 탔어.

남: 맞아. 줄을 서자.

여: 아, 줄이 꽤 길어 보여. 아무래도 먼저 먹어야겠어. 배가 고파지네.

남: 좋아. 간식을 좀 먹자.

여: 좋아. 그러고 나서 롤러코스터를 타면 되겠다.

[해설] 두 사람은 롤러코스터를 타려다가 대기 줄이 긴 것을 보고 먼저 간식을 먹기로 했다.

[어휘] amusement park 놀이공원 get in line 줄을 서다

12 ③

남: 실례합니다만, Joe's Place라는 식당을 아세요?

여: 네. 이 근방에서 유명하죠.

남: 그곳에 가는 길을 알려 주시겠어요?

여: 물론이죠. Queen 가까지 쭉 걸어가신 다음에 왼쪽으로 도세요. 그런 다음 한 블록을 더 걸어가세요. 왼편에 있어요.

남: Queen 가에서 좌회전해서 한 블록을 가라고요?

여: 아, 죄송해요. 제가 헷갈렸네요. Queen 가에서 두 블록을 가셔야 하고, 그러고 나면 왼쪽에 있어요. 쉽게 찾으실 거예요.

남: 고맙습니다.

해설 식당은 현재 위치에서 Queen 까지 직진한 뒤, 왼쪽으로 돌아 두 블록을 가면 왼편에 있다고 했다.

어휘 get confused 헷갈리다, 혼동되다

13 ⑤

남: 안녕하세요, 무엇을 도와드릴까요?
여: 요가 수업을 신청하고 싶어요.
남: 좋아요. 저희는 4시에 시작하는 수업이 있어요.
여: 제가 학교에서 3시 30분에 나가서, 시간에 맞출 수 있을지 잘 모르겠어요.
남: 5시에 시작하는 또 다른 수업이 있어요.
여: 더 늦은 수업들도 있나요?
남: 사실 오후 4시부터 7시까지 매시간 수업이 있어요.
여: 그럼 7시, 마지막 수업으로 할게요.
남: 좋아요. 이 양식을 작성해 주세요.

해설 여자는 마지막 요가 수업인 7시 수업에 등록하기로 했다.

어휘 sign up for ~을 신청하다 make it 시간 맞춰 가다 actually [ǽktʃuəli] 사실은

14 ④

여: James, 뭐 하고 있니?
남: 이집트에 관한 책을 읽고 있어.
여: 이집트에 관심이 있니?
남: 응. 나는 이집트의 역사와 문화를 좋아해서, 종종 이집트에 관한 정보를 찾아봐.
여: 그렇다면 너에게 좋은 소식이 있어.
남: 그게 뭔데?
여: 투탕카멘 왕 전시회가 전시 중이라고 들었어.
남: 국립 박물관에서? 나는 이미 지난 토요일에 그 전시회를 봤어.
여: 안타깝다. 네가 안 봤다면, 나랑 같이 가자고 했을 텐데.

해설 남자는 지난 토요일에 투탕카멘 왕 전시회를 봤다고 했다.

어휘 be interested in ~에 관심이 있다 look up (필요한 정보를) 찾아보다 on display 전시[진열]된

15 ②

남: 좋은 아침입니다. 이는 제주행 항공 123편에 탑승하시는 승객들께 드리는 공지입니다. 항공 123편은 현재 10번 탑승구에서 탑승하고 있습니다. 지금 특급 탑승권을 소지하신 승객과 어린 자녀를 동반한 승객을 안내하고 있습니다. 탑승권과 여권을 준비해 주십시오. 일반 승객은 사전 탑승이 완료될 때까지 자리에 남아 계시면 감사하겠습니다. 일반 탑승은 약 10분 후에 시작됩니다. 감사합니다.

해설 남자는 제주행 항공의 탑승 시작을 알리며, 사전 탑승 후 일반 탑승이 이어질 것이라고 말하고 있다.

어휘 announcement [ənáunsmənt] 공지 passenger [pǽsindʒər] 승객 board [bɔːrd] 탑승하다 gate [geit] 문; *게이트, 탑승구 invite [inváit] 초대하다; *안내하다 boarding pass 탑승권 appreciate [əpríːʃièit] 고마워하다 regular [régjələr] 일반적인 remain [riméin] 남아 있다

16 ③

여: 도와드릴까요?
남: 네, 지갑을 사고 싶어요.
여: 이건 어떠세요? 저희의 가장 인기 있는 지갑이에요.
남: 그게 얼마죠?
여: 90달러예요.
남: 좀 너무 비싸네요. 더 저렴한 것이 있나요?
여: 이 갈색 지갑은 어떠세요? 100달러였는데, 지금은 40% 할인 중이에요.
남: 좋아요, 그걸로 살게요.

해설 남자가 사려는 지갑은 원래 100달러였는데 40% 할인 중이라고 했으므로, 60달러를 지불해야 한다.

어휘 popular [pápjələr] 인기 있는 a bit 조금, 약간 off [ɔːf] 할인하여

17 ①

남: 그래서… 어떻게 생각해?
여: 솔직히 말하면, 여기는 내가 가 본 곳 중 최악의 식당이야.
남: 나도 동의해. 내 수프는 식었고, 스테이크는 너무 질겼어.
여: 그리고 웨이터 말이야! 너무 무례했어.
남: 알아. 나한테 물을 엎지르고 심지어 사과조차 하지 않았어.
여: 여기 오지 않았으면 좋았을 걸.
남: 우리 식사에 40달러를 지불해야 한다는 걸 믿을 수가 없어.
여: 항의해야 할까?
남: 응, 매니저를 찾자.

해설 두 사람은 식당의 음식과 서비스 문제에 대해 이야기한 후 여자가 이를 항의해야 할지 물었으므로, 항의할지 여부에 관한 응답이 가장 적절하다.
② 우리는 스테이크를 먹지 말았어야 했어.
③ 그래, 우리는 수프를 주문해야 할 것 같아.
④ 그래, 여기 또 와서 아이스크림을 사자.
⑤ 형편없는 식사에 우리가 그렇게 많은 돈을 쓴 게 유감이야.

어휘 to be honest 솔직히 말하면 worst [wəːrst] 최악의 (bad의 최상급) tough [tʌf] 질긴 rude [ruːd] 무례한 spill [spil] 엎지르다 apologize [əpálədʒàiz] 사과하다 [문제] ask for ~을 찾다

18 ③

남: 보세요, 엄마! 학교 신문이에요!
여: 진정해. 그게 뭐가 그렇게 신나니?
남: 1면을 보세요.
여: 알았다. 새 학교 식당에 관한 기사가 있구나.
남: 아니요! 그 밑을 보세요.
여: 그래. 얘, 네 사진이네.
남: 네, 그리고 제가 쓴 수필이에요. 그걸 1면에 실었어요!
여: 멋지다! 네가 너무 자랑스럽구나.

[해설] 남자는 학교 신문의 1면에 자신의 글이 실렸다고 했으므로, 축하나 칭찬의 뜻을 나타내는 응답이 가장 적절하다.
① 다음번에 다시 시도하면 돼.
② 두 페이지가 빠져 있구나.
④ 그들이 내 수필을 뽑았다니 믿을 수 없어!
⑤ 네가 왜 그것을 거기에 두었는지 이해할 수 없어.

[어휘] front page (신문의) 1면 article [áːrtikl] 글, 기사 essay [ései] 수필, 에세이 [문제] missing [mísiŋ] 없어진, 빠진 pick [pik] 뽑다, 고르다

19 ①

여: 와, 너 전자책 리더 샀구나! 멋져 보여!
남: 응. 소형으로 사서, 어디서든 읽을 수 있어.
여: 편리해 보인다.
남: 응, 그래. 나는 항상 이걸 가지고 다녀. 버스나 지하철을 타는 동안 전자책을 읽을 수 있고, 심지어 학교 공부에도 사용할 수 있어.
여: 다른 이점은 없니?
남: 음, 읽으면서 뭔가 이해되지 않을 때, 온라인으로 바로 찾아볼 수 있어. 아주 유용해. 너도 하나 사는 걸 추천해.
여: 실은, 나는 일반 책이 더 좋아.

[해설] 남자는 전자책 리더의 이점을 말하며 여자에게도 살 것을 추천했으므로, 추천을 받아들이거나 거절하는 응답이 가장 적절하다.
② 며칠간 네 책을 빌릴 수 있을까?
③ 너는 새 데스크탑 PC를 사야 할 것 같아.
④ 전자책을 읽는 이점이 뭐니?
⑤ 나에게 이 책을 추천해 줘서 고마워.

[어휘] compact [kəmpǽkt] 소형의 convenient [kənvíːnjənt] 편리한 benefit [bénəfit] 이점 immediately [imíːdiətli] 즉시 useful [júːsfəl] 유용한

20 ②

여: Jake는 고등학생입니다. 어느 일요일 오후에, 그는 기말고사 공부를 하러 집 근처에 있는 공공 도서관에 갔습니다. 도서관이 조용해서, 그는 잘 집중할 수 있었습니다. 그리고 나서 한 시간쯤 후에, 학생 두 명이 도서관에 들어와서 그의 옆 테이블에 앉았습니다. 그들은 큰 소리로 이야기를 나누기 시작했습니다. 그 모든 소음 때문에 Jake는 공부하기가 매우 힘들어졌습니다. Jake는 그들을 쳐다봤지만, 그들은 계속 이야기를 했습니다. 이런 상황에서, Jake는 그들에게 뭐라고 말하겠습니까?

Jake: 조용히 좀 해 줄래?

[해설] 도서관에서 두 학생의 대화 소리 때문에 공부에 집중할 수 없는 상황이므로, 조용히 해 줄 것을 요청하는 말이 가장 적절하다.
① 나 좀 도와줄래?
③ 시험 잘 봤니?
④ 내가 뭐 좀 사다 줄까?
⑤ 도서관에서는 음악을 들으면 안 돼.

[어휘] public [pʌ́blik] 공공의 concentrate [kánsəntrèit] 집중하다 chat [tʃæt] 이야기를 나누다 loudly [láudli] 큰 소리로, 시끄럽게 stare at ~을 응시하다[빤히 보다] [문제] pick up ~을 집다; *~을 사다 allow [əláu] 허락하다

Dictation Test ⑩   pp. 146~153

01 1) adopt a dog 2) want a medium-sized dog
    3) It has long fur

02 1) witch-shaped cake 2) is made of blueberries
    3) It was only $20

03 1) really big fan of yours 2) if I could interview you
    3) For a report

04 1) arrive by 6:40 2) leaves at 5:30
    3) takes about one hour

05 1) have a bad cold 2) Take three of these pills
    3) make your throat feel better

06 1) turn on the heater 2) do you like best
    3) Would you mind

07 1) such a long face 2) it's hard to study
    3) help me with math

08 1) have a special guest 2) for just $20
    3) for only two days

09 1) designing buildings
    2) have a good imagination
    3) safe and comfortable

10 1) begin in two weeks 2) How often do you go
    3) take it easy

11 1) going to ride next 2) get in line
    3) get some snacks

12 1) how to get there 2) walk one more block
    3) it's on your left

13 1) sign up for a yoga class
    2) there are classes every hour
    3) seven o'clock class
14 1) reading a book about Egypt
    2) look up information 3) saw that exhibition
15 1) announcement for passengers
    2) is now boarding
    3) boarding pass and passport ready
    4) Regular boarding will begin
16 1) most popular wallet 2) have a cheaper one
    3) it's 40% off
17 1) the worst restaurant 2) hadn't come here
    3) we should complain
18 1) so exciting about it 2) picture of you
    3) on the front page
19 1) can read anywhere 2) carry it with me
    3) look it up online immediately
20 1) study for his final exam
    2) started chatting loudly
    3) study with all the noise

실전모의고사 ⑪회

pp. 154~155

01 ⑤	02 ③	03 ①	04 ②	05 ④
06 ③	07 ⑤	08 ①	09 ①	10 ②
11 ⑤	12 ③	13 ④	14 ③	15 ③
16 ②	17 ⑤	18 ②	19 ④	20 ④

01 ⑤

여: 와. 이 벽은 아름답게 장식되었네.
남: 멋지지 않니? 우리 반 친구들 각자가 공룡을 하나씩 그렸어.
여: 너는 어느 것을 그렸어?
남: 내가 그린 것은 저 큰 나무 가까이에 있어.
여: 날개가 달린 공룡 말하는 거야?
남: 아니, 네 발로 걷고 있어.
여: 목이 긴 것과 뿔이 세 개인 것 중에 어느 거야?
남: 둘 다 아니야. 내 것은 등을 따라 뼈판이 있는 거야.
여: 오, 저거네. 멋지다!

해설 남자가 그린 것은 등을 따라 뼈판이 있는 공룡이라고 했다.

어휘 decorate [dékərèit] 장식하다 dinosaur [dáinəsɔ̀:r] 공룡
horn [hɔːrn] 뿔 bony [bóuni] 뼈의 plate [pleit] 접시; *(동물의 몸을 보호하는) 판 back [bæk] 등

02 ③

남: 크리스마스가 얼마 안 남았어. 우리 저녁 식사로 뭐 할까?
여: 집에서 바비큐 파티를 할 수 있지.
남: 응, 그렇지만 우리는 항상 그렇게 하잖아. 특별한 뭔가를 하는 게 어때?
여: 멋진 식당에서 파티를 하는 건 어때?
남: 그거 정말 좋겠다! 친구를 초대해서 함께 즐길 수 있어.
여: 하지만 인기 있는 식당은 지금쯤 완전히 예약이 차지 않았을까?
남: 그럴 수도 있어. 네가 몇몇 식당에 전화해서 알아봐 줄래?
여: 응, 지금 바로 할게.

해설 남자는 여자에게 크리스마스 파티를 하기 위해 몇몇 식당에 전화해서 예약 가능 여부를 알아봐 달라고 부탁했다.

어휘 just around the corner (어떤 시기가) 아주 가까워진
barbecue [báːrbikjùː] 바비큐 파티

03 ①

① 여: 한국 원화를 달러로 교환하고 싶어요.
   남: 네. 얼마나 교환하시겠습니까?
② 여: 계좌를 개설하고 싶어요.
   남: 이 양식을 작성하셔서 신분증과 함께 다시 제게 주세요.
③ 여: 저한테 조금 커 보여요. 이게 맞는 사이즈인가요?
   남: 네. 그렇게 맞도록 나온 거예요.
④ 여: 모두 합해서 8,000원이네요, 맞죠?
   남: 네, 맞습니다. 거스름돈 여기 있어요.
⑤ 여: 실례합니다. 은행에 어떻게 가죠?
   남: 저 길로 가세요. 길 끝에 있어요.

해설 여자가 환전하고 있는 상황이다.

어휘 exchange [ikstʃéindʒ] 교환하다, 환전하다 bank account (예금) 계좌 ID [àidíː] 신분증(= identification) in total 모두 합해서

04 ②

남: 시험 준비됐니? 안타깝게도 공부할 시간이 많지 않아.
여: 못 들었니? 월요일 시험이 모두 취소되었어.
남: 정말? 나는 몰랐어. 왜?
여: 우리 학교 50주년 기념일이잖아. 그래서 선생님께서 시험을 하루 연기하셨어.
남: 오늘이 목요일이네. 그건 우리가 공부할 날이 5일 있다는 뜻이지. 충분한 시간인 것 같아.

여: 나도 동의해. 나는 이번 토요일에 도서관에 갈 거야. 나랑 같이 공부
할래?

남: 그래. 좋아.

해설 오늘이 목요일이고 공부할 날이 5일 있다고 했으므로, 두 사람이 시
험을 치를 요일은 화요일이다.

어휘 cancel [kǽnsl] 취소하다 anniversary [æ̀nəvə́:rsəri] 기념일
postpone [pouspóun] 연기하다

05 ④

남: Baltimore 미술관에 오신 것을 환영합니다. 표를 보여 주시겠습니
까?

여: 여기 있습니다.

남: 고맙습니다. 입장하시기 전에, 휴대전화를 꺼 주십시오.

여: 아, 상기시켜 주셔서 감사합니다.

남: 또한 어떤 음식이나 음료도 가지고 들어가실 수 없습니다. 껌을 씹
는 것도 허용되지 않습니다.

여: 알겠습니다. 미술품 사진을 찍어도 되나요?

남: 죄송하지만, 안 됩니다.

여: 정말요? 실망스럽네요.

남: 로비에 기념품 가게가 있습니다. 그곳에서 미술품 사진들을 구입하
실 수 있습니다.

여: 알겠습니다. 그건 좋네요.

해설 미술관 실내에서 뛰지 말라는 내용은 언급되지 않았다.

어휘 chew [tʃuː] 씹다 disappointing [dìsəpɔ́intiŋ] 실망스러운
lobby [lábi] 로비 purchase [pə́:rtʃəs] 구입하다

06 ③

남: 실례합니다. 제 뒷사람에게 제 의자를 차지 말라고 해 주시겠어요?

여: 그렇게 하겠습니다. 불편을 드려 죄송합니다.

남: 고맙습니다. 그런데 베이징은 몇 시인가요?

여: 현지 시각은 아침 9시입니다.

남: 시차가 어떻게 되죠?

여: 저희보다 9시간 늦습니다.

남: 알겠습니다. 감사합니다. 물 한 잔도 부탁해도 될까요?

여: 네. 잠시만 기다려 주세요.

해설 남자는 여자에게 자신의 뒷사람이 의자 차는 것을 제지해 달라고 요
청하고 물을 가져다 달라고 했으므로, 두 사람이 대화하는 장소로 가
장 적절한 곳은 비행기이다.

어휘 inconvenience [ìnkənví:njəns] 불편 local [lóukəl] 현지의
time difference 시차

07 ⑤

① 남: 우리 내일 어디서 만날까?

여: 도서관 앞에서 만나자.

② 남: 경기는 어땠어?

여: 굉장히 흥미진진했어.

③ 남: 난 영어 말하기 대회가 걱정돼.

여: 걱정하지 마. 넌 잘할 거야.

④ 남: 네가 지난주에 내 역사 공책 빌려 간 거 기억하니?

여: 응. 내일 너에게 돌려줄게.

⑤ 남: 저 긴 머리의 키 큰 여자는 누구니?

여: 나는 그녀가 어제 어디에 있었는지 몰라.

해설 어떤 여자의 외모를 묘사하며 누구인지 묻는 질문에 그녀가 어제 어
디에 있었는지 모른다는 응답은 어색하다.

어휘 in front of ~의 앞에 borrow [bárou] 빌리다 give ~ back
~을 돌려주다

08 ①

남: 좋은 연기였어요, Banks 씨. 다음 장면을 촬영하기 전에 좀 쉬세
요.

여: 실은, 그렇게 좋았던 것 같지 않아요. 제가 더 감정적이었어야 해요.

남: 저는 괜찮아 보였어요. 감독님께 그 장면을 다시 촬영하자고 요청할
까요?

여: 네. 그런데 그러기 전에, 제가 준비할 시간을 좀 가질게요.

남: 연습하고 싶으세요? 제가 대본을 가져다드릴게요.

여: 아니, 괜찮아요. 저는 등장인물에 확실히 몰입할 몇 분이 필요할 뿐
이에요.

남: 알겠습니다.

해설 여자는 자신의 연기가 마음에 들지 않아 재촬영을 원하는데 그전에
준비할 시간이 필요하다고 했다.

어휘 shoot [ʃuːt] 촬영하다 scene [siːn] 장면 emotional [imóuʃənəl]
감정적인 director [diréktər] 감독 script [skript] 대본 get
into ~에 익숙해지다 character [kǽriktər] 등장인물

09 ①

남: 저는 기상 센터의 Jake Brown입니다. 자, 화창한 날들은 끝났으
니, 이번 주에는 야외에서 어떤 계획도 세우지 마십시오. 이 위성 사
진에서 볼 수 있듯이, 폭풍이 다가오고 있습니다. 오늘 밤 강한 비와
바람을 일으킬 것으로 예상됩니다. 이번 주 내내 비가 계속되겠으
니, 각별히 주의하시기 바랍니다. 내일 아침 기온은 15도까지 떨어
지겠습니다. 그러니 외출하실 때 따뜻한 재킷을 입으시고 우산을 챙
기시기 바랍니다. 감사합니다.

해설 폭풍의 영향으로 오늘 밤 강한 비와 바람이 예상되며 이번 주 내내
비가 계속될 것임을 예보하고 있다.

어휘 satellite [sǽtəlàit] 위성 storm [stɔːrm] 폭풍 approach
[əpróutʃ] 다가오다 temperature [témpərətʃər] 기온 drop
[draːp] 떨어지다

10 ②

여: 그래서 이 여행 패키지에 대해 어떻게 생각하세요?

남: 가격을 제외하고는 마음에 들어요. 약간 비싼 것 같아요.

여: 음, 그건 훌륭한 호텔과 활동을 제공하기 때문이에요. 하지만 덜 비싼 호텔을 포함한 더 저렴한 패키지를 추천해 드릴 수도 있어요.

남: 더 저렴한 건 얼마예요?

여: 가격은 700달러에서 1,000달러 사이예요. 선택하시는 날짜에 달려 있답니다.

남: 5월 10일에 출발하는 건 어떤가요?

여: 그때는 성수기가 아니라서, 여행 비용이 700달러입니다.

남: 아, 그건 가격이 적당한 것 같네요. 그걸로 할게요.

[해설] 남자가 여행 패키지에서 선택한 출발일이 성수기가 아니라서 비용이 700달러라고 했다.

[어휘] except for ~을 제외하고는 provide [prəváid] 제공하다 activity [æktívəti] 활동 range from A to B A에서 B까지의 범위에 걸쳐 있다 depend on ~에 달려 있다 high season 성수기 reasonable [ríːznəbl] 합리적인; *가격이 적당한

11 ⑤

남: 나 서점에 다녀왔어.

여: 찾고 있던 책은 샀어?

남: 아니, 품절이었어.

여: 아, 인터넷에서 그걸 찾아볼게. 책의 제목이 뭐였지?

남: 〈조선 왕조〉야.

여: 알았어. 내가 이 사이트에서 찾아볼게.

남: 그래. 거기에 있어?

여: 응, 찾았어. 그리고 10% 할인을 해 줘.

남: 내가 지금 그걸 주문하면 여기까지 오는 데 얼마나 걸릴까? 숙제 때문에 이번 주말에 필요하거든.

여: 이번 금요일이래.

남: 잘됐다. 지금 당장 한 권 주문해야겠어.

[해설] 남자는 서점에서 품절되어 사지 못한 책이 인터넷 사이트에 있다는 여자의 말에 당장 주문하겠다고 했다.

[어휘] dynasty [dáinəsti] 왕조 search [səːrtʃ] 찾다, 조사하다

12 ③

여: 슬라임을 손수 만들고 싶으신가요? 필요한 건 풀, 베이킹 소다, 물이 전부입니다. 매우 간단하며, 비용이 1달러에 불과합니다. 시작하기 전에, 슬라임이 피부에 직접 닿지 않도록 장갑을 착용하십시오. 그런 다음 그릇에 풀과 물을 붓고 젓는 것으로 시작하세요. 다음으로, 베이킹 소다를 첨가하고 그 혼합물을 다시 젓습니다. 잘 섞은 후, 손으로 문지르세요. 처음에는 끈적거리겠지만, 더 이상 끈적이지 않을 때까지 계속 문지르세요. 10분밖에 안 걸릴 것입니다. 그럼 끝입니다! 그것을 가지고 즐겁게 노세요!

[해설] 재료(풀, 베이킹 소다, 물), 비용(1달러), 제작 방법(풀, 물, 베이킹 소다를 넣고 잘 섞은 후 손으로 문지르기), 제작 소요 시간(10분)에 관해서는 언급되었으나, 구입처는 언급되지 않았다.

[어휘] homemade [hóumméid] 집에서 만든, 손수 만든 glue [gluː] 접착제, 풀 touch [tʌtʃ] 만지다; *닿다 skin [skin] 피부 directly [diréktli] 똑바로; *직접(적)으로 pour [pɔːr] 붓다 stir [stəːr] 젓다 mixture [míkstʃər] 혼합물 rub [rʌb] 문지르다 sticky [stíki] 끈적거리는 no longer 더 이상 ~ 아닌

13 ④

여: 얘, Jason. 나랑 파티에 갈래?

남: 어떤 파티?

여: 내 사촌 Kate가 한 살이 돼서, Lisa 숙모와 Danny 삼촌이 파티를 할 거야.

남: 멋지다. 두 분 집에서 열리니?

여: 아니. 4번가에 있는 해산물 음식점에서.

남: Golden Fish 말하는 거니?

여: 맞아. 파티는 4월 27일 오후 5시부터 8시까지야. 올 수 있니?

남: 4월 27일? 일요일이니? 난 일요일마다 축구 연습이 있거든.

여: 아니, 토요일이야.

남: 그렇다면, 가고 싶어.

[해설] 파티는 4월 27일 토요일에 열린다고 했다.

저녁 파티에 초대합니다!		
①	누가	Danny와 Lisa
②	왜	딸의 첫 번째 생일을 축하하려고
③	장소	4번가의 Golden Fish 음식점
④	날짜	4월 27일 일요일
⑤	시간	오후 5시부터 8시까지

[어휘] turn [təːrn] ~으로 바뀌다 seafood [síːfùːd] 해산물 [문제] celebrate [séləbrèit] 축하하다

14 ③

남: 이것은 네트와 공을 필요로 하는 인기 스포츠입니다. 공은 수박과 거의 같은 크기입니다. 두 팀이 경기를 합니다. 때로는 각 팀에 여섯 명씩 실내에서 경기를 합니다. 또 다른 경우에는, 각 팀에 두 명씩 해변에서 경기를 합니다. 한 선수가 네트 너머로 공을 서브합니다. 그리고 나서 두 팀은 공을 주고받으며 칩니다. 선수들은 손과 팔을 사용합니다. 공이 땅에 닿으면, 상대 팀이 점수를 얻습니다.

[해설] 두 팀이 손과 팔을 사용하여 공을 네트 너머로 보내는 스포츠는 배구이다.

[어휘] net [net] 그물, 네트 inside [insáid] 실내에서 serve [səːrv] 섬기다; *(공을) 서브하다 back and forth 앞뒤로, 왔다 갔다 ground [graund] 지면, 땅

15 ③

남: 어디 가니?
여: 프런트에 내려가는 길이야. 물어볼 게 있어서.
남: 알고 싶은 게 뭔데?
여: 호스텔에 세탁 서비스가 있는지 물어보려고.
남: 아, 이 층에 세탁기가 있어. 내가 전에 봤어.
여: 아, 잘됐다. 어디에 있니?
남: 모퉁이를 돌면 바로 세탁실이 있어. 하지만 동전을 좀 가져가야 할 거야.
여: 지금은 동전이 없는데.
남: 음, 프런트에 가면 분명 너한테 잔돈을 줄 수 있을 거야.
여: 그래, 맞아. 거기에 먼저 가야겠어.

[해설] 여자는 세탁기를 이용하려면 동전이 필요한데, 프런트에서 잔돈으로 바꿔 줄 것이라는 남자의 말에 먼저 프런트에 가겠다고 했다.

[어휘] front desk (호텔 등의) 프런트 hostel [háːstl] 호스텔(값싼 숙소) laundry [lɔ́ːndri] 세탁 washing machine 세탁기 coin [kɔin] 동전 change [tʃeindʒ] 변화; *잔돈

16 ②

남: 우리 뭐가 필요해?
여: 달걀과 시금치를 사야 해.
남: 여기 달걀이 있네. 이것들로 사자. 할인 중이야.
여: 꼭 유통 기한을 먼저 확인하도록 해. 가게들은 종종 오래된 품목들을 할인하거든.
남: 7월 14일까진 괜찮아.
여: 좋아. 사용할 수 있는 날이 5일이라는 뜻이네.
남: 아니. 실은 7일이야.
여: 아, 네 말이 맞아. 헷갈렸어. 그걸로 사자.

[해설] 유통 기한 7월 14일까지 7일 남았다고 했으므로, 오늘 날짜는 7월 7일이다.

[어휘] spinach [spínitʃ] 시금치 expiration date 유통 기한

17 ⑤

여: 얼마나 오래 아프셨나요?
남: 어젯밤 저녁 식사 때 아프기 시작했어요. 그러고 나서 오늘 아침에 양치할 때 또 아팠고요.
여: 입을 벌려 보시면 제가 한번 볼게요. [잠시 후] 음…
남: 심각한가요?
여: 유감스럽게도 좋은 소식은 아니네요. 충치가 세 개 있으세요.
남: 정말요? 제가 무엇을 해야 하죠?
여: 우선, 때워야 해요. 금이 가장 오래가기 때문에 금으로 때울 것을 권해 드려요.
남: 알겠어요, 지금 바로 해 주실 수 있나요?
여: <u>네. 준비하는 데 몇 분 걸립니다.</u>

[해설] 충치 치료를 바로 해 줄 수 있는지 물었으므로, 가능 여부를 말하는 응답이 가장 적절하다.
① 그리 오래 걸리지 않을 거예요.
② 더 천천히 하셔도 돼요.
③ 그걸 준비하셔야 해요.
④ 유감이지만, 비용이 너무 많이 들 것 같아요.

[어휘] pain [pein] 고통 cavity [kǽvəti] 구멍; *충치 (구멍) filling [fíliŋ] (치아의) 충전재 suggest [səɡʤést] 제안하다, 권하다 last [læst] 계속하다; *오래가다 [문제] take time 천천히 하다 cost [kɔːst] (값·비용이) ~ 들다

18 ②

남: 도와드릴까요?
여: 이 책들을 빌리고 싶어요.
남: 네. 몇 권이죠?
여: 여섯 권이에요. 괜찮나요?
남: 사실, 한 번에 다섯 권만 대출하실 수 있어요.
여: 아, 알았어요. 그러면 이 한 권은 돌려놓을게요.
남: 좋아요. 학생증 좀 보여 주시겠어요?
여: 여기요. 언제 반납해야 하나요?
남: <u>다음 주 금요일까지예요.</u>

[해설] 대출한 도서를 언제 반납해야 하는지 물었으므로, 구체적인 반납 기한을 말하는 응답이 가장 적절하다.
① 너무 어렵게 생각하지 마세요.
③ 합계가 8달러예요.
④ 물론이죠, 문제없어요.
⑤ 그것들을 더 일찍 반납하셨어야 했어요.

[어휘] check out (책 등을) 대출하다 at a time 한 번에 [문제] due 기한이 ~까지인

19 ④

남: 새 영화에 대해 말씀해 주시겠습니까?
여: 공상 과학 영화예요. 우주 전쟁에 관한 것이죠.
남: 흥미로운데요. 그것을 감독하는 데 있어 가장 어려운 부분은 무엇이었나요?
여: 전쟁 장면을 만드는 것이 어려웠어요. 많은 특수 효과를 사용했죠.
남: 그렇군요. 언제 극장에서 감독님의 영화를 볼 수 있나요?
여: 11월에 개봉될 예정입니다.
남: <u>얼마 안 남았네요.</u>

[해설] 여자가 감독한 영화를 언제 볼 수 있는지 묻는 남자의 질문에 여자가 개봉일을 답했으므로, 얼마 남지 않았다는 응답이 가장 적절하다.
① 그건 여태껏 최고의 영화였어요!
② 당신이 그 영화를 즐기길 바랍니다.
③ 가장 가까운 극장이 어딘가요?
⑤ 같이 영화 보러 갑시다.

어휘 science fiction film 공상 과학 영화 direct [dirékt] 감독하다 special effects 특수 효과 release [rilíːs] 놓아 주다; *(영화를) 개봉하다

20 ④

여: Carol은 몇 주 전에 새 카메라를 샀습니다. 그녀는 이번 주말에 휴가를 갈 예정이어서, 그에 필요한 모든 것을 싸고 있습니다. 짐을 싸는 동안, 그녀는 새 카메라가 사라진 것을 알아차립니다. 그녀는 모든 곳을 다 찾다가 남동생의 책상 서랍에서 그것을 발견합니다. 그는 사과를 하면서, 사용하고 나서 바로 돌려주려 했다고 말합니다. 그녀는 그가 그녀의 물건을 빌리기 전에 절대 물어보지 않기 때문에 화가 납니다. 이런 상황에서, Carol은 남동생에게 뭐라고 말하겠습니까?

Carol: 뭔가 빌리고 싶으면 나에게 먼저 물어봐 줘.

해설 남동생이 자신에게 물어보지 않고 물건을 빌려가서 화가 났으므로, 뭔가 빌리고 싶으면 먼저 물어보라는 말이 가장 적절하다.
① 나는 이미 새 카메라를 주문했어.
② 내 카메라를 찾아 줘서 고마워.
③ 왜 지금 나한테 이것에 대해 말하는 거니?
⑤ 나는 오늘 휴가에서 돌아오고 싶지 않았어.

어휘 pack [pæk] (짐 등을) 싸다, 챙기다 disappear [dìsəpíər] 사라지다 drawer [drɔːr] 서랍

Dictation Test ⑪   pp. 156~163

01 1) dinosaur with wings 2) walking on four legs
    3) the one with three horns

02 1) have a barbecue 2) doing something special
    3) be fully booked by now 4) call a few restaurants

03 1) exchange Korean won for dollars
    2) open a bank account 3) How can I get to

04 1) Monday classes are canceled
    2) postponed the exam 3) Today is Thursday
    4) have five days to study

05 1) turn off your cell phone 2) can't bring any food
    3) take pictures of the artwork
    4) can purchase pictures

06 1) stop kicking my chair 2) local time is nine
    3) bring me a cup of water

07 1) Where should we meet 2) What did you think of
    3) give it back

08 1) film the scene again 2) bring you the script
    3) need a few minutes

09 1) in the weather center 2) storm is approaching
    3) take an umbrella with you

10 1) except for the price
    2) range from $700 to $1,000 3) tour costs $700

11 1) back from the bookstore 2) search this site
    3) offer a 10% discount 4) order a copy

12 1) All you need is 2) it only costs $1
    3) pouring the glue and water
    4) take just 10 minutes

13 1) is turning a year old 2) at a seafood restaurant
    3) on April 27 4) have football practice

14 1) same size as a watermelon
    2) six people on each team 3) played on the beach
    4) use their hands and arms

15 1) have a washing machine 2) take some coins
    3) give you change

16 1) check their expiration date
    2) have five days to use 3) it's seven days

17 1) felt pain again 2) have three cavities
    3) suggest gold fillings 4) do that right now

18 1) borrow these books 2) put this one back
    3) need to return

19 1) about a war in space
    2) used lots of special effects 3) It'll be released

20 1) new camera has disappeared
    2) in her brother's desk drawer
    3) never asks before he borrows

실전모의고사 ⑫회   pp. 164~165

01 ⑤	02 ③	03 ④	04 ④	05 ⑤
06 ④	07 ④	08 ⑤	09 ⑤	10 ②
11 ⑤	12 ②	13 ④	14 ③	15 ④
16 ③	17 ⑤	18 ⑤	19 ③	20 ⑤

01 ⑤

남: 멋진 그림이다. 화가가 누구야?

여: 내가 직접 그렸어. 내가 바라는 집이야.

남: 이게 네가 바라는 집이라고? 나는 네가 아파트에 사는 것을 좋아한다고 생각했어.

여: 실은, 난 언젠가 나만의 2층 집을 짓고 싶어.

남: 이 그림에 있는 집처럼? 멋지다.

여: 응. 이 집의 가장 좋은 점은 앞에 있는 창이야. 나는 저 큰 창을 통해 햇빛이 들어오기를 원해.

남: 정말 멋지다. 누구라도 거기에 살면 행복할 것 같아.

[해설] 여자가 그린 집은 2층이고 앞쪽에 큰 창이 있다고 했다.

[어휘] apartment [əpáːrtmənt] 아파트 story [stɔ́ːri] 이야기; *(건물의) 층 front [frʌnt] 앞면 sunlight [sʌ́nlàit] 햇빛

02 ③

여: 안녕, Alex. 대학 생활은 어때?

남: 아주 좋아. 난 새 기숙사로 막 이사했어.

여: 정말? 이전 기숙사는 뭐가 문제였니?

남: 세 사람과 방을 같이 써야 했어. 하지만 이제 룸메이트가 한 명뿐이야.

여: 잘됐다.

남: 새 기숙사의 방이 더 크기도 하고.

여: 그래? 음식은 어때?

남: 캠퍼스에서 가장 맛있는 구내식당이 있어.

여: 와, 운이 좋다.

남: 그리고 무엇보다 좋은 건, 이전 기숙사보다 강의실에 더 가까워.

[해설] 룸메이트 수(한 명), 방 크기(더 큼), 구내식당 음식(캠퍼스에서 가장 맛있음), 강의실과의 거리(이전보다 더 가까움)는 언급되었으나, 비용은 언급되지 않았다.

[어휘] college [kálidʒ] 대학(교) dormitory [dɔ́ːrmitɔ̀ːri] 기숙사 share [ʃɛər] 공유하다, 함께 쓰다

03 ④

[휴대전화가 울린다.]

여: 여보세요?

남: 안녕, Alison.

여: 안녕, Walter. 무슨 일이니?

남: 컴퓨터로 숙제를 하고 있었는데, 갑자기 작동을 멈췄어. 뭐가 잘못됐는지 모르겠어. 나 좀 도와줄 수 있니?

여: 아, 나 이제 막 연극 동아리 모임에 가려고 했거든. 급한 거니?

남: 응, 오늘 이 숙제를 끝내야 하거든. 그래서 네가 들러서 이걸 고쳐 줄 수 있을까 궁금했어.

여: 알겠어. 모임 끝나고 바로 네가 있는 곳으로 갈게.

남: 좋아. 그럼 이따 봐.

[해설] 남자는 숙제를 하던 중에 컴퓨터가 고장이 나서 여자에게 고쳐 달라고 부탁했다.

[어휘] be about to-v 이제 막 ~하려고 하다 urgent [ə́ːrdʒənt] 긴급한 come over 들르다 fix [fiks] 수리하다

04 ④

[전화벨이 울린다.]

여: 안녕하세요, Dr. Baker's 의원입니다.

남: 안녕하세요. 제게 문제가 있어서요. 요즘 눈이 많이 충혈되고 건조해요.

여: 전에 여기 오신 적이 있나요?

남: 네. 전에 Baker 선생님께 치료받은 적이 있어요.

여: 알겠습니다. 언제 진료받길 원하세요?

남: 글쎄요, 선생님께 처방전만 받으면 돼요.

여: 네, 하지만 그래도 병원에 오셔야 해요.

남: 알겠습니다. 내일 아침 11시에 가도 될까요?

여: 죄송하지만, 11시에는 다른 환자를 진료 보세요. 11시 30분에 오실 수 있나요?

남: 네, 좋아요.

[해설] 병원에 오전 11시 30분에 올 수 있는지 묻는 여자의 말에 남자는 좋다고 대답했다.

[어휘] treat [triːt] 대하다; *치료하다 prescription [priskrípʃən] 처방전

05 ⑤

여: 안녕하세요. 뭘 도와드릴까요?

남: 네. 제가 오늘 아침에 35번 버스를 탔는데, 쇼핑백을 잊고 두고 왔어요.

여: 그러시군요. 어디에서 버스를 타셨나요?

남: 시청에서 타서 세 정거장 뒤에 내렸어요.

여: 몇 시에 내렸는지 기억하세요?

남: 정확하진 않지만, 오전 8시경이었던 것 같아요.

여: 알겠습니다. 쇼핑백을 설명해 주시겠어요?

남: 작은 검은색 쇼핑백이에요. 그리고 안에 새 영어 사전이 있어요.

여: 알겠습니다. 여기 있는지 확인하는 동안 잠시만 기다려 주세요.

[해설] 남자는 버스에 두고 내린 쇼핑백을 찾고 있으며 여자가 쇼핑백이 있는지 확인해 보겠다고 했으므로, 두 사람이 대화하는 장소로 가장 적절한 곳은 분실물 보관소이다.

[어휘] forget [fərgét] 잊다; *잊고 두고 오다[가다] get on (차·버스 등에) 타다 get off (차·버스 등에서) 내리다 exactly [igzǽktli] 정확하게 describe [diskráib] 묘사하다, 설명하다 dictionary [díkʃəneri] 사전

06 ④

① 남: 난 이 재킷을 온라인 쇼핑몰에서 주문했어.

여: 너한테 약간 커 보여.
② 남: 도와드릴까요?
　　여: 아니요, 그냥 둘러보는 중이에요.
③ 남: 이 재킷을 반품하고 싶어요.
　　여: 아, 뭐가 잘못됐나요?
④ 남: 조금 작아요. 이거 더 큰 치수로 있나요?
　　여: 네. 갖다 드릴게요.
⑤ 남: 난 이 색이 맘에 들어.
　　여: 그래, 그리고 너한테 잘 어울려.

해설 옷 가게에서 남자가 입어 보고 있는 재킷이 작아 보이는 상황이다.

어휘 a bit 조금, 약간　look around 둘러보다　suit [suːt] 어울리다

07 ④

여: Eddie, 어디 가니? 너 학교 밴드 보러 안 가니? 공연장은 저쪽이야.
남: 갈 건데, 과학 실험실에 먼저 들러야 해.
여: 왜? 20분 후면 공연이 시작할 거야.
남: 그래, 하지만 Dana가 방금 전화했는데, 도움이 필요하대. 몇 분이면 될 거야.
여: 알았어, 하지만 서둘러. 자리가 남아 있지 않을 거야.
남: Dana랑 나를 위해 두 자리 맡아 줄래? 우리 빨리 갈게.
여: 할 수 있을진 모르지만, 해 볼게!

해설 남자는 학교 밴드 공연을 보러 가기 전에 과학 실험실에 들러야 해서, 여자에게 Dana와 자신의 자리를 맡아 달라고 부탁했다.

어휘 drop by ~에 들르다　lab [læb] 실험실 (= laboratory)

08 ⑤

여: 이번 겨울 휴가에 할 무언가를 찾고 있나요? 아름다운 멕시코를 방문하는 건 어떨까요? Global Travel에는 여러분을 위한 완벽한 패키지여행이 있습니다. 해변에서 2분밖에 걸리지 않는 고급 호텔에서 4박 5일을 보낼 수 있습니다. 이 패키지는 전문 가이드와 함께 지역 시장과 마을을 방문하는 여행을 포함하고 있습니다. 하지만 항공권은 개별적으로 구입해야 합니다. 가격이나 더 많은 정보를 원하시면, Global Travel로 오늘 바로 전화 주세요.

해설 방문 국가(멕시코), 여행 기간(4박 5일), 호텔 위치(해변에서 2분 거리), 불포함 항목(항공권)에 관해서는 언급되었지만, 여행사 위치는 언급되지 않았다.

어휘 include [inklúːd] 포함하다　village [vílidʒ] 마을　professional [prəféʃənəl] 직업적인, 프로의

09 ⑤

남: 이 직업을 가진 사람들은 우주를 연구하고 탐험합니다. 그들은 우주로 여행하기 전에, 많은 정신적, 육체적 준비를 거쳐야 합니다. 예를 들어, 그들은 중력 없이 사는 것에 익숙해져야 합니다. 임무에 앞서, 그들은 또한 많은 조사를 해야 합니다. 그들은 많은 책을 읽고, 실험을 하고, 특별훈련 강습을 받습니다. 우주에 도착하면, 그들은 소행성과 다른 행성들 같은 것을 연구하는 많은 특별 과제들을 수행합니다.

해설 우주를 여행하며 우주를 연구하고 탐험하는 일을 하는 직업은 우주비행사이다.

어휘 explore [iksplɔ́ːr] 탐험하다　go through ~을 거치다　mental [méntal] 정신적인　physical [fízikəl] 육체적인　get used to v-ing ~하는 데 익숙해지다　gravity [grǽvəti] 중력　mission [míʃən] 임무　experiment [ikspérimənt] 실험　carry out ~을 수행하다　task [tæsk] 일, 과제　asteroid [ǽstərɔ̀id] 소행성　planet [plǽnit] 행성

10 ②

① 여: 넌 더 자주 운동해야 해.
　　남: 알아, 하지만 너무 바빴어.
② 여: 이 책은 몇 챕터로 되어 있나요?
　　남: 그것은 우리의 베스트셀러 책 중 하나예요.
③ 여: 우리 내일 소풍을 가는 게 어때?
　　남: 그건 좋은 생각이 아닌 것 같아. 종일 비가 올 예정이야.
④ 여: 아이스크림 더 먹을래?
　　남: 응, 하지만 조금만.
⑤ 여: 공원에 가는 게 어때?
　　남: 아니, 난 집에서 컴퓨터 게임을 하는 편이 낫겠어.

해설 책이 몇 챕터로 되어 있냐는 질문에 베스트셀러 책 중 하나라는 응답은 어색하다.

어휘 exercise [éksərsàiz] 운동하다　best-selling [béstséliŋ] 베스트셀러의　would rather ~하는 편이 낫다

11 ⑤

남: Julia, 잘 지내니?
여: 응, 하지만 크리스마스가 얼마 안 남았잖아! 할 일이 정말 많아.
남: 어떤 일? 너희 아파트에 놓을 크리스마스트리를 살 거니?
여: 응, 물론이지. 그걸 장식할 장식품과 전등도 좀 사야 해. 하지만 우선, 사야 할 모든 선물 목록을 작성하려고.
남: 그래. 맛있는 진저브레드맨 쿠키도 좀 구우면 좋겠다!
여: 그럴 거야, 하지만 오늘은 아니야.

해설 여자는 우선 사야 할 선물 목록을 작성할 거라고 했다.

어휘 ornament [ɔ́ːrnəmənt] 장식품　make a list 목록을 작성하다

12 ②

남: 우리 개집을 어디에 놓을까?

여: 정원 뒤쪽 문 옆 어때? 낯선 사람이 오면 우리 개가 짖을 수 있잖아.

남: 거긴 너무 멀어. 난 테라스에서 개를 보고 싶어.

여: 음, 그럼 테라스 바로 앞은 어때?

남: 그건 너무 가까워. 우리 개가 시끄러울 수도 있어.

여: 그럼 왼쪽, 나무 근처는 어때?

남: 완벽해. 너무 멀지 않고, 우리 개가 나무 그늘 아래에서 쉴 수 있어.

여: 좋아! 거기 놓자.

[해설] 두 사람은 테라스에서 너무 멀거나 가깝지 않으면서 나무가 근처에 있는 곳에 개집을 놓기로 했다.

[어휘] bark [ba:rk] 짖다 stranger [stréindʒər] 낯선 사람 terrace [térəs] 테라스 shade [ʃeid] 그늘

13 ④

여: 몇 시간 후면 네 경주가 시작하는구나, 그렇지? 기분이 어때?

남: 불안해요.

여: 너는 분명 잘할 거야.

남: 감사해요. 엄마가 경주로에서 저를 응원해 주시는 걸 볼 수 있다면 도움이 될 것 같아요.

여: 안타깝지만 네 경주에는 갈 수 없어. 오후 2시에 중요한 회의가 있거든. 경기장에 제시간에 도착할 수 없을 거야.

남: 회의가 얼마나 걸리나요?

여: 오래 걸리지는 않을 거야. 30분 안에 끝날 것으로 예상하고 있어.

남: 그러면 오실 수 있어요! 첫 경주는 1시에 시작하지만, 제가 뛰는 1,000미터 경주는 두 시간 후에 시작해요.

[해설] 첫 경주는 1시에 시작하고, 남자가 뛰는 1,000미터 경주는 두 시간 뒤에 시작한다고 했다.

[어휘] race [reis] 경주 cheer for ~을 응원하다 track [træk] 길; *경주로, 트랙 field [fi:ld] 들판; *경기장 in time 제시간에

14 ③

남: 안녕, Jane. 지난 며칠 동안 어디에 있었어?

여: 친구 Kate가 미국에서 온 이후로 바빴어.

남: 그 애와 뭘 했니?

여: 음, 쇼핑, 관광, 한국 음식 먹기 같은 많은 것들을 했어.

남: 네 친구는 여기를 마음에 들어 하니?

여: 물론이지. 어제 우리는 궁궐에서 한복을 입었는데, 그 애는 그걸 무척 좋아했어.

남: 좋다! 분명 그 애에게 좋은 경험이었을 거야.

[해설] 여자는 미국에서 온 친구와 어제 궁궐에서 한복을 입었다고 했다.

[어휘] sightseeing [sáitsì:iŋ] 관광 palace [pǽlis] 궁전, 궁궐 experience [ikspíriəns] 경험

15 ④

여: 안녕하세요, 학생 여러분! 사서 Emily Brown입니다. 지난 3일 동안 도서관 자원봉사자를 모집했지만, 아직 더 많은 도움이 필요합니다. 저는 여러분이 돕는 일에 자원하길 격려하고 싶습니다. 학교 도서관에서, 자원봉사자들은 반납된 책을 책꽂이에 다시 놓고, 학생들이 책을 찾는 것을 돕고, 청소를 하는 것으로 돕습니다. 자원봉사를 하고 싶다면, 도서관에 오셔서 자원봉사 양식을 작성해 주세요. 학급과 이름을 남겨주세요. 저는 이것이 여러분에게 좋은 경험이 될 것이라고 보증합니다. 감사합니다.

[해설] 여자는 도서관 자원봉사자를 모집했지만 아직 더 많은 도움이 필요하다며, 학생들에게 자원해 달라고 말하고 있다.

[어휘] librarian [laibrɛ́:əriən] 사서 recruit [rikrú:t] 모집하다 volunteer [vὰləntíər] 자원봉사자; 자원하다, 자원봉사로 하다 encourage [inkə́:riʤ] 격려하다 shelf [ʃelf] 책꽂이 promise [prámis] 약속하다; *단언하다, 보증하다

16 ③

여: 정말 귀여운 기념품이에요! 저 인형들은 얼마예요?

남: 이 인형들이요? 하나에 5달러예요, 손님.

여: 아니요, 저 큰 것들 말고요. 저쪽에 있는 작은 것들이요.

남: 아, 알겠어요. 저것들은 하나에 2달러예요.

여: 그렇군요. 저기에 있는 티셔츠들도 맘에 드네요.

남: 그것들은 아주 인기가 많아요. 흰색, 파란색, 그리고 초록색, 세 가지 색으로 나오고요.

여: 얼마인가요?

남: 하나에 10달러예요.

여: 좋아요. 작은 인형 두 개랑 티셔츠 한 장 살게요.

남: 알겠습니다. 가방에 넣어 드릴게요.

[해설] 작은 인형 두 개($2x2)와 티셔츠 한 장($10)을 사기로 했으므로, 총 14달러를 지불해야 한다.

[어휘] souvenir [sù:vəníər] 기념품 certainly [sə́:rtnli] 확실히; *(대답으로) 그럼요, 물론이죠

17 ⑤

[휴대전화가 울린다.]

남: 안녕, Sue. 무슨 일이야?

여: 안녕, Shawn. 별일 없어. 그냥 안부 전화했어. 우리 한동안 서로 못 봤다. 곧 만나야지.

남: 맞아.

여: 너 다음 주 금요일에 동창회에 갈 거니?

남: 아니, 못 갈 것 같아.

여: 왜 못 가?

남: 다음 주 금요일에 캠핑 여행을 가거든.

해설 여자는 남자에게 왜 동창회에 못 가는지 물었으므로, 그 이유에 관한 응답이 가장 적절하다.
① 너를 빨리 만나고 싶어.
② 너희 부모님께 내 안부 전해 줘.
③ 내가 모임에 참석할 수 있다면 좋겠어.
④ 네가 올 수 있는지 궁금해.

어휘 in a while 한동안 class reunion 동창회 [문제] say hello to ~에게 안부를 전하다

18 ⑤

남: 에어컨이 고장 났어?
여: 응, 수리 기사가 좋아 보이지 않는다고 했어.
남: 수리할 수 있대?
여: 수리할 수는 있지만, 너무 낡았대. 심지어 수리 후에도, 문제가 있을 수 있대.
남: 그럼 우리 어떻게 할까?
여: 새것을 사는 게 좋을 것 같아.
남: 하지만 새 에어컨을 사려면 비용이 더 들 거야.
여: 맞아. 수리 기사가 수리 비용은 많이 들지 않을 거라고 했어.
남: 음, 이번에는 수리하는 게 어때?
여: 알았어. 하지만 또 고장 나면 새것을 사자.

해설 남자는 새 에어컨을 사려면 비용이 더 들기 때문에 이번에는 수리하자고 제안했으므로, 제안을 받아들이거나 거절하는 응답이 가장 적절하다.
① 좋아. 내가 수리할 도구를 가져올게.
② 우리는 에어컨이 필요하지 않아.
③ 지금 전자 제품 매장으로 가자.
④ 좋아. 비용이 얼마가 들든 상관없어.

어휘 repairman [ripérmæn] 수리 기사 [문제] tool [tuːl] 도구 electronics store 전자 제품 매장

19 ③

남: 소희야, 내가 너한테 빌린 게임 기억해?
여: 응, 기억해. 재미있었니?
남: 솔직하게 말하면, 해 보지도 못했어.
여: 정말? 왜 못 했어?
남: 그걸 소파 위에 올려놨는데, 우리 개가 물어뜯었어.
여: 농담이겠지. 작동이 안 돼?
남: 응, 안 돼. 정말 미안해.
여: 괜찮아. 그 일은 잊으렴.

해설 남자는 여자에게 빌린 게임을 개가 물어뜯어 망가뜨린 것에 대해 사과하고 있으므로, 괜찮다는 응답이 가장 적절하다.
① 네가 재미있었다니 기뻐.
② 난 컴퓨터로 그걸 쓰면 돼.
④ 너의 개가 곧 회복하길 바라.

⑤ 기일까지 그것을 꼭 반납하렴.

어휘 chew [tʃuː] 씹다; *물어뜯다 [문제] due date 기일, 만기일

20 ⑤

남: Anderson은 배우입니다. 그는 뮤지컬 오디션을 많이 봤지만, 한 배역도 따내지 못했습니다. 그는 왜 자신이 계속 떨어지는지 모르겠습니다. 그는 분명히 어떤 이유가 있을 것이라고 생각합니다. 그의 친구 중 한 명인 Jen은 많은 뮤지컬에서 연기를 했습니다. 그는 그녀에게 조언을 구합니다. 그는 그녀 앞에서 노래를 부르고, Jen은 문제점이 보입니다. Anderson은 너무 긴장해서, 자연스럽게 호흡하지 못합니다. 이런 상황에서, Jen은 Anderson에게 뭐라고 말하겠습니까?
Jen: 너는 더 편안해지고 자연스럽게 호흡해야 해.

해설 Jen은 Anderson이 노래를 부를 때 너무 긴장해서 호흡이 자연스럽지 못한 문제점을 발견했으므로, 이에 대해 조언하는 말이 가장 적절하다.
① 네가 배역을 맡았다는 말을 들으니 기뻐!
② 내 다음 연극에서 너한테 역할을 하나 줄게.
③ 너는 다음 오디션에서 배역을 따낼 거야.
④ 넌 항상 관객을 똑바로 봐야 해.

어휘 part [paːrt] 일부; *배역 fail [feil] 실패하다; *(시험 등에) 떨어지다 perform [pərfɔ́ːrm] 공연하다, 연기하다 breathe [briːð] 호흡하다 naturally 자연스럽게 [문제] role [roul] 역할 audience [ɔ́ːdiəns] 관객

Dictation Test ⑫

pp. 166~173

01 1) living in an apartment
    2) build my own two-story house
    3) through that big window

02 1) only have one roommate
    2) the best cafeteria on campus
    3) closer to my classes

03 1) suddenly stopped working
    2) come over and fix it 3) right after the meeting

04 1) I've been treated 2) give me a prescription
    3) come to the office 4) seeing another patient

05 1) forgot my shopping bag 2) what time you got off
    3) describe the shopping bag 4) check to see

06 1) looks a bit large 2) just looking around
3) I'll go get one 4) suits you well

07 1) drop by the science lab
2) take just a few minutes 3) save a couple of seats

08 1) Why not visit 2) two minutes from the beach
3) must be purchased separately

09 1) study and explore space 2) living without gravity
3) take special training courses

10 1) How many chapters 2) have a picnic
3) Would you like 4) I'd rather play computer games

11 1) buy a Christmas tree 2) ornaments and lights
3) make a list

12 1) next to the gate 2) right in front of the terrace
3) near the tree

13 1) cheering for me 2) get to the field in time
3) finish in half an hour 4) two hours later

14 1) Where have you been
2) shopping, sightseeing, and eating
3) wore hanbok at the palace

15 1) recruiting library volunteers
2) volunteer to help out 3) fill out a volunteer form

16 1) $2 each 2) come in three different colors
3) $10 each 4) two of the small dolls

17 1) called to say hello 2) going to the class reunion
3) I'm afraid I can't

18 1) there will be problems 2) buy a new one
3) will cost more 4) fixing it this time

19 1) I borrowed from you 2) my dog chewed it
3) Isn't it working

20 1) never gets a part 2) asks her for advice
3) gets too nervous

15 구입하다
16 현지의
17 소형의
18 다가오다
19 직업적인, 프로의
20 실망스러운
21 사서
22 서랍
23 개별적으로
24 탐험하다
25 공유하다, 함께 쓰다
26 연기하다
27 장식품
28 정신적인
29 붓다
30 엎지르다
31 (예금) 계좌
32 세탁기
33 솔직히 말하면
34 천천히 하다
35 ~을 응시하다[빤히 보다]
36 ~을 제외하고는
37 ~을 거치다
38 이제 막 ~하려고 하다
39 ~을 수행하다
40 ~하는 데 익숙해지다

B

01 sticky
02 physical
03 satellite
04 imagination
05 prescription
06 subject
07 passenger
08 bark
09 emotional
10 glue
11 loudly
12 dictionary
13 legendary
14 naturally
15 treat
16 role
17 celebrate
18 shade
19 dynasty
20 sightseeing
21 disappear
22 breathe
23 useful
24 board
25 gravity
26 decorate
27 rude
28 script
29 concentrate
30 storm
31 dormitory
32 coin
33 adopt
34 perform
35 convenient
36 depend on
37 be interested in
38 cheer for
39 get along with
40 make a list

Word Test 10~12 pp. 174~175

A

01 목적
02 격려하다
03 떨어지다
04 똑바로; 직접(적)으로
05 보호소
06 세탁
07 소행성
08 긴급한
09 젓다
10 ~의 마음을 사로잡다
11 문지르다
12 활동
13 촬영하다
14 관객

실전모의고사 ⑬ 회

pp. 176~177

01 ①	02 ④	03 ②	04 ②	05 ③
06 ⑤	07 ⑤	08 ①	09 ②	10 ⑤
11 ②	12 ④	13 ②	14 ③	15 ⑤
16 ③	17 ⑤	18 ①	19 ⑤	20 ⑤

01 ①

여: 안녕하세요, 무엇을 도와드릴까요?

남: 안녕하세요, 제가 쓸 시계를 찾고 있어요.

여: 그러시군요. 요즘 이 모델이 인기 있어요. 동그란 것과 네모난 것 두 종류가 있어요.

남: 저는 네모난 것이 좋아 보여요.

여: 시곗줄은 금속과 가죽 중 어느 걸 선호하세요?

남: 저는 보통은 금속을 선호하는데, 가죽이 이 디자인과 더 잘 어울리 네요.

여: 그럼 줄무늬 가죽이 있는 이건 어떠세요?

남: 음… 저는 눈에 띄는 것을 좋아하지 않아서, 무늬 없는 이걸로 살게 요.

여: 좋은 선택이에요. 손님과 잘 어울릴 거예요.

해설 남자는 무늬 없는 가죽 줄이 있는 네모난 시계를 사기로 했다.

어휘 look for ~을 찾다 type [taip] 종류 watch strap 시곗줄 metal [métəl] 금속 leather [léðər] 가죽 stand out 눈에 띄 다 pattern [pǽtərn] 무늬 look good on ~와 잘 어울리다

02 ④

남: 주하야, 네 영어 실력이 크게 향상됐어.

여: 그렇게 말해 줘서 고마워.

남: 너는 영어 실력을 향상시키기 위해 뭘 하니?

여: 매일 영어 신문을 읽어.

남: 와. 영어로 된 TV 프로그램도 보니?

여: 응. 미국 드라마 보는 것을 정말 좋아해. 처음에는 이해하기 어려웠 지만, 지금은 자막 없이 이해할 수 있어.

남: 멋진데! 그 밖에는 뭘 하니?

여: 영어 일기를 쓰고 외국 친구들과 온라인에서 영어로 채팅을 해.

남: 좋은 방법들이네.

해설 여자의 영어 실력 향상을 위한 방안으로 영어 캠프 참가하기는 언급 되지 않았다.

어휘 improve [imprúːv] 향상되다, 향상시키다 subtitle [sʌ́btàitl] (영화 등의) 자막 keep a diary 일기를 쓰다 chat online 온라 인에서 채팅하다 foreign [fɔ́ːrin] 외국의

03 ②

[휴대전화가 울린다.]

여: 여보세요, John. 무슨 일이야?

남: 얘! 너 어디야? 밖이니?

여: 응, 언니랑 영화 보러 가는 중이야.

남: 그렇구나. 아무튼, 내가 수학 숙제 적는 걸 또 잊어버려서 전화했어. 뭐였지?

여: 사실, 나 적었는데, 지금 정확히 기억이 안 나. Max한테 전화해 보 는 게 어때?

남: 알았어, 그렇게.

여: 더 도움이 못 돼서 미안해.

남: 괜찮아! 재미있게 보내!

해설 남자는 수학 숙제 적는 걸 잊어버렸다며 무엇인지 물어보았다.

어휘 write down ~을 적다 exactly [igzǽktli] 정확하게

04 ②

여: 토요일에 클래식 음악 콘서트가 있을 거야.

남: 알아, 하지만 나는 못 갈 것 같아. 콘서트는 저녁 7시에 시작하는데, 내가 8시에 공항으로 친구를 데리러 가야 하거든.

여: 낮 공연에 가는 건 어때?

남: 낮 공연이 있어?

여: 응, 2시에. 그게 내가 가는 거야.

남: 잘됐다! 우리 같이 갈 수 있겠어.

여: 좋아. 그러면 지하철역에서 1시 30분에 만나자.

남: 좋아.

해설 남자는 저녁에 공항으로 친구를 데리러 가야 해서, 여자와 함께 낮 2시 공연을 보기로 했다.

어휘 performance [pərfɔ́ːrməns] 공연

05 ③

[휴대전화가 울린다.]

남: 여보세요?

여: 여보세요, Brown 씨와 통화할 수 있을까요?

남: 접니다. 누구시죠?

여: 안녕하세요, 길에서 선생님의 지갑을 주웠다는 걸 말씀드리려고 전 화했어요.

남: 아, 잘됐네요! 제 전화번호는 어떻게 아셨어요?

여: 선생님의 지갑 속 명함에 있었어요.

남: 아, 어떻게 감사를 드려야 할지 모르겠군요.

여: 지갑을 어떻게 받으시겠어요?

남: 어디에 계시는지 알려 주시면, 제가 가서 뵐게요. 직접 감사 인사를 드리고 싶습니다.

해설 남자는 자신이 잃어버린 지갑을 길에서 줍고 전화를 해 준 여자에게

고마울(grateful) 것이다.
① 걱정스러운 ② 희망에 찬 ④ 궁금한 ⑤ 실망스러운

(어휘) wallet [wάlit] 지갑 business card 명함 in person 직접

06 ⑤

① 여: 질문 있으세요?
   남: 네. 어느 것이 최신 모델인지 말씀해 주시겠어요?
② 여: 안녕하세요. 오늘 무엇을 도와드릴까요?
   남: 제 손가락 좀 봐 주시겠어요? 부러진 것 같아요.
③ 여: 도움이 필요하신가요?
   남: 이것을 반품하고 환불받고 싶어요.
④ 여: 서비스 센터에 어떻게 가나요?
   남: 한 블록 직진하셔서 모퉁이를 돌면 바로 있어요.
⑤ 여: 오늘 무엇을 도와드릴까요?
   남: 전화기 화면이 깨졌어요. 수리받고 싶어요.

(해설) 남자가 화면이 깨진 휴대전화를 들고 서비스 센터에 방문한 상황이다.

(어휘) latest [léitist] 최신의 broken [bróukən] 부러진, 깨진 return [ritə́ːrn] 반환하다 get a refund 환불받다 screen [skriːn] 화면

07 ⑤

여: 저녁 식사가 정말 근사했어요. 하지만 시간이 늦어지고 있으니, 아무래도 이제 집에 가야겠어요.
남: 여기 어떻게 왔어요?
여: 지하철을 탔는데, 두 번 갈아타야 했어요. 꽤 오래 걸렸어요.
남: 아, 그런데 당신 집까지 곧장 가는 버스가 있어요.
여: 정말이에요? 그게 어떤 버스예요?
남: 142번 버스요. 버스 정류장은 Standard 은행 근처예요.
여: 그게 어디인지 모르겠어요. 버스 정류장까지 데려다주시겠어요?
남: 물론이죠. 어두워지고 있어요. 갑시다.

(해설) 여자는 버스 정류장의 위치를 몰라서 남자에게 데려다달라고 부탁했다.

(어휘) head [hed] (특정 방향으로) 가다 transfer [trǽnsfər] 옮기다; *갈아타다

08 ①

여: 여러분, 좋은 아침입니다. 모두 와 주셔서 감사합니다. 저는 새로 오신 Jim Stewart 선생님을 소개하기 위해 이 회의를 소집했습니다. 이분은 영문학 학위를 가지고 대학을 졸업했습니다. 이분은 지난 10년간 여러 학교와 지역 문화 센터에서 영어 교사로 일했습니다. 이분은 우리 학교에서 영어를 가르칠 것입니다. 또한 우리 1학년 학급들을 지도하실 것입니다. 저는 이분이 우리 직원으로 함께 하게

되어 기쁩니다. 이분을 환영해 주세요!

(해설) 대학 전공(영문학), 경력(10년간 영어 교사로 일함), 담당 과목(영어), 담당 학년(1학년)에 관해서는 언급되었으나, 나이는 언급되지 않았다.

(어휘) call a meeting 회의를 소집하다 introduce [ìntrədjúːs] 소개하다 graduate from ~을 졸업하다 university [jùːnəvə́ːrsəti] 대학 degree [digríː] 학위 literature [lítərətʃər] 문학 community center 지역 문화 센터 decade [dékeid] 10년 lead [liːd] 이끌다, 지도하다 staff [stæf] 직원

09 ②

남: 이곳은 동물들을 기르고 대중에게 보여 주는 장소입니다. 이곳은 사람들에게 다른 곳에서는 아마 볼 수 없는 동물들을 관찰할 기회를 제공합니다. 이곳에서는, 동물들을 집안에 기릅니다. 우리와 울타리가 동물들이 탈출하지 못하게 합니다. 울타리는 또한 사람들이 동물들에게 너무 가까이 다가가지 못하게 합니다. 이곳의 동물들은 전문가들이 돌봅니다. 전문가들은 동물들의 집을 자연 서식지처럼 보이게 만들려고 노력합니다. 수의사는 동물들의 건강을 자주 확인하고 그들이 다치거나 아프면 즉시 치료합니다.

(해설) 우리에서 동물들을 기르고 대중에게 보여 주는 장소는 동물원이다.

(어휘) keep [kiːp] (동물을) 기르다 (keep-kept-kept) public [pʌ́blik] 대중의; *대중 observe [əbzə́ːrv] 관찰하다 cage [keidʒ] 우리 fence [fens] 울타리 keep ~ from v-ing ~가 …하지 못하게 하다 escape [iskéip] 탈출하다 care for ~을 돌보다[보살피다] expert [ékspərt] 전문가 natural habitat 자연 서식지 vet [vet] 수의사

10 ⑤

① 남: 음악 소리가 너무 커.
   여: 아, 미안해. 음량을 줄일게.
② 남: 어떻게 지냈어?
   여: 꽤 바빴어.
③ 남: 이건 내가 본 최악의 영화야.
   여: 왜 그렇게 말해?
④ 남: 어떤 음식점으로 결정했어?
   여: 은행 옆에 있는 새로 문을 연 프랑스 음식점으로.
⑤ 남: 도서관은 학교에서 얼마나 머니?
   여: 도서관은 매일 열어.

(해설) 도서관과 학교의 거리를 묻는 말에 도서관이 매일 문을 연다는 응답은 어색하다.

(어휘) turn down (소리를) 줄이다 volume [vάljuːm] 음량 decide on ~로 결정하다 far [faːr] 먼

11 ②

남: Sandy! 네가 새집을 샀다고 들었어. 언제 이사해?
여: 사실 이미 했어. 지난주에 이사했어.
남: 정말? 그래서 새집은 어때?
여: 방이 세 개야. 남편과 내가 쓸 방 하나, 그리고 우리 아이들이 쓸 방 두 개가 있어. 이제 우리 아이들도 자기 방이 있어.
남: 네 아들이 분명 그 점을 무척 좋아하겠네.
여: 맞아. 그리고 부엌이 커. 아주 마음에 들어!
남: 잘됐네. 정원이 있니?
여: 응! 그렇게 크진 않지만, 예뻐. 오늘 오후에 정원을 청소하고 꽃을 좀 심으려고 계획 중이야.
남: 그거 좋은 생각이야.

[해설] 여자는 오후에 정원을 청소하고 꽃을 심을 계획이라고 했다.

[어휘] own [oun] 자신의 clean up ~을 청소하다 plant [plænt] 심다

12 ④

[전화벨이 울린다.]
남: 안녕하세요, Holiday 호텔입니다.
여: 안녕하세요, 다음 주말에 2인용 침대 객실을 예약하려고요. 그러니까 8월 19일에서 21일까지요.
남: 알겠습니다. 성함을 말씀해 주시겠습니까?
여: Gillian Thompson입니다.
남: 산 전망을 원하세요, 아니면 바다 전망을 원하세요?
여: 음, 어느 쪽이든 괜찮을 것 같아요.
남: 알겠습니다. 확인해 볼게요. 하룻밤에 300달러로 이용 가능한 방이 하나 있습니다. 바다 전망인 방이에요.
여: 좋아요.
남: 네. 2인실로 2박 예약하셨습니다.
여: 정말 감사합니다.

[해설] 남자는 바다 전망의 객실로 예약을 해 주었다.

호텔 예약	
① 객실 타입	2인실
② 날짜	8월 19일 - 21일
③ 이름	Gillian Thompson
④ 전망	산 전망
⑤ 총액	600달러

[어휘] book [buk] 책; *예약하다 view [vju:] 전망 ocean [óuʃən] 바다 either [í:ðər] 어느 쪽도 available [əvéiləbl] 이용 가능한 reserve [rizə́:rv] 예약하다

13 ②

[전화벨이 울린다.]
여: 안녕하세요. ABC 치과입니다.
남: 안녕하세요, 저는 Harry Kane입니다. 예약하고 싶은데요.

여: 네. 내일 아침 9시는 어떠세요?
남: 약간 위급 상황인데, 오늘 방문하는 게 가능한가요?
여: 무슨 일인가요?
남: 축구를 하다가 이가 부러졌어요.
여: 그럼 오늘 오후 3시는 어떠세요?
남: 좀 더 빠를 수는 없나요? 상당히 아프거든요.
여: 오후 1시 괜찮으세요? 그게 제가 할 수 있는 최선입니다.
남: 좋아요. 정말 감사합니다.
여: 천만에요. 그때 뵐게요.

[해설] 남자는 이가 부러진 위급 상황이라, 여자가 예약이 가능한 가장 빠른 시간이라고 말한 오늘 오후 1시로 예약했다.

[어휘] make an appointment 예약하다 emergency [imə́:rdʒənsi] 비상, 위급 possible [pásəbl] 가능한 break [breik] (뼈를) 부러뜨리다 (break-broke-broken) hurt [hə:rt] 다치다; *아프다 quite a bit 상당히

14 ③

여: 얘, 뉴욕 여행은 어땠어?
남: 너무 재미있었어. 나는 빨리 또 여행하고 싶어.
여: 얼마나 오래 여행했어?
남: 2주 동안.
여: 어느 곳이 제일 좋았어?
남: 유명한 관광지 모두 좋았지만, 그냥 거리를 걷는 것도 좋았어.
여: 나도 뉴욕에서 걷고 싶어.
남: 그중 가장 좋았던 날은 어제였어. 내 친구 Mark가 나를 위해 깜짝 파티를 열어 줬거든.
여: 와, 정말 좋았겠다.

[해설] 남자는 어제 친구가 깜짝파티를 열어 줘서 좋았다고 했다.

[어휘] travel [trǽvəl] 여행하다 tourist spot 관광지 throw a party 파티를 열다

15 ⑤

여: 안녕하세요, 학생 여러분! 저는 교장입니다. 제가 전에 알려드린 대로, 오늘부터 학교 식당 공사가 시작됩니다. 공사는 다음 주 금요일까지 약 2주간 계속될 것으로 예상됩니다. 이 기간 동안, 학교 식당 근처 구역을 피해 주십시오. 공사 구역을 꼭 지나야만 한다면, 조심하십시오. 공사 소음에 대해 미리 사과드립니다. 여러분의 인내와 양해를 부탁드립니다. 고맙습니다.

[해설] 교장 선생님은 학생들에게 오늘부터 약 2주간 학교 식당 공사를 한다고 알리고 있다.

[어휘] principal [prínsəpəl] 교장 announce [ənáuns] 알리다 construction [kənstrʌ́kʃən] 공사 expect [ikspékt] 예상하다, 기대하다 continue [kəntínju:] 계속되다 period [píəriəd] 기간 avoid [əvɔ́id] 피하다 area [ɛ́əriə] 지역; *(특정 공간 내의)

구역 in advance 미리 patience [péiʃəns] 인내, 인내심

16 ③

남: 이 만화책들을 빌리고 싶어요.
여: 네. 한번 볼게요. [잠시 후] 책 다섯 권을 고르셨네요.
남: 네. 얼마예요?
여: 한 권에 2달러예요.
남: 그러면 모두 합해서 10달러인가요?
여: 아, 잠시만요. 그중 두 권은 신작이네요. 신작은 한 권에 3달러예요.
남: 그렇군요. 여기 15달러요.
여: 여기 거스름돈이요. 일주일 이내에 반납하는 것 잊지 마세요.

[해설] 신작 2권($3×2=$6)과 일반 책 3권($2×3=$6)을 빌렸으므로 총 12달러인데 15달러를 냈으므로, 남자가 받을 거스름돈은 3달러이다.

[어휘] rent [rent] 빌리다, 대여하다 release [rilíːs] (음반·책의) 발매된 작품 change [tʃeindʒ] 거스름돈 within [wiðín] ~ 이내에

17 ⑤

남: 너 시내에 새로 생긴 극장에 가 본 적 있니?
여: 아니 아직, 하지만 거기서 멋진 뮤지컬이 공연 중이라고 들었어.
남: 맞아, 〈Wicked〉야! 초연 배우들이 공연하고 있어. 너 그 뮤지컬 관람에 관심 있니?
여: 응. 하지만 표를 살 여유가 없어.
남: 있지? 나 그 뮤지컬 표가 두 장 있어.
여: 정말? 어디서 났어?
남: 우리 누나가 나한테 줬어. 나랑 같이 갈래?
여: 아주 멋져. 몇 시에 시작해?

[해설] 남자는 여자가 관심 있어 하는 뮤지컬에 함께 갈지 물었으므로, 제안을 받아들이는 응답이 가장 적절하다.
① 나는 거기가 어딘지 몰라.
② 너에게 부탁이 하나 있어.
③ 표가 너무 비싸.
④ 미안하지만, 나는 그 뮤지컬을 좋아하지 않아.

[어휘] original [ərídʒənəl] 원래의, 최초의 cast [kæst] 출연 배우 can't afford to-v ~할 여유가 없다 [문제] wonderful [wʌ́ndərfəl] 아주 멋진

18 ①

여: 실례합니다. 질문 하나 해도 될까요?
남: 물론이죠. 뭔가요?
여: 제가 여기 처음인데, 버스를 잘못 탔나 걱정이 돼서요.
남: 어디로 가시는데요?
여: Plaza 호텔에 가려고요.

남: 아, 맞는 버스를 타셨어요. 그 바로 앞에 설 거예요.
여: 오, 다행이에요. 얼마나 더 가야 하나요?
남: 여기서 다섯 정거장이에요.

[해설] 여자는 버스 안에서 자신의 목적지까지 얼마나 더 가야 하는지 물었으므로, 그곳까지 남은 정거장을 알려 주는 말하는 응답이 가장 적절하다.
② 다른 버스를 타셔야 해요.
③ 이 버스를 어디서 타셨나요?
④ 제가 당신이라면 거기에 가지 않을 겁니다.
⑤ 모퉁이에서 좌회전하셔야 해요.

[어휘] pass by ~ 옆을 지나가다 right [rait] 정면으로; *바로 farther [fáːrðər] 더 멀리 (far의 비교급) [문제] get on ~에 타다

19 ⑤

여: 넌 지난주에 있었던 체육 대회 어땠어?
남: 난 정말 좋았어.
여: 흥미진진했어, 그렇지 않니?
남: 그랬어. 모든 경기 보는 게 즐거웠는데, 특히 농구 경기가 재미있었어.
여: 나도. 그 경기는 정말 흥미진진했어. 그리고 Ted가 MVP였잖아! 그 애가 그렇게 잘하는 선수인지 몰랐어.
남: 나도 몰랐어. 나는 키가 큰 사람들만 농구를 잘한다고 생각했거든.
여: 그러니까 말이야! 그 애는 키가 크지 않아도, 정말 잘했어!
남: 완전히! 겉모습만 보고 판단하면 안 돼.

[해설] 키가 큰 사람들만 농구를 잘한다고 생각했다는 남자의 말에 여자가 체육 대회의 농구 경기에서 Ted는 키가 크지 않지만 정말 잘했다고 했으므로, 겉모습만 보고 판단하면 안 된다는 응답이 가장 적절하다.
① 물론이야. 연습이 완벽을 만들지.
② 농구 선수들은 대개 키가 아주 커.
③ 그는 MVP에 적합한 사람이 아닌 것 같아.
④ 키가 큰 선수들은 농구에서 이점이 많아.

[어휘] athletics day 체육 대회 event [ivént] 사건; *경기 especially [ispéʃəli] 특히 be good at ~을 잘하다 even though 비록 ~일지라도 [문제] judge [dʒʌdʒ] 판단하다

20 ⑤

남: Douglas는 아파서 수업에 빠졌습니다. 그의 반 친구 Eva는 그가 괜찮은지 알아보려고 전화를 합니다. 그녀는 그가 수업에서 놓친 것을 알려 줍니다. 그리고 나서 선생님께서 다음 주 시험에 나올 몇 가지 중요한 주제에 대해 말씀하셨다고 그에게 말합니다. Douglas는 이 주제들에 대해 더 알고 싶습니다. 이런 상황에서, Douglas는 Eva에게 뭐라고 말하겠습니까?
Douglas: 네가 필기한 것을 나한테 빌려주겠니?

[해설] Douglas는 아파서 빠진 수업에서 시험과 관련된 중요한 주제들을 배웠다는 Eva의 말을 듣고 그것에 대해 더 알고 싶다고 했으므로,

필기한 것을 빌려줄 수 있는지 묻는 말이 가장 적절하다.
① 좀 나아졌니?
② 너 시험 잘 봤니?
③ 너희 공부 모임에 함께 하고 싶어.
④ 다음 주에 너에게 이메일을 보낼게.

[어휘] miss [mis] 빠지다, 놓치다 ill [il] 아픈 classmate [klǽsmèit] 학급 친구 find out ~을 알아내다

Dictation Test ⓭

pp. 178~185

01 1) square one seems good 2) leather looks better
3) without a pattern

02 1) improve your English
2) love watching American dramas
3) keep an English diary

03 1) going to the movies
2) write down the math homework
3) Why don't you call 4) not being more helpful

04 1) pick up my friend
2) There's an afternoon performance
3) let's meet at 1:30

05 1) found your wallet 2) get my number
3) get your wallet 4) thank you in person

06 1) get a refund 2) just around the corner
3) have it fixed

07 1) head home now 2) had to transfer twice
3) goes straight to your home
4) walk me to the bus stop

08 1) introduce our new teacher
2) degree in English literature
3) lead our first-year classes

09 1) animals are kept
2) keep the animals from escaping
3) cared for by experts 4) checks the health

10 1) turn down the volume 2) have you decided on
3) How far is the library

11 1) moved last week 2) must be excited about that
3) clean up the garden

12 1) book a room 2) with a mountain view
3) one available for $300
4) double room for two nights

13 1) kind of an emergency
2) three o'clock this afternoon 3) a little sooner
4) Is 1:00 p.m. okay

14 1) How long did you travel 2) famous tourist spots
3) threw a surprise party

15 1) school cafeteria construction starts
2) continue for about two weeks
3) avoid the area around the cafeteria

16 1) rent these comic books 2) $10 in total
3) are new releases 4) return them within a week

17 1) interested in seeing 2) can't afford to buy
3) come with me

18 1) on the wrong bus 2) stop right in front of it
3) How much farther

19 1) enjoyed watching all the events
2) such a great player
3) Even though he's not tall

20 1) if he is all right 2) missed in class
3) know more about these topics

실전모의고사 ⓮ 회

pp. 186~187

01 ①	02 ④	03 ②	04 ③	05 ⑤
06 ⑤	07 ⑤	08 ⑤	09 ①	10 ②
11 ⑤	12 ③	13 ②	14 ②	15 ⑤
16 ⑤	17 ④	18 ⑤	19 ⑤	20 ③

01 ①

남: Sue, 가방에 있는 거 뭐야? 귀엽다.
여: 아, 내가 어제 가죽 작업장에 갔거든. 거기에서 이 열쇠고리를 만들었어.
남: 네가 직접 만든 거야? 멋지다.
여: 응. 만들기 정말 힘들었어.
남: 정말? 시간이 많이 걸려?
여: 응, 얼굴을 만드는 데 모든 시간을 써서, 몸은 만들 수도 없었어.
남: 얼굴만 있어도 괜찮아 보여. 디자인은 직접 선택했어?
여: 응. 처음에는 토끼 만드는 걸 생각했지만, 고양이로 결정했어.
남: 좋은 선택이야.

[해설] 여자는 가죽 작업장에서 고양이 디자인 열쇠고리 만들기를 선택했는데, 얼굴을 만드느라 시간이 오래 걸려서 몸은 만들지 못했다고 했다.

어휘 workshop [wə́ːrkʃɑ̀p] 작업장 key chain 열쇠고리

02 ④

여: 안녕하세요, 여러분. 오늘의 특별 초대 손님 Samuel Anderson
입니다.

남: 안녕하세요. 초대해 주셔서 감사합니다.

여: 주방장이 되는 건 어떤 것인지 저희에게 말씀해 주시겠어요?

남: 네. 주방장으로서, 저는 단지 손님들을 위한 음식을 만들지만은 않
습니다. 매일 아침, 요리에 쓸 모든 재료를 확인합니다. 다른 요리사
들을 관리하기도 합니다.

여: 와, 정말 많은 일을 담당하고 계시는군요! 그 밖에 하시는 다른 일들
도 있나요?

남: 주방은 항상 깨끗해야 해서, 매일 구석구석까지 점검하죠.

여: 그러니까 총책임자에 더 가깝네요.

해설 주방장인 남자의 역할로 손님 응대는 언급되지 않았다.

어휘 chef [ʃef] 요리사, 주방장 ingredient [ingríːdiənt] 재료 dish
[diʃ] 접시; *요리 manage [mǽnidʒ] 관리하다 cook [kuk] 요
리하다; *요리사 be in charge of ~을 담당하다 more like 오히
려 ~에 가까운[닮은] general [dʒénərəl] 전반적인, 총체적인

03 ②

여: 우리 가족은 이번 여름에 여행하려고 계획 중이야.

남: 아, 정말? 어디 갈 거니?

여: 아직 결정 못 했어. 몇몇 장소를 염두에 두고 있는데, 결정하기가 쉽
지 않아.

남: 음, 내가 너라면, 제주도를 가겠어. 유네스코에서 선정한 세계 문화
유산이잖아.

여: 아, 그곳은 우리의 선택지들 중 하나야. 거기 가 봤니?

남: 응, 지난여름에 거기 갔었는데, 환상적이었지. 경치가 아름답고, 할
것도 먹을 것도 많았어.

해설 남자는 지난여름 제주도에 갔을 때 좋았던 점을 이야기하며, 여자에
게 가족 여행지로 제주도를 추천하고 있다.

어휘 take a trip 여행하다 have ~ in mind ~을 염두에 두다, ~을 생
각하다 World Heritage Site 세계 문화유산 scenery [síːnəri]
경치

04 ③

남: 무엇을 도와드릴까요?

여: 용인행 버스표를 사고 싶어요. 어떤 버스가 가장 빨리 출발하나요?

남: 음… 오후 2시에 출발하는 버스가 있는데, 일반 버스예요. 용인행
급행 버스도 있어요.

여: 두 버스의 차이점은 무엇인가요?

남: 용인까지 가는 데, 일반 버스로는 1시간, 급행 버스로는 단 30분 걸

려요.

여: 급행 버스는 몇 시에 출발해요?

남: 3시에 출발해요.

여: 그건 너무 늦네요. 전 그냥 일반 버스 탈게요.

남: 알겠습니다.

해설 여자는 오후 2시에 출발하는 용인행 일반 버스를 타기로 했다.

어휘 leave [liːv] 떠나다, 출발하다 regular [régjələr] 일반적인, 보
통의 express [iksprés] 급행의 difference [dífərəns] 차이

05 ⑤

여: Tom, 기분은 어때요?

남: 괜찮아요. 그냥 좀 피곤해요.

여: 금방 나아질 거예요. 수술은 아주 잘됐어요.

남: 다행이네요. 저 언제 집에 갈 수 있나요? 배드민턴을 치고 싶어요.

여: 글쎄요, 일주일쯤 병원에 머물면서 치료를 받아야 할 것 같아요.

남: 아, 제가 한 달 후에 시합이 있어요. 연습을 해야 해요. 침대에 누워
서 시간을 낭비할 수는 없어요.

여: 이해는 하지만, 당분간은 배드민턴 치는 것을 허락할 수가 없네요.
수술은 성공적이었을지라도, 경과를 주의 깊게 살펴볼 필요가 있어
요.

해설 남자는 시합 준비를 위해 빨리 퇴원하고 싶었으나, 병원에서 치료를
더 받아야 하며 당분간 배드민턴을 치면 안 된다는 말을 들었으므로
실망스러울(disappointed) 것이다.
① 외로운 ② 신이 난 ③ 무서운 ④ 놀란

어휘 operation [ɑ̀pəréiʃən] 수술 receive [risíːv] 받다 treatment
[tríːtmənt] 치료 or so ~쯤 competition [kɑ̀mpətíʃn] 대회,
시합 progress [prágres] 전진; *경과 successful [səksésfəl]
성공적인

06 ⑤

① 여: 이 커피는 매우 뜨거우니, 조심하세요.
남: 고맙습니다. 조심할게요.

② 여: 제 커피 얼마나 기다려야 하죠?
남: 3분 후에 준비될 거예요.

③ 여: 이건 제가 주문했던 게 아니에요.
남: 죄송합니다. 제 실수였던 것 같아요.

④ 여: 내가 커피 마시기에 좋은 곳을 발견했어.
남: 그래? 가 보자.

⑤ 여: 정말 죄송해요. 괜찮으세요?
남: 괜찮아요. 걱정하지 마세요, 세탁하면 없어질 거예요.

해설 여자가 남자의 옷에 커피를 쏟은 상황이다.

어휘 order [ɔ́ːrdər] 주문하다 mistake [mistéik] 실수 wash [wɑʃ]
씻다; *세탁

07 ⑤

[휴대전화가 울린다.]

남: 여보세요, 엄마.

여: 오, Andy. 미안하지만, 직장에서 조금 늦을 것 같아. 긴급회의가 있어.

남: 얼마나 늦어요?

여: 회의가 언제 끝나는지에 달렸어. 늦어도 8시까지는 끝날 거야.

남: 8시요? 그건 정말 늦네요.

여: 미안해. 너 혼자 저녁을 먹어야 할 것 같아.

남: 괜찮아요, 엄마.

여: 냉장고에 피자집 전화번호가 있어. 무언가를 주문하고 배달시키렴.

남: 알았어요, 엄마.

[해설] 여자는 직장에서 늦을 것 같아 남자에게 피자집에 전화해서 음식을 배달시키라고 부탁했다.

[어휘] urgent [ə́:rdʒənt] 긴급한 depend on ~에 달려 있다 be over 끝나다 at the latest (아무리) 늦어도 alone [əlóun] 혼자 fridge [fridʒ] 냉장고 deliver [dilívər] 배달하다

08 ⑤

남: 타지마할에 오신 것을 환영합니다. 타지마할은 인도에서 가장 유명한 건물입니다. 그것은 Agra시에 위치해 있습니다. 그것은 17세기에 Shah Jahan 황제에 의해 건설되었습니다. 그는 사랑하는 아내가 죽은 후 그녀를 위한 거대한 무덤으로 그 건축물을 지었습니다. 타지마할은 세계에서 가장 아름다운 건물 중 하나입니다. 그것은 커다란 흰색 돔으로 알려져 있습니다. 이제 저를 따라 타지마할의 아름다움을 즐기십시오.

[해설] 위치(인도의 Agra시), 건축 시기(17세기), 건축 목적(아내를 위한 무덤), 색(흰색)에 관해서는 언급되었으나, 자재는 언급되지 않았다.

[어휘] century [séntʃəri] 100년, 세기 emperor [émpərər] 황제 structure [strʌ́ktʃər] 구조; *구조물, 건축물 tomb [tu:m] 무덤 beloved [bilʌ́vid] 사랑하는 be known for ~로 알려져 있다 dome [doum] 돔, 반구형 지붕

09 ①

여: 이것은 매우 유용한 제품입니다. 이것은 다양한 모양과 크기로 나오지만, 사용하는 건 간단합니다. 버튼을 눌러 이것을 켜고 끌 수 있습니다. 사람들은 날씨에 따라 이것을 사용합니다. 날씨가 더울 때, 이것은 우리에게 찬 공기를 제공합니다. 이것이 공기를 건조하게 할 수도 있기 때문에, 비 오는 날에 이것을 사용하기도 합니다. 이것은 실내 공기에서 열과 습기를 제거하고 원하지 않는 열과 습기를 외부로 이동시켜 작동합니다. 이러한 방식으로, 집 내부의 온도가 내려갈 수 있습니다.

[해설] 실내 공기에서 열과 습기를 제거하여 내부 온도를 낮춰 주는 제품은 에어컨이다.

[어휘] product [prɑ́dʌkt] 상품, 제품 a variety of 다양한 press [pres] 누르다 remove [rimú:v] 제거하다 humidity [hju:mídəti] 습기 temperature [témpərətʃər] 온도 lower [lóuər] 내리다, 낮추다

10 ②

① 남: 너 독서 동아리에 가입할 거니?

　여: 아니. 난 이미 연극 동아리 소속이야.

② 남: 지민이는 숙제를 제출했니?

　여: 응, 그 애는 그걸 아직도 하고 있어.

③ 남: 우리와 함께 할래?

　여: 나도 그러고 싶지만, 할 일이 많아.

④ 남: 얼마나 더 걸릴까요?

　여: 30분 정도요. 가능한 한 빨리 하고 있어요.

⑤ 남: 이 소포를 어디로 보내야 할까요?

　여: 제 사무실로요. 주소는 오하이오주 Springfield, Elm 가 22번지예요.

[해설] 지민이가 숙제를 제출했는지 묻는 말에 그렇다고 말한 후 아직도 하고 있다는 응답은 어색하다.

[어휘] turn in ~을 제출하다 package [pǽkidʒ] 소포

11 ⑤

여: 어디 가니?

남: 중고품 교환 시장에 가는 길이야. 그곳에서 사람들이 물건을 교환할 수 있거든. 나는 더 이상 필요하지 않은 오래된 옷들이 좀 있거든. 그걸 중고 전자레인지로 교환했으면 하고 있어. 내 것은 고장 났거든.

여: 아, 그래서 그 옷들을 가지고 가는 거야?

남: 응. 중고품 교환 시장에 가 본 적 있니?

여: 아니, 없어.

남: 나랑 같이 갈래?

여: 가고 싶지만, 나는 친구를 만나러 가는 길이야.

남: 아, 알겠어. 다음번에 와도 돼. 경찰서 앞에서 토요일마다 열리거든.

여: 잘됐어. 하지만 가기 전에, 내가 거기에서 교환할 것을 찾아보는 게 좋겠어.

[해설] 남자는 오래된 낡은 옷을 내놓고 중고 전자레인지를 구하기 위해 중고품 교환 시장에 가는 길이라고 했다.

[어휘] swap meet 중고품 교환 시장 trade [treid] 교환하다 used [ju:zd] 중고의 microwave oven 전자레인지 hold [hould] 들다; *개최하다, 열다 (hold-held-held) had better ~하는 게 낫다

12 ③

여: 우리 미술 전시회 준비를 하자. 초상화는 어느 구역이 가장 좋을까?

남: 내 생각에는 D 구역이 좋을 것 같아. 가장 큰 구역이잖아.

여: 음. 아마도 거기에는 풍경화가 더 나을 거야. 우린 그게 더 많잖아.

남: 네 말이 맞아. 음, A 구역과 E 구역은 너무 작아. C 구역은 어떨까?

여: 음, B 구역이나 C 구역 둘 다 괜찮을 거야. 그곳들은 같은 크기니까. 너는 어디기 더 나은 것 같아?

남: 난 출구 바로 옆에 있는 구역에 놓는 게 더 좋아.

여: 좋아! 우리 거기에 놓자!

해설 두 사람은 너무 작지 않으면서 출구 바로 옆에 있는 C 구역에 초상화를 놓기로 했다.

어휘 prepare for ~을 준비하다 exhibition [èksəbíʃən] 전시회 portrait [pɔ́ːrtrit] 초상화 landscape [lǽndskèip] 풍경; *풍경화 exit [éksit] 출구

13 ②

[휴대전화가 울린다.]

여: 여보세요?

남: 얘, Lisa. 오늘 저녁에 시간 있어?

여: 응, 무슨 일이야?

남: 형이 여행에서 돌아와. 형을 데리러 공항에 가는 게 어때?

여: 좋아. 우리 언제 만날까?

남: 7시 어때? 비행기는 저녁 8시에 도착하는데, 여기에서 공항까지 가는 데 1시간이 걸려.

여: 너무 빠듯하지 않아? 30분 더 일찍 만나지 않을래?

남: 좋아! 너희 집에서 보자.

여: 좋아.

해설 남자는 형을 데리러 공항에 가기 위해 7시에 만나는 게 어떨지 여자에게 물었는데, 여자가 30분 더 일찍 만나자고 했다.

어휘 pick ~ up ~을 데리러 가다 tight [tait] (여유가 없이) 빠듯한

14 ②

남: 얘, Jane. 너를 찾고 있었어.

여: 왜?

남: 너 영화 〈Blast Off〉에 관심 있다고 말하지 않았어?

여: 응, 기대하고 있어.

남: 금요일에 그게 개봉할 거라고 들었어.

여: 정말? 그럼 표를 확인해야지, 그런데… [잠시 후] 오 이런!

남: 무슨 일이야?

여: 남아 있는 표가 없어.

남: 걱정 마. 내가 어제 우리 표 두 장을 샀어.

여: 정말 좋은 친구구나! 금요일이 기다려져.

해설 여자가 영화표가 남아 있지 않다고 말하자, 남자는 어제 표를 두 장 샀다고 했다.

어휘 release [rilíːs] (영화 등을) 개봉하다

15 ⑤

남: 안녕하세요. 새 학년이 시작되었습니다. 우리는 올해 다양한 동아리 활동이 있음을 알려드리게 되어 기쁩니다. 현재 각 동아리에서 회원을 모집하고 있습니다. 각 동아리 활동 사진이 보고 싶으면, 체육관에 와서 확인할 수 있습니다. 우리 학교는 동아리 활동을 적극 지원하고 연말에 시상할 예정입니다. 여러분이 많이 참여하기를 바랍니다. 체육관에 들러서 다양한 동아리를 확인하고, 관심 있는 어떤 동아리에든 지원하는 것을 잊지 마십시오.

해설 학교에 다양한 동아리 활동이 있고, 현재 각 동아리에서 회원 모집을 하고 있음을 알리고 있다.

어휘 actively [ǽktivli] 적극적으로 support [səpɔ́ːrt] 지원하다 participate [pɑːrtísəpèit] 참가하다, 참여하다 apply for ~에 지원하다

16 ⑤

[전화벨이 울린다.]

남: 여보세요, Mega 해산물 뷔페입니다. 무엇을 도와드릴까요?

여: 다음 주 일요일에 Betty Summers 이름으로 점심 식사 예약을 하고 싶어요.

남: 네. 몇 명이죠?

여: 어른 두 명과 어린이 두 명입니다. 그리고 뷔페 가격이 얼마인지 알고 싶어요.

남: 물론입니다. 평일에 어른은 20달러, 13세 미만 어린이는 10달러입니다. 주말에는 한 사람당 5달러가 더 붙습니다. 아이들이 13세 미만인가요?

여: 제 딸만요.

남: 네, 그럼 어른 세 명과 어린이 한 명 가격이네요. 고맙습니다. 그때 뵙겠습니다.

해설 주말에는 한 사람당 5달러씩 추가되어 어른 세 명($25x3)과 어린이 한 명($15) 가격이므로, 지불할 금액은 $90이다.

어휘 make a reservation 예약하다 adult [ədʌ́lt] 어른 cost [kɔːst] (값·비용이) ~ 들다[이다] weekday [wíːkdèi] 평일

17 ④

남: 안녕, Carol. 다이어트는 어떻게 되어 가니?

여: 좋아, 내 생각에는. 벌써 5kg 줄였어.

남: 정말? 빠르다!

여: 응. 두 달 전만 해도, 난 60kg이 나갔어.

남: 멋지다. 하지만 넌 더 이상은 체중을 줄일 필요가 없어. 지금 좋아 보여.

여: 음, 고마워. 그런데 여름이 오고 있잖아. 그래서 3kg을 더 줄이고 싶어.

남: <u>조심해. 너무 마른 건 건강에 좋지 않아.</u>

[해설] 남자가 다이어트 중인 여자에게 지금이 좋아 보인다며 체중을 더 줄일 필요가 없다고 하자 여자는 더 빼고 싶다고 했으므로, 건강을 걱정하며 조언하는 응답이 가장 적절하다.
　① 그게 얼마나 걸렸니?
　② 너는 지금 체중이 얼마나 나가니?
　③ 네 식단에 유의해야 해.
　⑤ 지방을 너무 많이 먹으면 건강에 좋지 않아.

[어휘] weigh [wei] 무게가 ~이다　lose weight 체중을 줄이다
[문제] pay attention to ~에 주목[유의]하다　thin [θin] 마른
fat [fæt] 뚱뚱한; *지방

18 ⑤

여: 안녕하세요. 무엇을 도와드릴까요?

남: 안녕하세요. 제가 감기에 걸린 것 같아요.

여: 봅시다. 음, 열이 39도예요.

남: 그리고 두통이 있고 콧물이 나요.

여: 그 밖에는요?

남: 기침도 해요.

여: 여기 있습니다. 이 약을 드세요.

남: 얼마나 자주 그걸 먹어야 하죠?

여: <u>하루에 세 번씩, 매 식사 후에요.</u>

[해설] 약을 얼마나 자주 먹어야 하는지 물었으므로, 복용 횟수에 대한 응답이 가장 적절하다.
　① 휴식을 취하셔야 해요.
　② 체온을 확인할게요.
　③ 가능한 한 물을 많이 마시세요.
　④ 악화되면, 병원에 가세요.

[어휘] degree [digríː] (온도 단위인) 도　fever [fíːvər] 열　headache [hédèik] 두통　runny nose 콧물　medicine [médisn] 약
[문제] get worse 악화되다

19 ⑤

여: 점심 식사에 나를 초대해 줘서 고마워. 스파게티가 정말 맛있었어.

남: 네가 맛있게 먹었다니 기뻐. 후식으로 커피 한잔할래?

여: 좋아. 고마워.

남: 커피 어떻게 줄까?

여: 크림과 설탕을 넣어 줘.

남: 커피랑 같이 쿠키 좀 먹을래?

여: <u>고맙지만 괜찮아. 커피면 충분해.</u>

[해설] 음식을 권했으므로, 감사를 표하거나 사양하는 응답이 가장 적절하다.

　① 여기 거스름돈 있어.
　② 그건 식탁 위에 있어.
　③ 그건 그렇게 좋진 않았어.
　④ 나는 차보다 커피를 더 좋아해.

[어휘] dessert [dizə́ːrt] 후식　[문제] kitchen table 식탁

20 ③

여: 내일은 Kevin의 어머니에게 특별한 날입니다. 그녀의 생일입니다. Kevin은 어머니에게 파티를 열어 드리고 싶어서, 쇼핑을 하기 위해 쇼핑몰에 갑니다. 그는 생일 케이크, 꽃, 장식에 쓸 풍선을 포함해 많은 것들을 삽니다. 그가 돈을 내는데, 가격이 생각했던 것보다 더 비쌉니다. 그래서 그는 영수증을 확인하고 총액이 잘못된 것을 알아차립니다. 이런 상황에서, Kevin은 점원에게 뭐라고 말하겠습니까?

Kevin: <u>영수증이 잘못된 것 같아요.</u>

[해설] 가격이 생각했던 것보다 더 비싸 영수증을 확인하고 총액이 잘못된 것을 알게 되었으므로, 영수증이 잘못되었다는 말이 가장 적절하다.
　① 전액 환불을 원해요.
　② 다른 사이즈가 있나요?
　④ 내가 준 생일 선물이 마음에 안 들었니?
　⑤ 너 언제 생일 파티를 할 거니?

[어휘] including [inklúːdiŋ] ~을 포함하여　balloon [bəlúːn] 풍선
decoration [dèkəréiʃən] 장식　receipt [risíːt] 영수증　realize [ríːəlàiz] 깨닫다, 알아차리다　total [tóutl] 합계, 총액　clerk [kləːrk] (상점의) 점원　[문제] full refund 전액 환불

Dictation Test ⑭

pp. 188~195

01　1) made this key chain
　　2) couldn't even make a body　3) with just a face
　　4) decided on a cat

02　1) check all the ingredients　2) manage other cooks
　　3) in charge of　4) like a general manager

03　1) have several places in mind　2) if I were you
　　3) lots of things to do

04　1) leaves at 2:00 p.m.　2) one hour by regular bus
　　3) take the regular one

05　1) operation went very well　2) have a competition
　　3) can't allow you to play

06　1) be ready in three minutes　2) what I ordered
　　3) come out in the wash

실전모의고사 15회

pp. 196~197

01 ⑤	02 ④	03 ①	04 ②	05 ④
06 ⑤	07 ④	08 ④	09 ③	10 ③
11 ③	12 ②	13 ⑤	14 ④	15 ②
16 ④	17 ④	18 ⑤	19 ②	20 ④

01 ⑤

남: 다음 분이요.
여: 너무 추워서 뜨거운 음료가 필요해요. 추천 좀 해 주시겠어요?
남: 바닐라 우유는 어떠세요? 여기 저희 카페에서 인기 있는 음료예요.
여: 그거 정말 좋겠네요.
남: 어떤 사이즈로 드릴까요? 작은 것과 큰 것이 있어요.
여: 작은 것으로 주세요.
남: 여기서 드실 건가요, 포장하실 건가요?
여: 여기서 먹을게요.
남: 여기서 드시면 종이컵 대신에 머그잔을 받으실 겁니다. 괜찮으신가요?
여: 물론이죠.

[해설] 여자는 작은 사이즈의 뜨거운 바닐라 우유를 주문했고 머그잔에 받기로 했다.

[어휘] recommendation [rèkəməndéiʃən] 추천 instead of ~ 대신에

02 ④

여: 안녕, Nick. 너 아팠다고 들었는데, 지금은 굉장히 보기 좋다.
남: 고마워. 석 달 전에 수술을 받았는데, 지금은 괜찮아.
여: 너 정말 활기차 보여! 비결이 뭐니?
남: 굉장한 비결은 없어. 수술 이후에, 나는 모든 것에 대해 긍정적으로 생각하려 노력했고, 매일 밤 잠을 충분히 자.
여: 그게 다야?
남: 음, 채소를 많이 먹으려고 노력하고 있기도 해.
여: 그게 중요한 것 같네.
남: 그래. 그리고 규칙적으로 운동하는 것도 도움이 됐어.
여: 아, 그렇구나.

[해설] 남자가 건강을 되찾기 위해 한 일로 물을 충분히 마시는 것은 언급되지 않았다.

[어휘] surgery [sə́ːrdʒəri] 수술 energetic [ènərdʒétik] 활기찬, 기운찬 positively [pázitivli] 긍정적으로 regularly [régjələrli] 규칙적으로, 정기적으로

03 ①

[전화벨이 울린다.]

남: 여보세요?

여: 안녕, Charles. 나 Betty야.

남: 안녕, Betty. 잘 지내니?

여: 음, 문제가 있어. 한국에서 사촌이 찾아오거든.

남: 잘됐구나. 문제가 뭔데?

여: 그 애의 항공편이 화요일 밤에 도착해. 내가 공항에 그 애를 데리러 가야 해.

남: 화요일 밤? 우리 화요일 밤에 역사 시험공부를 하기로 했잖아.

여: 알아. 하지만 못할 것 같아. 미안해.

남: 괜찮아. 일정을 변경하면 되지.

여: 이해해 줘서 고마워.

해설 여자는 사촌을 데리러 공항에 가야 해서 남자와 함께 시험공부를 하기로 한 약속을 지키지 못한다고 했다.

어휘 flight [flait] 항공편 be supposed to-v ~하기로 되어 있다 reschedule [rìːskédʒuːl] 일정을 변경하다

04 ②

[휴대전화가 울린다.]

여: Go 여행사입니다. 무엇을 도와드릴까요?

남: 금요일에 부산에 가는데 항공편을 예약하려고 해요.

여: 편도인가요 아니면 왕복인가요?

남: 왕복으로 해 주세요.

여: 오후 1시, 2시, 5시 출발이 있습니다. 이 시간 중 어느 것이 괜찮으신가요?

남: 3시나 4시 정각 출발은 없나요?

여: 죄송하지만 없습니다.

남: 알겠어요, 그럼 2시 정각이 가장 좋네요.

여: 알겠습니다.

해설 남자는 3시나 4시 출발을 원했으나 항공편이 없어서 2시 출발 항공편을 예약하기로 했다.

어휘 round trip 왕복 여행 departure [dipáːrtʃər] 출발

05 ④

여: 너 몸이 안 좋아 보여. 무슨 일 있니?

남: 운전하면서 일이 있었어.

여: 정말? 무슨 일?

남: 택시 한 대가 내 차 앞에 끼어들었어. 나는 정말 간신히 제때 멈췄어. 서로 부딪치는 줄 알았어. 지금 심장이 정말 빠르게 뛰고 있어.

여: 괜찮아. 진정해. 어쨌든 사고 당하는 건 피할 수 있었으니 다행이야. 잠시 앉아서 긴장을 풀어.

남: 그래. 손이 아직도 떨려.

해설 남자는 택시와의 충돌 사고를 간신히 모면했으나 여전히 떨린다고 했으므로 무서울(frightened) 것이다.
① 외로운 ② 궁금한 ③ 지루한 ⑤ 실망한

어휘 barely [béərli] 간신히 manage to-v 간신히 ~하다 crash [kræʃ] 충돌하다 beat [biːt] (심장이) 뛰다 calm down 진정하다 fortunate [fɔ́ːrtʃənət] 운이 좋은, 다행인 get into an accident 사고를 당하다 relax [rilǽks] 쉬다, 긴장을 풀다

06 ⑤

① 여: 이 책은 얼마 동안 빌릴 수 있나요?
남: 일주일간 대출 가능합니다.

② 여: 어디 가니?
남: 도서관에 가는 길이야.

③ 여: 어떤 종류의 음악을 좋아하니?
남: 힙합을 정말 좋아해.

④ 여: 도와드릴까요?
남: 네, Blue Band의 새 CD를 찾고 있어요.

⑤ 여: 음악 소리 좀 줄여 주시겠어요?
남: 아, 네. 죄송합니다.

해설 도서관에서 남자가 이어폰으로 듣는 음악 소리가 밖으로 새어 나오는 상황이다.

어휘 check out (책 등을) 대출하다 head [hed] (특정 방향으로) 가다

07 ④

여: 이 프린터 좀 도와줄래? 작동이 안 돼.

남: 뭐가 문제야?

여: 전원을 껐다가 켜도, 계속 오류 메시지가 떠.

남: 문제가 뭔지 알아. 나도 전에 이런 일이 있었거든.

여: 어떻게 고칠 수 있어?

남: 드라이버를 재설치해야 해.

여: 난 그걸 어떻게 하는지 몰라. 네가 나 대신 해 줄래?

남: 물론이지. 그렇게 어렵지 않아.

해설 남자가 프린터 문제를 해결하려면 드라이버를 재설치해야 한다고 하자, 여자는 방법을 모른다며 남자에게 대신 해 달라고 부탁했다.

어휘 give ~ a hand ~을 도와주다 work [wəːrk] 일하다; *(기계·장치 등이) 작동되다 error [érər] 오류 reinstall [rìːinstɔ́ːl] 재설치하다

08 ④

여: 저는 오늘 유명한 판타지 소설가 J.K. Rowling에 대해 이야기할 겁니다. 그녀는 1965년 7월 31일 영국 예이트에서 태어났습니다. 그녀는 독서광이었고, 6살 때 첫 작품을 썼습니다. 그녀는 〈해리 포터〉 책 시리즈로 가장 잘 알려져 있습니다. 이 시리즈는 널리 읽혔

고 특히 어린이들 사이에서 많은 팬층을 가지고 있습니다. 〈해리 포터〉 책은 현재 80개 언어로 출판되고 전 세계적으로 5억 부 이상 판매되었습니다. 이 책의 인기 때문에, Rowling은 10억 달러 이상을 벌었습니다.

[해설] 출생지(영국 예이트), 대표작(〈해리 포터〉 시리즈), 주요 독자층(어린이들), 책 판매 부수(5억 부 이상)에 관해서는 언급되었으나, 수상 경력은 언급되지 않았다.

[어휘] novelist [návəlist] 소설가 bookworm [búkwə̀ːrm] 독서광 fan base 팬층 publish [pʌ́bliʃ] 출판하다, 발행하다 million [míljən] 100만 due to ~ 때문에 popularity [pàpjəlǽrəti] 인기 billion [bíljən] 10억

09 ③

남: 이것은 아메리카와 아프리카의 열대 지방의 나무에서 자랍니다. 이것으로, 우리는 전 세계 사람들이 즐기는 달콤한 간식을 만들 수 있습니다. 이것의 역사는 중앙아메리카에서 시작되었습니다. 마야인들은 오래전에 그 지역에 살았고, 차가운 음료를 만드는 데 이것을 처음으로 사용했습니다. 15세기에 유럽인들이 아메리카를 발견했을 때, 그들은 이것을 유럽으로 가져왔습니다. 우유와 설탕을 그 가루와 섞어 간식으로 만들어졌는데, 이는 현재 초콜릿의 탄생이었습니다. 그 이후로, 이것은 많은 유럽인들로부터 사랑받고 있습니다.

[해설] 열대 지방의 나무에서 자라며 우유와 설탕을 섞으면 초콜릿이 되는 것은 카카오이다.

[어휘] tropical region 열대 지방 treat [triːt] 간식 birth [bəːrθ] 탄생, 출생 discover [diskʌ́vər] 발견하다 powder [páudər] 가루 modern-day [mádərndèi] 현대의

10 ③

① 남: 뉴욕행 버스가 얼마나 자주 출발하나요?
　여: 두 시간마다 출발해요.
② 남: 이 알약을 하루 세 번 드시고 사흘 후에 다시 오세요.
　여: 그럴게요. 정말 고맙습니다.
③ 남: 점심을 먹고 나면 잠들 수밖에 없어.
　여: 점심 정말 맛있었어. 고마워.
④ 남: 저희 사진 좀 찍어 주시겠어요?
　여: 그럼요.
⑤ 남: 우리 숙제 같이 하는 게 어때?
　여: 좋아. 언제 만날까?

[해설] 점심 식사 후에 잠이 온다는 말에 점심이 맛있었다는 응답은 어색하다.

[어휘] can't help v-ing ~할 수밖에 없다 fall asleep 잠들다

11 ③

여: 얘, Jason. 주말 계획이 뭐니?
남: 난 꽤 바빠. 토요일에는 캠핑을 갈 거야.
여: 캠핑? 누구랑 가는데?
남: 우리 가족 전체. 누나를 위한 파티야. 누나가 막 고등학교를 졸업했거든.
여: 그렇구나. 음, 그럼 일요일은?
남: 그날 차를 수리하시는 걸 돕기로 아버지께 약속했어.
여: 음, 너랑 영화 보고 싶었는데, 너 상당히 바쁜 것 같아.
남: 미안해, 아마 다음 주에 영화 볼 수 있을 거야.

[해설] 남자는 일요일에 아버지가 차를 수리하시는 것을 돕기로 했다고 말했다.

[어휘] whole [houl] 전체의 promise [prámis] (남에게) ~을 약속하다 quite [kwait] 꽤, 상당히

12 ②

여: 무엇을 도와드릴까요?
남: 대구행 표를 사고 싶어요.
여: 네. 언제 출발하고 싶으세요?
남: 사실은 가능한 한 빨리 출발해야 해요.
여: 알겠습니다, 지금이 8시 30분이네요. 열차가 5분 전에 떠났다는 뜻이죠. 그리고 다음 열차는 저녁 8시 50분에 출발합니다.
남: 알겠습니다. 그러면 대구에 언제 도착하죠?
여: 저녁 10시에 도착합니다.
남: 괜찮을 것 같네요. 표 한 장 살게요. 요금이 얼마죠?
여: 15,000원입니다.
남: 네, 여기 있습니다. 어느 승강장에서 열차가 출발하나요?
여: 3번 승강장에서 출발할 거예요.

[해설] 남자는 저녁 8시 50분에 출발해서 대구에 10시에 도착하는 열차표를 구매했다.

열차표	
① 도착지	대구
② 출발 시각	저녁 8:15
③ 도착 시각	저녁 10:00
④ 운임	15,000원
⑤ 승강장	3

[어휘] leave [liːv] 떠나다, 출발하다 as soon as possible 가능한 한 빨리 fare [fɛər] 운임, 요금 platform [plǽtfɔːrm] 플랫폼, 승강장 depart [dipáːrt] 출발하다

13 ⑤

[전화벨이 울린다.]
남: 여보세요?
여: 여보세요. 토요일 콘서트 표가 아직 있나요?

남: 11월 10일 표를 말씀하시는 건가요?

여: 네.

남: 죄송하지만, 그 콘서트 표는 매진되었습니다.

여: 오, 이런. 유감이네요.

남: 일요일은 어떠세요? 11월 11일 공연에는 상당수 좌석이 남아 있습니다.

여: 괜찮겠네요. 다른 날은 남은 표가 있나요?

남: 평일에 콘서트를 가셔도 된다면, 모든 평일 공연은 구매할 수 있는 티켓이 있어요.

여: 잘됐네요. 그럼 11월 14일 수요일에 두 좌석을 예매할게요.

남: 알겠습니다.

[해설] 여자는 원래 11월 10일 토요일 티켓을 원했지만 매진되어서, 11월 14일 수요일 티켓을 예매하기로 했다.

[어휘] quite a few 상당수

14 ④

여: Tony, 다음 주 과학 경진 대회에 참가할 거야?

남: 물론이지. 나는 그날을 위해 거의 한 달 동안 준비했어.

여: 와, 한 달이나?

남: 응. 첫째 주에 발명품을 생각해 냈고, 둘째 주에는 그걸 만들었어.

여: 그럼 지난주에는 뭐 했어?

남: 지난주에는 보고서를 썼어.

여: 대단하다. 너 정말 준비됐구나.

남: 이번 주에 내가 해야 할 일은 발표 준비가 전부야.

여: 넌 분명 잘할 거야.

남: 그러길 바라.

[해설] 남자는 거의 한 달 동안 과학 경진 대회를 준비 중인데, 지난주에는 그것을 위한 보고서를 썼다고 했다.

[어휘] take part in ~에 참가하다 come up with ~을 생각해 내다 invention [invénʃən] 발명품 presentation [prì:zəntéiʃən] 발표

15 ②

여: 좋은 저녁입니다. 이제 교통 정보입니다. 만약 여러분이 도로에서 이것을 듣고 계시다면, 교통이 평소보다 훨씬 더 느리다는 것을 이미 알고 계실 겁니다. 오늘 오후 6시경 Hudson 가에서 교통사고가 있었습니다. 그 사고로 인해, 차량이 멈췄습니다. 이 문제가 해결되는 데 30분 정도 소요될 것으로 예상됩니다. 그 이후, 교통이 정리될 것입니다. 저는 교통 속보의 Ellen Burrell이었습니다. 감사합니다.

[해설] 앞서 있었던 교통사고로 인해 현재 교통이 평소보다 더 정체되고 있으며 30분 정도 후 교통이 정리될 것임을 알리고 있다.

[어휘] traffic [tréfik] 교통(량) vehicle [ví:ikl] 탈것, 차량 come to a halt 정지하다, 멈추다 resolve [rizálv] 해결하다 update

[ʌ́pdèit] 갱신; *최신 정보, 속보

16 ④

남: 도와드릴까요?

여: 새 셔츠를 하나 사고 싶어요. 뭘 추천하시나요?

남: 이 녹색 셔츠는 어떠세요?

여: 마음에 들어요. 얼마인가요?

남: 70달러였는데, 오늘은 50% 할인됩니다.

여: 아, 정말요?

남: 네, 오늘이 세일 마지막 날이에요. 운이 좋으시네요.

여: 그렇군요. 가격이 괜찮으니, 두 장 살게요. 하나는 언니에게 주려고요.

남: 알겠습니다. 잠시만 기다려 주세요.

[해설] 셔츠의 원래 가격은 70달러인데 50% 할인 중이고 2장을 산다고 했으므로($35×2), 70달러를 지불해야 한다.

[어휘] off [ɔ:f] 할인하여 sale [seil] 세일, 할인 판매

17 ④

남: 안녕, Cara. 뭐 하고 있니?

여: 아, 안녕. 배낭을 싸고 있어. 하이킹 가거든.

남: 이런 때 하이킹을 간다고? 밖이 정말 추워.

여: 걱정하지 마. 운동은 나를 계속 따뜻하게 해 줘서, 추위를 별로 느끼지 않아.

남: 그래도 난 네가 조심해야 한다고 생각해. 산은 훨씬 더 추워.

여: 그렇지. 제안할 거라도 있니?

남: 만약을 위해서 여분 옷을 가져가는 게 어때?

여: 그래. 걱정해 줘서 고마워.

[해설] 남자는 하이킹을 가는 여자에게 산은 더 추우니 조심하라며 여분 옷을 가져가라고 제안했으므로, 이를 받아들이며 고마움을 표현하는 응답이 가장 적절하다.
① 나는 정상에 오르고 싶어.
② 나는 전에 거기 가 본 적이 전혀 없어.
③ 나는 바다보다 산이 더 좋아.
⑤ 지팡이가 있으면 하이킹하는 게 어렵지 않아.

[어휘] suggestion [səʤéstʃən] 제안 extra [ékstrə] 여분의, 추가의 just in case 만약을 위해서 [문제] reach [ri:tʃ] ~에 닿다[도달하다] top [tɑp] 정상 prefer [prifə́:r] 더 좋아하다 concern [kənsə́:rn] 관심, 걱정 walking stick 지팡이

18 ⑤

여: 오늘은 선생님의 직업에 관해 이야기해 보겠습니다.

남: 네, 좋아요.

여: Stevens 선생님, 일이 상당히 힘들어 보이는데요. 그중 가장 어려

운 부분이 뭔가요?

남: 글쎄요, 저는 수술 전에 종종 긴장돼요. 하지만 긴장이 실수를 야기할 수 있기 때문에, 긴장을 풀려고 노력하죠.

여: 그렇군요. 어떤 종류의 수술을 하시나요?

남: 주로 심장 질병을 앓고 있는 사람들을 치료합니다.

여: 언제 선생님의 일이 가장 보람 있다고 느끼시나요?

남: 제 환자들이 회복될 때 제 자신이 자랑스러워요.

[해설] 여자는 남자에게 언제 일이 가장 보람 있게 느껴지는지 물었으므로, 의사로서 보람을 느끼는 때에 관해 말하는 응답이 가장 적절하다.
① 저는 늘 환자를 돕기 위해 최선을 다해요.
② 환자는 의사의 조언을 따라야 해요.
③ 의사가 되는 것이 최고의 직업 같아요.
④ 직업 선택에 있어 급여는 그리 중요하지 않아요.

[어휘] career [kəríər] 직업 tough [tʌf] 어려운, 힘든 nervousness [nə́:rvəsnis] 긴장, 초조 cause [kɔːz] 야기하다 perform [pərfɔ́ːrm] 수행하다 heart disease 심장 질병 rewarding [riwɔ́ːrdiŋ] 보람이 있는 [문제] follow [fálou] 따르다 salary [sǽləri] 급여, 월급

19 ②

여: 오늘 취업 면접에 와 주셔서 감사합니다. 간단히 자기소개를 해 주시겠어요?

남: 안녕하세요. 저는 Hunter Clinton입니다. 27살이고, 런던에서 왔습니다.

여: 좋습니다. 이런 종류의 업무에 경험이 좀 있으신가요?

남: ABC 은행에서 인턴으로 일했습니다.

여: 좋습니다. 그곳에서 경험은 즐거웠나요?

남: 네. 제가 대학에서 배운 것을 실제 업무에 적용하는 것이 흥미로웠습니다.

여: 알겠습니다. 대학에서 어떤 공부를 했죠?

남: 컴퓨터 공학을 전공했습니다.

[해설] 대학에서 어떤 공부를 했는지 물었으므로, 자신의 전공을 말하는 응답이 가장 적절하다.
① 3달 전에 졸업했습니다.
③ 4년 동안 학교에 다녔습니다.
④ 당신의 회사에서 일하고 싶습니다.
⑤ 제 성적은 평균보다 더 좋았습니다.

[어휘] briefly [brí:fli] 간단히 intern [intə́:rn] 인턴 apply [əplái] 적용하다 [문제] major in ~을 전공하다 computer science 컴퓨터 공학 grade [greid] 등급; *성적 average [ǽvəːrdʒ] 평균

20 ④

남: Dan과 Mira는 같은 스페인어 반입니다. Mira는 수업 동안 무척 조용합니다. Dan은 Mira에게 왜 아무 말도 하지 않는지 묻습니다. Mira는 수업 동안 스페인어를 말해야 하는데 잘하지 못하기 때문이

라고 말합니다. 그녀는 실수를 하고 비웃음을 당할까 봐 두렵습니다. Dan은 그녀가 그저 시도해야 한다고 생각합니다. 또한 스페인어로 생각을 공유하는 게 재미있으며 실수를 하는 것은 당연하다고 그녀에게 말하고 싶어 합니다. 이런 상황에서, Dan은 Mira에게 뭐라고 말하겠습니까?

Dan: 실패는 성공의 어머니야.

[해설] Dan은 실수하는 것은 당연하며 그저 시도해야 한다고 말하고 싶어 하므로, 실수를 통해 배운다는 의미의 말이 가장 적절하다.
① 쉽게 얻은 것은 쉽게 잃어.
② 아니 땐 굴뚝에 연기가 나겠니.
③ 엎지른 물은 다시 담을 수 없어.
⑤ 실력 없는 목수가 늘 연장을 탓하지.

[어휘] be afraid of ~을 두려워하다 make an error 실수하다 laugh at ~을 비웃다 share [ʃɛər] 공유하다 natural [nǽtʃərəl] 당연한 make a mistake 실수하다 [문제] blame [bleim] 탓하다, 나무라다

Dictation Test ⑮
pp. 198~205

01 1) need a hot drink 2) I'd like a small one
3) instead of a paper cup

02 1) had surgery 2) get enough sleep
3) eat a lot of vegetables 4) exercising regularly

03 1) pick her up 2) were supposed to study
3) I'm afraid I can't

04 1) book a flight 2) three or four o'clock departure
3) two o'clock is the best

05 1) cut in front of my car 2) beating so fast
3) avoid getting into an accident 4) are still shaking

06 1) How long can I borrow 2) Where are you heading
3) I'm looking for 4) turn down the music

07 1) It isn't working
2) keep getting an error message
3) reinstall the driver

08 1) was born in 2) is best known for
3) especially among kids
4) has earned over $1 billion

09 1) grows on trees 2) make sweet treats
3) make a cold drink
4) birth of modern-day chocolate

10 1) every two hours 2) can't help falling asleep
3) Would you mind

11　1) plans for the weekend　2) how about Sunday
　　3) help him fix his car

12　1) as soon as possible　2) leaves at 8:50
　　3) arrives at 10:00　4) How much is the fare

13　1) still have tickets available　2) are sold out
　　3) all of our weekday shows
　　4) seats for Wednesday, November 14

14　1) came up with an invention　2) wrote a report
　　3) prepare for the presentation

15　1) traffic is much slower　2) Due to the accident
　　3) take about 30 minutes

16　1) it's 50% off　2) last day of the sale
　　3) That's a good deal

17　1) packing my backpack
　　2) even colder in the mountains
　　3) take extra clothes

18　1) seems quite tough
　　2) feel nervous before an operation
　　3) is most rewarding

19　1) introduce yourself briefly　2) worked as an intern
　　3) study at university

20　1) very quiet during the class
　　2) afraid of making errors
　　3) it's natural to make mistakes

33 진정하다　　　　34 ~을 제출하다
35 파티를 열다　　　36 ~을 준비하다
37 ~할 여유가 없다　38 미리
39 악화되다　　　　40 ~와 잘 어울리다

B
01 exit　　　　　　02 billion
03 foreign　　　　04 humidity
05 reach　　　　　06 express
07 leather　　　　08 degree
09 popularity　　　10 temperature
11 successful　　　12 headache
13 treat　　　　　14 receipt
15 lower　　　　　16 rewarding
17 century　　　　18 vet
19 grade　　　　　20 salary
21 positively　　　22 scenery
23 emperor　　　　24 literature
25 patience　　　　26 metal
27 expert　　　　　28 million
29 difference　　　30 clerk
31 average　　　　32 suggestion
33 just in case　　34 major in
35 come up with　　36 graduate from
37 be known for　　38 keep a diary
39 turn down　　　40 as soon as possible

Word Test 13~15
pp. 206~207

A
01 소설가　　　　　02 기간
03 원래의, 최초의　　04 긴장, 초조
05 피하다　　　　　06 관심, 걱정
07 발견하다　　　　08 계속되다
09 탈출하다　　　　10 적극적으로
11 10년　　　　　　12 수술
13 탄생, 출생　　　14 공사
15 예약하다　　　　16 활기찬, 기운찬
17 지원하다　　　　18 발명품
19 규칙적으로　　　20 관찰하다
21 비상, 위급　　　22 충돌하다
23 출발　　　　　　24 여분의
25 직원　　　　　　26 직업
27 출판하다　　　　28 전진; 경과
29 탓하다, 나무라다　30 직접
31 ~을 돌보다[보살피다]　32 ~ 때문에

실전모의고사 16 회
pp. 208~209

01 ③	02 ④	03 ③	04 ⑤	05 ④
06 ⑤	07 ③	08 ④	09 ③	10 ②
11 ⑤	12 ②	13 ③	14 ①	15 ⑤
16 ①	17 ④	18 ④	19 ①	20 ①

01 ③

여: 안녕하세요, 무엇을 도와드릴까요?
남: 안녕하세요. 여권 지갑을 찾고 있어요.
여: 지갑이 부착된 것과 여권만 들어가는 것, 두 종류가 있어요.
남: 지갑이 있는 것이 더 좋을 것 같아요.
여: 어떤 디자인이 가장 좋으세요?
남: 이 체크무늬가 좋아 보이는 것 같아요. 줄무늬보다 더 멋지네요.

여: 좋은 선택이에요. 그것은 신상품이고 가장 많이 팔리는 품목 중 하나예요.

남: 그것을 살게요.

해설 남자는 지갑이 부착된 체크무늬의 여권 지갑을 사기로 했다.

어휘 passport holder 여권 지갑 attached [ətǽtʃt] 부착된 checkered [tʃékərd] 체크무늬의

02 ④

남: 그거 알아? 우리 가족 이사 가.

여: 아, 이런! 전학 가는 거야?

남: 아니. 이사 갈 집은 지금 사는 곳에서 겨우 두 블록 떨어져 있어.

여: 잘됐네. 그런데 왜 이사 가는 거야?

남: 지금 살고 있는 집이 너무 작아서. 이 집은 2층이고 방이 4개야.

여: 좋다. 새 집이야?

남: 아니. 20년 전에 지어졌어. 새 집은 너무 비싸.

여: 그렇지. 우리 삼촌이 얼마 전에 새 집을 샀어. 50만 달러였어!

남: 와! 그나저나, 네가 한번 봐야 해. 모퉁이에 있는 빨간 집이야.

해설 위치(지금 사는 곳에서 두 블록 거리), 방 개수(4개), 연식(20년 전에 건축됨), 색(빨간색)에 관해서는 언급되었으나, 가격은 언급되지 않았다.

어휘 cost [kɔːst] (값·비용이) ~이다[들다]

03 ③

[휴대전화가 울린다.]

남: 여보세요?

여: 안녕하세요, Thomas. 이웃 사람 Fiona예요.

남: 안녕하세요, Fiona. 잘 지내세요?

여: 좋지 못해요. 어젯밤에 잠을 잘 수가 없었어요.

남: 정말요? 아프세요?

여: 아니요. 당신의 개 때문예요. 밤새 짖더군요.

남: 아, 그거 정말 죄송해요. 창문 밖에 고양이가 있었나 봐요.

여: 이해해요, 하지만 매우 짜증 나게 하더라고요. 밤에 개를 조용히 시켜 주시겠어요?

남: 네. 이제 저희 개가 그렇게 많이 시끄럽게 하지 않도록 할게요.

여: 고마워요, Thomas.

해설 여자는 이웃집의 개가 짖는 소리에 밤새 잠을 잘 수 없었다며 밤에 개를 조용히 시켜 달라고 말하고 있다.

어휘 neighbor [néibər] 이웃 ill [il] 아픈 bark [baːrk] 짖다 annoying [ənɔ́iiŋ] 짜증 나게 하는

04 ⑤

남: 얘, 오늘 밤 나랑 저녁 먹을래?

여: 음, 내 일정을 확인해 볼게.

남: 오늘 바쁜 날이야?

여: 응. 오후 4시까지 수업이 있고, 오후 5시에 조 모임이 있어.

남: 모임이 몇 시에 끝나?

여: 한 시간 정도밖에 안 걸릴 거야.

남: 그러면 7시에 만나자. 괜찮니?

여: 응, 그럴 것 같아. 그때 봐.

해설 두 사람은 여자의 조 모임이 끝나고 7시에 만나서 저녁을 먹기로 했다.

어휘 or so ~ 정도

05 ④

남: 뭘 찾으시는 걸 도와드릴까요?

여: 네. 중간고사 때문에 책을 한 권 찾고 있어요.

남: 알겠습니다. 책 이름이 무엇이죠?

여: 〈남프랑스의 역사〉라는 책이에요.

남: 알겠습니다. 저자 이름을 아시나요?

여: 아니요, 그게 문제예요.

남: 괜찮습니다. 제가 컴퓨터로 찾아보면 돼요.

여: 잘됐네요. 도와주셔서 정말 감사해요.

남: 죄송합니다만, 그 책은 지금 대출 중이네요. 이번 주 목요일에 반납될 거예요.

여: 알겠습니다. 그때 다시 올게요.

해설 남자는 여자가 찾는 책의 대출 현황과 반납 예정일을 알려 주었으므로, 두 사람이 대화하는 장소로 가장 적절한 곳은 도서관이다.

어휘 author [ɔ́ːθər] 저자 appreciate [əpríːʃièit] 감사하다

06 ⑤

① 여: 내일 날씨가 어떨까?
   남: 뉴스에서 비가 올 거래.
② 여: 내 가방을 도서관에 두고 온 것 같아.
   남: 다시 가서 가져와야겠네.
③ 여: 책 반납했니?
   남: 아직. 수업 끝나고 반납할 거야.
④ 여: 네 비옷 정말 맘에 들어. 그거 어디서 샀니?
   남: 부모님께서 사 주셨어.
⑤ 여: 아, 우산 가지고 오는 걸 잊었네. 하나 사야겠어.
   남: 내 것을 같이 쓰는 게 어때?

해설 비가 오는데 여자는 우산 없이 서 있고, 우산을 든 남자가 이를 보고 있는 상황이다.

어휘 raincoat [réinkòut] 비옷

07 ③

남: 얘, 민주야. 그 가방 정말 크다! 어디 가는 거니?

여: 안녕, Mike. 부모님 댁에 가는 중이야. 일주일 동안 거기 머물 거야.

남: 부모님이 어디에 사셔?

여: 부산에 사셔. 나는 KTX를 타고 거기 갈 거야.

남: 아, 나 지금 시내에 가는 중인데. 내가 역까지 태워 줄까?

여: 고맙지만, 이미 택시를 불렀어. 그런데 Mike, 내 부탁 하나 들어줄래?

남: 물론이지, 뭔데?

여: 내가 없는 동안 내 우편물 좀 가져와 줄래? 요즘 빈집을 노리는 도둑이 많다고 들었거든.

남: 알았어. 문제없어.

[해설] 여자는 부모님 댁에 가 있는 동안 남자에게 자신의 우편물을 챙겨 달라고 부탁했다.

[어휘] downtown [dàuntáun] 시내 give ~ a ride ~을 태워 주다 station [stéiʃən] 역 do ~ a favor ~의 부탁을 들어주다, ~에게 호의를 베풀다 collect [kəlékt] 모으다; *가져오다 mail [meil] 우편; *우편물 thief [θi:f] 도둑 target [tɑ́rgit] 목표로 삼다 empty [émpti] 빈

08 ④

여: 이제 저는 유명한 멕시코 화가인 Frida Kahlo에 대해 이야기하려고 합니다. 그녀는 멕시코에서 태어났고 부모님과 6명의 자매와 함께 자랐습니다. 처음에 그녀는 의학을 공부했지만, 18세 때의 심각한 교통사고 때문에 진로를 바꿨습니다. 그녀는 자신의 초상화를 자주 그렸습니다. 그녀는 사람들에게 자신의 고통을 보여 주고 싶었습니다.

[해설] 출생지(멕시코), 가족 관계(부모님과 6명의 자매), 화가가 된 계기(의학을 공부했지만 심각한 교통사고로 진로를 바꿈), 작품 소재(주로 초상화)에 관해서는 언급되었으나, 수상 경력은 언급되지 않았다.

[어휘] medicine [médisn] 약; *의학 career path 진로 traffic accident 교통사고 suffering [sʌ́fəriŋ] 고통

09 ③

남: 이 직업을 가진 사람들은 음식이 제공되는 장소에서 일합니다. 그들은 음식에 관한 모든 것에 책임이 있습니다. 그들은 재료를 사고, 메뉴를 만들고, 음식을 준비합니다. 그들은 또한 주방의 운영을 관리합니다. 그들은 주방이 항상 깨끗한지 확인합니다. 이 직업을 가지려면, 식당에서 일한 경험이 필요합니다. 요리 학교에서 전문 교육을 받는 것도 도움이 됩니다.

[해설] 재료 구입, 음식 준비, 주방 운영 관리 등 음식에 관한 모든 것에 책임이 있는 직업은 주방장이다.

[어휘] serve [səːrv] 제공하다 be responsible for ~에 책임이 있다 create [kriéit] 만들다, 창조하다 operation [àpəréiʃən] 수술; *운영 education [èdʒukéiʃn] 교육

10 ②

① 남: 도와드릴까요?
   여: 아니요, 괜찮아요. 그냥 둘러보는 거예요.
② 남: 소금 좀 건네주실래요?
   여: 네. 이 수프는 약간 짜네요.
③ 남: 가장 가까운 은행이 어디인지 아세요?
   여: 네. 저기 붉은색 건물 옆이에요.
④ 남: 너 피곤해 보인다. 잠을 충분히 못 잤니?
   여: 응. 영화를 보느라고 늦게까지 깨어 있었어.
⑤ 남: 우리 여름 휴가에 대해 생각한 것 좀 있니?
   여: 캠핑 가는 게 어때?

[해설] 소금을 건네달라고 부탁하는 말에 알겠다면서 수프가 짜다고 말하는 응답은 어색하다.

[어휘] look around 둘러보다 stay up late 늦게까지 깨어 있다 thought [θɔːt] 생각

11 ⑤

남: 오늘 아내 생일이야. 그래서 오늘 밤 아내에게 생일 파티를 열어 주려고 해.

여: 준비를 다 끝냈니?

남: 거의. 집을 청소하고 아내가 좋아하는 꽃을 좀 샀어.

여: 케이크는?

남: 오븐에 있어. 초콜릿 케이크를 굽고 있거든.

여: 와, 너 정말 열심히 하고 있구나.

남: 응, 그래. 이제 난 저녁 준비를 시작해야 해.

여: 무엇을 만들 거니?

남: 페퍼로니 피자를 만들 거야. 아내가 가장 좋아하는 것들 중 하나거든.

[해설] 남자는 아내의 생일 파티를 위해 청소하고 꽃을 사고 케이크를 구웠고, 이제 저녁 식사 준비를 시작해야 한다고 했다.

[어휘] throw ~ a party ~에게 파티를 열어 주다 favorite [féivərit] 가장 좋아하는 (것)

12 ②

여: 안녕하세요. 지금 스터디룸을 사용할 수 있나요?

남: 네. 몇 명이시죠?

여: 세 명이요.

남: 네. 이 표를 확인하고 가능한 방들 중 하나를 고르세요.

여: 입구에서 가까운 방은 원하지 않아요. 전에 사용했는데, 약간 시끄

러웠어요. C방을 쓸 수 있나요?

남: 죄송하지만, 그 방은 여덟 명 이상의 단체를 위한 방입니다. 책장 가까이에 있는 방은 어떠세요? 책을 쉽게 이용하실 수 있어요.

여: 음… 실은, 복사기 바로 옆에 있는 방을 사용하는 게 더 좋은 것 같아요. 자료를 좀 복사해야 하거든요.

남: 알겠습니다. 이 양식을 작성해 주세요.

[해설] 여자는 입구에서 가깝지 않으면서 복사기 바로 옆에 있는 방이 좋다고 했다.

[어휘] entrance [éntrəns] (출)입구, 문 a bit 조금, 약간 access [ǽksès] 접근하다; *이용하다 copy machine 복사기 copy [kápi] 복사하다 material [mətíəriəl] 재료; *(특정 활동에 필요한) 자료

13 ③

여: 이 고속도로 휴게소는 정말 좋다.

남: 그래. 우리 지역 쇼핑몰보다 여기에 가게가 더 많은 것 같아.

여: 뭘 살 수 있는지 살펴보자.

남: 재빨리 둘러볼 시간밖에 없어. 우리 고속버스가 2시 정각에 출발해.

여: 지금 몇 시지?

남: 오후 1시 30분이야. 먼저 먹을 것을 사서 먹으면서 둘러보자.

여: 좋은 생각이야.

남: 보고 싶은 가게가 너무 많아. 버스가 30분 늦게 출발하면 좋겠어.

여: 내가 막 그 말을 하려던 참이었어.

[해설] 두 사람이 탑승할 고속버스는 오후 2시 정각에 출발한다고 했다.

[어휘] highway [háiwèi] 고속도로 rest stop 휴게소 be about to-v 막 ~하려고 하다

14 ①

남: 주말 어떻게 보냈어?

여: 매우 생산적이었어. 나는 많은 것을 했어.

남: 뭘 했는데? 가족 모임이 있다고 하지 않았어?

여: 사촌이 아파서 취소됐어.

남: 안됐다. 너 그걸 기대하고 있었잖아, 그렇지 않니?

여: 응, 하지만 대신 집안일을 했어.

남: 잘했네. 대청소를 했니?

여: 응. 구석구석 다 청소했어.

남: 분명 잘했겠지.

[해설] 여자는 주말에 사촌이 아파서 가족 모임이 취소되었고, 대신 대청소를 했다고 말했다.

[어휘] productive [prədʌ́ktiv] 생산적인 reunion [riːjúːnjən] 모임 cancel [kǽnsl] 취소하다 chore [tʃɔːr] 집안일 spring cleaning (봄에 하는) 대청소 from top to bottom 샅샅이, 구석구석

15 ⑤

여: 매일 우리는 세계 전역에서 일어나는 끔찍한 재앙들에 대해 듣습니다. 어느 것에도 대비하는 것이 최선입니다. 만일 지진이 엄습하고 여러분이 실내에 있다면, 건물에서 나가지 마세요. 대신 책상 밑에 숨거나 출입구 안에 서 계세요. 외부에 있다면, 높은 건물이나 나무로부터 떨어지세요. 그리고 운전 중이라면, 천천히 길가로 차를 대고 차에서 나오지 마세요. 기억하세요, 비상시에 무엇을 해야 할지 아는 것이 여러분의 생명을 구할 수 있습니다.

[해설] 여자는 지진이 일어났을 때 안전하게 대처하는 방법에 관해 설명하고 있다.

[어휘] terrible [térəbl] 끔찍한 disaster [dizǽstər] 재앙 prepare [pripέər] 준비하다; *대비하다 earthquake [ɔ́ːrθkwèik] 지진 hit [hit] 치다; *엄습하다 indoors [ìndɔ́ːrz] 실내에 doorway [dɔ́ːrwèi] 출입구 pull over (차를) 길가에 대다

16 ①

남: 놀이공원 입장권 한 장 주세요.

여: 30달러입니다. 회원 카드가 있으면, 30% 할인을 받으실 수 있습니다.

남: 카드는 없어요.

여: 학생 할인도 제공하고 있습니다. 학생이시면 20% 할인해 드립니다.

남: 아뇨, 학생도 아니에요. 전액을 지불해야 할 것 같네요.

여: 음, 오후 4시 이후까지 기다렸다가 구입하시면 반액 표를 사실 수 있어요.

남: 좋네요, 그렇게 할게요.

[해설] 놀이공원 입장권은 30달러인데 오후 4시 이후 반액 표를 사기로 했으므로, 남자가 지불할 금액은 15달러이다.

[어휘] offer [ɔ́ːfər] 제공하다 discount [diskáunt] 할인

17 ④

여: 진수야, 너의 내년 계획은 뭐니?

남: 나는 미국에 갈 거야. 그곳에서 공부할 계획이야.

여: 정말? 와, 굉장하다. 뭘 공부할 건데?

남: 컴퓨터 공학. 나는 프로그래머가 되고 싶거든.

여: 정말 흥미롭다! 언제 떠나니?

남: 학교는 9월에 시작하지만, 아파트를 구하기 위해 8월에 떠날 거야.

여: 아파트? 거기서 얼마나 오래 머물 계획인데?

남: 내가 학위를 따는 데 3년이 걸릴 거야.

[해설] 미국에서 얼마 동안 머물 계획인지 물었으므로, 구체적인 체류 기간을 말하는 응답이 가장 적절하다.
① 학위를 따기 쉽지 않을 거야.
② 나는 해외로 가기로 3년 전에 결심했어.
③ 거기 가는 데 14시간 정도 걸릴 거야.

⑤ 나는 떠나기 전에 영어를 공부할 계획 중이야.

어휘 plan on v-ing ~할 계획이다 programmer [próuɡræmər] 프로그래머 [문제] go abroad 해외로 가다

18 ④

남: 오늘 일은 어땠어요, 여보?
여: 좀 바빴지만, 나쁘지 않았어요.
남: 잘됐네요.
여: 그런데 집에 오는 길에 소방차를 몇 대 봤어요. 근처에 불이 났나요?
남: 네, Baker 씨 댁에 불이 났어요.
여: 정말이요? 큰불이었나요?
남: 다행히 그건 아니었어요. 소방차가 빨리 도착해서, 아무도 다치지 않았어요.
여: 감사한 일이에요. 그거 정말 다행이네요.

해설 이웃집에 불이 났지만 큰불이 아니었고 다친 사람도 없다고 했으므로, 안도의 뜻을 나타내는 응답이 가장 적절하다.
① 문 잠그는 것을 잊지 말아요.
② 며칠 동안 쉴 수 있다면 좋겠네요.
③ 우리는 그녀에게 병문안을 가야 해요.
⑤ 당신은 앞으로 더 조심해야 해요.

어휘 fire truck 소방차 neighborhood [néibərhùd] 근처, 이웃 catch fire 불이 나다 fortunately [fɔ́ːrtʃənətli] 다행스럽게도, 운 좋게도 [문제] lock [lɑk] 잠그다 take ~ off ~ 동안 쉬다

19 ①

여: 안녕하세요. 도와드릴까요?
남: 네. 약 5개월 전에 이 스마트폰을 샀는데요, 수리가 필요해요.
여: 네. 1년 동안은 전부 무상 수리입니다. 문제가 뭐죠?
남: 갑자기 작동을 멈췄는데, 이유를 모르겠어요.
여: 알겠습니다. 여기에 두고 가시면, 뭐가 잘못됐는지 저희가 알아보겠습니다.
남: 감사합니다. 언제 스마트폰을 돌려받을 수 있나요?
여: 며칠 후에요.

해설 남자는 언제 스마트폰을 돌려받을 수 있는지 물었으므로, 시기에 관한 응답이 가장 적절하다.
② 빠를수록 좋아요.
③ 갈색으로 살게요.
④ 기다리시게 해서 죄송해요.
⑤ 겨우 3주 전에 구입했어요.

어휘 find out ~을 알아내다 [문제] sooner [súːnər] 곧; *빨리 (soon의 비교급)

20 ①

남: Tim은 지난 3개월 동안 코딩 대회에서 우승하기 위해 열심히 노력했습니다. 그는 온라인 강의를 들으며, 매일 한 시간씩 문제를 풀었습니다. 주말마다 컴퓨터 공학에 관한 책을 읽었습니다. 그래서 그는 대회에서 우승할 것이라고 기대했습니다. 하지만 일어난 일은 예상 밖이었습니다. 그는 1라운드에서 탈락했습니다. 그는 매우 실망했지만, 긍정적으로 생각하기로 결심했습니다. 이런 상황에서, Tim은 자신에게 뭐라고 말하겠습니까?
Tim: 나는 실패로부터 배우고 계속 노력해야 해.

해설 Tim은 우승을 기대했던 대회에서 탈락해 매우 실망했지만 긍정적으로 생각하기로 결심했으므로, 실패로부터 배우고 계속 노력하겠다는 말이 가장 적절하다.
② 날마다 나 자신에게 동기 부여를 하기는 힘들어.
③ 내 미래에 대해 심사숙고해야 해.
④ 함께 일하는 것이 혼자 일하는 것보다 더 나아.
⑤ 내가 리더처럼 행동하면, 다른 사람들이 나를 따를 거야.

어휘 expect [ikspékt] 기대하다, 예상하다 unexpected [ʌ̀nikspéktid] 예상 밖의 eliminate [ilímənèit] 없애다; *탈락시키다 disappointed [dìsəpɔ́intid] 실망한 [문제] failure [féiljər] 실패 motivate [móutiveit] 동기를 부여하다

Dictation Test ⑯

01 1) looking for a passport holder
    2) ones with a wallet attached
    3) checkered pattern looks good

02 1) two blocks away from
    2) two floors and four bedrooms
    3) built 20 years ago
    4) cost half a million dollars

03 1) couldn't sleep last night 2) was barking all night
    3) keep him quiet 4) doesn't make so much noise

04 1) have dinner with me 2) have classes until 4 p.m.
    3) let's meet at seven o'clock

05 1) looking for a book 2) name of the author
    3) look it up 4) is checked out right now

06 1) How will the weather be 2) return your books
    3) forgot to bring my umbrella

07 1) will stay there 2) give you a ride
    3) do me a favor 4) collect my mail

08 1) was born in Mexico
    2) because of a serious traffic accident
    3) portraits of herself

09 1) places where food is served 2) prepare the food
    3) kitchen is always clean 4) at a cooking school

10 1) just looking around 2) pass me the salt
    3) stayed up late

11 1) throwing her a birthday party
    2) bought some flowers 3) baking a chocolate cake
    4) start making dinner

12 1) near the entrance 2) access the books easily
    3) right next to the copy machine

13 1) express bus leaves at two o'clock
    2) buy something to eat 3) 30 minutes late

14 1) there was a family reunion
    2) my cousin was sick 3) do a spring cleaning

15 1) don't leave the building
    2) get away from tall buildings 3) slowly pull over

16 1) get 30% off 2) offer a student discount
    3) pay full price 4) get a half-price ticket

17 1) plan on studying there 2) leaving in August
    3) How long do you plan

18 1) saw some fire trucks 2) Was it a big fire
    3) nobody was hurt

19 1) get it repaired 2) let us find out
    3) get my smartphone back

20 1) to win a coding competition
    2) he expected to win
    3) eliminated in the first round
    4) decided to think positively

실전모의고사 17회

01 ④	02 ③	03 ④	04 ⑤	05 ⑤
06 ③	07 ②	08 ④	09 ③	10 ⑤
11 ④	12 ③	13 ②	14 ③	15 ①
16 ③	17 ⑤	18 ⑤	19 ④	20 ③

01 ④

여: Jacob, 겨울이 다가오고 있어. 네 침대에 둘 더 따뜻한 담요가 필요해.

남: 그래요, 엄마. 저쪽에 담요들이 있어요. 같이 하나 골라요.

여: 그래. 난 이게 마음에 들지만, 넌 꽃무늬를 좋아하지 않을 것 같구나.

남: 맞아요. 좋아하지 않아요. 하지만 이 체크무늬가 좋네요.

여: 그래, 하지만 그건 너무 얇아. 너를 따뜻하게 하지 못할 거야. 대신 이건 어떠니?

남: 전 그 동그라미가 싫어요. 이 별무늬가 더 좋아요.

여: 어디 만져보자. 좋아, 이건 충분히 두꺼운 것 같구나.

남: 좋아요. 그럼 이걸로 사요.

[해설] 두 사람은 별무늬가 있는 담요를 사기로 했다.

[어휘] blanket [blǽŋkit] 담요 pick ~ out ~을 고르다 thin [θin] 얇은 thick [θik] 두꺼운

02 ③

남: 저기, Laura. 인터뷰는 이미 다 끝났나요?

여: 네, 방금 끝났어요.

남: 좋은 지원자가 있었어요?

여: 네, Nancy Bailey라는 사람이 있었어요. 그녀는 저와 같은 학교를 졸업했어요.

남: 그녀는 무엇을 전공했어요?

여: 신문방송학이요. 그녀는 신문사에서 일한 경험도 있어요.

남: 그녀가 우리 회사와 맞을 것 같아요?

여: 네. 그녀는 긍정적이고 열정적이에요. 그녀의 성격이 우리 회사 문화와 잘 맞을 것 같아요.

남: 잘됐네요.

[해설] 학교(여자와 같은 학교), 전공(신문방송학), 경력(신문사에서 일한 경험), 성격(긍정적이고 열정적)에 관해서는 언급되었으나, 나이는 언급되지 않았다.

[어휘] candidate [kǽndidèit] 후보자, 지원자 fit in 어울리다, 맞다 company [kʌ́mpəni] 회사 passionate [pǽʃənət] 열정적인 persanality [pàrsənǽləti] 성격, 인격 culture [kʌ́ltʃər] 문화

03 ④

[전화벨이 울린다.]

여: Pizza World에 전화 주셔서 감사합니다. 무엇을 도와드릴까요?

남: 안녕하세요. 제 이름은 Patrick인데요, 아르바이트 구인 광고를 봤어요. 아직도 사람을 찾고 계시나요?

여: 네. 저희는 피자를 배달할 사람이 필요해요.

남: 근무 시간은 어떻게 되나요?

여: 평일 하루에 4시간이고, 오후 5시부터 시작해요.

남: 아, 그거 좋네요. 그리고 급여가 얼마인지 말씀해 주실 수 있나요?

여: 한 시간에 10달러를 받으시게 될 거예요. 관심 있으시면 내일 잠깐 들르시는 게 어때요?

남: 좋아요. 그때 뵐게요.

해설 남자는 피자 가게의 아르바이트 구인 광고를 봤다며 근무 조건에 대해 문의했다.

어휘 advertisement [æ̀dvərtáizmənt] 광고 deliver [dilívər] 배달하다 pay [pei] 급여 come by 잠깐 들르다

04 ⑤

여: 발목이 너무 아파. 더 이상 못 가겠어.

남: 뭐? 힘내. 정상까지 가는 데 1시간도 안 걸릴 거야.

여: 미안하지만, 난 그만할래. 한 발짝도 못 딛겠어.

남: 알았어. 저기 쉼터에 가서 기다리는 게 어때?

여: 좋은 생각이야. 너 혼자 하이킹을 완주하면 되겠다.

남: 괜찮아? 두어 시간 걸릴 거야.

여: 난 괜찮을 거야. 2시간 뒤에 보자.

남: 알았어. 지금 오후 3시니까, 5시에 만나.

여: 좋아.

해설 두 사람은 남자가 정상에 다녀오는 2시간 뒤인 오후 5시에 만나기로 했다.

어휘 ankle [ǽŋkl] 발목 shelter [ʃéltər] 쉼터

05 ⑤

여: 내 열쇠를 못 찾겠어.

남: 마지막으로 어디에서 그걸 가지고 있었는지 기억 나니?

여: 아, 이런. 오늘 아침 열쇠를 차에 두고 잠근 것 같아. 믿을 수가 없어. 어떻게 해야 하지?

남: 다른 열쇠는 없니?

여: 집에 하나 있어. 하지만 집 열쇠도 차 안에 뒀어.

남: 자물쇠 수리 기사를 부르는 게 어때? 누군가를 빨리 보내 줄 거야.

여: 하지만 20분 후에 유치원에 딸을 데리러 가야 하거든. 자물쇠 수리 기사를 기다릴 시간이 없어.

해설 여자는 열쇠를 차 안에 두고 잠근 것 같은데 곧 딸을 데리러 가야 하므로 걱정스러울(worried) 것이다.

① 자랑스러운 ② 신이 난 ③ 질투하는 ④ 놀란

어휘 lock [lɑk] 잠그다, 넣어 두다 locksmith [lɑ́:ksmiθ] 자물쇠 수리 기사 kindergarten [kíndərgà:rtn] 유치원

06 ③

① 남: 실례합니다, 흰색 셔츠를 찾고 있어요.
　여: 저쪽 스웨터 옆에 있어요.

② 남: 신용 카드로 지불할 수 있나요?
　여: 죄송합니다, 현금만 받습니다.

③ 남: 이 셔츠에 구멍이 있어요.
　여: 아, 그 점 죄송합니다. 새것으로 교환하시겠어요?

④ 남: 가장 가까운 은행이 어디죠? 돈을 좀 인출하고 싶어요.
　여: 저쪽에 있는 ATM을 이용하시면 됩니다.

⑤ 남: 얼마예요?
　여: 30달러예요. 카드로 지불하실 건가요, 현금으로 지불하실 건가요?

해설 환불 창구에서 남자가 구멍 난 셔츠를 들고 점원과 이야기를 나누고 있는 상황이다.

어휘 accept [əksépt] 받다 cash [kæʃ] 현금 hole [houl] 구멍 exchange [ikstʃéindʒ] 교환하다 withdraw [wiðdrɔ́:] 인출하다

07 ②

남: 안녕, Amber. 무슨 일이야?

여: 우리 동아리가 학교 축제에서 연극 공연을 해.

남: 잘됐다. 그래서 뭐가 문제야? 좋은 배역을 맡지 않았어?

여: 실은, 내가 그 연극에서 주인공을 연기할 거야.

남: 잘됐네. 축하해.

여: 고마워. 하지만 상황이 좋지 않아.

남: 어려운 배역이야?

여: 그런 문제가 아니야. 우리의 연극 표가 거의 팔리지 않았어.

남: 걱정 마. 사람들이 곧 사기 시작할 거야.

여: 정말 그렇게 생각해? 어쩌면 네가 친구들에게 좀 팔아 줄 수도 있겠다.

남: 물론이지. 기꺼이 할 수 있지.

해설 여자는 학교 축제에서 자신의 동아리가 공연하는 연극 표가 거의 팔리지 않아서 남자에게 표를 팔아 달라고 부탁했다.

어휘 play [plei] 연극; 연기하다 role [roul] 역할; *배역 main character 주인공 Congratulations. [kəngrætʃəléiʃənz] 축하해.

08 ④

여: 학생 여러분, 주목해 주세요! 내일 우리는 현대 미술관으로 견학을 갈 겁니다. 여러분은 오전 9시까지 학교에 도착해야 합니다. 제시간

에 올 수 있도록 노력해 주시겠어요? 내일은 교복을 입을 필요가 없습니다. 평상복을 입어도 됩니다. 작은 공책과 펜을 가져와야 합니다. 자기 도시락도 가져와야 합니다. 우리는 오후 4시까지 학교로 돌아올 겁니다. 여러분 모두 내일 즐거운 시간을 보내길 바랍니다.

해설 장소(현대 미술관), 집합 시각(오전 9시), 복장(평상복), 준비물(작은 공책과 펜)에 관해서는 언급되었으나, 이동 방법은 언급되지 않았다.

어휘 field trip 견학, 현장 학습 on time 제시간에 uniform [júːnifɔ̀ːrm] 교복, 유니폼 casually [kǽʒuəli] (복장이) 편안하게 return [ritə́ːrn] 돌아오다

09 ③

남: 이것들은 인쇄된 간행물입니다. 이것들은 종종 고품질 종이에 인쇄됩니다. 이것들은 일반적으로 기사, 사진, 광고를 담고 있습니다. 각각은 고유한 특징이 있습니다. 어떤 것들은 가벼운 읽기 자료로 가득 차 있는 반면, 다른 것들은 더 전문적입니다. 이것들은 보통 매주 또는 매월 정기적으로 발행됩니다. 이것들은 서점에서 구입하거나 집으로 배달될 수 있습니다. 도서관이나 인터넷에서도 볼 수 있습니다.

해설 매주 또는 매월 정기적으로 발행되며, 고품질 종이에 기사, 사진, 광고를 담고 있는 것은 잡지이다.

어휘 publication [pʌ̀bləkéiʃən] 출판; *출판물, 간행물 high-quality [haikwáːləti] 고품질의 typically [típikəli] 일반적으로 contain [kəntéin] ~이 들어 있다, ~을 포함하다 article [ɑ́ːrtikl] 글, 기사 characteristic [kæ̀riktərístik] 특징 be filled with ~로 가득 차다 specialized [spéʃəlàizd] 전문적인 purchase [pə́ːrtʃəs] 사다, 구입하다

10 ⑤

① 여: 이 바지에 대해 항의를 해야겠어요.
　남: 문제가 뭔지 여쭤봐도 될까요?
② 여: 너 축구를 해 본 적 있니?
　남: 아니, 나는 스포츠를 좋아하지 않아.
③ 여: 너 어젯밤에 나에게 전화했었니?
　남: 응, 하지만 네 전화기가 꺼져 있었어.
④ 여: 영화에 관해 얘기해 줄래?
　남: 피카소의 삶에 관한 것이고, 아주 재미있어.
⑤ 여: 쓰레기를 어디에 둘까요?
　남: 조만간에요.

해설 쓰레기를 어디에 둘지 물었으므로, 구체적인 장소에 대한 응답이 와야 자연스럽다.

어휘 complain [kəmpléin] 불평[항의]하다 turn off ~을 끄다 life [laif] 삶 garbage [gɑ́ːrbidʒ] 쓰레기 sooner or later 조만간

11 ④

[전화벨이 울린다.]
남: 여보세요, 119입니다. 긴급 상황이 무엇입니까?
여: 저희 아버지가 계단에서 굴러 떨어지셨어요. 다리가 부러진 것 같아요.
남: 주소가 어떻게 되세요?
여: Main가 1123번지예요.
남: 네. 지금 구급차를 보내겠습니다. 하지만 수화기를 들고 기다려 주세요.
여: 서둘러 주세요. 아버지가 좋아 보이지 않으세요. 움직이지를 못하세요.
남: 구급차가 가는 중입니다. 누워 계실 수 있습니까?
여: 가능할 것 같아요.
남: 그럼 아버지를 눕히시고 움직이시지 말라고 하세요. 곧 구조원이 도착할 겁니다.
여: 알겠습니다.

해설 남자는 여자에게 아버지를 눕히고 움직이시지 않게 하라고 했다.

어휘 fall down the stairs 계단에서 굴러 떨어지다 address [ədrés, ǽdres] 주소 ambulance [ǽmbjələns] 구급차 stay on the line 수화기를 들고 기다리다 lie down 눕다[누워 있다] help [help] 도움; *도움이 되는 사람

12 ③

여: 무엇을 도와드릴까요, 손님?
남: 3월 30일 뉴욕행 항공편을 예약하고 싶어요. 이용 가능한 좌석이 있나요?
여: 네, 빈 좌석이 몇 개 있습니다. 일등석을 원하시나요, 아니면 일반석을 원하시나요?
남: 일반석이요. 짧은 비행이어서, 추가 비용의 가치는 없는 것 같아서요.
여: 알겠습니다. 그리고 창가 쪽 좌석으로 하시겠어요, 아니면 통로 쪽 좌석으로 하시겠어요?
남: 통로 쪽 좌석으로요. 출구 근처에 좌석이 있나요?
여: 네. 500달러입니다.
남: 좋아요, 그걸로 할게요.

해설 남자는 일반석 중에서 출구 근처에 있는 통로 쪽 좌석을 예약하기로 했다.

어휘 flight [flait] 항공편 several [sévrəl] 몇몇의 first-class [fə́ːstklǽs] 일등석(의) economy class 일반석 worth [wəːrθ] ~의 가치가 있는 aisle [ail] 통로 exit [éksit] 출구

13 ②

[전화벨이 울린다.]
여: 안녕하십니까, Beachside 호텔입니다.

남: 안녕하세요. 1월 13일로 예약을 하고 싶어요.
여: 좋아요. 트윈 침대가 있는 객실을 원하시나요?
남: 네. 체크인 시간은 언제인가요?
여: 오후 3시 이후 언제든지 체크인하실 수 있습니다.
남: 좋네요. 공항에서 호텔까지 가는 가장 좋은 방법은 무엇인가요?
여: 무료 셔틀 서비스가 있습니다. 항공편이 몇 시에 도착하나요?
남: 오후 1시에 도착할 거예요.
여: 저희 셔틀버스는 공항에서 오후 2시, 4시, 6시에 출발해요.
남: 좋네요. 2시 버스가 딱 맞을 것 같아요.

해설 남자는 항공편이 오후 1시에 공항에 도착하기 때문에, 2시에 출발하는 호텔 셔틀버스를 타면 딱 맞겠다고 했다.

어휘 arrive [əráiv] 도착하다 depart from ~에서 출발하다

14 ③

여: 안녕, Jake. 네게 토마토 몇 개 줄게.
남: 오, 나 토마토 좋아해. 고마워. 어디서 났어?
여: 내가 직접 재배했어.
남: 정말? 집에서 토마토를 재배해?
여: 아니. 우리 가족이 시골에 작은 채소밭을 가지고 있어.
남: 멋지다.
여: 응, 지난봄에 그 토마토들을 심었고 어제 첫 수확을 했어.
남: 멋지다. 나에게 나눠 줘서 고마워.

해설 여자는 지난봄에 토마토를 심고 어제 첫 수확을 했다고 했다.

어휘 countryside [kʌ́ntrisaid] 시골, 지방 harvest [háːrvist] 수확 share [ʃɛər] 공유하다; *나눠 주다

15 ①

여: 안녕하세요, 여러분! 주목해 주시겠습니까? 저는 저희 모든 여름 상품에 대한 대규모 할인을 알려 드리고자 합니다. 저희는 수영복, 슬리퍼, 비치타월, 자외선 차단제를 포함한 모든 바닷가 용품에 대해 40% 할인을 제공합니다. 하지만 이 대규모 할인은 오늘만 진행합니다! 모든 가격은 내일 정상으로 돌아갈 것입니다. 이 좋은 조건은 온라인으로도 제공되니, 꼭 이용하세요!

해설 오늘 하루 모든 바닷가 용품을 40% 할인 판매한다고 했으므로, 특별 행사에 대한 홍보임을 알 수 있다.

어휘 flip-flop [flípflàːp] (끈을 끼워서 신는) 슬리퍼 sunblock [sʌnblak] 자외선 차단제 normal [nɔ́ːrməl] 보통의; *정상 take advantage of ~을 이용하다

16 ③

남: 안녕하세요. 무엇을 도와드릴까요?
여: 다음 주 〈지킬앤하이드〉 표 2장 주세요.

남: 네. 한 장당 100달러입니다.
여: 저는 극장 회원 자격이 있어요. 할인받을 수 있나요?
남: 네, 받으실 수 있어요. 회원 카드를 보여 주시면, 30% 할인받으실 거예요.
여: 잘됐네요. 여기 제 회원 카드입니다.
남: 네. 원래 총액은 200달러인데, 이 금액이 30% 할인 후의 새로운 총액이에요.

해설 원래 표 두 장의 가격은 200달러인데 극장 회원 카드가 있어서 30% 할인된다고 했으므로, 여자가 지불할 금액은 140달러이다.

어휘 membership [mémbərʃip] 회원 (자격·신분) get a discount 할인받다

17 ⑤

남: 나 어때 보여? 오늘 밤에 파티에 가거든.
여: 어디 보자… 네 셔츠랑 바지가 아주 멋져 보여.
남: 고마워. 그리고 나는 이 재킷을 입을 거야.
여: 좋은 선택이야. 넥타이 맬 거니?
남: 응. 이 두 개 중에 결정하려던 참이었어.
여: 솔직히 말해서, 둘 중 어떤 것도 보기 좋을 것 같지 않아.
남: 정말? 넥타이를 고르는 건 항상 어려워. 날 위해 하나 골라 줄래?
여: **그래. 이 파란색 넥타이 어때?**

해설 남자는 여자에게 넥타이를 골라 달라고 부탁했으므로, 어울리는 넥타이를 제안하는 응답이 가장 적절하다.
① 나는 집에 있는 편이 낫겠어.
② 그 셔츠도 멋져 보이는구나.
③ 나는 그림을 꽤 잘 그려.
④ 아니, 나는 그곳에 너를 데리러 갈 수 없어.

어휘 choice [tʃɔis] 선택 decide [disáid] 결정하다 to be honest 솔직히 말해서

18 ⑤

여: 나 집에 왔어요!
남: 당신 행복해 보이네요. 뭐 좋은 일 있었어요?
여: 네. 직장에서 프로젝트가 끝났는데, 상사가 그걸 아주 마음에 들어 했어요. 난 정말 기뻐요.
남: 잘됐네요! 당신이 정말 자랑스러워요. 축하할 겸 저녁 외식을 하는 게 어때요?
여: 좋은 생각이네요. 생각한 곳이 있나요?
남: **시내에 있는 멕시코 음식점은 어때요?**

해설 저녁 외식 장소로 생각해 둔 곳이 있는지 물었으므로, 음식점을 제안하는 응답이 가장 적절하다.
① 미안하지만, 난 지금 바빠요.
② 신용 카드로 지불하고 싶어요.
③ 난 그곳이 싫어요. 거기는 너무 붐비거든요.
④ 내일 7시가 좋을 것 같아요.

[어휘] be proud of ~을 자랑스러워하다 celebrate [séləbrèit] 축하하다, 기념하다 have ~ in mind ~을 염두에 두다, ~을 생각하다

[어휘] midterm [mídtə̀ːrm] 중간고사 loud [laud] (소리가) 큰 concentrate [kánsəntrèit] 집중하다

19 ④

여: 안녕하세요, Drake. 자리에 앉으세요.

남: 감사합니다, Jones 씨.

여: 손님들로부터의 최근 불만에 대해 당신과 이야기를 하고 싶었습니다.

남: 아! 무엇에 관한 것들이었나요?

여: 음, 이번 주에 몇몇 손님들이 말하기를 당신이 그들에게 무례했다고 하네요.

남: 아, 죄송합니다. 제가 설명할게요. 제가 이번 주에 몸이 좋지 않았는데, 몇몇 손님들이 알아차렸을지도 모르겠어요. 하지만 다음에는 더 주의하겠습니다.

여: 알겠습니다. 하지만 당신의 몸 상태가 어떻든, 늘 손님들에게 정중해야 합니다.

남: 맞습니다. 다시는 그런 일이 없을 거예요.

[해설] 여자는 남자의 불친절에 대한 손님들의 불만을 들었다며 항상 손님들에게 정중할 것을 당부했으므로, 이를 수긍하고 시정하겠다고 말하는 응답이 가장 적절하다.

① 그게 그들의 잘못이라고 생각하지 않아요.

② 무슨 말씀인지 전혀 이해되지 않아요.

③ 그저 불평만 하는 것은 도움이 될 수 없어요.

⑤ 손님이 정말 많아서 제가 바빴어요.

[어휘] take a seat 자리에 앉다 recent [ríːsnt] 최근의 complaint [kəmpléint] 불평, 불만 customer [kʌ́stəmər] 손님 rude [ruːd] 무례한 explain [ikspléin] 설명하다 notice [nóutis] 알아차리다 polite [pəláit] 예의 바른, 정중한 [문제] fault [fɔːlt] 잘못

20 ③

남: Jessica는 고등학생입니다. 내일 중간고사가 있어서, 그녀는 학교 도서관에서 공부하고 있습니다. Jessica의 옆에 앉은 남자는 음악을 듣고 있습니다. 그의 헤드폰에서 나오는 소리가 너무 커서 Jessica는 집중할 수가 없습니다. 도서관이 꽉 차서, 이용할 수 있는 다른 좌석이 없습니다. 이런 상황에서, Jessica는 옆에 있는 남자에게 뭐라고 말하겠습니까?

Jessica: 음악 소리를 낮춰 주시겠어요?

[해설] 도서관에서 옆 사람의 헤드폰으로 들리는 음악 소리가 너무 커서 공부에 집중할 수가 없으므로, 음악 소리를 낮춰 달라는 말이 가장 적절하다.

① 힙합 좋아하세요?

② 이 노래 제목이 뭔가요?

④ 이 근처에 빈자리가 있나요?

⑤ 헤드폰을 어디서 사셨나요?

Dictation Test 🕗   pp. 220~227

01 1) like this checkered pattern 2) prefer these stars
     3) it's thick enough

02 1) graduated from the same school
     2) experience working for a newspaper
     3) positive and passionate

03 1) looking for someone
     2) need someone to deliver pizzas
     3) how much the pay is 4) how about coming by

04 1) take less than an hour 2) in two hours
     3) meet you at five o'clock

05 1) may have locked my keys 2) locked in the car
     3) supposed to pick up

06 1) only accept cash 2) exchange it for a new one
     3) withdraw some money 4) pay by card or cash

07 1) get a good role 2) things are not going well
     3) Almost no tickets 4) sell some to your friends

08 1) arrive at the school 2) may dress casually
     3) should bring your own lunch

09 1) printed publications
     2) contain articles, photographs, and advertisements
     3) are published regularly

10 1) want to complain 2) was turned off
     3) Sooner or later

11 1) fell down the stairs 2) sending an ambulance
     3) lay him down

12 1) any seats available 2) worth the extra money
     3) an aisle seat 4) near the exit

13 1) any time after 3:00 2) have a free shuttle service
     3) departs from the airport 4) two o'clock bus

14 1) grow tomatoes at home
     2) has a small vegetable garden
     3) got my first harvest

15 1) announce a big sale 2) offering a 40% discount
     3) huge sale is taking place

16 1) They're $100 each 2) get a 30% discount
     3) total was $200

17 1) How do I look 2) either one would look good
   3) pick one out
18 1) something good happen 2) so proud of you
   3) have a place in mind
19 1) recent complaints from our customers
   2) you were rude 3) haven't been feeling well
   4) no matter how you feel
20 1) studying at the school library 2) so loud that
   3) no other seats available

실전모의고사 18회

pp. 228~229

01 ③	02 ④	03 ③	04 ③	05 ⑤
06 ③	07 ①	08 ⑤	09 ③	10 ③
11 ④	12 ④	13 ④	14 ③	15 ①
16 ③	17 ⑦	18 ②	19 ⑤	20 ④

01 ③

남: Lucy에게 줄 선물을 찾고 있니?
여: 응. 이 보석함들 어떤 것 같아?
남: 멋지다. 그 애가 귀여운 것을 좋아하잖아.
여: 그중 몇 개는 음악이 나와. 음악이 있는 것과 없는 것, 어느 게 나은 것 같아?
남: 음악이 나오는 게 나은 것 같아.
여: 동감이야. 그리고 뚜껑을 열면 어떻게 되는지 봐.
남: 와! 발레리나가 음악에 맞춰 돌고 있네.
여: 이건 유니콘이 있고, 저건 인어가 있어.
남: 유니콘이 있는 게 제일 귀여운 것 같아.
여: 동의해. 그걸 사야겠다.

[해설] 여자는 뚜껑을 열면 유니콘이 음악에 맞춰 돌아가는 보석함을 사기로 했다.

[어휘] jewelry [dʒúːəlri] 보석 lid [lid] 뚜껑 spin [spin] 돌다
mermaid [mɔ́ːrmèid] 인어

02 ④

여: Gary, 무슨 일 있니?
남: 아무 일도 없어. 단지 내일 학교에서 발표를 해야 해.

여: 아, 좋겠다. 나는 발표하는 걸 좋아하거든.
남: 어떻게 너는 그렇게 자신감이 있니?
여: 음, 긴장을 푸는 게 중요해. 불안감을 극복하기 위해 노력해야 해. 그리고 많이 연습해야 해. 나는 항상 실제 발표 전에 가족들 앞에서 예행연습을 해.
남: 그렇구나. 하지만 발표하는 동안에 해야 할 말을 잊어버리면 어쩌지?
여: 메모 카드 몇 장에 모든 것을 적어. 반드시 읽기 쉽게 만들어. 색연필을 사용해서 중요한 사항을 강조해도 돼.
남: 좋은 생각이다! 조언 고마워.
여: 천만에. 네가 더 많이 준비되어 있을수록, 너는 더 편안함을 느낄 거야.

[해설] 발표 능력 향상 방안으로 거울 앞에서 연습하기는 언급되지 않았다.

[어휘] give a speech 연설하다, 발표하다 confident [kánfidənt] 자신감 있는 overcome [òuvərkʌ́m] 극복하다 anxiety [æŋzáiəti] 불안 rehearse [rihə́ːrs] 예행연습을 하다 actual [ǽktʃuəl] 실제의 what if ~? ~면 어쩌지? make sure 반드시 ~하도록 하다 highlight [háilàit] 강조하다, 눈에 띄게 하다

03 ③

남: 오늘은 어떻게 해 드릴까요?
여: 새로운 머리 모양을 시도해 보고 싶어요. 파마를 하는 게 보기 좋을 것 같아요.
남: 네, 제 생각에도 파마가 손님에게 잘 어울릴 것 같아요. 학생이세요?
여: 네, 서울 중학교에 다녀요. 왜요?
남: 파마를 특가로 해 드리고 있거든요. 학생은 학생증을 보여 주기만 하면 20퍼센트 할인을 받을 수 있어요.
여: 좋은데요! 그런데 제가 며칠 전에 학생증을 잃어버렸어요. 그래도 할인받을 수 있는 방법이 있을까요?
남: 죄송하지만, 학생증 없이는 할인해 드릴 수 없어요.

[해설] 남자는 학생증 없이 할인을 받을 수 있냐는 여자의 요청을 거절하고 있다.

[어휘] suit [suːt] 어울리다 student ID 학생증

04 ③

여: 오늘 우리 일정이 어떻게 되나요?
남: 첫 번째로 머무는 곳은 Royal 정원입니다. 그곳에서 오후 2시에 출발할 겁니다.
여: 그렇게 오래 머무르나요? 지금 오전 11시인데요.
남: 정원을 산책하는 데 두 시간 정도 보낼 겁니다.
여: 그 후에 무엇을 하나요?
남: 오후 1시부터 2시까지 점심을 먹을 겁니다.
여: 점심은 뭔가요?
남: 전통 현지 음식을 먹을 겁니다. 분명 그걸 좋아할 거예요.

여: 기대되네요.

남: 지금 첫 번째 목적지에 도착했습니다. 정원을 답사하고, 여기서 1시에 뵙겠습니다.

여: 네. 그때 봐요.

[해설] 지금은 오전 11시이고, 정원을 두 시간 정도 산책한 후 1시에 만나기로 했다.

[어휘] stop [stap] 멈추다; *체재, 머무름 stroll around 산책하다 destination [dèstinéiʃən] 목적지 explore [iksplɔ́:r] 답사하다

05 ⑤

남: 도와드릴까요?

여: 네. 제 고양이가 아픈 것 같은데, 이유를 모르겠어요. 많이 먹지 않고 거의 온종일 자요. 전에는 아주 활동적이었거든요.

남: 그렇군요. 제가 좀 살펴볼게요. [잠시 후]

여: 어떤가요?

남: 음, 가벼운 감기에 걸린 것 같네요. 하지만 더 자세히 봐야 할 것 같아요. 고양이를 하루 두고 가시겠어요?

여: 물론입니다. 괜찮아지면 좋겠네요.

남: 저희가 잘 돌봐 줄게요. 너무 걱정하지 마세요.

[해설] 남자는 고양이의 건강 상태를 더 자세히 살펴보기 위해 하루 이곳에 두고 가라고 했으므로, 두 사람이 대화하는 장소로 가장 적절한 곳은 동물 병원이다.

[어휘] used to-v ~하곤 했다, ~이었다 active [ǽktiv] 활동적인 come down with (병에) 걸리다 mild [maild] (정도가) 가벼운

06 ③

① 여: 너 숙제 다 했니?
   남: 네, 이미 끝냈어요.
② 여: 네 공 어디에 있니?
   남: 잊어버린 것 같아요. 학교에 두고 왔을 거예요.
③ 여: 창문 근처에서는 축구를 하지 말아야지.
   남: 죄송해요. 이제부터 더 조심할게요.
④ 여: 밖이 추워. 재킷을 입어야 해.
   남: 네. 그거 어디에 있어요?
⑤ 여: 내가 창문 닦는 것 좀 도와주겠니?
   남: 네! 이 천을 써도 되나요?

[해설] 남자아이가 축구공으로 유리창을 깬 상황이다.

[어휘] from now on 이제부터, 앞으로 cloth [klɔ:θ] 천

07 ①

남: 안녕, Jenny. 너 기분 좋아 보인다. 무슨 좋은 일 있었니?
여: 응. 내가 세계 리더십 프로그램 구성원이 됐어.

남: 와, 축하해.

여: 고마워. 첫 번째 리더십 워크숍에 참가하기 위해 다음 주에 일본에 갈 거야.

남: 잘됐네! 하지만 수업에 빠져야겠네.

여: 응, 맞아. 이미 그에 관해 교수님께 말씀드렸어. 일본에서 돌아온 후에 네 공책을 빌릴 수 있을까?

남: 물론이지, 문제없어.

[해설] 여자는 일본에 다녀오는 동안 수업에 빠지게 되어서, 돌아온 후에 남자의 공책을 빌려 달라고 부탁했다.

[어휘] accept [əksépt] 받다; *(구성원으로) 받아들이다 global [glóubəl] 세계적인 professor [prəfésər] 교수 borrow [bárou] 빌리다

08 ⑤

여: 블로그 하기나 보도하기, 시 쓰기를 좋아하나요? 어떤 것이든, 여러분의 감정과 경험을 저희와 공유해 주시길 바랍니다. 〈Teen News〉의 청소년 기자에 지원하세요. 10세에서 18세 사이의 누구나 지원할 수 있습니다. 청소년 기자로서, 여러분의 블로그 게시물을 저희 웹 사이트에 링크할 수 있습니다. 여러분의 콘텐츠이기 때문에 무엇을 쓸지 여러분이 결정합니다. 저희는 여러분의 글을 편집하는 데 도움을 드리며 저작물을 업로드할 때 도움을 제공합니다. 친구와 가족이 여러분의 게시물을 읽을 수 있을 뿐만 아니라, 여러분의 블로그에 메시지를 남길 수도 있습니다. 청소년 기자가 되기 위해 오늘 지원하세요!

[해설] 저작물 종류(블로그, 보도, 시), 지원 자격(10세에서 18세 사이의 누구나), 활동 내용(자신의 블로그 게시물을 웹 사이트에 링크), 혜택(글 편집 및 저작물 업로드 시 도움)에 관해서는 언급되었으나, 지원 방법은 언급되지 않았다.

[어휘] reporting [ripɔ́:rtiŋ] 보도 emotion [imóuʃən] 감정 youth [ju:θ] 젊음; *청소년 reporter [ripɔ́:rtər] 기자 content [kəntént] 내용(물), 콘텐츠 on hand (도움을) 구할[얻을] 수 있는 edit [édit] 편집하다 support [səpɔ́:rt] 지원, 도움

09 ③

남: 에너지 낭비를 줄여야 한다는 것에 모두가 동의합니다. 그런데 어떻게 할 수 있을까요? 방을 나갈 때는 항상 불을 끄는 것으로 시작할 수 있습니다. 또한, 겨울에 추우면, 실내 온도를 높이지 마세요. 대신, 스웨터를 입거나 따뜻한 양말을 신으세요. 먹을 것을 찾을 때, 냉장고 문을 열고 생각하지 마세요. 문을 열기 전에 결정하세요. 이 모든 사소한 것들이 시간이 지나면 결국 큰 절약이 될 수 있습니다.

[해설] 에너지 절약을 위한 실천 방안들을 말하고 있다.

[어휘] agree [əgrí] 동의하다 reduce [ridjú:s] 줄이다 waste [weist] 낭비 turn up the heat (실내) 온도를 높이다 add up to 결국 ~가 되다 saving [séiviŋ] 절약

10 ③

① 남: 난 이번 주 일요일에 암벽 등반을 하러 갈 계획이야.
　 여: 정말 조심해.
② 남: 내가 경기에서 져서 슬퍼.
　 여: 기운 내! 다음 달에 다시 해 볼 수 있어.
③ 남: 어떻게 지냈니?
　 여: 전에 중국에 가 본 적이 있어.
④ 남: 계좌를 하나 개설하고 싶습니다.
　 여: 네. 이 신청서를 작성해 주시겠어요?
⑤ 남: 호텔에 도착하는 데 얼마나 걸리나요?
　 여: 한 시간 반 걸릴 겁니다.

[해설] 어떻게 지냈는지 안부를 묻는 말에 중국에 가 본 적이 있다는 응답은 어색하다.

[어휘] match [mætʃ] 성냥; *경기, 시합 open an account 계좌를 개설하다 application form 신청서

11 ④

남: 엄마랑 아빠가 몇 시쯤 집에 돌아오셔?
여: 8시경이라고 말씀하셨어.
남: 음… 여행에서 돌아오시면 매우 피곤하실 거야. 도착하시기 전에 우리가 집을 청소하고 저녁 식사를 준비하는 게 어때?
여: 정말 좋은 생각이다. 기뻐하실 거야.
남: 맞아. 내가 거실을 청소하는 동안, 네가 요리를 하는 게 어때?
여: 좋아. 저녁으로 카레를 만들게.
남: 좋아, 부모님께서 좋아하실 거야. 시작하자.

[해설] 부모님이 여행에서 돌아오시기 전에, 남자는 거실을 청소하고 여자가 저녁 식사를 준비하기로 했다.

[어휘] clean up ~을 치우다[청소하다] pleased [pli:zd] 기쁜 curry [ká:ri] 카레

12 ④

여: 우리 어디서 피크닉 할까?
남: 저 나무 아래 어때? 그늘이 있어서, 시원하게 있을 수 있어.
여: 너무 추울 수도 있을 것 같아. 나는 양지에 앉고 싶어. 연못 옆에 앉는 건 어떨까?
남: 거기에는 사람이 너무 많아. 피크닉 하는 동안 성가신 걸 원치 않아.
여: 음… 나는 벤치에 앉고 싶은데, 이미 다른 사람들이 차지했네.
남: 그럼 아이스크림 트럭 옆에 앉는 건 어때? 벤치에 앉아 있는 사람들이 일어나면 우리가 거기로 쉽게 옮길 수 있어.
여: 좋아!

[해설] 벤치에 앉아 있는 사람들이 일어나면 두 사람이 쉽게 자리를 옮길 수 있도록 아이스크림 트럭 옆에서 피크닉을 하기로 했다.

[어휘] shade [ʃeid] 그늘 in the sun 양지에 bother [báðər] 성가시

게 하다

13 ④

남: 안녕하세요, Michelle. 사장님께 말씀드릴 게 있어요.
여: 죄송하지만, 사장님은 지금 회의 중이세요.
남: 회의가 언제 시작됐나요?
여: 3시에요. 그런데 회의는 곧 끝날 거예요.
남: 몇 시에 끝날 것 같아요?
여: 회의는 4시에 끝날 예정이에요.
남: 알겠습니다. 그러면 15분만 기다리면 되겠군요.
여: 네. 여기 앉으세요. 마실 것 좀 드릴까요?
남: 아닙니다, 괜찮습니다.

[해설] 회의가 4시에 끝난다고 하자 15분만 기다리면 되겠다고 했으므로, 현재 시각은 3시 45분이다.

[어휘] boss [bɔːs] 상관; *사장 be scheduled to-v ~할 예정이다

14 ③

남: 우리 다음 수업이 뭐야?
여: 체육이야.
남: 아, 이런! 체육복을 집에 두고 왔어.
여: 오늘 우리 체육이 있는 거 몰랐어?
남: 알았어. 하지만 어제 체육복을 세탁하고, 학교에 다시 가져오는 것을 잊었어.
여: 네 친구 중 한 명에게서 체육복을 빌려야겠다.
남: 좋은 생각이야. 만약 내가 늦으면, 선생님께 이유를 말씀드려 줘.
여: 알았어.

[해설] 남자는 어제 체육복을 세탁하고, 학교에 다시 가져오는 것을 잊었다고 했다.

[어휘] P.E. 체육(= physical education) gym clothes 체육복

15 ①

여: 안녕하세요, 학생 여러분. 학교 영양사 Phillips 박사입니다. 요즘 학생들이 학교 급식에서 채소만 빼고 뭐든 먹는 경향이 있습니다. 채소는 매일의 식단에 포함되어야 하는 필수 식품입니다. 비타민과 미네랄의 중요한 공급원이므로, 채소가 풍부한 식단이 여러분의 건강과 성장에 중요합니다. 우리 학교는 학생들에게 필수 영양소가 포함된 매일의 점심을 제공합니다. 그러니 학생들은 학교 급식에 포함된 채소를 먹어야 합니다. 감사합니다.

[해설] 채소는 건강에 중요한 영양소의 공급원이라고 말하며, 학생들에게 학교 급식에 포함된 채소 섭취를 장려하고 있다.

[어휘] nutritionist [nuːtríʃənist] 영양사 tend to-v ~하는 경향이 있다 vital [váitəl] 필수적인 mineral [mínərəl] 미네랄 rich in ~이

풍부한 essential [isénʃəl] 필수적인 nutrient [nú:triənt] 영양소

16 ③

여: 3월 7일 도쿄행 항공권을 구입하고 싶습니다.
남: 편도십니까, 아니면 왕복이십니까?
여: 왕복이요. 2주 후에 돌아오고 싶어요.
남: 알겠습니다. 일등석, 비즈니스석, 아니면 일반석을 타시겠습니까?
여: 비즈니스석은 얼마인가요?
남: 900달러입니다.
여: 생각했던 것보다 비싸군요. 일반석은 얼마죠?
남: 비즈니스석 표의 반값입니다.
여: 좋습니다, 일반석 표로 주세요.

[해설] 일반석은 비즈니스석(900달러)의 반값이라고 했으므로, 여자가 지불할 금액은 450달러이다.

[어휘] return [ritə́:rn] 왕복; 돌아오다 business class (여객기의) 이등석, 비즈니스석

17 ③

남: 얘, Lucy. 중요한 역사 시험에 대한 준비가 됐니?
여: 아니 아직. 아직도 공부할 게 많아.
남: 나도! 내일까지 준비가 될 것 같지 않아. 끔찍해.
여: 무슨 말이야? 소식 못 들었어?
남: 소식? 무슨 소식?
여: 시험이 다음 주로 연기되었다고 선생님께서 공지하셨어.
남: 확실해?
여: 응. 어제 학교 웹 사이트에 게시됐어.
남: 그 말을 들으니 정말 기뻐!

[해설] 남자는 시험이 내일인 줄 알고 있었는데 여자가 다음 주로 연기되었다는 소식을 알려 주었으므로, 기쁨이나 안도를 나타내는 응답이 가장 적절하다.
① 다시는 늦지 마.
② 너는 몇 등급 받았니?
④ 미안해. 너한테 말하는 걸 잊었어.
⑤ 내가 시험을 놓치다니 믿을 수 없어!

[어휘] announce [ənáuns] 알리다, 공지하다 delay [diléi] 연기하다 post [poust] 발송하다; *게시하다

18 ②

남: 너 무척 기분 좋아 보인다. 무슨 일이야?
여: 내가 요리 대회를 준비하던 것 기억하니?
남: 응! 우승했니?
여: 응. 일등상을 탔어.

남: 축하해! 넌 대회에서 뭘 만들었니?
여: 꿀 소스를 넣은 생선을 요리했어. 내가 그 소스의 요리법을 직접 만들었지!
남: 네가 우승했다는 건 놀랄 일이 아니야. 넌 정말 요리를 잘하잖아!
여: 그렇게 말해 줘서 고마워.

[해설] 남자는 여자가 요리 대회에서 우승한 게 놀랄 일이 아니라며 요리 실력을 극찬했으므로, 칭찬에 대한 감사의 응답이 가장 적절하다.
① 나는 네 말에 동의하지 않아.
③ 신경 쓰지 마. 모든 게 괜찮아.
④ 포기하지 마. 더 잘할 수 있어.
⑤ 대회에서 좋은 결과가 있길 바랄게.

[어휘] cooking contest 요리 대회 win [win] 우승하다 (win-won-won) win first prize 일등상을 타다 recipe [résəpì] 조리법 surprise [sərpráiz] 놀라게 하다 [문제] give up 포기하다

19 ⑤

남: 여행 안내 책자를 왜 읽고 있어? 여행을 갈 계획이니?
여: 응, 이번 여름에 3주 동안 두바이를 방문할 거야.
남: 와. 그곳에 오랫동안 머무네. 여행 계획은 이미 세웠니?
여: 아직. 그래서 내가 여행 안내 책자를 읽고 있는 거야.
남: 그렇구나. 거기까지 가는 데 얼마나 걸려?
여: 비행기로 10시간 정도 걸려.

[해설] 두바이까지 가는 데 얼마나 걸리는지 물었으므로, 소요 시간을 말하는 응답이 가장 적절하다.
① 거기에 빨리 가고 싶어.
② 3주는 그리 길지 않아.
③ 나는 아침 6시에 두바이로 떠나.
④ 항공권은 비싸.

[어휘] travel guide 여행 안내 책자 plan out ~에 대해 계획을 세우다

20 ④

남: Walter는 새 옷을 쇼핑하고 있습니다. 그는 '하나 사면, 하나가 공짜' 판촉의 일환으로 할인 중인 근사한 스웨터를 봅니다. 그 스웨터는 50달러이고, 그는 50달러에 스웨터 두 장이면 굉장히 좋은 가격이라고 생각합니다. 그는 파란색과 노란색 스웨터를 가지고 계산대로 갑니다. 점원이 물품을 스캔할 때, Walter는 금전 등록기 화면에 100달러가 나오는 것을 봅니다. 그는 등록기에 오류가 있는 게 틀림없다고 생각합니다. 이런 상황에서, Walter는 점원에게 뭐라고 말하겠습니까?
Walter: 가격에 오류가 있는 것 같아요.

[해설] Walter는 금전 등록기에 오류가 있어서 가격이 많이 나왔다고 생각하고 있으므로, 가격이 잘못된 것 같다는 말이 가장 적절하다.
① 환불받을 수 있나요?
② 저한테 이 가게에서 쓸 수 있는 쿠폰이 있는 것 같아요.

③ 이제 이 셔츠 두 장을 원하지 않아요.
⑤ 어느 것이 더 낫나요, 파란색 아니면 노란색?

어휘 promotion [prəmóuʃən] 판촉 counter [káuntər] 계산대
item [áitem] 물품 appear [əpíər] 나타나다 cash register
금전 등록기 [문제] mistake [mistéik] 실수, 오류

Dictation Test ⑱ pp. 230~237

01 1) these jewelry boxes 2) with or without music
    3) open the lid 4) the one with the unicorn

02 1) overcome your anxiety
    2) rehearse in front of my family
    3) on some note cards
    4) The more prepared you are

03 1) perm would suit you 2) get 20% off
    3) lost my student ID 4) can't give you a discount

04 1) leaving there at 2:00 2) from 1:00 to 2:00
    3) see you here at one o'clock

05 1) sleeps most of the day
    2) coming down with a mild cold
    3) take good care of her

06 1) I've already finished 2) might have left it
    3) will be more careful 4) help me clean

07 1) accepted to the global leadership program
    2) you'll have to miss class 3) borrow your notes

08 1) blogging, reporting, or writing poetry
    2) Anyone between the ages
    3) link your blog posts 4) edit your writing

09 1) turning off the lights
    2) put on a sweater or warm socks
    3) Make your decision

10 1) Be very careful 2) How have you been
    3) open an account 4) How long does it take

11 1) prepare dinner 2) clean up the living room
    3) make curry for dinner

12 1) can stay cool 2) next to the pond
    3) don't want to be bothered 4) already taken

13 1) speak to the boss 2) should be over soon
    3) wait for 15 minutes

14 1) left my gym clothes 2) forgot to bring them back
    3) borrow some gym clothes

15 1) except for the vegetables
    2) for your health and growth
    3) need to eat the vegetables

16 1) return two weeks later
    2) Nine hundred dollars 3) half the price
    4) take an economy-class ticket

17 1) got a lot to study 2) delayed until next week
    3) posted on the school's website

18 1) won first prize 2) made the recipe
    3) doesn't surprise me

19 1) this summer for three weeks
    2) planned out your trip 3) How long does it take

20 1) $50 for two sweaters 2) sees $100 appear
    3) must be a mistake

Word Test 16~18 pp. 238~239

Ⓐ
01 불안
02 특징
03 끔찍한
04 부착된
05 필수적인
06 잘못
07 모임
08 목표로 삼다
09 보석
10 저자
11 접근하다; 이용하다
12 (출)입구, 문
13 만들다, 창조하다
14 얇은
15 ~이 들어 있다, ~을 포함하다
16 후보자, 지원자
17 세계적인
18 짜증 나게 하는
19 쓰레기
20 나타나다
21 시골, 지방
22 실내에
23 받다; (구성원으로) 받아들이다
24 일반적으로
25 필수적인
26 생각
27 고통
28 전문적인
29 없애다; 탈락시키다
30 극복하다
31 성격, 인격
32 ~에서 출발하다
33 제시간에
34 잠깐 들르다
35 연설하다, 발표하다
36 자리에 앉다
37 ~을 이용하다
38 ~로 가득 차다
39 (병에) 걸리다
40 샅샅이, 구석구석

Ⓑ
01 withdraw
02 unexpected
03 recipe
04 professor
05 education
06 cash
07 thick
08 productive

09 worth	10 confident
11 disappointed	12 failure
13 passionate	14 checkered
15 motivate	16 disaster
17 nutritionist	18 chore
19 complaint	20 casually
21 ankle	22 address
23 harvest	24 normal
25 polite	26 lock
27 thief	28 weekday
29 kindergarten	30 rehearse
31 advertisement	32 copy machine
33 fire truck	34 be proud of
35 give up	36 tend to-v
37 look around	38 stay up late
39 pull over	40 be responsible for

고난도 실전모의고사 01회 pp. 240~241

01 ④	02 ⑤	03 ③	04 ⑤	05 ③
06 ④	07 ③	08 ③	09 ③	10 ②
11 ③	12 ①	13 ③	14 ⑤	15 ①
16 ②	17 ⑤	18 ④	19 ⑤	20 ④

01 ④

남: 지선아, 연극 보러 올래? 우리 연극 동아리에서 하는 공연이야.
여: 그래, 가고 싶어.
남: 내가 남자 주인공을 연기할 거야. 여기 표야. 맨 위에 연극의 제목을 볼 수 있어. 〈로미오와 줄리엣〉이야.
여: 이 표 멋져 보인다.
남: 정말? 사실 내가 직접 디자인했어.
여: 난 왼쪽에 있는 노란 장미가 마음에 들어.
남: 그건 우리 동아리의 상징이야. 기쁨을 뜻해. 우린 관객이 우리 연극을 보는 동안 기쁨을 느끼길 원해.
여: 정말 멋져. 연극이 언제니?
남: 날짜는 장미의 오른쪽에 있고, 장소는 그 아래에 있어.
여: 아, 이제 보여! 꼭 갈게.

해설 남자가 만든 표에는 맨 위에 연극 제목이 있고 왼쪽에는 노란 장미가 있으며, 장미 오른쪽에는 공연 날짜가, 그 아래에는 장소가 있다고 했다.

어휘 performance [pərfɔ́rməns] 공연 hero [hí:ərou] 영웅; *남자 주인공 symbol [símbəl] 상징 represent [rèprizént] 대표하다; *나타내다, 뜻하다 joy [dʒɔi] 기쁨 audience [ɔ́:diəns] 관객 definitely [défənitli] 분명히[틀림없이]

02 ⑤

남: 안녕하세요. 도와드릴까요?
여: 저희는 하룻밤을 묵을 곳이 필요해요.
남: 하룻밤만요?
여: 네, 아침에 떠날 거예요.
남: 알겠습니다. 저쪽에 텐트를 설치하시면 됩니다.
여: 어디요? 저 큰 나무 앞에요?
남: 아뇨, 저 피크닉 테이블 옆에요. 저 바위들 근처에 불을 지피시면 돼요.
여: 좋네요. 근처에 화장실이 있나요?
남: 네. 저 길 아래에 있어요.
여: 아, 알겠습니다. 감사합니다.
남: 별말씀을요. 자정 전에 모두 소등해 주시고 너무 시끄럽게 하지 말아 주세요. 마지막으로, 야생 동물에게 먹이를 주지 마세요.
여: 알겠습니다. 안 그럴게요.

해설 텐트 설치 위치(피크닉 테이블 옆), 불 사용 위치(바위 근처), 화장실 위치(길 아래쪽), 소등 시각(자정 전)에 관해서는 언급되었으나, 야생 동물 발견 시 신고 방법은 언급되지 않았다.

어휘 set ~ up ~을 설치하다 nearby [níərbái] 근처에 midnight [mídnàit] 자정 make a noise 시끄럽게 하다 feed [fi:d] 먹이를 주다 wild animal 야생 동물

03 ③

여: 안녕, 지훈아. 너 걱정스러워 보여. 무슨 일이야?
남: 형이 한국 방문 차 미국에서 와. 내가 공항에 마중을 나가겠다고 형에게 말했는데, 그렇게 할 수 없을 것 같아.
여: 아, 할 일이 있니?
남: 응, 중요한 업무 회의가 있어.
여: 형이 언제 도착하는데?
남: 이번 토요일 오후 4시에.
여: 토요일? 음, 난 아직 토요일에 아무 계획을 세우지 않았어.
남: 오, 정말? 그럼 네가 나 대신 형을 마중 나가 줄 수 있을지 모르겠네.

해설 공항에 형을 마중 나가지 못하게 된 남자는 여자에게 대신 가 줄 것을 부탁하고 있다.

어휘 pick ~ up (차로 사람을) 마중 나가다 wonder [wʌ́ndər] (정중한 부탁·질문에서) ~일지 모르겠다

04 ⑤

남: 월요일이 어버이날이야.
여: 알아. 부모님을 위해 멋진 선물을 사는 건 어때?
남: 좋은 생각이야. 오늘 쇼핑몰에 가서 선물을 사자.
여: 좋아. 방과 후 오후 4시에 만나는 게 어때?
남: 음… 조금 더 늦게 만날 수 있을까? 내가 4시 30분에 피아노 수업이 있어.
여: 그래. 언제 끝나는데?
남: 5시 30분에 끝나.
여: 그러면 거기에서 쇼핑몰까지 오는 데 30분쯤 걸리겠네.
남: 맞아.
여: 좋아. 쇼핑몰에서 그때 보자.
남: 이따 봐.

[해설] 두 사람은 남자의 피아노 수업이 끝나는 5시 30분에서 이동 시간을 고려하여 30분 후에 쇼핑몰에서 만나기로 했다.

[어휘] Parents' Day 어버이날

05 ③

남: 안녕하세요. 무엇을 도와드릴까요?
여: 이 소포를 우편으로 보내고 싶어요.
남: 네. 안에 뭐가 들었죠?
여: 그냥 책 몇 권이요. 호주에 있는 친구에게 보낼 거예요.
남: 어떤 걸로 보내시겠어요?
여: 보통 우편으로 보내면, 언제 도착하나요?
남: 10일 안에 도착할 겁니다.
여: 좋아요, 그러면 보통 우편으로 보낼게요.
남: 어디 봅시다… 2kg이네요. 13달러입니다.
여: 알겠습니다. 여기 있어요.

[해설] 남자는 우편으로 호주에 소포를 보내려는 여자에게 도착 예정일과 우편 요금을 알려 주었으므로, 두 사람이 대화하는 장소로 가장 적절한 곳은 우체국이다.

[어휘] regular mail 보통 우편

06 ④

① 여: 네 카메라 정말 좋다. 그거 어디서 샀니?
　남: 인터넷 쇼핑몰에서 샀어.
② 여: 와! 이 그림 정말 놀라워.
　남: 응. 피카소가 그렸어.
③ 여: 이 카메라를 반품하고 싶어요. 마음에 들지 않아요.
　남: 알겠습니다. 영수증을 보여 주시겠습니까?
④ 여: 여기서 사진을 찍으시면 안 됩니다.
　남: 아, 죄송합니다. 몰랐어요.
⑤ 여: 표를 보여 주시겠습니까?
　남: 여기 있습니다.

[해설] 사진 촬영 금지 표시가 있는 곳에서 남자는 카메라를 들고 있고 여자가 제지하고 있는 상황이다.

[어휘] amazing [əméiziŋ] 놀라운 receipt [risíːt] 영수증

07 ③

남: 아, 이런!
여: 무슨 일이야, Henry?
남: 내 노트북 컴퓨터가 갑자기 멈췄어.
여: 바이러스 때문인 것 같니, 아니면 배터리가 부족해서?
남: 모르겠어. 오늘 아침에 충전했으니까, 배터리 때문일 리는 없어. 수리점에 가져가야겠어.
여: 그래, 그래야겠네.
남: 그런데 오늘 오후에 수업 발표에 노트북 컴퓨터가 필요하거든. 네 것을 빌려도 될까?
여: 물론이야. 난 오늘 오후에 필요 없어.
남: 정말 고마워.
여: 그런데 과학 숙제를 하려면 오늘 밤에 그게 필요해.
남: 알았어. 발표 끝나자마자 돌려줄게.

[해설] 남자는 자신의 노트북 컴퓨터가 고장 났는데 수업 발표에 필요해서 여자의 것을 빌려 달라고 부탁했다.

[어휘] suddenly [sʌ́dnli] 갑자기 charge [tʃɑːrdʒ] 충전하다 assignment [əsáinmənt] 과제 as soon as ~하자마자

08 ③

여: 정원을 가꾸기 시작할 때, 결정할 가장 중요한 것은 위치입니다. 이상적으로, 정원은 가장 많은 햇빛을 받을 구역에 배치해야 합니다. 그 구역의 토질을 결정하는 것도 중요합니다. 계획을 세우는 것은 정원의 잠재력을 증가시키도록 돕는 또 하나의 방법입니다. 가장 키가 큰 식물들은 햇빛 차단을 방지하도록 정원 북쪽에 심어야 합니다. 정원의 크기도 중요합니다. 공간이 많지 않다면, 식물을 재배하는 데 용기들이 또 다른 선택지입니다.

[해설] 위치(가장 많은 햇빛을 받을 구역에 배치), 토질(구역의 토질 중요), 식물 배치(키가 큰 식물은 북쪽에 심기), 정원 크기(공간이 많지 않으면 용기들을 이용)에 관해서는 언급되었으나, 소요 시간은 언급되지 않았다.

[어휘] determine [ditə́ːrmin] 결정하다 location [loukéiʃən] 장소, 위치 ideally [aidíːəli] 이상적으로 soil [sɔil] 토양, 흙 draw up a plan 계획을 세우다 increase [ínkriːs] 증가시키다 potential [pəténʃəl] 잠재력 north [nɔːrθ] 북쪽 avoid [əvɔ́id] 방지하다, 막다 block [blɑk] 차단하다 container [kəntéinər] 그릇, 용기 option [ɑ́pʃən] 선택(할 수 있는 것)

09 ③

남: 이 장비는 이제 거의 모든 건물에서 발견됩니다. 사실, 많은 나라에서 모든 공공건물이 최소한 하나는 갖추도록 요구됩니다. 이것은 복도나 사무실과 같은 곳에서 볼 수 있습니다. 때때로 이것은 유리로 된 안전 상자 안에 보관되어 있습니다. 이것에는 기체, 액체, 거품이나 가루가 들어 있을 수 있습니다. 이것은 보통 빨간색입니다. 많은 사람들이 비상 상황에 이것을 사용하는 법을 배웁니다. 이것은 작은 불을 끄는 데 사용됩니다.

[해설] 기체나 액체, 거품, 가루 등이 들어 있고 불을 끄는 데 사용되는 빨간색 장비는 소화기이다.

[어휘] device [diváis] 장비, 기구 almost [ɔ́ːlmoust] 거의 require [rikwáiər] 요구하다 hallway [hɔ́ːlwèi] 복도 liquid [líkwid] 액체 foam [foum] 거품, 포말 powder [páudər] 가루 put out (불 등을) 끄다

10 ②

① 남: 날씨가 어때?
여: 비가 올 것 같아.
② 남: Sam은 어떻게 생겼니?
여: 그는 골프 치는 것을 좋아해.
③ 남: 그건 내가 본 것 중 최악의 영화였어.
여: 나도 동감이야.
④ 남: 넌 형제자매가 몇 명이니?
여: 난 외동딸이야.
⑤ 남: 넌 복권에 당첨되면 뭘 할 거니?
여: 난 근사한 자동차를 살 거야.

[해설] 다른 사람의 생김새에 관한 질문에 그 사람이 좋아하는 것을 말하는 응답은 어색하다.

[어휘] only child 외동(딸·아들) win the lottery 복권에 당첨되다

11 ③

여: 안녕, Arnold. 이번 주말에 과학 동아리 모임에 갈 거니?
남: 응. 내가 동아리 회장이니까 가야 해. 그런데 이번 주말은 아니야.
여: 아, 정말? 연기되었니?
남: 응, 대신 월요일에 모임을 할 거야. 이번 주말에는 몇몇 회원들이 현장 학습을 가거든.
여: 그렇구나. 너도 현장 학습 가니?
남: 아니. 난 대신 할머니 댁에 갈 거야. 너는?
여: 난 주말 내내 공부해야 해. 다음 주에 중요한 시험이 있거든.
남: 아, 안됐다.

[해설] 남자는 이번 주말에 과학 동아리 모임이 취소되어 대신 할머니 댁에 갈 예정이라고 했다.

[어휘] president [prézidənt] (클럽 등의) 회장 postpone [pouspóun] 연기하다, 미루다 instead [instéd] 대신에

12 ①

여: 이 지도를 봐. 이용할 수 있는 구역이 다섯 개 있어. 우리에게 어떤 구역이 가장 좋을 것 같아?
남: 우리는 팝콘과 음료를 팔 거니까, 화장실 옆에 있는 구역은 원치 않아.
여: 나도. E 구역은 어때?
남: 좋지 않은 것 같아. 영화가 상영될 강당에서 멀잖아. 영화를 보러 가는 사람들이 팝콘과 음료를 원할 텐데.
여: 그래, 그럼 강당 입구 옆의 구역이 가장 좋겠다.
남: 그게 바로 나도 생각한 바야.

[해설] 두 사람은 영화를 보러 가는 사람들이 팝콘과 음료를 원할 것이기 때문에 강당 입구 옆 구역을 선택하기로 했다.

[어휘] zone [zoun] 구역 beverage [bévəridʒ] 음료 auditorium [ɔ̀ːditɔ́ːriəm] 강당, 객석

13 ③

여: 얘, 진호야. 너 벌써 새집으로 이사했니?
남: 아직. 다음 주에 이사할 거야.
여: 다음 주 무슨 요일?
남: 화요일.
여: 화요일? 그날이 5월 14일이니?
남: 아니, 그날은 월요일이야. 우리는 그다음 날 이사해.
여: 아, 맞다. 그러면 이사하기까지 5일밖에 안 남았구나. 짐 다 쌌어?
남: 아니, 이번 주말에 싸기 시작할 거야.
여: 내가 도울 수 있는 일이 있으면 알려 줘.

[해설] 이사일인 5월 15일 화요일까지 5일 남았다고 했으므로, 오늘은 5월 10일이다.

[어휘] move [muːv] 움직이다; *이사하다

14 ⑤

남: 얘, Judy. 겨울 방학은 어땠어?
여: 아주 좋았어. 많은 아이들과 함께 보냈어.
남: 어떤 아이들? 아이 봐 주는 사람으로 일했어?
여: 아니.
남: 음… 친척들과 시간을 보냈니?
여: 아니.
남: 그럼 뭘 했어? 내가 계속 추측하게 하지 마.
여: 독서 프로그램을 돕기 위해 도서관에서 자원봉사를 했어.
남: 너에게 뭘 시켰어?
여: 미취학 아동들이 책을 읽는 것을 돕고 아이들이 읽은 책을 설명하는 것을 들었어.

해설 여자는 겨울 방학에 도서관에서 아이들의 독서 프로그램을 돕는 자원봉사를 했다고 했다.

어휘 babysitter [béibisìtər] 베이비시터, 아이를 봐 주는 사람 hang out with ~와 시간을 보내다 relative [rélətiv] 친척 guess [ges] 추측하다 preschooler [prìːskúːlər] 미취학 아동 describe [diskráib] 묘사하다, 설명하다

15 ①

여: 이것은 지역 학생 모두를 위한 공지입니다. 여러분도 아시다시피, 혹독한 날씨 때문에 지역 학교 모두 휴교하기로 결정했습니다. 온도가 영하 25°C로 떨어졌습니다. 그리고 거리에 거의 1미터의 눈이 쌓여서, 이동이 불가능해졌습니다. 이런 이유로, 우리는 모든 학생들이 학교에 가는 것보다 집에 있는 것이 더 안전할 것이라고 결정했습니다. 수업 시수는 방학 기간을 단축하여 조정할 것입니다. 휴교는 추후 공지가 있을 때까지 계속될 것입니다. 최신 뉴스를 잘 들어 주시고, 조심히 지내십시오.

해설 혹독한 날씨 때문에 지역 학교 모두 휴교하기로 결정했음을 공지하고 있다.

어휘 notice [nóutis] 공지 local [lóukəl] 지역의 severe [sivíər] 극심한; *혹독한 drop [drap] 떨어지다 nearly [níərli] 거의 travel [trǽvəl] 여행하다; *이동 impossible [impásəbl] 불가능한 adjust [ədʒʌ́st] 조정하다 shorten [ʃɔ́ːrtn] 짧게 하다, 단축하다 period [píːəriəd] 기간 closure [klóuʒər] 폐쇄 further [fɜ́ːrðər] 그 이상의, 추가의 take care 몸 건강해[조심해] (헤어질 때의 인사말)

16 ②

[전화벨이 울린다.]

남: 여보세요, 무엇을 도와드릴까요?

여: 제 예약을 확인하고 싶어요.

남: 알겠습니다. 성함과 예약 번호가 어떻게 되시죠?

여: Ruby Robinson이고, 제 예약 번호는 15366입니다.

남: 확인해 볼게요. 스포츠 세단을 5일간 예약하셨네요. 하루에 80달러입니다.

여: 네. 그리고 어린이용 시트도 요청했어요.

남: 맞습니다. 그건 하루에 10달러입니다. 저희 웹 사이트에서 쿠폰을 다운로드하시면, 총액에서 20%를 할인받으실 수 있습니다.

여: 알겠어요, 그럴게요.

남: 차를 가져가실 때 운전면허증 가져오시는 거 잊지 마세요.

여: 고맙습니다.

해설 하루에 80달러인 스포츠 세단과 하루에 10달러인 어린이용 시트를 5일간 빌리고($90×5=$450) 쿠폰으로 20% 할인($90)을 받았다고 했으므로, 여자가 지불할 금액은 360달러이다.

어휘 confirm [kənfɜ́ːrm] 확인하다 reserve [rizɜ́ːrv] 예약하다 ask for ~을 요청하다 driver's license 운전면허증

17 ⑤

여: Martin, 너 경주에 갈 거라고 들었어.

남: 응. 거기로 출장을 가.

여: 언제 가니?

남: 이번 주말에 KTX로 가. 돌아오기 전에 그 도시를 둘러보고 싶어.

여: 잘됐다. 경주에는 볼 게 많아.

남: 아, 거기 가 봤니?

여: 응, 기차 타고 경주에 여러 번 가 봤어. 조부모님이 거기에 사셔.

남: 정말? 가 볼 만한 좋은 장소들을 좀 추천해 줄 수 있니?

여: <u>불국사에 가 볼 것을 추천해.</u>

해설 경주에서 가 볼 만한 장소를 추천해 달라고 했으므로, 구체적인 장소를 말하는 응답이 가장 적절하다.
① 응, 거긴 정말 좋은 곳이야.
② 나는 언젠가 그곳에 가고 싶어.
③ 기차를 타면 더 저렴해.
④ 그곳에 가는 데 두 시간이 걸려.

어휘 business trip 출장 recommend [rèkəménd] 추천하다

18 ④

남: 엄마, Jimmy랑 제가 롤러코스터를 타도 되나요?

여: 그럼. 하지만 나는 같이 타지 않을게. 난 롤러코스터가 싫단다.

남: 괜찮아요. 엄마 없이도 탈 수 있어요.

여: 그래. 그게 어디 있는데?

남: 바로 저기요.

여: 아, 얘야. 저 표지판을 읽었니?

남: 아뇨. 아, 12세 미만의 어린이는 이 롤러코스터를 탈 수 없다고 쓰여 있네요.

여: 그래. 넌 나이가 충분히 되지만, Jimmy는 겨우 10살이잖아.

남: <u>그럼 저 혼자 타도 되나요?</u>

해설 롤러코스터를 타고 싶은데 동생은 나이 제한 때문에 탈 수 없다고 했으므로, 혼자 타도 되는지 묻는 응답이 적절하다.
① 제 나이가 더 많다면 좋을 텐데요.
② 표 있으세요?
③ 저 없이 가셔도 돼요.
⑤ 엄마가 롤러코스터를 싫어하시는지 몰랐어요.

어휘 ride [raid] 타다

19 ⑤

여: 안녕, Brad. 뭐 문제 있니?

남: 응. 스페인에 있는 친구에게서 방금 이메일을 받았어.

여: 아. 지난여름에 네가 그 애를 방문하지 않았니?

남: 그랬지. 정말 멋진 여행이었어. 그 애가 다음 달에 날 방문하기로 했었지.

여: 그런데 그 애가 오지 않는 거야?

남: 응, 안 온대. 그 애가 마침 박물관 일자리를 제안받았는데, 그 일을 다음 주부터 시작해.

여: 그렇구나. 그래서 아직 휴가를 낼 수 없겠구나.

남: 맞아. 그 애가 일자리를 구해서 기쁘지만, 그 애를 정말 보고 싶었거든.

[해설] 친구가 새로 일을 시작하게 되어 휴가를 낼 수 없어 방문이 취소되었다고 했으므로, 일자리를 구한 것은 기쁘지만 보지 못해서 아쉬운 심정을 말하는 응답이 가장 적절하다.
① 난 그 애가 새로운 일자리를 구할 수 있으면 좋겠어.
② 아마도 대신 네가 그 애를 다시 찾아갈 수 있을 거야.
③ 그게 좋겠지만, 난 시간이 많지 않아.
④ 난 박물관을 가는 걸 고대하고 있어.

[어휘] offer [ɔ́:fər] 제안하다 take time off 휴가를 내다

20 ④

남: Jake는 다음 달에 수학여행을 갈 때 입을 재킷이 필요했습니다. 그는 한 인터넷 쇼핑몰에서 멋진 것을 발견했습니다. 색과 스타일이 정확히 그가 찾던 것이었습니다. 그는 그것을 사기로 결정했습니다. 그는 보통 중간 치수의 재킷을 입기 때문에, 중간 치수를 주문했습니다. 이틀 뒤, 그는 재킷을 받았습니다. 그는 그것을 입어 보았는데, 그에게 조금 작았습니다. 그는 더 큰 재킷이 그에게 맞을 거라고 생각합니다. 그는 그것을 반품하고 큰 치수를 받고 싶습니다. 이런 상황에서, Jake는 고객 서비스 직원에게 뭐라고 말하겠습니까?

Jake: 이 재킷을 큰 치수로 교환할 수 있나요?

[해설] Jake는 더 큰 재킷을 원한다고 했으므로, 재킷을 큰 치수로 교환할 수 있는지 묻는 말이 가장 적절하다.
① 환불을 받고 싶어요.
② 제 주문을 취소하고 싶어요.
③ 이 재킷은 저한테 너무 커요.
⑤ 제게 어떤 색을 추천하시겠어요?

[어휘] exactly [igzǽktli] 정확히, 꼭 a bit 조금, 약간, 다소 customer service 고객 서비스 employee [implɔiíː] 직원

고난도 Dictation Test pp. 242~249

01 1) playing the hero 2) I designed it myself
    3) yellow rose on the left 4) on the right

02 1) set your tent up 2) make a fire
    3) turn all your lights off
    4) don't feed the wild animals

03 1) pick him up
    2) have an important business meeting
    3) haven't made any plans 4) I wonder if you could

04 1) shop for a gift 2) meet a little later
    3) finishes at 5:30 4) take you 30 minutes

05 1) mail this package 2) send it by regular mail
    3) in ten days 4) will be $13

06 1) bought it from 2) return this camera
    3) not supposed to take pictures
    4) show me your ticket

07 1) I charged it 2) take it to the service center
    3) Can I borrow yours 4) give it back

08 1) receive the most sunlight
    2) determine the soil quality
    3) avoid blocking the sunlight

09 1) have at least one 2) in emergency situations
    3) put out small fires

10 1) look like 2) can say that again
    3) won the lottery

11 1) Has it been postponed 2) going on a field trip
    3) going to my grandmother's house
    4) study all weekend

12 1) next to the restroom 2) far from the auditorium
    3) entrance of the auditorium

13 1) May 14 2) moving the next day
    3) only five days left 4) start packing this weekend

14 1) work as a babysitter
    2) hang out with your relatives
    3) volunteered at the library
    4) helped preschoolers read books

15 1) all of the local schools
    2) all students to stay home
    3) school closure will continue

16 1) confirm my reservation 2) for five days
    3) $10 a day 4) get a 20% discount

17 1) on a business trip 2) There's a lot to see
    3) some good places to visit

18 1) can go without you
    2) children under 12 can't ride 3) is only 10

19 1) was going to visit me 2) offered a job
    3) take time off

20 1) ordered a medium 2) a bit small 3) get a large

01 ①	02 ①	03 ④	04 ③	05 ⑤
06 ③	07 ⑤	08 ④	09 ③	10 ①
11 ③	12 ②	13 ②	14 ⑤	15 ④
16 ③	17 ⑤	18 ②	19 ⑤	20 ⑤

01 ①

여: 안녕하세요, 아이스크림을 사고 싶어요.
남: 네! 여기 여러 다양한 아이스크림이 많이 있어요.
여: 좋아요! 바닐라 두 스쿱이랑 딸기 한 스쿱 주세요.
남: 죄송하지만, 딸기가 너무 인기 있어서 다 떨어졌어요.
여: 아, 유감이네요. 딸기를 정말 좋아하거든요. 그럼 그냥 바닐라 두 스쿱 주세요.
남: 컵으로 드릴까요, 콘으로 드릴까요?
여: 컵으로 주세요.
남: 토핑 원하세요?
여: 네, 그 위에 초콜릿 소스 주세요.
남: 알겠습니다. 잠시 기다려 주세요.

[해설] 여자는 바닐라 아이스크림 두 스쿱 위에 초콜릿 소스를 얹어서 컵에 담아 달라고 했다.

[어휘] variety [vəráiəti] 가지각색, 가지가지 scoop [skuːp] 한 숟갈, 스쿱 run out 다 떨어지다 topping [tápiŋ] (음식 위에 얹는) 토핑

02 ①

여: 어제 축구 경기 보러 갔었니?
남: 응. 정말 좋았어.
여: 누가 경기를 하고 있었어?
남: 브라질과 독일.
여: 와! 누가 이겼어?
남: 브라질이 2 대 1로 이겼어.
여: 흥미진진한 경기였어?
남: 응, 경기가 정말 막상막하였어. 경기 후반까지 점수가 동점이었어.
여: 끝에 어떻게 됐어?
남: Anthony가 경기 종료 5분 전에 골을 넣었어. 극적이었어.
여: 와, 나도 봤더라면 좋을 텐데.

[해설] 출전 팀(브라질과 독일), 우승 팀(브라질), 최종 스코어(2 대 1), 결승 골을 넣은 선수(Anthony)에 관해서는 언급되었으나, 경기 날짜는 언급되지 않았다.

[어휘] tight [tait] 단단한; *막상막하의 tie [tai] 묶다; *동점을 이루다 score a goal 득점하다, 골을 넣다 dramatic [drəmǽtik] 극적인

03 ④

[전화벨이 울린다.]
여: Daily News에 전화 주셔서 감사합니다. 무엇을 도와드릴까요?
남: 안녕하세요. 제가 그곳 신문을 구독하는데요, 오늘 신문을 아직 받지 못했어요.
여: 아, 확인해 보겠습니다. 성함과 주소를 말씀해 주시겠습니까?
남: 제 이름은 Ben James이고, Westville의 Grand 가에 삽니다.
여: 아, Westville 지역을 담당하는 신입 배달 직원이 있는데, 실수를 한 것 같군요. 정말 죄송합니다.
남: 사실은 이번이 처음이 아니에요. 지난주에도 그랬어요.
여: 실수에 대해 사과드립니다. 즉시 댁에 신문을 배달해 드리고, 다시는 이런 일이 발생하지 않도록 하겠습니다.
남: 알겠어요. 감사합니다.

[해설] 남자는 신문을 구독하고 있는데 지난주에 이어 오늘도 신문이 배달되지 않았다고 했다.

[어휘] subscribe [səbskráib] (신문 등을) 구독하다 copy [kápi] 권, 부 in charge of ~을 맡고 있는 make a mistake 실수하다 actually [ǽktʃuəli] 사실은 apologize [əpálədʒàiz] 사과하다 immediately [imíːdiətli] 즉시

04 ③

여: 오늘 내 수업 시간표 받았어. 네 것은 받았니?
남: 응, 여기 있어. 여행을 계획하자.
여: 그래. 난 금요일 1시 이후에는 수업이 없어. 너는 어때?
남: 금요일 마지막 수업이 오후 5시에 끝나.
여: 그건 너무 늦어. 저녁 9시나 돼야 정동진에 도착할 거야.
남: 먼저 기차 시간표를 보자.
여: 좋아. 서울발 기차가 오후 2시부터 2시간마다 있어.
남: 내가 마지막 수업을 빠지면, 우리는 오후 4시에 출발하는 기차를 탈 수 있어.
여: 그래도 괜찮아?
남: 응. 현장 학습 보고서를 제출하면 수업을 빠질 수 있어.
여: 좋아. 그럼 내일 표를 구매할게.

[해설] 남자가 금요일 마지막 수업을 빠지고, 두 사람은 오후 4시에 출발하는 기차를 타기로 했다.

[어휘] skip [skip] 빼먹다 submit [səbmít] 제출하다 report [ripɔ́ːrt] 보고서

05 ⑤

여: 안녕, Eric. 너 새 목도리 필요하다고 했잖아. 우리 내일 쇼핑 가는 게 어때?
남: 나도 정말 그러고 싶은데, 그럴 수가 없어.
여: 할 일이 있니?
남: 아니. 사실은 음식에 내 용돈을 다 써서, 지금 돈이 전혀 없어.

102

여: 음식에 돈을 전부 다 썼다고?

남: 응. 나는 좀 더 현명했어야 했던 것 같아. 다음에는 내 용돈에 더 신중할 거야.

여: 그래, 네가 언제 그게 필요할지 절대 모르는 거야.

[해설] 남자는 음식에 용돈을 다 써서 필요한 물건을 살 돈이 없으므로 후회스러울(regretful) 것이다.
① 지루한 ② 기쁜 ③ 만족스러운 ④ 희망에 찬

[어휘] allowance [əláuəns] 용돈 should have p.p. ~했어야 했는데 (하지 못했다) wise [waiz] 지혜로운, 현명한 careful [kέərfəl] 조심하는, 신중한 spending money 용돈

06 ③

① 여: 맑은 날에 왜 우산을 가져왔니?
　남: 예보에서 비가 올 거라고 했어.
② 여: 눈이 와서 길이 미끄러워. 조심해.
　남: 알았어, 그럴게.
③ 여: 하늘에 먹구름 봐.
　남: 비가 올 가능성이 있어.
④ 여: 하늘에 구름이 거의 없어.
　남: 응, 선탠을 하기 좋은 날이야.
⑤ 여: 저 집에서 올라오는 연기 자욱한 것 보여?
　남: 불이 났을지도 몰라!

[해설] 두 사람이 먹구름을 보고 있으므로, 흐린 날씨에 관한 대화를 나누는 것이 자연스럽다.

[어휘] forecast [fɔ́ːrkæst] 예측, 예보 path [pæθ] 길 slippery [slípəri] 미끄러운 cloud [klaud] 구름; (먼지·연기 등이) 자욱한 것 chance [tʃæns] 기회; *가능성 barely [bέərli] 거의 ~ 아니게[없이] get a tan 선탠을 하다 rise [raiz] 오르다, 올라가다

07 ⑤

[전화벨이 울린다.]

여: Ace Car Parts입니다, 무엇을 도와드릴까요?

남: 안녕하세요. 지난주에 웹 사이트에서 차 시트 덮개를 주문했는데요.

여: 그러시군요. 제때 배송되었나요?

남: 네, 어제 도착했어요. 하지만 제 차 시트에 맞지 않아서요.

여: 정말요? 저희가 잘못된 걸 보내 드렸나요?

남: 아니요, 제가 잘못된 시트 덮개를 주문했어요. 더 작은 게 필요해요.

여: 알겠습니다. 색상과 모양은 어떤가요? 괜찮은가요?

남: 네, 좋아요.

여: 좋습니다. 안 맞는 시트 덮개를 되돌려 보내 주시기만 하면, 새것을 보내 드릴게요.

[해설] 남자는 구입한 차 시트 덮개가 자신의 차 시트에 맞지 않아 교환을 원하고 있다.

[어휘] cover [kʌ́vər] 덮개 send back ~을 되돌려 보내다

08 ④

여: 오늘은 박한나 씨를 인터뷰하겠습니다. 그녀는 올여름 최대의 영화 〈Panda Attack〉에서 주연을 맡은 젊은 여배우입니다. 박 씨는 20살밖에 안 됐지만, 많은 TV 프로그램과 광고에 출연했습니다. 하지만 〈Panda Attack〉은 그녀의 겨우 두 번째 영화입니다. 그녀는 한국에서 태어났지만, 이곳 로스앤젤레스에서 자랐습니다. 그녀는 현재 스탠퍼드 대학교에 재학 중이고, 4개 언어를 구사할 수 있습니다. 신사 숙녀 여러분, 박한나 씨를 환영해 주세요.

[해설] 나이(20세), 출생지(한국), 재학 중인 학교(스탠퍼드 대학교), 구사 가능 언어 수(4개 언어)에 관해서는 언급되었으나, 첫 출연 작품은 언급되지 않았다.

[어휘] actress [ǽktris] 여배우 star [stɑːr] (영화 등에서) 주연을 맡다 appear [əpíər] 나타나다; *출연하다 commercial [kəmə́ːrʃəl] (광고) 방송 currently [kə́ːrəntli] 현재 attend [əténd] 참석하다; *(~에) 다니다 language [lǽŋgwidʒ] 언어

09 ③

남: 이것은 한국에서 가장 중요한 전통 명절 중 하나입니다. 전국에서, 사람들이 추수를 축하하고 조상을 기리기 위해 고향으로 돌아갑니다. 가족 구성원들은 조상의 묘를 방문하고 경의를 표하기 위해 차례를 지냅니다. 그들은 음식을 나누고 떡과 같은 전통 음식을 먹습니다. 사람들은 또한 소원을 빌고 밤하늘에서 보름달을 보기 위해 늦게까지 깨어 있습니다. 이 명절은 음력 8월 15일에 기념됩니다.

[해설] 한국에서 가족들이 모여 추수를 축하하고 조상을 기리기 위한 차례를 지내는 음력 8월 15일은 추석이다.

[어휘] traditional [trədíʃənəl] 전통적인 harvest [hɑ́ːrvist] 추수 honor [ɑ́nər] 예우하다, 경의를 표하다 ancestor [ǽnsestər] 조상 tomb [tuːm] 무덤, 묘 memorial service 제사, 차례 pay one's respect 경의를 표하다 rice cakes 떡류 lunar month 음력 달

10 ①

① 남: 너의 가족에게 내 안부를 전해 줘.
　여: 우리 가족은 4명이야.
② 남: 그거 얼마 줬어?
　여: 돈 안 냈어. 무료였거든.
③ 남: 저 전화기를 이쪽으로 가져다줄래?
　여: 잠시만. 이것 먼저 끝내야 해.
④ 남: 나 열이 나. 어떻게 해야 하지?
　여: 더 심해지기 전에 진찰을 받는 게 어때?
⑤ 남: 오늘 밤에 컴퓨터로 게임할 거야?
　여: 아니, 친구들을 만나러 나갈 거야.

[해설] 가족에게 안부를 전해 달라고 했는데 가족 수를 말하는 것은 어색하다.

어휘 send one's love to ~에게 안부를 전하다 see a doctor 진찰을 받다

11 ③

남: 엄마, 저 집에 왔어요.
여: 잘 다녀왔니, Paul. 오늘 왜 이렇게 늦었니?
남: 방과 후에 친구들과 축구를 했어요.
여: 왜 나한테 전화를 하지 않았니? 저녁이 한 시간 전에 준비가 다 되었고, 우린 너를 기다리고 있었잖니.
남: 죄송해요, 엄마. 휴대전화 배터리가 나갔어요.
여: 앞으로는 추가 배터리를 가지고 다니렴. 그건 그렇고, 배가 많이 고프겠구나. 저녁 먹자.
남: 네. 하지만 먼저 샤워를 해야 할 것 같아요. 땀을 많이 흘렸거든요. 최대한 빨리 할게요.
여: 그래.

해설 남자는 축구를 하고 땀이 많이 나서, 저녁을 먹기 전에 샤워를 하겠다고 했다.

어휘 extra [ékstrə] 여분의, 추가의 take a shower 샤워를 하다 sweat [swet] 땀을 흘리다

12 ②

[전화벨이 울린다.]
여: 여보세요. 도와드릴까요?
남: 네, 제 이름은 Jason Han입니다. 일자리 때문에 전에 전화드렸어요.
여: 아, 맞아요. 나이가 어떻게 되시죠, Jason 씨?
남: 내년에 20살이 돼요.
여: 그렇군요. 동물 병원에서 일한 경험이 좀 있나요?
남: 아니요. 하지만 개 두 마리를 키우고 있고, 동물들을 정말 사랑해요.
여: 잘됐네요. 운전하실 수 있나요?
남: 음, 전 차가 없어요. 하지만 운전면허는 있어요.
여: 알겠습니다. 주말에 일하실 수 있나요?
남: 아니요. 평일 저녁 6시 이후에만 시간이 있어요.
여: 그렇군요. 매니저와 얘기해 보고, 다시 연락드릴게요.

해설 남자는 내년에 20살이 된다고 했다.

입사 지원		
①	이름	Jason Han
②	나이	20살
③	경험	있음 □ / 없음 ☑
④	운전면허	있음 ☑ / 없음 □
⑤	가능한 시간	평일 저녁 6시 이후

어휘 experience [ikspíəriəns] 경험 available [əvéiləbl] 이용 가능한; *시간이 있는

13 ②

남: 세연아, 너 새 개가 생겼다고 들었어.
여: 응, 귀여운 작은 강아지야. 이번 주에 방과 후에 와서 볼래?
남: 그러고 싶어. 너는 무슨 요일이 좋니?
여: 월요일이나 목요일 빼고 아무 날이나. 그때는 내가 수영하러 가거든.
남: 알았어. 나는 이번 주 금요일에 조부모님 댁에 가야 해서, 그때는 못 가. 그리고 우리 이번 주 화요일에는 Nate의 생일 파티에 가야 해.
여: 아, 파티는 화요일이 아니라, 수요일이야.
남: 맞다. 그럼 우리 둘 다 시간이 있는 날이 하루밖에 없네.
여: 그래. 그때 보자.

해설 여자가 수영하러 가는 월요일과 목요일, 남자가 조부모님 댁에 가는 금요일, Nate의 생일 파티가 있는 수요일을 제외하면, 남는 요일은 화요일이다.

어휘 come over ~에 들르다 except [iksépt] ~을 제외하고

14 ⑤

여: 얘, Alex. 다 괜찮아? 너 휴식이 좀 필요해 보여.
남: 응. 정말 휴식이 필요해.
여: 왜 그렇게 피곤해?
남: 어제 내 만화책들을 정리해서 일부를 자선 단체에 기부했어.
여: 정말? 넌 만화책 수백 권을 모아 왔잖아.
남: 맞아. 그리고 내가 가장 좋아하는 것들 일부를 제외하고 모두 기부했어.
여: 힘든 일이었겠다.
남: 응, 책 수백 권을 나르느라 지쳤어.

해설 남자는 어제 만화책을 정리해서 일부를 자선 단체에 기부했다고 했다.

어휘 organize [ɔ́ːrgənàiz] 정리하다 donate [dóuneit] 기부하다 charity [tʃǽrəti] 자선 단체 collect [kəlékt] 모으다, 수집하다 but [bət] ~을 제외하고 exhausted [igzɔ́ːstid] 지친, 기진맥진한

15 ④

여: 이전 수업에서 논의했듯이, 소셜 미디어는 전 세계 사람들을 연결합니다. 하지만 소셜 미디어의 부작용은 더 심각해지고 있습니다. 조사에 따르면, 십 대들 사이에서 소셜 미디어 사용이 점차 증가하고 있습니다. 소셜 미디어에 더 많은 시간을 보내는 것은 사이버 폭력, 우울증, 그리고 연령에 적절하지 않은 내용에의 노출로 이어질 수 있습니다. 소셜 미디어 중독은 무시할 수 없습니다. 소셜 미디어가 여러분의 삶을 해치고 있는 것을 발견한다면, 그것으로부터 잠시 쉬십시오.

해설 사이버 폭력, 우울증, 부적절한 내용에의 노출 등 소셜 미디어의 부작용에 대해 이야기하고 있다.

어휘 discuss [diskʌ́s] 논의하다 previous [príːviəs] 이전의 connect [kənékt] 연결하다 side effect 부작용 according to ~에 따르면 research [risə́ːrtʃ] 연구, 조사 usage [júːsidʒ] 사용 gradually [grǽdʒuəli] 점차 teen [tiːn] 십 대 lead to ~로 이어지다 cyberbullying [sáibərbuliŋ] 사이버 폭력 depression [dipréʃən] 우울증 exposure [ikspóuʒər] 노출 appropriate [əpróuprieit] 적절한 addiction [ədíkʃən] 중독 ignore [ignɔ́ːr] 무시하다

16 ③

남: 안녕하세요. 아들에게 줄 선물을 사려고 왔어요. 다음 주가 그 애 생일이거든요.

여: 판매 중인 컴퓨터 게임이 많습니다. 아이가 어떤 게임을 원하는지 아시나요?

남: 스포츠 게임을 좋아해요. 추천 좀 해 주시겠어요?

여: 이 농구 게임과 저 축구 게임이 가장 인기 있는 두 가지예요.

남: 얼마예요?

여: 각각 30달러예요.

남: 글쎄요, 그 둘 다 사고 싶지만, 60달러는 조금 비싸네요.

여: 아, 이번 주에 특별 할인을 하고 있어요. 두 개를 구매하시면, 두 번째 것은 50퍼센트 할인돼요.

남: 좋군요. 그럼 둘 다 주세요.

해설 남자가 사려는 게임은 각각 30달러인데 두 개를 사면 하나는 50% 할인이 된다고 했으므로, 지불할 금액은 45달러($30＋$15)이다.

어휘 thousands of 수천의, 많은 for sale 팔려고 내놓은 off [ɔːf] 할인되어

17 ⑤

남: 겨울 방학 동안 뭐 할 거니?

여: 아직 모르겠어. 너는?

남: 나는 봉사 동아리 회원이라, 자원봉사 일을 할 거야.

여: 아, 정말? 보통 어떤 일을 하는데?

남: 보통 커뮤니티 센터에 가서 아이들에게 영어를 가르쳐 줘. 가끔은 영어를 배우고 싶어 하시는 연세 드신 분들께 가르쳐 드리기도 해.

여: 와, 멋지다! 얼마나 자주 가르치니?

남: 일주일에 한 번. 하지만 우리는 방학 동안 횟수를 늘릴 거야.

해설 자원봉사로 얼마나 자주 영어를 가르치는지 물었으므로, 빈도를 말하는 응답이 가장 적절하다.
① 그냥 커뮤니티 센터에 가면 돼.
② 관심 있으면, 우리와 함께 하지 그래?
③ 그들을 가르치려면 영어를 유창하게 해야 해.
④ 가르치는 건 내가 생각했던 것보다 훨씬 어려워.

어휘 elderly [éldərli] 연세가 드신 [문제] fluently [flúːəntli] 유창하게

18 ②

여: 떠날 준비됐어?

남: 응, 하지만 우리 지하철을 타야 할 것 같아.

여: 왜? 역까지 걷기에는 너무 추워. 내 차가 바로 저기 있는데. 내가 운전할게.

남: 알아. 하지만 교통량이 많을까 봐 걱정돼.

여: 토요일이잖아. 토요일 오전에는 교통량이 많지 않아.

남: 하지만 방금 라디오를 듣고 있었거든. 시내에 큰 사고가 있었대. 영화가 시작하기 전에 극장에 도착할 수 없을 것 같아.

여: 그렇다면 지하철을 타자.

해설 남자는 시내에서 일어난 큰 사고 때문에 교통량이 많을까 봐 걱정하고 있으므로, 차 대신 지하철을 타자는 응답이 가장 적절하다.
① 걱정하지 마. 난 운전을 안전하게 하니까.
③ 맞아, 하지만 오늘은 토요일이야.
④ 우리는 라디오를 들을 시간이 없어.
⑤ 우리가 지하철을 탔어야 했다고 말했잖아.

어휘 traffic [trǽfik] 차량들, 교통량 downtown [dàuntáun] 시내에

19 ⑤

여: 안녕, 진수야. 왜 웃고 있어?

남: 안녕, 보라야! 내가 ABC 청소년 잡지의 십 대 기자로 뽑혔다는 걸 방금 알게 됐어. 이 자리를 얻기 위해 내가 정말 열심히 했기 때문에, 정말 기뻐.

여: 네가 정확히 뭘 하게 되는 거야?

남: 우리 학교에서 일어나는 일에 관해 쓰게 될 거야. 그 글들이 잡지에 실리게 되는 거지.

여: 와. 대단하다.

남: 응, 좋은 경험이 될 거야. 사실 난 언젠가 신문사에서 일하고 싶거든.

여: 아, 그럼 그게 너의 경력에도 도움이 되겠구나.

해설 남자는 청소년 잡지 기자로 뽑혔다며 나중에 신문사에서 일하고 싶다고 했으므로, 그 경험이 경력에 도움이 될 것이라는 응답이 가장 적절하다.
① 그래, 기꺼이 그걸 시도해 볼게.
② 네가 거기에서 일하는지 몰랐어.
③ 두 가지 직업을 갖는 것은 분명 어려울 거야.
④ 미안하지만, 나는 그 소식을 못 들었어.

어휘 position [pəzíʃən] 위치; *(일)자리, 직위 publish [pʌ́bliʃ] 출판하다; *게재하다[싣다] [문제] be willing to-v 기꺼이 ~하다 give it a try 시도하다 career [kəríər] 직업, 경력

20 ⑤

남: Katie는 영화를 보려고 합니다. 그녀가 오랫동안 보고 싶어 했던 영화입니다. 그녀는 영화관에 일찍 도착합니다. 그녀는 영화를 보는

동안 즐길 팝콘과 탄산음료를 삽니다. 그녀는 표에서 좌석 번호를 확인하고 어두운 객석으로 들어갑니다. 그녀는 자신의 자리를 찾습니다. 그녀는 금방 자리를 찾지만, 거기에 이미 한 남자가 앉아 있습니다. 그녀가 자신의 표를 다시 확인해 보니, 거기가 맞는 좌석입니다. 이런 상황에서, Katie는 남자에게 뭐라고 말하겠습니까?

Katie: 실례합니다. 제 자리에 앉아 계신 것 같아요.

[해설] 영화관에서 남자가 Katie의 자리에 잘못 앉아 있으므로, 자신의 자리임을 알려 주는 말이 가장 적절하다.
① 표를 어디서 사셨나요?
② 팝콘과 탄산음료 사셨나요?
③ 이 방이 너무 어두워서 표가 안 보여요.
④ 오늘 밤에 영화 볼래요?

[어휘] cinema [sínəmə] 영화관

고난도 Dictation Test 02 pp. 252~259

01 1) so popular that we ran out
    2) take a double scoop of vanilla
    3) chocolate sauce on it

02 1) Who was playing 2) won by a score of
    3) score was tied 4) scored a goal

03 1) haven't gotten today's copy
    2) get your name and address 3) made a mistake
    4) have a copy delivered

04 1) ends at 5:00 2) every two hours
    3) leaving at 4:00 4) submit a field trip report

05 1) spent all of my allowance 2) a little wiser
    3) careful with my spending money

06 1) made the path slippery
    2) chance that it will rain 3) get a tan

07 1) delivered on time 2) don't fit my car seats
    3) ordered the wrong seat covers
    4) have new ones sent

08 1) Only 20 years old 2) was born in South Korea
    3) speak four languages

09 1) important traditional holidays
    2) celebrate the harvest 3) watch the full moon
    4) 15th of the eighth lunar month

10 1) send my love to 2) pay for it 3) see a doctor
    4) going out to meet

11 1) played soccer with my friends
    2) My cell phone's battery died
    3) should take a shower

12 1) I'll be 20 next year 2) have any experience
    3) do have a driver's license
    4) available only on weekdays

13 1) come over and see him
    2) except Monday or Thursday 3) is on Wednesday

14 1) you need some rest
    2) organized my comic books
    3) donated all but some
    4) I'm exhausted from carrying

15 1) side effects of social media
    2) lead to cyberbullying
    3) Addictions to social media

16 1) the two most popular ones 2) $30 each
    3) a little expensive 4) get 50% off

17 1) do some volunteer work
    2) to teach children English
    3) How often do you teach

18 1) too cold to walk 2) be a lot of traffic
    3) There was a big accident

19 1) picked to be a teen reporter 2) get this position
    3) be a great experience 4) work for a newspaper

20 1) arrives at the cinema early
    2) checks her seat number
    3) man sitting there

Word Test 고난도 01~02 pp. 260~261

Ⓐ
01 조정하다   02 놀라운
03 음료   04 결정하다
05 용돈   06 연결하다
07 떨어지다   08 정리하다
09 과제   10 완전히
11 논의하다   12 확인하다
13 직원   14 차단하다
15 그릇, 용기   16 극심한; 혹독한
17 사용   18 이전의
19 제출하다   20 분명히[틀림없이]
21 기쁨   22 빼먹다
23 무덤, 묘   24 장소, 위치
25 점차   26 거의 ~ 아니게[없이]
27 (신문 등을) 구독하다 28 적절한
29 조심하는, 신중한   30 영화관
31 짧게 하다, 단축하다   32 그 이상의, 추가의

33	~을 설치하다	34	(불 등을) 끄다
35	~와 시간을 보내다	36	다 떨어지다
37	시끄럽게 하다	38	시도하다
39	계획을 세우다	40	경의를 표하다

Ⓑ

01	sweat	02	potential
03	north	04	liquid
05	ideally	06	language
07	performance	08	ancestor
09	charity	10	dramatic
11	feed	12	symbol
13	suddenly	14	increase
15	soil	16	teen
17	forecast	18	device
19	exhausted	20	relative
21	depression	22	slippery
23	ignore	24	impossible
25	actress	26	tie
27	experience	28	auditorium
29	publish	30	chance
31	exposure	32	addiction
33	fluently	34	wild animal
35	side effect	36	score a goal
37	win the lottery	38	take time off
39	lead to	40	according to